Police-Community Relations and the Administration of Justice

Eighth Edition

POLICE-COMMUNITY RELATIONS AND THE ADMINISTRATION OF JUSTICE

Ronald D. Hunter

Thomas Barker

Prentice Hall

Boston   Columbus   Indianapolis   New York   San Francisco   Upper Saddle River
Amsterdam   Cape Town   Dubai   London   Madrid   Milan   Munich   Paris   Montreal   Toronto
Delhi   Mexico City   Sao Paulo   Sydney   Hong Kong   Seoul   Singapore   Taipei   Tokyo

Editor in Chief: Vernon R. Anthony
Acquisitions Editor: Tim Peyton
Editorial Assistant: Lynda Cramer
Director of Marketing: David Gesell
Marketing Manager: Adam Kloza
Senior Marketing Coordinator: Alicia Wozniak
Marketing Assistant: Les Roberts
Project Manager: Holly Shufeldt
Senior Art Director: Jayne Conte

Manager, Cover Visual Research & Permissions:
   Karen Sanatar
Cover Designer: Suzanne Duda
Cover Photo: Superstock
Full-Service Project Management and Composition:
   Sadagoban Balaji, Integra
Printer/Binder: Hamilton Printing Co.
Cover Printer: Lehigh-Phoenix Color Corp.
Text Font: 10/12 Minion

Credits and acknowledgments borrowed from other sources and reproduced, with permission, in this textbook appear on appropriate page within text.

Library of Congress Cataloging-in-Publication Data

Hunter, Ronald D.
   Police-community relations and the administration of justice/Ronald D. Hunter, Thomas Barker.
      p. cm.
   Includes index.
   ISBN-13: 978-0-13-245778-1 (alk. paper)
   ISBN-10: 0-13-245778-4 (alk. paper)
   1. Police-community relations—United States.   2. Police—United States.   3. Criminal justice, Administration of—United States.   I. Barker, Thomas.   II. Title.
HV7936.P8H86 2011
363.2'30973—dc22

                                                            2010000679

10 9 8 7 6

Prentice Hall
is an imprint of

www.pearsonhighered.com

ISBN 10:   0-13-245778-4
ISBN 13: 978-0-13-245778-1

CONTENTS

PREFACE

Policing society, especially a free society, is too important an aspect of public policy to be left solely to the police. For that matter, the operation of the justice system is too important to be left solely to the practitioners. Citizen participation is crucial to the effectiveness of the criminal justice system. Every edition of this book has been organized around the same theme: Each criminal justice system (the police, the courts, and corrections) must develop and maintain meaningful, two-way communications among the agency, its service area, and populations served. This communication leads to community–agency partnerships that facilitate problem solving.

As the gatekeepers of the criminal justice system and the most visible representatives of our form of government, the police have a unique responsibility to engage in partnerships with their communities. These partnerships, once developed, can create a sense of safety, problem solving, and good quality of life for all served. This book addresses all the communities the police serve and discusses past, current, and future practices that can create and sustain meaningful and successful police–community relations.

This text is designed for use in a one-semester course on Police and the Community, Police–Community Relations, or Police and Society. It is an overview of the topics covered and much more can be said about every topic. We address the topics in the context of community relations and encourage the reader to pursue further study in areas of special interest.

Every edition of this textbook has had its friends. The current edition was written because much has changed since the seventh edition. The nation has its first African American president who was elected on a platform of change. Political, cultural, and social changes across the nation will continue. The makeup of the U.S. Supreme Court is changing. Technological advances are ongoing. Prosecutorial wrongdoing has become a focal concern in the administration of justice. And the police are expected to be better prepared for the challenges created by the preceding issues.

NEW TO THIS EDITION

The eighth edition of *Police–Community Relations and the Administration of Justice* represents an up-to-date discussion of police–community relations in the twenty-first century. It provides examples of innovative police–community partnerships in rural, suburban, and urban communities and the best police efforts in community policing and problem solving. The revision includes:

- An optimistic view of police–community relations in this century
- Additional boxes that detail police–community relations programs in large and small communities and in rural and urban settings
- The most current examples of community policing and problem-oriented policing
- Examples of community policing and problem-solving policing in other democratic societies where applicable
- A rewritten Chapter 10, "Community-Oriented Policing" (formerly "Community Policing"), that reflects the latest thinking on the concept
- A rewritten Chapter 11, "Police–Community Relations and the Media" (formerly "The Media Link"), that emphasizes the news media's importance to the marketing of the police agencies' community-oriented policing programs
- A rewritten Chapter 16, "Community Participation in the New Millennium," that reflects the importance of civilian oversight agencies and volunteer organizations in police–community relations

It is our fervent desire that this edition continue the tradition established by Pamela D. Mayhall of providing both instructors and students with an interesting and challenging overview of many issues relative to police–community relations.

Ronald D. Hunter
Georgia Gwinnett College

Thomas Barker
Eastern Kentucky University

ACKNOWLEDGMENTS

The professional staff at Prentice Hall is greatly appreciated, especially Lynda Cramer. Several law enforcement officers and agencies provided information, photographs, or other materials that greatly aided in this effort. We wish to thank Deputy Chief George Cooley and Chief Mike Coppage of the Birmingham Police Department; Captain E. A. Thomas and Chief D. Allan Wade of the Pelham Police Department; Ms. Julie Williams and Sheriff Clarence W. Dupnik of the Pima County Sheriff's Department; Chief Michael H. Zunk of the Indianapolis Police Department; Lt. David Graham of the Newport News Police Department; Detective Tom Bojo and Chief Hubert Smith of the Rome Police Department; Chief George Carpenter of the Wilmette Police Department; Ms. Diane McCarthy and Superintendent Terry G. Hillard of the Chicago Police Department; Commissioner Howard Safir of the New York Police Department; Chief Tom Johnson and Lt. Bob Scott of the Western Carolina University Police Department; Sheriff Jimmy Ashe of the Jackson County Sheriff's Department; the Gay Officers Action League of New England; and Ms. Jay Hern and Dr. Linda Lindsey of the North Carolina School for the Deaf.

We would like to sincerely acknowledge the contribution and support of our wives, Viola and Elizabeth (Betsy), who have been the "Wind Under Our Sails" since we both left law enforcement. Lastly, we acknowledge the BSJ who made it all possible.

POLICE-COMMUNITY RELATIONS AND THE ADMINISTRATION OF JUSTICE

CHAPTER 1

The Administration of Justice and the Police

"Injustice anywhere is a threat to justice everywhere."
—LETTER FROM BIRMINGHAM JAIL, APRIL 16, 1963.
—MARTIN LUTHER KING, JR.

KEY CONCEPTS

Civil Justice	Distributive Justice	Restorative Justice
Civil Liberties	Equality	Rule of Law
Common Law	Federalism	Social Justice
Commutative Justice	Human Rights	Social Stability
Criminal Justice	Justice	Symbolic Reassurance

LEARNING OBJECTIVES

Studying this chapter will enable you to:

1. Discuss the need for justice in order for nations and their governmental components to survive.
2. Define human rights and describe their importance to people living throughout the world.
3. Explain the importance of the Bill of Rights in protecting the civil liberties of American citizens.
4. Identify the different agencies responsible for protecting the civil rights of U.S. citizens.
5. Define justice and describe the different types of justice.
6. Explain the mission of a justice system.
7. Identify the four kinds of justice systems found around the world.
8. Discuss the challenges of administering justice within a democratic society.
9. Explain how federalism affects the administration of justice in America.
10. Present and discuss the various components within the U.S. justice system in addition to the police.
11. Describe how America's police system is structured.
12. Understand where the police fit within the U.S. justice system.
13. Be familiar with the "Four C's" of police–community relations.

INTRODUCTION

The majority of those reading this text have completed other courses about the criminal justice system and its processes. However, we are of the opinion that a brief refresher is in order to remind law enforcement students that the police do not exist in a vacuum. The myriad of agencies that comprise the "police" are integral components of a vital system of justice upon which social order and stability are dependent. The purpose, roles, and functions of the police within every nation on earth are interdependent with those of other governmental entities. To understand the police, one must understand the other components of the criminal justice system. To understand the criminal justice system, one must understand the concept of justice.

THE IDEA OF JUSTICE

To many of us, the concept of justice is relatively straightforward; the large numbers of people that comprise our societies require regulation to ensure peace and stability. Otherwise, competing interests and differing perspectives on what constitutes acceptable behavior would lead to chaos. The weak would be victimized by the strong, violence would become the social norm, and civilization would cease to exist. We often simplify this idea of justice into two words: "law and order." However, as we may easily note when viewing current world events, who determines what constitutes the law, who defines the nature of order, and how their views are imposed on the populace are not as clear-cut.

The Need for Justice

Nations and their components (states, territories, provinces, cities, counties, etc.) cannot exist without established systems of justice. These systems must not only ensure that domestic peace and tranquility are preserved, they must do so in a manner acceptable to those who are governed. This is true even in totalitarian societies. While those subject to governmental edicts may have little or no say in how laws are enacted and enforced, there must be a belief that subservience to their government is preferable to disorder. The reader may challenge this assertion by pointing to the arbitrariness and unfairness that may be found within the brutal dictatorships that have existed (and that unfortunately still exist) within our world. We agree. But even in those countries, one will find that those in power must present an appearance of justice. While these justice systems may be backed by repressive force, the masses of people must still feel that they and their families can reasonably exist. Otherwise, rebellion will take place.

Regardless of the nature of a society, social stability is not enough. Citizens must also feel that they are being treated "properly." What is viewed as proper is determined by historical and cultural influences. Governmental actions that would be totally acceptable in one nation would not be seen as such in others. As humankind has developed, its expectations have likewise developed. Two key components in evaluating the world's justice systems are the provisions for basic human rights and the extent of civil rights granted to citizens.

HUMAN RIGHTS   **Human rights** in its simplest term may be defined as a person's right to the basic necessities for survival. These include adequate food, shelter, medical care, and not being the victim of a government's or government-condoned group's efforts to commit genocide. Efforts on the part of the U.S. Army during the 1800s to annihilate Native Americans and by the Iraqi government during the rule of Saddam Hussein to eliminate the Kurds are clear examples of human rights violations. Modern human rights organizations would also charge that the existence of poverty and famine within third-world nations is another example. As this is being written, the United Nations is calling for the closure of the U.S. prison at Guantanamo Bay, Cuba, where terrorist suspects are being held, citing that these incarcerations are violations of human rights.

On December 10, 1948, the General Assembly of the United Nations adopted and proclaimed the Universal Declaration of Human Rights. Following this historic act, the Assembly called upon all member countries to publicize the text of the Declaration and "to cause it to be disseminated, displayed, read and expounded principally in schools and other educational institutions, without distinction based on the political status of countries or territories." (See Figure 1.1) This figure is the longest within the entire text, but we feel it warrants inclusion because (despite the fears of opponents of "world government," including the authors') the justice system in America will increasingly be held accountable to the edicts of international organizations.

CIVIL RIGHTS   As the reader can see within Figure 1.1, the U.N. Declaration goes beyond our definition of basic survival necessities to incorporate equal rights, freedom of speech, and protection from government abuse. In reality, many of the world's 191 nations do not adhere to

FIGURE 1.1   The U.N. Universal Declaration of Human Rights.

Preamble

Whereas recognition of the inherent dignity and of the equal and inalienable rights of all members of the human family is the foundation of freedom, justice and peace in the world,

Whereas disregard and contempt for human rights have resulted in barbarous acts which have outraged the conscience of mankind, and the advent of a world in which human beings shall enjoy freedom of speech and belief and freedom from fear and want has been proclaimed as the highest aspiration of the common people,

Whereas it is essential, if man is not to be compelled to have recourse, as a last resort, to rebellion against tyranny and oppression, that human rights should be protected by the rule of law,

Whereas it is essential to promote the development of friendly relations between nations,

Whereas the peoples of the United Nations have in the Charter reaffirmed their faith in fundamental human rights, in the dignity and worth of the human person and in the equal rights of men and women and have determined to promote social progress and better standards of life in larger freedom,

Whereas Member States have pledged themselves to achieve, in co-operation with the United Nations, the promotion of universal respect for and observance of human rights and fundamental freedoms,

Whereas a common understanding of these rights and freedoms is of the greatest importance for the full realization of this pledge,

Now, Therefore THE GENERAL ASSEMBLY proclaims THIS UNIVERSAL DECLARATION OF HUMAN RIGHTS as a common standard of achievement for all peoples and all nations, to the end that every individual and every organ of society, keeping this Declaration constantly in mind, shall strive by teaching and education to promote respect for these rights and freedoms and by progressive measures, national and international, to secure their universal and effective recognition and observance, both among the peoples of Member States themselves and among the peoples of territories under their jurisdiction.

Article 1.

All human beings are born free and equal in dignity and rights. They are endowed with reason and conscience and should act towards one another in a spirit of brotherhood.

Article 2.

Everyone is entitled to all the rights and freedoms set forth in this Declaration, without distinction of any kind, such as race, color, sex, language, religion, political or other opinion, national or social origin, property, birth or other status. Furthermore, no distinction shall be made on the basis of the political, jurisdictional or international status of the country or territory to which a person belongs, whether it be independent, trust, non-self-governing or under any other limitation of sovereignty.

Article 3.

Everyone has the right to life, liberty and security of person.

Article 4.

No one shall be held in slavery or servitude; slavery and the slave trade shall be prohibited in all their forms.

Article 5.

No one shall be subjected to torture or to cruel, inhuman or degrading treatment or punishment.

Article 6.

Everyone has the right to recognition everywhere as a person before the law.

Article 7.

All are equal before the law and are entitled without any discrimination to equal protection of the law. All are entitled to equal protection against any discrimination in violation of this Declaration and against any incitement to such discrimination.

Article 8.

Everyone has the right to an effective remedy by the competent national tribunals for acts violating the fundamental rights granted him by the constitution or by law.

(continued)

FIGURE 1.1   Continued

Article 9.

No one shall be subjected to arbitrary arrest, detention or exile.

Article 10.

Everyone is entitled in full equality to a fair and public hearing by an independent and impartial tribunal, in the determination of his rights and obligations and of any criminal charge against him.

Article 11.

(1) Everyone charged with a penal offence has the right to be presumed innocent until proved guilty according to law in a public trial at which he has had all the guarantees necessary for his defense.

(2) No one shall be held guilty of any penal offence on account of any act or omission which did not constitute a penal offence, under national or international law, at the time when it was committed. Nor shall a heavier penalty be imposed than the one that was applicable at the time the penal offence was committed.

Article 12.

No one shall be subjected to arbitrary interference with his privacy, family, home or correspondence, nor to attacks upon his honor and reputation. Everyone has the right to the protection of the law against such interference or attacks.

Article 13.

(1) Everyone has the right to freedom of movement and residence within the borders of each state.

(2) Everyone has the right to leave any country, including his own, and to return to his country.

Article 14.

(1) Everyone has the right to seek and to enjoy in other countries asylum from persecution.

(2) This right may not be invoked in the case of prosecutions genuinely arising from non-political crimes or from acts contrary to the purposes and principles of the United Nations.

Article 15.

(1) Everyone has the right to a nationality.

(2) No one shall be arbitrarily deprived of his nationality nor denied the right to change his nationality.

Article 16.

(1) Men and women of full age, without any limitation due to race, nationality or religion, have the right to marry and to found a family. They are entitled to equal rights as to marriage, during marriage and at its dissolution.

(2) Marriage shall be entered into only with the free and full consent of the intending spouses.

(3) The family is the natural and fundamental group unit of society and is entitled to protection by society and the State.

Article 17.

(1) Everyone has the right to own property alone as well as in association with others.

(2) No one shall be arbitrarily deprived of his property.

Article 18.

Everyone has the right to freedom of thought, conscience and religion; this right includes freedom to change his religion or belief, and freedom, either alone or in community with others and in public or private, to manifest his religion or belief in teaching, practice, worship and observance.

Article 19.

Everyone has the right to freedom of opinion and expression; this right includes freedom to hold opinions without interference and to seek, receive and impart information and ideas through any media and regardless of frontiers.

Article 20.

(1) Everyone has the right to freedom of peaceful assembly and association.

(2) No one may be compelled to belong to an association.

Article 21.

(1) Everyone has the right to take part in the government of his country, directly or through freely chosen representatives.

(2) Everyone has the right of equal access to public service in his country.

(3) The will of the people shall be the basis of the authority of government; this shall be expressed in periodic and genuine elections which shall be by universal and equal suffrage and shall be held by secret vote or by equivalent free voting procedures.

Article 22.

Everyone, as a member of society, has the right to social security and is entitled to realization, through national effort and international co-operation and in accordance with the organization and resources of each State, of the economic, social and cultural rights indispensable for his dignity and the free development of his personality.

Article 23.

(1) Everyone has the right to work, to free choice of employment, to just and favorable conditions of work and to protection against unemployment.

(2) Everyone, without any discrimination, has the right to equal pay for equal work.

(3) Everyone who works has the right to just and favorable remuneration ensuring for himself and his family an existence worthy of human dignity, and supplemented, if necessary, by other means of social protection.

(4) Everyone has the right to form and to join trade unions for the protection of his interests.

Article 24.

Everyone has the right to rest and leisure, including reasonable limitation of working hours and periodic holidays with pay.

Article 25.

(1) Everyone has the right to a standard of living adequate for the health and well-being of himself and of his family, including food, clothing, housing and medical care and necessary social services, and the right to security in the event of unemployment, sickness, disability, widowhood, old age or other lack of livelihood in circumstances beyond his control.

(2) Motherhood and childhood are entitled to special care and assistance. All children, whether born in or out of wedlock, shall enjoy the same social protection.

Article 26.

(1) Everyone has the right to education. Education shall be free, at least in the elementary and fundamental stages. Elementary education shall be compulsory. Technical and professional education shall be made generally available and higher education shall be equally accessible to all on the basis of merit.

(2) Education shall be directed to the full development of the human personality and to the strengthening of respect for human rights and fundamental freedoms. It shall promote understanding, tolerance and friendship among all nations, racial or religious groups, and shall

further the activities of the United Nations for the maintenance of peace.

(3) Parents have a prior right to choose the kind of education that shall be given to their children.

Article 27.

(1) Everyone has the right freely to participate in the cultural life of the community, to enjoy the arts and to share in scientific advancement and its benefits.

(2) Everyone has the right to the protection of the moral and material interests resulting from any scientific, literary or artistic production of which he is the author.

Article 28.

Everyone is entitled to a social and international order in which the rights and freedoms set forth in this Declaration can be fully realized.

Article 29.

(1) Everyone has duties to the community in which alone the free and full development of his personality is possible.

(2) In the exercise of his rights and freedoms, everyone shall be subject only to such limitations as are determined by law solely for the purpose of securing due recognition and respect for the rights and freedoms of others and of meeting the just requirements of morality, public order and the general welfare in a democratic society.

(3) These rights and freedoms may in no case be exercised contrary to the purposes and principles of the United Nations.

Article 30.

Nothing in this Declaration may be interpreted as implying for any State, group or person any right to engage in any activity or to perform any act aimed at the destruction of any of the rights and freedoms set forth herein.

Source: Adopted and proclaimed by General Assembly resolution 217 A (III) of December 10, 1948.

these standards. Even Western democracies have been slow to adopt them in their totality. Despite the protections of the Bill of Rights (the First Ten Amendments to the U.S. Constitution, written 150 years before the U.N. Declaration), it was not until the 1960s that full enforcement of civil rights began within the United States.

We view civil rights as moving beyond the basic necessities for survival to include equal participation in democratic elections, equal access to legal institutions, and equal protection by the government from both governmental and private abuse. Freedoms from government oppression or intrusive practices are also known as **civil liberties** (we will discuss them in more detail in a later section). The extension of these rights, based on gender and physical disabilities, was interpreted as being covered by the Bill of Rights during the 1970s (see Figure 1.2). Sexual orientation was included during the 1990s.

Federal civil rights violations may be investigated by the Civil Rights Division of the U.S. Department of Justice, by the Federal Bureau of Investigation (FBI), by civil suits filed by

FIGURE 1.2 The Bill of Rights.

Amendments 1–10 of the U.S. Constitution

The Conventions of a number of the States having, at the time of adopting the Constitution, expressed a desire, in order to prevent misconstruction or abuse of its powers, that further declaratory and restrictive clauses should be added, and as extending the ground of public confidence in the Government will best insure the beneficent ends of its institution.

Resolved, by the Senate and House of Representatives of the United States of America, in Congress assembled, two-thirds of both Houses concurring, that the following articles be proposed to the Legislatures of the several States, as amendments to the Constitution of the United States; all or any of which articles, when ratified by three-fourths of the said Legislatures, to be valid to all intents and purposes as part of the said Constitution, namely:

Amendment I

Congress shall make no law respecting an establishment of religion, or prohibiting the free exercise thereof; or abridging the freedom of speech, or of the press; or the right of the people peaceably to assemble, and to petition the government for a redress of grievances.

Amendment II

A well regulated militia, being necessary to the security of a free state, the right of the people to keep and bear arms, shall not be infringed.

Amendment III

No soldier shall, in time of peace be quartered in any house, without the consent of the owner, nor in time of war, but in a manner to be prescribed by law.

Amendment IV

The right of the people to be secure in their persons, houses, papers, and effects, against unreasonable searches and seizures, shall not be violated, and no warrants shall issue, but upon probable cause, supported by oath or affirmation, and particularly describing the place to be searched, and the persons or things to be seized.

Amendment V

No person shall be held to answer for a capital, or otherwise infamous crime, unless on a presentment or indictment of a grand jury, except in cases arising in the land or naval forces, or in the militia, when in actual service in time of war or public danger; nor shall any person be subject for the same offense to be twice put in jeopardy of life or limb; nor shall be compelled in any criminal case to be a witness against himself, nor be deprived of life, liberty, or property, without due process of law; nor shall private property be taken for public use, without just compensation.

Amendment VI

In all criminal prosecutions, the accused shall enjoy the right to a speedy and public trial, by an impartial jury of the state and district wherein the crime shall have been committed, which district shall have been previously ascertained by law, and to be informed of the nature and cause of the accusation; to be confronted with the witnesses against him; to have compulsory process for obtaining witnesses in his favor, and to have the assistance of counsel for his defense.

Amendment VII

In suits at common law, where the value in controversy shall exceed twenty dollars, the right of trial by jury shall be preserved, and no fact tried by a jury, shall be otherwise reexamined in any court of the United States, than according to the rules of the common law.

Amendment VIII

Excessive bail shall not be required, nor excessive fines imposed, nor cruel and unusual punishments inflicted.

Amendment IX

The enumeration in the Constitution, of certain rights, shall not be construed to deny or disparage others retained by the people.

Amendment X

The powers not delegated to the United States by the Constitution, nor prohibited by it to the states, are reserved to the states respectively, or to the people.

Amendment XIV

All persons born or naturalized in the United States, and subject to the jurisdiction thereof, are citizens of the United States and of the state wherein they reside. No state shall make or enforce any law which shall abridge the privileges or immunities of citizens of the United States; nor shall any State deprive any person of life, liberty, or property, without due process of law; nor deny to any person within its jurisdiction the equal protection of the laws.

Note: The Fourteenth Amendment warrants inclusion here because it is the mechanism by which the Bill of Rights became applicable as protections from state and local governments in addition to the national government.

FIGURE 1.3   **Mission of the U.S. Commission on Civil Rights.**

To investigate complaints alleging that citizens are being deprived of their right to vote by reason of their race, color, religion, sex, age, disability, or national origin, or by reason of fraudulent practices.

To study and collect information relating to discrimination or a denial of equal protection of the laws under the Constitution because of race, color, religion, sex, age, disability, or national origin, or in the administration of justice.

To appraise federal laws and policies with respect to discrimination or denial of equal protection of the laws because of race, color, religion, sex, age, disability, or national origin, or in the administration of justice.

To serve as a national clearinghouse for information in respect to discrimination or denial of equal protection of the laws because of race, color, religion, sex, age, disability, or national origin.

To submit reports, findings, and recommendations to the President and Congress.

To issue public service announcements to discourage discrimination or denial of equal protection of the law.

individuals, or by complaints filed with the U.S. Commission on Civil Rights (see Figure 1.3). They may also be enforced by lawsuits and criminal prosecutions filed under the constitutional protections of the states.

JUSTICE DEFINED

While everyone has his or her own concept of justice (usually determined by what we think is best for us), it is not as easily defined as one might think. According to Crank (2003), efforts at clarity tend to conflict with concerns over inclusiveness. Definitions are also determined by the perspective of the viewer. Reiman (2007) argues that our system of justice is biased against the poor and is, therefore, not just. Lawyers tend to view justice as the obligation that the legal system has toward the individual citizen and society as a whole. A common definition views justice as a concept involving the fair, moral, and impartial treatment of all persons (Wikipedia, 2007). To ensure that justice is seen from the relevant perspective of policing, we define **justice** *as the fair and equitable application of the rule of law by agents of social control regardless of the socioeconomic status of the individuals concerned.* While we admit that this is a rather idyllic view, we argue that it is, indeed, what a free society should strive for.

To accomplish justice, we feel that there are six components that the administration of justice must contain:

- *Compliance with the* **Rule of Law**. Codified legal standards must exist and must be followed. As noted in the Fourteenth Amendment of the U.S. Constitution, citizens can be deprived of life, liberty, or property only by due process of law.
- *Equity.* Laws must be applied in an equal manner to everyone subject to them. In addition, every person must be allowed equal access to the legal system. This is a subject of great debate in regard to the U.S. criminal justice system, and even greater debate in regard to the U.S. civil justice system.
- *Fairness.* Laws, as well as their application, must be fair and not single out groups or individuals for arbitrary or unfair treatment. As with equity, fairness is not easily monitored and can often become lost in legalities and legalese that govern the system's operations.
- *Accessibility.* There must be allowances for those individuals who do not have financial recourse to receive competent legal advice and support. This is dealt with in the criminal justice system by provisions for indigent defense. However, this is one component in which the U.S. civil justice system is very much lacking.
- *Effectiveness.* The system must work for common citizens in actuality as well as on paper. Like beauty, effectiveness is in the eye of the beholder. How well the U.S. justice system accomplishes this need is even more hotly debated than the previous components.

BOX 1.1
Alternative Definitions of Justice

Some satirical views of justice from Webster's online dictionary:

Justice. A commodity which in a more or less adulterated condition the State sells to the citizen as a reward for his allegiance, taxes and personal service.

Justice. Fair play; often sought, but seldom discovered, in company with Law.

Justice. A mythological character whose statue has been frequently erected. She had eye trouble.

Source: www.websters-online-dictionary.org/definition/justice.

• *Oversight*. There must be remedies for failures or misapplications of justice to be corrected. The checks and balances of the federal system, and judicial oversight in particular, are the mechanisms designed to correct injustices that occur. While far from perfect and frequently yielding unsatisfactory results, this process is as functional as any other that may be found within the world community.

Critics may correctly cite examples to argue that the above components are more idealistic than accurate. Indeed, the administration of justice (particularly within a democratic society of more than 300 million) will always be a subject of debate.

Types of Justice

Understanding the administration of justice is further complicated by the different types of justice found within our society and the meanings attached to them. While the police are predominately linked with criminal justice, the other types of justice impact on both how the police are perceived by others and how they function within society. Brief overviews of these other types of justice follow:

SOCIAL JUSTICE   Social justice is rendering to everyone that which is his or her due as a human being. Social justice is seen by its proponents as not just emphasizing equity and fairness in the application of jurisprudence but in regulating how a society's resources are allocated (Crank, 2003). Redistribution of wealth by the use of progressive tax systems, strict regulation of business, and extensive use of social interventions by government are principles embodied within social justice. Social justice seeks to see that people are treated both fairly and "morally" within all areas of society. Social justice may be either distributive or commutative.

Distributive justice seeks to distribute rewards and punishments so that neither equal persons have unequal things, nor unequal persons equal things. In other words, need is considered, but merit is rewarded. The U.S. system of welfare capitalism is based on distributive justice. Protections exist to ensure that the tenets of civil and human rights are provided but individual successes or failures are allowed.

Commutative justice seeks to ensure **equality** among citizens so that no one may be a gainer by another's loss. The fair and moral treatment of all persons, especially as regards social rules, is the part of a continued effort to do what is "right" (Crank, 2003; Reiman, 2007). Commutative justice places a greater emphasis on need rather than individual merit. Proponents of this perspective argue that biases due to class, ethnicity, gender, or other distinctions make capitalist society inherently unfair. Therefore, greater efforts by government in the redistribution of wealth and the enhancement of life for minorities and the lower class must be implemented to address social inequities. Until these occur, true justice is not attainable (Cole, 2004; Reiman, 2007).

CIVIL JUSTICE   Civil justice is the legal system that regulates the relationships between individuals. Distributive and commutative aspects do exist within the civil law system. However, the focus of civil law is to regulate noncriminal behaviors within society. Redress for harm from another's actions is not by criminal prosecution but by seeking legal intervention to regain that which was lost due to another's improper actions and/or to prevent further harm. Monetary compensation may be for the harm that was incurred. Punitive damages may also be awarded. Due to the complexities and costs of successful litigation, it is in the areas of civil law that the poor and the middle class are more likely to experience inequitable treatment.

The civil legal system is concerned with torts (private wrongs that are not deemed to be criminal). However, in cases of evictions and foreclosures, police officers (especially deputy sheriffs) may find themselves involved. Ill feelings and frustrations from civil actions may also lead to criminal activities on the part of those who feel that they have been wronged. Administrative law, rules, and regulations followed and/or enforced by governmental agencies are also dealt with by the civil law system. Some behaviors (such as cheating on your income tax, violating another's civil rights, and insider trading) may have both civil and criminal components.

RESTORATIVE JUSTICE   Yet another type of justice that may or may not involve the criminal justice system is the practice of restorative justice. As the name implies, **restorative justice** seeks to mitigate adverse relationships between individuals as well as certain behaviors that could be deemed to be criminal. Instead of seeking to punish based on criminal sanctions or imposing legal compensation, restorative justice seeks to avoid formal adjudication by using arbitration to resolve conflicts (Van Ness and Strong, 2006). Because it emphasizes the use of alternative means to restore relationships, this concept is also known as peacemaking (Fuller, 2005). Efforts at restorative justice usually involve issues of lesser monetary import and/or minor offenses. Restorative justice may take place in lieu of civil litigation, and it may also be used as an alternative to criminal prosecution.

CRIMINAL JUSTICE   **Criminal justice** is the system that the readers of this text are interested in. As we have noted above, it is not truly separate from the other systems of justice and actually interacts with them. We utilized Rush's (2004) definition of the criminal justice system as the "process of adjudication by which the legal rights of private parties are vindicated and the guilt or innocence of accused persons is established." Please note that the *criminal justice system is concerned not only with the enforcement of laws but with the protection of legal rights as well.* To ensure that laws are not arbitrarily imposed, the criminal justice system relies on procedural law as well as substantive law.

Substantive law defines behaviors (and in some cases, failures to act) that are deemed to be unlawful and establishes sanctions for their commission (or omission). Procedural law regulates how substantive law may be applied. The famous *exclusionary rule* (see Box 1.2) is one mechanism by which American courts ensure that a defendant's due process rights are protected.

BOX 1.2
The Exclusionary Rule

In 1914, the U.S. Supreme Court ruled in *Weeks* v. *United States* that evidence illegally obtained by federal officers must be excluded from admission at trial. In 1960, this rule was extended to state and local officers in the *Mapp* v. *Ohio* ruling. The exclusionary rule not only prevents evidence obtained from unreasonable searches and seizures from admission in trials, it also ensures that judicial integrity and the faith of citizens are upheld.

The protections of the Fourth Amendment as enforced by the exclusionary rule are also known as the "Fruits of the Poisonous Tree Doctrine." Searches, arrests, confessions, and other evidence-gathering activities that are obtained through improper or illegal techniques are deemed to be poisonous and must, therefore, be suppressed to keep the entire legal process from becoming tainted.

There are exceptions to the exclusionary rule. In *United States* v. *Leon*, the U.S. Supreme Court ruled that "evidence seized on a search warrant that was subsequently invalidated could not justify the substantial costs of exclusion." The key to this exception is that the efforts were, indeed, reasonable and in good faith. Good intentions are not enough.

Another exception to the exclusionary rule is the "Inevitable Discovery Rule." This rule was established by the U.S. Supreme Court in *Wong Sun* v. *United States*. This rule allows the admission of evidence if it would have been found and discovered legally at a later time.

Source: Adapted from Roberson, Wallace, and Stuckey (2007).

THE MISSION OF A CRIMINAL JUSTICE SYSTEM

Having reviewed several pages pointing out the complexities of justice, the reader may legitimately ask, "What then is the purpose of a criminal justice system?" The answer is simpler than our previous discussions may suggest. In a nutshell, *the U.S. criminal justice system exists to apply the rule of law as a means of providing social stability.* As we discussed previously, citizens must feel that their government is protecting them from crime and disorder. While the system need not be flawless, the public as a whole must have confidence in it.

The Rule of Law

Rule of law may be defined as government's establishment and imposition of legal processes to protect society from crime. It may also be defined as the mechanism by which government ensures the protection of individual rights. In order to accomplish these tasks, laws must provide for the following:

VENGEANCE/RETRIBUTION   When civilization evolved from tribal states to nation-states, government assumed responsibility for exacting vengeance on behalf of victims of crime. No longer would the strong be allowed to prey on the weak. Nor would victims or their families be permitted to conduct blood feuds to avenge themselves on those by whom they had been harmed. To keep citizens from "taking the law into their own hands," agents of social control must exact vengeance on behalf of victims.

ATONEMENT   Under the rule of law, those who commit crimes against others are seen as committing crimes against the state. In order to be allowed readmission to law-abiding society, offenders must atone for their crimes. The crime justice process is the means by which criminal offenders "pay their debt to society." While many ex-convicts may rightly argue otherwise, having been punished theoretically enables offenders to resume their place in society.

DETERRENCE/PREVENTION   The fundamental premise of the classical system of justice is that the imposition of punishment prevents further crime from occurring. Specific deterrence is the idea that by having received punishment, the offender will decide that the crime was not worth it. General deterrence is the concept that others contemplating similar crimes will be dissuaded from doing so by seeing the punishment of previous offenders (Hunter and Dantzker, 2005). Experienced police officers can point to the recidivism of offenders to question how well these premises work, but deterrence remains as the mainstay of the U.S. justice system.

TREATMENT   As part of the system's concerns to rehabilitate offenders so that they may reenter society and live productive lives, treatment is also an important component of justice in America. Like deterrence, the impacts of treatment are often disappointing, but fundamental fairness and social justice require that treatment be provided. Whether the treatments provided are appropriate or adequate will continue to be subjects of debate.

INCAPACITATION   In many cases, incarceration, as well as other means of incapacitation, is seen as legitimate goals of the U.S. justice system. Proponents of incapacitation argue that while offenders may return to crime later (except in the case of capital punishment—the ultimate incapacitation), they are prevented from doing so while under correctional control. A more correct version may be that they are impeded from committing crimes on the general public.

REPARATIONS   Lastly, a more humane means of applying the rule of law is to focus on the victim rather than society. Instead of punishing the offenders based on the harm they caused to society, they are ordered to make reparations to the victims of their crimes. This "restorative technique" is seen as not only helping those who have been harmed but also helping the offender.

Social Stability

Social stability is defined as the maintenance of order and the continuation of equitable social control by government. This requires government to not only repress criminal behaviors but to provide services (regulation of the private sector and the provision of public services) and to promote activities (such as public education and social programs) designed to benefit society as a whole.

MAINTENANCE OF ORDER   The maintenance of order involves many activities. Providing for democratic elections, collecting taxes, enforcing zoning regulations, collecting garbage, operating public utilities, providing crowd control at public events, enforcing parking regulations (including the issuing of parking tickets to students), and providing emergency services are but a few of the multitude of activities by government, many of which are performed by the police.

EQUITABLE SOCIAL CONTROL   One of the more controversial aspects of government is the need to address social inequities. While we may grouse at increasing government intrusion into our lives, providing social stability within a diverse nation of 300 million requires proactive government actions. As civil libertarians, the authors believe that citizens should be grudging in their tolerance of government interventions. However, we are also quick to note that these actions are necessary to ensure that all citizens are able to enjoy "life, liberty, and property." Government requirements such as progressive taxation, compulsory education, mandatory minimum wages, and protection of minority rights are examples of controversial government intrusions that are now seen as vital to public stability.

SYMBOLIC REASSURANCE   The last requirement of a justice system is what Hunter (see Hunter and Dantzker, 2005, p. 213) refers to as symbolic reassurance. **Symbolic reassurance** is the view that the criminal justice system not only provides guidelines for society to follow, it also punishes evil-doers to affirm law-abiding citizens' belief in the system. Universal conformity is not attained through threats of prosecution, but by reassuring law-abiding citizens that the system of justice is working. As long as a few offenders get occasional punishment (the more severe, the better), the public, especially the middle class, will remain compliant, even if they are not totally satisfied. Taken to an extreme, this concept implies that as long as the public perceives that "something is being done," even if it later proves to be faulty, the public will, for the most part, remain supportive.

THE CHALLENGES OF ADMINISTERING JUSTICE IN A FREE SOCIETY

We have discussed the protections of the Bill of Rights and the necessary components of a justice system within previous sections. This section will not repeat those arguments. However, we will stress the fundamental challenge that faces criminal justice practitioners within the United States. That challenge is quite simple: In a democratic and freedom-loving nation, how do we control crime while ensuring due process of law?

Crime Control versus Due Process

Crime control is the emphasis of justice system resources on the suppression of crime through the speedy enforcement of criminal laws. Advocates of the crime control model argue that the rights of society to be protected from crime should be the primary focus of the criminal justice system. Efficiency and effectiveness in criminal prosecutions are emphasized. In this model, the adjudication process is viewed as being an "assembly line." The counterpart to the crime control model is the due process model. In this model, the emphasis of the justice system is formal, adjudicative fact-finding that emphasizes the rights of the accused. The administration of justice is a slow and deliberate process that may be viewed as being an "obstacle course" (Packer, 1968).

BOX 1.3
Other Justice Systems

When seeking to study the U.S. system of justice, it is helpful to understand that our system is but one of many that exist within the world. While widely divergent in how they are comprised, most justice systems can be categorized into four distinct typologies:

Common Law Justice Systems

The common-law tradition evolved from the United Kingdom. Nations such as the United States that were formerly British Colonies tend to follow this legal tradition. Key elements of this tradition are the protection of individual liberties, concerns for equity, reliance on legal custom, and adversarial prosecution.

Civil Law Justice Systems

The civil law tradition (not the same as what is referred to as civil law in the United States) developed in Europe from Roman law and Catholic canon law. These systems are found in continental Europe and in nations around the world that emerged from European colonization. Key elements of this tradition are codified law, an emphasis on the protection of society, and inquisitorial prosecutions. France and Germany are leading exemplars of this tradition.

Islamic Justice Systems

The Islamic legal tradition is based on the Shari'a, law based on the Qur'an (the holy book of Islam) and the Sunna (the writings of the Prophet Mohammed). Varying interpretations of this system are found in Muslim nations. How strictly the Shari'a is applied within individual nations depends on cultural influences as well as the religious perspectives of the dominant Islamic sect within those nations.

Socialist Justice Systems

The socialist legal tradition evolved from the merger of Russian law and Marxist-Leninism following the revolution that led to the creation of the Soviet Union. This tradition viewed the law as artificial (meaning that rather than viewing the rule of law as binding, the edicts and rulings of the communist party, as well as adherence to Marxist philosophy, held precedence). Despite the breakup of the Soviet Union and the spread of democratic practices within its former satellites, the influence of this tradition may still be found in many of these nations. Currently, the Peoples Republic of China would be the leading example of this tradition.

Source: Adapted from Reichel (2005) and Dammer, Fairchild, and Albanese (2006).

RIGHTS OF SOCIETY According to Bohm and Haley (2005), the crime-control perspective is a reflection of traditional conservative values. Conservatives would probably agree with this assessment but argue that they are not seeking to deemphasize the protections of due process but to eliminate burdensome legal technicalities that neither protect individual rights nor protect society from crime. They point to other Western democracies that utilize the Civil Law System, in which the rights of society are deemed more important than those of any one individual. They may also accurately argue that most courts of limited jurisdiction in the United States operate in this manner.

RIGHTS OF INDIVIDUALS Bohm and Haley (2005) characterize the due process model as being a reflection of traditional liberal values. They point to the **common law** tradition of emphasizing the rights of individuals as safeguards from government oppression. They further argue that the protection of individual rights actually serves to protect societal rights.

Balancing the Rights of Society with Those of Individuals. As with most debates, the truth lies somewhere in the middle. Due process as defined by Roberson, Wallace, and Stuckey (2007, p. 454) is: "Those procedures that effectively guarantee individual rights in the face of criminal prosecution and those procedures that are fundamental rules for fair and orderly legal proceedings." In actual practice, individual rights are protected within the U.S. justice system, but the sheer volume of cases require that fair and orderly proceedings be expedited in lower-level courts and on less serious offenses. Capital cases and cases in which lengthy prison terms could be imposed rightly receive the greatest scrutiny.

This debate will continue as long as there is a U.S. justice system. During times of unrest and tension, the public will demand greater protections for society (the current dispute over the

BOX 1.4
The Civil Rights Act of 1871

The Civil Rights Act of 1871 (42 U.S.C. § 1983) is one of the most important federal statutes in force in the United States. It was originally enacted a few years after the American Civil War and consisted of the 1870 Force Act and 1871 Ku Klux Klan Act. One of the main reasons behind its passage was to protect Southern blacks from the Ku Klux Klan by providing a civil remedy for abuses then being committed in the South. The statute has been subjected to only minor changes since then but has been the subject of voluminous interpretation by courts.

Section 1983 does not create new civil rights. Instead, it allows individuals to sue state actors in federal courts for civil rights violations. To gain federal jurisdiction, that is, access to a court, the individual must point to a federal civil right that has been allegedly violated. These rights are encoded in the U.S. Constitution and federal statutes.

The statute reads:

Every person who under color of any statute, ordinance, regulation, custom, or usage, of any State or Territory or the District of Columbia, subjects, or causes to be subjected, any citizen of the United States or other person within the jurisdiction thereof to the deprivation of any rights, privileges, or immunities secured by the Constitution and laws, shall be liable to the party injured in an action at law, Suit in equity, or other proper proceeding for redress, except that in any action brought against a judicial officer for an act or omission taken in such officer's judicial capacity, injunctive relief shall not be granted unless a declaratory decree was violated or declaratory relief was unavailable. For the purposes of this section, any Act of Congress applicable exclusively to the District of Columbia shall be considered to be a statute of the District of Columbia.

For most of its history, Section 1983 had very little force. The legal community did not think the statute served as a check on state officials and did not often litigate under the statute. However, this changed in 1961 when the Supreme Court of the United States decided *Monroe* v. *Pape*, 365 U.S. 167. In that case, the Court articulated three purposes that underlay the statute: "1) 'to override certain kinds of state laws'; 2) to provide 'a remedy where state law was inadequate'; and 3) to provide 'a federal remedy where the state remedy, though adequate in theory, was not available in practice.'" Blum & Urbonya, Section 1983 Litigation, p. 2 (Federal Judicial Center, 1998) (quoting *Monroe* v. *Pape*). *Pape* opened the door for renewed interest in Section 1983.

Now the statute stands as one of the most powerful authorities with which federal courts may protect those whose rights are deprived. It is most often used to sue police and other state officials who allegedly deprived a plaintiff of constitutional rights within the criminal justice system.

Source: Adapted from Wikipedia (2007).

Patriot Act as a means of combating terrorism is a prime example). Civil libertarians see the Patriot Act as an encroachment on individual liberties. Advocates argue that it does not negatively impact law-abiding citizens and provides needed societal protections. Regardless of where you stand on the Patriot Act, the fact remains that the U.S. justice system will always have to juggle efficiency and effectiveness in protecting society from criminals with our traditional concern for individual rights. By the nature of their law enforcement responsibilities, the police will remain at the forefront of this debate (Walker, 2002).

THE COMPONENTS OF THE U.S. JUSTICE SYSTEM

The Federalist System

When discussing the U.S. justice system, one must be aware that there are in actuality several types of justice systems. The U.S. Constitution establishes a federalist system of government in which the national government shares power with the states and the states' political subdivisions (municipalities, townships, special districts, and counties). The magnitude of these systems may be realized by the knowledge that there are more than half a million elected officials within the United States. In addition to the state and national governments, these officials serve in more than 74,500 local governments, 20,000 municipalities, 16,500 townships, 3,000 counties, and more than 35,000 special districts (Fiorina et al., 2005: Chapters 1 and 3). At every level of government, you will find legislative bodies that make laws, executive agencies that enforce those laws, courts that interpret and apply the laws, and correctional organizations that carry out adjudicated sanctions. The criminal justice process utilized by every governmental level is displayed within Figure 1.4.

LAWMAKING   When we think of lawmaking within the United States, we generally think of the U.S. Congress or the 50 state legislatures. These legislative bodies (including the legislatures of American territories of the Virgin Islands, Guam, and American Samoa, as well as the Commonwealth of Puerto Rico and the council of the District of Columbia) enact laws that are known as statutes. The decisions of these bodies have considerable impact on the lives of their citizens. But it is at the local levels (among the approximately 74,500 local governmental bodies mentioned above) that most citizens have direct contact on a regular basis. Each of these entities has legislative bodies (usually referred to as councils, commissions, boards, or authorities) that enact lesser laws known as ordinances or codes (property taxes, sales taxes, zoning and building regulations, liquor sales and consumption, garbage collection, animal control, noise and nuisance abatement, etc.) that influence your daily life.

LAW ENFORCEMENT   In the following section, we will describe the police system in America in more detail. Suffice it to say at this point that if you are in need of police services, it is most likely that the officers that respond will be employed by a local government.

PROSECUTION   At the national level, the U.S. District Attorneys are responsible for the prosecution of federal cases within their respective jurisdictions. The numbers of cases that they prosecute are a mere fraction of those dealt with by state-level prosecutors. Depending on the state in which they serve, these prosecutors (known as District Attorneys or State's Attorneys) may deal only with violations of state laws, or they may also be responsible for enforcing local ordinances within their jurisdictions. In many states, local ordinances (as well as lesser state offenses delegated to them by the state legislatures) may be prosecuted by local attorneys (either the city attorney, an assistant city attorney, or a local attorney employed part-time), often known as solicitors. In many jurisdictions, this responsibility may actually extend to the police officers who made the arrests or issued the citations.

ADJUDICATION   At every level within the U.S. justice system, trial courts exist to adjudicate the cases within their respective jurisdictions. Ninety-four district courts try federal cases within the 50 states and territories. State trial courts of general jurisdiction try violations of state laws and civil cases within their judicial circuits or districts. These courts also try cases that are transferred or appealed from lower courts. Courts of appeal exist at both the state and federal levels. The U.S. Supreme Court is the highest court of appeal in America. While these courts are the ones that receive the greatest amount of media attention, it is in the courts of limited jurisdiction in which the vast majority of cases are tried. These courts may be lower-level state courts assigned to try lesser offenses and ordinance violations for the counties and municipalities within their area, or they may be separate county or municipal courts operated by those governmental entities. It is within these courts that the previously discussed "assembly line" may be found, with dozens of cases being tried within a single session.

CORRECTIONS   Correctional institutions exist at every level within the U.S. system. Federal prisons of every security category house convicted prisoners. State courts do the same. Municipal and county jails house prisoners awaiting trial, convicted prisoners awaiting sentencing, convicted prisoners awaiting transfer to state or federal facilities, and prisoners convicted of lesser crimes and ordinance violations. Community corrections programs are also found at every governmental level. Due to their costs, many counties and municipalities use private correctional organizations to provide community supervision. Local police agencies may find themselves supervising offenders assigned to community service and/or inmate work programs.

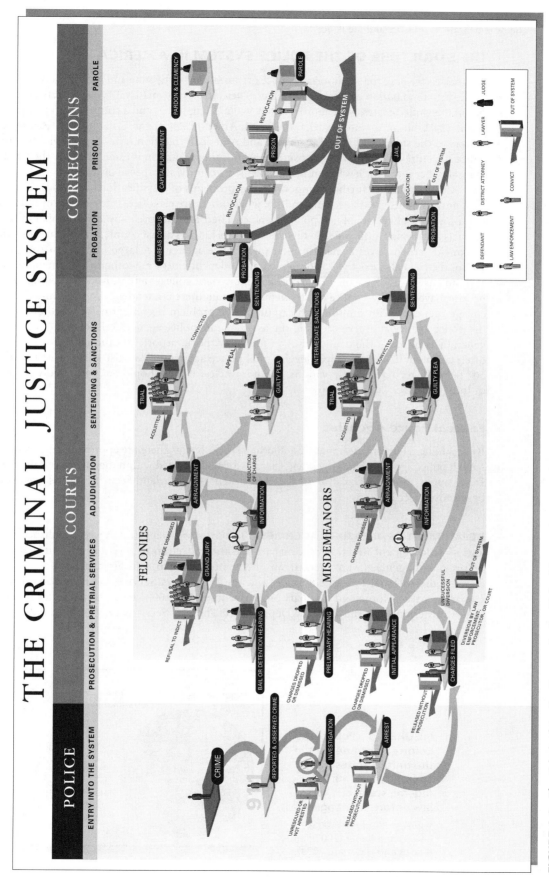

FIGURE 1.4 The Criminal Justice Process in the United States.

Source: www.ojp.usdoj.gov/bjs/flowchart.htm#efiles.

THE STRUCTURE OF THE POLICE SYSTEM IN AMERICA

In America, we have many important police organizations at the state and national levels. However, we are actually a nation of local police forces. There are approximately 18,760 separate police agencies in the United States, with approximately 940,275 employees and a combined annual budget of about $51 billion. As noted earlier, the Tenth Amendment of the Constitution reserves police powers to the states, and both **federalism** and American tradition have resulted in a fragmented police structure at lower levels of government; this fragmentation is exemplified by the separation of local police into four levels: municipal, township, county, and special districts.

Count totals are further compounded by problems of classification at the local level. Some local governments are true municipalities, while others are classified as townships or villages that may or may not have qualifying police agencies. There are a surprisingly large number of housing districts and transit authorities in the United States (34,684 at last count), which obviously do not all consider themselves as having their own police agencies. A large number of independent school districts also exist (13,726), which are independent of any other government authority, and can have or not have their own police agency. Many colleges and universities, both public and private, have their own police departments, although there is a tendency to not count the private college agencies. With multibranch campuses, the problem becomes one of whether you count the police agency at every academic site as a separate police agency. Railway police agencies are generally counted at the county level, but hospital, port, airport, and tunnel police agencies are often counted at the municipal level. Tribal police agencies also exist at many of the nation's 567 federally recognized reservations, and it is unclear if they should be considered state, county, or local police (O'Conner, 2006).

Federal Police Agencies

By including all units that have arrest and firearm authority, there are approximately 100 different federal police agencies. The largest agencies are formally located within the Justice and the Treasury Departments. Since the creation of the Department of Homeland Security, several agencies have been moved (see Box 1.5).

DEPARTMENT OF TREASURY AGENCIES   The Treasury Department was established in 1789, and its enforcement function revolves around the collection of revenue. Its four primary law enforcement agencies were the Bureau of Alcohol, Tobacco, and Firearms; the U.S. Customs Service; the Internal Revenue Service; and the U.S. Secret Service. With the creation of the Department of Homeland Security on November 25, 2002, three of these large agencies were transferred from the Treasury Department: The U.S. Secret Service and the U.S. Customs

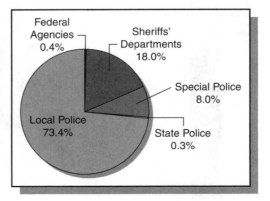

FIGURE 1.5   Public Law Enforcement Agencies in the United States (From approximately 18,760 federal, state, and local law enforcement agencies).

Sources: O'Conner (2006); Reaves and Bauer (2002); and Reaves and Hickman (2003).

BOX 1.5
Federal Law Enforcement Agencies

Administrative Office of the U.S. Courts
   Federal Corrections Supervision Division

Amtrak Police

Central Intelligence Agency
   Office of Security

Civil Aeronautics Board

Department of Agriculture
   Office of Inspector General
   U.S. Forest Service
   Division of Law Enforcement and Investigations

Department of Commerce
   Bureau of Industry and Security
      Office of Export Enforcement
   National Institute of Standards and Technology
      Office of Security
   National Oceanic & Atmospheric Administration,
      National Marine Fisheries Service
      Office of Law Enforcement
   Office of Inspector General

Department of Defense
   Defense Criminal Investigative Service
   National Security Agency
   Office of Inspector General
   Pentagon Force Protection Agency
   U.S. Air Force
      Office of Security Police
      Office of Special Investigations
   U.S. Army
      Criminal Investigation Command
      Intelligence and Security Command
      Military Police Corps
      Provost Marshall
   U.S. Marine Corps
      Military Police
   U.S. Navy
      Naval Criminal Investigative Service

Department of Education
   Office of Inspector General

Department of Energy
   Transportation Safeguards Division

Department of Health and Human Services
   Food & Drug Administration
      Office of Criminal Investigation
   National Institutes of Health
      Division of Public Safety
   Office of Inspector General

Department of Homeland Security
   Customs and Border Protection
      Border Patrol
   Federal Emergency Management Agency
      Security Division
   Immigration and Customs Enforcement
      Federal Protective Service
   Transportation Security Administration
   U.S. Coast Guard
      Intelligence and Law Enforcement Branch
   U.S. Secret Service
      Uniformed Division

Department of Housing and Urban Development
   Fair Housing and Equal Opportunity Division
   Office of Inspector General

Department of the Interior
   Bureau of Indian Affairs
      Division of Law Enforcement Services
   Bureau of Land Management
      Office of Enforcement
   Bureau of Reclamation
      Hoover Dam Police
   National Park Service
      Division of Ranger Activities & Protection
      U.S. Park Police
   Office of Inspector General
   U.S. Fish and Wildlife Service
      Division of Law Enforcement

Department of Justice
   Antitrust Division
   Bureau of Alcohol, Tobacco, Firearms, and Explosives

(continued)

Bureau of Prisons
Civil Rights Division
Drug Enforcement Administration
Federal Bureau of Investigation
Office of Inspector General
U.S. Marshals Service

Department of Labor
Occupational Safety and Health Administration
Office of Inspector General
Office of Labor-Management Standards

Department of State
Bureau of Diplomatic Security, Diplomatic
   Security Service
Bureau of Diplomatic Security, Protective
   Liaison Division
Office of Inspector General

Department of Transportation
Federal Aviation Administration, Police
Office of Inspector General

Department of the Treasury
Bureau of Engraving and Printing, U.S. Mint Police
Internal Revenue Service
   Criminal Investigation Division
   Inspection Service
   Office of Inspector General
   Office of the Regional Inspector

Department of Veterans Affairs
Office of Inspector General
Veterans Health Administration
   Office of Security and Law Enforcement

Environmental Protection Agency
Office of Criminal Investigations
Office of Inspector General

Federal Communications Commission

Federal Maritime Commission

Federal Trade Commission

General Services Administration
Office of Inspector General

Interstate Commerce Commission

Library of Congress
Police

National Aeronautics and Space Administration
Office of Inspector General

Nuclear Regulatory Commission
Office of Enforcement

Office of Personnel Management
Compliance and Investigations Group
Office of Inspector General

Securities and Exchange Commission
Division of Enforcement

Smithsonian Institution
National Zoological Park Police
Office of Protection Services

Social Security Administration
Office of Inspector General

Tennessee Valley Authority
Office of Inspector General
Public Safety Service

U.S. Capitol Police

U.S. Government Printing Office
Police

U.S. Mint
Police

U.S. Postal Service
Postal Inspection Service
Postal Security Force

U.S. Supreme Court Police

Sources: Barker, Hunter, and Rush (1994); Conser et al. (2005, pp. 91–92); Fuller (2005, p. 164); Reaves and Bauer (2003); and federal agency Web sites.

Service are now located within the Department of Homeland Security, and the Bureau of Alcohol, Tobacco, and Firearms is now located within the Department of Justice. While there are some smaller units that continue to have law enforcement authority, the only large federal police agency remaining within the Treasury Department is the Internal Revenue Service, which employs approximately 2,855 federal officers (Reaves and Bauer, 2003).

DEPARTMENT OF JUSTICE AGENCIES   The Justice Department was created in 1870 and is responsible for enforcing laws passed by the U.S. Congress (federal crimes). The largest Justice Department agency is the Bureau of Prisons. Since this is primarily a corrections organization, we will not discuss it. Other justice units having law enforcement authority are the Antitrust Division, the Civil Rights Division, and the Office of Inspector General. The organization of the Department of Justice is displayed in Figure 1.6. The four primary law enforcement agencies within the department are the Bureau of Alcohol, Tobacco, Firearms and Explosives; the Drug Enforcement Administration; the U.S. Marshals Service; and the FBI.

   Bureau of Alcohol, Tobacco, Firearms and Explosives.   The Bureau of Alcohol, Tobacco, Firearms and Explosives (ATF) performs the dual responsibilities of enforcing federal criminal laws and regulating the firearms and explosives industries. ATF's duties are to investigate and reduce crime involving firearms and explosives, acts of arson, and illegal trafficking of alcohol and tobacco products. Effective January 24, 2003, the Bureau of Alcohol, Tobacco, and Firearms (ATF) was transferred under the Homeland Security bill to the Department of Justice. The law enforcement functions of ATF under the Department of the Treasury were transferred to the Department of Justice. The tax and trade functions of the former ATF remained in the Treasury

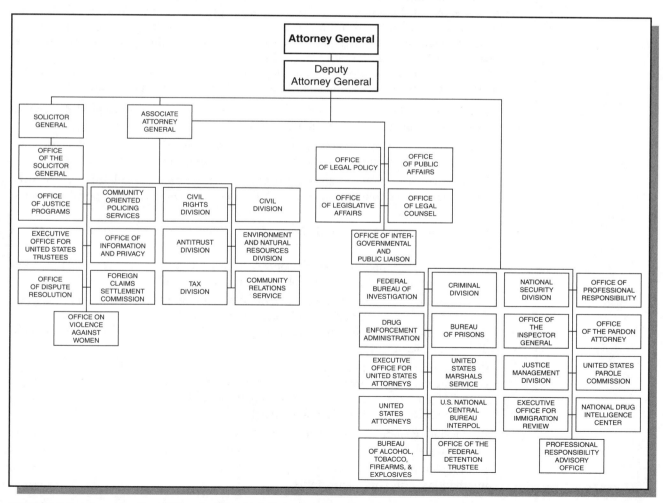

FIGURE 1.6   Organizational Chart of the U.S. Department of Justice.

Source: www.usdoj.gov/dojorg.htm.

Department with a new Alcohol and Tobacco Tax and Trade Bureau. At the time of its transfer to the Department of Justice, the agency's name was changed to the Bureau of Alcohol, Tobacco, Firearms and Explosives (ATF) to reflect its new mission in the Department of Justice.

In order to accomplish its mission, the Bureau of Alcohol, Tobacco, Firearms and Explosives works with local law enforcement to identify, arrest, and prosecute the most violent criminals in designated cities. ATF investigates fire and explosives incidents throughout the United States. ATF is also responsible for enforcing federal criminal laws relating to alcohol and tobacco diversion and trafficking. In addition, ATF's investigative efforts are directed at reducing the source of funding to criminal and terrorist organizations, and stemming the loss of revenue to affected states and the federal government.

Drug Enforcement Administration.   The Drug Enforcement Administration (DEA) was created in 1973 with the merger of the Bureau of Narcotics and Dangerous Drugs with several other federal drug regulation and investigative agencies. It is currently one of the larger federal law enforcement agencies, with 10,894 employees of which 5,296 are special agents. The mission of the DEA is to enforce the controlled substances laws and regulations of the United States and bring to the criminal and civil justice systems of the United States, or any other competent jurisdiction, those organizations and principal members of organizations involved in the growing, manufacture, or distribution of controlled substances appearing in or destined for illicit traffic in the United States; and to recommend and support nonenforcement programs aimed at reducing the availability of illicit controlled substances on the domestic and international markets (Drug Enforcement Administration, 2006).

In carrying out its mission as the agency responsible for enforcing the controlled substances laws and regulations of the United States, the DEA's primary responsibilities include:

Investigation and preparation for the prosecution of major violators of controlled substance laws operating at interstate and international levels.

Investigation and preparation for prosecution of criminals and drug gangs who perpetrate violence in our communities and terrorize citizens through fear and intimidation.

Management of a national drug intelligence program in cooperation with federal, state, local, and foreign officials to collect, analyze, and disseminate strategic and operational drug intelligence information.

Seizure and forfeiture of assets derived from, traceable to, or intended to be used for illicit drug trafficking.

Enforcement of the provisions of the Controlled Substances Act as they pertain to the manufacture, distribution, and dispensing of legally produced controlled substances.

Coordination and cooperation with federal, state, and local law enforcement officials on mutual drug enforcement efforts and enhancement of such efforts through exploitation of potential interstate and international investigations beyond local or limited federal jurisdictions and resources.

Coordination and cooperation with federal, state, and local agencies, and with foreign governments, in programs designed to reduce the availability of illicit abuse-type drugs on the U.S. market through nonenforcement methods such as crop eradication, crop substitution, and training of foreign officials.

Responsibility, under the policy guidance of the Secretary of State and U.S. Ambassadors, for all programs associated with drug law enforcement counterparts in foreign countries.

Liaison with the United Nations, Interpol, and other organizations on matters relating to international drug control programs.

U.S. Marshals Service.   The U.S. Marshals Service is the oldest federal law enforcement agency, having been created by Congress in 1789. While the 94 U.S. Marshals are appointed by the president and approved by Congress, in 1969, the agency's regulations, training, and duties were standardized to ensure uniformity and professionalism among its offices. The Marshals Service is one of the more diverse law enforcement agencies, with a variety of duties that once included conducting the U.S. Census. Today, the U.S. Marshals Service is responsible for apprehending fugitives, protecting federal judges and courts, managing and selling seized assets, transporting prisoners, managing prisoners, protecting witnesses, and serving court documents (United States Marshals Service, 2006).

Federal Bureau of Investigation.   The Federal Bureau of Investigation (FBI) is the primary investigative agency of the federal government and arguably the most famous of the federal law enforcement agencies. The primary responsibility of the FBI is to investigate violations of federal criminal law and to assist local and state agencies in investigations. These include crimes such as kidnapping, bank robbery, art and cultural property crime, jewelry and gem theft; white-collar crime, and organized crime. The FBI is also responsible for investigating corporate fraud, health care fraud, mortgage fraud, identity theft, insurance fraud, telemarketing fraud, Internet fraud, and money laundering.

In addition to the above crimes, the FBI is engaged in counterterrorism activities, counter-intelligence activities, and cyber crime investigations (including stopping those behind serious computer intrusions and the spread of malicious code as well as identifying and thwarting online sexual predators who use the Internet to meet and exploit children and produce, share, or possess child pornography). The FBI also counteracts operations that target U.S. intellectual property and endanger national security and competitiveness.

The FBI's other duties include investigating public corruption at all levels of government; investigating all allegations regarding violations of applicable federal civil rights laws (its Civil Rights program consists of the following subprograms: Hate Crimes, Color of Law/Police Misconduct, Involuntary Servitude/Slavery, and Freedom of Access to Clinic Entrances); and suppressing violent street gangs, motorcycle gangs, and prison gangs. In addition, the FBI has federal law enforcement responsibility on more than 200 of the nation's 267 Indian reservations.

DEPARTMENT OF HOMELAND SECURITY AGENCIES

The Department of Homeland Security was created on November 25, 2002, in an effort to better coordinate efforts to protect the United States from terrorism. Twenty-two federal agencies were either created or transferred into what immediately became the largest federal justice organization. The organizational chart for the Department of Homeland Security is displayed in Figure 1.7. The largest agencies transferred into the Department of Homeland Security were the U.S. Secret Service and the U.S. Customs Service (from the Treasury Department), the Immigration and Naturalization Service and U.S. Border Patrol (from the Department of Justice), the Federal Emergency Management Agency (formerly independent), and the Transportation Security Administration and the U.S. Coast Guard (from the Department of Transportation).

Customs and Border Protection.   U.S. Customs and Border Protection (CBP) is the unified border agency within the Department of Homeland Security (DHS). CBP combined the inspectional workforces and broad border authorities of U.S. Customs, U.S. Immigration, Animal and Plant Health Inspection Service, and the entire U.S. Border Patrol. CBP includes more than 41,000 employees to manage, control, and protect the nation's borders, at and between the official ports of entry. CBP's priority mission is preventing terrorists and terrorist weapons from entering the United States while also facilitating the flow of legitimate trade and travel.

U.S. Customs and Border Protection assesses all passengers flying into the United States from abroad for terrorist risk. The CBP regularly refuses entry to people who may pose a threat to the security of our country. This was not a focus prior to 9/11, but a shift in priorities and the formation of U.S. Customs and Border Protection have made this the top priority of the agency: keeping terrorists and terrorist weapons out of the country (Bureau of Customs and Border Protection, 2006).

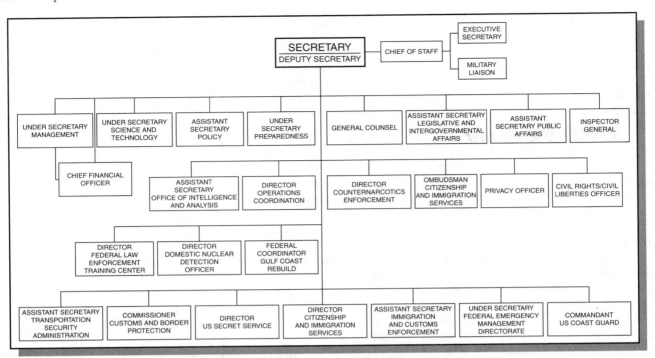

FIGURE 1.7 Organizational Chart of the Department of Homeland Security.

Source: Department of Homeland Security (2006).

Immigration and Customs Enforcement. Created in March 2003, the Immigration and Customs Enforcement (ICE) is the largest investigative branch of the Department of Homeland Security (DHS). The agency was created after 9/11, by combining the law enforcement arms of the former Immigration and Naturalization Service (INS) and the former U.S. Customs Service to more effectively enforce immigration and customs laws and to protect the United States against terrorist attacks. ICE does this by targeting illegal immigrants: the people, money, and materials that support terrorism and other criminal activities.

The ICE mission is to protect America and uphold public safety. ICE attempts to fulfill this mission by identifying criminal activities and eliminating vulnerabilities that pose a threat to our nation's borders, as well as enforcing economic, transportation, and infrastructure security. ICE seeks to eliminate the potential threat of terrorist acts against the United States, creating a host of new systems to better address national security threats and to detect potential terrorist activities in the United States (Bureau of Immigration and Customs Enforcement, 2006).

Transportation Security Administration. The Transportation Security Administration (TSA) was created in response to the terrorist attacks of September 11, 2001, as part of the Aviation and Transportation Security Act that was signed into law by President George W. Bush on November 19, 2001. TSA was originally in the Department of Transportation but was moved to the Department of Homeland Security in March 2003.

TSA's mission is to protect the nation's transportation systems by ensuring the freedom of movement for people and commerce. In February 2002, TSA assumed responsibility for security at the nation's airports and by the end of the year had deployed a federal workforce to meet congressional deadlines for screening all passengers and baggage (Transportation Security Administration, 2006).

The U.S. Coast Guard. The U.S. Coast Guard is a military, multimission, maritime service and may be considered one of the nation's five armed services. Its mission is to protect the public, the environment, and U.S. economic interests—in the nation's ports and waterways, along the coast, on international waters, or in any maritime region as required to support national security.

Its numerous cutters, aircraft, and boats carry out these functions. In wartime, the Coast Guard operates under the aegis of the U.S. Navy.

The U.S. Coast Guard is the nation's leading maritime law enforcement agency and has broad, multifaceted jurisdictional authority. The specific statutory authority for the Coast Guard Law Enforcement mission is given in 14 USC 2, "The Coast Guard shall enforce or assist in the enforcement of all applicable laws on, under and over the high seas and waters subject to the jurisdiction of the United States." In addition, 14 USC 89 provides the authority for U.S. Coast Guard active duty commissioned, warrant, and petty officers to enforce applicable U.S. law. It authorizes Coast Guard personnel to enforce federal law on waters subject to U.S. jurisdiction and in international waters, as well as on all vessels subject to U.S. jurisdiction.

The Coast Guard is responsible for protecting the U.S. Exclusive Economic Zone from foreign encroachment, enforcing domestic fisheries law, and developing and enforcing international fisheries agreements. It is the lead federal agency for maritime drug interdiction and shares lead responsibility for air interdiction with the U.S. Customs Service. As such, it is a key player in combating the flow of illegal drugs to the United States. The Coast Guard is also tasked with enforcing immigration law at sea. It conducts patrols and coordinates with other federal agencies and foreign countries to interdict undocumented migrants at sea, denying them entry via maritime routes to the United States, its territories, and possessions (United States Coast Guard, 2006).

U.S. Secret Service.   The U.S. Secret Service Division began on July 5, 1865, in Washington, D.C., to suppress counterfeit currency. In 1867, Secret Service responsibilities were broadened to include "detecting persons perpetrating frauds against the government." This appropriation resulted in investigations into the Ku Klux Klan, nonconforming distillers, smugglers, mail robbers, land frauds, and a number of other infractions against the federal laws. In 1902, the Secret Service assumed full-time responsibility for protection of the president. In the years since, Secret Service protections have been extended to include former presidents, the president's family, candidates for president, the president-elect, and the vice president.

The passing of the Patriot Act in 2001 (Public Law 107-56) increased the Secret Service's role in investigating fraud and related activity in connection with computers. In addition, it authorized the Director of the Secret Service to establish nationwide electronic crimes task forces to assist law enforcement, private sector, and academia in detecting and suppressing computer-based crime; increased the statutory penalties for the manufacturing, possession, dealing, and passing of counterfeit U.S. or foreign obligations; and allowed enforcement action to be taken to protect American financial payment systems while combating transnational financial crimes directed by terrorists or other criminals. In March 2003, the Secret Service was transferred from the Department of the Treasury to the Department of Homeland Security (United States Secret Service, 2006).

Uniformed Division.   The Secret Service Uniformed Division, initially a force comprised of a few members of the military and the Metropolitan Police Department, began formalized protection of the White House and its grounds in 1860. This unit was under the direction of the White House Military Aide until 1922 when President Warren G. Harding prompted the establishment of a White House police force.

In 1930, Congress placed the supervision of the White House police under the direction of the Chief of the Secret Service. In 1970, Public Law 91-217 expanded the role of the White House police, newly named the Executive Protective Service, to include protection of diplomatic missions in the Washington, D.C., area. Congress later added the protection of the vice president's immediate family as an Executive Protective Service's responsibility in 1974. After several name revisions, the force officially adopted its current name, the United States Secret Service Uniformed Division in 1977. While protection of the White House complex remains its primary mission, the Uniformed Division's responsibilities have expanded greatly over the years.

It now protects the following: the White House complex, the main treasury building and annex, and other presidential offices; the president and members of the immediate family; the temporary official residence of the vice president in the District of Columbia; the vice president and members of the immediate family; and foreign diplomatic missions in the Washington, D.C.,

metropolitan area, and throughout the United States and its territories and possessions, as prescribed by statute (United States Secret Service, 2006).

STATE POLICE AGENCIES   In the United States, state police are a police body unique to each state,
having statewide authority to conduct law enforcement activities and criminal investigations. State
police agencies exist in some form in all U.S. states except Hawaii. In general, they perform functions outside the normal purview of the city police or the county sheriff, such as enforcing traffic
laws on state highway and interstate expressways, overseeing the security of the state capitol
complex, protecting the governor, training new officers for local police forces too small to operate
an academy, providing technological and scientific support services, and helping to coordinate mul-
tijurisdictional task force activity in serious or complicated cases.

Twenty-three states actually call their state police by the term "State Police." In this case,
state police are general-power law enforcement officers with statewide jurisdiction who conduct
patrols and respond to calls for service and perform all the other aforementioned duties. These
states are Alaska, Arkansas, Delaware, Idaho, Illinois, Indiana, Kentucky, Louisiana, Maine,
Maryland, Massachusetts, Michigan, New Hampshire, New Jersey, New Mexico, New York,
Oregon, Pennsylvania, Rhode Island, Vermont, Virginia, and West Virginia.

In the other 25 states (Alabama, Arizona, Connecticut, California, Colorado, Florida, Georgia,
Iowa, Kansas, Minnesota, Mississippi, Missouri, Montana, Nebraska, Nevada, North Carolina, North
Dakota, Ohio, Oklahoma, South Carolina, South Dakota, Tennessee, Texas, Utah, Wisconsin, and
Wyoming) the state police are limited-function traffic enforcement agencies known by any of the fol-
lowing: State Highway Patrol, Highway Patrol, State Patrol State Troopers, or Department of Public
Safety. These agencies are usually complemented by limited-function investigative agencies.
Examples of such and their divergent names are the Arizona Criminal Investigations Bureau,
Colorado Bureau of Investigation, Florida Department of Law Enforcement, Minnesota Bureau of
Criminal Apprehension, Mississippi Criminal Investigation Bureau, North Carolina State Bureau of
Investigation, Ohio Bureau of Criminal Identification and Investigation, the Oklahoma State Bureau
of Narcotics and Dangerous Drugs, South Carolina State Law Enforcement Division, Texas Rangers,
and the Utah Bureau of Organized Crime and Criminal Information.

There are also many other special-purpose state police agencies, such as those devoted to
wildlife, fire, and alcoholic beverage control. Regional special-purpose task forces (e.g., for drug,
gang, or terrorist control) exist at all levels of government. New task forces are constantly being
created and old ones eliminated based on changes in criminal activity, political expediency,
and/or available resources. States that have highway patrols rather than general-service state
police have tended to create investigative agencies patterned after the FBI to investigate violations
of specific state laws and to assist local law enforcement agencies in complex or multicounty
investigations (Conser et al., 2005; O'Conner, 2006).

County Law Enforcement

When people think of county law enforcement, they usually think of a sheriff's office, and there
are about 3,100 sheriffs in the United States (Reaves and Hickman, 2002). Most of them are
elected officials who exercise political control and influence and go to a county board for money.
Some counties (like Orleans Parish in Louisiana) have two sheriffs: one criminal and the other
civil. Sheriffs, in general, have other duties besides law enforcement, such as running a jail,
collecting taxes, serving papers, and courthouse security. A contract system also exists where
cities contract with the sheriff's office for police services.

Not all counties have sheriff's offices. In many states, the larger counties have county police
departments run by a chief of police. In some metropolitan areas, city and county departments
have been consolidated. When such cases occur, there are usually funding problems in continuing
to maintain the sheriff's office, the workload becomes too much for the sheriff, or county officials
want to exert more power over law enforcement. Some counties have both a sheriff's office and
a county police department. In those counties, the sheriff's departments focus on running the

TABLE 1.1 State and Local Law Enforcement Agencies in the United States

Type of Agency	Number of State and Local Law Enforcement Agencies, June 2000
Total	17,784
Local Police	12,666
Sheriff	3,070
Primary State	49
Special Jurisdiction	1,376
Texas Constable	623

Source: Adapted from Reaves and Hickman (2002).

jails and serving civil process and warrants in a manner similar to those states that have general-service state police agencies (O'Conner, 2006).

Municipal Police

There are more municipal police departments (approximately 13,000) in the United States than any other kind of agency (Reaves and Hickman, 2002). This number includes transit, school, and housing police. There are about 800 departments that have only one officer, but NYPD is in a class by itself with about 40,000 regular officers and 13,000 special-purpose transit, school, and housing officers. A complete list of all "special-purpose" police agencies would include animal cruelty, beach, harbor, hospital, housing, port, railroad, sanitation, school, transit, and transportation authorities. These are usually separate municipal-level agencies and should not be confused with specialized units belonging to a single department, such as airborne, band, bicycle, bomb, D.A.R.E., detective, forensics, gang, graffiti, HAZMAT, intelligence, internal affairs, K9, marine, motorcycle, mounted, narcotics, operations, organized crime, sex crimes, SWAT, or traffic.

The vast majority of municipal departments are small, having 10 or fewer officers. The great number of these "micro" agencies helps keep the average size of all police departments in the United States around 25 sworn officers, not counting civilians, a measure of police strength (counting the civilians is a measure of professional growth). Larger, "macro" agencies with 1,000 officers or more usually have many specialized units. More "medium"- to "large"-size agencies with 26–999 (average 150) officers usually maintain extensive order/maintenance functions, assigned to municipal "peacekeeping" agencies in general.

TABLE 1.2 Ten Largest Police Departments by Number of Full-Time Sworn Personnel

Agency	Number of Sworn Officers, June 2000
New York City	40,435
Chicago	13,466
Los Angeles	9,341
Philadelphia	7,024
Houston	5,343
Detroit	4,154
Washington, D.C.	3,612
Nassau Co. (NY)	3,038
Baltimore	3,034
Miami-Dade Co.	3,008

Source: Adapted from Reaves and Hickman (2002).

WHERE THE POLICE "FIT" WITHIN THE U.S. JUSTICE SYSTEM

Where the police fit within the U.S. system of justice depends on who is making the determination. Americans are rightly jealous of their civil liberties, and allowing designated persons to have the authority to make arrests and carry firearms makes many people uneasy. For these reasons, police officers live in "glass houses." They are held to higher moral standards, and their professional actions are scrutinized on a daily basis by the legal community as well as laypersons. How the police are regarded is often influenced by factors over which they have little or no control.

Many citizens tend to view the police as heroes who risk their lives to protect and serve the public. These views are reinforced on those occasions when an officer actually loses his or her life while on duty. There are many others who see the police as abusive and corrupt villains who help maintain an unjust society. Unfortunately, these views are reinforced whenever a corrupt or brutal action on the part of a police officer becomes public knowledge. Fortunately, more enlightened citizens tend to view police officers as ordinary people doing a demanding, often thankless, and occasionally dangerous job.

The roles assigned to various police agencies affect how they are perceived. Local law enforcement agencies have the greater impact on the lives of larger portions of the populace than do state and federal officers. They also tend to be held in less awe than officers at the state and federal levels. How police officers are perceived is also determined by their roles. State and federal agencies generally perform duties that are considered "law enforcement" more than do local police agencies. At the local level, crime fighting is only a portion of a patrol officer's duties. Order maintenance and service responsibilities take up most of his or her time.

Because of their diverse duties, local agencies often have officers with the least experience, education, and training exercising greater discretion and performing some of the more challenging and dangerous duties. This is just one of the realities of police work. Another reality is that the nature of police work will naturally lead to conflict with certain groups of people. Civil libertarians, social activists, trial lawyers, and journalists will always provide challenges for the police. Members of the lower and working classes, young people, and ethnic minorities also provide challenges due to cultural factors as well as social and civil justice issues independent of the police.

The police are necessary for the success of the criminal justice system. As such, they are also vital to the stability of society as a whole. How well they perform as individual officers and as police organizations is determined by many issues that will be discussed within subsequent chapters. As we begin this journey, we wish to address four factors that will ultimately determine where the police fit within the administration of justice in the United States. These factors may be referred to as the *"Four C's" of police–community relations.* They are as follows:

Communication between the police and their communities must be two-way and continuous.

Cooperation between the police and their communities is crucial for success.

Competition between the police and their constituents is detrimental to success. And,

Complacency leads to corruption and cannot be tolerated.

BOX 1.6
To Protect and Serve

Perhaps the most commonly used cliché regarding police work is "to protect and serve." Along with the American flag, this adage may be found on police and sheriff's stationery, logos, and vehicles across the United States. If you wish to engage in an interesting classroom discussion, ask the following questions: Who is being protected? How are they being protected? Who are they being protected from? You will find that the responses are no longer so common. Then ask the following: Who is being served? How are they being served? And lastly, are the services rendered the same for every police organization? We think that you will find that once you move beyond the jargon, there is not as much agreement or understanding as one would suppose.

REALITY CHECK

The Murder of Derwin Brown

Police Captain Derwin Brown was a 23-year veteran of the DeKalb Police Department when he was elected to the position of Sheriff of DeKalb County, Georgia. The sheriff in DeKalb County runs the largest jail in the South, with a budget of $51 million. Brown had run on a platform of cleaning up the corruption and graft that had historically troubled the DeKalb Sheriff's Department. During the period between his election and his assuming office, Brown had announced plans to fire 38 jail employees, most of them appointed by the incumbent sheriff Sidney Dorsey. He had also vowed to conduct an investigation into allegations of racketeering and corruption on the part of Sidney Dorsey and many of his subordinates.

On the evening of December 15, 2000, Brown was shot in front of his home. He was hit 11 times with bullets fired from a Tec-9 handgun and died on the scene. For nearly a year, the investigation stalled and sputtered. But on November 30, 2001, investigators charged three men with his murder. The arrests came just days after former deputy Patrick Cuffy agreed to cooperate and pleaded guilty to a lesser charge in an unrelated shootout at his home in March that left one man dead. Cuffy and Paul Skyers—who worked for a security company owned by incumbent DeKalb County Sheriff Sidney Dorsey—told investigators that they and two other men spent several Friday nights rehearsing Brown's killing, making practice runs to the neighborhood to prepare for the attack and the getaway.

According to Cuffy and Skyers, they had drawn straws with ex-deputy Melvin Walker and David Isaiah Ramsey to determine who would be the triggerman. Walker drew the short straw. On the night of the assassination, Walker stepped from the shadows and opened fire with a Tec-9 semiautomatic pistol. Even more compelling was that Cuffy and Skyers told investigators the men took their orders from Sidney Dorsey, who was angry about losing the election to Brown. Cuffy told investigators that Dorsey had a hit list that included a district attorney and at least four others, and that Dorsey promised the men promotions and jobs if they helped him.

In an acrimonious trial, attorneys for Walker and Ramsey denied that the defendants had anything to do with Brown's death. They accused Cuffy and Skyers of concocting lies about their clients and Dorsey's involvement in order to avoid prosecution for a murder that they themselves actually committed. On March 25, 2002, Walker and Ramsey were acquitted. Dorsey's supporters hailed the verdicts as a victory and predicted that Dorsey would also be acquitted. The district attorney stated that he would honor the immunity deals that he had made with Cuffy and Skyers.

On June 10, 2002, the murder trial of Sidney Dorsey began. The trial was moved to Albany, Georgia, due to pretrial publicity. Jury selection was completed on June 14, 2002. Over the next four weeks, a bizarre story of corruption, extortion, racketeering, thefts, coerced sex, bribery, and misuse of office would emerge. The prosecution would present Sidney Dorsey as a bitter man who had sought revenge against the man who had defeated him and who also wanted to obstruct Brown's expected probe into corruption that occurred during his own tenure as sheriff.

During the trial, the jury learned that Dorsey routinely used deputies to conduct his personal business. He was said to have required deputies to work for his private security business while on duty. He coerced female subordinates and females seeking business contracts with the Sheriff's Department to have sex with him. He had employees run personal errands, including delivering "happy meals" to his son at school and driving his daughter to and from Tennessee, as well as driving family members on a Florida vacation. He also required employees to perform legal work for him and a woman with whom he was having a sexual relationship. According to District Attorney J. Tom Morgan, once he had proven to the jury that Dorsey was a thief, it was much easier to convince them that he was also a murderer.

On July 10, 2002, nearly 19 months after Derwin Brown's death, Sidney Dorsey was convicted of ordering Brown's assassination, two counts of racketeering, one count of violation of oath of office, and eight counts of theft by taking. He was sentenced to life in prison for the murder of

Derwin Brown and an additional 23 years for the other convictions. On May 12, 2004, Dorsey's attorney appealed his convictions. On July 1, 2005, the Georgia Supreme Court upheld the murder and racketeering charges against Dorsey.

On March 30, 2004, Melvin Walker and David Ramsey were indicted on federal civil rights charges of "depriving Derwin Brown of his life without due process of law" as well as gun posses-sion charges. Their federal trial began on July 8, 2005. On August 3, 2005, Walker and Ramsey were convicted on all charges. On November 21, 2005, Walker and Ramsey were each sentenced to life in prison with no chance of parole.

Conclusions

Nations must demonstrate to their citizens that they are able to provide justice in order for their governments to survive. While we may not feel that the justice systems of many nations are actually "just," they must not become too abusive or revolution will occur. Human rights and civil lib-erties are interpreted differently among the nations of the world. The Western democracies and the United States in particular have justice systems based on the protection of civil liberties that utilize due process of law to deprive indi-viduals of their lives, liberties, and properties. The mission of the U.S. justice system is to provide protection from crime and maintain social stability while respecting individ-ual rights. Compliance with the rule of law, equity, fairness, accessibility, effectiveness, and oversight is a fundamental component in achieving justice. We also noted that in order to administer criminal justice, nations must also promote social and civil justice.

The administration of justice in the United States is further complicated by the common-law traditions of indi-vidual liberties, rule of law, and an adversarial legal system. These due process considerations make crime control more difficult for the United States than in other nations. The fed-eralist system also complicates the administration of justice in America. The impacts of federalism and the common-law tradition are felt within all components of the U.S. system of justice. They have particular impacts on the structure and practices of America's police. They also influence where and how the police fit within the U.S. justice system.

Student Checklist

1. Understand why debates regarding the meaning of justice are relevant to students of the police.
2. Why should the police be concerned about protecting the civil rights of American citizens?
3. Explain the impact of the Civil Rights Act of 1871 on actions of police in America.
4. Describe the functions of a justice system in addition to providing "law and order."
5. Describe how the common law system of justice differs from other justice systems.
6. Provide an overview of how America's police system is structured.
7. Identify the more important federal police agencies and describe their responsibilities.
8. Describe how the police "fit" within the U.S. justice system.
9. Explain why the "Four C's" are relevant to police–community relations.

Topics For Discussion

1. Discuss the impact of the U.N.'s Declaration of Human Rights on the nations of the world.
2. Why must students of the police in America understand the importance of the Bill of Rights?
3. Should police officers in America be held criminally liable for violations of citizens' civil liberties?
4. Would the United States be better served by a more centralized system of policing, such as that found in other Western democracies?
5. Has the creation of the Department of Homeland Security enhanced or hindered the coordination of federal law enforce-ment efforts?

Bibliography

Barker, T., Hunter, R. D., and Rush, J. P. (1994). *Police Systems and Practices*. Upper Saddle River, NJ: Pearson/Prentice Hall.

Bohm, R. M., and Haley, K. N. (2005). *Introduction to Criminal Justice*, 4th ed. Boston, MA: McGraw-Hill.

Bureau of Customs and Border Protection. (2006). www.cbp.gov

Bureau of Immigration and Customs Enforcement. (2006). www.bice.immigration.gov

Bureau of Justice Statistics. (2006). www.ojp.usdoj.gov/bjs/

Cole, D. (2004). *No Equal Justice: Race and Class in the American Justice System*. New York: The New Press.

Conser, J. A., Russell, G. D., Paynich, R., and Gingerich, T. E. (2005). *Law Enforcement in the United States*, 2nd ed. Sudbury, MA: Jones and Bartlett.

Crank, J. P. (2003). *Imagining Justice*. Cincinnati, OH: Anderson Publishing.

Dammer, H. R., Fairchild, E., and Albanese, J. S. (2006). *Comparative Criminal Justice Systems*, 3rd ed. Belmont, CA: Thomson/Wadsworth.

Department of Homeland Security. (2006). www.dhs.gov

Drug Enforcement Administration. (2006). www.usdoj.gov/dea

Federal Bureau of Investigation. (2006). www.fbi.gov/hq.htm

Fiorina, M. P., Peterson, P. E., Johnson, B., and Voss, D. S. (2005). *The New American Democracy*, 4th ed. New York: Pearson/Longman.

Fuller, J. R. (2005). *Criminal Justice: Mainstreams and Crossroads*. Upper Saddle River, NJ: Pearson/Prentice Hall.

Grant, H., and Terry, K. J. (2005). *Law Enforcement in the 21st Century*. Boston, MA: Pearson/Allyn and Bacon.

Hess, K. A., and Wrobleski, H. M. (2006). *Police Operations, Theory and Practice*, 4th ed. Belmont, CA: Thomson/Wadsworth.

Hickman, M. J., and Reaves, B. A. (2002). *Local Police Departments, 2000*. NCJ 196002. Washington, D.C.: Bureau of Justice Statistics.

Hunter, R. D., and Dantzker, M. L. (2005). *Crime and Criminality: Causes and Consequences*. Monsey, NY: Criminal Justice Press.

King, M. L., Jr. (1963). *Letter from Birmingham Jail*, April 16.

O'Conner, T. (2006). http://faculty.ncwc.edu/toconnor/polstruct.htm

Packer, H. E. (1968). *The Limits of the Criminal Sanction*. Stanford, CA: Stanford University Press.

Reaves, B. A., and Bauer, L. M. (2003). *Federal Law Enforcement Officers, 2000*, NCJ 199995. Washington, D.C.: Bureau of Justice Statistics.

Reaves, B. A., and Hickman, M. J. (2002). *Census of State and Local Law Enforcement Agencies, 2000*, NCJ 194066. Washington, D.C.: Bureau of Justice Statistics.

Reichel, P. L. (2005). *Comparative Criminal Justice Systems: A Topical Approach*, 4th ed. Upper Saddle River, NJ: Pearson/Prentice Hall.

Reiman, J. (2007). *The Rich Get Richer and the Poor Get Prison*, 8th ed. Boston, MA: Pearson/Allyn and Bacon.

Roberson, C. R., Wallace, H., and Stuckey, G. B. (2007). *Procedures in the Justice System*, 8th ed. Upper Saddle River, NJ: Pearson/Prentice Hall.

Rush, G. (2004). *The Dictionary of Criminal Justice*, 6th ed. Guilford, CT: McGraw-Hill/Dushkin.

Transportation Security Administration. (2006). www.tsa.gov

United Nations. (2007). www.un.org/overview/rights.html

United States Coast Guard. (2006). www.uscg.mil

United States Commission on Civil Rights. (2007). www.usccr.gov

United States Department of Homeland Security. (2007). www.dhs.gov/interweb/assetlibrary/DHS_OrgChart.pdf

United States Department of Justice. (2007). www.usdoj.gov/dojorg.htm

United States Marshals Service. (2006). www.usdoj.gov/marshals

United States Secret Service. (2006). www.secretservice.gov

Van Ness, D., and Strong, K. H. (2006). *Restoring Justice: An Introduction to Restorative Justice*, 3rd ed. Cincinnati, OH: LexisNexis.

Walker, J. T. (2002). "Laws of the state and the state of the law: The relationship between police and law," in Walker, J. T. (Ed.), *Policing and the Law*. Upper Saddle River, NJ: Pearson/Prentice Hall.

Webster's Online Dictionary. (2007). www.websters-online-dictionary.org/definition/justice

Wikipedia. (2007). http://en.wikipedia.org/wiki/Justice

CHAPTER 2

Police Role Concept in a Changing Society

The Policeman is a "Rorschach" in uniform as he patrols his beat. His occupational accoutrements—shield, nightstick, gun, and summons book—clothe him in a mantle of symbolism that stimulates fantasy and projection.

—NIEDERHOFFER, 1967

Variation is basic to all human beings. We might fight less quickly if we looked at it this way and also we might put more energy into finding more harmonious ways to incorporate the differentness.

—SATIR, 1978

KEY CONCEPTS

Crime Control Role	Generalization	Perception
Crime-Fighting Model	Objectivity	Role Concept
Deletion	Order Maintenance	Service Role
Distortion	Role	Subjectivity

LEARNING OBJECTIVES

Studying this chapter will enable you to:

1. Define *perception* and *role conflict*.

2. Identify and explore conflicting perceptions that exist regarding the role of police officers in the community.

3. Identify major elements necessary to the success of programs designed to assist officers in achieving realistic role concepts and improved service to and participation in the community.

4. Describe the factors and conditions of change in our society.

5. Identify and describe some of the paradoxes and dilemmas that our changing society creates for the police officer.

In the previous chapter, we discussed where the police fit within the American system of justice as well as within society as a whole. The nature of police officers' relationships with members of various communities will be detailed in the following chapters. This chapter will examine how the police view themselves within our constantly changing and increasingly complex society. We will also discuss how individuals, groups, and organizations within society may view the police. These views of who officers are and what they do (or are supposed to do) may be defined as the roles of the police.

Roles are distinct behavior patterns acted out in connection with a particular social position. Roles are either *ascribed* (not under the person's control) or *achieved* (attained voluntarily). Examples of ascribed roles include male, female, and infant; examples of achieved roles include husband, wife, and teacher. Roles provide us with ways of categorizing and anticipating the behavior of others. They assist us in deciding how to act in relationship to others and help to give order to our world. One person plays many roles, and sometimes these roles conflict. The Hispanic American police officer, for instance, may be faced with role conflict because he or she is both Hispanic American and an officer, and he or she has difficulty in reconciling the two. Conflict might also occur in other ways: (1) the expectations of others regarding behaviors appropriate to a role may be different from the expectations of the role incumbent; (2) the expectations of others might vary widely, making it very difficult for the role incumbent to be successful in that role; or (3) the "official" and working definitions of the role are contradictory. The police role includes all of these contradictions.

Ask anyone. A police officer is a "crime fighter," or a "human service worker," or a "knight in blue," or the "power arm of the Establishment," or a "dumb cop," or a "competent professional." Ask a police officer. What will he or she say they are? This chapter identifies and accounts for some of the conflicting perceptions that exist regarding the police role.

GREAT EXPECTATIONS

Police officers in today's society are expected not only to apprehend bank robbers and murderers, but they are also expected to direct traffic, transport the sick and injured to the hospital, help schoolchildren cross streets, patrol polling places on election day, provide shelter and care for drunks and drug abusers, investigate accidents, settle family disputes, locate missing and runaway children, and a host of other things. They must be all things to all people. They are the only all-purpose emergency service in society (Doerner, 2004). As such, they respond to all situations in which "something-that ought-not-to-be-happening-and-about-which-someone-had-better-do-something-now!" (Bittner, 1970). They are expected not only to enforce the law, maintain order, and resolve disputes but also to do so in a scrupulously fair manner, no matter what sort of verbal or physical abuse might be directed toward them.

When they gather evidence or apprehend criminals, police must never violate an offender's constitutional rights under penalty of having the evidence suppressed in court. They must be professionally detached from the violence and tragedy that they encounter on their daily tour of duty. They are expected not only to be honest and fair in fact but also to give a constant appearance of honesty and fairness. They must have a professional knowledge of criminal law in order to ensure that the rights of those they apprehend are protected. They must be prepared to manage conflicts and to deal swiftly and appropriately with almost every manner of crisis our society has invented.

The relationship between police and the citizens they are sworn to serve is a close one. As the President's Commission on Law Enforcement and the Administration of Justice observed:

> It is hard to overstate the intimacy of the contact between the police and the community. Policemen deal with people when they are both most threatening and most vulnerable, when they are angry, when they are frightened, when they are desperate, when they are drunk, when they are violent, or when they are ashamed. Every police

action can affect in some way someone's dignity, or self-respect, or sense of privacy, or constitutional rights. As a matter of routine, policemen become privy to, and make judgments about, secrets that most citizens guard jealously from their closest friends: relationships between husbands and wives, the misbehavior of children, personal eccentricities, peccadilloes, and lapses of all kinds. Very often policemen must physically restrain or subdue unruly citizens. (President's Commission on Law Enforcement and the Administration of Justice, 1967, pp. 91–92)

Perhaps that is why the officer often is viewed so subjectively. The perception of what the role of a police officer in society is and should be varies considerably depending on who is doing the perceiving and under what circumstances judgment is made.

PERCEPTION

Seeing and Perceiving

Man is not disturbed by events, but by the view he takes of them.

—Epictetus

How often have you heard such statements as these?

Well, this is the way I see it.

I suppose that is just the way he sees it.

I have to respond the way I see it.

I suppose you have to act in accordance with the way you see it.

Perception is more than receiving visual stimulation, or sensing something. It is actually a process of creating meaning out of what we hear, see, smell, taste, and feel (our sensations, or sensory experience) and using the sense that we make of the world as the basis for our actions. As used in the examples above, the word "see" also implies more than a visual sensation. "To see" can mean to believe, to understand, and to make sense of, as well as to view. Sometimes we use the word "see" when we actually mean "perceive."

Perception Is Personal

It is unlikely that two people, even at a given time and place, will perceive the same event in exactly the same way. Every police officer knows that eyewitness accounts, however sincere, may vary widely and be inaccurate (Loftus, 1996; Zalman and Seigel, 1999). On occasion, mistaken eyewitness testimony can lead to wrongful convictions. In 1999, the Innocence Project examined the 62 DNA exonerations that had taken place up to that time and concluded that mistaken eyewitness testimony was a factor in 84 percent of those wrongful convictions (Poveda, 2001, pp. 689–708).

Creating meaning from sensations requires a judgment call. Several elements combine to set the context, or the frame of reference, within which a person makes such a judgment call. Attention, knowledge, past experiences, and present motives or needs all help to shape the way a person perceives (or perhaps misperceives). The relatively stable and predictable set of habits by which the person manages day-to-day living under ordinary conditions (personality) influences perception.

Behavior is closely linked to perception. Our actions are based on the world as we believe it to be.

Donna Allen pulls her van over to the curb and steps out to the sidewalk to ask directions from Joan Patrick, who is walking toward her. Before Joan finishes giving Donna the directions she asked for, both women look up simultaneously and see a huge lion approaching them. "A lion!" screams Joan, as she turns and runs in the opposite direction as fast as she can. "Stop!" yells Donna, but Joan is soon out of earshot. Donna then walks to the lion, gently strokes his mane to indicate that all is well, takes the lion to the back of the van, and orders him to leap into the van, which the lion does. Donna then closes the tailgate of the van, climbs into the driver's seat, and continues on her way, regretting that Joan did not take time to give her sufficient directions to reach her destination. She would undoubtedly have to stop again and ask directions, which might make her late for her performance at the circus.

In this example, the objective experience of the two women was the same, but they had different perceptual experiences. Objective experience can be standardized and agreed upon by most people. Donna and Joan would agree that they saw an animal approach and the animal was a lion. The lion's appearance on the sidewalk as the two women talked was an objective experience. The perceptual experiences of the two women can be implied by observing their behavior as the lion approached them. Joan saw the lion as dangerous and a threat to her well-being and ran away in fright. Donna did not see the lion as a threat but showed affection toward the lion and concern that the lion might be upset. Her behavior was to comfort the lion, and her most outstanding concern was to get to her destination as soon as possible.

It is possible to analyze this situation in terms of *knowledge, past experience*, and *need*. Donna was acquainted with the lion, and since she was the lion's trainer, she knew that the lion was not dangerous and was no threat to either of the two women. Joan did not have this knowledge and was therefore afraid of the lion. Donna had obviously had experience with this particular lion and perhaps other lions and probably tended to "see" lions in general in a different way than did Joan. Joan's past experience with lions primarily consisted of indirect experiences, such as seeing lions in the zoo, in movies, and on television; in most of those instances, the lions she had seen were portrayed as being dangerous and threatening. Those in the zoo were locked up, and those in the movies and on television were always attacking someone or some other animal. Joan had no need in relationship to the experiencing of the lion other than the need for survival. She perceived that her survival was threatened at that moment; thus, her need for survival was really why she chose to run. Donna's most outstanding need of the moment was related to her desire to put on a good performance at the circus and to reach the circus in time for that performance. Consequently, the temperament of the lion was very important to her, so she proceeded to comfort the lion, to load him back into the van, and to drive off as rapidly as she could, hopefully in the direction of the circus.

Richard Bandler and John Grinder theorized how perception comes about. They claim that **generalization**, **deletion**, and **distortion** are psychological processes common to all people. These are ways in which we make sense of and survive in the world. "The processes which allow us to accomplish the most extraordinary and unique human activities are the same processes which block our further growth if we commit the error of mistaking the model for the reality" (Bandler and Grinder, 1975, p. 14).

Generalization is the psychological process whereby a person detaches some part of one model from an original experience and then applies this model to represent an entire category. A common example is experiencing an ice cube. When a person touches an ice cube for the first time, he or she learns that ice cubes are cold. As part of learning about the world, it will be helpful to this person to generalize that other ice cubes are also cold. However, if he or she refused to touch ice cubes after that original experience, generalizing that cold is painful to touch, the generalization could be a hindrance.

"*Deletion* is a process by which we selectively pay attention to certain dimensions of our experience and exclude others" (Bandler and Grinder, 1975, p. 15). People have the ability to filter out experiences while concentrating on a model. The coach, for example, watching the video replay of his basketball team's victory, screens out (deletes) all the activity on the basketball court except the behaviors of the team members and the opponents. He deletes the behavior of the cheerleaders and everyone else in the gym. Although through deletion the coach is able to pinpoint specific information that he might have otherwise missed, he loses the flavor added by the spectators, the band, and the cheerleaders, because he has deleted this dimension of his experience. The coach's perception could get him into trouble when his wife, the band director, asks him later how he enjoyed the victory song played by the band and the coach has no recollection of the experience.

Distortion is the third modeling process, and it allows us to make shifts in our experience of sensory data (Bandler and Grinder, 1975, p. 16). An actress onstage distorts as she exaggerates her movements and sounds. This is a useful form of distortion because it allows the audience to experience the performance in a rich and fantasized fashion. If, however, once offstage, the same actress rushes to the telephone and tearfully reports to the police an exaggerated version of a disagreement between her and her husband, the shift in her experience of sensory data will not be positively useful.

Perception issues exist between police and community groups. In most cases, the officer on the beat perceives the behavior of citizens differently from the way they perceive their own situation, circumstances, and behavior. Citizens may perceive the police officer's role, purpose, and behavior quite differently from the way the police officer does. The factors responsible for such differences in perception are the same as outlined in the previous discussion:

1. Differences in past experience, and sets of habits.
2. Knowledge.
3. Individual needs relative to the situation in question through the modeling processes of generalization, distortion, and deletion.

Consider another example:

John, age twenty-five, has lived all of his life in a suburban area near a large U.S. city. Roy, also age twenty-five, has lived all of his life in an inner-city neighborhood of that same large U.S. city where confrontations between police and youth have escalated to violence several times in the last few years. John and Roy are walking together on a sidewalk within that inner-city area when they see a police officer, on foot, approaching them. As the officer draws nearer, he nods his head in greeting and smiles. John responds, "Good morning, Officer," and returns his smile. As the officer passes, John becomes aware that Roy looks uncomfortable. He recalls that Roy at first did not look at the officer. But after he had said, "Good morning," Roy had looked up at the officer with a tremendous frown on his face and a look of contempt in his eyes. Roy neither spoke to the officer nor returned his smile. John is puzzled; he cannot understand Roy's reaction. To John, the officer was obviously trying to be pleasant. He did not offend John or Roy, and he showed no indication of ill will toward them. Yet Roy finds it very difficult to understand John's behavior because just as Roy was beginning to trust John, John demonstrated to Roy that he was inclined to be friendly with police officers. John feels that Roy now believes John is "not to be trusted"; when the chips are down, John is on the side of the cop.

Is John's perception of Roy in this instance "true"? Or is Roy's perception of John "true"? Whether these perceptions are true or not, the perceptual experiences of the two men in this instance are nevertheless quite real, and capable of affecting their attitudes toward each other, their ability to trust each other, and the way they behave toward each other in the future.

Another question to be asked is this: Why did Roy and John react differently toward the same objective experience—the approaching of a police officer who greeted them with a friendly smile? First, although the police officer was looking at both of the men when he gave his nod of greeting and smiled, Roy perceived that he was not smiling at him at all. Throughout his life, Roy's only relationships with police officers have been negative ones. Roy has generalized from these experiences to avoid police officers at all costs. He has distorted reality and perceives that "the only purpose of the police is to control, not to protect." Roy perceives that what the police mean by control is to "keep people from the inner city in their place," "prevent them from expressing themselves," "deprive them of most of the nicer things in life," and so forth. Roy's past experiences with police officers have included their frequent questioning of him about crimes committed—crimes that he knew nothing about. In fact, Roy has never committed a crime in his life. In the past, however, police officers have taken him down to the precinct station and applied pressure to get him to "finger" friends who have been accused of crimes. On several occasions, when Roy indicated to them that he knew nothing about whether or not the person involved had committed a crime, he was told that if he did not cooperate, little or no mercy would be shown to him by the police when they caught him in a crime (which they seemed to feel was inevitable).

The police officers who have taken Roy down to the station to question him may be distorting objective reality in much the same fashion that Roy does. The officers may be generalizing from past experience, assuming that Roy's behavior will be similar to the behavior of others in their experience. The officers may be deleting the objective reality about Roy (that he is a law-abiding citizen, for instance) and, instead, be distorting the scowl that appeared on Roy's face when he saw the officers approaching to mean that Roy is guilty. In fact, Roy may be in the process of generalizing from his own past experience about police officers.

Moreover, Roy has never heard any of his friends indicate that they had ever been protected by police officers. His friends always talked about the police as the "enemy." Roy is often afraid as he walks down a street after leaving the movies. He is afraid of other people who might rob or take advantage of persons walking alone on the street late at night. Roy has caught himself on many occasions wishing that there were a police department that would protect him from such hoodlums. Yet, he has never felt that any police officer saw this as his role. Through his own experiences and conversations with his friends, Roy has come to view the police as the most definitive instrument of an oppressing society, deployed not only to protect the rest of society *from* him but to keep him *down* in every way.

In contrast to Roy's past experiences with the police, John had always been taught that police officers were his friends. John read about the helpful police in storybooks; police officers came to his schools, and even one of his father's best friends was a police lieutenant who lived in the area. John remembers the time when his family returned from a vacation and discovered that their house had been burglarized. They called the police, and after the house had been searched, it was discovered that the only missing item was $50, which John's mother had placed in an envelope and left on the coffee table before leaving. After the police had talked to John's parents, one of the officers said, "Don't worry, Mr. and Mrs. Jones, we have sufficient evidence. We will get the thief, and your $50 will be returned." As John grew up, he became friends with a few police officers, who went out of their way to be nice to him. On a few occasions, he had been stopped by police officers for speeding or committing some minor traffic violation. However, he seldom received a ticket, only a warning that usually ended in "I'm going to let you go this time, but be careful. We want you to get wherever you are going safely." In general, John has always thought of police officers as his friends and that the chief role of the police in the community is to protect citizens.

Because of these past experiences, John and Roy responded differently to the smiling policeman as he approached them on the sidewalk. Their different behaviors were obviously based on their different perceptions. Their different perceptions were in turn based on the differences between them in terms of past experiences with the police, their habits, knowledge of the situation that they were in at the moment, personal needs, distortion, generalization, and deletion.

John and Roy were both reacting to reality as it impinged upon them. Each person's perceptual experience is "reality." Because perceptual experience is not altogether a conscious phenomenon, many individuals would be at a loss if they were asked to explain why they understand life the way they do. In the case of the smiling police officer, Roy could not have readily explained to John why his perception of the officer's behavior was negative. Similarly, John could not have readily explained to Roy why he perceived the officer's behavior to be positive. Still, each one acted in what he believed to be his own best interest, based on his understanding of reality.

Perceptions of the police function differ in the ghetto, the middle- and upper-middle-class suburbs, the political arena, the police briefing room, and so on. Some people see the police as their personal instruments for ending or reducing crime on the street to ensure their personal safety. Others see police as an instrument of society with the somewhat broader aim of maintaining a degree of harmony, consistency, and peace (whatever the latter has come to mean in today's world). Some people have a more restricted view of the police, seeing them as an agency to suppress underprivileged and minority segments of society. Still others perceive the police as an agency by which dominant society confines and reinforces the boundaries of ghettos and minority groups. The police are also viewed as being so helplessly caught within social class, racial, and political factions that they are utterly stymied in their work but are made scapegoats for the ills that are inevitable in a society torn by conflict. It is doubtful that any two people selected at random would completely agree as to what a police officer does (or should do).

ROLE CONCEPT

A role may be defined as a set of behavioral expectations and obligations associated with a position in a social structure or organization (Cox and Fitzgerald, 1999). These expectations can be framed in an objective, dispassionate manner; a subjective, totally personal manner; or in some modification of these two approaches.

Objectivity as an approach requires the observer to determine, study, and weigh facts in an unbiased, scientific manner, setting aside preconceived notions and personal prejudices and preferences. In this approach, conclusions are drawn from the facts. Any conclusion not borne out by evidence that is objectively based is not acceptable.

Subjectivity, on the other hand, is not concerned with objective fact, and even an awareness by the subjective observer of such fact does not guarantee an objective conclusion. Facts are redefined by the observer in terms of his or her personal life experiences, biases, assumptions, dreams, and fears. Individual judgment is based on how a person feels about what he or she sees and how the person believes what he or she sees relates to him or her. Although others may consider his or her view unrealistic, given the world as he or she understands it, his or her expectations are logical. Most expectations held by most people are, to some degree, subjectively derived.

THE POLICE OFFICER'S ROLES

Crime Control

> Ask a retiring officer to tell you about his best memories. He'll probably recall stories of high-speed pursuits, shoot-outs, fights, or chasing someone on foot. Ask a new rookie what he likes about being a cop, and he'll say things like "putting the bad guys in jail." The fact is, most officers see their role as a crime fighter. (Trautman, 1991, p. 16)

Very few, if any, would argue with the statement that a core mission of the police is to control crime. The police do have, and we expect them to perform, a crime control role. However, the police and the public often see crime control as the total responsibility of the police. Furthermore, the police and the public see the crime control role of the police as the only role the police should perform. This myopic view of the police and their role has a significant impact on policing as an occupation and on the performance of individual officers as actors in the criminal justice system.

The exclusive image of the **crime control role** of the police embodied in the "crime fighter" image has serious consequences on the police and their behavior. Crime and its control are not the sole responsibility of the police. The police did not create nor can they control the social conditions that create crime. At best, the law and the criminal justice system are poor controllers of human behavior. As long as we see crime control as the primary role of the police, we fail to recognize that crime is a social phenomenon and that crime prevention is the responsibility of society, communities, and a host of other social institutions. In addition to creating unrealistic expectations about the police's ability to contend with crime, this narrow view prevents an informed analysis of the other important roles assigned to the police (Walker and Katz, 2002).

Order Maintenance

The crime control role involves all those functions of arrest and detection of law violators as well as those behaviors devoted to crime prevention (e.g., preventive patrol). However, as Wilson (1968, p. 4) pointed out, less than one-third of all police radio calls involve criminal matters that may result in an arrest, and only about 5 percent of all cases actually result in an arrest. It is the **order maintenance role** that is more central to the modern police officer's job than any other aspect of his or her behavior. Most recent studies support the assertion by Wilson that the role of a patrol officer "is defined more by his responsibility for maintaining order than by his responsibility for enforcing the law" (Wilson, 1968, p. 16).

Order maintenance activities may consist simply of officers being seen so as to provide a sense of security or as an aid in promoting the public peace. It may consist of monitoring the activities of individuals engaging in behavior that, if allowed to "get out of hand," could result in inconvenience or annoyance for other citizens. It can involve restoration of order in disorderly or potentially disorderly situations. It can be actual intervention into disputes between individuals or groups that, if unchecked, could lead to serious violations of the law. Most of these activities do not involve actual enforcement of laws. Those situations in which legal conditions for arrests do exist are dealt with through mediation or warnings in lieu of arrest (Wrobleski and Hess, 2006).

Service

In addition to their crime control and order maintenance roles, the police spend a great deal of time performing service activities. This role is second only to order maintenance in importance. The duties and responsibilities that fall within this category include many activities that may appear to be only peripherally related to the direct police services of patrol, investigations, traffic control, and the police mission of preventing crime and disorder (Barker, Hunter, and Rush, 1994). Providing emergency rescue services, working traffic accidents, unlocking locked cars, jump-starting stalled vehicles, and helping people in distress are but a few of the many services routinely provided by the police. Also, as we shall see in Chapter 12, the police as first responders provide numerous services to special populations, particularly the elderly. The **service role** is vitally important to the police in an era of community policing because it shows that the police and the law-abiding community can work together to solve problems and meet needs.

Many of the services performed by the police are not inherent to the police mission but have become police services by default. Because the police are available 24 hours a day and no one else has emerged to perform a specific task, that task may come to be seen within a particular community as a police responsibility. In addition to being the only 24/7 (hours/days), 365-days-a-year general emergency service public agency, they are society's only 24/7, 365-days-a-year all-purpose social service public agency.

Other Roles

In addition to the three roles discussed above, other duties are also performed by the police (see Table 2.1). Whereas Cordner (1992) argues that information gathering could legitimately be classified as a law enforcement duty, others argue that it is more appropriately a service or even an order maintenance function. Still others (Barker, Hunter, and Rush, 1994) consider information gathering to be a separate role that falls partially within all three. Since the majority of police reports are taken primarily for insurance purposes, we will classify information gathering as a distinct role.

Yet another police role that is contained partially within the duties of crime control, order maintenance, and service is that of protection of individual rights. The police in the United States and other democracies are responsible not only for protecting society from individual behavior but also for ensuring that the constitutional rights of all citizens are upheld (Conser et al., 2005).

TABLE 2.1 Twenty-Five Most Frequent Types of Calls for Service

Type of Call for Service	Frequency	Percent
1 Suspicious Activity Calls	13,436	10.2
2 Burglary Alarm Calls	8,867	6.7
3 Loud Music/Noise/Party Calls	8,586	6.5
4 Traffic Accident Calls	8,311	6.3
5 Check Welfare Calls	7,708	5.8
6 9-1-1 Hangup Calls	5,990	4.5
7 Theft/Burglary from Vehicle Calls	5,948	4.5
8 Criminal Information Calls	5,185	3.9
9 Agency Assist Calls	4,320	3.3
10 Theft Calls	3,888	2.9
11 Illegal Parking Calls	3,825	2.9
12 Criminal Damage Calls	3,228	2.4
13 Stolen Vehicle Calls	3,161	2.4
14 Family Fight Calls	3,128	2.4
15 Burglary Calls	2,974	2.3
16 Stranded Motorist Calls	2,852	2.2
17 Fight Calls	2,066	1.6
18 Subject Disturbing Calls	2,039	1.5
19 Trespassing Calls	1,697	1.3
20 Shoplifting Calls	1,509	1.1
21 Assault Calls	1,498	1.1
22 Incorrigible Juvenile Calls	1,449	1.1
23 Unwanted Guest Calls	1,304	1.0
24 Threat Calls	1,198	0.9
25 Traffic Hazard Calls	1,189	0.9
All Other Calls	26,692	20.2
	132,048	**100.0**

Source: What Police Do (Police Workload in Tempe, Arizona, 2003). Tempe Police Department, 2006 (http://www.tempe.gov/police/AnnualReport2003/CallsForServiceInfo03.htm).

POLICE ROLE CONFLICT

In the preceding section, we discussed the various roles assigned to police officers within a typical police agency. The extent to which these complex and often contradictory roles are carried out varies considerably among police agencies, due to their nature, tradition, size, location, mission, and the orientation of the community served. In addition, considerable variation within agencies is due to different role outlooks among individual officers. As discussed earlier, the police are affected by both external and internal groups. Individual perceptions and political ideologies also influence the behavior of police officers (Walker and Katz, 2002).

Traditionally, the literature on policing has focused on four individual styles that were derived from Wilson's (1968) departmental roles. This typology consists of *crime fighters, social agents, law enforcers,* and *watchmen* (Peak, 2006). The *crime fighter* or "cowboy" is an officer who views himself or herself as primarily a serious crime investigator. Lesser offenses and noncriminal duties are seen as trivial and not worthy of police attention. The *social agent* views policing as a combination of crime control, order maintenance, and provision of services; law enforcement duties are considered an important but only a minimal portion of their overall duties. The *law enforcer* or "legalist" is similar to the crime fighter in that he or she tends to emphasize crime control. However, the law enforcer differs from the crime fighter in that all statutes, ordinances, and regulations are felt to be important and require strict enforcement. The *watchman* is dedicated to preserving social and political order within the community. He or she will enforce the laws to the extent necessary to maintain the peace.

The four categories described above are not believed by many police scholars to adequately present the variations among individual officers in regard to role perceptions. In response to such criticisms, Broderick (1987) developed a classification scheme that attempts to categorize officers based on personality type rather than on a particular police style. His typology is useful in assessing individual behavior patterns but is less rigid in predicting performance. Broderick's categories include *enforcers, idealists, realists*, and *optimists*.

Enforcers are concerned primarily with keeping the streets "clean" and ensuring that citizens behave properly. They see themselves as protecting the "good people" from the "bad people." Most enforcers would be considered authoritarians who perceive citizens as either hostile or apathetic toward them. *Idealists* are committed to the law and the rights of citizens. They see themselves as professionals who better serve the public than do their more authoritarian and/or less dedicated colleagues. Frustration with the "system" often drives these individuals into other careers or causes them to become realists. *Realists* tend to be cynical and dissatisfied with society and the criminal justice system. As a defense mechanism, they have stopped caring about their role as police officers and generally do only what is required to stay out of trouble. Realists often seek transfers to assignments where they can "hide out" and be left alone by both the public and other police officials. *Optimists* see themselves as service providers who are performing an important societal function. They view themselves, their colleagues, and the public in a positive manner. Although aware that they alone cannot change the world, they are willing to do their part. Officers often do not fit in any one of these categories and may occasionally shift categories during their careers.

As if the contradictory perceptions on the part of individual officers were not complicated enough, debates regarding the role of the police in a democratic society confuse the issue further. As seen by Roberg, Novak, and Cordner (2005), these debates include the following:

Do rigid bureaucratic rules or responsiveness to political demands best serve the public interest?

Should police be concerned with preserving community norms or strict compliance with laws?

Is the police occupation a professional activity or a craft?

Are officers to emphasize their duties as crime fighters or social service workers?

Should the police be more concerned with crime prevention or the apprehension of criminals?

Should police activities be of a proactive or reactive nature?

The manner in which public officials, community leaders, and police officials resolve their differences in regard to these debates influences the organization's values and goals and determines those tasks and activities that will be emphasized by that police agency.

The consequences of contradictory views on the part of individual police officers, police administrators, public officials, and community leaders cause more confusion (and often conflict) than consensus in regard to the role of the police.

FORMATION OF ROLE CONCEPTS

The Sources of Role Concepts

Role concepts have their sources in needs and past experiences. Because both of these can vary widely from group to group and individual to individual, so can role concepts.

Three major factors affect the way individuals and groups in society perceive the role of the police officer:

1. The individual's or group's specific needs and problems.
2. The individual's or group's personal experiences with police officers.
3. The image of police officers created by various media.

If expectations are unrealistic, so is the role concept, and it will become further distorted if the unrealistic expectations are repeatedly unmet.

Some people, for instance, have often experienced oppression by the police. If a particular neighborhood has a severe crime problem and the police are not solving it, residents will conclude that police either cannot or do not want to fulfill the community's needs—in other words, unfulfilled needs and past experience have induced the community to expect little of the police. Based on that expectation, residents may withhold community cooperation from law enforcement, thus compounding the problem and further strengthening the negative role concept.

Lack of Information

Sometimes, lack of accurate citizen information regarding police efforts can lead to unreasonable expectations on the part of an individual or a group in the community. For example, an area of a city might be plagued with assaults and robberies. The police in that area may respond by increasing routine patrol, increasing foot patrol in business areas, and generally focusing most of their efforts on that current problem. Personnel shortages may prevent ideal service to other, less immediate problems, such as juveniles racing cars in the streets. The citizens may not be aware of the increased efforts of the police in the assault and robbery areas. When complaints are made about juveniles racing cars in the streets, the citizens may conclude that the police are negligent if they take longer than usual to respond to the call.

How Police Respond

To understand the problems involved in creating and maintaining positive role expectations for the police, consider the three outcomes that are possible when a law enforcement problem arises:

1. *The problem is confronted and solved.* This creates the expectation that the police will do the same again, if and when necessary. Note, however, that in the familiar area of enforcing traffic laws, the police often are attributed with a negative role concept due to their effective actions.
2. *The problem is confronted but not solved.* Naturally, this often has a negative impact on the police role concept, but the police may have no way of preventing certain problems (ranging from murder to domestic arguments); citizens who believe otherwise have unrealistic expectations.
3. *The problem is not confronted.* The usual reason is that the problem (trash removal, street and light maintenance, etc.) is the responsibility of some other agency. Nevertheless, the citizen may feel it is due to police failure to provide service.

Thus, in at least two of the three cases just described, observers are likely to adopt a negative role concept of the police, even though the expectations on which that concept is based are unrealistic or mistaken.

THE MEDIA AND ROLE CONCEPTS

In the United States today, the media play a very important part in forming expectations about the police. Thus, many people evaluate the actions of police officers against criteria formed by TV or movie scriptwriters. If preconceived ideas regarding the police role are challenged by a reality that contradicts what people believe to be true, will they choose to believe the reality? Unfortunately, the answer is not always yes.

The police officers of Hollywood lore are fictional images of police stereotypes that have been exaggerated to provide entertainment to a bored public. That public (and indeed, the police themselves) tend to accept the images created by scriptwriters and portrayed by actors and actresses who have little or no knowledge of what police officers actually do. The result is the creation of mythical police roles that have only a limited basis in reality.

Holden (1992) identified six police stereotypes that have either been created or perpetuated by the entertainment media. The first and perhaps oldest media image of the police is that of the buffoon. This characterization began in early movies such as *The Keystone Kops* and continues in present-day television and movie depictions. A second image is not as extreme as the buffoon but tends to present police officers as slow-witted and unprofessional dullards who need the guidance of smart citizens (à la Sherlock Holmes, Mrs. Columbo, or Jessica Fletcher of *Murder, She Wrote*) to solve crimes. A third type, the sadist, abuses his or her police authority to perpetuate evil acts. Such characters were aptly portrayed by Richard Gere in *Internal Affairs*, Ray Liotta in *Unlawful Entry*, and Michael Chiklis in *The Shield*. A fourth image is that of the hero who fights the bad guys (and often police superiors and the criminal justice system) to protect the innocent from evil. Mel Gibson in the *Lethal Weapon* series and Bruce Willis in the *Die Hard* series exemplify such heroes. A fifth character is the *wizard*, a supercop who solves challenging cases utilizing his or her superior intellect and/or technical expertise. These images are exemplified in the several *CSI* television shows in which individuals perform the tasks of investigators and forensic scientists. Finally, we are presented with the harassed professional who is highly competent but overworked and underappreciated. The characters of *NYPD Blue* and *Law and Order* would fall within this category.

In addition to the foregoing roles depicted by the entertainment media, the public is influenced considerably by the news media. Media attention (TV, newspapers, radio, and magazines) comes to police agencies for the police's crime-fighting role rather than its service role (the former makes better copy). Depicting the police negatively as misusing deadly force, police prejudice, or police corruption is also newsworthy. The amount of emphasis given to police actions and the media's interpretation of these actions as either proper or improper have a tremendous effect on the public's perception of the police. It has been argued that media coverage can transform a local incident into a national crisis (Grant and Terry, 2005). We doubt that anyone watching the media coverage of the 1999 murders of several students at Columbine High School in Littleton, Colorado, would question that assertion.

FACTORS AND CONDITIONS OF CHANGE

Reassessing the Dimensions

Traditionally, obedience to the law, ethical behavior, and moral decisions have been bound and intertwined into an absolute adherence based on extremes of legal versus illegal, good versus bad, and right versus wrong. Situations were black and white, or at least they appeared to be. In small rural, agriculturally based communities, a police officer could make decisions based on the relatively fixed value system of the majority. It was not that minorities did not exist, but rather that they were usually not vocal and, for the most part, not counted separately.

Since the end of World War II, however, the continuing struggle between tradition and change, between fixed values and no values, and between simple lives and complex living has seen tradition slowly dying. At the same time, people have not been able to adapt as quickly as the technology surrounding them. They are somewhat bewildered by a growing shrinkage of space and time and a negative relationship between the two. They find the so-called knowledge and information explosions threatening to overwhelm them. They find that the emergence of electronic controls creates what might be called "electronic amorality." The struggle for survival takes on new dimensions, and fixed value systems are seriously questioned and sometimes abandoned.

Never before have philosophers and peace officers, politicians, and the public been so carefully and sincerely reexamining the dimensions and limits of liberty, freedom, and democracy as living entities. Some years ago, George Orwell stated this:

> The point is that the relative freedom which we enjoy depends on public opinion, the law is no protection. The governments make laws, but whether they are carried out, and how the police behave, depends upon the general temper of the country. If large numbers of people are interested in freedom of speech, there will be freedom of speech even if the law forbids it; if public opinion is sluggish, inconvenient minorities will be persecuted, even if laws exist to protect them. (Orwell, 1963)

Milton Mayer, a philosopher and commentator on humankind in a democracy, in his *Liberty: Man versus State* commented on the many perceptual facets of liberty: "Plainly, what one man calls justice another man calls expropriation; and one man's security is another man's slavery, one man's liberty is another man's anarchy" (Mayer, 1969, p. 41). Mayer wondered if in our time the rule of law is not becoming the enemy of liberty.

Values have become relative to one another and to situations. "Policies" help to "bend" the law, and social conditions tend to confuse and confound the search for simple solutions and answers. From a quiet, relatively simple rural life with fixed values, we have moved to an involved, complex urban community where any sense of common union is difficult to find and where all groups wish to be counted. Increasingly in the last several decades, many of the formerly powerless groups in our society (African Americans, Hispanic Americans, Asian Americans, Native Americans, women, the elderly, and gays, to name a varied few) have demanded that their wants and needs be addressed (Figure 2.1). The influences of minority groups on policing are in evidence

FIGURE 2.1   An officer in Chinatown.

Courtesy of the New York City Police Department.

both inside and outside police organizations. Although most of the media and public attention regarding the police and minorities focuses on external relations, advocacy groups representing the views of minority officers are becoming commonplace.

In determining the will and consent of the people, all these factors must be considered in a given community, and absolutes are very difficult to find.

A World of Infinite Choices

A new era of development is occurring in the world. Changes are overwhelming and rapid. This time has been dubbed the "Information Age," and it is developing out of television, cable networks, microcomputers, the Internet, satellites, and other related information and entertainment resources. In many ways the tiny microprocessor (a silicon chip) has been at the center of the storm. Every field of human endeavor and most leisure activities have been or will be affected by it. Combined with various other scientific advances (particularly biomedical ones), this new era promises to move us into a world of choices we have never even imagined.

Those who attempt to predict the future disagree on whether the greatest impact of this new age will be positive or negative. Everyone agrees, however, that it will be great—perhaps greater than any revolution we have yet known.

Life is already being changed by these new technologies, and with change comes new opportunities and new problems. Some jobs are disappearing and others appearing as industries computerize. Social isolation, already a problem in our society, may be a by-product of our changed lifestyles as more work is done without ever leaving home. Intense interaction with machines is new to most of us. It will be a very different kind of communication. Some people will find the promised increase in leisure time satisfying, whereas others will find it boring. Boredom can bring about frustration, anger, and depression.

Biomedical advances have changed our lives for the better—and, in the opinion of some, for the worse. Artificial organs, prosthetic devices, birth control pills, test-tube babies, genetic engineering, and microsurgery at the level of DNA have all moved us into the twenty-first century.

New ethical problems must be confronted. When does life begin and end? What is "quality of life?" What limits are appropriate on creating and ending human life? How can we protect rights to privacy in an information age? Who is to monitor information systems? Can we prevent the dehumanization effect that so many people fear? Will private and governmental monitoring of our lives and activities take away or add to our freedom? What values are we modeling as the TV screen becomes an all-purpose display, and even a two-way communication instrument? What values do we wish to model?

These changes can make the job of police officers easier and more scientific. They can also bring new cooperation and integration among members of the justice community. Already new technologies have made it possible for officers to predict where and at what time crime will occur, match crime characteristics to offender characteristics quickly, increase the information that can be gathered and used from a crime or crisis scene, improve surveillance techniques, record calls and responses, and benefit from research in all areas of criminal justice training and function.

These same advances are changing the nature of the role of the police officer and the skills that an officer needs on the job. New technologies, especially the use of computers, will change policing in the twenty-first century. In 1999, all local police departments serving 25,000 or more residents used computers for administration purposes (Bureau of Justice Statistics, 2001). Seventy percent of these departments had computerized arrest records, 45 percent used computers for criminal investigation purposes, and 38 percent used computers for crime analysis. In the field, 31 percent used in-field computers, primarily laptops. The officers used these in-field computers to produce field reports and to access driving records, criminal histories, prior calls for service, and reports of stolen property. The improved skills in sorting and using the available information, problem solving, and knowledge of utilizing new technologies and resources may be just the beginning in the changing role of policing (Conser et al, 2005; Grant and Terry, 2005).

Although important to effective police function, technological sophistication cannot take the place of daily, one-on-one interactions between officers and the citizens they serve. As the trend toward computerization increases, police administrators will need to ensure that positive police–community relations, in the form of daily interaction between officers and the citizens they serve, continue to be a departmental priority.

THE PARADOXES OF POLICE PRACTICE

Individuals involved in our criminal justice system have to face paradox after paradox: They are very often confronted with situations in which they are "damned if they do and damned if they don't." This paradox is illustrated by the fact that society is just starting to recognize the contradictions and burdens placed on the police. They are expected to represent heritage in a changing time. They are expected to represent the controls of authority and the controls of tradition, yet they are faced with a hierarchy of ethical decisions in which they often must decide which law they may or may not allow the individual or criminal or the youngster to break or not break. The police are faced with the ethical problem of how far one can bend the law before it will break. In keeping with these paradoxical concepts, we find that police are expected to have a definite, if somewhat vague, role in society—a role tainted and tinged by stereotyping, prejudice, and an aura of unreality concerning this stressful profession.

Within this framework, in which police are considered to be on the side of our heritage and yet are expected to cope with change, we find that there is not just one "police officer"—a person involved in various aspects of law enforcement. Rather, we find that there are many "police officers" and that there are many emerging roles, styles, and skills involving the police. These include the police officer as a counselor, as a human services representative and member of the human services team, as a human relations expert, as a decision maker, as an agent for change, and as a trust builder between police agencies on the one hand and the various increasingly hostile segments of society on the other. The police officer is not only expected but is mandated to transmit, carry forward, control, and enforce those aspects of human existence that individuals, societies, nations, and civilizations have considered worthwhile, and which they have put into codes of law.

Community Relations: Residue from the Past

Often compounding the individual officer's problems is the police department's problem of poor community relations. Looking back into the recent history of policing, we can find many practices that were seemingly brutal and abusive, but which had the open or silent approval of most of the members of the community. Even though these practices of misconduct have been eliminated or greatly curtailed, the residents of the community may still have a tendency to view their police as somewhat less than sensitive, as well as unfair, oppressive, and perhaps even unaware of social needs and changes.

New officers who rid themselves of prejudicial attitudes or master their personal prejudices so that they do not affect their jobs are still perceived by the community as being insensitive, unfair, oppressive, and unaware of social needs and changes. The members of the community respond only to their perceptions of the uniform. As a group, they generally do not consider any officer's professional attributes. Members of the community may therefore act in a hostile manner, regardless of the individual officer's professional behavior. Some community members apparently have been conditioned to the concept that everyone who wears the uniform has certain prejudicial attitudes. Because the new officer is responded to with what he or she considers to be hostility, he or she is not given a chance to demonstrate to the community that he or she is an unbiased professional. Older officers will warn the new officer that his or her professional considerations are not the appropriate response for dealing with certain groups or individuals in the community, and that "There's only one way to handle those people." The typical response for the new officer is to become more and more like the experienced officers.

The chance the police department had of beginning a new era of excellent community relations is then stifled. The incoming officer is socialized to the standards of the past. Thus, the cycle of poor police–community relations seems to continue unbroken, even when the department has been fortunate enough to recruit an officer who did not bring unfavorable attitudes to the job or could control the negative attitudes he or she did have.

TOWARD A REALISTIC ROLE CONCEPT

The Police Officer's Working Personality and Reality

Skolnick's analysis of the police officer's "working personality" (discussed in more detail in Chapter 7) highlights three elements of the officer's task: danger, authority, and efficiency. According to Skolnick, these elements in turn generate three personality characteristics: suspiciousness, feelings of isolation, and police solidarity (Skolnick, 1975, p. 44). This context is supported by the paramilitary structure of the police organization, which discourages innovation and flexibility and encourages dependency (Doerner, 2004). As the rigidity of the structure increases, the degree to which these characteristics are emphasized also increases.

If more than 80 percent of the officer's time is spent in service-related duties, role concepts that stress danger, authority, and efficiency should be joined or replaced with one more in keeping with the service function.

Service versus Crime Fighting

Clearly, role concepts based on crime fighting and on the service model of police work will be quite different. Some of the most important contrasts between the two are presented below:

Crime Fighting	Service
Focus on law breakers	Focus on law abiders
Specialization	Decentralization
Strong hierarchical authority	Neighborhood involvement
High mobility	Foot patrol
Strict procedures	Wide discretion
Close surveillance and readiness to make arrests	Tolerance and willingness to handle problems by means other than arrest

Which model is more appropriate for police work? Many citizens and police officers would choose the **crime-fighting model**. Yet the objective realities of police work suggest that the service model must be given at least equal emphasis.

TOWARD A CONGRUENT ROLE

Police roles must be defined within the legal limits of authority and in relationship to the needs of the public. The National Advisory Commission on Criminal Justice Standards and Goals recognized the following list of functions that police agencies perform:

- Prevention of criminal activity
- Detection of criminal activity
- Apprehension of criminal offenders
- Participation in court proceedings
- Protection of constitutional guarantees
- Assistance to those who cannot care for themselves or who are in danger of physical harm
- Control of traffic
- Resolution of day-to-day conflicts among family, friends, and neighbors

(a)

(b)

(c)

FIGURE 2.2   **Differing Police Roles (a) A SWAT Team posing during training; (b) Sergeant Kent Davis delivering food items to North Carolina families displaced by flooding from Hurricane Floyd; (c) Jackson County Sheriff's Deputies taking needy children shopping during their annual "Shop with a Cop" activities.**

Courtesy of Jackson County Sheriff's Department (photos [a] and [c]) and Western Carolina University Police Department (photo [b]).

- Creation and maintenance of a feeling of security in the community
- Promotion and preservation of civil order (National Advisory Commission on Criminal Justice Standards and Goals, 1973, p. 72).

How much emphasis each function should receive is often a matter of controversy and varies from jurisdiction to jurisdiction. In every instance, however, working out the optimum mix of functions and priorities will require the active cooperation of local government, the police, and the community.

ELEMENTS OF CHANGE

The police–community relationship is vital to obtaining a realistic and mutually satisfactory role concept for police officers. For their part, police administrators must take steps to overcome the distrust and misunderstandings of the past and to develop internal and external programs that help officers to achieve the following: (1) serve the community more effectively, (2) view their

FIGURE 2.3 **The Rome Police Department appreciates the congruent roles of policing.**

Courtesy of Rome Police Department.

own roles in more favorable terms, and (3) participate in developing community relations. This will require sound planning based on the following elements:

1. Absolute commitment on the part of the police organization.
2. A law enforcement philosophy that recognizes that about 80 percent of police activity involves noncriminal matters.
3. Attempts to instill a professional service concept in existing personnel and in new recruits.
4. Proper balance between the academic and practical aspects of police education and training.
5. Using nonpolice personnel to teach police wherever appropriate (e.g., in areas such as sociology, psychology, and criminal law).
6. An organizational philosophy based on a behavioral approach to law enforcement goals (i.e., on modifying attitudes and behavior).
7. A reevaluation of recruitment methods.
8. Use of such methods as problem simulation, role playing, and group work to modify attitudes and behavior.
9. The realization that change is lasting only if it occurs at all organizational levels.

CRITERIA FOR CHANGE

The following criteria can be used to evaluate police education and training programs. These must be designed to promote needed change:

1. The education and training process should be lively and creative—an arena where ideologies, ideas, and points of view may clash and compete.

2. Attention must be given to a wide range of personal and institutional behavior. Being an effective and professional police officer involves at least the following attributes:
   a. a sophisticated understanding of the moral, social, political, and legal framework of the society.
   b. an intensive understanding of the community—its values, aspirations, difficulties, needs, and resources.
   c. considerable personal strength, autonomy, and self-understanding.
   d. the ability to understand, empathize, and communicate with others.
   e. a deep commitment to the basic ideals of justice and freedom within our society.
   f. a deep understanding and knowledge of the policies and practices of law enforcement organization.
3. Stress should be placed on the development of programs designed to give insight into the personal, social, legal, and cultural context of law enforcement service. The education and training function should be able to develop more sophisticated mechanisms for field training and greater articulation between the classroom and the real world.

POLICING IN A CHANGING SOCIETY

The conditions that affect society have their potential effect on the police officer as an ethical practitioner and as a human being. Police officers are not immune to the situations they must face. They are influencers and controllers of those situations. Whether they are facing problems of deadly force, problems of mixed ethical decisions, or problems involving the fundamental privacy of individual citizens, it all rubs off on them.

The alienation resulting from loneliness, inadequacy, despair, and helplessness found among many of the persons with whom they are in contact every day is bound to have its effect on the personality and psychological stability of every police officer. Many police officers sense that they are becoming withdrawn and distant because of the situations they have to face. There is no greater irony in law enforcement than to find attrition in the ranks of competent police officers as they paraphrase the adage "We have faced the enemy, and he is us."

Yet if this is a time of growing public and private cynicism and changing values, it is particularly challenging for people in law enforcement to avoid attempts to manipulate and distort daily police practice. Indeed, now more than ever before, it is essential for those sworn to represent and uphold the law to do exactly that.

The police officer is, for most people, their only contact with the law. What the officer says, thinks, and does reflects on the total community. A successful police department must be attuned to and have the respect and support of the community. The misuse of office or denial of justice to even one person, like ripples on a pond, spreads wider and wider until all are touched.

The National Advisory Commission's assessment of the situation remains as relevant today as it was in 1973:

> The communities of this Nation are torn by racial strife, economic chasms, and struggles between the values of the old and the viewpoints of the young. These circumstances have made it difficult for the policeman to identify with and be identified as part of a community of citizens. As communities have divided within themselves, there has been a breakdown in cooperation between the police and the citizens.
>
> The problem is particularly acute in large urban population centers. Here, the fibers of mutual assistance and neighborliness that bind citizens together have grown precariously thin. (National Advisory Commission on Criminal Justice Standards and Goals, 1973, p. 72)

The prescription recommended for improving the situation described is cooperation between police and community. As an essential element of cooperation, the police agency must constantly

FIGURE 2.4   An officer with children in a public housing area.

Courtesy of Rome Police Department.

seek to improve its ability to determine the needs and expectations of the public, to act upon those needs and expectations, and to inform the people of the resulting policies developed to improve the delivery of police services. This cooperation is a partnership between the community and its police agency. The partnership extends to mutual problem identification and problem solving.

On the other side of the relationship, the public must be informed of the police agency's roles so that it can better support the police in their efforts to reduce crime.

REALITY CHECK

A Lighter Side of Reality

A young patrol officer serving with the Tallahassee Police Department found himself assigned to do an "officer friendly" visit with a group of first graders at a local elementary school. At first unhappy that he would not be available for serious crime-fighting duties within his beat, the officer warmed up considerably when he met the excited students who had been eagerly anticipating his arrival. He spent a great deal of time telling the students how police officers were their friends and that they (the children) should feel free to talk to police officers and should never hesitate to contact the police if they became lost or frightened. During his presentation, the young officer described the many things that the police do for the public.

After talking to the children for about half an hour, the young officer asked if the children had any questions. He then spent the next several minutes answering a variety of questions about his uniform, his equipment, and his experiences, as well as listening to a myriad of comments and stories the children had heard about police officers. Reveling in the adoration of his young admirers, the officer was beginning to feel very good about himself and his role as a police officer.

During his interaction with the children, the officer had noticed that one young boy had hung back from the other students when they had crowded around to talk with him and that he had not participated when the other children were asking questions. Feeling very much the hero and wanting to make sure that every child had the opportunity to interact with him, the officer made a point of talking to the boy before he left the classroom. He walked over to the child and asked, "How are you?" The child replied, "Okay." The officer asked, "Is anything wrong?" The child sullenly responded, "No." The officer then said, "You didn't come up to talk to me. Do you know who I am?" To which the boy retorted, "My daddy says you're a son of a bitch!" Taken by surprise, the officer said, "Oh. Well, tell your daddy I said, Hi." He then made a hasty exit to resume his patrol duties. Reality had been restored.

Conclusions

Law enforcement often becomes the object of animosity against the establishment. Because of the police officer's traditional role, this may be an expected sociological or psychological occurrence. It seems clear that if new methods of reducing tensions are not found, an increased polarization in society will take place, which can only lead to more violence and retaliation. In an atmosphere of fear and distrust, the problems themselves lose proportion and cooperative solutions become impossible.

Police agencies generally reflect the community. If the community is progressive, its police agencies become progressive. If the entire community is belligerent, police agencies become belligerent. If a community has racist tendencies or is indifferent to the plight of minority groups, police agencies will almost always reflect the same tendencies. If the community is apathetic, police agencies become apathetic.

The police must make every effort to understand the needs and aspirations of all members of the community. There is also a great need for the public to understand the proper role to be played not only by police agencies but also by the entire criminal justice system within the community in our changing society. Such an understanding is impossible to achieve if it is forgotten that the police are essentially a service agency.

If progress is to be made, changes must be sought and initiated by all segments of the community, including the police. The progress of change always seems to begin with small things. Change must be based on an understanding of the community and an appreciation of what the community can be tomorrow and the day after.

Student Checklist

1. Define the terms *perception* and *role concept*.
2. How does a citizen's perceptions of the police affect the way the citizen acts toward a police officer?
3. List three factors responsible for differences in perception.
4. Describe the processes of generalization, deletion, and distortion.
5. Describe objective and subjective approaches to framing role expectations.
6. Identify and account for some of the conflicting perceptions that exist regarding the role of a police officer in the community.
7. Name several factors and conditions of change in our society.
8. Identify some of the paradoxes and dilemmas our changing society creates for the police officer.
9. What are some of the elements necessary to the success of programs designed to assist officers in achieving realistic role concepts and improved service to and participation in the community?

Topics for Discussion

1. What is your perception of the police in your community? What life experiences have brought you to that perception?
2. From your own community, suggest some specific examples of destructive perceptions between police and citizens (individuals or groups) that lead or could lead to poor police–community relations.
3. Suggest some ways to modify these destructive perceptions (see topic 2).

4. Survey students in the class individually as to their concepts regarding the role of police officers. Is there a consensus of views? To what degree are the concepts subjective? Objective? Are the views expressed representative of the views of identifiable groups in your community?

Bibliography

Bandler, R., and Grinder, J. (1975). *The Structure of Magic*, Vol. I. Palo Alto, CA: Science and Behavior Books.

Barker, T., Hunter, R. D., and Rush, J. P. (1994). *Police Systems and Practices: An Introduction*. Upper Saddle River, NJ: Prentice Hall.

Bittner, E. (1970). *The Functions of Police in Modern Society*. Rockville, MD: National Institute of Mental Health.

Broderick, J. J. (1987). *Police in a Time of Change*, 2nd ed. Prospect Heights, IL: Waveland Press.

Bureau of Justice Statistics. (2001). *Law Enforcement Management and Administrative Statistics: Local Police Departments 1999*. Washington, D.C.: U.S. Department of Justice.

Conser, J. A., Russell, G. B., Paynich, R., and Gingerich, T. E. (2005). *Law Enforcement in the United States*, 2nd ed. Boston, MA: Jones and Bartlett.

Cordner, G. W. (1992). "The police on patrol," in D. J. Kenney (Ed.), *Police and Policing: Contemporary Issues*, 2nd ed. New York: Greenwood Press.

Cox, S. M., and Fitzgerald, J. D. (1999). *Police in Community Relations: Critical Issues*, 4th ed. New York: McGraw-Hill.

Doerner, W. G. (2004). *Introduction to Law Enforcement: An Insider's View*, 2nd ed. Dubuque, IA: Kendall/Hunt.

Grant, H. B., and Terry, R. J. (2005). *Law Enforcement in the 21st Century*. Boston, MA: Pearson/Allyn and Bacon.

Greene, J. R., and Klockars, C. B. (1992). "What police do," in C. B. Klockars and J. R. Greene (Eds.), *Thinking about Police: Contemporary Readings*. New York: McGraw-Hill.

Holden, R. N. (1992). *Law Enforcement: An Introduction*. Upper Saddle River, NJ: Prentice Hall.

Loftus, E. (1996). *Eyewitness Testimony*. Cambridge, MA: Harvard University Press.

Mastrofski, S. D. (1990). "The prospects of change in police patrol: A decade in review," *American Journal of Police*, Vol. XI, No. 9, pp. 1–79.

Mayer, M. (1969). *Liberty: Man versus State*. Santa Barbara, CA: Center for the Study of Democratic Institutions.

National Advisory Commission on Criminal Justice Standards and Goals. (1973). *A National Strategy to Reduce Crime*. Washington, D.C.: U.S. Government Printing Office.

Niederhoffer, A. (1967). *Behind the Shield*. New York: Doubleday.

Orwell, G. (1963). *1984*. New York: Harcourt Brace Jovanovich.

Peak, K. J. (2006). *Policing in America: Methods, Issues, and Challenges*, 5th ed. Upper Saddle River, NJ: Pearson/Prentice Hall.

Poveda, T. G. (2001). "Estimating wrongful convictions," *Justice Quarterly*, Vol. 18, No. 3, pp. 689–708.

President's Commission on Law Enforcement and the Administration of Justice. (1967). *The Challenge of Crime in a Free Society*. Washington, D.C.: U.S. Government Printing Office.

Roberg, R. R., Novak, K., and Cordner, G. W. (2005). *Police and Society*, 3rd ed. Los Angeles, CA: Roxbury Press.

Satir, V. (1978). *Your Many Faces*. Millbrae, CA: Celestial Arts.

Skolnick, J. H. (1975). *Justice without Trial*, 2nd ed. New York: Wiley.

Trautman, N. (1991). *How to Be a Great Cop*. Dallas, TX: Standards and Training, Inc.

Walker, S. (1997). *Sense and Nonsense About Crime and Drugs: A Policy Guide*, 4th ed. Belmont, CA: Wadsworth.

Walker, S. (1998). *The Police in America: An Introduction*, 3rd ed. New York: McGraw-Hill.

Walker, S., and Katz, C. M. (2002). *The Police in America: An Introduction*, 4th ed. Boston, MA: McGraw-Hill.

Wilson, J. Q. (1968). *Varieties of Police Behavior*. Cambridge, MA: Harvard University Press.

Wrobleski, H. M., and Hess, K. M. (2006). *Introduction to Law Enforcement and Criminal Justice*, 8th ed. Pacific Grove, CA: Thomson/Wadsworth.

Zalman, M., and Seigel, L. (1999). "Psychology of perception, eyewitness identification, and the lineup," in L. Stolzenberg and S. J. D'Alessio (Eds.), *Criminal Courts for the 21st Century*. Upper Saddle River, NJ: Prentice Hall.

CHAPTER 3

Police–Community Relations: An Overview

The police are the public and the public are the police.

—PEEL'S PRINCIPLES

KEY CONCEPTS

Community–Police
   Relations
External Communities

Feedback (information flow)
Internal Communities
Overlapping Communities

People's Police
Police–Community
   Relations

LEARNING OBJECTIVES

Studying this chapter will enable you to:

1. Provide an overview of police–community relations and their impact on the police system.

2. Explain how police–community relations are complex interactions among a multitude of internal and external communities.

3. Define the *people's police* and *community*.

4. Describe the evolution of police–community relations programs in the United States.

5. Identify the current status of and prospects for police–community relations.

In the last few years, American law enforcement has accepted (begrudgingly at times) the notion that community relations is an important and even indispensable part of police work. In doing so, it has recaptured the old belief that a police force can and should be "the people's police"—an agency that is responsive to the public it serves.

    Philosophically, not every officer agrees, and practically, the nature of community relations varies widely from agency to agency, community to community, but change has occurred. Awareness and acceptance of community relations—the process of developing and maintaining meaningful communication among the agency, its service area, and specific populations served, aims to identify, define, and resolve problems of mutual concern—have increased.

THE POLICE–COMMUNITY ENVIRONMENT

Of all the issues that affect the police in the United States, none is more important than the manner in which the police and the public interrelate. Despite our democratic traditions (or perhaps because of them), we in the United States have been slow to accept the concept that "police are the public and the public the police." Yet the police and the community are not only interdependent, but are in fact inseparable from one another.

Readers, both police and civilian, may find it difficult to accept the assertion that police and community are inseparable. If one adheres to the traditional concept of police–community relations (as shown in Figure 3.1), such a statement may actually seem ludicrous. Typically, the police have responded to pressure from politicians and others who have reacted to complaints from groups or individual citizens regarding police procedures. Such an isolationist view has perpetuated an "us against them" mentality that has detracted from police–community interaction.

However, if one adheres to the more contemporary view that the individuals within various police organizations are but a microcosm of the general society and that this society is composed of numerous interrelated communities, the previous assertion is valid. Today's police organizations are not isolated monoliths that are impervious to the communities they serve. The police organization is not a unified community, nor is there a single community to which they respond. There are in actuality a myriad of sometimes cooperating, often competing communities that are constantly influencing and being influenced by one another.

Police organizations are in truth very responsive to this rapidly changing "community environment." To understand police–community interaction, it is necessary for the student of police to realize that there are constant exchanges among the various communities that exist both inside and outside the police organization. Figure 3.2 demonstrates how these "exchange relationships" (Cole and Smith, 2007) between communities occur.

As displayed in Figure 3.2, the police organization comprised a number of **internal communities** engaged in constant interaction with one another. These internal communities are engaged in numerous individual and group exchanges with a myriad of **external communities**. Within the **overlapping communities** displayed are those groups from which both the internal and external communities are comprised.

DEFINING POLICE–COMMUNITY RELATIONS

As argued in the preceding section, there is no one "community" that is served by the police. Instead, there are numerous communities that make up an often indefinable "public." As a result, "public opinion" is usually not a clear consensus of viewpoint within a nation, state, county, or municipality but a chorus of differing opinions from various communities.

Police–community relations are complicated and constantly changing interactions between representatives of the police organization and an assortment of governmental agencies, public

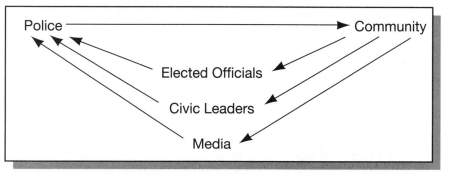

FIGURE 3.1   Traditional police–community relations.

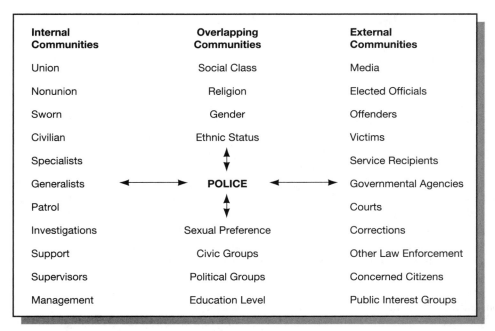

Internal Communities	Overlapping Communities	External Communities
Union	Social Class	Media
Nonunion	Religion	Elected Officials
Sworn	Gender	Offenders
Civilian	Ethnic Status	Victims
Specialists	↕	Service Recipients
Generalists	← POLICE →	Governmental Agencies
Patrol	↕	Courts
Investigations	Sexual Preference	Corrections
Support	Civic Groups	Other Law Enforcement
Supervisors	Political Groups	Concerned Citizens
Management	Education Level	Public Interest Groups

FIGURE 3.2   Contemporary police–community relations.

groups, and private individuals representing a wide range of competing and often conflicting interests.

Throughout this book we focus our discussion of police and community interaction on both the external communities outside the police organization and the internal communities within the police organization. Our primary contention is that successful police–community relations must take into account exchange relationships among community groups located both inside and outside the police organization. To be successful, these exchange relations depend on feedback from the internal and external community groups. Feedback leads to improvement and goal attainment. The isolated police agencies of the past failed to recognize that their success, however defined, required feedback from the community and the citizens served.

ACCEPTANCE OF THE CONCEPT OF POLICE–COMMUNITY RELATIONS

Secrecy and institutional separation have ceased to be defensible positions for police agencies to take in relation to the communities they serve. Although secrecy and institutional separation have not totally disappeared, it is valid to state that in less than two decades the most insular of all institutions in American society is becoming committed, at least in principle, to programs of ongoing exchanges with the community and with other agencies about its mandate and practices.

The concept of police–community relations has gained a secure level of acceptance in the law enforcement establishment and in urban government. Acceptance, in a working sense, means that proposals to establish and maintain such programs have a fair chance of success. There are no longer any organized factions publicly opposing police efforts to open and cultivate channels of communication with the public in general and with civic groups and social movements in particular. Whether those who were aligned against such attempts are now merely silent for the time being, or whether they have changed their views, is an open question. But there is no doubt that activities included under the heading of police–community relations are achieving respectability, and that a large and growing number of police officials in positions of responsibility have come to view them as indispensable for effective law enforcement and peacekeeping.

ACCEPTANCE AS A SIGN OF PROGRESS

This acceptance alone is a sign of progress, a remarkable achievement. It is, however, only a first step toward implementation. It is much easier to agree with the reasonableness and justice of a proposal than to implement it and live with the consequences of its implementation. Above all, when the task is to decide what must and can be done, it is important to measure aspirations against resistance, inertia, and regression. For example, despite the acceptance of the principle of police–community relations, few, if any, actually functioning police–community relations programs are fully deserving of the name. In an assessment that remains accurate, Moore (1992, p. 102) stated that "no police department in the United States can today be accurately characterized as community policing or problem-oriented policing departments."

A positive statement of present circumstances is that although newly functioning programs have been accepted in principle, the kinds of activities that total acceptance would lead one to expect have yet to be implemented. However, as we shall see, there is definitely reason to be optimistic. American policing in the twenty-first century has come a long way since it was transplanted from England. Nevertheless, the current "War on Terrorism," brought on by the 9/11 attacks on the United States, and the resulting economic crisis have had effects on American policing, particularly in the area of funding. Recent events also will increase the need for good police–community relations between the police and certain minority communities.

TIGHT FINANCES AND THEIR EFFECTS

In times of tight finances, new and existing programs must compete for reduced funding and for human resources with other programs that meet long-established police obligations (e.g., crime, traffic, and vice control). In such circumstances it becomes necessary to demonstrate a high level of cost-effectiveness in meeting police goals. Often, community relations programs become locked into quick and relatively safe ways of demonstrating success: (1) "busywork" activities, which show that something is happening and presumably goals are being accomplished and (2) solving easy problems and postponing (sometimes indefinitely) the more difficult ones (e.g., maintaining contact with civic and political groups that are receptive to the police and failing to reach out to those that are not receptive).

Such difficulties can arise with virtually any kind of program in which success is expected. The way police–community relations programs have developed seems to pose some unique difficulties for these programs in particular.

A HISTORICAL PERSPECTIVE

Nineteenth-Century Origins

The concept of police–community relations is not new. When Sir Robert Peel undertook the reorganization of the London police forces with the Metropolitan Police Act of 1829, he and the two key commissioners that he appointed, Charles Rowan and Richard Mayne, emphasized that the police should work in cooperation with the people and that members of the office should protect the rights, serve the needs, and earn the *trust* of the population they policed (Critchley, 1967; Reith, 1952).

Writing at the turn of the century, Melville Lee discussed Peel's principles of law enforcement. The following excerpts from Lee's text retain the flavor of the period in which they were written. They also reflect many of the concepts of police–community relations that are being proposed today. According to Lee, police officers are "public servants in the fullest sense of the term."

It should be understood at the outset that the principal object to be attained is the prevention of crime. To this great end every effort of the police is to be directed.

The absence of crime will be considered the best proof of the complete efficiency of the police.

. . . There is no qualification more indispensable to a police officer than a perfect command of temper, never suffering himself to be moved in the slightest degree by any language or threats that may be used; if he does his duty in a quiet and determined manner, such conduct will probably induce well-disposed bystanders to assist him should he require it.

. . . What is wanted is the respect and approval of all good citizens.

The wisdom of fostering cordial relations between the people and the civil defenders of their lives and properties seems so obvious, that it is a source of wonder that so little attention has been given to the study of how best to promote this desirable *entente cordiale.*

The police . . . are simply a disciplined body of men, specially engaged in protecting "masses" as well as "classes," from any infringement of their rights on the part of those who are not law-abiding.

. . . It is necessary also that they [the public] should be acquainted with the conditions that govern the mutual relationship.

We are well served by our police because we have wisely made them personally responsible for their actions.

. . . That is to say, the modern system rests, as the ancient one did, on the sure foundation of mutual reliance. (Lee, 1971)

These principles were imported into U.S. police departments. In a way, they had to be: There was strenuous opposition to establishing organized police forces on the grounds that they would be the exclusive organ of executive government and indifferent to public influence. They would function against the people, resulting in a "police state." Opposition was in part silenced by assurances that the new institution would be "the people's police" (Astor, 1971).

In many ways the institution focused on the needs of the people. Engaging in community service activities is a part of the American police heritage (see Figure 3.3). As Zumbrun (1983) noted, "During the early part of the 20th century, the New York City Police Department engaged in such non-stereotyped activities as massive Christmas parties for poverty-stricken children and their families, engaging in job hunts for released prisoners from Sing Sing prison and other non-crime fighting endeavors."

The "police state" issue did not die. World War II and many wars and cold war struggles before and since have been waged against so-called police states. In many European countries and

FIGURE 3.3 Service is part of the American police heritage.

in the United States, the police worked hard to disassociate themselves from such a label in the aftermath of World War II. Still, many Americans found adequate evidence to support the view that during their first century of existence in the United States, the police were often corrupt agents of boss-dominated urban governments (Berkley, 1969).

SELLING THE POLICE TO THE PEOPLE

The reformers of the 1950s felt that it was necessary to overcome the attitudes of contempt that middle-class citizens held toward police and, literally, to sell the police to the people. This was done by sending speakers to high schools, to business luncheons, to meetings of civil organizations, and so on. These speakers argued that the police are the "thin blue line," the last bulwark of defense against the dark forces of crime and disorder.

Three key elements were notable in these efforts:

1. At their best, the police employed highly sophisticated techniques of advertising, selling, and, of course, public relations.
2. To police the "public" in a public relations sense, meant, essentially, policing middle-class adults and youth ("solid citizens" and their offspring).
3. No attempt was made to improve the "product"; the programs were designed solely to improve the police "image"; there was little or no provision to recommend or effect needed changes in departmental policy or procedures.

Although these police–community contacts were chosen very selectively, in the 1950s they did constitute a movement away from the exclusive dominance of police departments by city-hall bosses.

The 1960s: From Public Relations to Community Relations

At the beginning of the 1960s, the police had reason to believe their public relations programs had been successful. But then minorities, disaffected young people, the poor, recent immigrants, antiwar activists, and street people made new claims and demands. Their quarrel was with the "system," or with society as a whole, but their confrontations were often with the police, who usually responded with force. One lesson should have been clear: Public relations programs designed to appeal to "solid citizens" were ineffective in dealing with the disadvantaged and the aggrieved—many of whom were openly hostile to the police.

Something else was needed—police–community relations—where *community* was defined realistically to include, as one anonymous reviewer of this text stated, all of the "stratified, segmentalized, unintegrated, and differential environments where police work." This focus includes precisely those segments of society ignored by the earlier public-relations approach. New police–community relations programs were built on the foundations of already existing public relations programs.

The San Francisco Community Relations Unit

In the mid-1950s, the Metropolitan Police Department of St. Louis, Missouri, established a public relations division that became known as one of the best-functioning programs of its kind in the country (School of Police Administration, 1967). The division contained a speakers' bureau, published a newsletter, organized citizens' councils, and maintained school contacts, all of which were considered to be effective in accordance with their aims. There were also police and community relations committees in housing projects, which, in the department's own estimate, did not function well even as late as 1966. Nevertheless, the undertaking as a whole had an enviable reputation. In 1962, Chief Thomas Cahill of San Francisco visited St. Louis to help obtain answers to his own problems. Chief Cahill realized that it was important to use other resources, not just physical force, to deal with outbreaks of discontent. His department was faced with student protests against hearings being conducted in San Francisco City Hall by the House Un-American Activities Committee. Chief Cahill took the new director of his community relations program, Lieutenant Dante Andreotti, to St. Louis to study that city's methods. Cahill and

Andreotti went to St. Louis to learn because they had a problem on their hands; their problem, however, was quite different from the situation that had motivated the St. Louis department. The St. Louis program was formulated primarily to address the "solid citizens." No one considered the program seriously impaired by the fact that the project that was directed toward working with the disadvantaged and the aggrieved did not function.

In the ensuing years, Lieutenant Andreotti developed a program in San Francisco that was vastly different from the St. Louis program. The direction of work that was permitted to lie fallow in St. Louis became the central interest of the San Francisco community relations unit. While Andreotti commanded the unit, "community relations" meant working primarily with the disadvantaged and the aggrieved segments of the population. The unit's officers were attached to organizations such as the Youth Opportunity Center, which served ghetto youngsters, and the Office of Economic Opportunity. They also exerted themselves to meet with, talk and listen to, and help people living in the Tenderloin, the city's skid row, and its ghetto. The activities of the San Francisco unit are illustrated by the following example:

> A robbery and beating of a white grocery store operator in a minority group neighborhood resulted in community-wide concern, and tension. As a result of the efforts of the police and the community relations unit, together with minority group leaders, a group of youngsters (many of whom had juvenile records) were organized into a picket line which marched back and forth in front of the store carrying signs condemning violence and stating that they were ashamed of what had happened. Although the boys picketing were not involved in the robbery or the beating, they offered verbal apologies to the family of the victim for the act done by members of their race. The publicity given this parade by the various media communications resulted in an almost immediate lessening of tensions. (School of Police Administration, 1967, p. 49)

This incident should not be taken as indicating the scope of the unit's program nor even its focal concerns. The routine work of the officers assigned to the unit concentrated much more on everyday kinds of predicaments, such as protecting persons who were not resourceful on their own or helping persons with police records find employment or lodging. The officers acted upon the realization that life in the city comprises many conditions, circumstances, and troubled people. They worked on the assumptions that ex-cons without jobs are likely to commit crimes again; intergroup tension may lead to violent confrontations; children without recreational facilities tend to get into mischief; and so on. When such potential is not checked, it leads to consequences that will sooner or later have to be handled by detectives, riot squads, or juvenile officers, depending on the specific situation.

Those in the San Francisco community relations unit were not the first police officers ever to help a former criminal find a job, nor were they the first to succeed in preventing a public disorder. Their innovation was in two additional aspects of their work. First, they did not simply go out to solve some problem; rather, they always dealt with problems in conjunction with other community resources. In the previous example, they worked together with minority group leaders. Cooperation was not simply a convenient expedient; it involved an established and ongoing mutually cooperative arrangement between members of the police and members of the community. Second, persons in the unit felt that providing services to citizens was their primary job. In the past such services were rendered on rare occasions and only after the officers took care of more demanding crime control problems.

The establishment of the community relations unit in San Francisco meant that personnel resources were specifically assigned to the task of working cooperatively with the people. More important, the chief of the department referred to the existence of the unit with pride. He claimed credit for creating it and gave weight to its importance by having its commanding officer report directly to the office of the chief, rather than through the chain of command. Nevertheless, some commanding officers and several line officers did not like the unit. Yet even without total acceptance within the department, the unit gained momentum. It soon was regarded locally and nationally as conspicuously successful.

Although others considered the unit to be a success, its commander, Lieutenant Andreotti, recognized the problems that still had to be faced and spoke about them at a law enforcement conference in 1968:

> It is my belief that there isn't a successful police-community program anywhere in the country today, in terms of commitment by all members of the law enforcement agency. There have been successful police-community relations units, but practically all of them have been frustrated in their efforts to get the rank and file involved to the point of a genuine, personal interest and commitment. (Andreotti, 1971, p. 120)

Police–Community Relations since the 1960s

The themes of the 1970s were Vietnam, the Watergate scandal of the Nixon administration, inflation, and the energy crisis. Compared with the 1960s, the 1970s were relatively subdued, except for a notable and disturbing increase in violence. It was a period of "finding" oneself, or, as it was called, the "Me Decade."

Out of the turmoil of the 1960s, and based on the findings of several presidential commissions, funding was made available through the Federal Law Enforcement Assistance Administration for research, education and training, and projects of criminal justice agencies designed to reduce crime. Law enforcement agencies had the opportunity to develop and implement new programs— and they did. Many were described as community relations projects, and some of those were innovative and elaborate. Many, in practice, were simply public relations activities. Few were carefully evaluated. As federal funding for them ended, many projects ended. Others, not necessarily as originally conceived, are still part of agency function today.

During the 1980s, the increasing fear of crime throughout U.S. society resulted in a transition of focus from enhancing relations with minority communities to providing reassurances to the general public that crime was not running rampant. Crime prevention units became popular with police agencies throughout the nation. These units served not only as a means of educating the public about crime prevention strategies but also became valuable tools for enhancing public perceptions of the police.

In addition to developing crime prevention units, the police also sought to enhance their relationships with the media. Specialized public information units sprang into existence across the country in agencies that previously had sought to suppress information. These units not only made information more accessible to the media and civic groups but also promoted support for police programs.

The results of the previous strategies led progressive police administrators to seek out new programs in which the public could become more actively involved with their police agencies. An array of community liaison units, school resource programs, joint police–community activities, and enhanced civilian oversight of police operations were experimented with. The culmination of these efforts is community-oriented policing, which is discussed in detail in Chapter 10.

Despite the advances in police–community relations since the 1960s, few programs receive the total support of their agencies. Andreotti's concern, first voiced in 1968, continues to be a community relations concern as we enter the new century. In terms of commitment by all members of law enforcement agencies, the status of police–community relations has not changed dramatically since 1968.

The rise of gangs in the inner cities and their rapid spread to suburban America, the detrimental effects of a flourishing illicit drug trade, the dramatic increase in hate crimes by both right-wing extremists and frustrated minorities, as well as the fear and instability produced by a declining economy demonstrate the need for enhanced police–community relations. The riots in Los Angeles and other major cities during the 1960s served to motivate police agencies to begin police–community relations. The distrust and resentment of police expressed in many U.S. cities following the Los Angeles riot of 1992, provoked by the acquittal of police officers charged with beating an African American motorist, also served as the catalyst for new developments in police–community relations.

A strong economy, a decline in violent crime, and more responsiveness on the part of the police to citizen complaints yielded positive results as the 1990s ended. However, the 1999 shooting death of an African immigrant by the New York City Police and the reactions of African American activists to that shooting have reignited tensions, in that city and elsewhere. The three-day riot (April 7–10, 2001) in Cincinnati, Ohio, following a police shooting of an unarmed black male demonstrates that there are still fragile relationships between the police and certain community groups. Currently, one of the major issues facing U.S. policing are claims that police officers and police departments are engaged in racial profiling or racially biased policing, particularly in the areas of traffic stops and searches. These events demonstrate that we still have far to go.

The Police and Social Work

Even under the best circumstances, community relations programs suffer both from neglect and from being given low priority by police departments. Many police officers have little interest in community relations programs, and even resist and condemn them. Social problems, as the thinking in police circles sometimes goes, are best left to social workers; they are not "proper" police business (i.e., they have little to do with preventing people from committing crimes and with bringing them to justice when they do). This view persists. Academy training often continues to focus predominantly on "crime fighting" behavior, even though it is generally known that the major portion of police work (some references note as high as 80 percent) is social service–related rather than "crime fighting" behavior.

To say that only social workers should deal with these problems is similar to arguing that a champion swimmer should not pull a drowning person from the water unless the swimmer has a Red Cross life-saving certificate. Commitment to the principles of police–community relations means acting on the assumption that the police are a service organization dedicated to keeping the peace, to the defense of the rights of the people, and to the enforcement of laws. In all these fields, they are not merely independent instruments of government; rather, they must work with individuals, community groups, and community institutions to achieve desired objectives.

It was this latter attitude that governed the intervention of the San Francisco community relations unit in the incident mentioned previously. This incident is a good example of commitment to the principles of police–community relations on the level of departmental organization. It is not clear in this case at which point community leaders would be told to stay out of it and let the experts take over (and the community relations unit would move on to the next case). Typically, that would be most likely to occur as procedures leading to the apprehension and trial of the assailants were set into motion.

Such a move may seem appropriate. Citizens are not expected to be involved in "catching criminals." In fact, when they insist upon becoming involved, police believe that they are likely to cause more harm than good. This is also the view of many judges, public prosecutors, city council members, and citizens. Thinking in terms of isolated offenses, it is difficult to reason otherwise.

Thus, even those who are in favor of genuine police–community relations are forced to agree that the work must be assigned to special units that work independently while the rest of policing takes its ordinary course. In other words, progressive departments establish external units to deal with their communities, but these units must follow the department's conditions. In still different terms, it appears that accepting the principles of police–community relations in its presently exclusively outward-oriented direction (somewhat in the way nations send envoys to other nations) does not mean that two-way police–community relations are the norm (or, to continue the analogy, that the other nations send them envoys).

This situation is not unique. The police are not alone in thinking that they can communicate adequately with the people by means of external ambassadors. Indeed, they have done better with this approach than have other institutions. The educational system, for example, keeps parents at arm's length while pretending to allow involvement by letting assistant principals of schools deal with the PTA. Similarly, institutions that deliver medical services often do not even pretend to communicate with the people they serve. In each of these cases, it is argued that lay people could not possibly contribute to solving the problems of a slow-learning child or a diabetic patient, just as it is said that lay people could not be helpful in solving a robbery.

All communities have educational needs, health needs, and law enforcement and peacekeeping needs. It is neither proper nor efficient for the specialists alone to define the nature of these needs nor the way in which they will be met. Specialists bring competence and skills to bear on meeting these needs, but they must communicate with lay citizens to determine what those needs are.

The Success of Police–Community Relations

The establishment of police–community relations units is a first, long step in recognition of the usefulness of bringing needs and special resources together in a harmonious relationship. Nevertheless, it is just that—a first step. The establishment of **community–police relations**, in a much broader sense, is a logical next step. An example might help in making clear what this involves.

It is commonly accepted that the ghettos of our cities produce a disproportionately large number of people who are arrested for criminal activities and that people living in these ghettos are exposed to a far greater risk of being criminally victimized than are other citizens. Finally, it is no secret that people living in these areas distrust the police and often are reluctant to help officers in their efforts to control crime. What would be more sensible, for the police to consider these three facts, together, with their present ways of dealing with suspects and victims, as systematically related? Joint consideration of the larger problem suggests that a successful attack on the problem can come only from the establishment of a program of trusting and fully cooperative relations between ghetto communities and the police.

The reversal of terms—from police–community relations to community–police relations—was not done simply to coin a new term. It does not matter what the arrangement is called. What matters is that the full effectiveness of the program cannot be attained merely by having a special unit to implement it. At best, such units can succeed only in doing an occasional good deed and putting out an occasional fire, while leaving the rest of the police department's work unaffected by even these accomplishments. Creating a special unit that has the responsibility for effective community relations has four adverse consequences (Moore, 1992, p. 135):

> First, by isolating the function in a special unit, the unit becomes vulnerable to organizational ridicule. The community relations units become known as the "grin and wave" or "rubber gun" squads.
>
> Second, after a special unit is formed, everyone else in the department is seemingly relieved of responsibility for enhancing community relations.
>
> Third, if the community relations unit should obtain important information about community concerns or ways in which the community might be able to help the department, it is difficult to make those observations heard in the department. Department members are not receptive to bad news or unwelcome demands; after all, that is the responsibility of the unit to stamp out dissent in the community.
>
> Fourth, the organization no longer looks for other ways to improve community relations.

Success of community–police relations requires a "people's police" attitude. Rank-and-file officers need to recognize that the police are a service organization dedicated to keeping the peace, defending the rights of the people, and enforcing the laws. Community–police relations is a broad, two-way program that involves every officer, not just a special unit.

INTERNALIZING COMMUNITY RELATIONS

Perhaps it would be easiest to explain the concept of incorporating community relations into police work by first discussing what it does *not* mean.

What "Community Relations" Does Not Mean

- *Making entire departments do what police–community relations units do now.* Special programs would remain the responsibility of the units, just as other units in police agencies also have special responsibilities. Although support for programs needs to be broadly based, it would be inefficient to have all units specializing in all programs.
- *Weakening law enforcement.* Viewing crime as a social problem does not imply that crime control would be "soft." Actually, police might become more strongly dedicated to crime control than they are now, and possibly become more effective in that task. Improved community relations would be a tool, or organizational strategy, used in crime control.
- *Close involvement with partisan politics.* Mobilizing support for police–community relations at state, county, and community levels may involve working with "political" figures and organizations, but it is a position that is not partisan, conservative, or liberal. It is a method for doing police work that considers the distribution of political forces in any community and seeks the cooperation of all.
- *"Bending" to community pressures.* Clearly, this is a danger in the face of conflicting demands, but risks can be contained provided that responsiveness to community needs and demands is not interpreted as bargaining away the police mandate. Because openness is reciprocal, the risk can become an opportunity for citizens to understand and respect the police mandate in society.
- *Turning police officers into social workers.* Social interaction is a critical part of police work, and police perform "social" work as part of their everyday tasks. The basic functions of social work are to develop, maintain, and strengthen the social welfare system so that it can meet basic human needs; to ensure adequate standards of subsistence, health, and welfare for all; to enable people to function optimally within their social institutional roles and statuses; and to support and improve the social order and institutional structure of society (Farley, Smith, and Boyle, 2006). Police also are involved in such a function as part of the overall mission of a service organization, dedicated to keeping the peace, defending the rights of the people, preventing crime, and enforcing laws. The common interests are apparent, but the professional specialty and the context within which each functions may vary (see also Morales, Sheafor, and Scott, 2007). Improving police–community relations in all aspects of police work will allow officers to be more effective public servants while exercising the full range of their proper police duties and service responsibilities.

What "Community Relations" Does Mean

- *Reviving the ideas of "the* **people's police**.*"* This is the basic notion on which modern, urban police departments were founded. Needs for police service must be determined on the basis of ongoing communication between the people and the police.
- *A more reasoned basis for police work.* Police officers usually operate with a repertoire of responses determined by penal codes, municipal ordinances, and demands of the often recurrent types of situations and emergencies with which they deal. The police–community relations concept encourages police to deal with complex problems in complex ways, going beyond traditional constraints and procedures where necessary (see Bittner, 1970).
- *A deeper, more comprehensive interest in human life.* To some, this phrase may sound sentimental, and to others, unnecessary, because many effective police officers now operate with humanity and compassion. Still, many police officers do not find it improper to adopt cynical attitudes toward human life. The police–community relations approach, by contrast, stresses that police are both entitled and required to take an interest in and help to resolve human problems.
- *An acceptance of the view that "relations" is a process, not a product.* It is vital, ongoing, and constantly changing. It requires mutual respect and mutual exchange and cannot be compartmentalized if it is to be effective. Feedback is a necessary ingredient of this process. The community and its groups must be encouraged to provide feedback to the people's police, and the police in turn must provide feedback to the community.

**FIGURE 3.4   An example
of good police–community
relations.**

Michael Newman, Photo Edit Inc.

SYSTEMS AND COMMUNITIES

A system is a set of elements, or components, interacting with each other. These elements may be physiological—as in organic systems in the human body, individuals within a family, groups of individuals as in a police department—or groups of systems, as in the criminal justice system. Systems, according to systems theory, are guided by major principles, which include the following:

1. The whole is greater than the sum of its parts.
2. Elements of a system interact in repetitive patterns.
3. A change in one part of the system will reverberate throughout the system (transactional reciprocity).
4. Interactions are governed by a set of rules.
5. Systems tend to maintain a balance among the elements.
6. Open systems exchange energy, or information flow, with the surrounding environment (Norgard and Whitman, 1980).

Feedback/Input

Important to the systems analogy, and the theme throughout this book, is the element of **feedback, or information flow** (mentioned in 6 above). Feedback/input separates public relations from police–community relations (discussed in Chapter 4) and is essential for improving the relationships between the police and their communities. As systems interact with their environments (internal and external), they receive feedback from these environments. In the past, police agencies ignored or set up shields to protect themselves from this feedback, not realizing the potential it had

FIGURE 3.5 Another example of good police–community relations.
Courtesy of Rome Police Department.

for system improvement or giving their "clients" the opportunity to act with and not merely be acted on. This feedback can be very useful in evaluating the operation or goal achievement of the system, particularly a social system such as a government agency. Feedback/input operates to allow the community or service clients to impact the operation and goal setting of the government agency, creating what the authors of the national best-selling book *Reinventing Government* called "Community-Owned Government" (Osborne and Gaebler, 1993). As an example of community-owned government, Osborne and Gaebler cite the efforts of Lee Brown when he became police chief of Houston, Texas, in 1982. In setting up "neighborhood-oriented policing," Brown believed that the police should do more than respond to incidents of crime by also helping neighborhoods solve problems that create crime and crime conditions. The police, particularly beat officers, solicited input from neighborhood residents because Brown recognized that police officers are the boundary spanners between the police department as a system and the community as the external environment. Good police–community relationships demand that feedback from the community is constantly solicited and evaluated by the police. Efforts to solicit feedback, to name a few, come in the form of community surveys, customer follow-ups (contacting and surveying those who have requested the police), customer contacts (beat patrol), customer councils (regularly scheduled community meetings), focus groups, involvement in police activities (ride-alongs and citizen academies), and complaint-tracking systems. As cited in the book, many police agencies are involved in these activities.

The police must also solicit and involve themselves in providing feedback/input to other systems. Police agencies are a part of several systems and are also a system within a system. They are part of the criminal justice, the human services delivery, and the community social systems. Each person in the police agency is part of a family system and of the police agency system. Police agencies and police officers are affected by systems principles in all of these contexts. They help to shape the systems in which they participate, and they are shaped by them. Each of these systems is, in effect, a community with which the police must relate. Community is defined as a group of people sharing common boundaries, such as common goals, needs, interests, and/or geographical location. The task of police–community relations appears more complex as each community is considered.

THE MANY COMMUNITIES IN COMMUNITY RELATIONS

In future chapters, each of these communities, and others, will receive individual attention. At this point, however, it is important to recognize a few of the many communities that make up the environment in which police work. Each has a distinct identity of its own; each has its own elements, and each interacts in some distinct way with police and with each other. Each community must be part of police–community relations if it is to be truly effective.

External Communities

THE JUSTICE COMMUNITY Other police agencies, jurisdictions, courts, and corrections departments existing at many levels of government are part of the justice community with which police must interact. The nature of the relationship between police and members of the justice community has a direct impact on police effectiveness in achieving goals. A lack of coordination, communication, and mutual respect within this community, or system, is legendary. Community relations includes relations with this community as a whole and with its individual members.

THE POLITICAL COMMUNITY As we stated, the early police reformers worked to extricate the police from domination by political bosses and their partisan politics. It is proper that partisan politics, in the form of interference in police personnel decisions and enforcement decisions, be eliminated. However, the police can never divorce themselves completely from politics and elected officials. Our current system of decentralized policing ensures that police departments "are closely tied to political and community interests, and that they be held politically accountable for their actions" (Cordner, Scarborough, and Sheehan, 2004). The political community—in the form of elected officials—is one of the ways that democratic societies keep police power

FIGURE 3.6 The best police–community relations is a product of caring: Deputies assisting with the local Special Olympics.

Courtesy of Jackson County Sheriff's Department.

in check. The political community also provides funding and other resources. Many police executives have failed to recognize the importance of the political community to their, and their agencies', success. The legendary battle between Los Angeles P.D. Chief Daryl Gates and Mayor Bradley is well known (Gates, 1992).

THE HUMAN SERVICES COMMUNITY   The human services umbrella includes many public and private social service resources: mental health and general medical services; media, civic, and religious groups; and educational services. These also form a community, and sometimes multiple communities, with which police officers and agencies interact. Mutual support and availability of services may be lacking because of poor police–community relations. Keeping the peace may depend on access to and coordination of such resources.

CITIZENS AND THE POLICE   Peel's principles state that (Critchley, 1967; Reith, 1952) "the police must secure the willing cooperation of the public in voluntary observance of the law to be able to secure and maintain public respect." Part of police–community relations is understanding the public that police serve and having the public understand police. That is no easy task. The public is many people, with many varying needs and hopes, who live in a changing society and bring to that society conflicting values and cultural rules. The police agency is relatively closed, somewhat secretive, and vague as to what the police role and the citizen role should be. Citizen participation in policing, particularly in crime-prevention aspects, has increased in recent years. The business community actively participates in police-designed crime-prevention programs. Neighborhoods operate effective block watches. Many of these efforts are models in cost-effective crime prevention. Citizen volunteers now participate in many areas of police work. Even those efforts that have been focused on little more than public relations could be redefined and expanded in the context of community relations.

Thus far, however, much of this redefinition and expansion is rhetorical rather than practiced, and those communities and neighborhoods most in need of improved police–community relationships are the ones least likely to be involved in such projects. The cooperation and support of other groups are much easier to gain and maintain.

Internal Communities

THE PERSONAL SUPPORT COMMUNITY   The officers' support groups, both in the sense of a family system and close personal relationships, affect the officers' perspective and effectiveness. Each officer has an impact on the support groups as well. This relationship may be one of the most critical in determining an officer's ability to cope with the human experience of being a cop. It also may determine to a large degree how the individual officer will relate with other communities.

THE POLICE COMMUNITY   The police officer must also be considered as a member of the police agency and police structure. It is this community that can determine whether police–community relations outside the agency will be supported or undermined both as a matter of policy and practice. The first positive relationship that must be formed in effective community relations is accomplished within the agency itself (Fischer, 1981, pp. 54–55).

REALITY CHECK

The Need to Emphasize Membership in Communities

As young police officers (which we freely acknowledge to have been many years ago), the authors found themselves increasingly socializing with officers with whom they worked. They also found that parties they attended were increasingly "cop parties" in which everyone present either was in, or affiliated with, law enforcement. The tendency for police to socialize within their own "comfort group" is very natural in that this can prevent them from confrontations with others who are biased against police officers, as well as avoiding unpleasant situations (such as parties where drugs are present) in which they might be forced to intervene.

Although this socialization phenomenon is not unique to policing, it can become a major impediment to good police–community relations because it helps to perpetuate the view on the part of many police officers that they are separate and distinct from "the public." This can lead to an "us versus them" perspective that Barker, Hunter, and Rush (1994) labeled as "Blue Blindness." This perspective not only creates a potential for abuse and intolerance on the part of the police, but leads to suspicion and distrust of the police by citizens. The dilemma faced by police administrators is how do they combat these views from developing? Common strategies are to ensure diversity in hiring and implement training programs that promote tolerance and understanding.

The uses of hiring to ensure minority representation and training to promote awareness are not only wise but necessary to comply with legal and social expectations. However, these strategies are not enough to prevent officers from becoming isolated from the many communities they serve. What is needed is to intervene during the early socialization of new officers to prevent blue blindness from occurring. This is done by encouraging officers to maintain their ties with people who are not in law enforcement (contrary to what some may think, there are plenty of "normal people" within the communities that an officer may belong to who do not engage in unlawful behavior). In addition, during their initial training, both at the academy and in field training, officers should be encouraged to engage in social and recreational activities that enable them to interact with people from other professions. Becoming involved in "external communities" is beneficial for both the officers and agencies in which they serve.

Conclusions

Police–community relations programs were built on the foundations of already existing public relations programs and, like those programs, involved working with the community in ways that leave little or no room for recommending or effecting changes in departmental policies or procedures. In other words, there was no allowance for essential feedback.

Police–community work concentrated on precisely the segments of the community (e.g., blacks, lower-class youth, and poor) that were most neglected by the earlier public-relations approach, a change that called for new attitudes and procedures.

Police–community relations (following a familiar tendency of our age and bureaucracies everywhere) has become a specialized function to be carried out by special units.

Programs were begun in the 1970s because it was apparent that some response to injustice, discrimination, and poverty was needed, but the response was rarely the result of careful analysis and planning.

Police–community relations work to date has revealed the isolation of the police in society, particularly their isolation from what is going on in ghettos, universities, hospitals, union halls, various government agencies, and, most important, other institutions of the criminal justice system.

If police wish to maintain ongoing dialogues with all members of society, community relations must be a part of every officer's job and the department's mission.

A police agency is part of several systems and is also a system within a system. Each of these systems is, in effect, a community with which the police must relate. These include the justice community, the political community, the human services community, the personal support community, the system within a system, and citizens and the police. The task of police–community relations appears increasingly complex as each community is considered. However, understanding the concept of police–community relations, the people who are involved in its processes, the systems in which they function, the problems they encounter, and the successes they achieve provides a basis for improving police–community relationships in all communities.

Student Checklist

1. Describe the different views of communities utilized within "traditional" police–community relations and "contemporary" police–community relations.
2. What is police–community relations as described in this chapter?
3. Define the *people's police* and *community*.
4. Describe briefly the impact of police–community relations on the police system.
5. Why is feedback necessary for effective police–community relations?
6. Describe briefly the evolution of police–community relations programs in the United States.
7. List some of the difficulties surrounding a new police–community relations program.
8. Identify several "communities" within which the police play important roles.
9. Describe the current status of and prospects for police–community programs in the United States.

Topics for Discussion

1. Describe some of the difficulties that might be encountered by a new police–community relations program in your community.
2. How can police, psychiatrists, social workers, and teachers be mutually helpful and yet not intrude into each other's professions?
3. Discuss the merit of formal meetings between police administrators and presiding judges, and compare this with the need to change attitudes in these areas of the criminal justice system.
4. Demonstrate that a police–community relations program is a process, not a product.
5. Discuss how overlapping memberships in various internal and external communities could facilitate both conflict and cooperation.

Bibliography

Andreotti, D. A. (1971). "Present problems in police-community relations," in C. R. Chromache and M. Hormachea (Eds.), *Confrontation: Violence and the Police*. Boston, MA: Holbrook Press.

Astor, C. (1971). *The New York Cops: An Informal History*. New York: Scribner.

Barker, T., Hunter, R. A., and Rush, J. P. (1994). *Police Systems and Practices: An Introduction*. Upper Saddle River, NJ: Prentice Hall.

Berkley, G. E. (1969). *The Democratic Policeman*. Boston, MA: Beacon Press.

Bittner, E. (1970). *The Functions of the Police in Modern Society*. Washington, D.C.: U.S. Government Printing Office.

Cole, G. F., and Smith, C. E. (2007). *The American System of Criminal Justice*, 11th ed. Pacific Grove, CA: Wadsworth.

Cordner, G. W., Scarborough, K., and Sheehan, R. (2004). *Police Administration*, 5th ed. Cincinnati, OH: Anderson Publishing.

Critchley, T. A. (1967). *A History of Police in England and Wales, 1900–1966*. London: Constable.

Farley, O. W., Smith, L. L., and Boyle, S. W. (2006). *Introduction to Social Work*, 10th ed. Boston, MA: Pearson/Allyn and Bacon.

Fischer, R. J. (December 1981). "Administration in law enforcement: Management in law enforcement viewed as a system of systems," *The Police Chief*.

Gates, D. F. (1992). *Chief: My Life in the LAPD*. New York: Bantam Books.

Goldstein, H. (1977). *Policing a Free Society*. Cambridge, MA: Ballinger.

Lee, M. (1971). *A History of Police in England*. Montclair, NJ: Patterson Smith. (Originally published in 1901 by Methuen and Co.)

Moore, M. H. (1992). "Problem-Solving and Community Policing," in M. Tonry and N. Morris (Eds.), *Modern Policing*. Chicago, IL: The University of Chicago Press.

Morales, A. T., Sheafor, B. W., and Scott, M. E. (2007). *Social Work: A Profession of Many Faces*, 10th ed. Boston, MA: Pearson/Allyn and Bacon.

Norgard, K. E., and Whitman, S. T. (1980). *Understanding the Family as a System*. Phoenix, AZ: Arizona Department of Economic Security.

Osborne, D., and Gaebler, T. (1993). *Reinventing Government*. New York: Penguin Books.

Reith, C. (1952). *The Blind Eye of History*. London: Faber & Faber.

School of Police Administration and Public Safety, Michigan State University. (1967). *A National Survey of Police and Community Relations*. Washington, D.C.: U.S. Government Printing Office.

Zumbrun, A. J. T. (June 1983). Manuscript comments.

CHAPTER 4

Public Relations and Community Relations: A Contrast

I think it is important for the police officer who works a beat to be involved in going to meetings of neighborhood associations and civic clubs, getting to know the people so they can know him. It is important for the managers (police supervisors) to do the same thing. Oftentimes there is a historical tendency to have kind of a one-way communications system. It's equally important for the police to receive feedback.

—L. P. BROWN, INTERVIEW IN THE *NATIONAL CENTURION*, AUGUST 1983

KEY CONCEPTS

Community Advisory
   Councils/Committees
Citizens Police Academy
Community Crime Watch
Community Relations
Crime Prevention

Foot Patrol Programs
Neighborhood Team
   Policing
Neighborhood Watch
Operation Identification
Police Auxiliary Volunteers

Problem-Oriented
   Policing
Ride-Along Program
Rumor Control
Speakers' Bureau
Storefront Centers

LEARNING OBJECTIVES

Studying this chapter will enable you to:

1. Describe the origin of police–community relations as a separate operational concept.
2. Distinguish between police–public relations and police–community relations.
3. Identify the major purposes of community relations activities.
4. Provide examples of existing programs.
5. Describe community relations issues regarding crime-prevention programs.

P olice–community relations programs in the United States have been built on already existing public relations programs. However, though community and public relations may be related, they are by no means the same. The differences become especially apparent when the two are compared with reference to their purposes, the activities they involve, and the type of citizen reaction or interest they presuppose. Public relations activities are designed to create a favorable environment for agency operations by keeping the public informed of agency goals and operations and by enhancing the police image; the target is a citizen who passively accepts (and approves) what the police department is doing. There is no feedback or input. **Community relations**, on the other hand, seeks to involve the citizen actively in determining what (and how) police services will be provided to the community and in establishing ongoing mechanisms for resolving problems of mutual interest to the community and the police—feedback and input.

PUBLIC RELATIONS AND/OR COMMUNITY RELATIONS?

During the short history of police–community relations, there has been little agreement on what it actually is. This lack of agreement among law enforcement professionals has resulted in the development of programs and approaches to community relations that reflect the personal views of local administrators more than they reflect any widely accepted body of knowledge. As a result, considerable confusion exists as to what community relations efforts should accomplish, and how they should do so.

It is generally accepted that police–community relations as a separate operational concept originated in the St. Louis Police Department in 1957. Since that time, the police–community relations concept has experienced sporadic growth throughout the nation. Although the need for community relations is widely accepted today as a crucial part of police administration, its current prominence is of short duration.

The rapid growth of community relations programs resulted from the violent confrontations of the mid- to late 1960s. In larger cities and urban centers, law enforcement administrators realized that they were confronting problems that traditional police tactics were not capable of solving. Administrators in smaller cities, usually on the urban fringes, recognized the possibility that violence might spill over into their communities. In both cases, the creation of specialized units, or the assignment of so-called community relations duties to specific officers, was the response. It was widely felt that such specialized responsibilities could help improve communications between increasingly activist minority groups and the police. In fact, the primary goal of such units at the outset was usually to serve as go-betweens, interpreting the attitudes, desires, and intentions of minority citizens and police agencies to each other.

Over the years, additional duties have been assigned to the community relations specialists. Thus, the community relations function has been variously described as a problem-avoidance methodology (International City Manager's Association, 1967), an "art" that is embodied in police administrative philosophy (Earle, 1980), a way of integrating police operations with community needs and desires (Brown, *n.d.*), and a way of accommodating the reality that the police are part of the political system (Attorney General's Advisory Commission on Community-Police Relations, 1973). In the early 1980s, it was often described as synonymous with police-organized community crime prevention. The concept of community policing has now added new meaning to the traditional understanding of police–community relations in the 1990s and beyond (Trojanowicz et al., 1998). The community policing philosophy broadens the scope of police–community interactions from a narrow focus devoted exclusively to crime to an examination of community concerns, such as the fear of crime, disorder of all types, neighborhood decay, and crime prevention. The philosophy seeks to change police–community relations from the traditional reactive approach of police agencies dealing with community problems as they define them to a proactive approach by partners in the definition and solving of community problems.

These diverse views have resulted in police involvement in remedial educational projects, employment counseling, encounter groups, intensive training in human relations, teaching school, inspecting residences for antiburglary campaigns, organizing block meetings, and dozens of other activities. This dispersion of effort both reflects and intensifies the lack of agreement on just what community relations is. However, most theoreticians and practitioners agree on one point: What community relations should not be. The President's Commission on Law Enforcement and the Administration of Justice stated that community relations is:

> not a public relations program to "sell the police image" to the people. It is not a set of expedients whose purpose is to tranquilize for a time an angry neighborhood by, for example, suddenly promoting a few Negro officers in the wake of a racial disturbance. (President's Commission on Law Enforcement and the Administration of Justice, 1967)

Despite this warning, and despite the fact that most professionals recognize that community relations must go further than mere image improvement on the part of law enforcement, there is still considerable confusion between the concepts of public relations and community relations.

The Relationship

There is a definite relationship between community relations and public relations. It is important, however, to recognize their differences and to practice both concepts in a way that will meet the needs of the contemporary police agency most effectively. Doing so requires (1) developing an acceptable definition of each; and (2) developing an analytical framework within which they can be examined and measured, which is no easy task in an area generally considered to be intangible.

Defining Community Relations

We have already noted the problems involved in defining community relations. However, for purposes of the following discussion, it is necessary to construct a definition that includes the most significant characteristics of those definitions discussed earlier. We also need a definition that can generally be applied to a wide range of police efforts. The following definition is suggested by the Attorney General's Advisory Commission on Community-Police Relations (1973):

> Community-police relations is a philosophy of administering and providing police services, which embodies all activities within a given jurisdiction aimed at involving members of the community and the police in the determination of: (1) what police services will be provided; (2) how they will be provided; and (3) how the police and members of the community will resolve common problems.

Such a definition includes the key characteristics of community relations. It must incorporate the following:

- Be a philosophy of police administration and service.
- Integrate police operations with community needs.
- Involve the police and community in problem solving.
- Be reciprocal.
- Be ongoing.

Defining Public Relations

Admittedly, the preceding definition is not too specific. It must be as broad as it is, however, to include the many activities that make up community relations. Any definition of public relations is also broad. It, too, must include the wide variety of operations carried out in its name. For example, *Webster's New Collegiate Dictionary* (2003) defines public relations as "The business of inducing the public to have understanding for and goodwill toward a person, firm, or institution."

A review of various texts on public relations reveals a variety of definitions. They all have one element in common: Each holds that public relations includes those activities that attempt to explain agency goals and operations to the public and to gain public support for those goals and operations.

These two definitions should not lead to the conclusion that either community relations or public relations can be isolated or explained easily. Neither concept is as simple as a basic definition might imply. Rather, the two are complex and can be understood only when several of their individual characteristics are examined.

COMMON FRAMEWORK FOR ANALYZING COMMUNITY AND PUBLIC RELATIONS

Because they are related and both properly part of police activity, the differences between community and public relations should be understood. A useful analytical framework for this purpose focuses on three characteristics of their activities:

1. The *purpose* of the activity.
2. The *processes* involved in the activity.
3. The extent of *citizen involvement.*

The Purpose of the Activity

All police operations have, or should have, a stated purpose or goal. The purpose of an activity generally embodies the values that the police agency intends to live by. Purpose is an administrative guide. It answers this question: Why has this activity been designed? Purpose, in this sense, is largely philosophical. It describes a hoped-for end. In practice, an activity may serve several purposes. Some activities may be given great administrative importance and others very little.

Why an activity actually takes place and what it accomplishes may have little to do with its stated purpose. Suppose that in an agency, fewer than 7 percent of the agency goals are to "improve the police image," yet some 30 percent of all programs described by the agency fit into a public information category in which most public relations or image-enhancement activities are contained. Officers who participated in the programs probably would rate their programs as highly successful. Their own goals for the programs have been met. The values that the police agency intended to adhere to have not. Understanding the purpose of an activity requires careful observation of what is actually being accomplished versus what was expected.

Public Relations

One common purpose of public relations activities is to develop and maintain a good environment in which to operate. For the police, this involves influencing attitudes in three areas of the environment. They must influence the public, from whom they need support (or, at least, noninterference). They must influence politicians, who are the source of funds. They must influence staff in other elements of the justice community who process those people the police usher into the system. Public information through the media can increase the preventive activity of the mass media when they cover security topics important to the public.

In order to achieve this purpose, the police must minimize obstacles and encourage support. The obstacles result from conscious opposition to what the police have done, are doing, or plan to do. They can include anything from subtle refusal to cooperate to overtly undermining police function. Support for police, on the other hand, could mean anything from passive acceptance to active support and cooperation. Passive acceptance may not be helpful, but neither is it harmful. Active support, such as that required for a campaign to target-harden a residence, is helpful to both the citizen and the police.

In general, the police have employed two ways of achieving their public relations purpose: public information and image enhancement. Public information is perhaps the most routine and widely applied public relations activity in which the police and most other organizations engage. Image enhancement is a logical extension of the public information effort.

PUBLIC INFORMATION　A strongly held value in our culture is that the informed and educated citizen is the best participant in democratic government. Applied to police performance, the theory is that if people understand why an agency (such as the police) performs as it does, they will be supportive of their performance. Information received by the public, however, often is misinformation, fostered in part by the popular entertainment media, which frequently spotlights and glamorizes the police crime-fighting role.

A check of TV listings for a one-week period in November 1982 revealed that 39 hours of prime-time (4:00–10:00 P.M.) scheduling were dedicated to police or police-related shows. The listings came from four major networks, one independent station, and one pay-TV station. In the six-hour period covered by the study, at least one hour was dedicated to newscasts (sometimes crime drama in themselves, but not counted as part of the 39 hours). Omitting that hour, a person conceivably could have watched police or police-related shows for the entire prime-time period on Saturday, Sunday, Tuesday, and Thursday, and for four hours on Wednesday. Mondays and Fridays offered less than three hours of this type of material. These shows ranged from serious drama/adventure to light, humorous entertainment programming. A reexamination of TV listings for a one-week period in April 1999 revealed similar results. In a check of TV listings from 5:00 to 10:00 P.M., 43 hours were devoted to police or police-related shows.

Complicating the effect of these programs on public information is the fact that the image portrayed is often distorted. Officers are most often white and criminals and suspects shown are more likely to be black or Hispanic. Police aggression is overplayed. Popular shows like *CSI, Law and Order, Without a Trace, Cold Case,* and *NCIS* exaggerate the occurrence of violent crimes such as stranger murders, kidnappings, and serial killings. The programs leave the impression that crimes are easily solved and justice always prevails. Many of the technologies portrayed are more fiction than fact. There is concern that jurors often have a distorted image of police evidence gathering because of television portrayals.

News coverage of police activities focuses on their crime-related duties because these are the most newsworthy. Such emphasis is understandable: Because much public information activity by police is in response to media inquiries about crime, police public information campaigns may underwrite misperception by stressing criminal themes, rather than the totality of the police job, which actually consists mainly of noncriminal responsibilities. Los Angeles Police Chief William Bratton has asked the media to stop providing real-time coverage of police chases because some run from the police to seek fame in the media spotlight. Television executives declined the request because police pursuits were newsworthy and popular.

IMAGE ENHANCEMENT　Promoting a positive image is a logical extension of public information activity. Police realize that community-wide respect and cooperation are difficult goals to achieve. There are many negative aspects to the role that society has assigned to the police. Police are charged with seeing that large numbers of people adhere to sometimes unpopular standards, and even the fact that a police force is necessary is distasteful to many citizens. Police need to promote a positive image of themselves whenever possible. In most cases, this is done by stressing the "helping" and "emergency" attributes of the police role. Public information campaigns that focus on an officer rescuing lost children, capturing armed robbers, and providing assistance at the scene of an automobile accident serve the image-enhancement purpose well.

Community Relations

Community relations programs can (and often do) share purposes and subpurposes with public relations efforts. In this context, however, public relations is a part of a broader, more complex goal. Community relations efforts are geared toward integrating community forces and law enforcement agencies into active partnerships for dealing with the many social and criminal problems assigned to the police. Within this framework are the following specific objectives of community relations programs:

- To determine the appropriate range of services the police will provide to the community.
- To determine how these services will be provided (in the sense of appropriate tactics and procedures).
- To identify and define potential problem areas and move to correct them.
- To establish ongoing mechanisms for resolving problems of mutual interest to the police and the community.

The philosophy of community relations stresses the interrelationships and mutual dependencies of police agencies and citizens. Community relations seeks to involve citizens actively in determining what (and how) police services will be provided to the community and establishes ongoing mechanisms for resolving problems of mutual interest. The police must depend on the community as a source of their legitimacy. If they cease to be the "people's police," they no longer achieve their basic mission. Protecting and serving must be defined in terms of the community's needs and wishes in order for the police function to be legitimate. The community is in turn dependent on the police to provide services essential to maintaining an atmosphere of stability. Ultimately, then, community relations serves to create and maintain mutually supportive relationships between police and citizens—something that is needed by both.

PROCESSES INVOLVED IN THE ACTIVITY

Several interesting differences arise when public relations and community relations activities are compared with respect to a set of process questions that apply to both:

1. To what degree are the activities standardized?
2. Is the activity agency oriented, community oriented, or both?
3. What is the direction of information flow?
4. What is the hierarchical level of police agency involvement?
5. What is the breadth of agency involvement?

Public Relations

STANDARDIZATION   Public relations activities tend to be routinized and specialized wherever possible. This makes them easier to control, facilitates their repetition, and prevents wasteful duplication or diversion of staff energy from other more highly valued tasks. An excellent example is the agency-initiated press release, which is the basic tool of the public information function. Preparing such a release is largely a matter of following a standardized form, taking clearly defined steps to obtain administrative sanction, and using regular distribution channels. These steps guarantee a logical, predictable base for the information function.

AGENCY ORIENTED, COMMUNITY ORIENTED, OR BOTH   Public relations activities are agency oriented. They include a range of services designed primarily to serve agency needs. Even services to those outside the agency are designed around the benefits that can be gained by the agency. The agency press release, for example, serves the news media by providing newsworthy information in a readily digestible form. The selection of material and its initial presentation, however, are structured to maximize their image-building or support-gathering potential for the agency.

INFORMATION FLOW   In public relations activities, information flows outward. This one-way pattern reflects the belief that if those in the agency's environment are properly informed about police operations, they will support them.

HIERARCHICAL LEVEL OF INVOLVEMENT   Because virtually all police agencies are hierarchical in nature, it is relatively easy to pinpoint management responsibility for agency activities once that responsibility has been assigned. Assignment is generally made in direct relationship to the importance given to a specific program by top administration. In other words, if the program is regarded as important, a high-ranking officer will be in charge of it.

BREADTH OF AGENCY INVOLVEMENT   Agency involvement in public relations is narrow. Public relations is a tool of police management, not an essential component of operating philosophy. It is an easily compartmentalized function, even though it attempts to represent all segments of departmental activity. Public relations activities are generally assigned to a specific unit, and they do not require heavy commitments from other elements of the department.

Community Relations

STANDARDIZATION   In general, community relations activities are difficult to routinize and standardize. Some of their elements may become routine, but the function they are supposed to perform—linking the police to a wide array of publics and interests—usually requires flexibility and capacity for rapid change. Police administrators who prefer the familiar "standard operating procedures" find the concepts of flexibility and capacity for rapid change difficult to understand and accept—and sometimes difficult to permit.

AGENCY ORIENTED, COMMUNITY ORIENTED, OR BOTH   If the function of the police is to protect and serve, then to be community oriented ultimately serves the needs of the agency, too. The aim of community relations is to provide services that are considered important (not by some police administrator but by the people) to the public served. For example, a police storefront center in an urban neighborhood can serve the police by being a place to collect information on criminal activity and by functioning as a complaint center, thereby improving communication with area residents. If the center is truly a community relations activity, it also will provide citizens with services that they identify as crucial, such as liaison with other government agencies, assistance in domestic crises, conflict mediation, and referral and counseling services. In this way, an intentional balance of self-serving and citizen-serving processes is achieved.

INFORMATION FLOW   Two-way information flow is critical to community relations. The communication process must publicize the police point of view, stimulate discussion of issues, and solicit feedback from members of the community or communities involved. In practice, many agencies continue to emphasize the outward flow of messages, sometimes undermining their own community relations efforts.

HIERARCHICAL LEVEL OF INVOLVEMENT   As in the case of public relations, the hierarchical setting of responsibility for community relations activities is so varied that it defies generalization. If community relations activities are specialized, their responsibility would undoubtedly be that of a ranking agency person. But if the activities are expected to pervade the entire organization or involve only specific, line-level units, responsibility might be assigned to lower levels. Each instance is evaluated independently.

BREADTH OF AGENCY INVOLVEMENT   The breadth of agency involvement is a different matter. Although certain aspects of community relations may be assigned to specific departmental units, involvement generally crosses divisional boundaries. This requires a distinction between *specialized programs*, which may have relevance only to a certain geographical or functional unit, and *general practices* aimed at accomplishing community relations objectives across the department and the community. The former are likely to be successful on a long-term basis only if the latter are part of the department's operating philosophy. Here, a reliable system of internal communication is essential in ensuring that the agency presents a "united" community relations philosophy, particularly in areas where news media take special interest in discovering and publishing contradictions among units of the department.

CITIZEN INVOLVEMENT

Although the police have either assumed or have been assigned responsibility for dealing with many of our more complex social problems, it is folly to think that they alone can solve any of them. In reality, the police are only able to provide limited specialized attention to the most crucial problems, usually in a crisis-reactive fashion. Real solutions require much broader efforts by many segments of the community. Even effective crisis reactions often require the involvement of nonpolice resources. In terms of citizen involvement, public relations and community relations activities provide a definite contrast.

Public Relations

In most public relations activities, citizen involvement is kept to a minimum. It is generally passive; the citizens receive information dispensed by the law enforcement agency or utilize services that primarily serve agency purposes. In most cases, citizens are reasons for, but not participants in, the activity.

Community Relations

Community relations activities often rely heavily on citizen involvement. The citizen is, by definition, an active participant. The police agency does not relinquish responsibility for administering agency programs or practices relating to community relations. It does, however, ensure that citizen resources are properly accommodated, both to provide assistance in accomplishing police goals and to stimulate feedback on issues and problems. Table 4.1 summarizes the characteristics of public relations as compared to community relations.

WHY PUBLIC RELATIONS IS NOT ENOUGH   Public relations activities can and should be part of a properly applied community relations program, but they cannot substitute for it. The analysis in the following section pinpoints some very real weaknesses of public relations programs.

TABLE 4.1 Characteristics of Public Relations as Compared to Community Relations

	Public Relations	Community Relations
Purpose	Attain/maintain good environment	Develop police–community partnership
	Inform public	Integrate community needs with police practices
	Enhance image	
	Minimize obstacles	
	Stimulate support	
Process	Routinized functions comprise activities	Flexible and adaptable functions comprise activities
	Agency-oriented services	Community-oriented services
	One-way (outward) information flow	Two-way information flow
	Responsibility compartmentalized	Responsibility dispersed throughout agency
Citizen Involvement	Consciously kept to a minimum	Actively sought and stimulated

BOX 4.1
Police–Community Relations Must Involve Citizens!

Philosophical Framework

To achieve its mission, a police agency needs the support and active participation of the citizens served. Such a mission requires that the agency seek to develop the following:

- A high level of police–community understanding and trust.
- Effective and meaningful two-way communication.
- Increased community awareness of crime problems and ways to reduce the probability of being victimized.
- Alternative resources for the agency that will increase productivity and more effective use of certified officers.

The list above constitutes the mission of the community relations section of the Pima County Sheriff's Office. Programs developed to fulfill this mission meet nationally recognized criteria for crime-prevention practices. They are also unique. They meet the specific needs of the agency and population served. They are innovative in recruitment, training, and utilization of citizen volunteers. The Pima County Sheriff's Office has received national recognition for seeking meaningful participation of citizens in almost every agency function.

Specific Projects and Programs

As Lewis and Salem (1981) stated, "Community crime prevention strategies prevent crime by altering the relations between the criminal, victim, and environment, reducing the opportunity for victimization." Programs developed seeking to apply these strategies with the help of citizen volunteers in the sheriff's office are listed below. Some of these exist in similar form in many communities in the United States. Others are unique to this agency.

- *Suspicious activity cards.* All sheriff's auxiliary volunteers participate by documenting their observations, which are then routed to the appropriate agency (see Figure 4.2).
- *Business identification program.* Citizen volunteers maintain a cross-indexed file of businesses and their owners or managers, allowing officers quick access to relevant information in the event of a fire or crime on the premises after business hours.
- *Emergency response program.* Certain volunteers have developed additional skills and have citizen band radio

FIGURE 4.1   Volunteer auxiliary teams involve citizens of all ages in police support activities.

Courtesy of Buffalo Police Department.

(continued)

SUSPICIOUS ACTIVITY CARD

SUSPICIOUS PERSON # ONE:			☐ DRIVER		☐ PASSENGER		☐ PEDESTRIAN	
Sex	Race	Hgt	Wgt	Hair	Eyes	Skin	Approx. Age	

SUSPICIOUS PERSON # TWO:			☐ DRIVER		☐ PASSENGER		☐ PEDESTRIAN	
Sex	Race	Hgt	Wgt	Hair	Eyes	Skin	Approx. Age	

Manner of Dress & Identifying Marks (Person # One)   ☐ Glasses   ☐ Moustache or Beard

Manner of Dress & Identifying Marks (Person # Two)   ☐ Glasses   ☐ Moustache or Beard

Possible Occupation or Activity of Subject(s)

Location of Suspicious Activity		Sub-Division	Time	Date

Type Veh	Make	Model	Year	Color	Lic No.	State or Color Plate

Additional Information:

Submitted by: C. Bear #

FIGURE 4.2   Suspicious activity card used by volunteers to report suspicious activity to appropriate agency.

Courtesy of Pima County Sheriff's Department.

capability. They have a call-out system devised to put "eyes and ears" into specific areas on request of the department.

• *Neighborhood Watch program.* The backbone of community involvement with crime prevention. Neighborhoods are organized into manageable groups that meet four times per year. Members are given initial and follow-up information on crime-prevention techniques. Neighbors are encouraged to be more observant and involved in their areas (Figure 4.3).

• *Home security survey.* All residential burglary victims are contacted by mail and offered a personalized survey of their home to help prevent being victimized again (Figure 4.4).

• *Operation Identification.* Normally included within home security checks or Neighborhood Watch presentations. Citizens who demonstrate compliance with suggested procedures receive free Operation Identification stickers.

• *Crime watch program.* A minicourse of instruction for public nonpolice officials and private/commercial organizations that have radio-equipped vehicles operating in the community. The course is aimed at making the operators more efficient observers and reporters of criminal or suspicious activity (Figure 4.5).

• *Interdepartmental people power assistance program.* Many volunteers have provided support to the depart-

ment by assisting with administrative duties. Help has been provided to the records section, burglary detail, auto theft detail, district level administration, and management services division, which is where the volunteer program is coordinated. The burglary and auto theft units use volunteers to maintain their multi-indexed intelligence files of stolen property.

Public Awareness Programs

The volunteers have participated in various crime-prevention awareness shows or programs. They have worked closely with other local crime-prevention groups, including the Crime Prevention Fair and Crime Resisters. At the crime fair, volunteers staff an informational display. This fair is a highly successful, countywide awareness event held for one week each October. At the annual county fair, held each spring, the volunteers staff and maintain an informational and recruitment display. Volunteers also assist local shopping malls in presenting specific crime-prevention themes during weekend expositions. Topics typically include auto theft, burglary prevention, and child safety.

Recruitment

The minimum age for adult citizen volunteers is 18. No upper age limit or restriction exists. A separate county volunteer program exists for teenagers through Explorer Scout posts.

FIGURE 4.3 Neighborhood watch sign.

David R. Frazier, Folio, Inc.

Sheriff's Auxiliary Volunteers
of Pima County, Inc.
P.O. BOX 910 • TUCSON, ARIZONA 85702

INFORMATION FOR ALL NEIGHBORHOOD WATCHES:

The Sheriff's Auxiliary Volunteers has a program in which we video tape the property inside of your home. This service is free and you are given the tape to be put in safety deposit box or in a safe place.

We also have home inspections. An inspector comes to your home and checks locks, windows, doors, etc.

We have an engraver to loan so you may etch your drivers license number on the TV, microwave, etc.

For more information call the phone numbers listed below.

George Meyers--741-4972
Home Inspections

Isabel Powers--741-4685
Crime Prevention

FIGURE 4.4 Sheriff's Auxiliary Volunteers information sheet regarding its home security survey.

Courtesy of Pima County Sheriff's Department.

(continued)

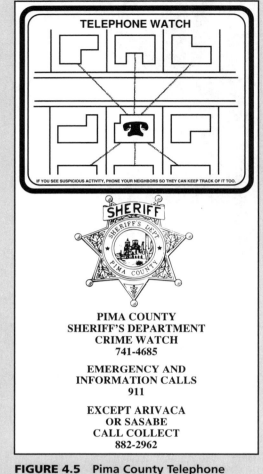

FIGURE 4.5 Pima County Telephone Watch program.

Courtesy of Pima County Sheriff's Department.

Recruitment is countywide. Both officers and volunteers are involved in recruiting efforts. There are no physical requirements for admission. Screening is thorough. A background check for arrest or prior contact with law enforcement is routine. Prior arrest does not automatically bar an applicant from participation. Circumstances surrounding the event and lapse of time since the offense are considered. The agency seeks responsible volunteers who are sincere in their service goals and who will fulfill the citizen volunteer standard of conduct.

Training

The foundation of a successful volunteer program is training. In addition to an orientation to the agency and crime prevention (four to six hours), each sheriff's office volunteer is trained in basic civil liability; the goals, structure, and procedures of

the volunteer programs; introduction to law enforcement systems and agencies; cardiopulmonary resuscitation; basic medical first aid care; identification of criminal or suspicious activity and reporting methods; and traffic accident scene assistance (20 hours).

Advanced skills training is offered in specialized areas. For example, a 44-hour advanced course is required for volunteers who wish to be crime-prevention instructors and program facilitators. This training includes the history and theory of crime prevention and risk management; the concept of creating barriers; security lighting; locks; alarm systems; how to do home security surveys; how to develop Neighborhood Watch programs; public speaking and instruction skills; how to facilitate citizen emergency response training; and civil liability for instructors.

Class members must demonstrate proficiency through oral board and written examination prior to certification by the department.

Identification

All volunteers who successfully complete the training are issued identification cards that remain the property of the department. Volunteers in specialized support programs may also wear identifying patches when on duty (Figure 4.7a).

Supervision of Volunteers

Effective supervision is critical to program success. Supervision is required to accomplish the following:

- Ensure that the skills and interests of the volunteer are matched to departmental needs.
- Facilitate acceptance of the volunteer by departmental personnel.
- Identify any problems early and work toward their solution.
- Encourage cooperation and teamwork among volunteers and between volunteers and agency personnel.
- Effectively coordinate the many volunteer programs and projects.
- Continue to challenge the interest and support of volunteers.
- Maintain the flexibility necessary to meet changing community and departmental needs.

Communication Connections

Information exchange, support, and recognition, always necessary to the success of volunteer programs, are facilitated through a regular newsletter. The *Community Connection* is published at least bimonthly.

Comments

The Volunteers in Prevention, Prosecution, Probation, Prison and Parole (VIP) division of the National Council on Crime

FIGURE 4.6   **Citizen Volunteer Standard of Conduct.**

Members shall conduct their private and professional lives in such a manner as to avoid adverse reflection upon themselves or this department.

Members shall obey all federal, state, and local laws as well as the rules and regulations listed herein.

Members knowing of any other member violating any laws shall report such violation to their District Volunteer Liaison Officer (DVLO) or District Commander.

Members shall treat their peers and associates with respect. They shall be civil and courteous at all times in their relationships with one another.

Members shall make no false reports or knowingly enter or cause to be entered in any departmental report or record any inaccurate or false information.

No member shall willfully misrepresent any matter. Members shall not release any official business of the department without the direct consent of the District Commander or their DVLO.

While acting in an official Sheriff's Auxiliary Team capacity, members shall not recommend to any person the employment of a particular attorney, bail bondsman, towing company, or any other service for which a fee is charged.

Members shall not solicit or accept any personal gift, gratuity, or reward for services rendered in the line of volunteer duty. No member shall purchase, consume, or be under the influence of any alcoholic beverage while acting in the capacity of a Sheriff's Auxiliary Team volunteer.

Members shall not possess or use any controlled substance, narcotic, or hallucinogenic except when prescribed by a physician or dentist.

Members shall keep their liaison deputy informed of any unusual activity, situation, or problem with which the department would logically be concerned.

Source: Pima County Maternal: Deputy L. R. Sacco, SAU Coordinator, Pima County Sheriff's Department.

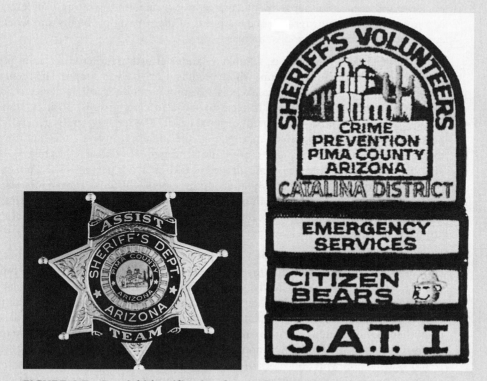

FIGURE 4.7   Special identification for auxiliary volunteers.
Courtesy of Pima County Sheriff's Department.

(continued)

and Delinquency (NCCD) estimates that at least 350,000 volunteers are currently active in direct-service juvenile and criminal justice programs. If volunteers in all capacities of criminal justice are included, the total number would be closer to 750,000 volunteers.

Not every justice agency has had the positive experience with volunteer programs that Pima County has had. What are the ingredients that make this and other volunteer programs successful? A study of programs in a variety of justice agencies in the United States suggests that the critical ingredients for success of volunteer programs are as follows:

1. Strong administrative commitment to the concept.
2. Clearly defined program goals and functions that relate to community and agency need.
3. Careful screening of volunteers.
4. A strong training program, including ongoing training in specialized areas.
5. Assessment of volunteer interests and skills and assignment of volunteers to meaningful tasks.
6. Sensitivity to the needs and fears of agency personnel regarding volunteer services and early resolution of problems in this area.
7. Development of support of agency personnel for the volunteer concept.
8. Effective supervision of volunteers and monitoring of volunteer activities.
9. Involvement of volunteers in recruiting and supervisory activities.
10. Feedback system that encourages recognition, evaluation, and recommendations for change from volunteers and staff.
11. Sensitivity to the needs of volunteers.
12. Willingness to encourage and accept change within the program that is necessary for its vitality.
13. Application of group dynamics principles in strengthening volunteer cooperation and coordination.
14. Strong personal commitment on the part of those who supervise the project.
15. Inclusion of line personnel in every phase of the program development and implementation.

Failing to Provide True Problem-Solving Mechanisms.   Public relations techniques aim to preserve and enhance a department's image, not cope with operating problems. In contrast, community relations programs make a point of identifying problems and working with the community to prevent or resolve them.

Reaching the Wrong Targets.   Public relations efforts are often directed at intermediaries, usually respected, organized groups whose members are likely to support the agency in any case. For example, providing public speakers is a common public relations device. The department thoughtfully provides informed officers to speak to civic groups, business concerns, clubs, schools, and so on, in basically an educational effort. The target group is generally already supportive of the police. The speaker may talk "at" the audience, answer a few questions, and return to headquarters. In most instances, everyone is pleased. No dialogue has taken place, however, and the citizens have rarely been encouraged to take an active part in solving police–community problems. The department hopes that group members will act as intermediaries, carrying the department's message to others, thus building support to avert future problems. In contrast, community relations programs are directed both to groups that are supportive of the police and groups that are not. Active citizen assistance and feedback are sought from both.

Alienating Concerned Citizens.   The pure public relations approach alienates concerned citizens by convincing them that the department is merely interested in image building, not in dealing with problems or in effective communication with the community. Similar feelings may disenchant intermediaries with their role. The community newspaper, for example, receiving only superficial news releases that fail to discuss significant issues of concern, will soon refuse to print them. Only limited descriptive material about training courses, medal-of-valor awards, and number of arrests made during a month will be printed if real problems of rising crime rates, citizen dissatisfaction with police performance, or similar issues are ignored. Alienating concerned citizens is one of the greatest inherent dangers of a pure public relations concept.

Dealing Ineptly with Crucial Issues.   The purpose of public relations is essentially to change perceptions, not to solve substantive operational problems. Thus, when internal change or real communication between police and community is needed, the superficiality of the public relations approach may simply aggravate matters.

Limited Decision-Making Power.   Public relations is a secondary element of police management, and it is compartmentalized. Those in charge of its activities have little power to influence policy or procedural decisions; their responsibility is merely to secure acceptance of the decisions others make.

How Public Relations Can Strengthen Community Relations

The public relations concept has a distinct and valuable place in agency operations as an element of an overall community relations program when the latter is truly part of administrative philosophy. There are at least five functions that are essentially public relations in thrust but which complement community relations efforts.

INFORMING THE PUBLIC ABOUT CRUCIAL ISSUES   The public relations purpose of informing the public can be valuable to both police and citizens if it extends to critical issues. The "whys" of police policies and procedures can be explained to the public. Alternatives to current practice, as seen by the agency, can be explained and any trade-offs outlined. These explanations must be straightforward and honestly portray the police intention to inform, not to sell the status quo. This is the point at which the public relations effort supports the community relations effort. Proper performance of police tasks, not public relations techniques, must do the selling.

DEVELOPING COMMUNITY SUPPORT   Public relations can work to stimulate active citizen support, including cooperation in crime control and prevention activities. This is a change from the traditional public relations orientation. Generating support must be part of an overall mission of involvement, and it must be done with scrupulous honesty. The agency will need to be wary of passive lip service that has characterized purely public relations approaches in the past. Stimulating true citizen involvement can secure the strongest support any criminal justice agency can promote.

SUPPLEMENTING AGENCY OPERATIONS AND PROGRAMS   As an outgrowth of a balanced community relations philosophy, police agencies may implement special operations and programs. Public relations techniques can be used to explain the reasons for and goals of these activities, to stimulate discussion, and to elicit feedback about them.

For example, both public and community relations techniques are useful in initiating a Neighborhood Watch program. The former can help to sell the concept, and the latter can help to define a specific neighborhood's needs and develop and maintain community feedback and support.

PRESENTING AN ACCURATE PICTURE OF THE AGENCY AND ITS FUNCTIONS   The modern police agency performs a confusing variety of tasks, from catching criminals to providing on-site assistance in serious emotional crises. The mundane and sensational, the dull and controversial—and how they relate to one another—are important aspects of agency function. By presenting an accurate and balanced picture of the police organization, public relations efforts can promote true public understanding of the police role and mission. This is perhaps the most important function that public relations can perform as part of a community relations effort.

ENHANCING THE AGENCY'S IMAGE   Public relations can continue to perform many of its traditional functions, even when operating in a community relations mode, but these functions become subordinated to the principles of the broader concept. For example, it is unrealistic to ask any bureaucratic organization to abandon its efforts to achieve support for its programs. The realities of competing for scarce operating resources—money, personnel, and material—preclude such simplistic proposals. Nevertheless, the achievement of support, including image enhancement, must be accomplished in accordance with a strict set of guidelines requiring honesty and integrity in the tactics used. Building the agency's image should be a conscientiously controlled means of providing better service, not the ultimate goal of the agency's community relations program.

PROGRAM EXAMPLES

Thus far, this chapter has focused on the differences between the concepts of public relations and community relations as they are commonly applied by the contemporary law enforcement agency. In this final section, attention will turn to examining several public relations and community relations programs. There are few "pure" programs, just as there are few agencies that embody only the characteristics associated with the concept in the preceding pages. Any evaluation of an agency's orientation must be made by examining the total structure of its operations. Some representative examples of community outreach efforts are described in the following pages.

PUBLIC RELATIONS PROGRAMS   Whether or not a program is purely public relations oriented or is part of a larger community relations thrust is often determined by its long-range goals and the population it seeks to reach. Although most of the programs listed below as public relations could possibly be incorporated into community relations, they frequently exist for short-term enhancement and reach a population that is already supportive of the police.

SPEAKERS' BUREAU   Most law enforcement agencies are ready on request to provide speakers to civic groups, business concerns, schools, and other organizations. The speakers usually give a short, informative talk on a topic such as drug abuse, traffic safety, or crime and protection. They may also distribute descriptive literature to an audience.

RIDE-ALONG PROGRAM   Another common program is the citizen ride-along. This program allows members of the general public to accompany a police officer on routine patrol. Although some jurisdictions place few restrictions on the **ride-along program**, many require that the rider be free of a criminal record or meet requirements of age, occupation, or other significant conditions. The ride-along program does have elements of mutual education for both citizen and police officer, but its primary purpose is to help the citizen "understand" the difficulties of modern police work.

POLICE STATION TOURS   Guided tours of police stations have become standard fare for civic organizations and school groups. Depending on the size and sophistication of the agency, such tours include visiting the jail, crime lab, lineup room, communications center, records center, and various operating bureaus or divisions. Tours are often arranged in conjunction with "police week" ceremonies.

SAFETY LECTURES   Lectures on traffic laws, crossing streets, and other safety topics—usually geared toward children—are conducted in shopping centers and schools and are often accompanied by films and demonstrations.

CITIZEN RECOGNITION   Many agencies give awards to citizens who provide particularly helpful services to the police. Such awards may be given for bravery or merely for reporting a suspicious person who turns out to be a burglar or armed robber. In either case, the agency makes a formal presentation of a plaque or some other suitable award to show its appreciation for an informed and involved citizenry.

CITIZENS ACADEMIES   One of the most popular public relations programs at all levels of police agencies in the United States, Canada, and the United Kingdom are citizens academies.

They are, like many U.S. police innovations, a cultural transplant from Great Britain. In 1977, the British Constabularies of Devon and Cornwall established a "Police Night School" to familiarize citizens with their police agencies. Today, citizens academies are found in the United States in state police agencies, sheriff's agencies, and local police agencies of all sizes. The Royal Canadian Mounted Police (RCMP) also has citizens academies throughout Canada. All citizens acadmies have the common purpose of creating a better understanding and communications between the agency and the citizens through education. Citizens academies produce informed citizens. They show how police officers perform their duties and serve the community. In many communities, they are strictly public relations efforts, although the departments refer to them as community relations; in others they are a part of the overall community relations strategy of the agency.

Programs with a Major Community Relations Focus

Successful community relations programs also serve a public relations function. Improved public relations is a by-product of these programs, not the sole or even primary goal of these (Trojanowicz et al., 1998, p. 15). The following programs were designed as community relations programs. Although they are not universally implemented in ways that realize their optimum effectiveness, the dominant focus of each is community relations. They generally share the common characteristics of community partnership and reciprocal police community feedback/input.

RUMOR CONTROL   The **rumor control** program is most often used during violent street confrontations, generally between the police and residents of racial and ethnic minority neighborhoods. It involves developing networks for gathering, sorting, and clarifying information. Unfounded or exaggerated rumors are identified and exposed. Facts are provided before the rumors can precipitate disturbances. Local civic leaders such as businesspeople, teachers, and religious leaders usually assist in this process. In some communities, the rumor control operation has been used ineffectively simply to provide information to the community by the police. Where it has been optimally used, however, the control network has developed into a useful forum for discussing common police problems in many neighborhoods. The prevention of civil disorder requires that police leadership and management recognize rumors and the problems that caused them in order to put into place a speedy and effective response through their community networks.

COMMUNITY ADVISORY COUNCILS/COMMITTEES   Community Advisory Councils/Committees are known by several names in the United States, Canada, and the United Kingdom but they all have the common purpose of offering community groups and individuals a forum to discuss community issues with the police. Community groups with members on these councils include representatives from all ethnic and cultural populations, as well as business and social welfare agencies depending on the diversity of the community. The groups provide input and feedback on the policies, programs, and practices of the police agency.

STOREFRONT CENTERS   **Storefront centers**, a well-publicized method of bringing the police officer closer to the people, have been complaint reception centers, mini-precinct houses, and meeting places and have served many other purposes. Their effectiveness depends on whether they embody the one-way principles of public relations or the two-way principles of community relations.

NEIGHBORHOOD TEAM POLICING   Community-based teams, under a team commander, have been used to deliver police services to particular neighborhoods. The team has responsibility for deployment, assignments, methods of operations, and other organizational and operational decisions, and offices for team members are located within the policed area. This policing style provides several community relations opportunities. These opportunities include closer, more stable ties with neighborhood residents; citizen participation in planning and delivery of services; and participation and input from all team members with regard to team management and activities. Effectiveness of community-based teams varies widely. Those that are most effective work as a team and consider themselves part of the community they serve.

BOX 4.2
Neighborhood Policing in the United Kingdom and the United States

Neighbourhood Police Teams (United Kingdom)

Neighbourhood Policing is provided by teams of police officers and Police Community Support Officers (PCSOs) [nonsworn constables who assist police officers and handle incidents not requiring full police powers] often together with Special Constables, local authority wardens, volunteers, and partners.

It aims to provide people who live or work in a neighborhood with:

- **Access**—to local policing services through a named point of contact.
- **Influence**—over policing services through a named point of contact.
- **Influence**—over policing priorities in their neighbourhood.
- **Interventions**—joint action with partners & the public.
- **Answers**—sustainable solutions & feedback on what is being done.

This means that neighbourhood teams:

- publicize how to get in touch with them
- find out what the local issues are that make people feel unsafe in their neighbourhood and ask them to put them in order of priority
- decide with partners and local people what should be done to deal with those priorities and work with them to deliver the solutions
- let people know what is being done and find out if they are satisfied with the results.

Source: National Policing Improvement Agency, www.neighbourhoodpolicing.co.uk/

Neighborhood Police Teams (United States)

Ferguson, Missouri Police Department (54 sworn officers)

The Neighborhood Enforcement Team (N.E.T. squad) formed in 2004, identifies neighborhood public safety concerns and crime problems. Policing strategies and action plans are then developed to address these concerns and problems. . . . Citizen input, data analysis, and interdependent communication help the N.E.T. Squad concentrate their enforcement activities to make Ferguson neighborhoods safer and minimize crime. The N.E.T. Squad engages in numerous policing activities from traffic enforcement to criminal arrests to quality of life issues, such as issuing summons or taking suspects into custody for noise violations, manner of walking in the roadway, and other disruptive behaviors.

Source: www.fergusoncity.com

Spokane, Washington Police Department (300 sworn officers)

Starting in 2008, the Spokane Police Department will begin its implementation of a Neighborhood Policing Plan. In a series of several phases, the current north/south patrol response format will be separated into four precincts, each composed of two districts. Partnering with local Community Policing Services (COPS) Shops, patrol officers will be permanently assigned to these smaller geographical areas, creating the opportunity to build lasting partnerships with community members. Each precinct will have at least one Neighborhood Resource Officer (NRO) and each precinct will have one crime analyst specifically examining crime trends for that precinct.

Source: www.spokanepolice.org/patrol/beats

St. Louis County, Missouri Police Department (465 sworn officers)

Neighborhood Policing is a philosophy—one of a partnership between police and law-abiding citizens to create permanent solutions to problems that lead to crime. . . . Neighborhood policing is a partnership of the police, the community, and other agencies of St. Louis County government. Armed with the philosophy of neighborhood policing, these groups come together to identify, analyze, and solve the crime and disorder problems that are unique to each area neighborhood . . . a knowledgeable team of neighborhood beat officers is formed, to serve and provide service 24 hours a day, 7 days a week. This team is assigned to each of the St. Louis County Police Department's police beats. Each beat is grouped together to form a neighborhood policing sector.

Source: www.co.st-louis.mo.us/police

FOOT PATROL PROGRAMS   The reestablishment of police foot patrol in many cities has reintroduced a traditional method for intensifying the interaction between citizens and police. A strict reliance on motorized patrol creates a situation where there is little or no face-to-face interaction between citizens and the police and prevents the development of communication and trust. Skolnick and Bayley reported that their observations of foot patrol and research studies pertaining to it revealed four meritorious effects:

1. Since there is a concerned human presence on the street, foot patrol is more adaptable to street happenings and thus may prevent crime before it begins.
2. Foot patrol personnel may make arrests, but they are also around to give warnings either directly or indirectly, merely through their presence.
3. Carried out properly, foot patrol generates goodwill in the neighborhood, which has the derivative consequence of making other crime-prevention tactics more effective. This effectiveness in turn tends to raise citizen morale and reduce citizen fear of crime.
4. Foot patrol seems to raise officer morale (Skolnick and Bayley, 1986, p. 216).

PHYSICAL DECENTRALIZATION OF COMMAND   Many police organizations are decentralizing the police bureaucracy to provide for quality interaction between the police and the community and, as in neighborhood policing, a heightened identification between the police and specific areas. This has led to the creation of fixed substations, ministations, and the creation of additional precincts.

Although these programs share some of the characteristics and objectives of neighborhood team policing, they are quite different, in that they provide for the creation of small autonomous commands and involve the assignment of police personnel to specific areas for long periods of time.

PROBLEM-ORIENTED POLICING   **Problem-oriented policing**, which includes a number of different programs undertaken in a large number of police agencies, provides for a new approach to the delivery of police services. In this approach the police go beyond individual crimes and reactions to calls for service by attacking the problems that caused them. It moves the police from a reactive response to individual incidents to a proactive approach to citizen concerns.

In practice, police examine the reasons why particular crimes or calls for service occur in certain locations or at particular times and then map out a strategy for dealing with them. The strategy for dealing with these events involves active participation by the community members affected. The following are four features of problem-oriented policing:

1. As part of their work, officers identify groups of similar or related events that constitute problems.
2. Then they collect, from a variety of sources, information describing the nature, causes, and consequences of each problem.
3. Officers work with private citizens, local businesses, and public agencies to develop and implement solutions.
4. Officers evaluate solutions to see if the problems were reduced (Spelman and Eck, 1986, p. 4).

Crime Prevention: Another Name for Community Relations?

Almost all of the program examples mentioned could be included under a broad crime-prevention umbrella, and many others could be added to the list. Several hundreds of millions of federal and local funds have been spent on crime-prevention projects in recent years. There is no doubt that **crime prevention** is a well-advertised, whether or not a well-executed, focus of police function. Citizen demand for crime-prevention programs continues to grow. A National Crime Prevention Institute has been established to provide specialized prevention training and consultation.

Some of these programs are oriented toward community relations and have become citizen action–centered. In these, citizens and police are involved in defining what crime problems exist in a particular area and population and what actions can be taken to prevent such crimes from occurring. Implementation and evaluation are part of the prevention program.

Most programs that are tagged as "crime prevention," however, continue to be, at least in practice if not in original purpose, almost entirely informational—from the police to the citizen. As Krajick stated, "in what some crime prevention experts term a 'knee-jerk reflex,' popular programs like brochure distribution and security surveys are picked up by police departments without any study as to whether those programs address a particular problem in their jurisdictions" (Krajick, 1979, p. 7).

Some programs are considered very successful, and their success is defined in terms of several criteria. These include (1) the number of neighborhood crime watch teams formed; (2) number of volunteers in the program; (3) measurable decrease in a particular type of crime in a given neighborhood; (4) number of brochures distributed; (5) number of presentations made; and (6) number of households following the security advice of police representatives.

Some projects have not been successful by the most generous, short-term criteria for success. Even the design or methodology of program evaluations are sometimes suspect.

Do successful crime-prevention programs also meet long-range community relations goals? The answer is difficult to determine from the short-term rationale used to test for a program's success. Involving the community in an ongoing program of crime prevention requires an underlying community relations perspective. The characteristics of neighborhoods and their problems must be considered. Two-way communication must exist, and a structure must be provided that will encourage continuing involvement of the community.

Even this level of crime prevention will be easier to achieve when working with neighborhoods that already have a positive view of the police. It is much more difficult (and therefore seldom attempted) to build the same relationship in neighborhoods that have had more negative confrontations with police. However, it has been found that police efforts that help minority parents protect their children (DARE, McGruff, Safe Kids, etc.) are more positively received.

In recent years, many agencies have defined police–community relations in terms of their crime-prevention activities. Given the criteria discussed in this chapter for true community relations programs, for prevention services to qualify, they would have to be broadly based, meet long-range goals, and be set up to address far more than just "crime-specific" problems. Rarely is this the case in practice. Therefore, where crime prevention has been substituted for community relations, the community relations concept has usually been narrowed. Crime-prevention activities can support a total police–community relations effort, but they are only part of it.

The following are crime-prevention programs that are among the most public relations oriented:

- *Security surveys* in which the police, by invitation or request, visit a home or business and suggest ways in which security can be improved.
- *Clinics* in which individual citizens and businesses are advised how to prevent specific types of crime (e.g., rape, shoplifting, bank robbery, and burglary).
- *Awareness-alertness programs* in which bulletins about particular crime problems occurring in the community are issued. During the holiday season, many police agencies will issue to businesspeople circulars pointing out various shoplifting techniques. Some agencies also insert burglary-prevention messages in public utility billing statements or bank statements. Although these awareness notices often call upon the citizen to help the police by making it hard for the criminal to consummate an unlawful act, they seldom follow up on such requests, nor do they provide any realistic means for helping the citizen to do so.

Under the umbrella of crime prevention are several programs that include both the elements of public relations and community relations. The ultimate impact of these programs depends on the emphasis placed on the various elements and on the context in which they are applied.

Neighborhood Watch

The many varieties of area watch programs range from those in which residents of a neighborhood are asked to watch for strange activities at their neighbors' homes to those in which citizens are mobilized into committees to work with local police units in identifying local problems and developing responses to them. In the first instance, the police ask citizens to report any suspicious activities occurring in the neighborhood. The citizen merely becomes an extension of the police patrol apparatus. In the latter instance, the police officer on the beat and the citizen endeavor to perfect their partnership responsibilities in identifying those problems that can ultimately be corrected by police intervention. Neighborhood Watch programs can successfully reduce crime. For example, a Neighborhood Watch program was created in the Korbow subdivision in Fayetteville, North Carolina, in 2006. In the initial month of creation, the subdivision reported 63 crimes; in their first anniversary month, five crimes were reported; and in the second anniversary month, only two crimes were committed (Barksdale, 2009).

OPERATION IDENTIFICATION   In an **operation identification** program, police encourage citizens to mark their possessions with their Social Security numbers or other identification recognizable as belonging to them, in order to discourage theft and to increase the possibility of apprehending the offender and restoring the goods to the original owner. Usually, citizens can bring items to the station for identification marking or they will be provided with an etching tool so that they can mark items at home.

POLICE AUXILIARY VOLUNTEERS   The elderly are a prime target of crime today. Senior volunteer programs combine police expertise and elderly citizen volunteers, who work together to find ways in which the elderly can assist in preventing crime and in providing support and assistance to elderly victims. Many volunteer auxiliary programs involve citizens of all ages in a broad range of police support activities. (See Reality Check for a discussion of this project.)

FIGURE 4.8   A crime-prevention billboard.
Joe Rowley, AP Wide World Photos.

COMMUNITY CRIME WATCH   In some communities, public utilities, such as telephone, gas, and electric companies, have been trained and organized as part of a crime-watch team. Because of the extent of their community access and their frequent opportunity for "patrol," employees of such agencies can provide a unique community service. Once trained in what to look for, they become an excellent police support group. If they observe suspicious behavior or circumstances, they are asked not to intervene but to report.

CRIME STOPPERS   The programs included in this category are known by several names: Crime Stoppers, Crimes Solvers, Secret Witness, Crime Line, and so on. These programs join the news media, the community, and the police in a concerted effort to enlist private citizens in the fight against crime. The program is based on the premise that some citizens who know of or observe crimes will not report them because of apathy or fear but will report them for a cash reward.

The first Crime Stoppers Program was begun by police officer Greg MacAleese in Albuquerque, New Mexico, in 1976. Since that time the number of such programs has steadily increased in the United States and in Canada and New Zealand. In 1985 there were 600 programs, resulting in 92,000 felony arrests, 20,000 convictions, and the recovery of $500 million in stolen property (Rosenbaum, Lurigio, and Lavrakas, 1987).

REALITY CHECK

The Need for Discretion within Community Programs

Within this chapter, and throughout this text, you will see examples of numerous citizen and community programs that police agencies are encouraged to utilize in order to enhance police–community relations. We wholeheartedly endorse the programs discussed within this text. However, as with everything in life, discretion is necessary. There must be adequate screening mechanisms for these programs to ensure they do not create liability and/or embarrassment for the agency. In addition, if citizens are going to be involved in positions of trust, background checks and training should be mandatory. Three examples of good intentions that went awry follow:

1. When a Florida police department first began ride-along programs, any interested citizen was invited to participate. They merely had to complete a card that freed the agency from liability if they were injured during their ride-along. One young man (who had stated that he was interested in becoming a police officer when he graduated from college) became a frequent rider with the midnight shifts. He was good company on slow nights and did as he was told when required to stay back from hazardous or delicate situations. This came to a halt several months later after he was arrested for burglary. At his booking we learned that he had an extensive record of thefts and burglary that a background check would have revealed. When questioned about his activities, he stated that he had really enjoyed his interactions with the police officers and also had gained very useful information for his occupation.

2. In an effort to help the families of police officers gain insights into their loved ones' occupations, children and spouses were encouraged to participate in the (now more restrictive) ride-along program with their wives or husbands. One officer brought his wife to ride with him almost every weekend. All went well until one night when the officer was injured in a traffic accident. His wife accompanied him in the ambulance to the hospital where he was treated for minor injuries. Not knowing that his wife was riding along, a dispatcher called

his home to inform his family that he had been injured. Imagine the surprise of the police supervisor when the officer's real wife showed up at the hospital and found another woman by the officer's bedside. Clearances to participate in ride-alongs suddenly became even more restrictive.

3. Another Florida agency developed a senior volunteer program somewhat like the examples provided from Pima County, but without the training and oversights that they utilize. One elderly lady was found to be quite useful within the Records Section where her typing and filing skills were greatly appreciated. She volunteered several hours each week and was quickly accepted into the police "internal community." Unfortunately, after confidential information from a controversial child abuse case became public knowledge, it was learned that the dear lady had seen nothing wrong with regaling the members of her quilting club with the inside information that she gained from her access to police reports.

Conclusions

The difference between public relations and community relations is not always clear-cut. The guidelines presented in this chapter can help an observer to make informed judgments about the nature and purpose of police activities, but only if the activities are studied in the context in which they occur. To what extent do primarily self-serving principles and practices affect a police agency's receptivity to community input? The answer to this question ultimately determines whether the agency is operating under a public relations or community relations philosophy.

Public relations by itself can often prove valueless and even harmful to police agencies because its activities are agency oriented (and thus basically self-serving). Public relations officers are not agents of change and may gloss over or misrepresent crucial issues. On the other hand, every police agency must rely on public relations to some extent to help ensure its position in relation to other forces at work within the community. Public relations activities can play a valuable role in community relations programs provided they follow strict guidelines of honesty and integrity and make a goal such as image enhancement subordinate to providing better service.

Crime prevention has become a household phrase, although not necessarily a household effort. For crime prevention to be synonymous with police–community relations, crime-prevention efforts will need to meet police–community relations goals, something that seldom occurs in practice.

Student Checklist

1. Describe how police–community relations originated as a separate operational concept.
2. Describe the difference between police–community relations and police–public relations.
3. What is the major purpose of police–community relations activity?
4. List three examples of police–public relations programs.
5. List three examples of crime-prevention programs.
6. List three examples of programs with a major community relations focus.
7. Describe the characteristics of a crime-prevention program that meets police–community relations goals.

Topics for Discussion

1. Discover what activities and programs your local police agencies participate in. Are these oriented predominantly toward public relations or community relations? Whom do they serve and involve?
2. Devise a community relations project in crime prevention that could be initiated in your community. What are the characteristics that make your project oriented toward community relations rather than toward public relations?
3. What are the disadvantages of community relations programs?

Bibliography

Attorney General's Advisory Commission on Community-Police Relations. (1973). *The Police in the California Community.* Sacramento, CA: State of California.

Barksdale, A. (April 5, 2009). Fayetteville police chief to unveil plan to fight crime. *The Fayetteville Observer*, www.fayobserver.com

Brown, L. P. (*n.d.*). Police-community evaluation project (unpublished manuscript).

Earle, H. H. (1980). *Police-Community Relations: Crisis in Our Time*, 3rd ed. Springfield, IL: Charles C Thomas.

International City Manager's Association. (1967). *Police Community Relations Programs.* Washington, D.C.: ICMA.

Krajick, K. (1979). "Preventing crime," *Police Magazine*, November, pp. 7–13.

Lewis, D. A., and Salem, G. (1981). "Community crime prevention," *Crime and Delinquency*, July, pp. 405–421.

Merriam-*Webster's 11th New Collegiate Dictionary*. (2003). Springfield, MA: Merriam-Webster.

President's Commission on Law Enforcement and the Administration of Justice. (1967). *The Challenge of Crime in a Free Society*. Washington, D.C.: U.S. Government Printing Office.

Rosenbaum, D. P., Lurgio, A. J., and Lavrakas, P. J. (1987). *Crime Stoppers: A National Evaluation of Program Operations and Effects*. Washington D.C.: National Institute of Justice, U.S. Department of Justice.

Skolnick, J. H., and Bayley, D. H. (1986). *The New Blue Line: Police Innovation in Six American Cities*. New York: Free Press.

Spelman, W., and Eck, J. E. (1986). *Problem-Oriented Policing*. Washington, D.C.: Police Executive Research Forum.

Trojanowicz, R. C., Kappler, V. E., Gaines, L., and Bucqueroux, B. (1998). *Community Policing: A Contemporary Perspective*, 2nd ed. Cincinnati, OH: Anderson.

CHAPTER 5

The Public and the Police: A Consortium of Communities

The criminal justice system is, in reality, if not in appearance, a system. . . . You are most likely to accept [it] as a system if you recognize that society is in the process of imposing the system concept on an existing criminal justice apparatus that for years has been loosely tied together.

—CHAMELIN, FOX, AND WHISENAND

I pick up a guy for car theft; he kicks me and calls me everything but an upstanding citizen all the way to the jail. While I'm still doing the paperwork, he's on his way home, free to steal another car. I don't know why I bother.

—A FRUSTRATED COP

KEY CONCEPTS

Civic Organizations

Community Interest
Organizations ·

Economic/Business
Organizations

Ethnic/Racial
Minorities

External Communities

Government Agencies

Internal Communities

Labor Unions

Political Organizations

Public Service
Organizations

Religious Organizations

LEARNING OBJECTIVES

Studying this chapter will enable you to:

1. Discuss how relations between the police and the public are in reality complex relations among many overlapping communities.

2. Identify and describe the external communities that comprise the public.

3. Identify and describe the internal communities that comprise the police.

4. Describe how exchange relationships among various communities affect police–community relations.

In Chapter 3, we stated that "police–community relations are complicated and constantly changing interactions between representatives of the police organization and an assortment of governmental agencies, public groups, and private individuals representing a wide range of competing and often conflicting interests." In these interactions, those communities that are most vocal, like the proverbial squeaky wheel, often receive more attention and wield more influence. Some receive moderate attention and have moderate influence. Still others are seemingly neglected. Due to constant variations within society, the attention given to individual communities by the police and the influence they have on the police vary considerably over time.

In this chapter, we focus our discussion of police and community interaction on both the external communities outside the police organization and the internal communities within the police organization. Our primary contention is that successful police–community relations must take into account exchange relationships among community groups located both inside and outside the police organization (Figure 5.1).

In the following sections, we introduce many of the communities, both external and internal, which exert influence on and are in turn influenced by the police. Understanding the complexity of the interactions among the many communities that comprise the public and the police will enable the reader to better grasp the difficult challenges involved in establishing and maintaining true police–community relations.

Know 5 ⟶

EXTERNAL COMMUNITIES

Ethnic/Racial Minorities

The difficulties that the police and various ethnic groups have had in relating to one another are not of recent origin. Long before the New World was discovered, police forces were being used to control dissident groups. Usually, these groups were comprised of individuals whose homelands had been conquered by another group. The fictional warfare between the Sheriff of Nottingham and Robin Hood was based on actual difficulties that the Normans had with the Saxons following their conquest of England. Today, similar difficulties are all too apparent in

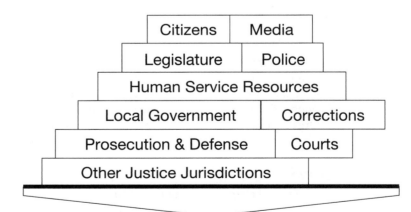

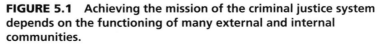

FIGURE 5.1 Achieving the mission of the criminal justice system depends on the functioning of many external and internal communities.

Israel, Northern Ireland, and Eastern Europe. However, one need not leave the United States to explore this phenomenon.

There are many ethnic minorities within the United States. With the exception of Hispanics (defined by heritage and language), ethnic concerns in the United States focus primarily on racial rather than national, cultural, or religious memberships. The numbers and the extent to which ethnic minorities differ from the white majority affect how these minorities are treated within society. Interestingly, discrimination against minority groups is often perpetuated by other minority groups. The worst urban riots that took place in the United States during the 1980s occurred in Miami, Florida, and pitted African Americans against Hispanic Americans, and the Los Angeles riot of 1992 produced bitter conflicts between African Americans and Asian Americans.

BOX 5.1

Operationalizing the System Concept

Assessing a Local System

This process may be used for assessing either the local justice system, including all key components, or one local agency as a subsystem, or system within a system of that larger system.

  I. System Mission
    A. What is the mission of the system?
      1. As defined by legislative and judicial guidelines
      2. As defined by written policy statements
      3. As defined by present agency administrators
      4. As defined by line personnel
      5. As defined by the communities served
      6. As defined by those whose lives are directly affected by the system, the victims and offenders
    B. Assess the mission in system terms.
      1. Is there agreement among these definitions?
      2. If agreement does not exist, what is the nature of the disagreement and where does it exist?

  II. System Components
    A. Identify the key internal system components.
    B. Identify the key functions of each component.
      1. As defined by policy
      2. As defined by procedure
      3. As defined by practice/perception of line personnel
    C. Analyze the ways in which these functions accomplish or undermine system mission.

  III. Interaction in Repetitive Ways
    A. Identify ways that each component interacts with each other.

    B. Identify the written (explicit) rules that guide the interactions of each component with other components.
    C. Identify the unwritten (implicit) rules that guide interactions.
    D. Analyze the ways in which these rules for interaction are constructive or destructive to the system mission.

  IV. Structural Variables
    A. Use of power
      1. How is power manifested in the system and in components?
      2. Where is power centered?
      3. What influence do individual components and individuals have on the system?
      4. What sort of leadership evolves from the power structure?
      5. How is power achieved?
      6. How is influence maintained?
      7. How is power balanced among system (or subsystem) components?
    B. Autonomy
      1. How much autonomy (to be self-directing) is given to each component in the system?
      2. How much autonomy is given to each individual?
      3. How is interdependence affected by the autonomy existing in the system?
    C. Coalitions
      1. How do components and individuals within a system form alliances for joint action?
      2. Are the alliances rigid or flexible?
    D. Negotiation
      1. How are agreements made and mutual problems solved within the system?
      2. Is negotiation open and goal oriented?

(continued)

E. Syntax: The Quality of Connections
(This aspect is difficult to evaluate. Some key questions relating to affect, empathy, respect, and bonding might include the following.)
1. Is the prevailing mood in an agency or the system trusting, affectionate, hopeful, cynical, or depressing?
2. Do system members demonstrate a willingness to understand the functions and problems of other system members?
3. Do police extend positive regard to corrections (and vice versa)?
4. Are emotional bonds among system members strong or weak?
5. Are existing emotional bonds healthy or destructive?

V. Internal Process
A. System communication
1. Permeability
   a. To what degree are system members open to messages from others?
   b. Do system members make certain that messages are mutually understood?
   c. Do system members discount messages from others?
2. Communication style
   a. Do system members balance consideration of personal needs, the needs of others, and the requirements of the situation?
   b. Is anyone discounted or omitted?
3. Information processing
   a. Is there congruence in the way different members/components process information?
   b. Are misunderstandings expressed and resolved?
4. Coherence and flow
   a. Are messages confused in transmission?
   b. Is attention among members focused or scattered?
   c. Does communication flow or is it chaotic and disjointed?
B. The change process
1. Impose change, or select an example of imposed change. Analyze the impact on other components of change in one component based on this example.
2. How do system components deal with change?
C. Self-esteem
1. How do members (candidly) value others within the system?
2. How do members (candidly) value themselves within the system?

VI. External Relationships
A. The external systems
1. Identify local systems that impinge on (have major influence on) this system.
2. What is the function of each as it relates to the system?
B. The relationship
1. What is the nature of the relationship of the system/system components with external systems in general (open or closed)?
2. What is the nature of the relationship of the system/system components with each external system?
C. How do system relationships with external systems/ individuals affect the achievement of system goals?

VII. Summary of Strengths and Weaknesses
A. In what ways is this system working effectively as a system?
B. In what ways is this system working ineffectively as a system?
C. Given the legal structure, where can change be best applied to effect positive change in the total system?

VIII. System Planning
Robert Cushman (1980) states:
Local criminal justice decision-making should be guided by planning efforts at three levels: criminal justice agency planning, city or county level criminal justice planning, and comprehensive interagency and intergovernmental planning for the criminal justice system as a whole. Planning can help individual criminal justice agencies become more efficient, more productive, and more effective. Planning can help officials of general government—the city mayor, the board of supervisors, and county commissioners—evaluate and make decisions about the criminal justice system and its cost and performance. Many local governments also are finding that comprehensive system-wide planning (interagency and cross-jurisdictional) can help to streamline the entire system of criminal justice, eliminate duplication and fill service gaps, and generally improve the quality of service while minimizing costs.
A. Based on your analysis of the system mission and the reality of systems practice, determine what agencies/individuals should be involved in system planning.
B. Determine an approach to resolving system weaknesses and building on system strengths.

Regardless of the minority group in question, the primary issues that are faced by police are the same. First, police must provide services to all communities in a fair and equitable manner. Second, they must convince each community that they are actually doing so. Often, the second portion of the community relations formula is more difficult to attain than the first. The best means of enhancing relations with minority communities is not slick public relations programs presented by specialized units but the development of police forces that are carefully selected, well trained, highly disciplined, and representative of all communities served (Shusta et al., 2005).

Women

Sexism, like racism, has led the police into conflict with a sizable portion of the American populace. The treatment of women has differed historically from the treatment of minority groups, in that they were not necessarily the targets of physical brutality or verbal abuse. However, they have suffered as a gender group from discrimination in the forms of condescension and insensitivity on the part of a male-dominated occupation (Fuller, 2006).

The women's movement and the resulting assertion of women's rights in the workforce and the political process have brought about tremendous changes within a relatively short period of time (Peak and Glenser, 2004). Male police are becoming highly sensitized to issues that affect females as clients (whether as victims, witnesses, offenders, or concerned citizens) and as colleagues. The increasing number of women in law enforcement is accelerating this awareness as police forces become more representative of their communities.

Gays and Lesbians

Homosexuals have long experienced discrimination from police officers. Police have zealously enforced laws against homosexuality, which have existed in every state. As those laws have been eliminated (or ignored), gay people no longer suffer from such blatant persecution but in many areas continue to be treated as second-class citizens (Carter and Radelet, 2002). Contempt and derision for the gay lifestyle have led to difficulties in providing the police services to which all citizens are entitled. Confrontations with gay-rights protesters have further heightened tensions between police communities and gay communities. This issue is being addressed through training and regulations that promote equitable treatment for gay citizens. Some cities, such as San Francisco, actively recruit gay people to join their police forces in order to become more representative of the communities they serve. However, as long as the status of homosexuals in the United States remains unclear, the tensions between gays and police will continue.

Youth

Although most young people never experience any actual difficulties with the legal system, as a group they come into conflict with police at a higher rate than do middle-aged or older people (Walker and Katz, 2002). Much of this conflict is nothing more than the age-old dispute that naturally occurs between youths and adults. As young people mature from childhood into adolescence, their potential for conflict increases. Teenagers who are mobile and interested in having fun become even more likely to experience difficulties with police (as well as with other authority figures). Young adults become more conforming as they mature and find their place within society. The greatest challenge for the police is to allow youth to enjoy being young but to keep them from doing harm to themselves or others.

The Elderly

"Persons sixty-five and older comprise the largest part of the nation's live-alone population, and this proportion is growing steadily" (Carter and Radelet, 2002). As the number of elderly Americans increases, they are all too frequently becoming the victims of serious crimes. The living conditions of our elderly citizens and their relative susceptibility to crime have caused many to find that their "golden years" are filled with terror. Law enforcement must rise to the challenge of providing services that, along with other governmental assistance, will enrich the lives of our older citizens. Enrichment programs are necessary not only to reduce the victimization of elderly citizens but also to halt the increasing number of elderly engaged in drunkenness, drunken driving, and theft. Public awareness of the needs of the elderly has increased, but there is much to do to alleviate the impact of crime and the fear of it among older Americans.

The Poor

Members of the lower class often view police in a different light than do members of the middle and upper classes. Rather than seeing police officers as protectors of their rights and property, the poor tend to see police as the protectors of others' rights and property. In short, many lower-class people think of the police as their oppressors rather than their defenders. This perspective is easily understood. Although the lower class comprises predominantly honest and hardworking individuals, it is dramatically overrepresented within the ranks of lawbreakers. People who feel they have been wronged by society have less commitment to the laws of that society. People who are in desperate situations are more likely to commit desperate acts. Those who feel they have nothing to lose are more willing to risk being arrested (Reiman, 2001).

No matter how fair our society becomes—whether we adopt socialistic programs comparable to those of several European nations or whether the standard of living for all Americans greatly improves—there will always be a sizable lower class and members of this class will be overrepresented within the criminal community. Therefore, we cannot eliminate conflict between the police and the lower class. However, we can reduce the amount of conflict by developing procedures and regulations that ensure that lower-class citizens receive fair and equitable treatment and services from the police.

The Media

The relationship between the police and the media is a complicated one. The police are interested in serving the public and protecting their reputations. The media are interested in serving the public and making profits. The police are obligated at times to withhold information that they feel would be detrimental to the public good (names of victims, case specifics, etc.). The media are obligated to release information that they feel the "public has a right to know." Too often, though, deciding what information should be released or withheld is based on self-interest on the part of the media or the police rather than on what is in the public interest (Grant and Terry, 2005).

Because of conflicting views on what is best for the public and because of self-serving motives, the media and the police are often adversaries. How this adversarial relationship is handled is of the utmost importance for the police, the media, and the public. Quite frankly, some secrets must be kept, and the media grudgingly realize this. However, the police must also realize that only those secrets that would cause public harm (this does not include embarrassment of police officials or concealment of improper practices) can be legitimately withheld from the media. Therefore, the relations between media and police personnel should be based on openness, honesty, and accessibility. Anything less will only exacerbate an already difficult relationship.

Religious Organizations

The influence of **religious organizations** may be seen throughout U.S. society. Historically, the United States has been viewed as a Christian country, with most religious disputes occurring between Catholics and the various Protestant denominations. Minority religions were (and are) protected by the U.S. Constitution but have not necessarily been tolerated by its peoples. "Blue laws" were passed in many states and communities to force Catholics and non-Christians to comply with Protestant practices. Religious groups, such as Jews, Muslims, Hindus, and Buddhists, often found themselves the objects of hatred and intolerance. During the nineteenth century, Mormons were driven out of several states before finding a safe haven in what would become the state of Utah. At that time also, Native Americans were prevented from practicing their religions.

Today, the relationship between the police and religious organizations is, for the most part, amicable. Most of the traditional religions are supportive of police efforts to provide "law and order" for their communities. However, some nontraditional religions are built around practices that might bring them into conflict with law enforcement, and religious organizations are often split on social issues such as civil rights, war, and abortion. In the resulting conflicts, police officials may be placed in the unpopular position of arresting community members who are convinced that they are doing "God's will." As with ethnic minorities, fair and equitable treatment is the key to building and/or maintaining positive relations.

Civic Organizations

Civic organizations such as the Kiwanis, Rotary, Exchange, Civitan, Masons, Shriners, Jaycees, and Lions are less likely to come into conflict with law enforcement than are religious organizations. They, along with the many other reputable organizations dedicated to community service, often comprise persons who are thought to be "mainstays" of a community. However, as with any organizations, individual members may engage in unlawful behavior, and local organizations may be created under the guise of civic service that are actually fronts for illegal activities. Police officials should take care to ensure that their membership (or lack of membership) in these organizations does not affect any dealings they may have with them.

Public Service Organizations

Public service organizations are nonprofit associations directed toward accomplishing community goals. The Salvation Army, Goodwill Industries, and the American Red Cross are three of the better-known charities. The Boy Scouts and Girl Scouts are two of the better-known youth-development associations. Many local groups that offer family support, crisis counseling, and emergency aid can be valuable allies for the police in rendering assistance to people in need. Police officials need to identify and establish communications with those organizations to enhance their ability to serve the public.

Political Organizations

Politics and policing have been difficult bedfellows for many years. The linkage between politics and police corruption has been a problem not only within the nation's larger cities (Reppetto, 1978; Walker, 1977), but among rural law enforcement as well (Bopp and Schultz, 1977; Johnson and Wolfe, 2003). To "get politics out of the police and the police out of politics" (Walker and Katz, 2002) has been a goal of reformers for more than a century.

Unfortunately (or perhaps, fortunately) the simple truth is that politics cannot be eliminated from policing or any other governmental agency (Carter and Radelet, 2002). Efforts to regulate police membership in opposition parties or to prohibit their involvement in political campaigns have traditionally resulted in abuses on the part of "reformers" (Walker, 1977). As citizens, police officers are entitled to belong to political parties and other political organizations. However, their behavior can be regulated through clear and concise policies and procedures to ensure that their political outlook or activity does not affect their job performance.

Labor Unions

The historical relationship between police organizations and **labor unions** has been one of hostility and mistrust. The police were frequently used as strikebreakers in the labor disputes of the early twentieth century (Reppetto, 1978). Today, the police are prohibited by state and federal laws from violating the rights of striking workers. However, this does not mean that tensions between the police and union members are eliminated. The police are still responsible for the property and safety of industrial management. They must also see that the rights of those workers who do not participate in union activities are protected. Fair and impartial law enforcement remains essential.

Economic/Business Organizations

The relations that the police have had with the business community have not been as physically violent as with labor unions, but they have not always been pleasant. Often, business leaders have felt that they are "above the law" and should be exempt from police "intrusion" into their affairs. Similarly, many expect preferential treatment when they do need police services. Cooperative relations with business organizations such as the local chamber of commerce, builders' associations, food services, and the trucking industry are necessary. But the neutrality of the police organization in enforcing laws must be stressed.

Community Interest Organizations

The number of watchdog organizations dedicated to maintaining surveillance over governmental agencies continues to increase. Organizations such as the American Civil Liberties Union and Common Cause are nationally known and respected. Others may consist of only one or two people within a specific community. These organizations may exist for a variety of reasons: to ensure that individual rights are protected; to guard against governmental waste and inefficiency; to protect citizens from hazardous conditions; to attract attention to a particular issue; or just to satisfy individual egos. Regardless of their motivation, law enforcement agencies are advised to cooperate with them to the extent that departmental procedures, governmental regulations, and state laws will allow.

Clients

The interrelationships between the police community and the **external communities** are vitally important. However, most individuals hold memberships within several communities at the same time. Furthermore, there may be additional factors that influence how they interact with various police communities.

Many citizens may never have direct contact with police officials. The latest figures from a 1999 national survey show that only 21 percent of U.S. residents had a contact with the police (see Table 5.1). Individual perceptions of the police are based on citizens' memberships within their respective communities. Those perceptions may be reinforced or altered if and when direct contact occurs. A victim who feels that his or her case received only minimal attention from police may be very understanding or very dissatisfied. A victim who feels that he or she was treated with respect and the case handled properly may become an enthusiastic supporter. The same holds true for witnesses, concerned citizens, and sometimes even offenders. Courteous and professional treatment by a police officer can overcome many preconceptions about police. Similarly, one inconsiderate or rude officer can undermine the efforts of many. Once again, fair and equitable treatment of all people with whom the police come into contact, regardless of the situation or the person's station in life, is the key to good relations.

Governmental Agencies

Law enforcement agencies are but one group out of a myriad number of organizations at all levels of government. The police must interact on a daily basis with representatives of these **government agencies**: elected officials, top administrators, midlevel bureaucrats, and frontline employees. These agencies may be subunits of the same political entity as the police organization, such as agencies charged with maintaining the streets, utilities, public housing, educational

TABLE 5.1 Contacts between Police and the Public—2005

In 2005:

19 percent of U.S. residents age 16 or older had contact with the police

56 percent of contacts were in traffic stops

24 percent of contacts were to report a problem

1.6 percent of contacts involved police use or threat of force

83 percent of those who had force used against them thought it was excessive

White, black, and Hispanic drivers were stopped at similar rates, although blacks and Hispanics were more likely to be searched

11.6 percent of all searches found evidence of criminal wrongdoing

Male drivers were three times more likely than female drivers to be arrested, and black drivers were twice as likely to be arrested.

86 percent of stopped drivers thought they were pulled over for a legitimate reason.

Overall, 9 out of 10 persons who had contact with the police thought they acted properly.

Source: Duprose, M. R., and Langran, P. A. Contacts between Police and the Public: Findings from the 2005 National Survey, Bureau of Justice Statistics, U.S. Department of Justice, 2005.

facilities, parks, and public transportation. They may be emergency organizations such as fire departments, ambulance services, and civil defense. They may be local, state, or federal regulatory agencies. They may be legislative bodies: city councils, county commissions, state or federal legislatures that pass laws these agencies are responsible for abiding by and enforcing. In short, the police do not operate in a governmental vacuum (Cole and Smith, 1997). They are dependent on and are depended upon by many other governmental organizations equally dedicated to serving their respective publics.

FOR BETTER, FOR WORSE The concept of "system"—a set of communities interacting with each other—is imposed on the fragmented, sometimes chaotic and dysfunctional process of justice in which the police are active participants. No one has ever suggested that the justice system works efficiently as a system. As a committee of the American Bar Association observed:

> The American criminal justice system is rocked by inefficiency, lack of coordination, and an obsessive adherence to outmoded practices and procedures. In many respects, the entire process might more aptly be termed a nonsystem, a feudalistic confederation of several independent components often working at cross purposes. (American Bar Association, Committee on Crime Prevention and Control, 1972, p. 7)

Even in a dysfunctional system, system principles apply. The members of the justice system are interdependent and interrelated in their mission and their functions. If police dramatically increase their arrests, other components of the system will feel the strain. If corrections does not correct, other components of the system will have to process repeat offenders. If police do not investigate thoroughly (sometimes even if they do), their efforts will be wasted because the case will be dismissed. If prosecution is not adequate, even a perfect investigation will be of little benefit. There are times that police might understandably wish for divorce from this system. Even in the case of murder, the crime that is most likely to be reported in our society and for which police are most likely to make an arrest (86 percent of the cases), only 64 percent of those apprehended are actually prosecuted, and only 43 percent of these are convicted.

For better or worse, open or closed, functional or dysfunctional, exchange will occur among members of this system. Each may declare at times to be an independent agent within the system, owing loyalty and consideration to no one, but this is more an exercise in self-deception than fact. Worse, the deception itself increases the problem of fragmentation. The greater the fragmentation, the less likely system goals will be achieved. Understanding how system principles relate to the justice community will help us to gain a better understanding of this community, assess its needs, and improve its relationships.

Know →

INTERNAL COMMUNITIES

Minorities

Initially, minority representatives, regardless of their race or ethnicity, were treated as "tokens" by both police and public (Dulaney, 1996). The few minority officers who were employed often had restricted powers and served only in "their" communities. Nevertheless, the employment of the first black police officer in Atlanta, Georgia, in 1948 was the occasion for a parade in the black community. However, the great reform police chief, Herbert Jenkins, had to assure Atlanta citizens that "the Negro policemen would arrest only Negro persons" (Jenkins, 1970, p. 26). Since the 1960s, as a result of the Civil Rights Movement, Affirmative Action requirements, federal lawsuits, increased political activities on the part of minorities, and heightened awareness on the part of the white majority, minority representation has increased. Although U.S. policing is still dominated by whites (76.4 percent), blacks (11.7 percent) and Hispanics (7.8 percent) are now represented within the system. Other groups, such as Asians and Native Americans, appear to remain underrepresented (Bureau of Justice Statistics, 2006).

Despite having achieved more equitable membership within the ranks of the police organization, minorities within supervisory and administrative positions have progressed at a slower rate. However, progress is occurring. As of 1996, former chief Reuben Greenberg—a black Jew—of the Charleston Police Department in South Carolina, reported that blacks had held "the top positions in most of the largest cities in the nation: New York, Chicago, Houston, Dallas, Washington, D.C., Los Angeles, Philadelphia, Detroit, Miami, New Orleans, Baltimore, Oakland, Atlanta, and Memphis" (Dulaney, 1996, p. ix). In addition, two blacks have served as president of the International Association of Chiefs of Police. Lee P. Brown, the former mayor of Houston, Texas, has been the police chief in Atlanta, Houston, and New York City, as well as National Drug

FIGURE 5.2 A police check-on that reflects modern ethnic and gender diversity.
Courtesy of Birmingham Police Department.

Czar for the Clinton administration. When he was the chief in Houston, the legendary police reformer Patrick M. Murphy said that Brown was "the best police chief in the nation" (Dulaney, 1996, p. 94). At this writing, minority (African American and Hispanic American) members hold many leadership positions within law enforcement at the local, state, and federal levels.

Although there has been substantial progress in racial and ethnic representation within law enforcement, it has not been easy or without pain. Resentments have occurred within the police ranks. Charges of discrimination by minorities often have been answered with charges of reverse discrimination by white officers (Roberg, Kuykendall, and Novak, 2002). Addressing past inequities has created stressful situations for all concerned. These concerns can be dealt with only through organizational policies and procedures that are fair to both minority and majority members.

Gender

Many of the issues discussed in the preceding section are also applicable to women. Actually, female representation in law enforcement has progressed at a slower rate than has that of ethnic minorities. In 1999, females accounted for 6.3 percent of white officers, 2.5 percent of black officers, and 1 percent of Hispanic officers in local police departments (BJS, 1999). In 2000, women comprised 13 percent of all sworn law enforcement positions nationwide (National Center for Women and Policing, 2001). The National Center for Women and Policing (2001, p. 2) reports "that [13 percent] is a paltry four percentage points higher than in 1990, when women comprised 9 percent of sworn officers." In 2001, there had not been substantial improvement. Women accounted for 12.7 percent of all sworn law enforcement officers in large police agencies (i.e., those over 100 sworn officers). In agencies under 100 sworn personnel, women accounted for 8.1 percent of all sworn personnel. The combined figures show that women represent only 11.2 percent of all sworn police personnel, even though they are 46.5 percent of the total workforce (National Center for Women and Policing, 2002). It was not until the 1972 Amendments to the Civil Rights Act of 1965 that women obtained the opportunity to choose law enforcement as a profession (Martin, 1989, pp. 312–330). Prior to those amendments, female representation in law enforcement was minimal, and assignments were usually to positions thought to be "properly suitable" by their male supervisors.

Only through legal actions and the perseverance of a group of exceptional pioneers did women break down the barriers within this traditionally male occupation. The first woman police chief in a major police force, Portland, Oregon, suffered personally and professionally as she shattered the bulletproof glass ceiling (Harrington, 1999).

Today, women have long since proven that they can perform well in all areas of law enforcement. Like ethnic minorities, they have experienced discrimination, resentment, and allegations of preferential treatment. In addition, they have endured the difficulties of sexual harassment from police and public alike. Despite these challenges, women have earned their place in policing.

Sexual Preference

Just as gay men and women have struggled for equitable treatment within the external communities, so too have they struggled within the law enforcement communities. Previously, gay police officers were required to keep their sexual preferences secret, not only to avoid ostracism but to avoid prosecution for violating laws against homosexuality. This has changed in many cities and police departments. The Gay Officers Action League (GOAL) was recognized in New York City in 1992 (Goalne, 2006; Goalny, 2006). Since then it has expanded to chapters throughout the nation and overseas.

As the nation has become more enlightened, laws regulating sexual relations between consenting adults have become more permissive. However, attitudes toward gays and lesbians in general and in law enforcement have softened only slightly. Whether gay people deserve the special protections accorded to ethnic minorities and females is a matter of debate (they are, after

FIGURE 5.3 A sign at the front entrance of the Southern States PBA, a police labor organization that provides protections similar to yet distinct from a police union.

Courtesy of Southern States Police Benevolent Association, Inc.

all, not recognizable as gay unless they indicate their sexual preference). That their private lives may be infringed upon by others who may disapprove of their sexual preference is not a debatable issue. Like religion, sexual preference should have no bearing on how people do their jobs or how they are treated while on the job. Gay officers must be accorded the same protections from harassment and discrimination as are accorded heterosexual police employees.

Police Unions

Employee organizations have a variety of names, such as leagues, fraternal organizations, federations, and benevolent associations, and differing degrees of employee representation (Whisenand and Ferguson, 1989). Whatever their name or their affiliation with external employee groups, their mission is to protect and promote the interests of their constituents. While they are categorized as an internal community due to their membership and influence within the police organization, they are often perceived by police administrators as being an external community (Cordner, Scarborough, and Sheehan, 2004). Police unions are discussed in detail in Chapter 6.

REALITY CHECK

Harmless Spoof or Insult?

In February 2006, a video made by officers of the San Francisco Police Department's Bayview Station was posted to the Internet and immediately caused a major controversy. Some of the scenes within the video depicted a homeless African American woman being run over by a patrol car, officers receiving simulated sex within an Asian massage parlor, officers making homoerotic advances to one another, female officers dressed provocatively, and a male officer dressed as a transgendered person.

The major television networks included portions of the video on their national newscasts. Civil rights activists in San Francisco and around the country decried the video and called for its participants to be punished. Declaring the video to be racist, sexist, and homophobic, Mayor Gavin Newsom ordered an investigation not just by SFPD, but by the city's Human Rights Commission and the city's Commission on the Status of Women. He also created a blue ribbon commission to study the SFPD's personnel policies and standards of conduct and training. Police Chief Heather Fong declared the video "a dark day in the history of the department" and immediately suspended 20 officers for misuse of city resources.

The officers involved in making the video argued that it was a spoof of the stresses of police work that was made for private showing at a party. Officer Andrew Cohen, who made the video, declared that the film was satire and should be viewed as such. San Francisco Police Officers Association president Gary Delagnes called the responses to the video to be hypocritical in a city that allegedly promotes freedom of expression and the tolerance of others' rights. He also pointed out in his argument that among the officers who willingly participated in making the video were gays, females, African Americans, and Asians.

The consensus among San Francisco police officers from other stations who were interviewed appeared to be that although they did not condone the video, they understood it as an attempt to mock the pressures that officers face on a daily basis, and they felt the reactions by city officials were extreme. One openly gay officer, who had previously worked at the Bayview Station, stated that he personally wasn't offended and that the video should not be used to judge a very progressive department. However, local gay and transgender activists did not share his opinion.

What do you think?

Conclusions

In this chapter, we have proposed that police–community interaction is not a simple relationship between a police organization and the community it serves but is instead a series of complex and constantly changing relationships between internal police communities and external communities. These communities influence and are influenced by one another on a daily basis. The relationships that exist among various communities are usually competitive, often cooperative, and frequently conflictive.

External communities include ethnic minorities, women, gays, youth, the elderly, the poor, religious organizations, civic organizations, public service organizations, labor unions, business groups, community interest groups, governmental agencies, the courts, corrections, legislative bodies, the other law enforcement agencies, the media, citizens directly served by the police, and a myriad of other community groupings.

The internal police communities consist of the following: administrative personnel, support personnel, operational personnel, management, civilians, political groups, minorities, males, females, gays, religious groups, college graduates, union members, and other typologies by which individuals and groups may be categorized.

To deal effectively with this complex hodgepodge of humanity, the police organization must be managed in a fair and competent manner that provides equal access and equitable treatment to all communities. Communication is the key not only to the police organization's success in police–community relations but also to its survival.

Student Checklist

1. Discuss how relations between the police and the public are in reality complex relations among many overlapping communities.
2. Identify and describe the external communities that comprise the public.
3. Identify and describe the internal communities that comprise the police.
4. Describe how exchange relationships among various communities affect police–community relations.

Topics for Discussion

1. Identify and describe all the communities of which you are a member. Which could be considered a subsystem of others?

2. Identify and describe all the communities of which a police officer might be a part. Could these overlapping memberships result in conflict for the officer?

Bibliography

American Bar Association, Committee on Crime Prevention and Control. (1972). *New Perspectives on Urban Crime*. Chicago, IL: American Bar Association.

Bopp, W. J., and Schultz, D. O. (1977). *A Short History of American Law Enforcement*. Springfield, IL: Charles C Thomas.

Bureau of Justice Statistics. (2006). *Sourcebook of Criminal Justice Statistics*. Washington, D.C., Table 1, p. 53.

Carter, D. L., and Radelet, L. A. (2002). *The Police and the Community*, 7th ed. Upper Saddle River, NJ: Prentice Hall.

Cole, G. F., and Smith, C. E. (1997). *The American System of Criminal Justice*, 8th ed. Belmont, CA: Wadsworth.

Cordner, G. W., Scarborough, K. E., and Sheehan, R. (2004). *Police Administration*, 5th ed. Cincinnati, OH: Anderson Publishing Co.

Cushman, R. C. (1980). *Criminal Justice Planning for Local Governments*. American Justice Institute, Washington, D.C.: U.S. Department of Justice (LEAA).

Dulaney, W. M. (1996). *Black Police in America*. Bloomington, IN: Indiana University Press.

Fuller, J. R. (2006). *Criminal Justice: Mainstream and Cross Currents*. Upper Saddle River, NJ: Pearson/Prentice Hall.

Goalne. (2006). Gay Officers Action League of New England, http://www.goalne.org

Goalny. (2006). Gay Officers Action League of New York, http://www.goalny.org

Grant, H. B., and Terry, R. J. (2005). *Law Enforcement in the 21st Century*. Boston, MA: Pearson/Allyn and Bacon.

Harrington, P. (1999). *Triumph of Spirit*. Chicago, IL: Brittany Publications.

Jenkins, H. (1970). *Keeping the Peace: A Police Chief Looks at His Job*. New York: Harper & Row.

Johnson, H. A., and Wolfe, N. T. (2003). *History of Criminal Justice*, 3rd ed. Cincinnati, OH: Anderson Publishing.

Martin, S. E. (1989). "Female officers on the move? A status report on women in policing," in R. Dunham and G. P. Alpert (Eds.), *Critical Issues in Policing: Contemporary Issues*. Prospect Heights, IL: Waveland Press.

National Center for Women and Policing. (2001). *Equality Denied*. Los Angeles, CA: Feminist Majority Foundation.

National Center for Women and Policing. (2002). *Equity Denied*. Los Angeles, CA: Feminist Foundation.

Peak, K., and Glenser, R. W. (2004). *Community Policing and Problem Solving*, 4th ed. Upper Saddle River, NJ: Prentice Hall.

Reiman, J. (2001). *The Rich Get Richer and the Poor Get Prison: Ideology, Class and Criminal Justice*, 6th ed. Boston, MA: Allyn and Bacon.

Reppetto, T. A. (1978). *The Blue Parade*. New York: Free Press.

Roberg, R. R., Kuykendall, J., and Novak, K. (2002). *Police Management*, 3rd ed. Los Angeles, CA: Roxbury Press.

Shusta, R. M., Levine, D. R., Wong, H. Z., and Harris, P. R. (2005). *Multicultural Law Enforcement: Strategies for Peacemaking in a Diverse Society*. Upper Saddle River, NJ: Pearson/Prentice Hall.

Walker, S. (1977). *A Critical History of Police Reform: The Emergence of Professionalism*. Lexington, MA: Lexington Books.

Walker, S., and Katz, C. M. (2002). *The Police in America: An Introduction*, 4th ed. Boston, MA: McGraw-Hill.

Whisenand, P. M., and Ferguson, F. (1989). *The Managing of Police Organizations*, 3rd ed. Upper Saddle River, NJ: Prentice Hall.

CHAPTER 6

Relations within the Police Organization

Police officers do not do what they do by themselves or on their own; they do so within the framework of an organization, an agency—a police agency.

—BARKER, HUNTER, AND RUSH, 1994

KEY CONCEPTS

Auxiliary Service	Formal Organization	Police Insiders
Civilian Personnel	Informal Organization	Staff Personnel
Communications	Line Personnel	Sworn Personnel

LEARNING OBJECTIVES

Studying this chapter will enable you to:

1. Discuss the structure and organization of police agencies.
2. Describe the various interdependent work groups that exist within police organizations.
3. Identify and describe the complex relationships between individuals and units that determine the success of the police organization.
4. Describe how the change process is influenced by good communication and coordination of efforts.
5. Discuss the impact of unions within police organizations.
6. Develop recommendations on how officers should deal with other police "insiders."

In order to perform successfully within the police bureaucracy, a police officer must be able to recognize and cope with the interaction among the overlapping (and often competing) groups into which "police insiders" may be divided. In this chapter, we identify and discuss some of the more prevalent organizational groupings found within police agencies and various issues that impact their interactions.

LIFE INSIDE A POLICE ORGANIZATION

A police organization is often viewed by outsiders as a single community of like-minded individuals dedicated to the performance of specifically defined tasks. In actuality, a police organization is a conglomerate of many individuals and groups that cooperate in varying degrees in their attempts to accomplish a variety of complex and often ill-defined tasks. These groups are contained within a bureaucratic structure designed to maintain discipline and accountability.

Despite its quasi-military structure, the police organization is not a closed system (Roberg, Kuykendall and Novak, 2002). How well the police agency functions depends on how well police officers contend with the many influences—both from inside and outside the organization—that impact employee performance. The various types of influences on employee behavior are displayed in Figure 6.1.

THE FORMAL ORGANIZATION

Despite decades of proposed managerial approaches (including community-oriented policing), police organizations remain quasi-military hierarchies. Efforts to change their organizational structures have been met with only limited success. No alternative structure has yet emerged that is perceived as a system for managing the performance of the many police groups. The reason for the endurance of the quasi-military structure is that it facilitates communications, coordination, and control—all of which are vital to the success of the police mission.

Communications and Accountability

Of all the skills needed to be an effective officer, leader, and/or supervisor, skill in communicating is the most vital (Bennett and Hess, 2007). To be successful, officers must be able to clearly articulate their decisions and the responses expected from others. They must also ensure that their interpretations of communications from superiors, peers, subordinates, and

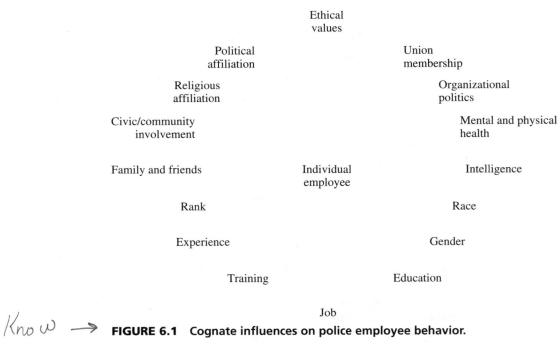

Know →   **FIGURE 6.1** Cognate influences on police employee behavior.

others from both inside and outside the police agency are accurate. Communications within the organizational setting are too frequently misconstrued by those who fail to verify that they understand or have been understood by others.

Although communication skills vary from officer to officer, even the best communicators cannot be effective unless they are in the "loop." The police bureaucracy attempts to ensure that managers are not bypassed by establishing a chain of command and formal communications (Lynch and Lynch, 2005). Although the purpose of formal communications is to ensure that commands are relayed and that coordinated decision making is facilitated, recurrent breakdowns do take place. The frequency of these communication failures and their negative impact can be effectively curtailed by examining and revising (1) the existing informational exchange network and (2) job assignments to ensure functional grouping of work units in both physical and organizational proximity.

If there is no means of verifying accountability for actions taken (or not taken) within the organization, goals and objectives will not be met. There must be a clear chain of command within the organization that delineates who has the authority to give orders and who is responsible for compliance with those orders. It is of vital importance that the chain of command not be limited to a mechanism for pushing orders downward. Rather, it should be a responsive communication network that channels information and ideas in both directions and facilitates feedback. In addition, the span of control for each police officer must be restricted to an appropriate number of subordinates, units, and/or duties for which they may be reasonably held accountable (Barker, Hunter, and Rush, 1994).

Structure

As discussed in the previous sections, police organizations are quasi-military hierarchies designed to maintain command and control over subordinates. This heavily centralized structure is frequently criticized as being outdated and ineffective. Performance within the traditional police organizational structure all too often degenerates into a bureaucratic quagmire that stifles productivity and overwhelms **line personnel** with excessive paperwork. However, it is our view that the coordination of interactions within the structure—not the overall organizational structure itself—usually leads to problems in performance. The communication and accountability enhancements suggested in the previous section can be readily incorporated into the organizational structures utilized within most law enforcement agencies without dramatic changes.

The traditional police hierarchy is a pyramid-type structure comprising those components deemed necessary to achieve the agency's mission. In small police agencies, two or three components may address all the duties for which the organization is responsible. The organizational structure for a typical small police agency is displayed in Figure 6.2. Larger police agencies require more complex organizational structures in order to accomplish the increasingly intricate and specialized duties required in metropolitan areas. The tasks assigned and the lines of authority necessary to ensure coordination of efforts and compliance with regulations determine how the organization is divided. An organizational structure indicative of the typical medium-size police department is given in Figure 6.3. An extremely large department is shown in Figure 6.4.

ORGANIZATIONAL UNITS

Every police organization (excluding the small agencies that perform the required functions but have no separate units) is divided into operations, administration, and auxiliary services. Administration may consist solely of the chief administrator, or it may comprise many units made up of numerous employees. Auxiliary services may be limited to a single dispatcher who also performs other duties, or it may include ancillary units that involve many individuals performing

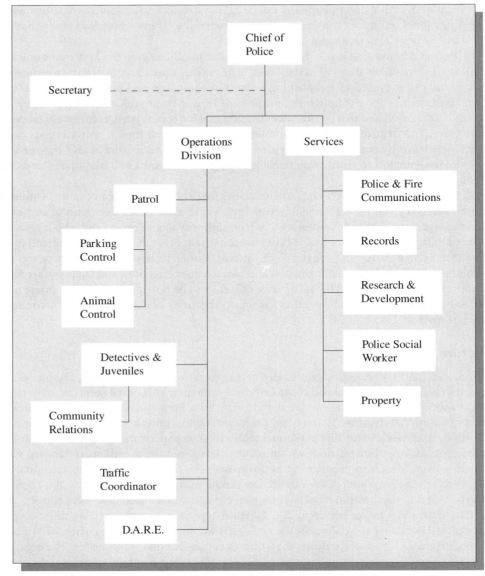

FIGURE 6.2 **A small-size police department: Wilmette, Illinois (sworn personnel: 42).**
Courtesy of Wilmette Police Department.

specialized functions in a variety of work locations. Operations may be one or two patrol officers performing all direct-to-the-public services during a particular work shift, or it may consist of several thousand patrol officers, investigators, and specialists within a metropolitan department.

The number of units within a police organization, where they are located within the system, as well as the duties assigned to those units vary considerably from agency to agency. In addition to size, such factors as available resources, administrative priorities, demands for service, and organizational tradition determine how the agency will be structured. Table 6.1 indicates the typical work units and the component within which the observer might reasonably expect to find them. It should be noted that in many midsize police organizations, administration and auxiliary services (often called "technical services") are frequently combined within a support services bureau.

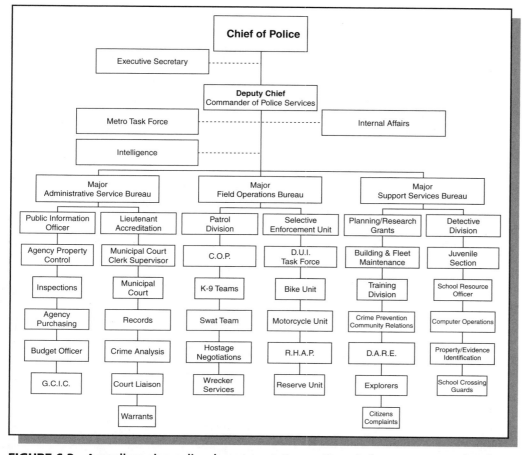

FIGURE 6.3 A medium-size police department: Rome, Georgia (sworn personnel: 98).

Courtesy of Rome Police Department.

Operations

Operations units are those components within a police organization that provide direct services to the public. The most important operations unit is the patrol unit. Indeed, in many small departments, patrol is the only operations unit. Patrol is charged with providing a first response to virtually all calls for police services. It is the only unit within the typical police agency responsible for all three functions of policing: crime control, order maintenance, and service delivery (Barker, Hunter, and Rush, 1994). Therefore, regardless of agency size, patrol should receive first priority in the allocation of both personnel and resources.

In larger departments, criminal investigations is the operations unit that follows patrol in value. As agency size and workload increase, patrol officers do not have the time to conduct lengthy and complicated follow-up investigations as well as to remain accountable for their assigned beat. Criminal investigations assumes the responsibility for continuing investigations initiated by patrol officers that cannot be readily concluded and/or require additional resources due to their severity or complexity.

The other tasks shown in Table 6.1 may be conducted as part of either patrol or criminal investigations or may be assigned to specialized units. The size of these units, the nature of their duties, and their location within the organizational structure are wholly dependent on the agency being examined. It is essential that they be located near other units with whom they

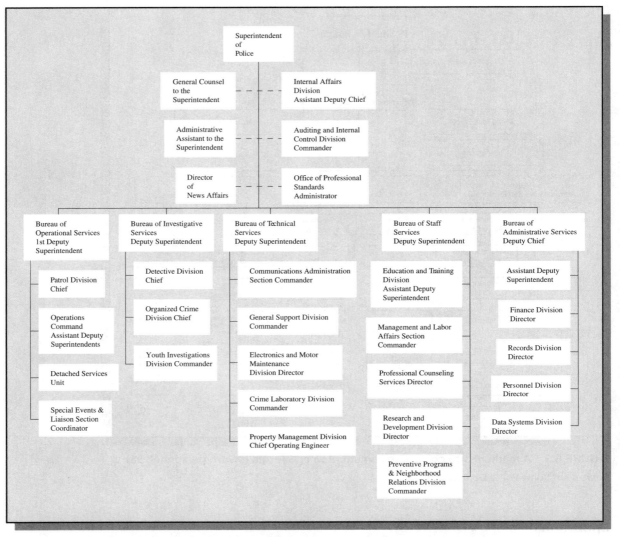

FIGURE 6.4 **An extremely large police department: Chicago, Illinois (sworn personnel: 13,000+).**
Courtesy of Chicago Police Department.

interact (e.g., patrol officers and investigators must have ready access to crime analysis or that unit's worth is severely impaired).

Administration

Table 6.1 lists subdivisions of administration responsible for the processes by which police personnel are selected, trained, advised, regulated, evaluated, transferred, promoted, demoted, disciplined, rewarded, compensated, and terminated. The responsibility for performing these functions may be with a single administrator in a small agency or may require the efforts of many units in a large metropolitan organization.

The many tasks involved in administration and their impact on both individuals and the entire organization cannot be stressed too much. Although individuals in operations are the

TABLE 6.1 Typical Police Organizational Components

Operations	Administration	Auxiliary Services
Patrol	Personnel	Records
Traffic	Training	Communications
Investigations	Planning and analysis	Property and evidence
Vice and narcotics	Budget and finance	Crime lab
Organized crime	Legal assistance	Detention
Juvenile services	Public information	Identification
Crime prevention	Internal affairs	Facilities maintenance
Crime analysis	Intelligence	Equipment maintenance
Special operations	Computer services	Departmental supply

backbone of the department and should be duly recognized as such, administration is the nerve center that ensures that operations personnel are able to perform their tasks adequately.

Auxiliary Services

Support units responsible for providing direct assistance to operations personnel are often referred to as being auxiliary, ancillary, or technical services units (Barker, Hunter, and Rush, 1994; Cordner, Scarborough, and Sheehan, 2004). Although administrative units are necessary in order to maintain the police organization, auxiliary units are essential in order to provide police services to the public. The most important **auxiliary service** is communications. Communications, which provides the vital link to the public and to other police units, is second only to patrol in importance to the police organization. The other auxiliary units indicated in Table 6.1 are also required for the success of operations personnel and the accomplishment of the organization's mission.

THE INFORMAL ORGANIZATION   ←—*Know*

Informal communication networks exist that often circumvent the organization's formal structure. This **informal organization** is both advantageous and disadvantageous to a police agency. Although official business is conducted by the **formal organization**, the informal organization often determines which decisions will be made and the manner in which these decisions will be carried out (Thibault, Lynch, and McBride, 2004). The informal organization plays an important role in ensuring that things get done when the formal structure or individuals within it are found to be lacking. Unfortunately, the informal organization can also be utilized to inhibit the success of programs, impede the enforcement of policies and procedures, and resist organizational change.

Activities and Effects

The informal organization is made up of many different communications networks, which crisscross the department's formal organizational structure. These networks may expedite agency performance by permitting individuals to utilize their political skills to interrelate with one another in order to better accomplish their respective tasks. Being aware of who exerts influence on which decision makers, who should be avoided on specific issues, who can be contacted within a particular unit, and who is on friendly terms with whom can greatly enhance an individual's ability to get things done.

Those same contacts that enhance performance can also become detrimental when misused by personnel who are more concerned with their own self-interests. Leaking privileged information to curious friends, calling on "contacts" to inhibit actions proposed by perceived competitors, organizing opposition to policies or program changes, and seeking assistance in concealing misconduct are but a few examples of the adverse effects of the informal organization. In addition, organizational performance will be severely impaired if these informal networks lead to the development of cliques and rivalries, which too frequently degenerate into petty feuds that detract from work efforts.

Know →
All 5

POLICE ORGANIZATIONAL CONSIDERATIONS

There are many factors within the police organization that influence or directly determine how well that organization will accomplish its stated goals. None are more important than the relations among individuals and units within the organization.

Staff versus Line Personnel

Police organizations, like all bureaucracies, are divided into those performing specific tasks and those facilitating those performing the tasks. Individuals and units assigned to perform specific police tasks are categorized as line personnel, or operations personnel. Individuals assigned to facilitate the performance of police tasks (administration and auxiliary services) are categorized as **staff personnel**, or support personnel.

Students of the police (and often the police themselves) frequently fail to grasp that both operations and support are "real police work." These separate units are totally dependent on one another. Unfortunately, in their concerns with individual or unit goals, individuals within these respective work units often tend to lose sight of the organizational mission. When this occurs, mutual cooperation and benefit become competition and conflict, which undermine the effectiveness of both the individual units and the overall organization.

Sworn versus Civilian Personnel

Demands for enhanced governmental efficiency by taxpayers and community-interest groups have affected the police as well as other public organizations. One means of increasing police efficiency has been to utilize civilians in those positions that do not require sworn police officers. The vast majority of support services can be provided by **civilian personnel** (Swanson, Territo, and Taylor, 2005). Use of civilians may also be extended to many operations duties that can be performed by nonsworn (and less expensive) community service officers.

The use of civilians may be threatening to some **sworn personnel**, particularly those who occupied positions that have since been "civilianized." In addition, the difference in status between sworn and nonsworn may lead to resentment and conflict (Roberg, Kuykendall, and Novak, 2002). The importance of all employees to the overall departmental mission, regardless of their assignment or position, must be constantly stressed by management.

Interunit Competition

Just as myopic views regarding the importance of one's work group and the lack of importance of other units can lead to problems between operations and support personnel, such views can also affect relations within operations units. This view of "us versus them" frequently leads to competition and conflict, particularly between patrol and investigation units. During their respective law enforcement careers, the authors observed that individuals who resented other units tended to do so regardless of their assignments. If transferred from one unit to another, they soon joined with those whom they earlier opposed in criticizing those with whom they recently served. Unfortunately, supervisors and unit managers often instigate conflict among organizational units in the mistaken belief that they are promoting "healthy competition."

FIGURE 6.5 Virginia PBA members attend a Hampton City Council meeting en masse.
Courtesy of David Graham.

Union Issues

A labor union is a legally recognized employee organization that has the authority to bargain with employers on behalf of its membership. Labor unions have existed in this country for nearly two centuries but did not become forces to be reckoned with in policing until the 1960s (Bennett and Hess, 2007).

Despite strong opposition on the part of police administrators and elected officials, police unions have developed in response to desires for better economic benefits, enhanced working conditions, fair treatment, and input into policymaking. Today, nearly three-fourths of all American police officers are members of unions (Walker and Katz, 2002).

Collective bargaining is the term by which the negotiation process between the police union and the employing organization is known. Within the negotiation process, representatives of the union and representatives of the governmental entity that employs them seek to reach agreement on issues such as salaries, work conditions, job assignments, promotional policies, disciplinary procedures, health coverage, pensions, and paid leave, as well as other relevant concerns. Once an agreement has been reached (either through negotiations or, following their breakdown, arbitration or court settlement), the union and governmental agency enter into a legally binding contract that specifies the rights of both sides regarding their interaction with one another. Failure of either side to comply with the contractual agreement is dealt with administratively or, if necessary, through litigation.

In addition to collective bargaining, police unions provide representation for individual employees in disciplinary proceedings. They also represent employees who have filed grievances against supervisory actions or administrative policies that are perceived as improper or unfair. Police unions assist in providing legal representation for members. They participate in political campaigns in order to strengthen the police influence on lawmaking and governmental policies. They lobby local, state, and—occasionally—the federal government on law enforcement issues. In addition, they serve as social organizations that sponsor activities for and on behalf of their memberships.

The impact of police unions on policing has often been negatively depicted by police administrators and civilian reformers, who see the unions as promoting employee issues at the expense of the police organization. Unions are believed to have impeded organizational progress due to (1) their concerns about seniority, which frequently conflicted with affirmative action and merit programs; (2) their resistance to civilian review boards, which would enhance community relations; (3) their desire to participate in decision making, which restricts managerial discretion in the achievement of the police mission; and (4) their concern with economic benefits, which restricts funds needed in other areas (Cole and Smith, 2007).

However, police unions are also seen as having a positive impact on policing in that they require police organizations to become more professional. Police administrators have defined professionalism as bureaucratic enforcement of strict rules and regulations. Unions have required managers to become more sensitive to employee issues and to permit employees to have input into departmental decision making. Involving the rank and file in decision making has improved police effectiveness and has required police administrators to enhance their own performance.

Professionalism is now being defined by progressive police administrators as developing competent personnel capable of interacting with the community to provide desired services. The sense of belonging fostered by increased participation in the organization's success (and subsequent increased responsibility) has heightened police performance. Limiting the potential for administrative mismanagement has benefited not only the internal communities but the external communities as well (Whisenand, 2005).

Managing Change

Change is an inevitable manifestation of organizational life. It cannot be ignored. It is a reality of the working environment in which policing is done. Although change may make us uncomfortable, it is certain to occur. In fact, it is vital to the positive growth of a law enforcement agency (Cordner, Scarborough, and Sheehan, 2004). Efforts to implement changes within the police organization (such as community policing) that do not take into account the interaction of the various work groups (as well as the internal communities discussed in the previous chapter) will produce only short-term benefits. Those individuals who feel threatened by proposed changes will undermine such efforts (Bennett and Hess, 2007). Therefore, proponents of change must fully understand the interactions within a police organization before they begin to implement their programs.

FIGURE 6.6 Dr. Ron Hunter presenting officer satisfaction survey results to the Hampton, Virginia, City Council.

Courtesy of David Graham.

Every officer who has been transferred to a new assignment has heard the words "But we've always done it this way!" Human beings are creatures of habit who do not welcome changes in their established routines. As a result, implementing change can be a very difficult and frustrating ordeal for all concerned. It challenges those whose work efforts and procedures are being altered from familiar methods to new and potentially threatening processes (which are often viewed as being counterproductive if not outright unnecessary). It also requires those overseeing the implementation of change to provide fair but firm leadership.

The key to managing change within a police organization is understanding the following:

1. *Why change must occur.* (It could be mandated by outside influences such as court decisions, the passage of new laws, or community demands; prescribed by superiors seeking to enhance departmental performance; or based on the individual supervisor's desires to increase individual or unit productivity.)
2. *What the effects of the proposed change might be.* (What are the intended results? What are the effects, both beneficial and adverse, on individuals and units? Who will be affected? How will they be affected? How extensive will the impact be?)
3. *How change is to occur.* (What is to be done? Who is to do it? Where will the changes occur? When are they to occur?)

Once a police manager has obtained answers to the aforementioned questions, he or she should convey that understanding to subordinates. Much resistance to change within the organization is due to lack of communication on the part of management about why change is occurring, what its effects will be, and what employees are supposed to do. In addition, the police supervisor or manager should relay reasonable concerns and recommendations regarding the implementation of change to superiors.

DEALING WITH OTHER EMPLOYEES ← *Know*

The pressures and challenges of the varying responsibilities held by police officers (whether patrol officers, investigators, first-line supervisors, middle managers, command staff, or top administrators) require not only task competence but also understanding of subordinates, superiors, and counterparts. If either of these qualities is lacking, difficulties will naturally occur. In the following section, we examine the varying issues that impact the manager's relations with these different groups.

Dealing with Superiors

The management styles of police executives vary considerably due to work assignment, experience, education, training, individual personality, and the policy requirements of the agency and/or superiors. How well administrators and supervisors relate to other individuals within the organization depends on the appropriateness of their particular management styles. In order to deal effectively with managers in superior positions, officers and/or lower-ranking managers must accurately comprehend others' leadership styles as well as their own.

Cordner, Scarborough, and Sheehan (2004) identified four general styles of leadership found among police managers. These styles of leadership are ideal types; some police leaders exhibit just one style, while other leaders may represent combinations of one of more styles. The key to understanding each style is how the police leader orients himself or herself to the internal and external communities.

1. *The Administrator.* The administrator adheres to the traditional/professional model of police administration. He/she believes that education, training, and technology are the keys to maintaining police autonomy and ensuring effective administration. Administrators' efforts are directed primarily to the internal communities and management duties. Management duties are important and cannot be ignored, but often these administrators

ignore the importance of external communities and the equal importance of police–community relations. The ideal-type administrator is not likely to embrace community-oriented policing.

 ✳ 2. *The Top Cop.* This police leadership style emphasizes leadership over management. He or she is internally oriented and very popular with the troops. They are often seen on the scene of major crimes and disturbances. Sometimes they become the major defenders of their cops even when they are wrong.

 ✳ 3. *The Politician.* Politicians leave internal management to subordinates while they cater to civic, political, and community groups. They may be very successful in creating good relations with external communities; however, they will not provide organizational guidance and stability. Furthermore, placing internal management in the hands of incapable or incompetent subordinates can be disastrous.

 ✳ 4. *The Statesman.* The statesman recognizes the importance of leadership internally and externally. He or she recognizes the importance of the troops, the entire organization, and the community. While the statesman will delegate management duties throughout the organization, he or she recognizes being solely responsible for its operation. A statesman charts the course and provides the values for the agency. The statesman also provides leadership in the community. The statesman recognizes that he or she is always accountable to the public and adhere to the principle of "policing by consent" in democratic societies.

The first three leadership styles have their own strengths and weaknesses. The fourth style, the statesman, is superior to the others. Those who fit this style—and they may be rare as an ideal type—recognize the importance of the internal and external communities. No police executive can succeed without recognizing the importance of both the internal and external communities. Neither should they forget that the police in a democratic society receive their authority from the people.

Immediate Superiors

The superior with whom the officer must be most familiar is his or her immediate supervisor. Successful officers must establish working rapport with their immediate superiors despite any differences in personal perspectives and/or administrative philosophies. Even though the relationship may not be warm and trust may be minimal, it is imperative for both current and future success that such differences be quickly and satisfactorily resolved. Regardless of personal conflicts, an immediate supervisor is entitled to the respect that the position deserves and to the loyalty desired if positions were to be reversed.

Most disagreements with superiors can be mitigated through understanding and compromise. When there are disputes that are not readily reconciled, officers must remember their responsibilities to the agency, their colleagues, and to themselves. Unhappy superiors can do considerable harm to an officer's career, so one should ensure that one's actions are both correct *and necessary* before challenging superiors. If such action is legally and/or ethically unavoidable, the officer should immediately request an audience with his or her superior's supervisor, seeking redress. If the direct supervisor is also the agency's top administrator, the only recourse may be legal action.

Distant Superiors

The same considerations just given also apply to superiors who are higher in the chain of command and to those outside the chain of command. There is a tendency on the part of police officers to focus on dealing with their peers and their immediate supervisors and to overlook relations with other superiors. Although one should not become fixated on developing political contacts, building goodwill whenever opportunities arise is a prudent strategy. (Those who try to play politics in order to enhance their careers are easily recognized and either held in contempt or manipulated by others.) The superior whom your current boss detests and encourages you to dislike could very well be your boss next month. Treat everyone with the respect they are due and hope that in the future it will be returned.

DEALING WITH SUBORDINATES

Much of the discussion regarding superiors is also applicable to dealing with subordinates. A professional, caring demeanor in which subordinates are treated with respect and a leadership approach that approximates the statesman style as closely as the work environment permits are recommended. In addition, it is important that the officer who attains supervisory rank understand not only the duties assigned within the work unit but also the tasks involved in performing those duties. He or she must also understand the employees being supervised.

Immediate Subordinates   ← *Know*

Roberg, Kuykendall, and Novak (2002) identified six employee types that police managers may encounter. Our adaption of these employee types follows:

1. *Rookies.* Neophytes seeking to prove themselves within the organization. They tend to be highly motivated and have high commitment to organizational goals but are initially lacking job competency. They require constant monitoring and direction.
2. *Workers.* Experienced employees who are moderately motivated, have high commitment to organizational goals, and have moderate-to-high job competency. They require only minimal monitoring and direction.
3. *Stars.* Talented, hardworking, ambitious employees who are highly motivated, have moderateto-high commitment to organizational goals, and high job competency. They require very little direction and only minimal monitoring unless they begin to view themselves as superior to and more deserving than other employees.
4. *Cynics.* Pessimistic and suspicious employees who commonly feel that they have been wronged by the organization. They often display low motivation and low commitment to organizational goals even though they have moderate-to-high job competency. They require very little direction, but frequent monitoring is necessary, except when assigned to tasks they feel to be interesting or important.
5. *Retirees.* Long-term employees who have become disenchanted with or have lost interest in their jobs. They have low motivation and low commitment to organizational goals despite moderate-to-high job competency. They require frequent direction and constant monitoring, with little hope of inducing more than marginal performance.
6. *Depleted.* "Burned out" employees who display no energy and no interest in the job and who are prone to mistakes. They have no motivation, no commitment to organizational goals, and low job competency. They cannot be effectively managed and should be removed from the operational environment and referred to appropriate professionals.

With the exception of the depleted employee, a good manager can successfully direct the performance of all the employee types discussed above. The purpose is providing leadership that is fair and equitable to all concerned. Fairness dictates that subordinates receive neither preferential nor discriminatory treatment. Equitable means providing attention to employees, which is not necessarily equal in detail or duration but is equal in effect.

Distant Subordinates

Although supervisory officers are concerned primarily with their own immediate subordinates, they must also consider lower-ranking employees within their chain of command and from other units within the organization. No individual or unit within a law enforcement agency operates in a vacuum. Just as wise officers consider the political expediency of maintaining good relations with distant superiors, they should also consider relations with distant subordinates. Providing appropriate consideration to distant subordinates may result in no direct benefit to any officer (although it might, because they could later become direct subordinates or direct supervisors), but such behavior might be beneficial to an officer's subordinates or to the overall mission of the department.

Know →

DEALING WITH PEERS

In addition to superiors and subordinates, an officer must also consider relations with individuals of equal rank. These individuals have the potential to either aid or inhibit an officer's current efforts within the organization. In addition, they may be future superiors or subordinates on whom the officer must rely. The ambitious officer would be well advised to monitor his or her conduct during the competition that inevitably develops during promotional and transfer processes. If rivalries are allowed to become too intense, they could be detrimental to the career ambitions of all concerned.

In dealing with peers, there are three types that should be considered:

1. *Allies.* Individuals with whom the manager has developed a mutually beneficial working relationship. These individuals need not be close personal friends, but they are inclined to view the manager in a positive manner and would not hesitate to render reasonable assistance if called upon.
2. *Adversaries.* Individuals with whom the manager has experienced difficulty in the past or whose past behavior toward others would cause the manager to be suspicious of their motivations.
3. *Neutrals.* Individuals with whom the manager has established neither an adversarial nor a beneficial working relationship. This may be due to changing circumstances that cause a manager to reevaluate a previous relationship or the result of little or no previous contact with the individual in question.

Interrelations with all three types of peers should be considered when making managerial decisions. As with superiors and subordinates, a police employee should contemplate who else is affected by his or her actions. Allies can be easily lost due to a selfish or thoughtless action. Neutrals can become adversaries, and adversaries can become hardened in their resolve to do harm should the opportunity arise.

Interrelationships

One of the quickest means of alienating other police employees is to claim credit for their accomplishments and/or to downplay their contributions to a project or event. If others (subordinates, peers, or superiors) aided you or assisted in a successful activity, ensure that proper credit is given. This may range from a simple thank-you to a written letter of appreciation, a public acknowledgment of contribution, or even a formal recommendation of award for meritorious conduct. Sharing glory for successful accomplishment is not only the right thing to do, it is also the smart thing to do.

In addition to sharing credit for success, an officer must also know how to deal with blame for failure. Despite the best intentions and efforts, things occasionally go wrong. When this occurs in a bureaucracy, there is too often a tendency to roll the blame as far down the organizational structure as possible. A good officer will not only be quick to identify and correct improper performance but will also be willing to accept responsibility for his or her own failures. Correcting mistakes is an integral part of police management. The officer should face this task with courage and fairness. Do not scapegoat others for your mistakes. Do not allow yourself to become a dupe for blunders made by superiors or peers. Never allow a subordinate to bear blame that is undeserved.

Before engaging in combative or controversial activities, the officer should ask, if the gain—on behalf of self, subordinates, superiors, peers, or the department as a whole—is worth the anticipated costs. If the answer to that question for any of the parties is no, don't do it!

FIGURE 6.7 **Officers receiving commendations.**

Courtesy of Chief Tom Johnson.

REALITY CHECK

You Just May Reap What You Sow

Approximately 20 years ago, a sergeant who supervised a dual-agency investigative task force approached his supervisor in a large Florida police department about a problem with one of the police investigators assigned to the task force. The sergeant had received a complaint from a 17-year-old clerk employed at the sheriff's department (who also participated in the task force) that a married police investigator had been having an affair with her. She alleged that the investigator would go to her apartment when he was supposed to be working evening shifts (every fourth week) and would spend the time in bed with her. She stated that they had broken up but that he was still coming by when on evening shift and still trying to get her to have sex with him.

To the surprise of the sergeant, his supervisor (a politically connected lieutenant with ambitions to become police chief) ordered that he not take any actions and was not to refer the matter to Inspectional Services (internal affairs). The lieutenant asserted that he would deal with the investigator personally to prevent embarrassment to the department and everyone involved. He threatened to punish the sergeant for poor supervision if he did not let the matter drop. This was extremely surprising in that the lieutenant was known for being a zealot in enforcing the rules. Well aware that the lieutenant had the chief of police's ear and that both were very vindictive, the sergeant did as he was ordered.

In time, the lieutenant advanced to the position of police chief. The investigator, who was now publicly known to be a protege of the former lieutenant, had also been promoted as his mentor had achieved rank. He was now a lieutenant himself assigned as a shift commander within Patrol Division.

A few months later, the police chief found himself having to deal with a scandal. A probationary police officer had filed a complaint of sexual harassment against the police department. Her allegation was that she had been pressured into having sex with her shift lieutenant. She further alleged that when she tried to end the relationship, she had been told that if she did not continue, the lieutenant would see that she did not satisfactorily complete her probationary period. A lawsuit was filed and the department was embarrassed by negative news coverage. The police chief's credibility was seriously damaged by this incident.

Guess as to the identity of the police lieutenant involved.

Conclusions

Police "insiders" include *all* departmental members, regardless of the typologies by which individuals and groups are categorized. In order to accomplish the tasks relative to the agency's mission, a successful police officer must understand not only the mission of his or her particular department but also how the agency is organized. There are a variety of groups contained within the police organization. Their relationships with one another are complex and constantly changing. Individual and group roles within both the formal and the informal organization influence the activities and effects of each. The different tasks performed within operations, administration, and auxiliary services must also be considered when evaluating the police organization.

There are a number of organizational considerations that are important to the police officers: staff versus line conflicts; sworn versus civilian conflicts; interunit competition; and how to manage change. The issues and impacts of police unions must also be considered. The categories of insiders with whom the officer must deal (e.g., superiors, subordinates, and peers) must not be overlooked. Each category of individual may require different responses on behalf of the officer.

Each section of this chapter conveyed a simple message: To be successful, police officers (regardless of rank) must be thoughtful, caring individuals who both understand their place within the organization and effectively interact with other people in the organization. This understanding and interaction are enhanced by a bureaucratic structure designed to facilitate communications, coordination, and control within the police organization.

BOX 6.1

What to Do

To deal effectively with the complex assortment of individuals and groups that comprise the police community, a police organization must be managed in a fair and competent manner that provides equal access and equitable treatment to all individuals. Police officers (regardless of rank) must be loyal to the agency and their colleagues within the agency. However, loyalty is based on what is both morally and legally correct. An officer's determination of his or her duty should be based on what is best for the organization but should not be at the expense of ethical principles.

Police officers must comprehend the interdependence of organizational components and promote cooperation among their peers, supervisors, and subordinates. The importance of every individual and work group within the department should be consistently emphasized. To ensure cooperation and maintain control within the organization, police managers must be effective communicators. Communication is the key not only to the police organization's success, but also to its survival.

What Not to Do

It is imperative that police officers understand where they fit within their organizations and how their work unit contributes to an agency's overall mission. They should not let personal desires or individual goals impact their unit's performance or its relations with other organizational components. Competition may aid in bolstering egos but must be controlled to prevent conflicts, which negatively impact both morale and performance.

Officers must not become aloof or isolated from other police insiders; they should not allow friendship or personal dislike to influence their decisions. In addition, police managers must be willing to delegate authority and responsibility to subordinates. In doing so, they must not forget to credit those responsible for the success of delegated duties. Too frequently, police managers seek to avoid blame that they should accept and claim glory that rightfully belongs to other people.

A police officer cannot be effective if other insiders are not treated properly. In order to be successful, officers must win the respect of their supervisors, peers, and subordinates. They cannot do so unless they demonstrate both personal integrity and respect for others.

Student Checklist

1. Discuss the structure and organization of police agencies.
2. Describe the various interdependent work groups that exist within police organizations.
3. Identify and describe the complex relationships between individuals and units that determine the success of a police organization.
4. Describe how the change process is influenced by good communication and coordination of efforts.
5. Discuss the impacts of unions within police organizations.
6. Develop recommendations on how officers should deal with other police insiders.

Topics for Discussion

1. Describe the organizational structure of your local police agency. How is it similar to those discussed within this chapter? How is it different from them?
2. Identify whether your local police agency has a collective bargaining agreement with a police union. If so, discuss the effect of the union on the police organization. If not, discuss what changes such a collective bargaining agreement would have on the organization.

Bibliography

Barker, T., Hunter, R. D., and Rush, J. P. (1994). *Police Systems and Practices: An Introduction.* Upper Saddle River, NJ: Prentice Hall.

Bennett, W. W., and Hess, K. M. (2007). *Management and Supervision in Law Enforcement,* 5th ed. Pacific Grove, CA: Thomson/Wadsworth.

Cole, G. F., and Smith, C. E. (2007). *The American System of Criminal Justice,* 11th ed. Pacific Grove, CA: Thomson/Wadsworth.

Cordner, G. W., Scarborough, K., and Sheehan, R. (2004). *Police Administration,* 5th ed. Cincinnati, OH: Anderson Publishing.

Lynch, R. G., and Lynch, S. (2005). *The Police Manager,* 6th ed. Cincinnati, OH: Anderson Publishing.

Roberg, R. R., Kuykendall, J., and Novak, J. (2002). *Police Management,* 3rd ed. Los Angeles, CA: Roxbury Publishing.

Swanson, C. R., Territo, L., and Taylor, R. W. (2005). *Police Administration: Structures, Processes and Behavior,* 6th ed. Upper Saddle River, NJ: Pearson/Prentice Hall.

Thibault, E. A., Lynch, L. M., and McBride, B. R. (2004). *Proactice Police Management,* 6th ed. Upper Saddle River, NJ: Prentice Hall.

Walker, S., and Katz, C. M. (2002). *The Police in America: An Introduction,* 4th ed. Boston, MA: McGraw-Hill.

Whisenand, P. M. (2005). *Managing Police Organizations,* 6th ed. Upper Saddle River, NJ: Prentice Hall.

CHAPTER 7

Coping with the Human Experience of Being a Cop

A good officer doing his job is a textbook example of burnout in progress.
—Daviss, 1982

A good police officer is like the transmission of a fine highway tractor—10 speeds forward, 3 in reverse, with a clutch that makes it possible to move from one to another smoothly and virtually at will.
—Delattre, 1981

KEY CONCEPTS

Emotional Distress
Family Programs
Health Hazards

Mental Illness
Physical Wellness
Social Hazards

Socialization
Wellness Programs
Working Personality

LEARNING OBJECTIVES

Studying this chapter will enable you to:

1. Identify and discuss factors that make it difficult for police officers to cope with change.
2. Discuss how the police working personality contributes to community isolation.
3. Identify and discuss the social hazards of police work.
4. Identify and discuss the health hazards of police work.
5. Identify and discuss strategies for reducing the stressors of police work.

The real or perceived role of the police in a changing society (see Chapter 2) directly affects the human experience of being a cop. A career in law enforcement can be exciting, challenging, and rewarding for those who are people oriented and committed to public service. Yet it can also be devastating for those who are not prepared for its rigors. Thousands of well-meaning, dedicated individuals who thought that police work was the career for which they were destined have discovered that the mental, physical, social, or economic costs of continuing such a career were too high. Many others have persisted within the field but at considerable expense to them and to others.

Police work is a hazardous craft that requires strong, caring individuals who can consistently deal with stressful situations. Over time, the impact of the dangers and stressors inherent to policing affects individual police officers differently. Some, perhaps most, go through their entire careers without suffering personally in any unusual or specific way. For others, policing appears to take a special toll on their lives. The sense of community isolation, the potential dangers, and the unique police lifestyle all seem to work together to adversely affect certain officers' physical, mental, and social well-being.

CHANGE AND THE POLICE   ← Know

Changes of recent years have had especially strong impact on police work. They include the following:

- Unprecedented advances in technology
- Biomedical advances
- Rethinking of moral issues
- Erosion of the sense of community or neighborhood solidarity
- Breakdowns in traditional social roles and institutional arrangement (especially those involving the family)
- Demands for a more just distribution of wealth and civil, social, and political rights
- Economic instability

The police frequently are caught in the middle, between those who want change and those who want to preserve the status quo. Individual police officers feel the conflict daily. The officer who is attacked by a group of angry youths as he attempts to arrest one of them for speeding understands the problem of being caught in the middle. So does the officer who, in a time of high unemployment, must serve an increasing number of eviction notices to families who cannot make mortgage payments on their homes, or who must supervise an auction of the family's possessions.

WHAT POLICING DOES TO THE POLICE

The Working Personality

Jerome Skolnick presented an analysis of how certain features that he identifies in the police officer's environment interact with the paramilitary structure of the typical police organization to produce what he calls a **working personality** (Skolnick, 1975, pp. 42–70). The danger present in the police officer's environment makes police officers suspicious people. They must respond to reported assaults against property and persons. As a result of their preoccupation with violence, they develop a stereotyping "perceptual shorthand" to identify "symbolic assailants": for example, "black equals danger." The individual police officer's suspiciousness does not necessarily result from personal experience. It may develop through identification with fellow officers who may have been victims of violence in the line of duty. Officers may feel socially isolated from a community that may consider them to be similar to occupation troops in an occupied country. The police band together with a solidarity surpassing that found in most occupational groupings.

The authority invested in the police further isolates police officers from a public that resents their direction in such activities as traffic and sports events or their regulation of public morality. Police officers are further accused of hypocrisy for having taken part in some of the activities (such as drunkenness) that they are called upon to suppress.

Since Skolnick's working personality of the police officer was first presented, the subject of the police personality has been discussed and analyzed from several different perspectives. Much of the literature tends to support, expand, and/or clarify elements of Skolnick's original thesis (Alpert, 1997; Burbeck and Furnham, 1985).

Selection or Socialization

Policing has great impact on those who choose it as a career. Some authors suggest that people who choose police work as a career are in a sense predisposed toward formulating a police personality. In other words, they may exhibit personality traits that are accepted and possibly rewarded in a law enforcement occupation.

This predispositional viewpoint may be interpreted in two different manners. The first interpretation is that those who seek to enter police work are authoritarian personalities who desire to have power and control over other citizens. This view or "myth" (Wrobleski and Hess, 2006) now receives little support from police scholars. A second predispositional interpretation is "that the behavior of a police officer is primarily explained by the characteristics, values, and attitudes that the individual had before he or she was employed" (Roberg, Kuykendall, and Novak, 2002). An example of this interpretation is Holden's argument (1992, p. 164) that police values are for the most part the lower-middle-class values that the majority of police officers bring into police work.

Know → A police behavioral perspective that competes with predispositional theory is that of **socialization**. Socialization theory holds that police behavior is learned from interactions with other police officers. Proponents of this view argue that as new police officers learn the "skills of policing" they also adopt the attitudes and values of their peers (Bayley and Bittner, 1997; Crank, 1998). In fact, those interested in a career in policing may actually begin to acquire police values and beliefs prior to entering police work (Roberg, Novak, and Cordner, 2005). Socialization is thought to occur as a result of the formal police organizational structure with its rigid rules and discipline, the informal "police subculture" into which the new officers are gradually assimilated, and the inherent nature of police work.

If one assumes, as we do, that human behavior is a product of lifelong learning experiences, an integrated perspective that considers the effects of socialization both prior to and after entering police service provides a more satisfactory explanation of police behavior. The values and beliefs that the individual officer takes into police work may or may not be compatible with those held by other officers. The new officer must then reassess his or her personal perspective in order to determine whether or not to adopt what appear to be "police norms." It is our view that the extent to which police officers accept or reject these norms is determined by the influence of the various community groups to which they belong.

Know → 3 ## SOCIAL HAZARDS OF POLICING

✳ Alienation from the Public

The police officer's role in society tends to alienate the officer from society as a whole. Police are given considerable authority by society to protect life and property and to keep public order; they are expected to risk their lives if necessary to discharge these duties. However, the police feel that they receive little prestige and support for such actions. Only recently has compensation in terms of salary increases and fringe benefits begun to be more closely commensurate with the responsibility and authority of the police, and those increases have not occurred uniformly throughout the United States or even from agency to agency in a given state or community.

Isolation and rejection of the police from society result in a sense of alienation. This pressures the police to develop their own subculture with norms that provide them with a basis for self-respect independent to some degree of civilian attitudes. Thus, many police officers look upon themselves as an oppressed minority, subject to the same kind of prejudice as other minorities.

Police as a Minority Group

A minority is a social group whose members experience, at the hands of another social group, various disabilities in the form of prejudice, discrimination, segregation, or persecution (or any combination of these). People tend to exclude police from their circle of friends because of the nature of the law enforcement occupation and its responsibilities. Such social discrimination is illustrated by the comments of a police officer to one of the authors.

> The business where my wife works recently had a picnic. My wife and I attended. I joined several other men at the barbecue pit to assist with the cooking. As we drank a beer or two, the discussion drifted to what occupations were represented in the group.
>
> I said that I was a police officer. One person turned to me and asked, "What kind? A detective?" I replied, "No, a traffic officer."
>
> The other man then became very interested. "What do you think of the new law that requires you to take away an individual's license when they have an accident until they can prove liability coverage?"
>
> I replied that it was a step in the right direction, but not enough. He exclaimed: "Aha! See, guys, what I told you! These guys are all alike. Give them a badge, a gun, some authority, and it goes to their head. They want to play storm troopers and abuse citizens!"
>
> By this time a larger group had gathered because the man had become very loud and argumentative. I told him quietly, "Listen, I don't want an argument. You asked for my opinion. Let's drop it. I just came over for some fun. I don't want any trouble." But he wouldn't stop.
>
> I walked over to my wife, informed her we were leaving. We spent the evening in our own backyard eating hamburgers that we had picked up on the way home. The evening was ruined for both of us. I'm not sure it is worth the trouble we have to go through just to be sociable.

Police are more likely to isolate themselves than to be isolated by others. Neighbors and friends have difficulty separating the person from the badge. When guests at a party discover there is a police officer present, they typically tell about the "crooked cops" they knew or how unfairly a friend of theirs was treated by a police officer. Most veteran officers grow weary of defending the police and withdraw into close associations with other officers. Given a choice, they would prefer to relax in the company of their fellow officers. In addition, the irregular hours created by shift work make it difficult for police to mesh their off-hours with those of neighbors who have "normal" occupations. A police officer is never "off duty." Many departments require an officer to carry a gun when not working and make arrests in outstanding cases.

Discrimination also affects the police officer's spouse and children.

> After I joined the force, the department started a program that allowed the officers to take their vehicles home. Since this program began, I have been asked on several occasions to speak to neighborhood youth who were racing up and down the street on dirt bikes. Everyone in the neighborhood now knows that I am an officer.
>
> Since beginning to bring the unit home, I have had my mailbox torn down several times. Excrement has been placed in it. Obscene phone calls are made frequently to my home. Beer bottles and empty cans have been thrown on my property. Trash cans have been turned over and the contents spilled on the ground.
>
> We are avoided by our neighbors, even though the neighborhood in which I live is a fine—so-called middle-class—area.
>
> My family is very unhappy. We are considering moving to another area—one where other police officers live. There we can have some peace and an opportunity to socialize without problems.

A sense of community isolation then emerges as the result of the job and the socialization process that occurs upon becoming a police officer. Police officers and their families develop strategies to cope with isolation from the community, which tends to lead to further isolation. They withdraw into the police subculture, which provides "protective, supportive, and shared attitudes, values, understandings and views of the world" (Grant and Terry, 2005). The product of this withdrawal is the exclusion of nonpolice associates, which leads to the development of a myopic (and therefore hazardous) view of society that Barker, Hunter, and Rush (1994) define as "blue blindness."

Isolation from the Family

All too often, policing becomes a disruptive influence for the family. The potential for danger, the authoritarian nature of the job, around-the-clock shifts, constantly changing shifts, and accommodations that must be made in family life all work together to increase tension in the law enforcement family. As a result, many believe that marital problems are endemic to law enforcement.

A high divorce rate is often linked to the police occupation itself (Terry, 1981). However, when policing is compared with other occupations and professions, it is found that the divorce rate is not that high (Peak, 2006). In many cases, the divorce rate among police officers is lower than anticipated (Doerner, 2004).

In some cases, this lower rate may be the result of more women involved in policing; there are now more two-officer families. In other cases, the spouse (particularly the wife) may have grown up in a police household, and this may be familiar with the strains attributable to policing. Finally, it may be that police families simply cope as well as or better than nonpolice families (Elliott et al., 1991). Further, when there is a divorce in a police family, it probably is for the same reasons that divorce occurs in any other family and not because of "the job." In divorce, as with many other aspects of policing, all too often the job gets blamed when the cause is elsewhere. However, a cautionary note comes from findings of a study conducted by researchers at the University of Buffalo, one of whom is a 23-year veteran of the New York State Police. The researchers found that female officers in their study were under more stress because policing is still a male occupation and women have more responsibilities to worry about such as family and child care (Violanti et al., 2008).

Know → 4 ## ECONOMIC HAZARDS OF POLICING

Salary Limitations

Before accepting or rejecting law enforcement as a career, potential candidates should carefully weigh the pros and cons of other occupations for which he or she might qualify. Although there are many other issues to consider in selecting one's life work, financial considerations cannot be ignored. If one's goal in life is to accumulate great wealth, one should not become a law enforcement officer. Despite the education, training, and professionalism of such a career, unless one rises to a top administrative position, becomes corrupt, or wins the lottery, one will experience a lower-middle-class existence.

Significant progress was made in the area of law enforcement wages and benefits during the 1980s, especially in large departments. Despite this, inadequate pay remains a problem for law enforcement officers nationwide. In performing their duties, officers believe that they are performing an important role in the community (i.e., protecting life and property). They also believe, especially in light of the dangerous nature of their work, that they should be paid commensurate with that role and the benefits they are providing to society. Overall, officers are simply frustrated at not being paid what they feel they are worth (Conser et al., 2005).

Career Limitations

Yet another issue that should be considered in pursuing a law enforcement career is this: Where does a person expect to be at the peak of his or her career? Not everyone can become the chief of police in a large metropolitan agency. Nor will all those who wish to become supervisory federal agents do so. Whether one's career is successful depends on how one defines success. Many officers who have spent their entire careers as patrol officers in small or midsize law enforcement agencies are rightly proud of their accomplishments. Similarly, many frustrated individuals (at all ranks and levels of policing) feel that they never received a fair chance. They might have felt this way no matter what occupation they chose. As in any job, perseverance and a good work ethic help things to happen.

Liability Issues

In a democratic society, the police are limited in what they can do. The public has both civil and criminal recourse to protect against police abuses. In addition, police bureaucracies have administrative processes that regulate the behavior of police personnel. Failure to act in a manner that is felt to be consistent with proper law enforcement procedures could result in a minor reprimand. More serious violations could result in more severe disciplinary actions, such as suspensions, compulsory transfers, demotions, or even terminations. Violations that are felt to have infringed on the legal rights of others could result in costly civil litigation at state or federal levels. Violations thought to constitute criminal actions could result in arrest, conviction, and imprisonment at state or federal levels. Whether they are convicted or subsequently acquitted of all charges, the economic impact of legal costs and career damages can be devastating to officers and their families.

HEALTH HAZARDS 4 ← Know

Violence

Danger is an inherent part of police work, and this danger is reinforced by the element of authority. Police are required to enforce laws that are often either more conservative or more liberal than the community or individual against whom it is being enforced. Notes Bittner (1992, p. 37), "the policeman is always opposed to some articulated or articulable human interest." In addition, police are almost always interacting with individuals in a moment of crisis. Thus the police are, more often than not, perceived more as adversaries than as friends.

All too often the scenario described above results in an act of violence in which the police officer is either the victim of violence or is forced to use violence to defend himself/herself or others. During the years 1998 through 2007, 594 law enforcement officers were felonioulsy killed within the United States (FBI, 2007a). These numbers indicate a slight trend toward fewer officer deaths from felonious assaults. However, we must point out that 2001 was an anomaly in that there were more officers killed (70) than in the years immediately before or after. When we include the officers of the New York Police Department that were killed (72) at the World Trade Center on September 11, 2001, it becomes the year with the highest number of officers feloniously killed as recorded by Uniform Crime Reports. While the numbers of officers slain in the line of duty do not reach the proportions depicted by the United States entertainment media, the potential for being murdered is a real threat with which police officers and their loved ones must contend. Table 7.1 contains information regarding officers killed in recent years.

TABLE 7.1 Law Enforcement Officers Feloniously Killed within the United States, 1998–2007

Year	1998	1999	2000	2001	2002	2003	2004	2005	2006	2007
Officers Killed	61	42	751	70*	56	52	57	55	48	57

*The 72 officer deaths resulting from the events of 9/11 are not included.

Source: FBI (2007a).

While the potential for violent death is relatively low for law enforcement officers within the United States, the possibility of being injured due to violence is not. In 2007, 59,201 out of 517,875 police officers in America were assaulted (FBI, 2007b). More than 30 percent were injured as a result of those assaults. The number of assaults on American police officers and the types of weapons utilized in those assaults are displayed in Table 7.2.

TABLE 7.2 Law Enforcement Officers Assaulted, Number of Assaults, and Percent Injured by Type of Weapon, 1998–2007

Year	Total Assaults/ Percent Injured	Firearm	Knife or Other Cutting Instrument	Other Dangerous Weapon	Personal Weapons	Number of Reporting Agencies	Population Covered	Number of Officers Employed
1998								
Total	60,673	2,126	1,098	6,414	50,034	8,153	193,098,427	452,361
Percent	30.7	20.7	23.7	30.2	31.3			
1999								
Total	55,971	1,772	999	7,560	45,640	9,832	207,124,112	462,782
Percent	38.0	11.9	17.5	27.1	29.0			
2000								
Total	58,396	1,749	1,015	8,132	47,502	8,940	204,598,589	452,531
Percent	28.1	11.4	15.2	26.9	29.2			
2001								
Total	57,463	1,841	1,168	8,233	46,221	9,773	213,645,308	471,096
Percent	28.3	10.3	15.3	26.1	29.7			
2002								
Total	59,526	1,927	1,061	8,526	48,012	10,164	219,424,713	491,009
Percent	28.2	11.4	15.1	25.7	29.7			
2003								
Total	58,600	1,879	1,084	8,180	47,457	10,539	225,769,768	501,738
Percent	28.2	10.7	13.4	25.4	29.7			
2004								
Total	59,373	2,109	1,121	8,598	47,545	10,459	225,597,839	499,396
Percent	27.9	9.6	14.1	25.7	29.4			
2005								
Total	57,820	2,157	1,059	8,379	46,225	10,119	222,873,755	489,393
Percent	27.4	9.0	12.8	25.6	29.4			
2006								
Total	58,600	2,157	1,055	8,611	47,440	10,596	227,360,586	504,147
Percent	26.7	9.5	12.7	23.6	28.4			
2007								
Total	59,201	2,176	1,023	8,507	47,495	10,856	231,763,568	517,875
Percent	26.1	9.4	11.4	22.2	27.9			

Source: FBI (2007b).

TABLE 7.3 Law Enforcement Officers Accidentally Killed within the United States, 1998–2004

Year	1998	1999	2000	2001	2002	2003	2004
Officers Killed	81	65	83	76	75	81	82

Source: FBI (2007c).

The threat of death and injury due to violence as well as the psychological impacts of possibly having to cause death or injury to others are facts with which law enforcement officers must contend. The keys to coping with these hazards are personnel selection and training (Doerner, 2004). Law enforcement personnel must be rigorously screened to recruit people who can be taught how to respond properly to dangerous situations. This must be followed by extensive training and education of officers as to the potential threats they will face and the proper responses to those threats (Conser et al., 2005).

Accidents

Law enforcement officers are more likely to lose their lives due to accidents than due to homicides. For example, in 2007, 57 officers were murder victims, while 83 were killed in accidents that took place while performing their duties (FBI, 2007c) (see Table 7.3). Automobile accidents, motorcycle accidents, aircraft crashes, being struck by vehicles, accidental shootings, falls, and drownings tend to be the more common causes for accidental deaths among officers. The number of officers who are injured due to accidents is not readily available, but it is not unrealistic to suppose that several thousand of such events occur each year (Figure 7.1). Broken bones, burns, animal bites, abrasions, back injuries, and any number of other physical maladies are incurred by officers daily.

As with violence prevention, accident prevention depends on education of law enforcement officers as to potential threats and proper solutions. In particular, training in pursuit driving and emergency responses (emphasizing the dangers of such actions to the officers and the public, as well as the need to limit such pursuits to life-threatening situations that justify the risks) is imperative (Barker, 1998). Additionally, training in traffic direction techniques, animal control techniques, and proper responses to hazard situations such as fires and chemical spills is necessary.

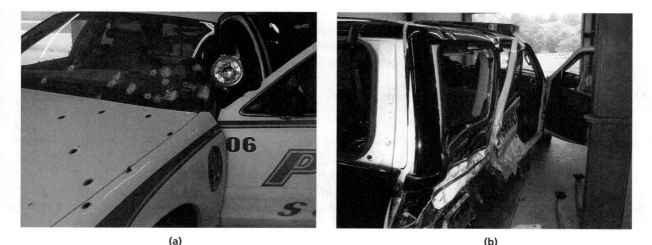

(a)   (b)

FIGURE 7.1   Police vehicles showing the dangers of law enforcement: (a) a police car with bullet holes from ambush attack; (b) sheriff's department SUV after being hit by a drunken driver. Fortunately, the drivers of both vehicles survived.

Courtesy of Lt. Bob Scott and Jackson County Sheriff's Department.

✴ Contagious Diseases

During the latter half of the twentieth century, police officers had relatively little to fear from contagious diseases. It was hoped that some of the more common communicable diseases, such as gonorrhea, herpes, and syphilis, would not be contracted while on duty. Outbreaks of the old horrors of earlier times—such as diphtheria, polio, tetanus, smallpox, and whooping cough—were then being controlled through vaccinations. Meningitis, mononucleosis, scarlet fever, salmonellosis, and tuberculosis remained threats, along with a variety of childhood diseases such as mumps, measles, and chickenpox, but the possibility of infection was rare.

During the 1980s, police officers became aware of a threat that was not only highly communicable but also lethal. Most citizens until then felt that AIDS (acquired immune deficiency syndrome) was a disease that threatened only homosexuals, prostitutes, and drug users. While learning that there were indeed "high-risk groups," police officers also learned that the potential to contract the human immunodeficiency virus (HIV), which causes AIDS, was present for anyone who might somehow exchange bodily fluids with an infected person. Since the demands of police work not only place officers in contact with high-risk individuals but also in situations in which bodily fluids can be exchanged (contact with open wounds, blood, saliva, etc.), it is imperative that officers be informed as to the facts and fictions regarding AIDS and the proper precautions that should be taken (Blumberg, 1997). One fact is that while police officers do face a risk of HIV infection, as of 2000 the Centers for Disease Control and Prevention had reported no confirmed cases of workplace exposure resulting in HIV infection (Flavin, 2000, p. 11). Table 7.4 contains responses to law enforcement concerns regarding AIDS. As with other communicable diseases, common sense and knowledge from proper training are the best defenses.

TABLE 7.4 Responses to AIDS-Related Law Enforcement Concerns

Issue/Concern	Educational and Action Messages
Human bites	Person who bites usually receives the victim's blood; viral transmission through saliva is highly unlikely. If bitten by anyone, milk wound to make it bleed, wash the area thoroughly, and seek medical attention.
Spitting	Viral transmission through saliva is highly unlikely.
Urine/feces	Virus isolated in only very low concentrations in urine; not at all in feces; no cases of AIDS or AIDS virus infection associated with either urine or feces.
Cuts/puncture wounds	Use caution in handling sharp objects and searching areas hidden from view; needle-stick studies show risk of infection is very low.
CPR/first aid	To eliminate the already minimal risk associated with CPR, use masks/airways; avoid blood-to-blood contact by keeping open wounds covered and wearing gloves when in contact with bleeding wounds.
Body removal	Observe crime scene rule: Do not touch anything. Those who must come into contact with blood or other body fluids should wear gloves.
Casual contact	No cases of AIDS or AIDS virus infection attributed to casual contact.
Any contact with blood or body fluids	Wear gloves if contact with blood or body fluids is considered likely. If contact occurs, wash thoroughly with soap and water; clean up spills with one part water to nine parts household bleach.
Contact with dried blood	No cases of infection have been traced to exposure to dried blood. The drying process itself appears to inactivate the virus. Despite low risk, however, caution dictates wearing gloves, a mask, and protective shoe coverings if exposure to dried blood particles is likely (e.g., crime scene investigation).

Source: Hammett (1987, p. 6).

BOX 7.1
Cops on Steroids

When we think of the dangers of drugs for law enforcement officers, we tend to think of assaults from drug users or traffickers, or toxic harm from raiding methamphetamine labs. However, another health hazard also exists in regard to police officers and drugs. In a recent article in *Men's Health* by Sabrina Rubin Erdely (http://articles.health.msn.com/id/10011139/site/100000000), the use of steroids by police officers was examined. In what appears to be a phenomenon that has spread across the nation, the Drug Enforcement Administration has determined that *juicing* has become a significant problem among police officers.

It appears that in order to obtain the strength and the size they feel they need to effectively deal with problems on the streets, many officers are using steroids to gain muscle mass. Although the gains from steroid use are indeed significant, the mental and physical effects are often devastating. Officers not only risk their own well-being from the inherent physical dangers, but also actually endanger themselves, other officers, suspects, and the public at large from the irrational and often bizarre thinking known as "roid rage."

In addition to the health issues, the knowledge that police officers are engaging in unlawful behaviors (condoned by, and sometimes encouraged by, fellow officers) is a major concern.

Emotional Distress Resulting from On-the-Job Stress

← Know

Due to the hazards that are inherent in law enforcement, *all* officers will, on occasion, experience **emotional distress.** While other occupations may be far more dangerous, the constant exposure to stressful stimuli makes policing one of the most difficult occupations. The threat of violent death and injury, the constant exposure to human tragedies, the responsibility for others, the feelings of alienation and helplessness, the demands of shift work, the limited career opportunities, and the lack of input in administrative decision making all combine to create stress for even the most stable and well-adjusted persons (Kroes, 1985; National Institute of Justice, 2000; Smith, 1982).

The impacts of stress can be temporary depression, extreme anguish, paranoia, cynicism, authoritarianism, denial, or just about any other means by which human beings try to cope with their feelings. Despite what some may think, police officers are human beings with the same frailties and weaknesses as other human beings. When the amount of stress to which they are exposed becomes too heavy, police officers will become emotionally distressed (Copes, 2005). According to the National Institute of Justice (2000, p. 20), police officers report that stress leads to the following:

- cynicism and suspiciousness
- emotional detachment from various aspects of life
- reduced efficiency
- absenteeism and early retirement
- excessive aggressiveness (which may trigger an increase in citizen complaints)
- alcoholism and other substance abuse problems
- marital or other family problems (e.g., extramarital affairs, divorce, or domestic violence)

BOX 7.2
The Murder of Officer Steve Taylor

Pensacola Police Officer Steve Taylor, who had been talking with friends about getting out of law enforcement to pursue a career in architecture, responded to a bank robbery alarm on October 19, 1982. He and another officer apprehended a suspect who had exited from the front door of the bank. While they were handcuffing the first suspect (Cliff Jackson), a second suspect (Clarence Edward Hill), who had exited the bank through a rear door, ran around from the back of the bank with the intention of shooting the officers and freeing his partner. Hill shot both officers at close range. Taylor, who was struck in the side, died shortly afterward. The other officer survived.

On September 20, 2006, Clarence Hill was executed by lethal injection for the murder of Steve Taylor.

- posttraumatic stress disorder
- heart attacks, ulcers, weight gain, and other health problems
- suicide

The National Institute of Justice (2000, p. 20) also reports that officers' spouses report that they feel stress from the following:

- shift work and overtime
- concern over the spouse's cynicism, need to feel in control in the home, or inability or unwillingness to express feelings
- fear that the spouse will be hurt or killed in the line of duty
- officers' and others' excessively high expectations of their children
- avoidance, teasing, or harassment of the officer's children because of the parent's job
- presence of gun in the house
- officer's 24-hour role as a law enforcer
- perception that the officer prefers to spend time with coworkers
- too much or too little discussion of the job
- family members' perception of the officer as paranoid or excessively vigilant and overprotective of them
- problems in helping the officer cope with work-related problems
- "critical incidents," or the officer's injury or death on the job

It is of vital importance that law enforcement administrators and their employees realize the sources and consequences of stress. Before officers can learn to cope with the stress that is inherent in policing, they must first be taught to overcome the "John Wayne mentality," which refuses to acknowledge any weaknesses (Darrow, 1988). Once officers have learned to acknowledge the existence of stress, they can be taught how to identify and neutralize those stressors with which they as individuals must contend (National Institute of Justice, 2000).

FIGURE 7.2 The National Law Enforcement Officers Memorial.
Courtesy of Tom Bojo.

The best means for officers to learn to cope with stress is for their agencies to develop programs that promote mental wellness. These may include providing counseling services for employees and their families and developing peer counseling programs, enhanced training programs, and enlightened management policies. Approaches to reduce or prevent stress in police agencies have included the following, among others:

- Services provided by a private mental health practice or an individual working with one or more law enforcement agencies.
- Peer support and referrals from specially trained police officers.
- Psychological services set up in the agency through the union, chaplaincy, or employee assistance program.
- A combination of these arrangements (National Institute of Justice, 2000, p. 22).

The following additional stress-reduction techniques have been suggested to reduce stress or as a means to cope with stress:

1. More efficient preemployment screening to weed out those who cannot cope with a high-stress job.
2. Increased practical training for police personnel regarding stress, including the simulation of high-stress situations.
3. Training programs for spouses so that they can better understand potential problems.
4. Group discussions where officers and perhaps their spouses can ventilate and share their feelings about the job.
5. A more supportive attitude by police executives toward the stress-related problems of patrol officers.
6. A mandatory alcoholic rehabilitation program.
7. Immediate consultation with officers involved in traumatic events such as justifiable homicides.
8. Complete false arrest and liability insurance to relieve the officer of having to second-guess his decisions.
9. The provision of departmental psychological services to employees and their families (Territo and Vetter, 1981, p. 272).

Mental Illness *← Essay pg 135–137*

If the distress discussed in the preceding section is not dealt with appropriately, it may escalate into behaviors that threaten the welfare of the officer and/or others. The individual officer may come to suffer from relatively mild emotional disturbances that require only counseling and reassurance, or he or she may be plagued by severe mental disorders that are career threatening or even life threatening in nature.

Law enforcement agencies must not only have assistance programs designed to help officers contend with emotional distress but must also develop strategies to aid those whose problems become too severe for continued police service. Medical pensions, extended health coverage, and family support services are only fair for those who have paid too high a price for their police careers.

Suicide

Being a police officer is also thought to increase one's risk of falling victim to suicide. Preliminary studies (Lester, 1983; Wagner and Brzeczek, 1983) identified higher levels of suicide among police officers than among other occupations. One study suggested a rate three times as high as the general population (Violanti, Vena, and Marshall, 1986). In Chicago, alcohol abuse was linked to 60 percent of the police suicides (Wagner and Brzeczek, 1983). Although these higher rates have been challenged by a more recent suicide study among Los Angeles officers (Josephson and Reiser, 1990), increases in officer suicides were noted.

Given the general nature of police work, many officers who feel suicidal are either afraid or have no one to turn to in discussing their feelings. This leads to an even greater sense of isolation, with many believing suicide to be the only way out. Fortunately, programs in stress reduction, marital and mental health counseling, and wellness programs are aiding many departments in addressing this concern. Unfortunately, suicide is expected to remain higher for law enforcement personnel than for the general populace (Copes, 2005).

Post-Traumatic Stress Disorder (PTSD)

The National Institute of Mental Health defines post-traumatic stress disorder (PTSD) as "an anxiety disorder that can develop after exposure to a terrifying event or ordeal in which grave physical harm occurred or was threatened" (www.nih.gov/health). They list violent personal assaults, natural or human-caused disasters, accidents, and military combat as some of the traumatic events that may trigger PTSD. Obviously, traumatic events in police work, such as line-of-duty deaths, suicide of a coworker, failed rescue attempts, mass casualty (it does not have to be on the magnitude of 9/11), deaths of children, and responding to incidents where the officer knows the victim, may be the precursor to PTSD among officers. People with PTSD have persistent frightening thoughts and memories of the traumatic events and feel stressed or frightened even when they are not in danger. This can be particularly debilitating to someone in an occupation such as police work.

The shooting of a suspect under any circumstances is an event that has the potential to create PTSD in any officer; however, what is commonly known as "suicide by cop" always leads to heightened levels of stress and trauma. In such a case, a police officer is chosen, for whatever reason, to be the instrument of death. The person who chooses this method of suicide may be angry, depressed, or mentally ill. If he or she cannot be disarmed or controlled by nonlethal methods, there may be no other option left open to the police but to take the life of the offender to protect the officer/s or others. That does not lessen the feelings of hopelessness or guilt for the officer/s involved or soften the accusations that follow from the "should have" and "what if" choir.

Substance Abuse

Police administrators frequently report that alcohol is a severe problem with officers and often report the existence of alcohol-related behavioral problems (Bennett and Hess, 2007). As early as 1972, Skolnick reported that officers drink heavily and with other officers. Fifteen years later, Carson (1987) found that officers involved in cases of excessive force and use of firearms drank more than officers who avoided such activities. Farmer (1990) found that alcohol use was an acceptable coping mechanism for both male and female police officers. In another study, both male and female officers reported drinking more alcohol than the general population (Pendergrass and Osgrove, 1986).

BOX 7.3

Is Shooting and Killing Suspects Just Part of the Police Job?

In one of the first court cases dealing with the issue of whether PTSD affects police officers, Arizona State Trooper David D. Mogel was said to be suffering from PTSD due to the killing of a shotgun-armed car thief wanted for a robbery after the suspect attempted to shoot him. Trooper Mogel claimed that because of the trauma caused from the incident, he could no longer function as a police officer. His claim was denied by the Arizona Department of Public Safety and Worker's Compensation, which ruled that shooting suspects was part of the job and not an "unexpected" event as required by Arizona law. The administrative law judge hearing the case disagreed and stated in her 2002 ruling—"I find that shooting and killing another human being in the line of duty is an extraordinary stress related to employment" (Kates, 2008). Any police officer who has had to shoot and kill a suspect would agree with the judge and add that it is something that is never forgotten.

The use and abuse of alcohol among police officers is apparently one way of coping with the problems inherent in "the job" (Violanti, Marshall, and Howe, 1985). Alcohol is the only and best coping mechanism some police officers believe they have. Clearly, then, with this belief system at work, police officers are at a high risk for alcoholism.

Although alcohol is the "drug of choice" among police officers, caffeine and nicotine are also extremely popular. It is not unusual for officers to drink several cups of coffee, glasses of tea, or soft drinks during their workday. Similarly, many officers use tobacco products while on duty. In addition to being chemically addictive, these drugs are also psychologically addictive in that they often develop as a means of killing time during periods of tedium.

The drugs mentioned above are not the only ones with which officers might experiment. The use of illicit drugs may also develop (or be continued). Dealing with these abuses is problematic because they are not only considered to be physically and psychologically harmful, they are also unlawful to possess or use. The abuse of such drugs by officers is not only potentially harmful to the officer but to the reputation of the law enforcement agency as well.

As with the hazards discussed in the preceding section, substance abuse is best dealt with by departmental programs designed to inform officers of the dangers involved, the policies and regulations of the department in regard to those issues, and the types of assistance available for those who seek help.

Physical Wellness Issues

In addition to substance abuse, a number of other **health hazards** exist for police officers. Stress, poor nutrition, and lack of exercise also contribute to poor physical health. Terry (1981) documented numerous physiological effects of police stress. These problems include headaches, indigestion, ulcers, lower back pain, and high blood pressure. In addition, Norvell, Belles, and Hills (1988) found that police officers have a higher risk of mortality associated with cancer, diabetes, and heart disease than do nonpolice. It is evident that a strong relationship exists between job-related stress and physical illnesses.

In addition to physical hazards attributed to stress, police officers are noted for having poor eating habits. Fast-food diets and limited exercise result in poor conditioning, which over time leads to obesity and/or other physical ailments. In combination with stress, these health problems can range from minor irritants to life-threatening illnesses.

The role of the police agency in providing for the physical health of its employees is crucial. Just as programs have been developed that assist in providing for the mental health of law enforcement officers, so are programs needed to promote **physical wellness**. Education as to proper nutrition and recreational needs must be provided. Whenever possible, incentives should be provided to encourage employees to maintain physical fitness. Assistance should be readily available for those seeking help from chemical dependency. In addition, these programs should be available to family members.

COPING WITH BEING A COP

In recent years, law enforcement administrators have increasingly recognized that they must do more to protect their employees from the hazards described previously. The results have been better selection procedures, more extensive training, and the development of employee programs designed to aid both sworn officers and nonsworn police personnel in coping with the challenges inherent in contemporary law enforcement (Figure 7.3). In the following sections, we highlight some of the procedures that are being utilized by progressive police agencies.

Selection

Since the days of August Vollmer's pioneering efforts in California, police reformers have called for the use of selection criteria to screen out those persons who were "unfit" for police work.

(a)　(b)

(C)　(D)

FIGURE 7.3 A law enforcement officer who leads a full life in addition to his or her police duties is less likely to succumb to the social and health hazards of police work. One such example is Detective Tom Bojo, who leads a busy, challenging, and balanced life. Detective Bojo is shown (a) with his family on vacation, (b) gardening with his daughter, (c) fishing with his son, and (d) playing softball.

Courtesy of Tom Bojo.

Initially, this procedure consisted of eliminating applicants who had criminal records and/or histories of violence. As policing has become more complex and demanding, the need for effective employee screening procedures has become even more important. Modern police officers must be intelligent, articulate, diplomatic, and compassionate. They must be sensitive to the needs of individuals and groups, yet be forceful and direct when circumstances dictate intervention. They must be dedicated to serving their community and enforcing laws. They must be able to use their considerable discretion in a fair and unbiased manner. They must be adaptable to any situation that might arise, and they must be able to endure the continuing stressors of police work. Choosing such a person is no easy task.

The task of selecting qualified officers is complicated by the need to make police forces more representative of the community being served. Height and weight requirements that were supposed to ensure physical competence were found to have little validity and were discriminatory toward women and Hispanic Americans (Martin, 1997). The requirement of a college education was thought to discriminate against African Americans and other minorities (Sapp and Carter, 1992). Other screening procedures, such as psychological testing, were also feared to be biased (Alpert, 1997). The product of these conflicts has been the gradual development of selection procedures designed to eliminate gender or ethnic bias while ensuring that competent individuals are employed.

Currently, progressive police agencies use a variety of selection procedures, such as written examinations, oral interviews, physical agility tests appropriate for both males and females, medical examinations, polygraph examinations, situational testing, background investigations, and psychological profiling. The emphasis is to eliminate the truly unfit without being biased against particular individuals or groups. Many agencies also use educational requirements that are now considered to be less discriminatory as more minorities obtain a college education (Carter and Sapp, 1992) (Table 7.5).

While these techniques are useful, perhaps the best means of obtaining competent officers is aggressive recruiting, developing attractive financial packages and retirement benefits, providing for career development, and establishing a reputation of concern for employees. These strategies, in conjunction with sound supervision, extensive training, and support programs, not only ensure that qualified applicants will compete for the available positions but that most of those selected will remain with the organization.

Training

Traditionally, training has been an area of weakness within police organizations. Police officers were sworn in and immediately put to work. They learned the job through trial and error, by observing other officers, and by listening to "war stories." Since the early 1970s, recruit training—or "basic training"—has become the norm throughout the United States. This training is provided at police academies that are either run by or comply with standards mandated by state police training commissions. The type of curriculum and hours required vary considerably from state to state. Initially, the focus of police academies was to teach recruits the technical knowledge required for police work (e.g., legal requirements, report writing, first aid, defensive tactics, and firearms proficiency). In recent years, the curricula have been lengthened to include a broader spectrum of subjects relative to the needs of modern police officers. Communication skills, sensitivity to cultural and ethnic diversity, conflict management, and liability concerns inherent in providing police services are now being taught in addition to the traditional "law enforcement" topics.

In addition to academy training, new police officers in many departments now receive additional training in a field training officer (FTO) program. The "rookie" rides with an experienced

TABLE 7.5 Education Levels by Race/Ethnicity

	Average Level of Education (years)	Percent Completing		
		No College	Some Undergraduate Work	Graduate Degree
African American	13.6	28	63	9
Hispanic American	13.3	27	68	5
White	13.7	34	62	4
Other	13.8	19	73	8

Source: Adapted from Carter and Sapp (1992, p. 11).

officer who has been carefully selected and trained to become an FTO. Over a period of several weeks (and frequently several months), the FTO teaches the rookie how to apply his or her academy training to handle real-world situations. As the rookie is being taught, his or her progress is monitored and evaluated. A person whose performance within the program is consistently unsatisfactory will be terminated. Those who complete the FTO program successfully are assigned to a regular patrol shift. They will continue to be closely monitored by senior officers and supervisors throughout their probationary period (usually one year from time of employment). The benefits of the FTO programs are not only in preparing new officers for a demanding job but are also seen in improved community relations and enhanced morale within police organizations (Doerner, 2004).

Yet another area of training that is of benefit to both the police and the community is in-service training. Too frequently, the needs of veteran officers have been ignored by police organizations. By developing periodic in-service training programs, all police personnel can be kept abreast of changes in laws and departmental procedures, be taught new police skills and techniques, be prepared for career development, be informed of community concerns, and be reassured in regard to their importance to the organization.

Family Programs

Police departments have also instituted programs to assist officers experiencing marital or family problems. An example of one such program may be found in Tallahassee, Florida, where a mental health counseling program in which departmental members (sworn and civilian) and their families may anonymously participate has been operating for several years. It is the view of the Tallahassee Police Department's administration that any stress inducers (personal or familial) that could affect their employees' well-being are legitimate concerns. Therefore, not only police employees but their spouses and dependents are eligible for free counseling at a mental health facility with whom the city of Tallahassee contracts.

In addition to family counseling programs as exemplified above, many departments provide support groups for the families of departmental employees. Periodically, employees and their families are offered seminars on such topics as nutrition, stress reduction, physical fitness, and financial planning. A number of other activities designed to promote family-member inclusion within the organization and their understanding of the work that their loved ones perform may be found within many police organizations. These include but are not limited to the following: ride-along programs, departmental dinners and banquets, and recreational associations. In some agencies, spouses are even allowed to participate in portions of recruit training in order to better understand what their spouses are going to be involved in.

Wellness Programs

In addition to the programs discussed in the preceding section, many agencies have also started treatment programs for officers with substance abuse problems, along with suicide-intervention and stress-reduction programs. The mere fact that agencies are now recognizing these problems and offering assistance rather than ignoring them or terminating employees is a major step. In addition, many departments have established "smoke-free" environments or have instituted preventive health programs to assist officers who wish to get in better physical condition.

Know →

Nonprofit Police Assistance Groups

In recent years several nonprofit organizations have taken on the task of providing assistance to police personnel, their families, and survivors of police officers killed in the line of duty. Concerns of Police Survivors (C.O.P.S.), organized in 1984 with 110 members, is now a national organization with a membership of 15,000 families (www.nationalcops.org). The members include spouses, parents, siblings, significant others, and affected coworkers of officers killed in the line of duty. The C.O.P.S. mission is to assist in the rebuilding of the lives of surviving families and affected coworkers. The national organization, recognizing that the survivor's level of distress is directly affected by the agency's response to the tragedy, provides training and assistance to law enforcement agencies throughout the United States.

The *Police Stress Unit* is a nonprofit volunteer organization formed by New Jersey police officers for themselves in 1983 (www.policestressunit.org). This volunteer organization has a 24-hour Crisis Intervention Hotline providing confidential supportive assistance that includes peer counseling and referral services for police officers, their spouses, and family members. The *Central Florida Police Stress Unit* is a nonprofit organization that is not affiliated with any police department or law enforcement agency (www.policestress.org). The organization uses volunteers from licensed mental health counselors, marriage and family therapists, clinical social workers, and consulting police psychologists. It has a 24-hour hotline and addresses the following areas:

- relationship and marital difficulties
- alcohol and substance abuse
- domestic violence and spouse abuse
- trauma associated with shootings, accidents, injury, and death
- difficult relationships with management and coworkers
- health and wellness issues
- financial problems and debt management
- issues related to retirement

Community Policing

Community policing (discussed in detail in Chapter 10) is yet another attempt to have police officers become more involved with the communities they serve. By seeking to become a part of the community, attending community meetings, talking to residents, seeking community input into police decision making, and so on, it is hoped that the community will become more accepting of police officers and that officers will feel less isolated from the community.

REALITY CHECK

A Hero on and off Duty

Sergeant Quentin Miller of the Asheville Police Department works with children every day as a school resource supervisor. Between his work and having raised five children (four grown, one still at home), one would think that he would spend his off time avoiding adolescents and their many issues. Not so. During his career at the Asheville Police Department, Sergeant Miller has found the time to create a midnight basketball program to keep kids off the streets. He also has coordinated a street ministry program, as well as a job-training program. During the summer of 2005, he cofounded a camp called *Back to Basics* in which kids were taught real-world skills that introduced them to different career opportunities and resulted in their obtaining summer jobs.

As if the above activities were not demanding enough, Sergeant Miller and his wife, Karen, have become certified as foster parents. It is their intention to make their home available to troubled children who have nowhere else to go. As this was being written, they were in the process of adopting a 14-year-old girl who had recently been released from juvenile detention. Not one to rest on his laurels, Sergeant Miller is currently working on plans to expand his *Back to Basics* program to offer opportunities to a greater number of children.

We have stressed the need within this chapter for police officers to develop other interests in order to ease the stresses of their jobs in law enforcement. In this case, it is obvious that the key to a happy and balanced life is to give more to the cause you love.

Source: Adapted from the *Asheville Citizen-Times*, January 3, 2006.

Conclusions

All of the aforementioned programs and others being developed are designed to help deal with whatever problems might affect the officer. These traumas of police work are real regardless of the officer's gender, race, or age. They do not affect all officers—perhaps not even a majority—but for those that are affected, the consequences are enormous, for the officer, for the department, and for society. To keep and maintain a solid, well-trained police force, departments and individuals alike must be aware of the potential for problems, identify existing problems, and seek out or provide adequate treatment. To do any less is unacceptable. Police officers are human beings first, facing the same problems that anyone else might face, indeed having a greater propensity for some than for other occupations. Fortunately, departments and officers are recognizing this and taking steps to prevent or deal with such problems.

Student Checklist

1. Describe the factors that make it difficult for police officers to cope with change.
2. Identify and describe job stressors of police work and their consequences for police officers.
3. Describe some ways in which stress can be reduced.
4. Describe the social hazards of police work.
5. Describe the health hazards of police work.

Topics for Discussion

1. How does the working personality contribute to community isolation?
2. What is the primary cause of police officer deaths?
3. What are some effects of stress on police officers?
4. What is the primary substance abused by police officers? Does gender play a role in its abuse?
5. How are police agencies dealing with the hazards of police work?
6. What is meant by career limitations, and what does it mean for police work?

Bibliography

Alpert, G. P. (1997). "The role of psychological testing in law enforcement," in R. G. Dunham and G. P. Alpert (Eds.), *Critical Issues in Policing: Contemporary Readings*, 3rd ed. Prospect Heights, IL: Waveland Press.

Barker, T. (1998). *Emergency Vehicle Operations: Emergency Calls and Pursuit Driving*. Springfield, IL: Charles C Thomas.

Barker, T., Hunter, R. D., and Rush, J. P. (1994). *Police Systems and Practices: An Introduction*. Upper Saddle River, NJ: Prentice Hall.

Bayley, D. H., and Bittner, E. (1997). "Learning the skills of policing," in R. G. Dunham and G. P. Alpert (Eds.), *Critical Issues in Policing: Contemporary Readings*, 3rd ed. Prospect Heights, IL: Waveland Press.

Bennett, W. W., and Hess, K. M. (2007). *Management and Supervision in Law Enforcement*, 5th ed. Pacific Grove, CA: Thomson/Wadsworth.

Bittner, E. (1992). "The functions of police in modern society," in C. B. Klockars and S. D. Mastrofski (Eds.), *Thinking about Police*, 2nd ed. New York: McGraw-Hill.

Blumberg, M. (1997). "The AIDS epidemic and the police: An examination of the issues," in R. G. Dunham and G. P. Alpert (Eds.), *Critical Issues in Policing: Contemporary Readings*, 3rd ed. Prospect Heights, IL: Waveland Press.

Burbeck, E., and Furnham, A. (1985). "Police officer selection: A critical review of the literature," *Journal of Police Science and Administration*, Vol. 13, pp. 58–69.

Carson, S. (1987). "Shooting, death trauma and excessive force," in H. More and P. Unsinger (Eds.), *Police Managerial Use of Psychology and Psychologists*. Springfield, IL: Charles C Thomas.

Carter, D. L., and Sapp, A. D. (January 1992). "College education and policing: Coming of age," *FBI Law Enforcement Bulletin*, pp. 8–14.

Conser, J. A., Russell, G. B., Paynich, R., and Gingerich, T. E. (2005). *Law Enforcement in the United States*, 2nd ed. Boston, MA: Jones and Bartlett.

Copes, H. (2005). *Policing and Stress*. Upper Saddle River, NJ: Pearson/Prentice Hall.

Crank, J. (1998). *Understanding Police Culture*. Cincinnati, OH: Anderson Press.

Darrow, T. L. (December 1988). "Addressing stress," *Police*, pp. 46–49.

Doerner, W. G. (2004). *Introduction to Law Enforcement: An Insiders View*, 2nd ed. Dubuque, IA: Kendall/Hunt.

Elliott, M., Bingham, R. D., Neilsen, S. C., and Warner, P. D. (1991). "Marital intimacy and satisfaction as a support system for coping with police officer stress," *Journal of Police Science and Administration*, Vol. 14, No. 1, pp. 40–44.

Erdely, S. R. (2006). "Cops on steroids," *Men's Health* by http://articles.health.msn.com/id/10011139/site/100000000.

Farmer, R. (1990). "Clinical and managerial implications of stress research on the police," *Journal of Police Science and Administration*, Vol. 17, pp. 205–218.

Federal Bureau of Investigation. (2007a). *Law Enforcement Officers Killed and Injured, 2007.* http://www.fbi.gov/ucr/killed/2007/table2.htm.

Federal Bureau of Investigation. (2007b). *Law Enforcement Officers Killed and Injured, 2007.* http://www.fbi/gov/ucr/killed/2004/table47.htm.

Federal Bureau of Investigation. (2007c). *Law Enforcement Officers Killed and Injured, 2007.* http://www.fbi.gov/ucr/killed/2004/table68.htm.

Flavin, J. (2000). "(Mis)representing risk: Headline accounts of HIV-related diseases," *American Journal of Criminal Justice*, Vol. 25, No. 1, pp. 119–136.

Grant, H. B., and Terry, R. J. (2005). *Law Enforcement in the 21st Century.* Boston, MA: Pearson/Allyn and Bacon.

Hammett, T. M. (1987). "AIDS and the law enforcement officer," *NIJ Reports*, Vol. 206, pp. 2–7.

Holden, R. N. (1992). *Law Enforcement: An Introduction.* Upper Saddle River, NJ: Prentice Hall.

Josephson, R. L., and Reiser, M. (1990). "Officer suicide in the Los Angeles Police Department: A twelve-year follow-up," *Journal of Police Science and Administration*, Vol. 17, pp. 227–229.

Kates, A. R. (2008). "Surviving Posttraumatic Stress Disorder (PTSD)," *CopShock*, 2nd ed. www.copshock.com/copshock_ptsd_lawsuit.htm.

Kroes, W. H. (1985). *Society's Victims: The Police,* 2nd ed. Springfield, IL: Charles C Thomas.

Lester, D. (1983). "Stress in police officers: An American perspective," *The Police Journal*, Vol. 56, pp. 184–193.

Martin, S. E. (1997). "Female officers on the move? Status report on women in policing," in R. G. Dunham and G. P. Alpert (Eds.), *Critical Issues in Policing: Contemporary Readings,* 3rd ed. Prospect Heights, IL: Waveland Press.

National Institute of Justice. (January 2000). "On-the-Job Stress—Reducing It, Preventing It," *National Institute of Justice Journal*, pp. 18–25.

Norvell, N., Belles, D., and Hills, H. (1988). "Perceived stress levels and physical symptoms in supervisor law enforcement personnel," *Journal of Police Science and Administration*, Vol. 16, pp. 75–79.

Peak, K. J. (2006). *Policing in America: Methods, Issues, and Challenges,* 5th ed. Upper Saddle River, NJ: Pearson/Prentice Hall.

Pendergrass, V., and Osgrove, N. (1986). "Correlates of alcohol use by police personnel," in J. Reese and H. Goldstein (Eds.), *Psychological Services for Law Enforcement.* Washington, D.C.: U.S. Government Printing Office.

Roberg, R. R., Kuykendall, J., and Novak, K. (2002). *Police Management,* 3rd ed. Los Angeles, CA: Roxbury Press.

Roberg, R. R., Novak, K., and Cordner, G. W. (2005). *Police and Society,* 3rd ed. Los Angeles, CA: Roxbury Press.

Sapp, A. D., and Carter, D. L. (1992). "Police and higher education" in R. N. Holden (Ed.), *Law Enforcement: An Introduction.* Upper Saddle River, NJ: Prentice Hall.

Skolnick, J. (1975). *Justice without Trial,* 2nd ed. New York: Wiley.

Smith, D. (1982). "Sources and consequences of stress for the police," *American Journal of Police*, Vol. 1, No. 2, pp. 114–148.

Territo, L., and Vetter, H. J. (1981). "Stress and police personnel," *Journal of Police Science and Administration*, Vol. 9, No. 2, pp. 195–207.

Terry, W. C., III. (1981). "Police stress: The empirical evidence," *Journal of Police Science and Administration*, Vol. 9, No. 1, pp. 61–75.

Violanti, J., Charles, L. F, Hartley, T. A., Mnastsakanova, A., Andrew, M. E., Fededulegn, D., Vila, B., and Burchfield, C. M. (2008). "Shift-work and suicide ideation among police officers," *American Journal of Industrial Medicine*, Vol. 51, No 10, pp. 758–768.

Violanti, J., Marshall, J. R., and Howe, B. (1985). "Stress, coping and alcohol use: The police connection," *Journal of Police Science and Administration*, Vol. 13, pp. 106–110.

Violanti, J., Vena, J., and Marshall, J. R. (1986). "Disease, risk and mortality among police officers: New evidence and contributing factors," *Journal of Police Science and Administration*, Vol. 14, pp. 17–23.

Wagner, M., and Brzeczek, R. (1983). "Alcoholism and suicide: A fatal connection," *FBI Law Enforcement Bulletin*, Vol. 52, pp. 8–15.

Wrobleski, H. M., and Hess, K. M. (2006). *Introduction to Law Enforcement and Criminal Justice,* 8th ed. Pacific Grove, CA: Thomson/Wadsworth.

CHAPTER 8

The Communication Process

More powerful than mace, the night stick, or the gun, effective rhetoric is an officer's most useful tool in the field.

—THOMPSON, 1982

KEY CONCEPTS

Articulation	Jargon	Proxemics
Discrimination	Kinesics	Scapegoating
Distortion	Nonjudgmental Listening	Symbolic Cues
Effective Listening	Personal Space	Tabloid Thinking
Empathy	Prejudice	

LEARNING OBJECTIVES

Studying this chapter will enable you to:

1. Define the communication process.

2. Contrast modes of communication.

3. Demonstrate effective listening skills.

4. Describe the communication process in police practices.

5. Identify several common blocks to effective communication in police–community relations.

Communication is basic to the world we know. We transmit and receive information in our world, often without even being aware that we are doing so. Because communication is a process that is shared by everyone and is constantly with us, it is easily taken for granted. Communication skills supposedly just "come naturally."

Yet it is faulty communication that generates misunderstanding and helps to build social barriers among people. The result of poor communication can be anything from poor job performance to war. Effective communication encourages healthy relationships between two people, within a family, between the police and the community, between employer and employee, among nations, and so on.

It is the function of this chapter to define and describe the process of communication in action and to identify some specific ways whereby persons, such as police officers, can increase the effectiveness of their communication with others. The ultimate aim is to describe the relationship between communication and police–community relations.

COMMUNICATION IN ACTION

Communication is a process through which messages are exchanged. It is effective only when these messages are mutually understood by the sender and receiver.

Communication operates in many dimensions, the most commonly recognized being intrapersonal, interpersonal, and person to group. Because the nature of work in the administration of justice process requires volumes of written reports (many of which will become legal records of the system), we include an additional dimension in this chapter: official communications.

Intrapersonal communication takes place within the person. We "talk to ourselves" as we solve problems or perform tasks. We may even write messages to ourselves. The academic community has just begun to speculate about the intrapersonal communication of criminal justice professionals. What happens to the thinking processes of the new recruit? Some suppose that the stresses of the occupation may distort the intrapersonal process, resulting in cynical, tough patrol officers; high divorce rates; and even illness.

Interpersonal communication takes place person to person. Whether or not we are able to form and maintain caring connections with others depends largely on our effective interpersonal communication skills. Police officers may stop or start fights, increase or decrease tension, gain or lose the cooperation of a witness, victim, or suspect through the exercise of interpersonal communication skills. This is the dimension to which most discussion regarding communication skills is addressed and to which definitions of the communication process most directly refer. This dimension is a major focus of this chapter. Much that is said in this context, however, can be generalized to other dimensions of communication in action.

Person-to-group communication implies a structured situation in which one person addresses a group on a predetermined subject. Public speaking engagements, a witness before a jury, and a minister before a congregation are all examples of person-to-group communication.

Some specific skills concerning group dynamics, presentation, and public speaking are related to this dimension of communication. To the extent that a group response is sought and received, people in the group reflect a group identity as they hear and respond to the message sent. In addition to this group dimension, however, every individual–group communication is also a person-to-person communication. The speaker is actually communicating individually with each person in the group, and the message received by one person will differ to some degree from the message received by any other person. This is true even though group consensus regarding some of the elements of the message may exist, and group response may provide feedback to the sender that the message sent was (or was not) received.

Official communication is usually written and can appear to be person to person or person to group. Actually, however, it usually is a "public" documentation of policy or procedure, or an official report or evaluation of events. It may be an in-house memo or a formal communication with other agencies. Lack of effectiveness in this dimension of communication has a sometimes subtle but very high cost. Administrators may lose the cooperation of staff members; agencies and individual officers may lose community support; prosecutors may lose convictions in court; and children and adults may be mislabeled, misdiagnosed, and mistreated. Official communication is an important part of communication in action. Some of the specific basic writing skills involved in this dimension of communication are not within the scope of this chapter. Official communication is discussed here in the context of effective police–community relations.

THE PROCESS OF COMMUNICATION

Achieving Effective Communication

Communicating effectively requires ongoing effort to sharpen communication skills. It does not happen by chance, nor is it something that can be tucked away in a uniform pocket and pulled out at the appropriate opportunity. Skills learned must be applied in many different ways and in as many different situations. What works best in one situation may not be the best choice in another.

One thing is certain, however: Effective communication is essential to positive police–community relations. Its power can scarcely be overestimated. Its success is incredible; its failure disastrous.

Know →

The Elements of Communication

The process of communication, as described in Figure 8.1, begins with a source who has an idea (meaning) that he or she wishes to transmit to a receiver. The idea cannot be transmitted as an idea. It must be encoded into symbols (spoken or written words, gestures, pictures, etc.). Once encoded, the message is transmitted and received. The receiver must decode the message (the symbols) into meaning. The receiver's response, or feedback, to the source is based on the receiver's perception of the meaning of the message sent. Feedback is encoded, transmitted, and decoded, and so the process continues.

Sources of Distortion

Know →

Distortion can occur at any and all stages of the process. Perhaps the symbols used were not mutually understood. Perhaps the message sent was confused at the source. Perhaps the receiver received only a part of the message or, because of distorted perception, was not open to receiving a clear message.

Because messages are sent and received in some situational context, other elements outside the source and the receiver may contribute to or distort the message. A noisy room, a crowd of people, poor lighting, interruptions in the sending or receiving elements of the process, and even the passage of time (particularly if the message is written) can affect what is sent and received.

A Continuing Process

Communication has no beginning or end; it is a continuing process. As we analyze the process and provide its "elements" with names and functions, we may sometimes give the false impression that the communication process does have a beginning and an end and that only one message is dealt with at any given time. As a matter of fact, communication in action does occur in sequence but never so simply as it may appear in a diagram. Messages are received and sent simultaneously. Messages

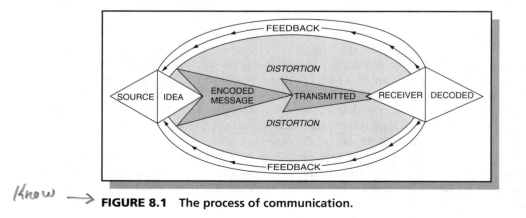

Know →

FIGURE 8.1   The process of communication.

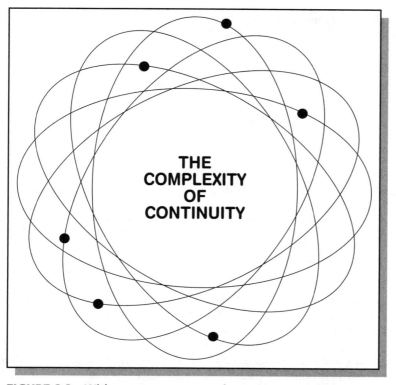

FIGURE 8.2   **With so many messages bouncing around at once, effective communication is a miracle.**

from other sources are received in addition to the message received from the identified source, and these other messages may influence the transmission or reception of the original message.

A single message may be received by one receiver, by several individual receivers (some of whom neither the source nor the receiver knew were receiving), or by a group receiving as a group and/or as individuals. Several messages may be sent at once by one source and received as one or many messages by all or some of the above-mentioned receivers. Considering the opportunities for distortion of the message and the number of messages bouncing around at any given time, it is a miracle that we are able to communicate effectively with one another at all (see Figure 8.2).

MODES OF INTERPERSONAL COMMUNICATION ← *Know*

There are three interpersonal channels or modes of communication: verbal, nonverbal, and symbolic.

Verbal communication refers almost totally to the words and combinations of words used in the message transmitted (or in feedback, which may again be a message transmitted). Words have no meaning in and of themselves. Meaning is derived from the person and from the context in which words are used.

✗ The nonverbal mode can be divided into three subgroups: paralanguage (vocal characteristics), kinesics (body language), and proxemics (personal and social space). Paralanguage includes such elements as diction, the rate and pitch at which a person is speaking, the loudness or softness of speech, and changes in these characteristics during communication (Table 8.1). Kinesics includes gestures, body positioning, facial expressions, and movement. Proxemics becomes a mode of communication in the manner in which **personal space** is used. Space may become a territorial issue, an intrusion into privacy; how it is used can increase or decrease social distance.

TABLE 8.1 Tone, Rhythm, and Tempo

Statement	Meaning
"I don't care what you do."	Personally, I don't care.
"*I* don't care what you do."	But someone else might.
"I *don't* care what you do."	I really *don't*.
"I don't *care* what you do."	Just do as you please, will you?
"I don't care *what* you do."	You have the choice, do what you want.
"I don't care what *you* do."	It doesn't matter to me what you do, but I care about what others do.
"I don't care what you *do*."	It's what you don't do that I'd like to talk about. Just get out of here and leave me alone.

Note: Tone, rhythm, and tempo of speech provide nonverbal cues to the listener as to the meaning being expressed by the speaker. The same words may have a wide variety of meanings.

Source: Adapted from materials developed by Cynthia Roed, Tucson, Arizona.

Symbolic communication, which is often included as a category of the nonverbal mode rather than as a separate channel of communication, occurs continuously at a passive level. We send and receive symbolic messages of which we are not always aware. We make judgments regarding other people based on symbols to which we have assigned meaning and which may have nothing to do with the individual observed. Because symbolic communication is passive, judgments are based on symbolic data that are seldom checked out for their validity. Almost anything can be a meaningful symbol to an individual, but usually symbolic communication includes messages relating to style of dress, place of residence, place (and type) of employment, type of car driven or transportation preferred, jewelry worn (or not worn), and so on (he wears a beard; all persons who wear beards are . . . ; therefore, he is . . .).

Know → ## VERBAL AND PARALANGUAGE CUES

Articulation

Ralph Waldo Emerson wrote, "I learn immediately from any speaker how much he has already lived, through the poverty or the splendor of his speech." Lazy speech can be corrected. Pronunciation depends primarily on correct **articulation**. Articulators are the teeth, tongue, lips, and hard palate. Sounds to pay particular attention to are those of *f*, *p*, *b*, and *v*. These sounds are hard to pronounce correctly. As our society becomes more educated, police begin to deal with a larger population possessing a certain standard of pronunciation. Each of us lapses into an occasional "yeah," and there may be situations in which more casual diction or word usage would be appropriate. However, as a norm, sloppy articulation can be annoying, and it is extremely unprofessional. Words such as "Kinda," "jist," "gonna," "cause," and "dere," or sentences filled with "you know," "and uh," or "sorta," are examples of sloppy articulation that can be easily corrected if the speaker is aware of the problem. As students among a captive audience, we notice these patterns in an instructor, but it is more difficult to examine our own speech habits objectively and to change them.

Volume and Rate

Everyone has an "Aunt Maude." When she calls, you hold the telephone six inches from your ear, and every word is still clearly audible. Coupled with a military uniform, a loud voice will prolong the "redneck cop" stereotype. What is your reaction to a raised voice? If you are like most people, you raise your own, but the police officer has the power to declare a citizen's raised voice disorderly conduct. What if the police officer begins a transaction with a louder tone than normally used socially and the situation escalates into a shouting match? Is the citizen really at fault?

Our society equates fast speech with excitement. Fight narratives delivered in a staccato nonstop rate add excitement to even a dull match. For police officers, consideration of this fact makes the rate of their speech all-important. As an example, consider this hit-and-run accident: The victim's motorcycle was demolished, and the victim lay sprawled in the middle of rush-hour traffic, bleeding profusely from the head. Despite the obvious necessity for speed, the veteran sergeant at the scene communicated slowly and calmly with witnesses before calling in a report. Therefore, he did not heighten an already excited situation. He slowed down the witnesses' rates of speaking and increased the intelligibility of the communication he was receiving. Rate of speech can also be too slow, in which case words may sound disconnected. When this occurs, the listener may lose both interest and the trend of the thoughts expressed.

Language

Human beings have the almost unconscious ability to turn thoughts into words. The words we choose and how we string them together to express our thoughts are very important to effective communication. Meanings are in people, not in the words themselves. Unless the people involved in interpersonal communication have common meaning for the language used, the message will not be mutually understood. Language, then, can become a barrier to communication as well as a tool for effectively achieving it.

Language and its meaning vary from culture to culture. Traditionally, to say that a person is "multilingual" has meant that the person can communicate in several languages, such as Spanish, English, Chinese, or German. Today we also include sign language and computer languages in this list. We also recognize (painfully sometimes) that Spanish is not Spanish and that English is not English. Meaning and phrasing vary from locale to locale, profession to profession, street to agency, children to adults.

Jargon, the special or technical language used by a group or discipline, probably impedes communication more often than it helps. Officers who employ police jargon when communicating with citizens are likely to confuse and annoy them. They may even create problems for themselves at home. Erma Bombeck chose the topic of "Fluent Law Enforcement" for one of her columns. She humorously envisioned the following conversation begun by a wife as she greets her police officer-husband at the door:

> "Hi, honey. Dinner will be ready in a few minutes. Who was that I saw you waving to?"
> "The white Caucasian adult, approximately 62 inches tall, weighing 119 pounds, green eyes, brown hair, and no visible distinguishing marks?"
> "That's the one."
> "She has been identified tentatively as our new neighbor, but we'll have to check it out. By the way, where is 11–83?"
> "I wish you'd stop referring to our son as the code number for 'accident.'"
> (Bombeck, 1982, p. 16)

Profanity can be useful for gaining attention or expressing verbal hostility, but, in the final analysis, it reduces the user's power to negotiate. Those who want their profanity to upset hearers (or readers) should remember that the more they use a profane expression, the less shocking it is.

Research has shown that the use of profanity by police officers occurs almost exclusively during interactions with certain citizens or categories of citizens (e.g., racial and ethnic minorities, lower- and working-class citizens, and other powerless and devalued persons). The use of such language is likely to be restrained and controlled in the presence of persons of power and influence (White, Cox, and Basehart, 1994). The use of such language is deliberate and represents previously learned tactics and strategies for the performance of their duties with such categories of people. White, Cox, and Basehart also point out that simplistic explanations of officer profanity, such as "lack of verbal skills" or "loss of personal control," do not fit reality because it is inconceivable to believe that a police officer would use profanity or obscenities during a deposition or in court testimony when tensions, stress, frustration, or anger-provoking conditions are high (White, Cox, and Basehart, 1994).

There are at least three interactive contextual dimensions in which the officer might use profanity in his or her dealings with citizens. The first is a personal dimension. That is, an officer uses profanity or obscenity to satisfy his or her own psychological or personal agenda. The officer may build up tensions, frustrations, and anger on the job and find catharsis in verbal expressions. A second dimension is a situational one. Officers use profanity or obscenities as a means of dealing with a variety of stressful situations, such as perceived danger, provocation, and resistance.

The third dimension involves the socialization experiences of the officers. It may be that the socialization experiences of the officer, including his or her training, provides formal and informal definitions of persons or groups as deserving of less-than-civil treatment. Van Maanen (1978) suggested that some citizens are labeled as "assholes" by the police and treated accordingly.

Intercultural distortion of words can cause great harm. In Spanish *tu madre* means "your mother." In colloquial (street) Spanish, it is an offensive phrase. A better choice of terms would be "mama" (Quintanilla, 1983, p. 5). There are many other similar examples. Perhaps the best distortion example involves the Japanese response to our warning in 1945 that we possessed a powerful new weapon, the atomic bomb. The response contained the word *migugostu*, which can mean either abrupt dismissal or "We shall consider it." The American interpreter read it as a rebuff, perhaps wrongly, with tragic consequences for Hiroshima and Nagasaki.

Tone of Voice

In situations where communication is repetitive, it is easy to present a bored, monotonous tone. This insulates the speaker from other people and produces a feeling of coldness. Clergy repeating the same ritual each week encounter this, as do actors in a long run of a play.

Television viewers can affirm that there are many tones of voice in which the Miranda rights can be delivered. The police dispatcher sighing, "Yesss, lady," into the telephone communicates a very clear but nonverbal message to her of exasperation.

If we feel depressed, angry at the world, or hungover, our voice patterns will reflect our feelings in inflection and intonation of words. A professional police officer deals largely with a "captive" clientele. However resistant clients may feel, they must relate in some way to the officer. What the officer expresses in paralanguage may not be reported to superiors but may have great impact on the police department's image in the community.

Telephone Cues

Victor Strecher, discussing police conduct on the telephone, states, "Voice, diction, reaction to the citizen's call, approach to the problem, and basic etiquette are the criteria of judgment. Here again, negative evaluations cannot be reversed. The police telephone response can easily predispose a complainant to a favorable or unfavorable reception of the radio-car officers who later respond to this request. Those who neglect telephone courtesy will not overcome the deficiency in police image through the correctness of their uniform and their approach to service calls" (Strecher, 1971, p. 104).

Listening to one's own voice over a tape recorder is effective feedback for analyzing presentation. Objective self-criticism is difficult but necessary. Just as officers must check their uniforms and equipment, a periodic evaluation of voice is equally important. It is a matter of training the ear to hear what is and is not of value.

The telephone voice characterized as bad is expressionless, mechanical, indifferent, impatient, and inattentive. Although the officer may come across as "tough" in the station, in turn, the receiver of the communication may come across as a bristly, hostile citizen the next time he or she encounters an officer. The police officer seeking information by phone might find citizens more receptive to providing it if positive telephone communication techniques are used by the officer.

Following are the basic rules of police telephone conduct:

1. Be courteous at all times, especially when things are a mess.
2. Avoid slang.
3. Be brief, but clear and concise. Use complete sentences. Organize your thoughts in advance, particularly if you are initiating the call.
4. Speak clearly in as relaxed a voice as possible, directly into the mouthpiece.
5. Do not eat or drink when making a phone call to a client or receiving one.
6. Picture the person at the other end of the line sympathetically. Talk to that person, not to the telephone.
7. Keep the receiver close to your ear, and listen to what is being said verbally and nonverbally.
8. If you must consult with someone, put the client on hold if such equipment is available. Nothing is more aggravating, nor presents a more unprofessional image, than monitoring a shouted conversation.
9. Letters and numbers will obviously play a crucial part of police phone communication. Take care when pronouncing them, thus avoiding incorrect spelling, misunderstanding, and repetition. Effective enunciation requires that every sound be given its proper value.
10. As much as humanly possible, refrain from interrupting the other person; allow the person to finish what he or she wants to say. However, emergency phone calls that involve agitated citizens may require firmer guidance to get the proper information.

KINESICS AND PROXEMICS CUES   *← Essay*

Correct interpretation by officers of cues communicated by suspects through body language and use of social and personal space has saved many police lives and prevented many crimes. Without the use of such cues, a major police function that is sometimes taken for granted—directing traffic—could not be accomplished.

Best-seller lists have featured several books on nonverbal cues. These books concentrate primarily on three concepts: body motion and positioning (**kinesics**) as a communication device; the use of personal and social space (**proxemics**); and the influence of certain clothing (symbolic) on ourselves and on others. Much of how we perceive ourselves is modeled in these ways.

Body Language

Julius Fast, author of *Body Language*, noted that sometimes our body cues reinforce our words, and at other times, they may contradict one another. For example, a calm, emotionless face that is accompanied by active arms, hands, legs, and feet is a distinctive feature of deception no matter what is said (Brougham, 1992, p. 16). The human body is the least controllable nonverbal channel of communication.

The Kinesic Interview Technique—taught at seminars throughout the country; the former U.S. Army Military Police School at Fort McClellan, Alabama; numerous police academies; and law enforcement agencies at the local, state, and federal levels—relies on unconscious verbal and nonverbal behaviors to reveal deception (Link, 1993). The first rule of this technique is to watch for breaks in eye contact as an indication that the interviewee is lying. This body language cue is hard to control when one is talking to another.

THE MEANING OF THE MESSAGE   Stress is often demonstrated in nonverbal ways, particularly in body language. Anger, too, denied verbally, may be "clearly" stated in kinesics (and proxemics) through clenched fists, muscle tautness, abruptness of manner, perspiration in the palms, and shaping of personal space (becoming very territorial, pacing back and forth, etc.). Many interrogators and polygraph examiners suggest that some of the same symptoms may occur in the person who is lying—willingly and knowingly relating something other than the truth. They also describe other changes in physiological and biological processes, such as change in pulse rate, perspiration flow, and change in skin color (Abrams, 1989).

Although changes in body language do have meaning, the meaning is not always apparent. What may seem to be evidence of a lie may be concern for a loved one; what may appear to be staggering and falling from drunkenness may instead be caused by a physiological disorder. We may accurately recognize a symptom, but not correctly assess what it is a symptom of. Lie detection through the use of the polygraph is supported by psychophysiologist David Raskin and challenged by psychologist David Lykken. Both agree, however, that in verifying the truthfulness of innocent subjects, "The lie detector turns up more innocent people found guilty—false positives—than guilty people found innocent" (Meyer, 1982, p. 26). As discussed in earlier chapters, what we see, hear, and smell is personalized through our perception process. Officers should not only be very aware of kinesics but also be very cautious in drawing conclusions regarding the meaning of messages received without checking out their hunches through other feedback options.

THE OFFICER'S MESSAGE   In addition to being aware of messages received through the body language of others, police officers need to be very aware of the messages transmitted through their own body language. Police officers may express boredom, interest, disgust, disrespect, anger, frustration, acceptance, authority, nervousness, and any number of other emotions through body language alone. An officer's body language may calm or ignite a situation. A youth gang member

FIGURE 8.3   The art of communication.

Courtesy of Birmingham Police Department.

may act on what he interprets in an officer's body language to be an insult. It is a rare veteran offender who does not guess, before any words are exchanged, who the new police officers and correctional service officers are and then proceed to test those people.

Personal Space

A TERRITORIAL IMPERATIVE   Nonverbal cues are probably displayed most prominently in Western peoples' use of proxemics, personal space. People tend to establish, or stake out, their own territory. Robert Ardrey (1966) traced this concept to biological inheritance, examining how animals establish certain territories. Fast (1981) relates a delightful anecdote in his book in which he experimented with a friend in a restaurant by moving his silverware and dishes, piece by piece, as if inadvertently, into the other man's table space. His friend became noticeably upset. Establishing territorial space is also illustrated by the behavior of students in the classroom: After high school, the "assigned-seat–alphabetical-order" arrangements cease, but notice how students tend to occupy the same territory in college classrooms. You may find yourself slightly irritated when someone occupies "your space."

IDENTIFYING TERRITORY   We identify territory as ours by spreading our books or dishes over a table, putting our pictures on the wall, putting our name on the mailbox, or displaying graffiti on a neighborhood boundary. Even on the job, we attempt to maintain a work area that is ours; if it is not respected, we are uneasy, somewhat confused, and at least mildly annoyed.

Territory in police work is identified in many ways: jurisdictional boundaries, district boundaries, the agency's organizational structure, job description, and so on. Territory can also be defined in the sense of level of discretionary decision making, or which car an officer drives.

The very need for territory sometimes interferes with the need for change. Change can be viewed as territorial infringement, and it may require that new boundaries be set. The issue of territory and change may become a major problem of police–community relations. It can be an issue for an individual officer or team, for two warring youth gangs, or for a neighborhood threatened by new freeway construction.

Interpersonal Space

Generally, the rules that regulate our use of personal space are implicit. Formal business requires a different use of distance than does friendship. What is comfortable and acceptable may depend both on the nature of the activity and the relationship. Hall (1966) identified four basic personal space zones:

1. *Intimate distance*, extending to about 18 inches from the skin. This is reserved space. Intimate activities include lovemaking, cuddling, and massaging.
2. *Personal distance*, about 11/2–4 feet from the body. Interactions with friends and people we care about are allowed in this space.
3. *Social distance*, about 4–12 feet. Impersonal and casual business is conducted at this distance.
4. *Public distance*, more than 12 feet. Formal interactions, lectures, and speeches take place at this distance.

THE MESSAGE OF PROXEMICS   Police officers violate, or invade, a person's space, sometimes deliberately and sometimes without intending to, causing the invaded person to move away or become (sometimes act) defensive. Brougham (1992, p. 16) reports that successful police interviewers create a high level of anxiety in a suspect by beginning an interview at a comfortable distance when discussing general information. Then the interviewer will move closer to the suspect when questioning on key points and will back off during desired responses. Brougham states that this practice serves to program a person to cooperate with the interviewer's line of questioning.

Physical obstacles may prevent effective communication. The authority figure sitting behind a desk places an obstacle between self and client. This use of proxemics says, "You must obey me. I am your superior." As Fast observed, "We learn certain tricks of domination to control a situation. We can arrange to be higher than our subordinates, or we can allow our boss to be higher than we are. We can be aware that we dominate our children when we hover over them" (Fast, 1981, p. 90). The act of stopping a vehicle is structured to place the police officer in an authoritative position. The citizen remains seated in his or her car, while the officer occupies "territory" over the individual.

Movement across social distances in our culture also distorts communication and causes feelings of anxiety. Huseman and McCurley (1972), in a study of police communication behaviors, found that police officers experience most of their problems in communicating with minority groups.

SYMBOLIC CUES

From birth we are taught to attach great importance to **symbolic cues**. A symbol is something that stands for something else. They carry a meaning that is recognized by members of a culture (Macionis, 1993, p. 65). Virtually all interactions among human beings involve the use of symbols. We are constantly looking for "clues" about the appropriate behavior in social situations.

The criminal justice system makes use of a number of symbols. The scales of justice convey the meaning that the system is blind to personal distinctions as it goes about evaluating evidence and judging guilt or innocence. Flashing blue or red lights signal the presence of an emergency vehicle. Traffic signs present various symbols that tell us what to do as we drive. Police officers use a variety of socially understood symbols, uniforms, nightsticks, other weapons, badges, and so on.

FIGURE 8.4 Sometimes words aren't necessary: It is obvious without written explanation that Deputy Holder and Sonja had a "good day."

Courtesy of the Jackson County Sheriff's Department.

Generally speaking, the police uniform is a symbol of authority. In situations where the officer is regarded as the person who can take command of a situation and solve a crisis, the uniform speaks positively in the police–citizen interaction. In situations where the officer is regarded as the enemy or as the scapegoat, the uniform becomes a negative symbolic cue, interfering with positive interaction between the officer and citizen. A veteran officer in a police–community relations class remarked, "If I approach a citizen to give a ticket, and push my hat back on my head, hook my thumb in my belt buckle, and smile, I'm in for trouble."

Realizing that the uniform itself is sometimes a negative symbolic cue to citizens, some departments have experimented with dressing officers in blazers, thus softening their image. Although studies regarding the practice have been inconclusive, interviews with police administrators indicate that street experience in most areas has led them to vary the use of the blazer and uniform depending on a number of factors. Key factors mentioned include (1) type of activity and (2) characteristics of citizens involved (e.g., age and level of initial hostility to police).

OFFICIAL COMMUNICATION

Verbal, nonverbal, and symbolic cues have relevance in the dimension of official communication. Awareness of language, its usage, and its impact are very important in written communication. The opportunity to gain immediate feedback (and therefore to determine whether or not the message received was the one sent) is not available. Certain words carry more importance than others in writing.

Paralanguage, the power of what is not said, is also critical in official communication. Written words are read without the sender's inflection. They should be reviewed carefully by the sender for any unintended ambiguity and fragmented statements.

Proxemics, in the sense of social space, may be expressed or challenged implicitly or explicitly in official communication. Territorial issues may be generated or resolved in intradepartmental memos. Reports may make positive or negative use of jurisdictional power and limitations.

Symbolic meaning is attached to whether or not official communication is written on letterhead (or on which letterhead) and in a proper format, as well as its length, the quality of paper it is on, whether it is an original or a copy, by whom it is signed, and so on.

EFFECTIVE LISTENING

Listening as a Mental Exercise

Hearing is the act or power of perceiving sound. Hearing with normal ears is an automatic process, but listening is a mental exercise. Radio and television broadcasters are continually concerned with how many people are hearing their programs. However, the question "Does anybody listen?" seems immaterial to them. This is a radically different question. It asks this: Does anyone understand my idea, my intention, my message? Does anybody care?

Americans are not effective listeners. In general they talk more than they listen. As one theorist states, "It is really not difficult to learn to listen—just unusual." Many of us, while ostensibly listening, are actually preparing a statement to "stun" the company when we gain the floor. A good relationship between listener and speaker is necessary in a conversation—in fact, an effective *listener* leads the conversation. John F. Kennedy was famous for the incisive questions he asked and the way he listened to replies. Robert Saudek, who conferred with him at the White House while producing "Profiles in Courage" for television, later told friends, "He made you think he had nothing else to do except ask you questions and listen—with extraordinary concentration—to your answers. You knew that for the time being he had blotted out both the past and the future. More than anyone else I have ever met, President Kennedy seemed to understand the importance of *now*." We all crave good listeners. Sporadic or half-attentive listening is easily detected through nonverbal feedback cues received by the source.

Effective listening is important in any occupation. However, it is especially important in police–community relations. Miscommunication between citizens and police officers can have disastrous, if not fatal, consequences.

Nonjudgmental Listening

Carl Rogers outlined the idea of **nonjudgmental listening** in his book, *On Becoming a Person*: "I would like to propose, as an hypothesis for consideration, that the major barrier to mutual interpersonal communication is our very natural tendency to judge, evaluate, to approve or disapprove the statement of the other person or the other group" (Rogers, 1961, p. 328). Rogers goes on to state that real communication occurs when one listens with understanding, trying to place oneself in another person's position. This is most difficult in highly emotional situations—the kinds of situations often dealt with by criminal justice personnel. When a police officer encounters similar situations, such as quarrels in the same family again and again, the officer may have a strong desire to "tune out." It is precisely that behavior that is ineffective.

In many Wisconsin communities, suburban police departments employ a "court officer" who serves as liaison between the district attorney and the police department. One such officer encountered continued friction with a fellow officer over the matter of ticket dismissals. "The law is the law," the second officer adamantly stated. It did not matter to him whether or not the defendant had good reason for clemency from the judge; he would not listen to explanations but merely delivered lengthy tirades. Suddenly the duty roster rotated the men, and this officer became—you guessed it—the court officer. In a few weeks, his attitude changed completely. He learned to listen to complete explanations.

Weaver summarizes, "All this really means is that in order to understand a verbal message well, you must understand the talker to some degree. This makes communicating with a total stranger somewhat difficult when you get above the level of asking or giving directions or talking about the weather" (Weaver, 1972, p. 88). In *Future Shock*, Toffler (1970) spoke of the increasing number of short-duration relationships, particularly in service occupations, and pointed out the difficulty of a professional attempting to listen and communicate with increasingly large numbers of people.

Listening Efficiency

Tests on listening show repeatedly that people have an average listening efficiency of only 25 percent. (This varies—some people can retain up to 70 percent and others only up to 10 percent.) Listening is not an easy, passive process. It is hard work, characterized by faster heart action, increased circulation of the blood, and a small rise in body temperature.

Most people talk at a speed of about 125 words a minute. Strong evidence exists that indicates if thought were measured in words per minute, most of us could think easily at about four times that rate. It is extremely difficult to slow down thinking time; thus we normally have about 400 words of thinking time to spare during every minute a person talks to us. What do we do with that excess thinking time while someone is speaking?

In interpersonal relationships, we too often prepare our next comment; in formal situations, as the speaker bores us, we become impatient and turn our thoughts to something else. Soon the side-thought trips become too enticing, and when we attempt to return to the speaker, we are lost. Effective listeners use their thought speed to advantage, not for side trips. They constantly apply their spare thinking time to what is being said.

SOME EFFECTIVE LISTENING FACILITATORS

1. Be prepared to listen. Rid yourself of as many distractions as possible.
2. Be an attentive listener. Observe the speaker for verbal and nonverbal cues that will increase your understanding of the speaker and the subject.

3. Be willing to risk becoming involved as a participant in, not just as an observer of, the communication.
4. Avoid prejudging what is being said and interrupting to offer criticism or advice.
5. Genuinely accept the other person's feelings and recognize his or her right to have views that differ from yours.
6. Offer feedback to the speaker, not in the form of judgments as to the "rightness" or "wrongness" of what was said, but in the form of a restatement and clarification of what was said both in terms of objective reality and in terms of the speaker's perceptions of and feelings about that reality: "What I am hearing is. . . ." "Are you saying that . . . ?"

EMPATHY

The squad car is repeatedly cited as the great insulator in police work, as are heavy caseloads for probation and parole officers. Given the police officer in the squad, the changing nature of neighborhoods, and the number of people dealt with in human relations occupations, people in these professions will need to develop high degrees of trust quickly, as will society. In reply to a questionnaire, one police officer answered, "I do my work impartially and without emotion."

Imagine that you are an elderly woman. Your only income is your social security check, which is very small. As you are walking to the grocery store, a man attacks you from behind and takes your purse, containing the only money you have. You are knocked to the ground. You sit there, dazed and bewildered. Someone calls the police, and soon two officers arrive. They begin immediately to fill out their report. They take information from you, asking you short and specific questions. The officers are doing their job impartially and without emotion. They are not sharing themselves with you, and were they to take the time to understand your feelings, they would not only have to spend more time with you, but they would also have to deal with their own feelings. The method used by the police officers insulates them from their own emotional involvement with you and is expeditious and efficient. But how are you feeling about their humaneness?

People entering the criminal justice profession need to possess a very special communication quality. Unlike the development of voice or listening skills, this concept has a rather vague aesthetic nature. It is called **empathy**, and theorists maintain that those entering people-oriented professions need to have large amounts of it. It is a caring attitude, the developed capacity to understand another, and to comprehend another's feelings, attitudes, or sentiments.

In its most extreme example, those persons who are unable to comprehend another's feelings, attitudes, or sentiments are sociopathic or psychopathic personalities. They are incapable of experiencing normal amounts of love or empathy (Levin and Fox, 1985, pp. 71–72). Psychologists speculate that some people become sociopaths because they have been rejected in their family relationships and cannot form social bonds. They often engage in various forms of misbehavior, cheating, lying, and, among the most severely affected, rape and murder (Ressler, Burgess, and Douglas, 1988).

BLOCKS TO EFFECTIVE COMMUNICATION

When community relations efforts fail, at least one of the following blocks has contributed to that failure: (1) community distrust of the police; (2) police distrust of community members; (3) poor training of police; (4) the organizational structure of the police agency; and (5) scapegoating.

Community Distrust of Police

If the citizens do not trust the police, they will avoid police contact and they will not talk to them. Therefore, if distrust causes avoidance and failure to communicate, the implications for the police organization are very dramatic. Citizens will not report crime; they will not give statements to officers who are investigating crimes; and they will not testify in court. The result is inefficiency and an unsafe community.

Police Distrust of Community

If the police view the community or some geographical part of the community they have sworn to protect as dangerous and full of people who are hostile to them, police will react in a negative way. They will not feel free to communicate with the community and will be guarded and cautious when they come in contact with those they are protecting. As a result, police officers will contribute to widening the gap between themselves and the rest of the community. Their belief system will be reinforced by negative community contacts. Eventually police officers will become fearful and hostile toward the very people they are supposed to be protecting and serving.

Poor Training

The training of police officers has significantly improved in recent years. However, the training curriculum of most police academies is heavily weighted on those skills necessary to perform the law enforcement task, a task that occupies a small portion of the officers' time. The majority of the time is often spent on police procedures, law, weapons training, driver training, self-defense, and first aid. These topics will still need to be taught. However, in the twenty-first century, law enforcement is facing a changed society—one that has become more culturally diverse—and police training must incorporate these changes. Training must develop interpersonal skills, such as active listening and de-escalation techniques, and proactive problem-solving skills. The training must stress cultural diversity and the need for the police to become part of the community not apart from the community (Coderoni, 2002). The police must incorporate community policing into their training. The police officer of the twenty-first century will be someone capable of critical and independent thinking and who can work with other agencies and culturally diverse community members to solve community problems.

Organizational Structure

The majority of U.S. police departments are paramilitary organizations, with chains of command, defined areas of responsibilities, volumes of rules and regulations, and a clear hierarchy of membership. Police organizations have chiefs, deputy chiefs, captains, sergeants, and patrol officers, and many large police organizations carry the military tradition even further, using the ranks of colonel, major, and corporal in the organizational structure.

The results of the paramilitary structure being used for a police service organization are well described by Egon Bittner:

> Another complex of mischievous consequences arising out of the military bureaucracy relates to the paradoxical fact that while this kind of discipline ordinarily strengthens command authority it has the opposite effect in police departments. This effect is insidious rather than apparent. Because police superiors do not direct the activity of officers in any important sense, they are perceived as mere disciplinarians.
>
> Contrary to the army officer who is expected to lead his men into battle—even though he may never have a chance to do it—the analogously ranked police official is someone who can only do a great deal to his subordinates and very little for them. For this reason supervisory personnel are often viewed by the line personnel with distrust and even contempt. (Bittner, 1970, p. 59)

An even more important consideration is that the paramilitary organizational structure not only blocks effective communication within the organization because of the superior–subordinate relationship, but the same working relationship inevitably is transferred to contacts between patrol officers and citizens.

Scapegoating

Allport (1954) defined **scapegoating** as "a phenomenon wherein some of the aggressive energies of a person or a group are focused upon another individual, group or object; the amount of aggression and blame being either partly or wholly unwarranted."

In more specific terms, police have often focused their attention on particular groups or individuals when such attention was really unwarranted.

A number of steps precede scapegoating. If we are aware of the progression, we will be able to spot the danger signs and take action before a serious problem occurs. These steps are (1) simple preferences; (2) active biases; (3) prejudice; (4) discrimination; and (5) full-fledged scapegoating.

SIMPLE PREFERENCES   We all have preferences—we like people who agree with us, who have similar backgrounds, and who share our value system. Our socialization process in many overt and subtle ways teaches us to prefer spaghetti or curry, gefilte fish or soul food, blondes or brunettes, Cadillacs or Fords. This simple preference for one food or one type of person is both natural and inevitable. A technical term for this simple preference is *predilection*.

ACTIVE BIASES   Here the simple preference turns stronger. People state their preference in negative terms. Instead of saying "I prefer spaghetti to curry," the statement might be "I don't like curry" or "I don't like Jewish food." An active bias is the stepping-off point toward a closed mind, an ineffective person, and an uninformed person. It immediately precedes a full-blown prejudice.

PREJUDICE   Many people have **prejudices**, which means that they have a tendency to prejudge certain groups, persons, or events. A prejudice is a prejudgment that is rigid and inflexible. Although a prejudice does no great social harm as long as it is not acted out, in the case of people involved in public service, it is extremely difficult not to let a prejudice affect judgment.

DISCRIMINATION   **Discrimination** is an act of exclusion prompted by prejudice. The most commonly accepted examples are discrimination against blacks and Hispanics by white society. This discrimination has manifested itself in different areas, including employment, housing, health care, and other social institutions. Although significant progress has been made, discrimination is one of the most significant social problems in the United States and one that profoundly affects U.S. police and their level of professionalism.

Racial and ethnic groups have, in the past, been systematically excluded from police service and from promotional appointments. Affirmative action programs have had an impact on this systematic exclusion. According to a study commissioned by the Police Executive Research Forum (PERF), estimates of blacks, Hispanics, and other racial/ethnic groups in 486 police agencies serving populations of 50,000 or more were very close to the current U.S. Census Bureau estimates for the population (Carter, Sapp, and Stephens, 1989, p. 39). Although this is cause for optimism, it does not signal an end to discrimination in the hiring practices of police agencies or in discriminatory behavior on the part of individual officers. Some police officers still look upon minorities as unworthy, unwanted, and unacceptable as human beings. The shooting of an unarmed African immigrant by New York police and allegations of arbitrary traffic stops by the New Jersey State Police again raise the specter of police discrimination against minorities.

FULL-FLEDGED SCAPEGOATING   Scapegoating manifests itself after all the preceding steps are fulfilled. It consists of concentrated aggression in both word and deed. The victim is abused both physically and verbally. The persons or groups being scapegoated are often given credit for astounding power and evil, as in the following examples: "The Jews are ruining America"; "Ship all blacks back to Africa and crime will stop"; "Wetbacks (Mexicans) are responsible for all of California's labor problems"; and "All teenagers are inherently lazy." When such statements are seen in print they are easily identified as simplistic statements by anyone with average intelligence. Yet many people make these statements day after day and, unfortunately, believe what they are saying.

Why Scapegoating Occurs

Allport (1954) identifies a number of reasons for the phenomenon of scapegoating. Among them are "tabloid thinking," self-enhancement, peer pressure and conformity, fear and anxiety, and displaced aggression. Some of these are discussed in more detail in the following sections.

TABLOID THINKING   This is the process in which people simplify a problem by blaming a group or class of people. For example, some people blame crime on illegal drug abuse; they feel that most crime is committed by drug-dependent people trying to get money to feed their habits. Although these people do commit crime, in reality they are responsible for only a small percentage of the crime rate. This tabloid-thinking process allows people to overlook real issues while they focus on the wrong cause.

Illegal drugs are sometimes scapegoated by **tabloid thinking**. Illegal drugs are those that we frequently define as dangerous substances. These substances include heroin, cocaine, LSD, ECTASY, angel dust, marijuana, certain prescription drugs, and many others. These represent a wide assortment of substances with many different sources, prices, and resulting behaviors. However, the most damaging, commonly abused drug in our society is not included in the list: It is alcohol. Under most circumstances, alcohol is not illegal to use; in tabloid thinking, it is not even recognized as a drug.

Considering the extent of the problem, efforts to prevent the crime, injury, and death caused by alcohol are very limited in the United States, with the exception of a recent tightening of laws relating to DWI/DUI (driving while intoxicated/driving under the influence) behavior. We are more likely to use our resources fighting illegal drug use. Tabloid thinking is a type of tunnel vision that, by omitting all the facts, may encourage us to focus all our energies on the wrong battle.

SELF-ENHANCEMENT   Some people have inferiority complexes. People who are experienced in interviewing police applicants often discover individuals who want to join the police department because they feel that having a badge and a gun will make them something they are not—that is, strong, more respected, or allowed to exercise control or authority over other people. Such applicants are serious liabilities to the police profession if they slip through the screening process. They will cause many communication blocks with the community through their scapegoating of others to cover their own feelings of inferiority. This type of person is also dangerous because he or she is often afraid; this personal fear often results in the use of excessive force. The use of such force when it is not warranted leads to a breakdown in communication between the police and the community.

PEER PRESSURE AND CONFORMITY   The need to belong to a group or organization is very strong in most people. New officers who join an organization that engages in scapegoating will find themselves joining with their fellow officers just so they can be part of the group. This is particularly evident when a new officer is coupled with an old-timer. Too often the officer ends up acting like the trainer.

STRATEGIES OF CHANGE

Achieving Mutual Respect

Mutual respect is achieved best in an atmosphere in which everyone counts. If I make promises that I cannot keep or make decisions that affect your life without considering your needs or your views, I am discounting you. If you treat me as if I am a category rather than a person, you discount me.

Strategies for overcoming blocks in the area of mutual respect include establishing programs that encourage honest, open exchange and positive personal contact between citizens and officers. Some of the options include the following:

- Increasing the number of walking police beats.
- Decentralizing functional police units.
- Implementing police–community projects in which shared decision making actually occurs.
- Ensuring that ride-along programs involve not only the youth and adults who already have respect for the police but also those who are distrustful.
- Establishing and supporting creative educational liaison projects.
- Initiating projects that survey citizen input and make changes based on the results of the survey.
- Participating in a community communication network designed to decrease problems with rumors and misunderstandings.
- Participating in a proactive social service action program.
- Involving volunteers in most areas of the police process.
- Assisting individual officers to increase their skills in analyzing the factors existing in each situation and selecting an interpersonal communication approach that is most congruent with existing needs.

In 1997 the police department of Roanoke, Virginia, began an outreach project to build relationships between the police and the community's growing Vietnamese community. Sponsored by the Bureau of Justice Assistance, the project was designed to provide services to the Vietnamese community and cultural awareness training to police officers. Criminal justice terminology was translated into Vietnamese and 22 different legal and criminal justice brochures were produced and distributed to the community. Police officers continue to conduct sessions at community meetings and 250 police officers have participated in a four-hour cultural awareness training program (Coventry and Johnson, 2001). It is anticipated that the project will lead to Vietnamese joining the police department. This is a program that could be replicated in other police departments with expanding immigrant populations.

Improving Training

Police training is an intense experience that has improved immensely over the years. Ways in which training can change to improve effective communication in police–community relations include the following:

- Building the academy and in-service training content upon a basic humanistic philosophy.
- Incorporating the teaching of more effective communication skills in ongoing workshops for officers.
- Placing a greater emphasis and more academy hours on service concepts and issues.
- Encouraging educational goals of officers, especially in seeking professional and liberal arts and sciences degrees.
- Ensuring that street training experience for new officers supports the philosophy and content of the academy.
- Increasing cultural awareness training, especially training centered on identifiable community groups.

Rethinking Police Organization

Realistically, reorganization in police agencies is traumatic, and it is difficult to conceive, achieve, and retain. Some communication blocks seem inherent in the organizational structure. Small system changes, however, can help to reduce the number and influence of these blocks. Suggestions include the following:

- Requiring management training seminars for all key management personnel.
- Using noncertified personnel in some key positions.

- Developing a reward system that places a high agency value on effective individual communication efforts.
- Increasing opportunities for exchange between line officers and top administration.
- Incorporating a "quality-circle" concept into the organization to ensure that all personnel in the organization are valued.
- Committing the organization to a single (rather than a contradictory) philosophy that encourages personal growth and community service.

Preventing Scapegoating

Efforts that will increase mutual respect also will help to decrease scapegoating. Humanistic training efforts help, sometimes by screening out recruits whose actions already demonstrate discrimination and scapegoating attitudes. Organizational changes that encourage personal growth and community service help to discourage scapegoating. Other strategies that focus on the individual officer might include the following:

- Providing opportunities for the officer to become more self-aware.
- Increasing opportunities for personal values clarification.
- Rewarding actions that demonstrate a lack of bias.
- Providing counseling opportunities.
- Providing opportunities for the officer to experience exceptions to stereotypes.

BOX 8.1
Fact or Inference? A Communication Game

A *statement of fact* is an observation that is verifiable. An *inference* is a conclusion or opinion; a subjective evaluation. Both are a necessary part of police work. Some of our greatest problems occur when we confuse the two. This exercise* will help you learn the difference between statements of fact and inferences and gain a better understanding of the ways in which inferences are made.

In this game, you will read three reports and answer questions about them. Then you will have an opportunity to check your answers.

Testing Your Skills

Directions: After reading each report twice *and without returning to the report for review*, answer the questions related to that situation below by circling the correct response. Mark "T" if the statement is definitely true on the basis of the information given in the report. Mark "F" if the statement is definitely false. Mark a "?" if you cannot be certain on the basis of the information given in the report. If any part of the statement is doubtful, mark "?".

Situation A

John and Betty Smith are awakened in the middle of the night by a noise coming from the direction of their living room. Smith investigates and finds that the door opening into the garden, which he thought he had locked before going to bed, is standing wide open. Books and papers are scattered all over the floor around the desk in one corner of the room.

Statements about Situation A

T F ? **1.** Mrs. Smith was awakened in the middle of the night.

T F ? **2.** Mr. Smith locked the door from his living room to his garden before going to bed.

T F ? **3.** The books and papers were scattered between the time Mr. Smith went to bed and the time he was awakened.

T F ? **4.** Mr. Smith found that the door opening into the garden was shut.

T F ? **5.** Mr. Smith did not lock the garden door.

T F ? **6.** Mr. Smith was not awakened by a noise.

T F ? **7.** Nothing was missing from the room.

T F ? **8.** Mrs. Smith was sleeping when she and Mr. Smith were awakened.

T F ? **9.** The noise did not come from their garden.

T F ? **10.** Mr. Smith saw no burglar in the living room.

T F ? **11.** Mr. and Mrs. Smith were awakened in the middle of the night by a noise.

Situation B

A businessperson had just turned off the lights in the store when a man appeared and demanded money. The owner opened a cash register. The contents of the cash register were scooped up, and the man sped away. A member of the police force was notified promptly.

Statements about Situation B

T F ? **1.** A man appeared after the owner had turned off the store lights.

T F ? **2.** The robber was a man.

T F ? **3.** The man did not demand money.

T F ? **4.** The person who opened the cash register was the owner.

T F ? **5.** The store owner scooped up the contents of the cash register and ran away.

T F ? **6.** Someone opened a cash register.

T F ? **7.** After the man who demanded the money scooped up the contents of the cash register, he ran away.

T F ? **8.** Although the cash register contained money, the report does not state how much.

T F ? **9.** The robber demanded money of the owner.

T F ? **10.** The report concerns a series of events in which only three persons are referred to: the owner of the store, a man who demanded money, and a member of the police force.

T F ? **11.** The following events were included in the report: someone demanded money, a cash register was opened, its contents were scooped up, and a man dashed out of the store.

Situation C

Members of the 12th Street Gang are planning an assault on the 4th Avenue Gang. Two days ago a 4th Avenue Gang member was in 12th Street territory. Tires on a car were slashed.

Statements about Situation C

T F ? **1.** One of the boys from the 4th Avenue Gang was in 12th Street territory.

T F ? **2.** The 4th Avenue Gang is a youth gang.

T F ? **3.** The leaders of the 12th Street Gang are planning an assault.

T F ? **4.** Three tires on a car were slashed.

T F ? **5.** The car in the story was in 12th Street Gang territory.

T F ? **6.** One of the 12th Street Gang members was in 4th Avenue territory.

T F ? **7.** The tires were slashed by a 4th Avenue Gang member.

T F ? **8.** The car belongs to a 12th Street Gang member.

T F ? **9.** The 12th Street Gang is a youth gang.

T F ? **10.** The slashing of the tires was a deliberate attack on the 12th Street Gang.

T F ? **11.** The member of the 4th Avenue Gang was in 12th Street territory to challenge the 12th Street Gang.

*This exercise is based on a game entitled "Inference versus Observation," in *Interpersonal Communication: A Guide for Staff Development*. Athens, GA: Institute of Government, University of Georgia, 1974.

REALITY CHECK

Correcting a Wrong Perception

While residing in a small Georgia town, I served as the part-time municipal judge for seven years. One of many cases I dealt with during that time involved a local who felt that he needed to drink at least a quart of beer each day in order to keep his kidneys functioning. Unfortunately, this medical precaution had not served him well when he had been arrested for DUI (driving under the influence). It had been exacerbated in that he was stopped by the police while hauling off the body of a neighbor's dog that he had shot after another neighbor had complained to him that it had chased her chickens. I had dealt with this situation as leniently as possible, allowing him to pay his fine over an extended time and placing him under the supervision of a local businessman who had interceded on his behalf.

A couple of years later, I was working in my backyard when I heard a gunshot and then observed a dog run yelping through the yards behind my house. The dog collapsed while running and then lay totally still, obviously dead. I turned to see several small neighborhood children watching what had happened. Indignant that someone had committed such an atrocity in the middle of our neighborhood, I immediately went over to the neighboring street to find out what was occurring. Upon my arrival, I saw my former dog-shooting friend sitting in his truck with a rifle beside him. He stated to me, "I'm watching that dog there."

I asked, "Haven't you been in enough trouble for shooting dogs? You'd better not shoot another one."

He stated, "I haven't shot any dog."

To which I replied, "Really, what about the one that just ran from here and died across from my house?"

He repeated, "I haven't shot any dog."

I replied that I was going to have to contact the police and that he better not shoot the dog he was watching.

As I was going to the police station, I saw that a patrol car had pulled up beside the dead dog. An officer was trying to distract the children while the body was loaded into a county truck. I asked the officer how he had responded so quickly, to which he replied that he had been with "them" when the dog was shot. I asked what he meant by them. I added that I had seen Bill (not his real name) with a gun in his truck on the next street and assumed that he had done the shooting. The officer replied with some distaste, "No, animal control had complaints on this dog and shot him when they couldn't catch him. That's them hauling him off."

Aware that I had wrongly accused Bill of shooting the dog, I went looking for him. I located him at the local grocery store where he had gone to seek help from his son. In front of his son and several customers, I said, "You were telling the truth, and I was wrong. I apologize for wrongly accusing you."

Bill was stunned. Then he stuck out his hand and thanked me for being "big enough" to apologize to him. Bill's son and the bystanders smiled and nodded in agreement.

This incident reinforced two things that I already knew. Don't jump to conclusions even if they appear to be obvious. And it really doesn't hurt to apologize when you are wrong.

Conclusions

The quality of police–community relations depends on the quality of police–community communication, and vice versa. This chapter has focused on the continuous, ongoing communication process and possible blocks to this process. Communication occurs on many levels: intrapersonal, interpersonal, person-to-group, organizational, and written. It includes the elements of sender, receiver, and message in a situational context.

The three basic modes of interpersonal communication are (1) verbal; (2) nonverbal (paralanguage, kinesics or body language, and proxemics or communication through the use of personal or social space); and (3) symbolic (the messages conveyed by style of dress, personal appearance, one's possessions, etc.). Cues exist for each mode that an effective communicator must learn to recognize and use. For example, a police officer who wants to use language and paralanguage well must pay attention to articulation of words, volume and rate of speech, tone of voice, choice of language, and (when necessary) telephone manner. The officer must also be aware of the effect of body positions, use of personal space, clothing, and personal appearance on communications.

An effective communicator is someone who not only sends but also receives messages well. Unlike hearing, listening is a mental exercise. People can "think" words much faster than they can speak or listen to them; effective listeners are those who apply their spare thinking time to what is being said—and who try to place themselves "in the speaker's shoes" in a nonjudgmental way.

Effective communicators are aware of themselves and others in a situational context. They determine what messages are appropriate to send and then couch them in an approach they feel will most effectively achieve their goals. A communication quality that is especially important in the administration is empathy. Free, open communication with other members of the community is possible only for the person who can empathize with others.

There are five common blocks to effective communication in police–community relations: community distrust of the police, police distrust of the community, poor training, police organizational issues, and scapegoating. There also are strategies for change that can eliminate or lessen these blocks to communication. Many of these strategies will be further explored in later chapters.

Student Checklist

1. Identify and describe three levels of communication.
2. Define and diagram the communication process.
3. Identify and give examples of the modes of communication.
4. What is effective listening?
5. What is the role of empathy in communication?

6. List the blocks to effective communication most frequently encountered in police–community relations.
7. List the strategies for change that could eliminate or lessen the blocks to effective police–community communication.

Topics for Discussion

1. Why is nonjudgmental listening an important skill for police officers to have?
2. When would it not be useful to be an effective listener?
3. How can you be ensured of getting feedback in the communication process?
4. Discuss the common blocks to effective communication between police and citizens mentioned in this chapter in relationship to your own community.

5. What programs identified in strategies for change might remove the blocks to effective communication that exist in your community?
6. Discuss the difference between active bias and simple preference.

Bibliography

Abrams, S. (1989). *The Complete Polygraph Handbook*. Lexington, MA: Lexington Books.

Allport, G. W. (1954). *The Nature of Prejudice*. New York: Doubleday.

Ardrey, R. (1966). *The Territorial Imperative*. New York: Atheneum.

Bittner, E. (1970). *The Functions of the Police in Modern Society*. Bethesda, MD: National Institute of Mental Health.

Bombeck, E. (August 1982). "He spoke fluent law enforcement," in *Vanguard, Official Publication of the San Jose Peace Officers Association II*.

Brougham, C. G. (July 1992). "Nonverbal communication: Can what they don't say give them away?" *FBI Law Enforcement Bulletin*, pp. 15–18.

Carter, D. L., Sapp, A. D., and Stephens, D. W. (1989). *The State of Police Education: Policy Direction for the 21st Century*. Washington, D.C.: Police Executive Research Forum.

Coderoni, G. R. (November 2002). "The relationship between multicultural training for police and effective law enforcement," *FBI Law Enforcement Bulletin*.

Coventry, G., and Johnson, D. (2001). "Building relationships between police and the Vietnamese community in Roanoke, Virginia," *Bureau of Justice Assistance Bulletin*. U.S. Department of Justice.

Fast, J. (1981). *Body Language*. New York: Pocket Books.

Hall, E. T. (1966). *The Hidden Dimension*. Garden City, NY: Doubleday.

Huseman, R., and McCurley, S. (December 1972). "Police attitudes toward communication with the public," *The Police Chief*, Vol. 39, No. 12, pp. 68–73.

Institute of Government. (1974). *Interpersonal Communication: A Guide for Staff Development*. University of Georgia, Athens, GA.

Levin, J., and Fox, J. A. (1985). *Mass Murder: America's Growing Menace*. New York: Plenum Press.

Link, F. (1993). *The Interrotec® Kinesic Interview Technique: A Short Course in Detecting Deception Behaviorally*, February 27 seminar at Fort McClellan, AL.

Macionis, J. (1993). *Sociology*, 4th ed. Upper Saddle River, NJ: Prentice Hall.

Meyer, A. (June 1982). "So lie detectors lie?" *Science*, Vol. 82, pp. 24–27.

Quintanilla, G. (February 1983). "Cross-cultural Communication: An Ongoing Challenge," *FBI Law Enforcement Bulletin*, pp. 1–8.

Ressler, R. K., Burgess, A. W., and Douglas, J. E. (1988). *Sexual Homicide: Patterns and Motives*. Lexington, MA: Lexington Books.

Rogers, C. (1961). *On Becoming a Person*. Boston, MA: Houghton Mifflin.

Strecher, V. (1971). *The Environment of Law Enforcement*. Upper Saddle River, NJ: Prentice Hall.

Toffler, A. (1970). *Future Shock*. New York: Random House.

Van Maanen, J. (1978). "The asshole," in P. K. Manning and J. Van Maanen (Eds.), *Policing: A View from the Street*. Santa Monica, CA: Goodyear Publishing Co.

Weaver, C. H. (1972). *Human Listening: Processes and Behavior*. New York: Bobbs-Merrill.

White, M. F., Cox, T. C., and Basehart, J. (1994). "Theoretical consideration of officer profanity and obscenity in formal contacts with citizens," in T. Barker and D. L. Carter (Eds.), *Police Deviance*, 3rd ed. Cincinnati, OH: Anderson.

CHAPTER 9

Police Discretion and Community Relations

Attached to our democracy by the glue of necessity is a continuous and pervasive delegation of authority which empowers man to use his best judgment in governing others.

—REED, 1980, P. 54

KEY CONCEPTS

Abuse of Power	Internal Review	Racially Biased Policing
Community Input	Legal Authority	"Rule of Silence"
Discretion	Legislative Review	Selective Enforcement
Discriminatory Enforcement	Personal Autonomy	Situational Factors
Environmental Factors	Professionalism	Police Work Rules

LEARNING OBJECTIVES

Studying this chapter will enable you to:

1. Define *discretion* and its role in the system.
2. Explain some of the justifications for selective enforcement.
3. Identify the legal authority for selective enforcement.
4. Describe some of the dangers inherent in selective enforcement.
5. Discuss racially biased policing.
6. Demonstrate a strategy for structuring discretion.

The exercise of discretion in the administration of justice is inevitable and, within bounds, desirable. It has existed in every legal system in history (Davis, 1970, pp. 58–59).

Discretion occurs at every decision point in the justice process. How it is exercised by members of one component in the justice system affects how it can be exercised by members of other components. The exercise of discretion by police and citizens helps to shape what occurs throughout the entire process.

Police, through their discretionary judgments, are street interpreters of law. In a practical sense, police selectively determine what and how law is to be enforced. They determine what services they will offer and under what circumstances and to whom they will offer them. Police discretionary decisions are most frequently street decisions, directly affecting individual citizens and neighborhoods. Conversely, discretion exercised by those same citizens affects what is reported to police, whether or not witnesses will testify, and how much support and cooperation the police will receive. Mutual respect and support between the police and the community they serve are often defined in terms of how fairly, objectively, and impartially police discretionary judgment calls are made.

In this chapter we address the following topics:

- The role of discretion in the justice system.
- The nature of selective, and sometimes discriminatory, law enforcement.
- Factors influencing decision making.
- Justifications and legal authority for selective enforcement.
- Dangers of selective enforcement, including racially biased policing.
- Strategies for structuring discretion.

DISCRETION IN THE SYSTEM

Our society is based on freedom of choice, and that freedom requires the exercise of **discretion**. Against a backdrop of a government based on the rule of law and equality of all people under the law, one of the most perplexing problems confronting the administration of justice is that of discretionary, or selective, enforcement of laws.

For a system of justice to function humanely, flexibility and discretion must exist within the system. The more flexibility in the system, the greater the possibility that individualized justice may be served—and the more the system is vulnerable to abuse. According to Atkins and Pogrebin (1978):

> The invisible system of justice that lies beyond the formal scriptures of the law derives its energy from the failure of statutory law or any administrative code of regulation to specify all contingencies of decision-making. The essential problem becomes that of discovering the elusive balance between structuring decisions and providing for individualized justice. (p. 2)

Defining Discretion

Discretion is an exercise of individual choice or judgment. The range of choices may be limited by certain legal, administrative, or ethical bounds, or it may appear to be limitless. Discretion requires discerning or distinguishing among options. As the Commission on Accreditation for Law Enforcement Agencies (1987) points out:

> Because the concept of discretion defies rigid codification, officers should be trained in how to exercise the broad discretionary authority they have been granted. (1.1)

The Elements of Discretion

Discretion is personal, which means that individual experience, education, style, goals, and ethics are all involved in the decision-making process.

- Discretion requires *judgment*, which means that some choice is made among perceived options.
- Discretion often grants both **personal autonomy** and personal influence over the lives of others.

The ability to discriminate, in the sense of discerning or distinguishing among options, is a part of the exercise of discretion. To discriminate, as we commonly use the term—or in other words, to treat differently or favor on a basis other than individual merit—is an abuse of discretion.

Exercising Discretion in the System

The exercise of discretion in one part of the justice system affects all other parts. A few of the discretionary choices available to system members are as follows:

Police, many times during the working day, will make decisions that, in effect, suspend or modify statutory laws. Sometimes police administrators informally and unofficially institute policies that involve selective enforcement. Yet this use of discretion—although well known to prosecutors, judges, legislators, and some members of the public—is rarely acknowledged openly by police. The power of the police is great as a practical interpreter of the law. Police officers also have much discretionary power in their public service and order maintenance roles. In fact, every situation confronting the officer requires the use of discretion (Barker, Hunter, and Rush, 1994).

Citizens can choose whether or not to report crimes, testify in court, press charges, and support the police. Citizens determine through their discretionary judgment what level of crime will be tolerated.

Defendants and their attorneys can choose whether or not to cooperate with others in the system, what strategies will be employed in the defense.

Prosecutors choose whether or not to file, what charges to bring, what bargains are reasonable, and what strategies to employ in the prosecution.

Judges determine legal questions, review cases and reports, and sentence offenders.

Corrections officials choose to a large degree what happens to the convicted offender in terms of custody and treatment so long as the offender is in their jurisdiction.

SELECTIVE AND DISCRIMINATORY ENFORCEMENT

A Modern Tightrope

The modern police officer walks a tightrope between the right of the community to be protected and the right of the individual to be left alone by government. Our legal justice system is based on the concept that most people voluntarily obey the law and police themselves. In a free society, every citizen is responsible for his or her own behavior, and the police are considered to be agents of the citizenry they serve, enforcing laws and maintaining order in the interest of "liberty and justice for all." This is a humanitarian ideal. In this context, law applied without discretion may actually conflict with justice.

Our burgeoning urban population centers are composed of many different cultures and subcultures with many different views as to how laws should be enforced. This factor makes the process by which police try to match selective law enforcement decisions with priorities of the public served increasingly complex.

The police officer's judgment on whether or not a violation of law has taken place is not the major topic of our discussion in this chapter. Certainly, there are many occasions on which a patrol officer must decide whether to take action to enforce the law (i.e., whether an act of omission has occurred, is occurring, or will occur). The activity that concerns us most in this chapter, however, is perhaps an even more controversial one with direct and ongoing impact on community relations. It involves the decision *not* to enforce laws when there is no doubt that a violation occurred.

The Administrative Choice

Police organizations rarely make explicit policies that require **selective enforcement** of laws. Yet, on occasion, they do sacrifice "strict enforcement" to other values or principles, and police officers soon learn of unstated departmental policies to this effect. James Q. Wilson, in *Varieties of*

Police Behavior, describes the development of departmental policies through weighing strict enforcement against accommodations that will serve other values. He suggests that at times a department may have to sacrifice strict application of laws to achieve the values of "order" and "service giving," that are also part of the police mission (Wilson, 1968).

Even though they may not be subject to direct disciplinary action for failing to adhere to these policies, officers who disobey them will undoubtedly find themselves receiving less direct, but very displeasing penalties (lost opportunities for promotion, undesirable work or shift assignments, letters of reprimand, etc.). In this way, administrators can make informal or unofficial policies as binding as formal or official ones.

Operational-Level Choices

THE POLICE OFFICER AS LEGISLATOR, PROSECUTOR, AND JUDGE In day-to-day contact with citizens, police officers have discretion to "bend" the law—or even fail to enforce it altogether—as they see fit. In particular, they can play three important roles.

As legislators, they can specify what enacting legislatures stated in general language; they can establish classes of exceptions that are not specifically provided for in statutory law.

As prosecutors, they may decide not to proceed against a suspect in exchange for cooperation that may have a value for law enforcement.

As judges, they may determine that a suspect deserves a "suspended sentence" (i.e., release with a warning) or some on-the-spot punishment at the officer's own discretion (e.g., confiscation of contraband and participation in a social program).

The Invisibility of the Police Officer's Choices

When a police officer chooses to act as legislator, prosecutor, or judge, few people ever learn about or review the decisions. There is no record for supervisors to review. The suspect is unlikely to say

FIGURE 9.1 Discretion may involve determining how to allocate resources.
Courtesy of Birmingham Police Department.

anything, especially if the officer has been lenient. In those cases where the officer does not work alone, the officer's partner (who is usually at the same level of authority) will remain silent unless some very severe abuse occurs (Barker and Carter, 1994).

DECISION MAKING AT AN ADMINISTRATIVE LEVEL

Considering the quantity and breadth of laws they are supposed to enforce, police administrators sometimes conclude, quite reasonably, that they do not have the budgetary or personnel resources to enforce all laws fully. Consequently, they have to find some basis for choosing which laws to enforce.

Finding the Optimum Law Enforcement Level

When resources and/or personnel are limited, a sensible way to decide which laws to enforce is to find the mix that provides the most law enforcement with the officers, funds, and material available. Working out the optimum mix is not easy though. First, every administrator will want to enforce some laws, regardless of cost. With regard to other laws, the administrator can make decisions about which ones to enforce and how strictly to enforce them—after determining the time, effort, funds, and personnel that different options would entail. In matters such as these, however, which touch the public so deeply, basing decisions purely on cost and efficiency considerations is impossible.

Community Input

No administrator can afford to ignore public opinion when deciding which laws to enforce. For one thing, on purely practical grounds, laws opposed to the community are likely to be far more expensive to enforce than those that are not. Moreover, trying to enforce such laws may lead to lack of cooperation in other enforcement efforts (Reiss, 1971, pp. 68–102).

But who is the "community" or the "public"? Sometimes, the police are going along with the general sentiments of the population of a neighborhood. At other times, they are bowing to the desires and interests of the powerful, the vocal, or some other segment of the community.

As Wilson (1977) noted:

> The administrator becomes attuned to complaints. What constitutes a "significant" citizen demand will, of course, vary from city to city. In some places, a political party will tell the police whom to take seriously and whom to ignore; in other places, organized community groups will amplify some demands and drown out others; in still other places, the police themselves will have to decide whose voices to heed and how to heed them. Whatever the filtering mechanism, the police administrator ignores at his peril those demands that are passed through. (p. 70)

Administrators will not always choose the policy that produces the greatest amount of successful law-enforcement effort at the lowest unit cost. They may determine, instead, that the cost of losing support of some community groups because of police efforts may be compensated for in the value of enforcement to the larger community. An example is a strong enforcement campaign directed against drug dealers. The campaign might alienate the community of drug users and be much more expensive to maintain than an intensified effort against parking-ticket scofflaws. On the other hand, value to the larger community in terms of property crime reduction and general community support resulting from the reduction in drug activities would likely outweigh the cost of enforcement.

Bargaining and Law Enforcement

The politically powerful residents of the community may not want selective enforcement of laws but may instead prefer that the laws be applied only in limited situations. Thus, parking laws may be strictly enforced in some areas, but during holiday shopping seasons, the police may adopt a policy of "forgiveness" in areas surrounding shopping centers. Selective enforcement also occurs in the application of laws against prostitution. For example, police arrests of prostitutes and their clients may cause business convention planners to avoid some cities. When convention business is lost as a result of strict enforcement of vice laws, members of the business community may exert considerable pressure on police officials to relax enforcement of these laws. At the same time, the police administrator may recognize that there is strong support in the community as a whole for laws against prostitution; if this were otherwise, the legislature would have changed the law. The result of these opposing pressures on the administrator may lead him or her to adopt law enforcement policies that limit prostitution to a controlled level of practice. Prostitution flourishes, but it becomes hidden from the public view. Therefore, it is not likely to cause mobilization of citizens who would favor full suppression. The police administrator's objective in adopting a selective enforcement policy would be to strike a bargain with the citizens who support limited prostitution in exchange for their support of "more important" law enforcement objectives.

A hidden danger to law enforcement in this kind of balancing act is loss of integrity in the public eye. General public knowledge of selective and discriminatory patterns of law enforcement will produce, at the very least, an attitude that justice can be negotiated.

BOX 9.1
The Decision to Authorize the Use of Stun Guns and Tasers

Stun guns and Tasers have been utilized by police officers for many years. They are useful nonlethal devices that enable officers to subdue violent offenders without causing extreme physical injury. However, like any other weapon in the police arsenal, they have the potential to cause harm to suspects and innocent people if used improperly. They also can result in litigation, criminal prosecutions, and major damage to police–community relations.

One of the first initiatives that police administrators should take when contemplating whether to allow (or issue) these weapons to officers is to determine if they are indeed necessary and appropriate for use within their jurisdiction. If it is decided that these weapons are needed, then the department should develop a policy regulating use and a mandatory training program in their proper use before authorizing them to be carried.

While the policy and training programs are being developed, the agency should work to educate police officers, the media, and community leaders about stun guns and Tasers. One important piece of this education is to inform the media about the differences between the two. Currently press reports tend to refer to both weapons as being stun guns. Although they both use electrical shock to temporarily disable offenders, they are totally different devices.

Stun guns are small, hand-held devices that can be carried on an officer's duty belt. They have two electrical prongs on one end that transmit 7–14 watts of electricity. When activated they transmit a mild shock (mild being a relative term, the temporary pain from the shock is not pleasant). The result is that the suspect's muscles (in most cases) relax for a brief period, during which the officer seeks to gain physical control. This device is very safe and does not cause harm to people with weak hearts or pacemakers. Since it is hand-held, the officer must come in close contact with the suspect. For this reason, it has limited benefits but is a useful tool for officers who are trained in its use and properly supervised.

Tasers (electrical weapons named after the original manufacturer) are larger devices that require holsters similar to those used for handguns. They fire probes that pierce the skin of the suspect. These probes are connected to the Taser by small wires approximately 15 feet in length. When fired, the device provides a strong charge of approximately 18–26 watts of electricity for a period of five seconds. This provides a severe (and more painful) shock to resisting suspects. This weapon has an advantage in that it does not require the officer to be too close to a violent individual. Unfortunately, Tasers also have a much greater potential to harm and (depending on whose data one reads), in some rare cases, could cause death. For these reasons, we recommend that this device be used only on extremely violent suspects in lieu of more lethal alternatives. Departments would be wise to restrict their carry to supervisors and/or specially trained officers.

The Rule of Silence

Police administrators rarely issue orders or make public statements listing the criteria for selective law enforcement policies. Administrators expect subordinates to develop the "right" kinds of priorities without specific direction. This method of operation is undoubtedly reinforced by the fact that legislators, courts, and prosecutors rely on the police to use discretion when applying laws. These assumptions, although never formally stated, bear an important relationship to the laws that will actually be enforced in the community. There have been exceptions to the administrative-level **"rule of silence"** on selective enforcement policies.

Exceptions to the Rule

Written policy guidelines sometimes set standards for the use of alternatives to arrest. Under such standards, people who could be charged with drunk and disorderly offenses are sometimes referred to clinics where treatment can be offered. Recently, a county sheriff, concerned about the already overcrowded local jail, requested publicly that both city and county officers stop arresting people for misdemeanor offenses. He recommended that violators be cited instead of arrested.

   Although in the instance above no public comments of support or concern were forthcoming from other police agencies, public statements encouraging selective enforcement may receive much criticism from other agencies, especially if local community support is divided or uncertain. When Connecticut State Police Commissioner Cleveland Fuessenich announced a policy in 1971 that would allow his officers to use discretion in determining whether an arrest should be made in cases involving the possession of small quantities of marijuana, other Connecticut police chiefs reacted with criticism. Their comments reflect a conventional public position: "The law says a crime has been committed. . . . Who is to say which law will be enforced?" "It is the court system which has the discretion over cases brought before it . . . the system should remain that way." "It is not the job of the law enforcement agency to pick out which laws shall be enforced and for which people" (*New Haven Register*, December 2, 1971, p. 1). Support for such a policy would vary with time and place. Today possession of small quantities of marijuana has been decriminalized in some areas and is overlooked in other jurisdictions. In California, a police chief who used to be a zealous enforcer recently proclaimed his support for the medical use of marijuana.

DECISION MAKING AT AN OPERATIONAL LEVEL

Police officers are charged with responding directly to citizens' requests for service and the need to maintain public safety and order in the community. In most cases, police decide what action to take. They may observe an event, consider several alternative courses of action, and make a decision without recording it or doing anything that anyone else could report. For example, a police officer might observe a motorist drive through a red traffic signal and decide not to give chase. In this type of situation, not even the citizen knows that he or she has been the focus of law enforcement discretion. This kind of decision making is among the least visible of the criminal justice processes.

   When being observed by a suspect, a complainant, a fellow police officer, or a supervisor, the officer will be very aware of the observer's expectations as he or she chooses a course of action. The literal application of the law to the situation might be of only secondary importance.

   Operational-level decision makers' judgments are governed by the same influences that affect the decisions of higher-level administrators. Because officers operate within a much smaller political sphere, they find their relationships with the more limited community potentially more intense. The reciprocal impact of both officer and community becomes clearer. It is easier to "bargain" within these more intimate relationships.

Community Input

If citizens do not report crimes to the police or summon an officer when service is needed, police will intervene only in those situations that they personally observe. Witnesses and victims who do not cooperate with the police limit police discretion.

A common reason why citizens do not report auto accidents or burglaries to the police is that their insurance might be canceled or their rate increased if the report is made. Conversely, they might report if they believe such a report is necessary for them to collect on insurance. The relationship between the victim and the offender and the attitude of the citizen toward police also have a great influence on the willingness of the citizen to report (Reiss, 1971, pp. 42–43). In a sense, the community members express their expectations to police in their interactions with them. The clearer the statement, the better police can structure their discretion to meet the community's needs.

Situational Factors

Several studies have found specific **situational factors** to be influential in discretionary decision making. Major factors include the attitude and appearance of the offender, as well as political factors such as community attitudes, pressures, and biases (Carlson, 2005; Shusta et al., 2005; Walker and Katz, 2002). As mentioned earlier, who else is present (victims, witnesses, other officers) also may influence decision making (Doerner, 2004; Peak, 2006).

Another important factor is whether the situation is on view (one that the officer has seen and in which he or she intervenes without invitation) or is one to which the officer was summoned by citizens. Wagner reports that more complaints occur against officers who intervene in on-view situations than against those who intervene at citizen request. Officers in two-officer vehicles also appear to be more susceptible to citizen complaints (Wagner, 1980).

Environmental Factors

Siegal and Senna (2007) suggest that certain **environmental factors** influence discretionary power, including (1) personal values, (2) pressure of police supervisors and peers, and (3) personal perception of what alternatives to arrest are available. An officer who grew up in a conservative environment may find decision making in a liberal environment uncomfortable. Routinely, the officer will be required to "assess cultural norms accurately and to be, in effect, the cultural and social engineer at that moment" (Greenlee, 1980, p. 51). Lester (1981), in his discussion of police use of deadly force, points to an apparent correlation between attitudes of violence in a community and use of deadly force. Where high rates of police violence existed, he found high rates of citizen against citizen and citizen against police violence also. He suggests that often police attitudes toward violence may reflect those of the community (pp. 56–57).

Educational and Experiential Factors

Carter, Sapp, and Stephens (1989) found that college-educated police recruits were slightly more likely to choose alternatives to arrest. Their findings suggest that education does have some effect on discretionary decision making. Finckenauer (1976) found that the primary factor that characterized all the situations that seemed to influence how discretion was exercised was the desire of the police to maintain a certain public image of the police role. Experience, too, in the sense of "street wisdom," seemed to influence discretionary decision making (Finckenauer, 1976a, pp. 92–93).

Police Work Rules

Anyone who has ever been a police officer for any length of time knows that random patrol is not random per se and that certain work rules exist in every police organization, or in the occupation as a whole, that structure or guide selective law enforcement practices. Some of these rules are

FIGURE 9.2 Discretion could involve dealing with a potentially explosive situation such as a labor strike.

Courtesy of Newport News Police Department.

known to the public in general: people who commit the offense of C.O.P. (contempt of cop) or P.O.P. (pissing off the police) get tickets instead of warnings or go to jail instead of other alternatives. It is well known that there is generally a tolerance zone for speeding infractions (5–10 mph) except in residential areas or school zones. Stroshine, Alpert, and Dunham (2008) document the existence of "working rules" on police suspicion and discretionary decision making in an observational study of Savannah, Georgia, and Miami-Dade, Florida, police officers.

The work rules were divided into 12 substantive categories:

1. The importance of time and place. Officers look for people who are out of place or vehicles and people in areas at times they shouldn't be (e.g., in warehouse areas at night).
2. The importance of appearance.
3. The importance of information. Police look for vehicles on stolen vehicle lists or for people that the community has identified as trouble.
4. The importance of behavior. For example, cars of people connected to known drug houses.
5. "Do unto others"/fairness. Do not stop or give people tickets for behavior they engage in.
6. Threshold. This is where the tolerance zone for speeding violations come in.
7. P.O.P.—Pissing Off the Police.
8. Safety.
9. "One act evolves into another." Examples include stopping stolen cars or those driven by known criminals because it leads to detection of other offenses.
10. "Keeping busy." This rule stresses the need for production in the form of tickets and arrests.
11. Work shirking. Those officers guided by this rule avoid becoming involved with the public.
12. Other. A catch-all category of rules.

JUSTIFICATIONS FOR SELECTIVE ENFORCEMENT

Justification by Administration

Generally, police administrators justify selective enforcement by arguing that they do not have the personnel, financial support, or support from the community or the criminal justice system to enforce the laws strictly. As we have discussed, selective enforcement in itself may be justified, and indeed be desirable, so long as reasonable boundaries of discretion are established that help to prevent abuse.

Justification for keeping selective enforcement policies secret, on the other hand, may serve to increase abuse and community distrust and to lower officer morale. Administrators commonly offer five arguments for secrecy. Each is considered below in terms of police–community impact:

1. *If the policies were stated, administrators would have to defend the quality of their decisions.* Responsible police administrators owe the community explanations for decisions that directly affect it. It follows, then, that if an administrator's decisions are indefensible, they should be changed, not hidden.

2. *Acknowledgment of such decisions would cause police administrators to lose the image of impartiality.* Perpetuating a false image of impartiality is of little or no positive value to the police–community relationship. In fact, once discovered, deluding the public creates a sense of distrust that may be very difficult to overcome.

3. *Statutory law prohibits the development of such policies.* The force of this argument is that the policies may be needed, even though the law forbids them, but it is the policies, not the secrecy, that the law forbids. As noted earlier, legislatures and courts recognize that police officers make discretionary selective decisions about the law. If administrators state their policies and the reasons for them openly, the chance of accommodation by legislatures and courts is great.

4. *Discretion breeds corruption.* If so, discretion would tend to breed corruption, whether open or secret. In fact, officially developed and publicly defended policies, together with procedures to review and control the use of discretion, could minimize corruption.

5. *There is a danger that stated policy, not statutory enactment, would become the limit of the law.* The inference here is that citizens might argue that the law is suspended by discretionary policy. According to most authorities, however, this defense in individual cases is appropriate only if citizens can show that imposition of policy resulted in an obvious injustice. Such defense would be available whether the policy is stated or unstated. (See the final sections of this chapter for further discussion of this point.) The issue, then, is whether the policy is justly applied, not whether it is stated or unstated.

Justification by Officers

A QUESTION OF INJUSTICE   Selective enforcement decisions are justified by police officers most frequently by the statement "Strict enforcement of the law could result in injustice." It is instructive to discuss some of the ways in which police officers believe this result might occur.

1. *The legislature did not intend for some laws to be applied literally; the law was intended to apply only to the situation where wrong occurs.* As a matter of fact, legislatures cannot make each law specify every case or situation to which it applies; it is just not practical. A police officer might conclude from this fact that the legislature assumes that those who enforce the law will exercise reasonable judgment in doing so. Given this view, the officer believes that he is really carrying out the legislative mandate when he decides that someone who violates the letter of the law has not violated its "spirit," and thus has done nothing wrong.

2. *The statute in question is out of date; to apply it to a contemporary situation would work an injustice.* Over the years, many states have accumulated laws that do not apply to the realities of modern life, but they have never been repealed. Were police officers to enforce them, people in the community would be outraged.

3. *Sure, the behavior violates the law, but if I arrest the perpetrator, the official system will not handle the matter justly.* This position is argued when the officer feels that the person who committed a violation is not "really" a criminal and therefore should not undergo the trauma of being processed through the criminal justice system or bear the stigma of a criminal record. The officer may administer a reprimand or some form of corrections (e.g., doing some "good deed," making restitution of some kind, or seeking counseling).

4. *If an arrest is made, the official system will not treat the offense seriously enough.* Police officers may feel that the criminal justice system (especially the courts) is too "soft" on criminals and affords them too many protections. Instead of arresting certain offenders, then, police may feel that confiscating contraband, repeatedly stopping the offenders for questioning, and imposing other forms of harassment are more effective ways of enforcing the law.

5. *The community does not support enforcement of the law in some cases.* Police officers sometimes feel that the neighborhoods they serve have a greater tolerance for certain types of behavior than does the community at large. For example, an officer may believe that assaults between two citizens residing in a barrio are both common and acceptable forms of social contacts within that community. The officer may also believe that the assault complaint made by a wife in this neighborhood against her husband is similar to the complaint that a wife in a more affluent neighborhood might take to a family counselor. Consequently, the police officer may overlook an assault case that would almost certainly result in arrest in another area.

The reasoning above is dangerous, and it may be the source of disharmony between a community and the police. Studies conducted in many ethnic neighborhoods echo the findings of a 1968 study by the National Advisory Committee on Civil Disorders. Lack of satisfaction by African American ghetto communities with the level of services they received from police was voiced in their concern: "The police maintain a much less rigorous standard of law enforcement in the ghetto, tolerating their illegal activities like drug addiction and prostitution and street violence that they would not tolerate elsewhere" (*Report of U.S. National Advisory Committee on Civil Disorders*, 1968, p. 161).

One study of child abuse cases has revealed that the police were more likely to report child abuse cases involving white families than those involving African American families (Willis and Ward, 1988). They believe that the officers included in their research took this action because (1) police officers view a situation involving a white victim as more deserving of official action than a situation involving an African American victim or (2) police officers may hold negative stereotypes of African American family life, which include the notion that violence and abuse are normal.

On the other hand, a decision not to raid a poker game in the basement of a citizen's home or not to arrest juveniles "tossing quarters" in the alley may be accurate personal interpretations of community norms. Accurate or not, police reasoning usually follows this pattern:

1. The activity in question is prevalent.
2. The community does not view the activity as wrong.
3. The community would view enforcement of the law in relation to the viewed activity as wrong. Enforcement may elicit negative responses from the community in the form of political pressure to cause the officers to be either reprimanded or transferred; social ostracism from the community and treatment with great incivility; lack of cooperation in other aspects of the police mission; and physical threats to their well-being.
4. The value of enforcement against the observed activity may be outweighed by the general loss of police effectiveness to render law enforcement services in higher priority areas; this loss of effectiveness results when the community withdraws its support.

Four Other Common Justifications

In addition to asserting that strict enforcement of the law could result in injustice, police officers note at least four other common justifications for selective enforcement:

1. *The community may want laws to be applied discriminatorily against "objectionable" persons whose general conduct and presence are not illegal.* Occasionally, a community may expect police to enforce infrequently used laws against specific individuals or groups. Officers are expected to overlook violations committed by other community members against these

same individuals or groups. In this situation, the selective enforcement and nonenforcement of law becomes an expression of community bias.

2. *Other parts of the criminal justice system have suspended the operation of some laws.* If a supervisor complains about an officer's attempts to enforce a given law, or if a judge or district attorney feels that certain offenses are trivial or perhaps should not be offenses at all (especially regarding so-called victimless crimes such as gambling), then the police officer will feel little motivation to enforce the laws in question. In this way, discretionary judgment made by a judge or district attorney can have a great impact on the discretion of others in the system—in this case, the police.

3. *There may be a trading advantage of law enforcement value in the decision not to enforce the law.* In many cases, police can "bargain" with an offender after apprehension. Officers might treat the offender leniently and even fail to arrest if the offender will, in turn, help to solve a more important case or apprehend a more important offender. Skolnick's study of criminal investigators found that burglary detectives often permitted informants to commit narcotics offenses, whereas narcotics detectives allowed informants to steal (Skolnick, 1993).

   Undercover techniques must be innovative and yet not corrupt, but the line between the two is sometimes blurred for police and offenders. Undercover techniques, by necessity, include deception, trickery, temptation, and coercion. Informants are a major part of the process, and they are often able to use the system to personal advantage. For example, informers in the ABSCAM case were able to exploit their roles. One swindled West Coast businessmen. (The FBI did nothing to stop him until ABSCAM was publicized.) Another informant acknowledged publicly that he made more than $200,000 from his activities and an advance for a book regarding his exploits (Marx, 1982, pp. 179–180).

4. *It may be inconvenient to enforce the law.* Officers may hesitate to enforce the law if it might involve personal inconveniences such as losing a day off, working overtime, or missing a meal.

THE QUESTION OF PROFESSIONALISM

The claim to **professionalism** made by police officers requires an assumption of the obligations of a profession. Reiss (1971) said that an attribute of a profession is "the making of decisions that involve technical and moral judgments affecting the fate of people" (p. 123). Police make these kinds of decisions. As Reiss suggests, if the police do not develop adequate discretionary guidelines, external controls will be developed to govern the police use of discretion. Should this occur, professionalism would be negatively affected. Mark's (1976) observation remains accurate:

> The public acceptance of police discretion . . . is crucial to professional growth. The public served must see the need for police discretion and acknowledge the competency of the practitioner to use discretion constructively and in the public interest. It is largely by the level of public acknowledgment of the police practitioner's competency to exercise discretion for the public good that one may sense the real impact of and progress toward true professionalization. (p. 361)

LEGAL AUTHORITY FOR SELECTIVE ENFORCEMENT

What the Law Says

Statutory law is usually clear on the duty of police officers when they are confronted with what they believe to be a violation of the law. For example, Section 16-1-3 of the Official Code of the State of Georgia (*Georgia Criminal Justice and Traffic Law Manual*, 1999) states the following:

> (11) "Peace Officer" means any person who by virtue of his office or public employment is *vested with a duty to maintain public order or to make arrests for offenses*, whether that duty extends to all crimes or is limited to specific offenses. [italics added]

The Georgia statute is representative of most state statutes that prescribe a peace officer's duty. The officer is not given any authority to discriminate between cases that appear to fall under the literal terms of a statute. An exception to this rule would be where an officer has knowledge of a court decision holding a portion of a statute or ordinance to be unconstitutional or in some other way limiting its literal application. If the law allows for tempering its application with mercy or with any other quality, it does not appear that statutory law provides the police officer with the authority to do it. The California statute is an exception to this rule, however. It appears to direct peace officers to use judgment to discriminate between apparent violations of the law.

"The rule of the common law, that penal statutes are to be strictly construed, has no application to this code. All its provisions are to be construed according to the fair import of their terms, with a view to effect its objects and to promote justice" (California Penal Code, Section 4). In California Penal Code (CPC) 836 the so-called "Law of arrest" states that a "peace officer *may* make an arrest." *May* is a term that provides for discretionary judgment; in contrast, *shall* is a term that allows for no choice.

In the police officer's world, the essence of the arrest process is judgment (Wilson, 1989). The situations that the police encounter are not all alike, and the people involved also vary. Therefore, the officer on the street must decide within certain often ambiguous statutes whether or not to make an arrest or take some other action.

What the Courts Say

Acknowledging that discretion is exercised at all is important, but it is only the first step in the reform of selective-enforcement decision-making policies. Even though the legal duties of police may be clearly stated, numerous instances of selective law enforcement at both the administrative and operational levels of policing exist in every jurisdiction. Furthermore, the courts have carefully avoided responding to any reference to these kinds of practices. A defendant is not ordinarily allowed to raise, in his or her defense in a criminal prosecution, the fact that authorities knowingly ignore hundreds of similar violations. The issue, if raised, is usually treated as being irrelevant to the question of the defendant's guilt. Clearly, the question of whether or not the defendant committed certain acts is not answered by the assertion that other persons may have done the same thing.

BOX 9.2

Legal Guidelines for Public Drunkenness Arrests in Georgia

16-11-41 Public Drunkenness

(a) A person who shall be and appear in an intoxicated condition in any public place or within the curtilage of any private residence not his own other than by invitation of the owner or lawful occupant, which condition is made manifest by boisterousness, by indecent condition or act, or by vulgar, profane, loud, or unbecoming language, is guilty of a misdemeanor.

40-6-95 Pedestrian Under Influence of Alcohol or Drug

A person who is under the influence of intoxicating liquor or any drug to a degree which renders him a hazard shall not walk or be upon any roadway or the shoulder of any roadway. Violation of this Code section is a misdemeanor and is punishable upon conviction by a fine not to exceed $500.00.

A police officer in Georgia was presented with this set of circumstances. He encountered a person who was so intoxicated that he could not stand or walk without assistance. The man was not loud, profane, or boisterous; in fact, he was too intoxicated to talk. Therefore, he did not fall within the definition of public drunkenness statute 16-11-41; however, the man's condition certainly falls within the parameters of a hazard under statute 40-6-95. Unfortunately, for the officer and the man, this took place in an open parking lot some 25 feet from the roadway. Therefore, the officer could not arrest the man for being a pedestrian under the influence of alcohol or drugs. The end result was that the officer did not arrest this severely intoxicated and incapacitated person, and his alternative to arrest was inappropriate for the circumstances and is the basis for a wrongful death action in federal court.

In relation to fact finding in the individual case, it would appear that the court's treatment of such matters is reasonable, but important issues are avoided. Does the "law," as it is applied to a given community, appear to single out particular people and their acts? Does this method of applying laws result in unequal protection of citizens, in violation of the Constitution? Setting the legal issues aside, it is fundamentally unfair for any agency to reserve statutes for application only to unlucky people who fall into a special, but not legally defined, class. The U.S. Supreme Court has attempted to deal with the issue of unequal protection under the law raised by discriminatory law enforcement. The case of *Yick Wo* v. *Hopkins* (118 U.S. 356, 1886) is the most frequently cited case in this area. It dealt with the situation of Chinese laundry operators who were subjected to regulations that apparently were never enforced against Caucasians. The regulations in question did not provide for differentiation by race, but patterns of enforcement during a period of several years made the discrimination obvious. The Court said the following:

> Though the law itself be fair on its face and impartial in appearance, yet, if it is applied and administered by public authority with an evil eye and unequal hand, so as practically to make unjust and illegal discrimination between persons in similar circumstances, material to their rights, the denial of equal justice is still within the protection of the Constitution.

Although the *Yick Wo* case would appear to provide for the victim of discriminatory law enforcement, it has been used in the courts in a very narrow manner. *Yick Wo* is generally held to be applicable only to situations where a contending party can show that there has been a systematic program of discrimination focused specifically on him or persons easily identifiable with him as members of the same class. This is an almost impossible fact for a defendant to prove in most cases, and it would not apply to the many discriminatory law enforcement decisions that are made by individual police officers every day. In another case, the Supreme Court avoided dealing with the issue of discriminatory enforcement of a vagrancy ordinance against the defendant when there were many other violators present at the time of his arrest. The defendant alleged that he was arrested not so much for vagrancy but because his previous public statements were unpopular with the police officers present (*Edelman* v. *California*, 344 U.S. 357, 1953).

The U.S. Supreme Court in *Whren et. al.* v. *U.S.* (1996) in a rare 9-0 decision rendered a verdict which has implications for selective and discriminatory enforcement, particularly racial profiling (discussed below). The defendant (Whren) was sitting a stop sign for what plainclothes police officers in an unmarked car thought was a long time. The officers watched as the defendant sped off from the stop sign and stopped him for the traffic violation. The defendant was holding bags of crack cocaine when the officers approached the car and was subsequently arrested for federal drug offenses. Whren's lawyer moved to suppress the evidence contending that the officers had used the traffic violation as a pretext for stopping the vehicle because they did not have the necessary probable cause or reasonable suspicion to stop for possible drug violations. The court in its ruling said that pretextual stops were not a violation of the Fourth Amendment's protection against unreasonable searches and seizures (Tillyer, Engel, and Wooldredge, 2008). However, the court said that selective stops that show "discriminatory purpose" and "discriminatory effect" are constitutional violations under the equal protection clause. This could come into play when it is shown that groups of people of certain race or ethnicity are stopped for minor traffic offenses, such as equipment violations, driving 1–2 miles over the speed limit, and failure to signal lane changes, disproportionately.

WRITS OF MANDAMUS

In addition to defendants in criminal cases, other citizens may also be concerned with the problem of selective law enforcement. The only way they can correct selective law enforcement policies they do not like is through the political system. Some effort to use *writs of mandamus* have been made. *Mandamus* is available by statute in most American jurisdictions. It is an action that can be brought against a public official to compel the official to perform specified ministerial acts that are directed by statute. Because *mandamus* is generally only applicable to ministerial acts that do not involve the use of judgment by the party to whom it is directed, courts have been unwilling to use the remedy to tell police departments how to conduct their business. The courts will not involve themselves in supervising the operation of the function of policing, which requires continuous attention and the exercise of judgment.

Other attempts have been made to seek court orders compelling police to do their duty. These efforts have failed, for the most part, because the courts are unwilling, except in the most abusive cases, to substitute their judgment for that of an agency under the executive branch of the government.

SELECTIVE ENFORCEMENT AND APPROPRIATE GUIDELINES

Abuse of Power

If a practice that represents a major portion of police work is not recognized as existing, it is excluded from police academy and in-service training programs. The officer is left to make decisions without guidance. This fact alone increases the possibility that decisions will vary widely and often will be made arbitrarily on subjective factors, without the benefit of adequate information. Decision making of this sort is most likely to reflect bias and favoritism. The officer is in effect given increased power to abuse power. The lack of guidelines also inhibits an agency's ability to deal with substantial questions of corruption and the abuse of citizens.

A potential for problems exists in undercover work. Illegal activity may be committed by police agents; privacy may be unduly invaded. However, the most abuse of power may, and can, occur in the basic police–citizen encounters when police decision making is guided by race or ethnicity. Thus, there exists a need for recognition of the problem and explicit policies to deal with it.

RACIALLY BIASED POLICING   Racial profiling is most frequently defined as "law enforcement activities (e.g., detentions, arrests, searches) that are initiated *solely* on the basis of race" (Fridell et al., 2001, p. 3). Racial profiling in police work to some degree has existed since the first police agencies were created as minority groups were singled out by race and ethnicity for police attention as potential criminal suspects. Early eastern police singled out dangerous classes, such as the Irish and other immigrant groups and the police in the South targeted blacks. The practice became common within some police agencies with the "war on drugs," when officers in those states where drug trafficking was rampant were trained to stop suspects based on a drug courier profile developed by the Drug Enforcement Administration (DEA) (Harris, 2002). The drug courier profile included the race and ethnicity of the driver as a characteristic. It was not long before attention on this practice spread beyond drug traffickers to include race and ethnicity of any driver or pedestrian as a reason for police attention. Since the 1990s, the term "racial profiling" has generated more debate and controversy than any other issue in policing. Former President Bill Clinton and President George W. Bush have called for an end to "racial profiling" by American police. Former U.S. Attorney Generals Janet Reno and John Ashcroft denounced the practice. U.S. Senator Russ Feingold (D-Wisconsin) and Representative John Conyers (D-Michigan) sponsored a bill entitled End Racial Profiling Act, S 989 and HR 2074. Col. Carl A. Williams, superintendent of the New Jersey State Police, was forced to resign over comments he made about his agency's involvement in racial profiling. Twenty-nine states have enacted laws that include data collection on the possibility of racial profiling. Law enforcement agencies (Cincinnati, Ohio; Columbus, Ohio; Highland Park, IL; Los Angeles; Montgomery Count, MD; New Jersey State Police; Pittsburgh Police Bureau; Steubenville, Ohio, Police Department; and Village of Mount Pleasant, IL) have entered into consent decrees with the U.S. Department of

Justice to end racial profiling in their agencies. The Montgomery County Sheriff's Department in Maryland has entered into an agreement with the U.S. Department of Justice to keep records of the drivers in traffic stops, to implement a new tracking system of complaints and investigations, and to provide training for officers and supervisors (Anonymous, 2001a). LAPD officers are required to complete a written or electronic report for each motor vehicle or pedestrian stop. The allegations usually are that members of the police department target persons on the basis of race or ethnicity for surveillance, stops, detentions, interrogations, and requests for consent to search and seizure or that excessive force is used against individuals based on race, color, national origin, or ethnicity (Racial Profiling Data Collection Resource Center at Northeastern University, 2009).

The existence of racial profiling has not escaped the attention of professional law enforcement. The Commission on Accreditation for Law Enforcement Agencies (CALEA) (Box 9.3) has adopted new standards dealing with racial profiling and made them mandatory for all agencies seeking accreditation (Anonymous, 2001b). The International Association of Chiefs of Police has passed several resolutions condemning racial profiling. The Police Executive Research Forum has recently released a report discussed below on racially biased policing, including racial profiling. A recent report by NOBLE (National Organization of Black Law Enforcement Executives) examines racial profiling and provides recommendations for "Creating Blindfolds of Justice," which will eliminate or reduce the incidents of racial profiling and other forms of "bias-based policing" (NOBLE, 2001).

Numerous police executives throughout the United States have responded to racial profiling. These actions have been voluntary or forced by state or court action (Tillyer, Engel, and Wooldredge, 2008). Police departments have written policies and procedures prohibiting racial profiling. Police departments have included or increased racial sensitivity training in the academy or in-service training. As of August 28, 2008, all Missouri peace officers who make traffic stops are required to have one hour of racial profiling training every year (www.dps.mo.gov/POST/Main/RacialProfilingTrainingRequirements.htm). In the bill, House Bill 2224, authorizing this training, the objective is stated as: "This training shall promote understanding and respect for racial and cultural differences and the use of effective non-combative methods for carrying out law enforcement duties in a racially and culturally diverse environment." Police departments throughout the nation collect data on traffic and pedestrian stops. These same executives are developing early warning systems to identify and discipline officers engaging in racial profiling.

In their report, Fridell and her colleagues (2001) expand the concept of racial profiling to **racially biased policing**. They point out that racial profiling confined to police actions based

---

BOX 9.3
The Commission on Accreditation for Law Enforcement Agencies

About CALEA

The Commission on Accreditation for Law Enforcement Agencies, Inc. (CALEA) was established as an independent accrediting authority in 1979 by the four major law enforcement membership associations: International Association of Chiefs of Police (IACP), National Organization of Black Law Enforcement Executives (NOBLE), National Sheriffs' Association (NSA), and Police Executive Research Forum (PERF). The executive directors of these four associations appoint members to the Commission annually; an endorsement requires a majority vote for each appointment.

The Commission has 21 members; 11 members are law enforcement practitioners; the remaining 10 members are selected from the public and private sectors. Commissioners are appointed to a term of three years. The position of Commissioner is voluntary and receives no salary, although travel and per diem expenses are provided when conducting Commission business.

CALEA maintains a small, professional staff managed by an executive director. The staff conducts all administrative and operational duties as directed by the Commission. Commission staff is available to assist applicant and accredited agencies through a toll-free telephone number.

CALEA produces a newsletter and offers workshops to explain the accreditation process and standards during the Commission Conference held three times annually.

(continued)

The Commission's Authority

CALEA derives its general authority from the four major law enforcement membership associations mentioned above. Their members represent approximately 80 percent of the law enforcement profession in this nation. The Commission derives its accreditation authority from those agencies that voluntarily participate in the accreditation program.

The Purpose of the Commission

The overall purpose of the Commission's accreditation program is to improve delivery of law enforcement service by offering a body of standards, developed by law enforcement practitioners, covering a wide range of up-to-date law enforcement topics. It recognizes professional achievements by offering an orderly process for addressing and complying with applicable standards.

The Voluntary Nature of the Accreditation Program

Successful completion of the accreditation program requires commitment from all levels of the organization, starting with the chief executive officer. To foster commitment, a decision to participate should be voluntary. To this end, the Commission ensures that law enforcement accreditation is and will continue to be a voluntary program.

Benefits

Besides the recognition of obtaining international excellence, the primary benefits of accreditation provides management model, better services, controlled liability insurance costs, administrative improvements, greater accountability from supervisors, and increased governmental and community support.

Source: Adapted from CALEA Online, http://www.calea.org/neweb.aboutus/aboutus.htm.

solely on race would not "include activities that are legally supportable in terms of reasonable suspicion or probable cause, but are nonetheless racially biased (Fridell et al., 2001, p. 4). Therefore, racially biased policing, as they define it, occurs when police officers inappropriately consider race or ethnicity in deciding with whom and when to engage in an enforcement capacity (Fridell et al., 2001, p. 5). Their studies show that police and citizens have different perceptions of the problem. The police define the problem as racial profiling (police actions based solely on race) and the citizens define the problem more broadly (racially biased policing). Again, we see how important perceptions are in police–community relations. Fridell and her colleagues recommend that each police agency adopt a policy that does the following:

- Emphasizes that arrests, traffic stops, investigative detention, searches, and property seizures must be based on reasonable suspicion or probable cause. (They recognize that not all detentions or all searches require either reasonable suspicion or probable cause. This provision addresses those that do.)
- Restricts officers' ability to use race/ethnicity in establishing reasonable suspicion or probable cause to those situations in which trustworthy, locally relevant information links a person or persons of a specific race/ethnicity to a particular unlawful incident(s).
- Articulates that the use of race and ethnicity must be in accordance with the equal protection clause of the Fourteenth Amendment.
- Includes provisions related to officer behavior during encounters that can serve to prevent perceptions of racially biased policing (Fridell et al., 2001, p. 50).

In addition to this policy recommendation, they provide recommendations to eliminate or reduce racially biased policing, covering all areas of policing from hiring and selection to management, supervision, and leadership. A study by Gaines (2006) provides evidence that policy writing, increased supervision, and training can have an effect on racial profiling. He examined traffic stops in Riverside, California, and concluded that the stops were in line with population and crime data in the city. Gaines attributes his findings to the department's extensive training in cultural diversity, increased supervision, and a comprehensive written directive system (policies, procedures, and rules) outlining the department's position on racial profiling. A content analysis of federal-level racial profiling civil suits found that the filing of these suits has drastically dropped since the high point in 2002 (24 cases) to one case in 2006 (Gabbidon, Marzette, and Peterson, 2007). They conclude that the reduction is the result of the "decade long attention and recent changes in recording requirements and police practices in general" (Gabbidon, Marzette, and Peterson, 2007, p. 236.).

Lack of Support

If police administrators make secret policies and if individual officers are called upon to tailor justice on a daily basis, officers, for lack of clear policy, can only guess what their supervisors want them to do. They are in a very ambivalent position; in most instances, they improvise. When officers make selective enforcement decisions, their confidence in their own integrity may be undermined by the feeling that they are part of an illicit conspiracy. Believing that they should make exceptions in the application of laws, they are unable to act openly because special accommodation is not supposed to be made. The necessity that all must be unspoken taints the contact of the officers with citizens and even with fellow officers. Also, officers may feel that no matter what they decide, they will be wrong. Should they make an unpopular decision, they may face the consequences alone. Because they acted "independently of written policy," they may not have agency support.

Impact on Public Image

A conspiracy of silence presents to the public a negative image of the entire system. Evasiveness and defensiveness on the part of the agency undermine credibility.

STRUCTURING POLICE DISCRETION

Recognizing Discretion in Law Enforcement

The American Bar Association, experts on law enforcement such as James Q. Wilson, numerous commissions, and others have urged the importance of open recognition by all parties (legislatures, the courts, the public, and, most important, police agencies themselves) that selective law enforcement is a fact. Of course, the public (and others) implicitly know this already; professional law enforcement officers should now admit it and develop controls over its use (American Bar Association, 1972, pp. 13, 116–144; Barker, Hunter, and Rush, 1994; Wilson, 1968, pp. 83–88).

Enforcement Policy Boards

One approach to providing discretionary guidelines for police was suggested by Stephen Schiller. He recommended that police departments establish enforcement policy boards to develop selective policies where needed. Statements of the policies, together with the reasons for them, would be made public and given to line personnel along with their training materials (Schiller, 1972).

BOX 9.4
Barker's Mechanisms for Controlling Police Unethical Behavior

Self-Control

Self-Control is the idea that officers will regulate their own behavior out of a sense of ethical correctness. Screening of applicants, promotion of ethical standards, and socialization by ethical officers are seen as ways to develop self-control.

Peer Group Control

Peer Group Control is the idea that ethical officers will use shaming and other socialization techniques to promote ethical behavior among their colleagues.

Supervisory Control

Supervisory Control is the means by which police supervisors seek to instill in their subordinates a "moral compass" based on enforcement of rules and laws as well as their own ethical examples as leaders.

Early Warning Audit Systems

Early Warning Audit Systems are mechanisms in which departments track complaints against officers and seek to intervene with those who receive multiple complaints.

(continued)

Administrative Reaction

Administrative Reaction refers to the prompt and strict enforcement of policies and procedures on the part of the police organization in order to send a clear message that unethical behavior is not tolerated.

External Accountability

External Accountability refers to the prosecution of unethical officers for unlawful behaviors as well as legal actions for inappropriate behaviors. It also refers to the use of mechanisms such as external review boards to determine the appropriateness of officer behaviors.

Since no single control mechanism will be effective for all officers, Barker (while acknowledging that unethical behaviors by some officers will still exist) calls for the use of all of the above controls in efforts to reduce unethical behaviors.

COMPOSITION OF THE BOARD   The presiding officer of the board would be the chief of police. It seems clear (even though Schiller does not suggest it) that the board might also include civic or community representatives and that some procedures would be set up for citizen input. The board would not get involved with individual citizen complaints, however; these would be handled by the courts or police internal affairs units.

POLICY IMPLEMENTATION UNITS   Every board would have a policy implementation unit to collect data on the use of policy at the operational level, to record inquiries by police officers, and to record difficulties in understanding policies in operational settings. These data would guide field personnel in interpreting policy in particular cases, and they would be reviewed periodically by the board.

The Courts

What functions should the courts play in implementing openly selective law enforcement policies? First, if a citizen is charged under a statute that is subject to the policy, the courts should decide if the statute really applies to the defendant under the policy (and the prosecution will have the burden of proving that it does).

Second, the courts might also determine whether or not a policy is arbitrary. If it is ruled arbitrary, the policy should be nullified (although the policy board should have the right to appeal the ruling to a reviewing court).

Review

INTERNAL REVIEW   A police **internal review** unit should be available to answer citizen complaints about nonenforcement or selective enforcement of laws. Where appropriate, the policy implementation unit would determine whether the complaints indicate violations of departmental policy. The policy implementation unit should collect and review data on all reported incidents to see if a policy is meeting the expectations of the policy board. If it is not, the unit should recommend that the board review the policy.

LEGISLATIVE REVIEW   Once selective law enforcement policies have been stated by the police department, legislators can act on them, clarifying any misunderstanding through committee proceedings or more definitive statutes. If the legislature rejects the law enforcement agency's interpretation of a statute, the agency must follow suit, even though it disagrees. Out of this disagreement, however, may come a clearly developed issue for review by the electorate.

THE COMMUNITY   Police have a great deal of legitimate coercive power and influence in the community. As Finckenauer suggests, such coercive influence can be legitimate only if it is consistent with community expectations. "It is therefore incumbent upon the community and its representatives to make known to the police what their expectations are" (Finckenauer, 1976b, p. 94).

LOOKING TOWARD TOMORROW

Some Recommendations

Presidential commissions, state advisory groups, and several distinguished scholars agree on the need for official police recognition of selective law enforcement policies, but they have not always agreed on exactly what this would involve. However, the following projects can be recommended:

1. Statutory revision so that the description of the peace officer's duty indicates that he or she is to arrest "if the circumstances are such as to indicate to a reasonably prudent person that such action should be taken." (Other phrasing could be used so long as it indicates a recognition that the officer has discretion in enforcing the law.)

    Judging an officer's behavior by the standard of what a "reasonably prudent person" would do under the same circumstances often comes into play when a police officer exercises or fails to exercise his or her discretion without considering the consequences of his or her action on the individuals involved. Such an incident occurred when Dallas, Texas, police officer Robert Powell briefly chased a vehicle with its lights flashing into a hospital parking lot and threatened to arrest the driver for running a red light while the driver's mother-in-law was dying inside the hospital. During the course of the 15–20 minutes encounter in the parking lot, the officer pulled his gun on the daughter of the dying woman and her friend in an attempt to stop them from exiting the vehicle and going into the hospital. They ignored his commands and went into the hospital. The officer pointed his gun at the driver and began lecturing him. The officer also ignored another police officer and a nurse's request to allow the son-in-law to go inside the hospital and see his mother-in-law before she died. Dallas Police Chief David Kunkle in commenting on Officer Powell's behavior stated: "His behavior, in my opinion, did not exhibit the common sense, the discretion, the compassion that we expect our officers to exhibit." The chief also complimented the driver and his wife, who he said "exercised extraordinary patience, restraint in dealing with the behavior of our officer" (Associated Press, 2009). The fact that the occupants of the car were black and the officer was white also raised the specter of racially biased policing. The officer was placed on administrative leave while the department examined his behavior for misconduct. He resigned before the investigation was complete. The authors doubt that charges of misconduct would have been sustained as the officer probably acted within the law and policy as currently written. The officer stated to police supervisors that he did nothing wrong and that he was just doing his job. Even though he failed the commonsense test, in all likelihood, he did not violate any department policy. The authors are not aware of any police policies, procedures, and rules that call for police officers to examine their actions based on the "reasonably prudent person" standard. The tape from the police cruiser's video camera was shown for days on all the TV news networks and the Internet, sparking a spirited debate on police discretionary decision making.

    It is fairly easy to put into law and train police officers as to the elements and circumstances under which arrests can be made; however, it is much more difficult to outline and train police officers when not to make an arrest. The chief later said that it would be difficult to train police officers for these circumstances and that the better course of action would be to hire people with good common sense and people skills. That is certainly a good recommendation for a number of police–community relations problems. Furthermore, introducing the "reasonably prudent person" standard into statutes, police policies, and training would go a long way toward eliminating incidents such as occurred in Dallas.

2. Structures within the department for policy articulation and policy implementation; both should be open and make provision for getting input from and reporting to the public. Discretionary limits will need to be clearly defined and updated as necessary to meet changing public need.

3. Police selection, training, and supervisory models that reflect the place of selective law enforcement in police work.

4. Articulation with other decision makers in the justice system to ensure that planning, implementation, and evaluation occur in the context of the whole system rather than in just the police component.

BOX 9.5
Making a Decision

Stage One

You are dispatched to 3321 N. Maryvale Road to the Janns residence. The dispatcher says that a family fight is reported to be in progress. Upon arrival, you hear yelling and screaming coming from inside the residence. You are joined by Deputy Slick. The two of you go to the front door and request permission to come inside. Mrs. Debra Janns invites you inside the residence.

As you step inside, Mr. Paul Janns, age 30 years, yells at his wife and you. He says to you and Deputy Slick: "Get the hell out of my house! I didn't call you, and you don't belong here."

Answer the following questions:

1. What is your primary goal at this point?
2. What are your options for accomplishing this goal?
3. Looking at each option, were you to act on it, what would be the probable outcome (both short term and long term)?
4. Which option will you choose, and how will you act on it?

Stage Two

Because at least one of your immediate goals would be to defuse the volatile situation, you might do the following:

In a calm, even voice you ask Mr. Janns to calm down and either to step outside or go into another room with you to talk about the situation. Mrs. Janns, at this point, yells at her husband, "Get out of here! I don't ever want to see you again." Mr. Janns says he isn't leaving. He turns to you and Deputy Slick and says that he and his wife can solve this problem without your help.

What should you do?

1. Leave? Why or why not?
2. Arrest him? Why or why not?

3. Arrest them both? Why or why not?
4. Try another calming approach? Why or why not?
5. Do you have as many options as you did at Stage One?

Stage Three

You place a hand on Mr. Janns's arm. He pulls away from you. Deputy Slick quickly steps in. He orders Mr. Janns to step outside. Mr. Janns says, "I don't want to go. I don't have any place to go."

Mrs. Janns says that she would like to file a complaint against her husband for assault. At this statement, Mr. Janns begins yelling again. He lunges at his wife.

1. What is your goal at this point?
2. Is the goal different from the one you expressed at Stage One?
3. What are your options for achieving it?
4. Are your options more limited at this point than in Stages One and Two? Why or why not?

Stage Four

Hopefully, you will have avoided this very common outcome to this scenario:

You and Deputy Slick move quickly to restrain Mr. Janns physically, because that seems to be your only remaining option. You arrest him, read him his rights, and take him into custody.

1. Did you have other options at this point?
2. What would you recommend to officers as guidelines for discretion in such situations?
3. How do the guidelines you suggest protect both you and the family and encourage solution at Stage One or Stage Two?
4. Compare your suggested guidelines with those established for a law enforcement agency in your community.

A Lesson from the Past

Police secrecy and indecisiveness about the issue of selective law enforcement is reminiscent of the way issues of abuses in interrogating suspects were handled by police in the past. Instead of developing guidelines and controls to prevent these abuses, the police did little to correct them. Finally, it fell to the U.S. Supreme Court—notably in the *Miranda* v. *Arizona* (384 U.S. 436 (1966)) decision and others—to correct abusive police practices. The lesson can be applied to the selective law enforcement issue. If professional law enforcement officers do not deal with important policy issues such as selective law enforcement in an open and straightforward manner, others will do it for them.

REALITY CHECK

Too Much Discretion?

On the morning of July 20, 2001, Le Thu Nguyen drove into a parking lot in Aurora, Colorado. She was arriving for work at a local beauty salon. As she pulled into the lot, a man ran across the lot toward her car. When Ms. Nguyen saw the man approaching, she tried to drive away, squealing her car's tires. The man lunged through the window and forced his way into the car. The car stopped in the lot for a short time before driving from the lot. A bystander, John Cauvin, immediately called 911, reporting that a black guy had jumped into an Asian lady's car. Despite Mr. Cauvin's statements that the woman had squealed her tires attempting to drive away and that the man had forced his way into the car, the police dispatcher who answered would not accept his report that a carjacking was taking place.

At first, she told the witness, " . . . if they come back, give us a call and let us know." She then said, "Ok, well, you would think she would be fighting or something . . . she would be fighting, screaming, or something if she needed help." She later said, "They may have just been playing around." When the witness insisted that he thought it was an emergency, the dispatcher cut him off and ended the call by saying that she would have someone check the area. She did not send an officer.

At the same time that John Cauvin was talking to the dispatcher, a coworker at the salon saw that the man who had forced his way inside the car was Ms. Nguyen's ex-fiance, Omar Green. When there was no police response to Mr. Cauvin's 911 call, she called Ms. Nguyen's mother, Susan DuVall. Ms. DuVall immediately called 911. The same dispatcher, Jeannette Price, who had talked to Mr. Cauvin answered the telephone. Ms. DuVall stated that her daughter had been carjacked and explained that the suspect was her daughter's ex-fiance who had previously abused her and against whom she had a restraining order.

Ms. Price replied, "I talked to people there. She was not fighting. She was not screaming. She did not ask for help." She then continued, "I mean a lot of times they end up making up."

Ms. DuVall then stated, "Right, well, that's not this case . . . "

Ms. Price then said, "Ok, well, we don't know because we haven't talked to her . . . "

Forty-six minutes after John Cauvin's original call, and 20 minutes after Ms. DuVall's call, a police officer arrived at the scene. No police search was initiated for the car. Ms. Nguyen's car and body were found by a friend the next day. Omar Green was later convicted of her murder. Both John Cauvin and Susan DuVall believe that Ms. Nguyen could have been saved if their 911 calls had been taken seriously. Due to the Colorado Government Immunity Acts, the City of Aurora is immune from lawsuits. Ms. Duvall is currently suing Ms. Price for failing to send help.

Source: Adapted from a 9news.com story by Chip Yost, reported on 12/4/2005.

Conclusions

Police administrators rarely admit the existence of selective law enforcement policies, yet they often implement such policies without stating them officially or acknowledging them publicly. The very nature of law and our criminal justice system gives operating police officers wide discretion in deciding when and how the law should be enforced. On both the administrative and the operating levels, there are often very good reasons for selective law enforcement (e.g., budgetary constraints on what can feasibly be done and the existence of outdated statutes) and, on occasion, some very bad reasons (e.g., bias against a segment of the community).

Police discretion is an important aspect of police–community relations and an integral part of community policing. It appears that in police departments that espouse a community policing philosophy, officers make less arrests than in departments pursuing aggressive police strategies. Therefore, police discretion is a necessary evil that must be structured properly. The abuse of discretion is the problem, not discretion itself. To prevent abuses, selective law enforcement policies should be formulated and implemented in an open, orderly manner. The means for accomplishing this exists. Such action would benefit both the police and the community and would increase the positive nature of their ongoing relationship.

Student Checklist

1. Define discretion and its role in the justice system.
2. Explain some of the administrative and operational justifications for selective enforcement.
3. Identify the legal authority for selective enforcement.
4. Describe some of the dangers inherent in selective enforcement.
5. Describe the difference between racial profiling and racially biased policing.
6. Based on the strategies discussed in this chapter, develop a strategy for structuring discretion in a police agency. Describe its strengths and weaknesses.

Topics for Discussion

1. Debate the use of selective law enforcement.
2. What will happen if police agencies are open in regard to their use of selective and discriminatory law enforcement?
3. How do the police agencies in your community (1) define policy regarding discretionary decision making and (2) provide controls to eliminate abuse?
4. What effect could introducing the "reasonably prudent person" standard into police training have on police discretionary decisions?

Bibliography

American Bar Association. (1972). *The Urban Police Function*. New York: Institute of Judicial Administration.

Anonymous. (2001a). "Special report II: Racial profiling," *Law and Order*, Vol. 49, No. 4, pp. 94–101.

Anonymous. (2001b). "CLEA adopts three new rules," *Crime Control Digest*, Vol. 35, No. 13, p. 7.

Associated Press. (March 27, 2009). Dallas Officer Detains NFL Player Rushing to Dying Mother-in-Law's Bedside. www.foxnews.com.

Atkins, B., and Pogrebin, M. (Eds.). (1978). *The Invisible Justice System: Discretion and the Law*. Cincinnati, OH: Anderson.

Barker, T., and Carter, D. L. (1994). *Police Deviance*, 3rd ed. Cincinnati, OH: Anderson.

Barker, T., Hunter, R. D., and Rush, J. P. (1994). *Police Systems and Practices*. Upper Saddle River, NJ: Prentice Hall.

CALEA Online. (2006). About *US*, http://www.calea.org/neweb.aboutus/aboutus.htm.

Carlson, D. P. (2005). *When Cultures Clash*, 2nd ed. Upper Saddle River, NJ: Pearson/Prentice Hall.

Carter, D. L., Sapp, A. D., and Stephens, D. W. (1989). *The State of Police Education: Policy Direction in the 21st Century*. Washington, D.C.: Police Executive Research Forum.

Commission on Accreditation for Law Enforcement Agencies. (1987). *Standards for Law Enforcement Agencies*. Fairfax, VA: CALEA.

Davis, K. C. (1970). "Discretionary justice," *Journal of Legal Education*, Vol. 23, pp. 58–59.

Doerner, W. G. (2004). *Introduction to Law Enforcement: An Insiders View*, 2nd ed. Dubuque, IA: Kendall/Hunt.

Finckenauer, J. (1976). "Some factors in police discretion and decision-making," *Journal of Criminal Justice*, Vol. 4, pp. 382–386.

Finckenauer, J. (1976a). "Higher education and police discretion," *Journal of Police Science and Administration*, Vol. 3, pp. 450–457.

Finckenauer, J. (1976b). "Some factors in police discretion and decision-making," *Journal of Criminal Justice*, Vol. 4, pp. 29–46.

Fridell, L., Lunney, R., Diamond, D., and Kubu, B. (2001). *Racially Biased Policing: A Principled Response*. Washington, D.C.: Police Executive Research Forum.

Gabbidon, S. L., Marzette, L. N., and Peterson, S. A. (August 2007). "Racial profiling and the courts: An empirical analysis of federal litigation, 1991–2006," *Journal of Contemporary Criminal Justice*, Vol. 23, No. 3, pp. 226–238.

Gaines, L. K. (2006). "An analysis of traffic stop data in Riverside, California," *Police Quarterl*, Vol. 9, pp. 210–233.

Georgia Criminal Justice and Traffic Law Manual. (1999). Charlottesville, VA: The Michie Company.

Greenlee, M. R. (February 1980). "Discretionary decision making in the field," *The Police Chief*, pp. 50–51.

Harris, D. A. (2002). *Profiles in Injustice: Why Racial Profiling Cannot Work*. New York: The New Press.

Lester, D. (December 1981). "An alternative perspective: The use of deadly force by police and civilians," *The Police Chief*, pp. 56–57.

Mark, J. A. (1976). "Police organizations: The challenges and dilemmas of change," in A. S. Blumberg and A. Neiderhoffer (Eds.), *The Ambivalent Force: Perspectives on the Police*, 2nd ed. Hinsdale, IL: Dryden Press.

Marx, G. T. (April 1982). "Who really gets stung? Some issues raised by the new police undercover work," *Crime and Delinquency*, pp. 165–193.

New Haven Register. (December 2, 1971). New Haven, CT.

NOBLE. (2001). "A NOBLE Perspective: Racial Profiling—A Symptom of Bias-Based Policing," Alexandria, VA: National Organization of Black Law Enforcement Executives.

Peak, K. J. (2006). *Policing in America: Methods, Issues, and Challenges*, 5th ed. Upper Saddle River, NJ: Pearson/Prentice Hall.

Racial Profiling Data Collection Resource Center at Northeastern University. (2009). www.racialprofilinganalysis.neu.edu.

Reiss, A. J., Jr. (1971). *Police and the Public*. New Haven, CT: Yale University Press.

Report of U.S. National Advisory Committee on Civil Disorders. (1968). Washington, D.C.: U.S. Government Printing Office.

Schiller, S. A. (1972). "More light on a low visibility function," *Police Law Quarterly*, Vol. 6. See also October 1972, January 1973, and April 1973 issues.

Shusta, R. M., Levine, D. R., Wong, H. Z., and Harris, P. R. (2005). *Multicultural Law Enforcement: Strategies for Peacemaking in a Diverse Society*. Upper Saddle River, NJ: Pearson/ Prentice Hall.

Siegel, L. J., and Senna, J. J. (2007). *Essentials of Criminal Justice*, 5th ed. Pacific Grove, CA: Thomson/Wadsworth.

Skolnick, J. (1993). *Justice Without a Trial*, 3rd ed. Upper Saddle River, NJ: Prentice Hall.

Stroshine, M., Alpert, G., and Dunham, R. (January 2008). "The influence of 'Working Rules' on Police Suspicion and Discretionary Decision Making," *Police Quarterly*, Vol. 11, No. 3, pp. 315–337.

Tillyer, R., Engel, R. S., and Wooldredge, J. (2008). "The intersection of racial profiling research and the law," *Journal of Criminal Justice*, Vol. 36, pp. 138–153.

Wagner, A. E. (1980). "Citizen complaints against the police: The accused officer," *Journal of Police Science and Administration*, Vol. 8, pp. 373–379.

Walker, S., and Katz, C. M. (2002). *The Police in America: An Introduction*, 4th ed. Boston, MA: McGraw-Hill.

Willis, C., and Ward, R. (1988). "The police and child abuse: An analysis of police decisions to report illegal behavior," *Criminology*, Vol. 26, pp. 695–716.

Wilson, J. Q. (1968). *Varieties of Police Behavior*. Cambridge, MA: Harvard University Press.

Wilson, J. Q. (1977). *Thinking About Crime*. New York: Random House.

Wilson, J. Q. (1989). *Bureaucracy: What Government Agencies Do and Why They Do It*. New York: Basic Books.

CHAPTER 10

Community-Oriented Policing

Community policing is a philosophy and process that creates partnerships between the police and the community to solve problems related to crime, fear of crime and quality of life issues. It is a philosophy not programs.

—LEE P. BROWN, MARCH 18, 2009

KEY CONCEPTS

Broken Windows Hypothesis	Crime Analysis Programs	Team Policing
CAPRA Model	Mini-Stations	Volunteers in Policing
Community-Oriented	Neighborhood Foot Patrol	Service
Policing	Peelian Model	Weed and Seed Programs
Computer-Aided Dispatching	Problem-Oriented Policing	Zero-Tolerance Policing

LEARNING OBJECTIVES

Studying this chapter will enable you to:

1. Understand the evolution of police service delivery models within the United States.
2. Describe the difference between police–community relations and community-oriented policing.
3. Describe the development of community policing models.
4. Discuss the philosophy and role of community-oriented policing.
5. Describe the strengths and weaknesses of community-oriented policing.
6. Assess the future of community-oriented models in U.S. policing.

We have stressed the need for the police to develop relationships with the public that are based on mutual respect and trust in order to provide proper police services to that public. Such a relationship is not created merely by soliciting support from the public but by establishing lines of communication that enable the police to become an integral part of the community being served. As noted in Chapters 1 and 2, this is a difficult undertaking.

The police are drawn in many directions by the complex and frequently competing groups that comprise each "community." These relationships are further complicated by the organization of the police system in the United States and the restrictions that are placed on it.

In this chapter, we discuss how American police organizations have evolved in their efforts to maintain law and order within a democratic society. Community-oriented policing, first known as community policing, is seen as the product of this evolutionary process. Community-oriented policing is best expressed by the concept that it is what the police do with a community, not what they do to the community. Community-oriented policing seeks to form partnerships with the community to identify and arrest offenders, prevent crime and disorder, recognize and solve problems, and foster and maintain mutual respect and trust. Community-oriented policing is best seen as a policing model that believes that the community (geographic focus) is best served by working with direct clients—those that the police interact with in their service delivery. The ultimate goal is to create as safe a community as possible. Improving the citizens' quality of life is also the goal of community-oriented policing. Community-oriented policing is the end result of a long history of police service models.

THE EVOLUTION OF POLICE SERVICE MODELS

The current state of policing within the United States is the product of a series of developments that have taken place over the past two centuries. While considerable progress has occurred, the reader may observe that in many ways, policing has not moved far from its roots. In fact, some would argue that in community-oriented policing, the concept of policing where all members of the community are responsible for the welfare and safety of all has returned to its roots.

The Watch and Ward

As English society evolved during the later Middle Ages, the decline of feudalism brought significant changes in law enforcement. The migration of serfs from the manors to towns and cities and the rise of a merchant class created a need for a more formal police system. In the ninth century,

---

BOX 10.1

Types of Police Clients—Royal Canadian Mounted Police (RCMP)

Direct Clients

Direct clients are those you interact with at various points in your service delivery or investigations. These would include callers, complainants, witnesses, victims, those affected by the harm done to victims (e.g. family), suspects, prisoners, and community groups. From a community policing perspective, police are expected not simply to ask how these people can help achieve police objectives. Rather, once we view them as clients, we also ask how we as police can best serve their needs in a manner consistent with public interest.

Indirect Clients

Indirect clients are those not directly involved in an incident or its investigation but who have an interest in its outcome either because of the way it was handled or because of the association of the incident to similar incidents. They include taxpayers, the public (public is captured in our Constitution), interest groups (e.g. victims' groups, women's groups, cultural groups) other government agencies or departments whose work may be impacted by your own. These clients may never interact with you personally. They, however, represent the public interest and it is your interest to understand their concerns if you are to successfully address them. They may send letters to the press. They may use incidents, through the press to draw attention to their concerns. They may represent the public interest to the RCMP as an organization or to other government departments.

Sometimes, indirect clients, such as interest groups, may approach you with a problem which they would like you to assist in solving. At this point, they become direct clients as you would be interacting with them directly.

Source: www.rcmp-learning.org

Alfred the Great established the "frankpledge" system (Beckman, 1980; Cole and Smith, 1997). Under this Saxon system, the head of each family was responsible for the conduct of all family members over the age of 12. Ten landless families grouped together into a "tithing" were responsible for one another. The "Tithingman" was responsible for raising a "hue and cry" if a criminal act occurred. Tithing members were then required to join in the apprehension of the offender(s). Ten tithings constituted a "hundred," which was headed by a "reeve" appointed by a local magistrate. Several hundreds made up a shire, which was overseen by a "shire reeve" (Beckman, 1980; Siegal and Senna, 2007).

The Statute of Winchester, enacted in 1285, replaced the frankpledge with the "watch and ward." This military system established parish "constables" (successors to the old Saxon reeves) to assist the sheriffs by maintaining order in the cities and towns. All males between ages 15 and 60 were required to assist the constable by (1) keeping an assize of arms; (2) maintaining the peace; (3) participating in the apprehension of criminals; and (4) serving as a member of a night watch (Critchley, 1977).

The system described above remained in effect in England for the next 600 years. As England conquered the remainder of the British Isles, its system of law enforcement was imposed on the inhabitants of Wales, Scotland, and Ireland. When the United Kingdom began expanding its empire to North America, it was this system, augmented by martial law, that was implemented. In the towns and cities that sprang up, the constable and watch were used to enforce the laws of the community, the colony, and England. A sheriff was elected by the populace or appointed by government officials to provide law enforcement for those areas outside the cities. In remote areas, the citizens in small settlements relied on the militia for protection. Those families and individuals living alone in isolated parts of the frontier had to rely on themselves and any neighbors who might be close enough to render assistance (Bopp and Schultz, 1977; Johnson, 1981).

The Peelian Model

The system of law enforcement that had existed in Great Britain performed reasonably well within the small towns and rural areas for several centuries. However, by the eighteenth century, the collapse of feudalism and the onset of the Industrial Revolution had led to congestion and social disorder within the large cities. The old system of law enforcement could not contend with the resulting chaos. London was a particularly troubled city in which there was almost a total breakdown of law and order (Cole and Smith, 2007).

Robert Peel was an ambitious young politician who was elected to Parliament in 1809 at the age of 21. By the age of 24, he was Chief Secretary to Ireland (then a British possession), where he established the Royal Irish Constabulary to bolster English rule in Ireland (Miller, 1977). This military force, commonly called "Peelers," had only limited success, due to fierce opposition from the populace. When Peel left Ireland in 1818, it was with an understanding that the police must work to achieve and maintain legitimacy from the public (Miller, 1977). This lesson would serve him in good stead when as Home Secretary to England he guided an "Act for Improving the Police In and Near the Metropolis" (Cole and Smith, 2007) through Parliament. Peel saw the creation of a "New Police" as necessary to contend with the increasing crime, class conflict, and social disorder that threatened England in general and metropolitan London in particular (Reppetto, 1978).

Due to Peel's efforts, the Metropolitan Police Act passed in June 1829 (Critchley, 1977). The act established a force, initially of 1,000 men and soon expanded to 3,400, to police the London metropolis with the exception of the one-square-mile area within the old City of London. The mission of the Metropolitan Police was crime prevention (Walker, 1998). They sought to accomplish this task by providing continuous "preventive patrols" throughout the metropolis. To stress that the police were there to serve rather than repress the public, it was

FIGURE 10.1 Peelian Principles.

1. To prevent crime and disorder, as an alternative to their repression by military force and severity of legal punishment.
2. To recognize always that the power of the police to fulfill their functions and duties is dependent on public approval of their existence, actions and behavior, and on their ability to secure and maintain public respect.
3. To recognize always that to secure and maintain the respect and approval of the public means also the securing of the willing cooperation of the public in the task of securing observance of law.
4. To recognize always that the extent to which the cooperation of the public can be secured, diminishes, proportionately, the necessity of the use of physical force and compulsion for achieving police objectives.
5. To seek and preserve public favor, not by pandering to public opinion, but by constantly demonstrating absolutely impartial service to law, in complete independence of policy, and without regard to the justice or injustice of the substance of individual laws, by ready offering of individual service and friendship to all members of the public without regard to the justice or injustice of the substance of individual laws, by ready offering of individual service and friendship to all members of the public without regard to their

wealth or social standing; by ready exercise of courtesy and good humor; and by ready offering of individual sacrifice in protecting and preserving life.
6. To use physical force only when the exercise of persuasion, advice and warning is found to be insufficient to obtain public cooperation to an extent necessary to secure observance of law or to restore order; and to use only the minimum degree of physical force which is necessary on any particular occasion for achieving a police objective.
7. To maintain at all times a relationship with the public that gives reality to the historic tradition that the police are the public and that the public are the police; the police being only members of the public who are paid to give full-time attention to duties which are incumbent on every citizen in the interests of community welfare and existence.
8. To recognize always the need for strict adherence to police-executive functions, and to refrain from even seeming to usurp the powers of the judiciary of avenging individuals or the State, and of authoritatively judging guilt and punishing the guilty.
9. To recognize always that the rest of police efficiency is the absence of crime and disorder and not the visible evidence of police action in dealing with them.

Source: Reith (1952, p. 154).

agreed that constables would not carry firearms. While the organization itself was structured after the military, Peel went to great lengths to ensure that it was perceived as a civilian force. With the exception of the rank of sergeant, no military titles were used in the police organizational structure (Reppetto, 1978). Strict discipline was enacted to ensure that no actions (i.e., excessive force or unnecessary interventions) were taken that might alienate the public (Cole and Smith, 2007).

The Metropolitan Police gained acceptance so rapidly and served so effectively that Parliament passed the "County and Borough Police Act of 1856" (Stead, 1985). This act required that every borough and county in England form its own police force. In time, the Metropolitan Police came to be the model not only for British forces but for police forces in democracies throughout the world.

The Traditional Model

In the nineteenth century in the United States, the larger cities of the North were experiencing chaos similar to that which Britain had gone through. As in Britain, the old system of policing could not cope with the wave of riots and disorders that swept through the large cities. The combined effects of industrialization, urbanization, and immigration transformed the northern cities into hotbeds of economic, ethnic, racial, and cultural strife (Walker, 1977). Crime was rampant in the streets, and mob violence was a frequent occurrence.

To the leaders of America's large cities, it was all too apparent that the police system had to be changed if control were to be regained. The same difficulties that had slowed the creation of the Metropolitan Police arose in such cities as New York, Boston, and Philadelphia. There was uncertainty about creating a "police state," political groups feared that rival factions would use the police to repress them, and there was reluctance to bear the financial costs (Grant and Terry, 2005). Despite these concerns, political leaders began to explore the various options available to them. The Metropolitan Police model was the alternative of choice (Johnson and Wolfe, 2003).

The creation of police forces within the large northern cities helped regulate social disorders but did not alleviate the underlying problems of congestion and class conflict. Within a relatively short period, the police had become a tool with which politicians rewarded their friends and punished their enemies. In New York, Boston, Philadelphia, and Chicago, politics and corruption dominated the police (Reppetto, 1978). Recent immigrants, particularly the Irish and Germans, gained considerable influence in the political machines that dominated the large cities throughout the nineteenth century. Subsequently, the police departments in cities such as Boston, New York, Philadelphia, Chicago, St. Louis, Cincinnati, and Milwaukee became the domains of the dominant ethnic groups. The amount of law enforcement received, if any, was dependent on one's political connections (Walker, 1977). Crime and social tumult plagued the metropolitan areas. Once again, it was obvious that the police systems of the large cities needed overhauling.

The second half of the century saw a number of efforts at police reform. In New York and a number of other cities, the state legislatures seized control of their police forces (Reppetto, 1978). The majority of these efforts were designed to wrest control of the police from the ethnic groups and return to the "higher morality" of the upper-class Anglo-Saxon Protestants (Berman, 1987). The reforms actually accomplished very little in improving

FIGURE 10.2   A driver's license checkpoint exemplifies a traditional (and still appropriate) police strategy.

Courtesy of Pelham Police Department.

police performance. In effect, they only replaced control by one political faction with that of another (Walker, 1977).

The Professional Model

In the early years of the twentieth century, the need for police reforms continued. There was still a call to "get politics out of the police and get the police out of politics" (Walker, 1998). This continued to be based on political competition to control city governments, but now the focus was on hiring professional administrators in order to limit political influence.

In addition to hiring professional administrators, advocates for reform, such as Richard Sylvester, police chief of Washington, D.C., and founder of the International Association of Chiefs of Police, called for personnel standards for police officers. One person, August Vollmer, police chief of Berkeley, California, and future founder of the American Society of Criminology, would spread the message across the nation that police officers needed to have higher education, extensive training, professional integrity, and a clearly defined organizational structure to regulate their activities (Carte and Carte, 1975; MacNamara, 1977).

Orlando Winfield Wilson attended the University of California and became a protegé of Vollmer. He became a Berkeley police officer and, through Vollmer's influence, later obtained positions as police chief in Fullerton, California, and Wichita, Kansas. His success in Wichita serves as yet another model for police reform. He would later become dean of the School of Criminology at the University of California, where he wrote *Police Administration*, the text that would become the bible for U.S. police chiefs. Wilson was later called upon to reform the Chicago Police Department, an effort that resulted in only modest success but laid the groundwork for future improvements (Carte and Carte, 1975).

Political turbulence dominated the United States in the 1960s. War protests, the civil rights movement, street crime, union actions, and unrest on college campuses created problems for city police. These problems were accentuated by the abuses of the Chicago police while "maintaining order" at the 1968 Democratic convention, the tactics that the Los Angeles police used in quelling racial unrest in that city, and by the discovery of "rampant corruption" in the New York City Police Department (Johnson and Wolfe, 2003). Once again the call for reform was heard.

THE DEVELOPMENT OF COMMUNITY-ORIENTED POLICE MODELS

A new group of reformers, led by New York City Police Commissioner Patrick Murphy, began to emerge during the 1960s and 1970s. New techniques that emphasized community relations and enhanced service delivery became popular (Walker and Katz, 2002). New procedures regulating the discretion and conduct of the police began to take effect. These changes, in conjunction with rulings of the U.S. Supreme Court that dramatically expanded the rights of those accused of criminal behavior, significantly affected the role and performance of law enforcement officers in general and of big-city police in particular.

U.S. police forces became more representative of their communities, and more disciplined than ever before. Administrators were constantly experimenting with ways in which to enhance the delivery of police services. The public and the media became more aware of what the police should be doing and, more important, what they should not be doing.

Today the mission of police is recognized as going beyond "crime fighting"—catching bad guys—and "order maintenance"—minimizing threats to the peace (Conser et al., 2005). Service to the public through community awareness and crime prevention programs is now in vogue. The police and the public are once again learning that law enforcement requires a cooperative effort, not alienation from one another. To achieve this cooperative goal, U.S. police agencies have experimented with a number of community-oriented models.

Team Policing

The professional model of policing had sought to move away from the favoritism, corruption, and inefficiency of the contextual law enforcement provided by the traditional model. Effectiveness in reducing crime rates and in apprehending criminals was stressed. Later, efficiency and accountability in providing police services became a focus. Although these efforts resulted in "better law enforcement," they did so at the expense of community relations. "Professional officers" were better disciplined, less biased, less corrupt, and more efficient. They were also more effective in fighting crime. However, their fixation with crime fighting and the strictly legalistic provision of services viewed as necessary for professional accountability caused them to become isolated from the communities they served (Barker, Hunter, and Rush, 1994). **Team policing** was an attempt to restore those needed ties to the community while maintaining the standards of the professional model.

Team policing sought to enhance police–community relations by increasing police–citizen interaction within designated communities. Patrol officers, with some assistance from specialists, were assigned to specific geographic areas. These areas were to become "their community." Service delivery would become more personal and would gain community support as a result of this interaction. Team policing concepts varied from conventional patrol delivery in the following aspects:

1. Geographic stability of the patrol team.
2. A combination of patrol and investigative functions.
3. Lower-level flexibility in policymaking.
4. Maximum interaction among team members.
5. Maximum communication among team members and the community (Roberg, Kuykendall, and Novak, 2002).

Although the intentions of team policing were commendable, the attempts to turn large-city policing into small-town policing failed. Community relations were somewhat improved, but lack of support from middle managers who perceived the decentralized geographic areas and team concept as threatening to their control, lack of dispatching technology that resulted in patrol movement within geographic communities, a lack of clarity as to the role of team officers, and resentment from other officers who perceived the teams as being elitist doomed the early efforts of team policing (Walker and Katz, 2002).

Integrated Criminal Apprehension Program

In 1975, the Law Enforcement Assistance Administration began funding of the Integrated Criminal Apprehension Program (ICAP) that would eventually be implemented, in varying degrees, in more than 500 cities. Originally developed as the Patrol Emphasis Program, ICAP was intended to direct patrol resources toward crime problems that were identified through intensive crime analysis. It was envisioned as an operations support concept that would enhance patrol operations, thus providing more efficient service delivery and more effectively addressing community needs (Carter, 1994; Hunter, 1991).

ICAP was both a program and a process for enhanced service delivery. It was a program in that it sought to establish key components that would structure service delivery efforts. These components were crime analysis, operations analysis, secondary receiving, directed patrol activities, managing criminal investigations, career criminal monitoring, and tactical crime prevention. ICAP was a process in that it sought to enhance the provision of services based on data collection, analysis planning, service delivery, and feedback (Grassie and Crowe, 1978).

The success of ICAP was limited due to the complexity of the concept, the requirement for sophisticated planning and analysis, and resistance to change on the part of police officials (Carter, 1994). While many of the components of ICAP were implemented by the participating agencies, most tended to utilize only those portions that fit within their particular service delivery schemes, rather than adopting the overall process. As a result, benefits to the communities being served were limited (Hunter, 1990). However, the emphasis on problem identification and response through crime analysis would influence the development of later service enhancement strategies, most notably that of problem-oriented policing.

Neighborhood Foot Patrol

Neighborhood foot patrol emerged during the 1970s as an effort to correct the deficiencies of team policing. Like team policing, this police service delivery style utilized teams assigned within a geographical area. Unlike team policing, it was not an attempt to change overall service delivery strategies within that area. Nor did it require organizational changes to implement its tactics. Instead, the teams emphasized foot patrols within designated neighborhoods. These patrol generalists were to interact within the small communities that they served. The regular patrol and investigations service delivery within the larger geographical area surrounding the designated neighborhoods was not affected (Carter, 1994).

Two of the early foot patrol programs were experimental programs in Newark, New Jersey; and Flint, Michigan. The primary efforts of these programs were to deter crime by maintaining a police presence and to involve citizens in crime prevention efforts. The successes of those programs led to the development of similar programs in Madison, Wisconsin; Baltimore County, Maryland; and Houston, Texas. It also led to the establishment of the National Neighborhood Foot Patrol Center at Michigan State University (Trojanowicz and Bucqueroux, 1990).

The reports from the early neighborhood foot patrol programs of enhanced community involvement and reduced crime rates have resulted in expansion of the program to many other cities, as well as expansion of the community involvement concept. Foot patrol is not a necessary part of community-oriented policing, nor does a police agency have to adopt community-oriented policing to utilize foot patrols. However, the neighborhood foot patrol concepts of police and citizens working together, developing trust, and sharing power became the basis for community-oriented policing (Trojanowicz and Bucqueroux, 1990).

Community-Oriented Policing

The successful implementation of neighborhood foot patrol led to the development of more comprehensive strategies designed to enlist community support within designated geographical areas. These strategies have become identified as **community-oriented policing**. What actually is community-oriented policing and how is it different from other models of policing? To answer this question we must first define community policing, as community-oriented policing was first known as. Dr. Robert C. Trojanowicz was the founder of the National Center of Community Policing at Michigan State University in 1983 and was its director until his untimely death in 1994. He was the leading proponent of community policing and was among the first to define the concept. His definition of community policing was:

> Community Policing is a new philosophy of policing, based on the concept that police officers and private citizens can work together in creative ways to solve contemporary community problems related to crime, fear of crime, social and physical disorder and neighborhood decay. The philosophy is predicated on the belief that achieving these goals requires that police departments develop a new relationship with the law-abiding people in the community, allowing them a greater voice in setting local priorities and involving them in efforts to improve the quality of life in their neighborhoods. It shifts the focus of police work from handling random calls to solving community problems. (Trojanowicz and Bucqueroux, 1990, p. 5)

The U.S. Department of Justice, Office of Community Oriented Policing Services (COPS) was created through the Violent Crime Control and Law Enforcement Act of 1994. It awards grants to tribal, state, and local law enforcement agencies "to hire and train community policing professionals . . . and provides training and technical assistance to advance community policing at all levels of law enforcement, from line officers to law enforcement executives" (www.cops.usdoj.gov). The COPS Office's definition of community policing is found in its mission statement:

> Moving from a reactive to proactive role, community policing represents a shift from more traditional law enforcement practices. By addressing the root causes of criminal and disorderly behavior, rather than simply responding to crimes once they have been committed, community policing concentrates on preventing both crime and the atmosphere of fear it creates. Additionally, community policing encourages the use of crime-fighting technology and operational strategies and the development of mutually beneficial relationships between law enforcement and the community. . . .

A succinct definition of community policing is provided by the California Attorney Generals Office (http://safestate.org).

> Community policing is a philosophy, management style, and organizational strategies that promotes pro-active problem solving and police-community partnerships to address the causes of crime and fear as well as other community issues.

Gary Cordner says that community policing has four major dimensions: the philosophical dimension, the strategic dimension, the tactical dimension, and the organizational dimension (http://www.kycops.org).

THE PHILOSOPHICAL DIMENSION   Most of its most thoughtful and forceful advocates emphasize that community policing is a new philosophy of policing, perhaps constituting even a paradigm shift away from professional-model policing, and not just a particular program or specialized activity. The philosophical dimension includes the central ideas and beliefs underlying community policing. Three of the most important are citizen input, broad function, and personal service.

THE STRATEGIC DIMENSION   The strategic dimension of community policing includes the key operational concepts that translate philosophy into action. These strategic concepts are the links between the broad ideas and beliefs that underline community policing and the specific programs and practices by which it is implemented. They assure that agency policies, priorities, and resource allocations are consistent with the COP philosophy. Three important strategic elements are re-oriented operations, preventive emphasis, and geographic focus.

THE TACTICAL DIMENSION   The tactical dimension of community policing ultimately translates ideas, philosophies, and strategies into concrete programs, tactics, and behaviors.
Even those who insist "community policing is a philosophy, not a program" must concede that unless community policing eventually leads to some action, some new or different behavior, it is all rhetoric and no reality. Indeed, many commentators have taken the view that community policing is little more than a new police marketing strategy that has left the core elements of the police role untouched. Three of the most important tactical elements of community policing are *positive interaction, partnership, and problem solving* [emphasis added].

THE ORGANIZATIONAL DIMENSION   It is important to recognize an Organizational Dimension that surrounds community policing and greatly affects its implementation. In order to support and facilitate community policing, police departments often consider a variety of changes in organization, administration, management, and supervision. The elements of the organizational dimension are not really part of community policing per se, but they are frequently crucial to its successful implementation. Three important elements of COP are structure, management, and information.

Community-oriented policing is seen by its advocates as the solution to the reactive practices of traditional service delivery models. The community-oriented model utilizes a flexible philosophy of community involvement that transcends community relations but is not strategy specific. The nature of the problems identified by problem solvers (community members and beat officers) sets the strategy. This flexibility is the greatest asset of community policing. Unfortunately, it is also its greatest weakness. Police practitioners, as well as police scholars, often do not understand how to apply this concept successfully. The results are attempts to classify all community relations efforts as being true community policing.

Problem-Oriented Policing

Another innovative operational style that has been utilized by police in recent years is **problem-oriented policing**. While community policing is a broad effort to develop new relationships within all or designated parts of a community, problem-oriented policing is a narrower effort to deal with a specific problem (Goldstein, 1990). However, problem solving using the problem-oriented policing approach is often used in community policing. In problem-oriented policing, there are no demands for the total restructuring of police organizations, nor is there insistence that decision making be shared with the community (Webster and Conners, 1993). Community involvement is encouraged, but it is noted that those areas of cities that require the greatest police attention often have little sense of community (Goldstein, 1990).

Problem-oriented policing attempts to engage productively with the community by "(1) assigning officers to areas for longer periods of time to enable them to identify the problems of concern to the community; (2) developing the capacity of both officers and the department to analyze community problems; (3) learning when greater community involvement has the potential for significantly reducing a problem; and (4) working with those specific segments of the community that are in a position to assist in reducing or eliminating the problem" (Goldstein, 1990, pp. 26–27).

Problem-oriented policing is considered to be superior to traditionally reactive service delivery in that, like the previously discussed ICAP, proactive planning and analysis govern resource allocation decisions. In this model, "problem solving is a central element, not a peripheral activity as in traditional policing. Everyone in the department contributes to its mission, not just a few innovative officers or a special unit. And, this problem solving approach places special emphasis on careful analysis of problems before developing solutions and seeks to avoid instant answers that are unsupported by good information" (Eck and Spelman, 1989, p. 96).

According to its proponents, problem-oriented policing is also superior to community policing in that it does not require departments to decentralize decision making or abandon crime control and service functions (Eck and Spelman, 1989; Goldstein, 1990). (Unfortunately, problem-oriented policing has been wrongly associated with community policing to the point that both police practitioners and police scholars are hesitant to embrace it.)

Like community policing, the application of problem-oriented policing suffers when police administrators adopt the terminology without understanding the concept or its applications. To be successful, problem-solving efforts, which address the needs of the public, not the police administration, should become the standard method of policing rather than an occasional tactic. And police administrators should attempt to get all department members involved in solving problems based on thorough analysis. The creation of special "POP squads" or encouraging specific officers to utilize problem-solving techniques is not enough (Eck and Spelman, 1989).

There are several approaches to problem solving currently used by police agencies. They include the following:

> *The Capra Model*: Many departments use the **CAPRA model** (clients, acquiring & analyzing info, partnerships, response, assessment) as a guide to the problem solving process for all kinds of crime and noncrime problems [see Box 10.2].
>
> *Guardians*: when searching for solutions to problems, it is often helpful to identify the so-called guardians, who are people who have an incentive or the opportunity to help rectify the problem (e.g., landlords and school principals)
>
> *Beat Meetings*: some departments utilize meetings between neighborhood residents and their beat officers to identify problems, analyze them, and brainstorm possible solutions.
>
> *Hot Spots*: many departments analyze their calls for service to identify locations that have disproportionate numbers of calls, and then do problem solving to try to lower the call volume in those places.
>
> *Multi-Agency Teams*: some jurisdictions use problem solving teams comprised not just of police but also of representatives of their [*sic* other] agencies (public works, sanitation, parks and recreation, code enforcement, etc.) so that an array of information and resources can be brought to bear once problems are identified.
>
> *Source*: www.kycops.org

Problem solving, especially as part of the agencies' community-oriented policing agenda, has many benefits for the police and the community. Although the police will always respond to emergencies, there are calls that are of a noncrime nature and could be handled more effectively by other government or social agencies. Decreasing the number of nonemergency calls would result in the following benefits, according to the San Diego Police Department (www.sandiego.gov/police):

- Officers are able to spend more time working with citizens to solve crime and disorder problems.
- With better police–citizen communication, officers can more effectively use and share crime information with the public.
- Officers who know both a community's problems and its residents can link people with other public and private agencies that can help solve community concerns.
- No single agency can solve complex social problems alone. A combined community-police effort restores the safety of our neighborhoods and business districts.

BOX 10.2
RCMP CAPRA Problem-Solving Model

Problem solving is the lynchpin of the RCMP's definition of Community Policing.

Community policing is defined by the RCMP as problem solving in partnerships with clients/communities to ensure continuous improvement in service delivery.

CAPRA (C = Clients, A = Acquire/Analyze Information, P = Partnership, R = Response, A = Assessment of Action Taken) is intended to promote discussion in small groups of employees, clients, and partners of the Royal Canadian Mounted Police.

BOX 10.3
Problem-Solving Awards

Herman Goldstein Award

The award honors Professor Herman Goldstein, who conceived and developed the theory of problem-solving. . . .

The Goldstein Award. . . . recognizes innovative and effective problem-oriented (POP) projects that have achieved measurable success in resolving specific crime, disorder or public safety problems faced by police and the community. . . .

Problems may range in scope from a very specific problem in a specific neighborhood, to one that affects many people over a wide area. While many successful POP projects are geographically focused, other problems affect certain types of people or occur at a certain time. The award program seeks projects that successfully resolved any type of recurring crime or disorder problem faced by the police. Examples from past projects include drug dealing in a strip mall, loitering day laborers, trespassers at a high school, 911 hang-ups, prostitution on a major thoroughfare, drug-dealing and gang activity in a neighborhood, drunk driving throughout a large metropolitan region, disorder and criminal activity in an apartment complex, gun violence, and thefts from construction sites.

Eligibility for Goldstein Award

All employees of governmental policing agencies *worldwide* who directly deliver police services to the public are eligible for the award. . . . While problem-oriented policing is frequently associated with the term "community policing," this award is not designed to honor all policing initiatives that some believe may fall under the "community policing" heading. Rather, the Goldstein Award recognizes problem-oriented approaches to specific crime and disorder problems. Submissions must address all four phases of the SARA problem-solving model [italics added].

Source: Adapted from Center for Problem-Oriented Policing; www.popcenter.org/goldstein.

The Tilley Awards

[Named after Professor Nick Tilley of Nottingtham Trent University, who developed POP in the United Kingdom.]

Rewarding the best policing work in the UK

Presented annually, the Tilley Awards for Problem-Oriented Policing recognizes the best police work out there, and reward the most intelligent, courageous, and effective approaches to dealing with the problems police encounter on the streets.

Scope of the award

We award three prizes . . . to projects that demonstrate excellence in applying problem-oriented principles to crime and disorder.

Entries can focus on any aspect of police or their partnership work including, for example:

- projects undertaken to reduce specific crime and disorder problems. In these cases judges will not simply be looking for a reduction in crime and disorder, but also for evidence of the approach being used on a consistent basis, applied to all calls for service.
- work to support problem-solving at an operational level, such as, freeing up resources to focus on problem-solving, or demonstrating improvements to problem-solving. . . .
- The winners will be awarded financial assistance to enable them to attend the International Problem-Oriented Policing Conference in the US in late autumn.

Source: Adapted from www.met.police.uk

TECHNOLOGICAL ADVANCES AND COMMUNITY POLICING

In addition to the operational and managerial strategies discussed within the previous section, community policing has also been impacted by technological advances in computerization and crime-prevention strategies. Three of the more significant advances include crime analysis, computer-aided dispatching, and crime mapping.

Crime Analysis Programs

Within the previously discussed ICAP, we mentioned the components of crime analysis, operations analysis, secondary receiving, directed patrol activities, managing criminal investigations, monitoring career criminals, and tactical crime prevention. The combined benefits of these operations may also be included within problem-oriented policing. These efforts may therefore be referred to as problem solving or simply as crime analysis. Peak and Glensor (2004, p. 80) define crime analysis as "a set of systematic, analytical processes providing timely and pertinent information to assist operational and administrative personnel." They divided crime analysis into three components: *tactical crime analysis*, used to identify crime trends and patterns; *strategic crime analysis*, for preparation of statistics and summaries designed to aid in long-term operational planning; and *administrative crime analysis*, used to aid in administrative decision making on social, economic, and geographic information.

Computer-Aided Dispatching

Computer-Aided Dispatching, also known as Computer-Assisted Dispatching, or simply as CAD, began in the late 1970s. Initially it was a means of reducing the volume of paperwork in creating dispatch cards that documented police activities on incidents that did not result in reports being written, in manually indexing police reports for retrieval, and in manually collecting statistics on calls for service. In addition to saving considerable time in filing and retrieving reports and complaint information, CAD enabled police departments to capture and retrieve many types of crime and operational data that had previously been unavailable or extremely time-consuming to generate.

The next generation of CAD added global positioning information that enabled dispatchers to track the movements of police cars in order to make better decisions in assigning calls for service. Initially these systems were resented by officers who felt they were spy devices designed so that management could constantly monitor their activities. While some officers may still resent the electronic intrusion into their work lives, the benefits in effective call dispatching and, more importantly, in sending aid to officers in trouble have been invaluable. The current generation of global positioning systems (GPS) that can even be worn by officers, have made CAD not only a great mechanism for easing administrative burdens and guiding operational decisions, but invaluable in advancing crime analysis and enhancing officer safety. Augmented by the latest versions of global information systems (GIS), dispatchers and officers also are able to expeditiously find locations within their jurisdictions and, in many cases, even within public buildings.

Crime Mapping

As children watching "Westerns" on television, we often would see maps of territories or counties displayed on walls in various sheriff's offices depicted. The good guy would often consult these maps in determining how or where to "cut them off at the pass." Later "cop thrillers" would often display a city map with pins on it in a fictitious detective squad room. The good guys would view the pins to decide where to do stakeouts or searches in order to "nab the bad guys." Thanks to the above technologies, the good guys no longer have to depend on hunches made from viewing potential travel routes or "hot spots" determined from clumpings of pins. Highly sophisticated computer graphics now enable investigators and crime analysts to obtain accurate and detailed maps of past, present, and potential crime areas within their jurisdictions.

THE CURRENT STATUS OF COMMUNITY POLICING

The emphasis in policing today is on community-oriented operational skills that will bring the community and the police together in a concerted effort to prevent disorder. Unfortunately, the success of such a service model is hampered by the lack of community consensus within a diverse and increasingly fragmented nation. There is no single geographical community with whom the police must relate; instead police face a complex system of overlapping and frequently competing internal and external communities in constant interaction.

The community policing approaches are further hampered by the lack of clarity provided by their proponents in regard to application. Police agencies have great difficulty implementing these models because many police administrators see community policing as programs, not a philosophy. In addition, community policing terminologies have been usurped by many police administrators who desire to appear progressive and wish to enhance community relations but who have neither the desire nor the intent to abandon the contemporary reactive model of delivering police services. To do so would require enhanced fiscal resources, a consensus of public support, and widespread acceptance by rank-and-file police officers and by police administrators. Therefore, "Political leaders and, unfortunately, many police leaders latch onto the label for the positive images it evokes, but do not invest in the concept itself" (Goldstein, 1999, p. 27).

Despite these difficulties, community policing has become a viable operational model for many police agencies throughout the United States. It has many advantages over traditional policing (see Table 10.1), and the prospect of returning to Peel's joint police–community cooperation has great appeal within our democratic society. As indicated earlier, the problems of community policing have been due not to the philosophy but to practitioners who usurp the title while still utilizing traditional policing strategies and who seek to implement changes without

TABLE 10.1 Traditional versus Community Policing: Questions and Answers

Question	Traditional	Community Policing
Who are the police?	A government agency principally responsible for law enforcement	Police are the public and the public are the police: The police officers are those who are paid to give full-time attention to the duties of every citizen
What is the relationship of the police force to other public service departments?	Priorities often conflict	The police are one department among many responsible for improving the quality of life
What is the role of the police?	Focusing on solving crimes	A broader problem-solving approach
How is police efficiency measured?	By detection and arrest rates	By the absence of crime and disorder
What are the highest priorities?	Crimes that are high value (e.g., bank robberies) and those involving violence	Whatever problems disturb the community most
What, specifically, do police deal with?	Incidents	Citizens' problems and concerns
What determines the effectiveness of police?	Response times	Public cooperation
What view do police take of service calls?	Deal with them only if there is no real police work to do	Vital function and great opportunity
What is police professionalism?	Swift, effective response to serious crime	Keeping close to the community
What kind of intelligence is most important?	Crime intelligence (study of particular crimes or series of crimes)	Criminal intelligence (information about the activities of individuals or groups)
What is the essential nature of police accountability?	Highly centralized; governed by rules, regulations, and policy directives; and accountable to the law	Emphasis on local account ability to community needs
What is the role of headquarters?	To provide the necessary rules and policy directives	To preach organizational values
What is the role of the press liaison department?	To keep the "heat" off operational officers so they can get on with the job	To coordinate an essential channel of communication with the community
How do the police regard prosecutions?	As an important goal	As one tool among many

Source: Sparrow (1988, pp. 8–9).

knowing what they are doing. These problems can be overcome—and have been overcome—by many contemporary police agencies.

Today, community-oriented policing is used to refer to police service delivery systems that utilize the concepts of the previously discussed problem-oriented and community policing models. The more successful applications are those in which police planners utilize those POP and COP strategies that best suit their particular agencies and the communities that they serve. Community-oriented policing moves from merely responding to reports of crime and/or requests for assistance to developing a proactive organization that works with its clients to determine what police services (not just crime control and order maintenance, although these are not ignored, but all services) are needed and how to best provide these services.

The newest incantations of community policing try to merge the best elements of all the previous strategies and technologies discussed on the previous pages into comprehensive and systematic models. These models include Community-Oriented Policing and Problem Solving (COPPS) and the Computerized Statistics Program (COMPSTAT).

Community-Oriented Policing and Problem Solving (COPPS)

Community-Oriented Policing and Problem Solving (COPPS) is basically a new and improved version of community policing that seeks to integrate the best aspects of community-oriented policing with the strong points of problem-solving policing. As defined by Peak and Glensor (2004, pp. 78–79), "Community Oriented Policing and Problem Solving (COPPS) is a proactive philosophy that promotes solving problems that are criminal, affect our quality of life, or increase our fear of crime, as well as other community issues. COPPS involves identifying, analyzing and addressing community problems at their source."

Perhaps the most commonly cited example of a successful COPPS program is the Chicago Alternative Policing Strategy (CAPS). In 1993 the program began in selected areas of the city. Police officers were assigned to fixed beats and trained in problem-solving strategies. Neighborhood meetings were held and citizen committees created to advise area police managers. From this beginning grew the concept that ". . . the entire department rather than just a specialized unit should become uniquely involved with and partner with the community" (Walker and Katz, 2002, p. 15).

The Salinas, California, Police Department on their Web site list what they consider to be the key concepts of the community-oriented policing and problem-solving philosophy (http://www.salinaspd.com). They are worth repeating here as they show how a police department attempts to put a philosophy into practice.

KEY CONCEPTS OF COMMUNITY-ORIENTED POLICING AND PROBLEM SOLVING

1. Commitment to customer (public) satisfaction.
2. An emphasis on solving chronic problems.
3. Empowering the beat officer to be the problem solver.
4. Determining the actual needs and desires of the community, and responding to these needs as priorities.
5. Working in partnership with the community to solve problems.
6. Utilizing all available resources to impact problems.
7. Personalizing police service response (beat responsibility).
8. Becoming proactive, as opposed to reactive.
9. Changing traditional measures of police effectiveness.
10. Managing calls for service and available resources.

The superiority of COPPS over previous models is that it gives equal emphasis to the need to use available technologies to efficiently and effectively address crime and/or operational problems and it does so without overlooking the need for citizen involvement in arriving at solutions to the identified problems and in assessing the impacts of those solutions.

Computerized Statistics Program (COMPSTAT)

Just as CAPS is a success story for Chicago, so is the Computerized Statistics Program (COMP-STAT) for the city of New York. Like CAPS, COMPSTAT seeks to incorporate the best of both problem-oriented policing and community-oriented policing. Some feel that this program is tainted in that its zero-tolerance policing has at times been utilized as one of its crime-control strategies. One could argue, however, that it was the benefits of COMPSTAT that actually created the decline rates in crime and violence that some have credited to zero-tolerance policing.

Where COMPSTAT differs from previous programs is that it seeks to enhance the results of COPPS and CAPS discussed above by incorporating the latest computer technologies as well as elements of TQM. Each police precinct is expected to use the technologies available to them to analyze crime and develop appropriate prevention and/or control strategies. Offender targeting and targeting geographic areas of the community where problems have been identified through crime analysis are integral to the success of COMPSTAT. While police subordinates are involved in the decision-making processes, it is the local police commanders that are held accountable. They meet weekly in "Crime Strategy Meetings," where they must consistently account for crime events that take place within their precincts. Unsatisfactory achievements within their precincts will result in reassignments to other duties (NYPD, 2006; Peak and Glensor, 2004).

COMMUNITY-ORIENTED POLICING APPLICATIONS

Despite the fact that COP is a philosophically driven concept designed to change how policing occurs in our society, it is often observed as a program, or a component of a program, in a police agency. Although the true advocates of COP renounce the component or program approach, COP is actually meant to be a problem-solving approach for reducing crime, reducing citizens' fears of the police and improving quality of life. How this is accomplished differs from site to site, and its success or failure also differs. Although police agencies have tried numerous ways to implement COP, there still are only a handful of legitimate means by which COP functions. These include forms of patrol other than by automobile, substations, the officer residency program, community action groups (a newer version of Neighborhood Watch), and problem-specific techniques.

Forms of Patrol

One of the most popular tools of COP appears to be the use of foot patrol. Although not a modern concept, at times it seems as if it is. In any case, foot patrol is employed by assigning officers to a given area in which they patrol on foot in an effort to better learn about the problems and people in their assigned beats or neighborhoods.

> In order to gain intimate knowledge of the neighborhood, patrol officers must interact both formally and informally with the people of the community: residents, business operators, workers, even people who are just passing through the area. (Watson, Stone, and DeLuca, 1998, p. 145)

The best means of accomplishing this interaction is through foot patrol. However, it is not the only method of patrol being employed as part of a COP approach.

Another growing and popular form of patrol is by bicycle. Many major metropolitan police agencies have bicycle patrols, which appear to have been fashioned after the Seattle, Washington, police department's unit. One of the most successful implementations is in Las Vegas, Nevada.

In an effort to reduce thefts, robberies, and prostitution along its famous "strip," the Las Vegas Metropolitan Police Department created a bicycle unit, which comprises several pairs of officers patrolling one of the busiest stretches of traffic in the country. Using a bicycle, officers can

FIGURE 10.3 **A bicycle patrol officer at work exemplifies a more community-oriented approach.**

Courtesy of Pelham Police Department.

better patrol the Strip, which has led to a reduction in crime. Bicycle patrols seem to be popular in downtown and business areas of many major cities.

Although foot and bicycle patrols appear to be the most popular form of COP patrol, other forms have included roller blades and three-wheel cycles. Ultimately, it is not necessarily the means of patrol but what is done during patrol. If officers still refuse to stop and interact except when necessary, no form of patrol will be successful. Then again, sometimes patrolling is not enough, no matter how interactive officers are. This has led to other means of reaching citizens, such as establishing substations.

Substations

Sometimes it is just too difficult for a person to reach police headquarters, which is supposedly the reason a person might not report a crime or might refuse to cooperate in an investigation. Having officers meet at a central location and then disperse throughout the city has also been identified as causing problems related to police investigations, citizen cooperation, and response time. To improve all such problems, police agencies, where appropriate, are creating substations as part of the COP effort. These substations range from full-fledged, miniature police stations housing both patrols and investigators assigned to a particular part of a city (e.g., the Ft. Worth, Texas, P. D. has substations located in the four main sections of the city: north, south, east, and west) to storefronts where one or more officers are assigned during specific times to allow citizens to walk in with complaints, give information about a crime, make an inquiry, or simply say hello. These substations also give officers a place to write reports or track down information through a computer (e.g., the Statesboro, Georgia, P. D. has a storefront station located in the

FIGURE 10.4 Canine officer with neighborhood kids.

Courtesy of Pelham Police Department.

local Wal-Mart because the main police station is on the opposite side of town). In essence, substations bring policing and officers closer to the community. The Anne Arundel County, Maryland, Police Department has a 2,000 square feet substation located in the Arundel Mall in Hanover. The substation has 12 officers assigned with a Community Relations Division stationed there. Six of the officers work during the day as part of the Community Relations Division. The other six officers patrol the area on bicycles.

The New Haven, Connecticut, Police Department as part of its community policing effort divided the city into 10 policing districts (www.cityofnewhaven.com/Police/CommunityPolicing. asp). Each of these districts has a district manager, a lieutenant or sergeant, who ensures that community policing objectives are met. The districts have neighborhood substations which act as "drop in" or "resource centers" where citizens meet, speak to city agencies, and participate in crime prevention activities. An important part of the community policing effort is the substation management teams. The substation management teams identify and examine neighborhood problems and identify strategies to deal with them. The composition of the teams varies from neighborhood to neighborhood but generally comprises a police supervisor, beat officers, block watch members, alderpersons, representatives of neighborhood-based agencies, and interested citizens.

Citizens Police Academies and Citizen Volunteers

Citizens police academies as a community policing concept were first developed in Great Britain in 1977 and spread to the United States in 1985. Since then they have become an integral part of the community policing efforts of police agencies at all levels of government, including the FBI. There is also a National Citizens Police Academy Association (NCPAA) with 344 members throughout the United States and Canada. NCPAA holds an annual meeting and publishes a quarterly newsletter. The overall objective of all citizens police academies is to foster better communication between the police and the citizens in their community. Generally all interested eligible citizens are encouraged to apply; however, some stress that they are looking for community leaders. Eligibility varies by agency and includes minimum age (18 or 21), residence in community, no felony convictions, and no misdemeanor arrests within the last three years. A background check is conducted on all applicants. The instruction varies from 7 to 15 weeks and includes an overview of the department and its function and operational procedures taught by agency personnel. Ride-alongs are often required for all who attend. Upon graduation from the citizens police academy, many departments encourage the citizens to join their volunteer programs.

The Glendora, California, Police Department requires that volunteers for their police auxiliary must attend the citizens police academy and an additional police auxiliary academy. These volunteers perform duties at the police station and for special events in the community, including fingerprinting job applicants, directing traffic, answering phones, assisting the records division, and issuing dog licenses. They may also be called out as an emergency response force during disasters (www.ci.glendora.ca.us/police/auxiliary.html).

After completing the citizens police academy, citizens of Plano, Texas, can join the department's Citizens Assisting Plano Police (CAPP) program (www.plano.gov/Departments/Police). These volunteers complete at least four hours of patrol per month. The volunteers wear CAPP uniforms and patrol in specially marked vehicles with the CAPP logo. Their duties include conducting "Open Garage Door" patrol; providing security at community events; assisting in lost child and adult incidents; monitoring the SkyWatch program (sky towers set up in shopping areas to deter thefts and provide security); aiding in crime scene security; providing assistance during festivals and parades; acting as "victims" in training scenarios; and discharging administrative duties such as working the front desks. In 2008, 60 CAPP volunteers contributed more than 7,000 hours of volunteer time (http://scntx.com/articles).

The **VIPS** (Volunteers in Policing) program, managed and implemented by the International Association of Chiefs of Police in partnership with the White House Office of the USA Freedom Corps, created after the terrorist attack of September 11, 2001, and the Bureau of Justice Assistance, Office of Justice Programs, U.S. Department of Justice, is the most extensive citizen volunteer program in American policing (www.policevolunteers.org). Law enforcement agencies start their own programs with assistance and funding from the national VIPS office. For example, graduates of the Chico, California, Police Department's Citizens Police Academy are encouraged to become a Volunteer in Police Service. They assist the department at community and special events. The VIPS volunteers also take police reports, assist in the police station, watch problem areas, and engage in community patrol (www.chico.ca.us/Police/Citizens_Academy.asp).

Resident Officer Program

One of the more innovative COP approaches is the resident officer program, in which a police agency either purchases or helps an officer purchase a home in the area where the officer works. Under this program, the resident officer is a neighbor who attempts to gain the trust of his or her neighbors, usually by making it known that he or she is available 24 hours a day should a problem arise. This approach cuts out the middle person—dispatch—by allowing individuals to contact officers directly. Living in the neighborhood makes an officer "one of us" and increases trust and cooperation. The Joliet and Elgin, Illinois, police departments have successfully used such a program for more than ten years. Still, it takes more than an officer to bring about positive changes.

Community Action Groups

For years, community action groups, more readily known as Neighborhood Watch groups, have been an essential element of COP. Such community involvement does not mean attending "gripe" sessions; rather, it involves participation in a group that actually responds to or assists the police in solving problems. Although it is one of the most important elements of COP, it is often the most difficult to establish. People seldom wish to get involved; in the past, that has been acceptable to most police officers. However, a successful COP relies on and receives public assistance through better reporting, keeping alert to unusual happenings in neighborhoods, and simply pitching in to physically address problems. (For instance, an empty corner lot that has turned into a dump and hangout is cleaned up and maintained by members of the neighborhood.)

Forms of patrol, substations, resident officers, and community action groups are four main ways to implement COP. However, the reality of COP comes down to what individual officers are allowed to do to address particular problems in their given neighborhoods.

Problem-Specific Techniques

The centerpiece of COP is problem solving. The problem can be anything from a simple one (e.g., a streetlight out in a busy business area) to a complex one (e.g., gang activity involving drugs). Because each city and police agency is different, how officers go about solving problems may differ slightly, but ultimately the approach is the same: the SARA model. The SARA model emphasizes four phases of the problem-solving process: scanning, analysis, response, and assessment (Bynum, 2001, p. 3).

> **Scanning** is the initial identification of the problem, where problems are identified as a group of related or recurring incidents or a particular concern of the community. Scanning is the most important step in the SARA model. The likelihood of solving problems is dependent on identifying problems in observable and measurable terms (Watson, 1998, p. 331).
>
> **Analysis** is an in-depth exploration of the problem and its underlying causes. If a problem is properly identified, an analysis will indicate why the problem is occurring and should reveal elements of an appropriate response (Watson, 1998, p. 331).
>
> **Response** implements an analysis-driven strategy to address the problem, focusing on the factors identified in the analysis phases.
>
> **Assessment** consists of ongoing review and monitoring of the process of the response in achieving its objectives. The primary goal of assessment is to determine if the response is having the desired effect on the problem. Unfortunately, it is the most neglected step in the SARA process. Police officers and agencies spend the least amount of time and effort on this step (Watson, 1998, p. 332).

The San Diego Police Department states on its Web site that "Problem Oriented Policing is the primary strategy of Community Oriented Policing. The community and police work together analyzing community problems and developing customized responses to them" (www.sanidego. gov/police). The department follows the SARA approach and lists brief examples of its use and success:

- The police, community, and City council worked to attack drug and gang problems in the Skyline and Meadowbrook community. Those efforts led to an organized community association, and a reduction in community activity.
- A trolley station was the location of gang fights, violent crimes, and narcotic activity. A squad of officers collected information to show the local transit board that the design of the station contributed to crime. Based on the careful work of the officers, the board agreed to provide funds to redesign the station.
- Calls of narcotic activity at an 80-unit apartment complex alerted officers to try a problem solving approach. Working with residents, the on-site manager, the management company, the Housing Commission, and other police units, the officers were able to evict problem residents and stop the drug dealing.
- The Drug Abatement Response Team (DART) involves the City Attorney, Housing Inspection and the police in identifying properties that have a long history of ongoing narcotics activities. In a six-month period, over 70 drug houses were targeted for abatement action.

The preceding are just a small sample of problems facing today's police officers. In general, COP attempts to address crime, citizen fears of both crime and the police, and quality of life. How this is accomplished varies from city to city, but the most popular trend is community-oriented policing, which forces the police and citizens to interact on an equal level to address potential and existing problems cooperatively. Otherwise, no solution for any problem can be achieved. To reach the goals of COP, police must begin by implementing it as a complete philosophical change and not through piecemeal programs.

RECOMMENDATIONS FOR IMPLEMENTING COMMUNITY-ORIENTED POLICING

Due to the growing popularity of community-oriented policing, more and more guides or manuals for implementation are being published. Most seem to focus more on program implementation than a complete philosophical implementation. The following offers what were perceived to be the implementation stages for a successful change to community-oriented policing but may also be followed for individual problem solving. The stages include preparation, initiation, implementation, preliminary evaluation, full implementation, and evaluation and monitoring (Dantzker, 1994).

Preparation

Probably the most important part of implementing COP or problem solving is preparation. It is a common shortcoming of agencies trying to address problems or implement changes, such as implementing COP, to rush the process without fully preparing for either the outcome or the change. Before a problem can be solved or change can occur, the police agency or individual officer should be well prepared. To do so, it is suggested that the preparation process begin with a focus on three main areas: (1) gathering information; (2) organizational review; and (3) the community.

GATHERING INFORMATION   One of the most crucial aspects of problem solving is gathering information. This is particularly true when it comes to COP. The first step is learning what community-oriented policing is and what it is not. An agency preparing to implement COP should obtain all it can of the explanatory literature, of which there is an abundance, and make sure that the literature is thoroughly reviewed and understood by the individual or group leading the department's change to COP. We suggest that a team consisting of members from the police agency, the political body, and the community be formed to gather and review this information. In addition to gathering information, the COP team can benefit by visiting at least one similar city that has implemented community-oriented policing.

ORGANIZATIONAL REVIEW   It is extremely important that the agency pursuing COP be able to answer this question: What will community-oriented policing mean to this agency? Furthermore, it should be decided quickly whether COP will become a complete organizational philosophy or simply program tools. Primarily, the agency needs to perform a self-assessment, during which such topics as organizational, administrative, and managerial structure; officer accountability (i.e., evaluations and discipline); training; and recruitment relative to community-oriented policing are reviewed. Furthermore, important issues such as budgeting, personnel, unions, 911/communications systems, and departmental expectations must be examined.

THE COMMUNITY   One of the most important tenets for the success of community-oriented policing is citizen involvement. Yet one of the more difficult aspects of community-oriented policing is determining how the community should be involved. We suggest such ideas as open forums, formation of citizen and police groups, and citizen advisory boards. Publicity, public relations, and educating the citizenry are key to COP. An important issue will be to identify and clarify citizen expectations and determine how to socialize police and citizens to community-oriented policing.

INITIATION   Once all the initial groundwork has been laid (completion of the preparation), it is time to begin introducing all concerned parties to community-oriented policing and begin making changes that will allow its implementation. This requires accomplishing three primary aspects of COP implementation: agency reorganization, public education, and training.

REORGANIZATION   Reorganization is probably the most difficult task for most agencies planning to implement community-oriented policing. Reorganization should involve staffing, command structure, and support services. We suggest that the agency planning to implement COP examine other agencies and their organizational efforts, the problems and solutions they encountered, and their continuing efforts to meet the organizational demands of community-oriented policing.

EDUCATION   Before any element of community-oriented policing hits the streets, it is imperative that both police personnel and citizens understand what is going to take place, how it is going to work, and what everyone's role is. Therefore, efforts must be made to educate citizens and police officers about the philosophy, service elements, and benefits of community-oriented policing.

TRAINING   Before the first officer is assigned as a community-oriented policing officer, an in-depth training program should be designed, implemented, and completed by all officers. This should not be taken lightly. Officers need to understand their new roles and expectations and how they will be evaluated before they begin practicing COP, or COP will most likely fail.

IMPLEMENTATION   Implementing community-oriented policing requires examining such topics as where community-oriented policing should begin (i.e., beats, districts, or entire city), when it should begin (i.e., time of year or particular shifts), who should be involved initially (i.e., all patrol officers, a select number of officers, or a special unit), and what activities should occur in what sequence. Once all these issues have been addressed, implementation will be fairly easy.

PRELIMINARY EVALUATION   Once COP has had a chance to take root, preliminary monitoring and evaluating of the process of community-oriented policing are extremely important. It is at this point that organizational and administrative glitches will be discovered that could thwart further implementation efforts if not properly resolved. The discovery of such impediments is normal and should not lead to disenchantment on the part of the implementers.

FULL IMPLEMENTATION   In cities whose size requires that COP be implemented in phases, time should be allowed for pilot areas to be fully evaluated and for the steps preceding full implementation to be completed. In smaller cities, COP may be implemented citywide in one phase, provided that the groundwork (completion of the previous steps) has been properly laid.

Evaluation and Monitoring

The final step in implementing community-oriented policing is the recognition of the need for monitoring and evaluations. Monitoring should include continual feedback from the individual officers involved, departmental administrators, and selected community members. Evaluations should include the information periodically obtained from personnel throughout the police agency, the individual officers involved, and the community as a whole. The importance of continual assessment, reappraisal of strategies, planning new strategies, and implementation of such strategies cannot be overemphasized. For COP to succeed, constant updating of procedures, ongoing training of officers, and enhanced communication between police and citizens are crucial.

Analysis of Efforts

Despite what is known about COP efforts in other cities, it is important that every police agency implementing COP realize that what works in one place will not necessarily work in another. However, the philosophy remains constant. It is also important to recognize that COP is not a panacea; it will not cure all that ails us. Yet when implemented and practiced correctly, COP can go a long way toward problem solving and enhancing police services to the community.

Furthermore, it is imperative that everyone involved be made aware of their roles and what is expected of them. COP is a philosophy and practice that will take time to implement and even more time before it effects change within society. It should not be rushed, and it cannot happen overnight. It must be cultivated thoroughly and slowly. We salute those agencies that seek to implement community-oriented policing. However, we caution them that what they are embarking on is not a quick fix but rather a total overhaul of their system of delivering police services.

REALITY CHECK

What's in a Name?

During the 1990s numerous police organizations across the nation benefited from federal funding of innovative community-oriented policing programs. One fairly large agency in northern Alabama developed an exemplary program within several of their larger public housing projects. The program, which established police mini-stations* within selected housing projects, was hugely successful. It was headed by a very dedicated police lieutenant who was allowed to select the best and brightest officers to serve within the program.

COP officers worked out of apartments that had been transformed into **mini-stations**. They walked beats within the housing projects, worked with neighborhood groups to solve problems, and strove to promote cooperation and understanding within the public housing communities that they served. Crime rates within the areas served by the COP officers declined considerably. Police–community relations across the city were at an all-time high. Civic, religious, and minority community leaders hailed the success of the program.

Because of the program's success, the lieutenant in charge was soon promoted and transferred to another assignment. Several of the officers within the program were also rewarded with promotions and/or transfers to other units. Another lieutenant was assigned to head the project. He soon replaced the officers within the program with officers whom he knew and trusted.

Unfortunately the new lieutenant was a former vice unit supervisor, and many of the officers whom he selected had worked for him in the vice unit. This would not have been a problem in and of itself. The insights gained from their vice experiences could have been quite useful for the program. However, within a few months, the program was transformed into a **"Weed and Seed" program**** in which the COP officers used their mini-stations as headquarters for aggressive "get tough on drugs" operations. The neighborhood foot patrols were replaced with drug sweeps and secretive intelligence gathering projects. COP officers no longer handled the routine calls for police assistance that arose within the housing projects.

Within six months the COP program within the housing project became an enigma. Community support evaporated. Public housing residents became distrustful of the officers involved. Instead of being members of the community, they were viewed as occupiers and oppressors. Crime rates (including drug offenses) escalated as the program became increasingly controversial. Within another few months the program was abandoned due to intense criticisms from civic, religious, and minority community leaders.

*Police substations.
**Weed and Seed programs are programs supported by federal grants. They have the following components: strict law enforcement in an area, community-oriented policing initiatives, prevention intervention and treatment through local social service agencies, and neighborhood revitalization efforts. Unfortunately, in many cases the other components are ignored while strict law enforcement is emphasized.

Conclusions

The provision of police services in the United States has seen considerable change during the past two centuries. Initially, citizens were responsible for policing themselves, due to the lack of adequate police organizations capable of providing police services. As police organizations have evolved, they have utilized a variety of service delivery styles. Unfortunately, efforts to enhance discipline, effectiveness, and efficiency have too frequently resulted in isolation from the communities being served. Today's community-oriented policing strategies seek to restore the ties to those communities.

Like its predecessors, community-oriented policing as a model of police service delivery is in a constant state of evolution. Problems of conceptual complexity and difficulty of implementation have yielded mixed results among the strategies utilized thus far. Police scholars and practitioners are currently seeking to develop a community-oriented policing model that addresses these issues. Despite these challenges, community involvement in the delivery of police services is the police style of the future.

Student Checklist

1. Describe the evolution of police service delivery styles in the United States.
2. Discuss the differences among the traditional model of policing, the professional model of policing, and community-oriented policing.
3. Contrast the differences between community-oriented policing and problem-oriented policing.
4. What are the strengths and weaknesses of community-oriented policing?
5. What must be done to make community-oriented policing work in the United States?
6. Describe the SARA model and problem-oriented policing.
7. Describe the role that POP plays in community-oriented policing.

Topics for Discussion

1. What degree of community involvement in policing do you believe is appropriate in your community?
2. If you were a police chief in a large city, would you attempt to implement community-oriented policing? Why or why not?
3. Assume that you are a police chief in a large city and you have been ordered by the city council to initiate some form of community-oriented policing. What strategies would you choose, and how would you seek to implement them?
4. Discuss the ways that a problem-solving approach to non-emergency calls could benefit the police agency and the community. In your discussion give examples not provided in the text.

Bibliography

Barker, T., Hunter, R. D., and Rush, J. P. (1994). *Police Systems and Practices: An Introduction*. Upper Saddle River, NJ: Prentice Hall.

Beckman, E. (1980). *Law Enforcement in a Democratic Society*. Chicago, IL: Nelson-Hall.

Berman, J. S. (1987). *Police Administration and Progressive Reform: Theodore Roosevelt as Police Commissioner of New York*. New York: Greenwood Press.

Bopp, W. J., and Schultz, D. O. (1977). *A Short History of American Law Enforcement*. Springfield, IL: Charles C Thomas.

Bynum, T. S. (2001). *Using Analysis for Problem-Solving: A Guidebook for Law Enforcement.* Washington, D.C.: Office of Community Oriented Problem Solving, U.S. Department of Justice.

Carte, G. E., and Carte, E. H. (1975). *Police Reform in the United States: The Era of August Vollmer, 1905–1932.* Berkeley, CA: University of California Press.

Carter, D. L. (1994). "Community policing," in T. Barker, R. D. Hunter, and J. P. Rush (Eds.), *Police Systems and Practices: An Introduction.* Upper Saddle River, NJ: Prentice Hall, Chapter 13.

Cole, G. F., and Smith, C. E. (1997). *The American System of Criminal Justice*, 8th ed. Belmont, CA: Wadsworth.

Cole, G. F., and Smith, C. E. (2007). *The American System of Criminal Justice*, 11th ed. Pacific Grove, CA: Thomson/Wadsworth.

Conser, J. A., Russell, G. B., Paynich, R., and Gingerich, T. E. (2005). *Law Enforcement in the United States*, 2nd ed. Boston, MA: Jones and Bartlett.

Critchley, T. A. (1977). "Peel, Rowan, and Mayne: The British model of urban police," in P. J. Stead (Ed.), *Pioneers in Policing.* Montclair, NJ: Patterson Smith.

Critchley, T. A. (1985). "Constables and justices of the peace," in W. C. Terry, III (Ed.), *Policing Society: An Occupational View.* New York: Wiley.

Dantzker, M. L. (May 1994). "The future of municipal law enforcement is community-oriented policing: Suggestions for implementation," *Texas Police Journal*, pp. 15–17.

Davis, E. M. (April 1977). "Developing police involvement," *The Police Chief.*

Eck, J. E., and Spelman, W. (1989). "A problem-oriented approach to police service delivery," in D. J. Kenney (Ed.), *Police and Policing: Contemporary Issues.* New York: Praeger.

Goldstein, H. (1990). *Problem-Oriented Policing.* New York: McGraw-Hill.

Goldstein, H. (July 1999). "The new policing: Confronting complexity," in (Attorney General) Bill Lockyer, *COPPS: Community Oriented Policing and Problem Solving*, Crime and Prevention Center Office of the Attorney General, California Department of Justice.

Grant, H. B., and Terry, R. J. (2005). *Law Enforcement in the 21st Century.* Boston, MA: Pearson/Allyn and Bacon.

Grassie, R. G., and Crowe, T. D. (1978). *Integrated Criminal Apprehension Program: Program Implementation Guide.* Washington, D.C.: U.S. Department of Justice.

Holden, R. (1992). *Law Enforcement: An Introduction.* Upper Saddle River, NJ: Prentice Hall.

Hunter, R. D. (1990). "Three models of policing," *Police Studies*, Vol. 13, No. 3, pp. 118–124.

Hunter, R. D. (1991). "The failure of ICAP at the Tallahassee Police Department," Paper presented at the Southern Criminal Justice Association Annual Meeting, Montgomery, AL.

Jacobs, J. (1966). *Prelude to Riot.* New York: Vintage Books.

Johnson, D. R. (1981). *American Law Enforcement: A History.* St. Louis, MO: Forum Press.

Johnson, H. A., and Wolfe, N. T. (2003). *History of Criminal Justice*, 3rd ed. Cincinatti, OH: Anderson Publishing.

MacNamara, D. E. J. (1977). "August Vollmer: The vision of police professionalism," in Phillip John Stead (Ed.), *Pioneers in Policing.* Montclair, NJ: Patterson Smith.

Miller, W. R. (1977). *Cops and Bobbies: Police Authority in New York and London, 1830–1870.* Chicago, IL: University of Chicago Press.

New York Police Department. (2006). "COMPSTAT Process." *NYPD—Official New York City Police Department Web Site.* http://www.nyc.gov/html/nypd/chfdept/compstat-process.html

Peak, K., and Glensor, R. W. (2004). *Community Policing and Problem Solving: Strategies and Practices*, 4th ed. Upper Saddle River, NJ: Prentice Hall.

Reith, C. (1952). *The Blind Eye of History.* London: Faber and Faber, Ltd.

Reppetto, T. A. (1978). *The Blue Parade.* New York: Free Press.

Roberg, R. R., Kuykendall, J., and Novak, K. (2002). *Police Management*, 3rd ed. Los Angeles, CA: Roxbury Press.

Sampson, R. (2001). *Drug Dealing in Privately Owned Apartment Complexes.* Washington, D.C.: Office of Community Oriented Policing Services, U.S. Department of Justice.

Siegel, L. J., and Senna, J. J. (2007). *Essentials of Criminal Justice*, 5th ed. Pacific Grove, CA: Thomson/Wadsworth.

Skolnick, J., and Bayley, B. H. (1986). *The New Blue Line: Police Innovation in Six American Cities.* New York: Free Press.

Sparrow, M. K. (1988). *Implementing Community Policing.* Washington, D.C.: U.S. Department of Justice, National Institute of Justice.

Stead, P. J. (1985). *The Police of Britain.* New York: Macmillan.

Trojanowicz, R., and Bucqueroux, B. (1990). *Community Policing: A Contemporary Perspective.* Cincinnati, OH: Anderson.

Walker, S. (1977). *A Critical History of Police Reform.* Lexington, MA: Lexington Books.

Walker, S. (1998). *The Police in America: An Introduction*, 3rd ed. New York: McGraw-Hill.

Walker, S., and Katz, C. M. (2002). *The Police in America: An Introduction*, 4th ed. Boston, MA: McGraw-Hill.

Watson, E. M., Stone, A. R., and DeLuca, S. M. (1998). *Strategies for Community Oriented Policing.* Upper Saddle River, NJ: Prentice Hall.

Watson, T. S. (1998). "Assessing problem-solving efforts using graphical displays," in T. Shelley and A. C. Grant (Eds.), *Problem Oriented Policing: Crime-Specific Problems, Critical Issues, and Making POP Work.* Police Executive Research Forum.

Webster, B., and Conners, E. F. (1993). "Police methods for identifying community problems," *American Journal of Police*, Vol. XII, No. 1, pp. 75–101.

CHAPTER 11

Police–Community Relations and the Media

The media represents a powerful mechanism by which to communicate with the community. They can assist with publicizing community concerns and available solutions, such as services from government or community agencies or new laws or codes that will be enforced in addition, the media can have a significant impact on public perceptions of the police, crime problems, and fear of crime.

—OFFICE OF COMMUNITY ORIENTED POLICING SERVICES

It is the philosophy of the Boise Police Department to respond to media inquiries as quickly, completely and accurately as possible. This media policy is only part of the department's general philosophy to operate in an open, cooperative partnership with the community [emphasis added].

—BOISE POLICE DEPARTMENT—MEDIA GUIDE

KEY CONCEPTS

Commitment to Crime
    Coverage
Competing Rights of the
    Media

Crisis Guidelines
Exploitation of Crime News
Police Information Officer/
    Public Information Officer

Restricting Coverage Argument
Heavy Coverage Argument
Marketing Police Community
    Relations

LEARNING OBJECTIVES

Studying this chapter will enable you to:

1. Overview media commitment to the reporting of crime news.
2. Contrast the responsibility of the press and the police.
3. Justify the need for guidelines in reporting.
4. Establish police–media guidelines for routine information release, crisis situations, and hostage situations.
5. Identify ongoing blocks to positive police–media relations and strategies for resolving them.

6. Contrast individual constitutional rights and the public's right to know.

7. Recognize the importance of the media in police–community relations.

The police and the media need each other. The police want a positive public image and the media want quick and reliable crime information. The media represent a principal link between police agencies and the public they serve. This link provides the police with a means to communicate successfully with, not to, its external environment. Again, as we said earlier, police–community relations is what the police do with, not to, their community. Whether or not that relationship is successful often depends on the relationship that the police department has with its local media representatives. Media impact on virtually every citizen is enormous, and crime news is a major media topic. Except for the relatively few people who become directly involved with the police, private citizens learn of police activity, of crime prevention, of the pursuit and apprehension of criminals and their disposition in the courts by what they read in their newspapers and see and hear on television and radio. True or not, positive or negative, what a citizen reads, hears, and observes in the local media largely defines the citizen's perception of the police.

The relationship between the police and the media is sometimes one of conflict and contention. Efforts of the press to transmit the truth as they see it may help or hinder the efforts of the police. They may endanger an individual or group; increase public fear, the intensity of riots, and the credibility of terrorists; and according to some observers, create a criminal environment. They may invade privacy or defame character of individuals. They may interfere with the rights of defendants to a fair trial. On the other hand, efforts of the press may uncover crimes and criminals, exonerate those convicted unjustly, protect the public from corruption in public service, encourage public involvement in crime prevention and other special emphasis programs, decrease danger to individuals or groups, and allay excessive public fear, usually through education.

COMMUNITY RELATIONS CONTEXT

Any discussion of the mass media involves the print and electronic media, including the newspapers, magazines, television, movies, radio, and the Internet. Each separately and collectively has an impact on police–community relations. In Chapter 9, we concentrated on police discretion and selective enforcement of law, something that is often hidden from public view. In this chapter, we address police–media relations, something that is rarely hidden from the public. Some approach police–media concerns in a narrow public information or public relations context and that does have its place. We approach it, instead, in the broader context of community relations because the nature of the police–media relationship in a community is integrally related to the nature of the larger police–community relationship. The average citizen's secondhand experience of crime and the police through the media affects their attitudes toward and expectations of the police (Morgan and Newburn, 1997, p. 109).

COMMITMENT TO CRIME COVERAGE

Statistics on massive media impact would be of little interest to police if it were not for the fact that media **commitment to crime coverage** is great. Some difference of opinion exists as to how much news about murder, robbery, rape, and larceny the public really wants or demands. Yet there can be little doubt that, with or without clear public demand, maximum coverage of crime is offered. Recent surveys place the proportion of crime news to total newspaper space at anywhere from 3 to 10 percent. In an individual issue, crime news may represent 30–35 percent. Moreover, this news often is given priority space.

The Subjectivity Factor

Newspapers can emphasize crime (grossly overemphasize, the critics of the press argue) by the placement of stories on page one; by large, black, and often lurid headlines; and by other attention-getting devices. "In weighing the effect on justice," Lofton, author of *Justice and the Press*, wrote, "The play and the slant of crime news are even more important than the amount of space allotted to the subject. . . . The large and dramatic headline on the front page gets more attention from readers than a small, unprovocative item buried on the back pages" (Lofton, 1966). In large-city newspapers in particular, sensational crimes are often given more space than significant news of national and international events. The story of a $15 robbery in a small community often occupies more space in the local newspaper than the expenditure by the local government of hundreds of thousands of dollars.

Some people question whether or not a news story can ever be totally objective. Paul Harvey, the well-known radio commentator, was asked on ABC television's *Good Morning, America*, why he chose to call his newscasts commentaries rather than news reports. He explained that news reports are assumed to be objective, yet, realistically, all such reports include some elements of subjectivity (in what is reported and omitted, what is accented, the tone in which it is reported, etc.). Saying that a report is objective, then, may be misleading. Paul Harvey would rather not mislead his listeners. Because news commentary makes no claims to objectivity and is, by definition, a subjective comment on the news, Mr. Harvey stated that he felt more comfortable with that format (1983). For the same reason, Dan Abrams, NBC News legal analyst and the CEO of Abrams Research, says that there is no need for him or any citizen to presume that the swindler Bernie Madoff or Caylee Anthony's mother, Casey, is innocent (Abrams, 2009). The facts as reported in the news would suggest otherwise in both cases. However, this may complicate both cases when they go to trial, where the presumption of innocence is objective, not subjective. Anyone who watches Nancy Grace on CNN TV knows that she appears to presume that every defendant is guilty.

Restricting Coverage Argument

Although some media sources choose individually to restrict crime coverage in some specific category of crime for a specific period of time, rarely has a general policy to restrict crime coverage been made and adhered to.

In the 1930s, Curtis H. Clay, editor of the *Post-Tribune* of La Salle, Illinois, made such a policy. Although crime news was not entirely omitted from the newspaper, it was relegated to less than front-page priority for a period of two or three years. Ownership of the paper has changed. It is now called the *Daily News-Tribune*, and this policy no longer exists. Mr. Clay's rationale for his restrictive policy is instructive, however:

> The intelligent criminal enters his career deliberately, with eyes open to chances of beating the law. He believes he is smarter than the police. Publicity encourages him; he likes to see his name in the headlines. He laughs at the "dumb cops" and contin-ues his outlawry, glorying in his notoriety. If and when he gets caught, he is ready to face the music. Wasn't his name on the front page for weeks, months? . . . Publicity can't stop him. It will not injure his reputation. It will enhance it. (MacDougall, 1964, p. 389)

The above rationale continues to have merit today. Within a few days of the media sensa-tionalization of the April 1999 massacre at Columbine High School in Littleton, Colorado, a copycat incident occurred in Alberta, Canada, as did a rash of bomb and gun threats across the United States.

Heavy Coverage Argument

Using Al Capone as his central character, Thomas S. Rice, a student of the press, argued an opposite view—that of sensationalizing crime in order to fight it:

> It is far, far better for the safety of our citizens and their families that we should have too much crime news instead of too little. . . . Every improvement in police administration and methods has followed newspapers playing up crime. Constant harping on Al Capone, with the definite object of bringing him to book, was not making a hero out of him. The Chicago newspapers which led the fight against that contamination of their city had the definite purpose of causing his fall. . . . Capone and other lawbreakers have come to grief from systematic sensationalizing of their personalities as well as their deeds until the public rose in revolt. (MacDougall, 1964, p. 391)

Rice claimed that what he called "systematic sensationalizing" led not only to Capone's downfall but also to the creation of the Chicago Crime Commission, which helped improve the administration of criminal justice in that city. Similar "sensationalizing" by newspapers, Rice said, led to the creation of similar commissions in Cleveland, Baltimore, and Philadelphia.

Certainly the press often can cause public outrage that, in turn, will bring about political pressures needed to motivate appropriate police action (Barker and Carter, 1994). The media and anti-gun forces argue that the Columbine High School incident warrants heavy coverage so that the nation can show its sympathy and develop strategies to prevent the future occurrence of similar events.

EXPLOITATION OF CRIME NEWS

Whatever one thinks of the relative merits of the conflicting arguments of Clay and Rice, it is the latter's views that are practiced by virtually all publishers, editors, and reporters of the daily newspapers of America. Newspaper coverage that followed the 1946 arrest of a 17-year-old Chicago youth, William Heirens, for several brutal murders was reasonably typical: The five Chicago newspapers gave, in total, much more coverage to the Heirens case, from arrest to sentencing, than to critical national events. A study of 85 issues of Chicago newspapers during that period revealed 62 banner headlines for the Heirens case, 11 to the operations of the Office of Price Administration (which affected the pocketbooks of virtually every person in America), and only 4 to atomic bomb tests.

Whether or not the readers of U.S. newspapers share this preoccupation, a favorite topic of the media, newspapers in particular, is violent crime. And although the degree of sensationalizing in American newspapers has diminished in the last 50 years, there is more than enough evidence that the press relies heavily on crime news. There is also evidence to suggest that some newspapers exploit what they claim to be public interest in crime in order to sell their newspapers. Ed Murray, managing editor of the *Los Angeles Mirror*, wrote of the Marilyn Sheppard murder case, "This case has mystery, society, sex, and glamour," thus explaining the massive coverage U.S. papers gave to an event that was really a rather ordinary homicide (Lofton, 1966, p. 182). Herbert H. Krauch, editor of the *Los Angeles Herald and Express* (2,000 miles from the murder and trial site) said of the trial of Sam Sheppard, "It's been a long time since there's been a murder trial this good."

There are other editors who, like Murray and Krauch, are convinced that crime news sells, and there is evidence to support them. In 1956, for example, two sisters were raped and murdered, and the resultant stories boosted total circulation of the city's daily newspapers by 50,000 copies. One year later when a rapist ran wild in San Francisco, that city's four newspapers had a field day. The *Chronicle* called the attacker the "Torture Kit Rapist" (the victims had been manacled and tortured by the rapist who had used a knife, adhesive tape, manacles, and scissors). The

News called the murderer the "Fang Fiend" because he had been described by one would-be victim as having "canine teeth, which protruded fang-like over his lower lip." A 23-year-old warehouse clerk was arrested as the rapist-murderer; when another man confessed, the press abandoned the case, but the coverage had been profitable. During each day of the almost two-week coverage of the case, each San Francisco newspaper sold about 15,000 more copies than normal.

Crime news is the most frequently reported news and there are several reasons for this (Chermak and Chapman, 2007). Newspapers must attract and maintain a pool of readers, and crime news is uncomplicated and can be easily lengthened or shortened to fill needed space. Furthermore, it can be gathered from police organizations at little cost.

Along this same line, many argue that the current fascination with reality-based television programs, such as *Cops, First 48, Dallas SWAT, FBI,* and *American Detective*, leads to the beliefs that policing is an action-packed profession and criminals are predominantly violent; that crime is the work of minorities, particularly African Americans; and that the police are regularly successful in their crime-fighting activities (Worral, 2000). Equally disturbing are the incidents of questionable practices (e.g., unreasonable force and violations of constitutional rights) shown being committed by real police officers as they execute warrants and make arrests during these pseudo news events.

Morgan and Newburn (1997) state that in both Great Britain and the United States "crime is our major source of entertainment" (p. 108). The film industry relies on crime stories; the more violent the better. Newspapers, television, and radio news broadcast crime accounts. Television dramas, particularly serial programs such as *CSI* and *Law & Order*, are very popular. "True crime" reconstructions are popular in Great Britain and the United States; every night, citizens of both countries can be entertained by flashing lights and wailing sirens.

An interesting phenomenon has occurred in recent years: As serious crime has decreased, media coverage has increased. Staszak (2001) says that three reasons are responsible for this paradox:

> First, for years the media has given priority to this type of news, and old habits are hard to break. Second, consumers of electronic and printed media still follow crime coverage. Polls show that this information still holds people's interest. Third, crime coverage is easy, loaded with good visuals and sound bites, and relatively inexpensive to cover. (p. 10)

PUBLIC REACTION TO MEDIA COVERAGE

Much has been said about the impact of television programming—sometimes including the news—particularly on young members of the viewing public. This impact is behind the recent move of the television networks to restrict the amount of violence shown on TV. This voluntary movement by the television networks came about because Congress was going to examine the issue. The average American child watches more than 20 hours of TV a week, and studies have shown that youths exposed to violence and aggression on television and in the movies are more likely to copy that behavior (Siegel and Senna, 2007). Controlled laboratory studies have not confirmed this link, however, so there is a need for more research on this issue.

The media, particularly television, has been criticized by citizens, acting independently of these organizations, for what the citizens have perceived as exploitation of crime coverage. For example, a television documentary on the life of Gary Gilmore, the convicted murderer who made national news for choosing to be executed, was angrily denounced by many as a poor use of airtime. It was suggested that the time and money spent developing and airing such a product could be better spent on documentaries about people who had made positive contributions to our civilization.

NBC's 1983 program *Special Report* generated even more anger among many citizens. *Special Report* was actually a work of fiction realistically portrayed on television, using NBC's

Special Report format. The story was a modern version of H. G. Wells's *The War of the Worlds*. It ended depicting massive destruction by terrorists in South Carolina. Although disclaimers were broadcast frequently, many people believed that the story was a special news report. The anger directed at the network, however, was for what citizens viewed as network irresponsibility in presenting a realistic model for terrorists to follow.

Coverage by media of the Tylenol poisonings in Chicago in 1982 received mixed reviews by the public. Some people seemed to feel that the coverage sensationalized events and encouraged "copycat" crimes. Others expressed an appreciation of the coverage, calling it restrained and geared toward the protection of the public because the cause of the problem was not immediately apparent.

The 1992 Pepsi tampering scare led to more than 50 complaints in 23 states within days of the first complaint in Tacoma, Washington. By the end of the first week, many of these complaints had been exposed as hoaxes, and at least a dozen people had been arrested. Forensic psychiatrist Park Dietz, consultant to the FBI, states that "each nationally publicized incident generates on average 30 more seriously disruptive crimes," and asks that news organizations limit their coverage of tampering (Toufexis, 1993). N. G. Berrill, a psychologist with the New York Forensic Health Group, states that the classic tamperer is an angry, antisocial person who "gets a real sense of power from devising a plan and seeing it blossom in the media" (Toufexis, 1993).

When ABC undertook its 1983 *Crime in America* series, the network demonstrated awareness of crime coverage issues by taking great care to avoid sensationalism. The series was presented with documentation and reserve. Balance was provided by presenting issues from many points of view. The current interest in such shows as *America's Most Wanted* and *Cops* would be open to charges of crime exploitation, especially when they portray actual victims and witnesses, if it were not for their crime-fighting credentials.

The coverage of crime-related issues by the media (both print and television) is often filled with irony. Efforts to condemn and exploit crime may actually appear within the same publication or presentation. As an example, the day after the Columbine High School assault, *The Anniston Star* had a detailed story on what had transpired, along with an editorial expressing support for the citizens of Littleton and concern as to how such a tragedy could occur. In that same edition of the newspaper was an article telling how funny MTV's *Death Match* (a show in which caricatures of celebrities fought to the death) was to watch.

CONFLICT BETWEEN MEDIA AND POLICE

It is clear that accounts of sensational, violent crimes sell newspapers and draw attention to radio and television news. But do attempts by the media to report crime help or hinder police efforts to fight crime? The record does not supply a clear answer.

BOX 11.1

How TV Creates Better Criminals and Unrealistic Juries

According to a story carried in the September 30, 2005, issue of *The Week*, shows like *CSI* and *Law & Order* are teaching criminals how to avoid being caught. British police have experienced cases in which car thieves dumped bins full of cigarette butts into cars they had abandoned, effectively flooding the crime scene with DNA samples. American police have found that suspects are using gloves, condoms, and other protective gear to avoid leaving physical evidence behind. Suspects also are wiping crime scenes down and removing items they once would have overlooked.

As if savvier criminals weren't enough of a problem, prosecutors are finding that jurors have heightened expectations about the evidence presented at trials. The oversimplification of evidence collection and forensic analyses on shows such as *CSI* has created unrealistic expectations on the part of jurors. It appears that jurors who watch crime dramas expect every case to have forensic evidence to support the charges. Even in relatively straightforward cases, juries are citing the lack of physical evidence in acquitting defendants.

A Hindrance and a Help

From the point of view of the police, overcoverage and sensationalizing of crime may not in themselves produce law enforcement problems. Occasionally, however, the press works at cross-purposes with the police, and law enforcement is hindered. This is particularly true in kidnapping cases, where the relationship between press and police is the most critical; the safety of the victim often depends on the cooperation given by the press to the police. Former FBI Director J. Edgar Hoover once compiled a list of cases in which he claimed the media had seriously hindered the work of his agency. One such case cited by Hoover was the Mattson kidnapping. Newspaper reporters prevented contact with the kidnappers of young Charles Mattson by refusing to leave the neighborhood of the Mattson home in Seattle. The boy's father received a letter from the kidnappers containing a newspaper picture of reporters around the house and said there would be no contact until they left. The Mattson boy was later found dead, obviously murdered by the kidnappers. In the kidnapping of Peter Levine, a reporter who was trying to verify rumors that the boy was missing phoned the boy's father who, caught off guard, admitted that his child was missing and said that he was willing to pay ransom. Warned by the kidnapper to prevent publicity, the father tried to persuade the newspapers to suppress the story, but the papers refused. Later, the headless body of the kidnapped boy was found floating in Long Island Sound.

A more recent case demonstrates how the media can hinder police operations and endanger the lives of others. In 1998, in Tampa, Florida, a three-time cop killer was chased to a convenience store, where he took a hostage. The police were unable to contact the hostage taker because a radio reporter had called the store and was conducting a live interview on the air. To further complicate matters, live television coverage of the event was describing the movements of the tactical unit, and there was a TV in the store (Rosenthal, 2001a). The event was finally resolved when the cop killer released the hostage and committed suicide. This event led to a voluntary agreement between the police and the local media (described later).

In another recent hostage case, news stations in Baltimore, Maryland, refrained from revealing information, conducting interviews, or showing images while the police conducted a four-day effort to resolve the situation and free three hostages, including a 12-year-old boy (Trigoboff, 2000). Agreements between the police and the media, whereby the media agrees not to provide live coverage of incidents involving hostages and barricaded suspects, have been in place in Portland, Oregon, since 1998 and in Boston, Massachusetts, since 1999 (Rosenthal, 1999a). Media cooperation with the police has also drawn criticism from some in the media. During a potential suicide attempt in Denver, Colorado, two television stations provided equipment complete with station logos and allowed two police officers to pose as TV journalists to talk a mentally disturbed person off a downtown statue (Sotelo, 2000). The TV stations were criticized by some in the media.

In other cases, the press has shown restraint and cooperation with the police. In the Lindbergh baby kidnapping case, the press voluntarily suppressed the contents of the original ransom note and the fact that the U.S. Treasury Department had sent the serial numbers of the bank notes used as ransom to banks across the country. The press also refrained from following Lindbergh on his futile trips to meet the kidnapper and deliberately misled the kidnapper by publishing false information about police activity. However, such cooperation did not save the Lindbergh infant. The media cooperation eventually led to the capture, trial, and execution of Bruno Richard Hauptmann for the kidnapping and murder of young Lindbergh.

Generally, the press has become more sensitive in kidnapping cases. In 1954, a 60-hour "conspiracy of silence" by all San Francisco newspapers, wire services, and broadcasters was credited with saving the life of a kidnapped realtor. A year later, however, the *New York Daily News* was widely, and properly, condemned by police and others for failing to go along with other New York–area newspapers that had refrained from publishing accounts of the kidnapping of one-month-old Peter Weinberger (MacDougall, 1964, p. 395). Frightened by the crowd at the site selected for the transfer of the ransom money, which had been reported in the *Daily News*, the kidnapper killed the baby.

The press has occasionally thwarted police work in other cases as well. By reporting detailed clues discovered by the police or announcing the time and place of a planned investigation, the press can—and in some cases actually does—tip off the criminal, who may destroy the evidence and avoid capture. Again, though, the record of the press is mixed, for persistent, imaginative reporters have helped the police to solve crimes and, in some cases, have solved the crimes themselves. The brutal murder of Bobby Franks in Chicago in 1923 was solved by the detective work of two reporters of the *Chicago Daily News*, whose suspicions led to the arrest and conviction of Nathan Leopold and Richard Loeb. In 1930, the *Kansas City Star* solved the murder of Mrs. A. D. Payne by her husband. Ku Klux Klan leader D. C. Stephenson went to prison for the murder of Madge Oberhalzer as a result of the investigative efforts of the *Indianapolis Times* and the *Vincennes Commercial*. The *Chicago Daily News* won a Pulitzer Prize for uncovering the stealing of millions of dollars from the Illinois State Treasury by the state auditor, Orville Hodge.

Other media exposés include the Watergate findings that ended the presidency of Richard Nixon and brought charges against his aides, and the revelation of President Bill Clinton's affair with Monica Lewinsky that ultimately led to his 1999 impeachment trial for perjury and obstruction of justice. The media's coverage of the Clinton presidency and its several scandals has led to charges by Clinton supporters that he, his wife, and staff have been harassed by the media. Interestingly, the coverage of leaks of a CIA operative's identity and the investigation of payoffs by lobbyists led to similar allegations by supporters of former president Bush.

The complete list of similar exposés of crime is long, evidence that the press and police are not necessarily natural adversaries.

Champions of the Innocent

The press has uncovered crime and criminals, and it can point to a long record of exonerating people already convicted of crime. In 1932, Joe Majczek was sent to prison for life for a murder he insisted he had not committed. Twelve years later, a series of articles in the *Chicago Times* revealed that he had been convicted largely on the testimony of a witness who had been threatened with prosecution for violating the Prohibition law unless she identified Majczek as the murderer. Majczek thereupon was freed from prison, fully pardoned, and compensated by the state for his twelve years in prison. The same year that Majczek was freed, a young, inarticulate black, Willie Calloway, was sentenced to life imprisonment for murder. His case came to the attention of reporter Ken McCormack of the *Detroit Free Press*, who wrote a series of articles that helped to exonerate Calloway. Calloway was then released after eight years in prison for a crime he did not commit. The scathing attack on death penalty convictions in Illinois by the *Chicago Tribune* from January 10 to 14, 1999, is widely believed to have led to Illinois Governor George Ryan's moratorium on executions until the state's death penalty procedures were reviewed. The highly successful Innocence Project owes much of its success to investigative reporters who have pursued witnesses and uncovered evidence. Barry Scheck, the cofounder of the Innocence Project, was recently quoted as saying: "When procedural mechanisms begin to fail, the press is the last resort for the public to find out the truth" (Arango, 2009).

A CLEAR NEED FOR GUIDELINES

The Background

Essentially, police and the media have different functions, and the difference can bring them into conflict. The police's task is to prevent crime, maintain law and order, protect the citizens of the community, and apprehend lawbreakers and bring them to justice. The media in a free society have an obligation to seek out and report the truth, even though the truth may embarrass or hinder the police. The information becomes a product that they package and sell in competition with other media. Nevertheless, the Society of Professional Journalists has had a Code of Ethics since 1926 (see Figure 11.1). This code does not specifically cover all the incidents that may arise in the reporting of crime-related information (protection of rape victims, juveniles, hostage and

Society of Professional Journalists

Code of Ethics

Preamble

Members of the Society of Professional Journalists believe that public enlightenment is the forerunner of justice and the foundation of democracy. The duty of the journalist is to further those ends by seeking truth and providing a fair and comprehensive account of events and issues. Conscientious journalists from all media and specialties strive to serve the public with thoroughness and honesty. Professional integrity is the cornerstone of a journalist's credibility.

Members of the Society share a dedication to ethical behavior and adopt this code to declare the Society's principles and standards of practice.

Seek Truth and Report It

Journalists should be honest, fair and courageous in gathering, reporting and interpreting information.

Journalists should:

► Test the accuracy of information from all sources and exercise care to avoid inadvertent error. Deliberate distortion is never permissible.

► Diligently seek out subjects of news stories to give them the opportunity to respond to allegations of wrongdoing.

► Identify sources whenever feasible. The public is entitled to as much information as possible on sources' reliability.

► Always question sources' motives before promising anonymity. Clarify conditions attached to any promise made in exchange for information. Keep promises.

► Make certain that headlines, news teases and promotional material, photos, video, audio, graphics, sound bites and quotations do not misrepresent. They should not oversimplify or highlight incidents out of context.

► Never distort the content of news photos or video. Image enhancement for technical clarity is always permissible. Label montages and photo illustrations.

► Avoid misleading re-enactments or staged news events. If re-enactment is necessary to tell a story, label it.

► Avoid undercover or other surreptitious methods of gathering information except when traditional open methods will not yield information vital to the public. Use of such methods should be explained as part of the story.

► Never plagiarize.

► Tell the story of the diversity and magnitude of the human experience boldly, even when it is unpopular to do so.

► Examine their own cultural values and avoid imposing those values on others.

► Avoid stereotyping by race, gender, age, religion, ethnicity, geography, sexual orientation, disability, physical appearance or social status.

► Support the open exchange of views, even views they find repugnant.

► Give voice to the voiceless; official and unofficial sources of information can be equally valid.

► Distinguish between advocacy and news reporting. Analysis and commentary should be labeled and not misrepresent fact or context.

► Distinguish news from advertising and shun hybrids that blur the lines between the two.

► Recognize a special obligation to ensure that the public's business is conducted in the open and that government records are open to inspection.

Minimize Harm

Ethical journalists treat sources, subjects and colleagues as human beings deserving of respect.

Journalists should:

► Show compassion for those who may be affected adversely by news coverage. Use special sensitivity when dealing with children and inexperienced sources or subjects.

► Be sensitive when seeking or using interviews or photographs of those affected by tragedy or grief.

► Recognize that gathering and reporting information may cause harm or discomfort. Pursuit of the news is not a license for arrogance.

► Recognize that private people have a greater right to control information about themselves than do public officials and others who seek power, influence or attention. Only an overriding public need can justify intrusion into anyone's privacy.

► Show good taste. Avoid pandering to lurid curiosity.

► Be cautious about identifying juvenile suspects or victims of sex crimes.

► Be judicious about naming criminal suspects before the formal filing of charges.

► Balance a criminal suspect's fair trial rights with the public's right to be informed.

Act Independently

Journalists should be free of obligation to any interest other than the public's right to know.

Journalists should:

► Avoid conflicts of interest, real or perceived.

► Remain free of associations and activities that may compromise integrity or damage credibility.

► Refuse gifts, favors, fees, free travel and special treatment, and shun secondary employment, political involvement, public office and service in community organizations if they compromise journalistic integrity.

► Disclose unavoidable conflicts.

► Be vigilant and courageous about holding those with power accountable.

► Deny favored treatment to advertisers and special interests and resist their pressure to influence news coverage.

► Be wary of sources offering information for favors or money; avoid bidding for news.

Be Accountable

Journalists are accountable to their readers, listeners, viewers and each other.

Journalists should:

► Clarify and explain news coverage and invite dialogue with the public over journalistic conduct.

► Encourage the public to voice grievances against the news media.

► Admit mistakes and correct them promptly.

► Expose unethical practices of journalists and the news media.

► Abide by the same high standards to which they hold others.

Sigma Delta Chi's first Code of Ethics was borrowed from the American Society of Newspaper Editors in 1926. In 1973, Sigma Delta Chi wrote its own code, which was revised in 1984 and 1987. The present version of the Society of Professional Journalists' Code of Ethics was adopted in September 1996.

FIGURE 11.1

terrorist incidents, etc.). However, as we have seen, the police and the media have entered into voluntary agreement (described later).

Competing Rights

Conflict between police and media often arises because the police are caught in the crossfire of competing rights under two key amendments to the U.S. Constitution. On one hand, the First Amendment guarantees an almost absolute right to print virtually anything, free of legal restraint. The Sixth Amendment, however, guarantees every person the right to a fair trial, which means a trial by peers who have not been influenced by prejudicial publicity before or during trial. Individuals in our society have a right to privacy and, within limits, not to have their character defamed. How can these competing rights be resolved fairly?

According to the U.S. Supreme Court in *Branzburg* v. *Hayes* [408 U.S. 665, 682–685, 92 S.Ct., 2646, 2657–2658, 33 LEd 2nd. 626 640–642 (1972)], "Newsmen have no constitutional right of access to the scenes of crime or disaster when the general public is excluded and they may be prohibited from attending or publishing information about trials if such restrictions are necessary to ensure a defendant a fair trial before an impartial tribunal."

Recognizing the Need for Guidelines

The necessity for developing guidelines for resolving or controlling conflicts involving the responsibilities or rights of the media, the police, and citizens (victims and defendants) has not always been recognized. However, four sensational cases were largely responsible for spotlighting or demonstrating this need.

THE BRUNO HAUPTMANN TRIAL   Before 1935, there was comparatively little concern for the rights of suspects and defendants, some of whom were badly treated by the police or the press, or by both. Then came the trial of Bruno Hauptmann for the kidnap-murder of the Lindbergh infant. The press, which had shown such commendable restraint before Hauptmann's capture, treated the trial at Flemington, New Jersey, as a combination circus and passion play, as did the prosecution, the defense, and the public. The prosecutor told a reporter that he "would wrap the kidnap ladder around Hauptmann's neck," a threat that was duly carried in the newspapers of the day. The defense counsel ordered stationery for Hauptmann to answer his "fan mail"; the letterhead carried a facsimile of the kidnap ladder. The press allied itself with the prosecution, charging once that the defendant was making "senseless denials" and, on another occasion, with being "a thing lacking in human characteristics." Although photographs had been forbidden in the courtroom, not only still pictures but motion pictures as well were taken and displayed to the public.

It was the Hauptmann trial that first compelled the organized bar to consider the need for a code of conduct that might prevent the improprieties and excesses of that trial. An 18-member committee of newspaper reporters, broadcasters, editors, publishers, and lawyers agreed on a general code of conduct to guide prosecutors, defense counsel, and the press in future criminal trials. The code drawn up by this committee was accepted by the American Bar Association but, except for Canon 35 (which prohibited photographs in the courtroom), the guidelines were generally ignored until two events many years later—the assassination of President John F. Kennedy and the Supreme Court decision in the Sam Sheppard case.

THE ASSASSINATION OF PRESIDENT JOHN F. KENNEDY   The aftermath of the Kennedy assassination in 1963 did more than anything since the Hauptmann trial to spur new remedies for the injustices of pretrial publicity. "From the moment of his arrest until his murder two days later," the American Civil Liberties Union concluded, "Lee Harvey Oswald was tried and convicted many times over in the newspapers, on the radio, and over television by the public statements of the Dallas law enforcement officials. Time and time again, high-ranking police and prosecution officials stated their complete satisfaction that Oswald was the assassin. As their investigation uncovered one piece of evidence after the other, the results were broadcast to the public" (Lofton, 1966, p. 130). The Warren Commission reached similar conclusions in its 1964 report and also criticized District Attorney Henry Wade and Police Chief Jesse E. Curry for their statements to the press which, the commission believed, were potentially harmful to both the prosecution and the defense. The commission criticized the press, too, for its lack of self-discipline, which created general disorder in the police and court buildings in Dallas. The events in Dallas that weekend, the commission said, "are a dramatic affirmation of the need for steps to bring about a proper balance between the right of the public to be informed and the right of an individual to a fair and impartial trial" (Lofton, 1966, p. xii).

THE TRIAL OF DR. SAM SHEPPARD   The need for definitive guidelines did not become critical until 1966 when the Supreme Court, in the Sam Sheppard decision, told the bench, the bar, the police, and the press that every defendant in a criminal case was entitled to a trial unpolluted by prejudicial pretrial publicity. It is widely held that the 1955 trial of Dr. Sheppard is one of the most flagrant examples of irresponsible behavior, not only by the news media but by the judiciary and law enforcement officials as well. The Supreme Court, in reversing Sheppard's conviction, agreed.

In its Sheppard decision, the Court offered explicit guidance on how trial courts and police should seek to preserve the defendant's right to a fair and impartial trial, preventing interference by the press. Many of these strictures were incorporated into guidelines that were later drawn up by joint bench–bar–press committees in various states, although many of the Supreme Court "rules" were already contained in such guidelines established prior to 1966.

THE TRIAL OF O. J. SIMPSON   The 1995 trial of former football star O. J. Simpson for the murder of Nicole Brown Simpson and Ronald Goldman received extensive media coverage. The nation was to a large degree divided along racial lines. African Americans celebrated when the defense's allegations of police incompetence and possible planting of evidence by a racist police officer led to an acquittal. Many European Americans felt that Simpson's $10 million legal "dream team" had used race to defeat compelling hair, fiber, and blood evidence that proved him guilty. Ultimately, both critics and supporters complained about the media's coverage.

MORE RECENT CASES   Due perhaps to the media's attention to the "War on Terror," political unrest, and the impacts of natural disasters such as Hurricane Katrina, there have not been as many sensational trials that received national attention in recent years. However, there have been at least three cases that have received scrutiny from the nation's media.

The first case is the murder of Jonbenet Ramsey. On December 25, 1996, 6-year-old Jonbenet was abducted from her bedroom, sexually assaulted, and murdered in the basement of her parents' home. Media from across the country followed the investigation for months. Speculation ran rampant as to who had committed the hideous crime. The use of the Ramsey's writing utensils in the preparation of a ransom note and references within the note that only a family insider would have been aware indicate that the killer was someone with intimate knowledge of the family. The hiring of an attorney and their perceived lack of cooperation with the police and district attorney's office created a cloud of suspicion that follows the Ramsey family to this day. The Boulder Police Department worked for years interviewing hundreds of witnesses to no avail. At the time of this writing, despite a series of books, television specials, and the employment of some of the nation's foremost investigators and forensic scientists, the case remains unsolved.

The second case has a much happier ending. On June 5, 2002, 14-year-old Elizabeth Smart was abducted from her bedroom in Salt Lake City, Utah. Her younger sister, who was in the same bedroom and witnessed the abduction, reported that a man with a gun had taken Elizabeth. Despite a thorough investigation on the part of the police, efforts to find Elizabeth or even determine what had happened to her were futile. The national media closely followed the case, and many comparisons were made to the Ramsey case. The willing cooperation from the child's parents did help dispel the type of suspicions raised in that case. Initial investigative efforts focused on a young drifter from West Virginia who had a history of bizarre behavior and who had been in the area. He was later removed from the list of likely suspects. Handyman Richard Ricci, who died in prison while serving a sentence for having burglarized the Smarts' home at another time, would remain a suspect. In October 2002, the younger sister would tell her parents that she thought she might know who the kidnapper was. She stated that he resembled a transient whom the family had employed for a few hours in 2001. The man had called himself Emmanuel. On March 12, 2003, police received calls that "Emmanuel" had been seen in the nearby city of Sandy, Utah, accompanied by two women. Police located Emmanuel and discovered that Elizabeth Smart, disguised in a wig, sunglasses, and an overcoat, was one of the women with him. Emmanuel, actually self-described prophet Brian David Mitchell, and his wife, Wanda Eileen

Barzee, had kept the child with them through threats of death if she attempted to escape. Elizabeth, was happily reunited with her family.

The third case, the murder of Caylee Anthony, is still in the news and has the potential for becoming the most publicized in U.S. history. The child's mother, Casey, is the chief suspect in the case, and several crime news commentators, such as Nancy Grace, appear to be convinced of her guilt as are many members of the public due to the media coverage. The broad Florida public-records laws have allowed thousands of pages of legal documents to be released to the media (Edwards, 2009). Those documents have included forensic-evidence reports, transcripts of detectives' interview, and details about parties and clubs she frequented, as well as information about her family's financial difficulties. Every aspect of the 22-year-old mother's life has become public. The authors cannot recall a case that has received this much media attention. The outcome of all this media attention on future court action is unpredictable at this time.

In addition to the issues raised earlier about reality-based television programs (overemphasis on violence, misrepresenting the nature of police work, overrepresentation of minorities, etc.), there are numerous constitutional issues involved. At issue in a U.S. Supreme Court decision in 1999 (*Wilson* v. *Layne*, U.S. Lexis 3633) was whether or not police–media ride-along programs violated the Fourth Amendment rights of parties inside private areas. The Supreme Court ruled that the presence of the media at the invitation of law enforcement officers during a search violated the Fourth Amendment rights of the Wilsons (Crawford, 2000). This decision will cause a reexamination of police–media ride-alongs and the presence of other third parties during police operations.

Complicating Issues

CONCERNS OF VICTIMS AND WITNESSES   Publication of a victim's name and address may increase potential danger to that person and lessen his or her ability to resolve the personal emotional trauma related to the event. This is especially true for rape victims. There are times when witnesses also may be endangered in much the same way by media coverage. Media restraint in these areas requires guidelines. Only recently have the concerns of victims and witnesses been considered in any organized way by the media.

The highly publicized 10-day rape trial of William Kennedy Smith in 1991 raised two issues concerning media coverage: the use of TV cameras in the courtroom and media protection of the privacy rights of the rape victim. The legal community was deeply divided over the issue of TV coverage (*USA Today*, 1991). Nevertheless, TV coverage was allowed in this trial, and the privacy issue became a source of controversy. CNN News hid the face of the alleged rape victim, but it was not long before she was identified. The same issues were raised in the highly publicized 1992 rape trial of heavyweight boxing champion Mike Tyson. The state of Indiana, which normally does not allow courtroom TV coverage, allowed the use of closed-circuit TV to accommodate more than a hundred news organizations that covered the trial.

It is easy to imagine the horror of learning of the death of a loved one by way of the media news. Because the news may be broadcast or published before next of kin can be notified of the death of a family member, guidelines for release of the name and address of the deceased are necessary.

THE NEED TO GET THE FULL STORY   A counterargument to the above is the need for the media to get the story right. Although the need to protect victims and witnesses is of vital importance, so is the need to see that justice is being carried out correctly. If the media publishes only what they are provided by the police and prosecutors, miscarriages of justice, systemic problems, and questionable practices could be overlooked. Sometimes the suspect's story needs to be told as well.

Crisis Situations

DISTURBANCES AND UNREST   The advent of militancy in the 1960s, urban guerrilla warfare, student unrest and demonstrations, civil rights protests, riots, and fire bombings have created new problems for the police. Effective working arrangements with the mass media in these situations are critical.

One commentator said, "Nothing, but nothing, ever happens the same way after you put a television or movie camera on it." Television, with its capacity for instantaneous reporting, has often incited violence, usually unintentionally, by attracting those who seek attention. Both rioters and police have been known to perform for the media. Occasionally the media has manufactured the news. During the riots in Newark, New Jersey, for example, a newspaper photographer from a New York newspaper was seen urging, and finally convincing, a young black boy to throw a rock for the benefit of the cameras. In Chicago in the late 1960s, a television camera crew was seen leading two "hippie" girls into an area filled with National Guardsmen. As the cameras started rolling, one of the girls cried on cue, "Don't beat me, don't beat me!" Virtually all the media outlets have their own rules against this sort of staging, but occasionally the rules tend to be forgotten during a major upheaval.

A less violent confrontation was described by an observer in the 1960s after a three-man television crew arrived at a labor picket line. Although the crew chief was disappointed because, from a pictorial standpoint, it was not much of a demonstration, he decided to film it anyway ("We may as well get it."). As the observer related, "The light man held up his 30-foot lamp and laid a 4-foot beam of light across the picket line. Instantly, the marchers' heads snapped up, their eyes flashed. They threw up their arms in the clenched-fist salute. Some made a V with their fingers, and they held up their banners for the cameras." The event was transformed into something substantially different than it would have been had not the television crew arrived to record it.

Immense damage can result during a civil disturbance as a result of a lack of restraint by press or police, by inaccurate reporting, by journalistic sensationalizing, by police overreaction, or by a breakdown in communication between the press and the police. A false rumor that police had killed a black cab driver in Newark, New Jersey, and an unfounded report of the killing of a 7-year-old boy in Plainfield, New Jersey, fanned major disturbances in those cities. In Tampa, Florida, a deputy sheriff died in the early stages of a riot that intensified after both the Associated Press and United Press International reported that he had been killed by rioters when, in actuality, he had suffered a heart attack.

Much concern was expressed by the media and the public regarding a man who "performed" a suicide for the camera. Many observers believed that no suicide would have taken place if the media had not covered the "event." Some local television stations, acknowledging that "acting" for the camera during disturbances adds to existing problems, use unmarked units on the scene, and thus maintain a low profile (Figure 11.2).

Although television coverage does provide incentive to violence, police should realize that coverage can also have the opposite effect. No one, including demonstrators, wants his or her unlawful acts recorded on camera (Figure 11.3). The presence of cameras can also have a restraining influence on overzealous police authorities; during the late 1950s and early 1960s, the U.S. Justice Department encouraged media coverage of civil rights demonstrations in the belief that it would inhibit violence by unsympathetic police in the Southern states.

Except in the rare instance when police intend to engage in improper conduct, it is in their interest to have reporters present. In Chicago in the 1960s, comedian Dick Gregory complained that police had been "brutal" in arresting him. Station WMAQ-TV carried Gregory's statement without comment, then reran the film showing Gregory being arrested, a film that did not bear out his claim. The Chicago Police were grateful.

Media representatives have long been aware of their grave responsibilities during riot situations. As far back as June 1963, in anticipation of confrontations in Selma, Alabama, Richard Salant, president of CBS News, sent a memorandum to his news personnel at Selma. He warned of "the unsettling effect on a stimulated crowd that the TV camera has" and requested that personnel and equipment be as unobtrusive as possible and that cameras be turned away or covered when there was any danger that their presence might aggravate tensions. In the 1980s in Miami, Florida, the media helped both to increase and decrease tensions in that already tense community.

FIGURE 11.2 How could press coverage help or hinder police efforts in resolving this crisis?

Getty Images, Inc.-Stone Allstock.

In December 1979, Arthur McDuffie was involved in a high-speed chase with the police in the streets of Liberty City, a ghetto area of Miami. When he was stopped, a struggle ensued from which McDuffie emerged in a coma. He died four days later from massive skull injuries. Four officers were charged with his death and were acquitted in May 1980. In the riot that followed this decision, 18 more deaths occurred in the Liberty City ghetto. The media in this instance helped to increase the tensions in Liberty City. The case became a major national media event, and many officials believe that the coverage contributed to the problems that already existed (Katzenbach, 1980). In contrast, in early 1983, when blacks were again prepared to riot over another incident, media coverage helped to prevent more violence. Leaders were televised advising restraint. Community administrators were covered promising an investigation that was forthcoming. This strategy has been emulated in other cities during the 1980s and 1990s with positive results. A noted exception is the Los Angeles riot of 1992 (discussed previously).

Hostage and Terrorist Activity

Of growing concern is the disturbing frequency of hostage and terrorist activity involving mass media and local police in almost free-for-all, three-sided confrontation. This has been exacerbated by technological advances in communications such as satellites, microwave relays, and portable cameras and recorders. Most disturbing of all is the occurrence of the "media events" that are staged by various terrorist groups or lone psychotics solely to attract mass public attention to their particular demands or problems. A particularly disturbing event of this nature took place in Berkeley, California, in 1990. Mehrdad Dashti held 33 hostages in a hotel bar while he

FIGURE 11.3 Although television coverage of scenes of potential disorder may provide an incentive to violence, it may also deter violence, since neither demonstrators nor police wish to have unlawful acts recorded on camera.

Courtesy of Birmingham Police Department.

made a series of barely coherent demands and statements defining his purpose. Even though there was a television set in the bar, TV crews broadcast the event live and reported on what the police were doing outside. The hostage situation was finally resolved with eight hostages shot, one fatally, and Dashti shot dead by the police. This event resulted in a debate over media disclosures of police operations (Goodman, 1990).

Vetter and Perlstein (1991) stated that the 1977 Hanafi Muslim siege in Washington, D.C., is a good example of how the media can be used to make a big story out of a minor terrorist incident. On March 9, 1977, Hamaas Abdul Khaalis, a Hanafi Muslim leader, and 12 members of his religious sect seized 134 hostages. Khaalis's demands were that the murderers (rival religious sect) of his family members be handed over to him so that he could exact justice. He also wanted the movie *Mohammed, Messenger of God* banned in the United States because it was blasphemous. Television reporters began broadcasting live from the scene, and journalists tied up telephone lines by interviewing the terrorists. According to Schmid and DeGraaf (1982), during the three days of the incident, NBC spent more than 53 percent of its evening news on the story, CBS spent more than 31 percent, and ABC spent 40 percent. One news reporter, seeing the police bringing food to the terrorists, reported erroneously that the police were preparing to assault the building. Another reporter called Khaalis and told him that the police were trying to trick him.

In 1993, the entire world was mesmerized by the siege of the Branch Davidian compound in Waco, Texas, and the deaths of four federal officers during the initial siege. There are allegations that the cult members were tipped off about the assault by media representatives. However, no evidence has been found to support these charges.

Of major concern and frustration to the police in these events is the apparent erosion of police control over the situation as a result of the presence of an aggressive, emotion-charged press corps. At times, the terrorist–media contact becomes more amiable than the police–media contact. The obvious presence of physical danger to hostages, police, and others heightens the frustration felt by police.

Since the 1977 Washington, D.C., situation occurred, many attempts have been made to resolve differences between police and press. Negotiations have taken place in many cities between news media and police in an effort to establish workable guidelines for both "sides," should such crisis occur in their city. At the time of this writing, the authors are aware of four police–media agreements that establish voluntary guidelines for live media coverage of critical incidents (Portland, Oregon; Tampa, Florida; Miami/Fort Lauderdale/Palm Beach, Florida; and Sahuarita, Arizona). Such agreements set out guidelines for the media and the police. They are not, nor can they be, one-sided restrictions on either party.

SETTING GUIDELINES

Information Release

Guidelines—or statements of principles, as they are called in some states—do exist. Some examples include a Bar-Press-Broadcasters Joint Statement of Principles in Oregon; in Massachusetts, a Guide for Bar and News Media; in Kentucky, a Press Association Statement of Principles for Pretrial Reporting; in New York, a Code on Fair Trial and Free Press of the New York County Lawyers Association; and in Philadelphia, a Statement of Policy of the Philadelphia Bar Association. In 1965 the U.S. Department of Justice adopted rules, later to be known as the Katzenbach Guidelines (after the then attorney general), which dealt with release of information relating to criminal proceedings by police personnel of the department and its agencies, such as the Federal Bureau of Investigation.

Most such guidelines, particularly as they apply to police, are basically similar. The following discussion is of two sets of guidelines. The first was developed in 1968 by the Wisconsin Advisory Commission on Pretrial Publicity (including a local police chief, a county sheriff, a district attorney, newspaper reporters and broadcasters, several academicians, and a trial judge). The second set was first developed in 1975 by the Professional Standards Division of the International Association of Chiefs of Police, with input from public information officers from all regions of the United States. These are relatively typical of those developed by other states and in local communities.

The Wisconsin Guidelines

These guidelines acknowledge that the media have the right to publish, and the public has the right to have, the truth about the administration of criminal justice. On the other hand, law enforcement officials have the right and responsibility to protect the individual's right to a fair trial. The guidelines, therefore, were to aid these officials in deciding what information should or should not be released.

WHAT CAN BE RELEASED   After arrest, the police can make public the following information under the Wisconsin guidelines:

- The text or substance of the charge.
- The name of the investigative and arresting agency.
- The length of the investigation.
- The defendant's name, address, age, employment, and marital status.

In most states, the police cannot by law release the name of a juvenile defendant. During an investigation, the police can release photographs of suspects' "wanted" posters and other information deemed necessary to the investigation or the apprehension of suspects.

WHAT CANNOT BE RELEASED   The Wisconsin guidelines advise that the police not release the following kinds of information:

- Any confessions, admissions, or incriminating statements by the suspect.
- The results of investigative procedures (e.g., polygraph tests, fingerprint identification, and ballistics tests).
- Any statement by police officers that might reflect on the credibility of witnesses and expected testimony.
- Any expression of opinion by police officers regarding the character or the guilt or innocence of the accused.

PROBLEM AREAS   On some matters, guidelines have been somewhat difficult to formulate, and different codes take different positions on what is to be done.

1. *Interviews.* Under the Wisconsin guidelines (and most others) the police will allow the media to interview a defendant only if the person in custody requests it and has been advised of the right to counsel. If the defendant already has an attorney, that attorney must be advised of the request for interview.
2. *Photographs.* Should the police grant media requests to photograph or televise suspects while in custody? The Wisconsin guidelines position is that the practice should neither be encouraged nor discouraged. The police should not deliberately pose the suspect, but they may give out a current photo of the suspect.
3. *The circumstances of arrest.* Like most guidelines, those in Wisconsin allow the police to make *a factual, unadorned* statement of the circumstances surrounding an arrest (e.g., possession of contraband or weapons, and resistance to arrest).
4. *Previous criminal record.* The appearance of a suspect's prior record in the press could influence a potential juror; on the other hand, the record is supposed to be public. The Wisconsin guidelines (and most others) resolve the dilemma by instructing police not to volunteer the information, but to make it available on specific inquiry about it.

Police Operational Response

Guidelines like those adopted in Wisconsin indicate what information should or should not be released to the media, but they do not indicate who in police agencies should make the relevant decisions. Nevertheless, the following rules seem sensible:

1. Statements relating to crime should be made by the ranking member of the department who is present before representatives of the media.
2. If no ranking officer is present, the police officer at the scene of the crime should be entitled to supply "basic and unelaborated information."
3. Where there is doubt as to whether information should be released or withheld, police officers should always choose to withhold it. (If the decision proves wrong, it can be corrected later; a decision to release, on the other hand, cannot be corrected later.)

Advantages of Guidelines

Measures to restrict the flow of prejudicial pretrial publicity may be implemented as a result of statute or court order. The police, press, and members of the bar, however, are free to take such measures on their own as the four departments mentioned earlier have done with critical incidents. Of course, such voluntary guidelines are not legally binding; nevertheless, by properly disciplining violators, a police agency can ensure that members of the department observe the guidelines.

BOX 11.2
CALEA Guidelines on Public Information

54.1 Public Information

54.1.1 A written directive states that the agency is committed to informing the community and the news media of events within the public domain that are handled by or involve the agency.
  Commentary: To operate effectively, law enforcement agencies must obtain the support of the public they serve. By providing the news media and the community with information on agency administration and operations, the agency can foster a relationship of mutual trust, cooperation, and respect. (Mandatory for all agencies)

54.1.2 A written directive establishes a public information function, to include:

- assisting news personnel in covering routine news stories, and at the scenes of incidents;
- being available for on-call responses to the news media;
- preparing and distributing agency news releases;
- arranging for, and assisting at, news conferences;
- coordinating and authorizing the release of information about victims, witnesses, and suspects;
- assisting in crisis situations within the agency; and
- coordinating and authorizing the release of information concerning confidential agency investigations and operations.

  Commentary: The agency's written directive should address how the agency will handle potential situations in which the news media are interested in agency operations, as well as situations in which the agency wishes to generate media interest. (Mandatory)

54.1.3 A written directive specifies a position in the agency responsible for the public information function.
  Commentary: The intent of the standard is to ensure that the agency has a point of control for disseminating information to the community, to the media, and to other criminal justice agencies.
  In smaller agencies these activities may be assigned as part-time responsibilities; in larger agencies the activities may be assigned to a full-time public information officer or component.
  The directive should also establish procedures to guide the actions of the public information officer in daily operations, as well as at the scene of crimes, catastrophes, special events, and unusual occurrences. (Mandatory)

54.1.4 A written directive establishes the procedures for press releases, to include:

- frequency of press releases;
- subject matter; and
- media recipients.

  Commentary: The agency should have procedures that address the criteria to be used in determining (1) the need for press releases on a daily or weekly basis, or as necessitated by specific occurrences in the agency's service area, and (2) the content and the extent of coverage of agency activities.
  The directive should also include policy on disseminating material in such a manner as to ensure that first-release information is equally available to all news media. Press releases may be issued in bulletin form or through tape-recorded messages, as long as the agency has addressed the equal-access issue. (Optional)

54.1.5 A written directive identifies—by name or position held—those within the agency who may release information to the news media:

- at the scene of an incident;
- from agency files;
- concerning an ongoing criminal investigation; and/or
- at any time that the public information officer is not available.

  Commentary: Situations may arise when the agency's public information officer is not available or events at the scene of an incident or other fast-breaking event require an immediate agency spokesperson. (Mandatory)

54.1.6 A written directive establishes criteria and procedures for issuing and revoking credentials to news media representatives.
  Commentary: Because of the unique relationship between agencies and news media personnel, agencies should develop procedures governing the issuance and the revocation of credentials, as well as criteria for the conduct of news media representatives. The agency policy should not attempt to limit the number of credentials issued but should make media representatives aware of their obligations and responsibilities as they cover daily assignments and special events. Credentials should be revoked only when the criteria governing conduct have been violated. If credentials are revoked, a statement should be sent to the concerned individual's employer citing the specific violation. (Optional)

54.1.7 A written directive governs the access of news media representatives, including photographers, to the:

- scenes of major fires, natural disasters, or other catastrophic events; and
- perimeter of crime scenes.

  Commentary: News media representatives should not be in a position to interfere with law enforcement operations at the scene of an incident. The guidelines for news media access, including access by photographers, to the scene should be communicated to the media to help ensure their cooperation. (Mandatory)

54.1.8 A written directive establishes procedures for involving the news media in the development of changes in policies and procedures relating to the news media.

Commentary: By allowing media representatives to participate in the process of developing policies and procedures relating to the news media, agencies can demonstrate that they value good rapport with the media and appreciate the problems such persons confront in their daily work. (Optional)

54.1.9 A written directive specifies the information held by the agency regarding ongoing criminal investigations that may be released to the news media.

Commentary: The intent of the standard is that the agency provide specific guidance to personnel regarding the release of information about (1) the prior criminal record, character, or reputation of the accused; (2) mugshots of the accused; (3) the existence of any confession, admission of guilt, or statement made by the accused or the failure or refusal by the accused to make a statement; (4) the results of any examinations or tests conducted or refusal by the accused to submit to any examinations or tests; (5) the identity, testimony, or credibility of any prospective witness; (6) any opinion of agency personnel regarding the guilt or innocence

of the accused; (7) any opinion of agency personnel regarding the merits of the case or quality of evidence gathered; (8) personal information identifying the victim; (9) information identifying juveniles; and (10) information received from other law enforcement agencies without their concurrence in releasing that information. (Mandatory)

54.1.10 A written directive requires that information released under standard 54.1.9 be reported to the agency's public information officer as soon as possible.

Commentary: The person responsible for the public information function should not have to rely on the media to be informed of newsworthy events involving the agency that occur within the agency's service area. Moreover, such information should be conveyed in a timely fashion. (Optional)

54.1.11 A written directive establishes agency procedures for releasing information when other service agencies are involved in a mutual effort.

Commentary: The word *agencies* as used above is meant to refer to all public service agencies (e.g., fire departments and coroners' offices). In instances in which more than one agency is involved, the agency having primary jurisdiction should be responsible for releasing, or coordinating the release of, information. (Optional)

_____

Source: From the Commission on Accreditation for Law Enforcement Agencies (1991, pp. 54–1 to 54–3).

In criminal cases police officers at all levels may face a great deal of media or public pressure to release information that should be withheld. If joint press–bar–police guidelines are in effect, they relieve pressure by pointing to what the police and the press have both agreed to. If only the police have adopted the guidelines, the individual officers can still take themselves "off the hook" by emphasizing that they are only following "policy."

CRISIS GUIDELINES FOR THE MEDIA

As a result of evidence that the presence of the news media, especially television, can encourage violence, the National Advisory Commission on Civil Disorders urged news organizations to develop guidelines for responsible coverage of riots. Some of the results are listed below with the news agencies that had them at the time. (The initials used indicate the three major networks—NBC, CBS, and ABC.)

1. Use of unmarked or camouflaged cars and equipment (NBC and CBS).
2. Extreme care in using inflammatory words and phrases (e.g., "police brutality," "angry mob," "racial," and "riot") and in estimating the size and intensity of crowds (all three networks).
3. Prohibitions against giving the exact location of disturbances or specifics about weaponry; "capping" cameras and lights if they seem to be contributing to disorder or interfering with the police (all three networks).
4. No "live" coverage of disturbances (ABC and CBS).
5. Agreement that media representatives would ask for police protection when needed and that the police are entitled to ask for special credentials from press representatives (all three networks).

Local stations and network affiliates may have individual policies that vary from these guidelines. Police officials need to work closely with local media.

Some suggestions made by a committee of the Northern California chapter of the Radio and TV News Directors Association fill some of the gaps in the network codes:

1. Competition between broadcasters should continue, but the focus should be changed from dynamic impact to calm reporting of vital information to the public, with maximum assistance in reestablishment of control as the primary goal.
2. Police authorities should take necessary steps to ensure that adequately informed staff members will be on duty at command posts and available to supply properly identified broadcast newspeople with pertinent information about the disorder.
3. Reports should be calm and objective and should present the overall picture. They should be devoid of sensationalism, speculation, and rumors that could incite or further extend disturbances or stir news breaks.

A Common Interest

The interests of the police and the media sometimes conflict, but they both want to see order restored as quickly as possible in riot situations. The media need the police to get the facts, and the police need the help and the restraint of the media. Thus, they have a second basis for cooperation and for working out, together, plans for dealing with disorders.

A Proposal for Hostage–Terrorist Situations

The following specific guidelines were first suggested by District of Columbia Police Chief Maurice J. Cullinane in 1977 after several major incidents. These suggestions give increased authority and discretion to the police negotiator.

1. Live minicamera broadcast should be limited to distance shots.
2. Media should remain in a special "broadcast area" apart from the police line, where they could receive briefings from police. (The police negotiator might allow the press into the command center where negotiations are conducted, if circumstances allow.)
3. Telephone calls to people holding hostages should be banned.
4. Live broadcasts showing police stationed around a hostage situation would be barred.

POLICE–COMMUNITY RELATIONS

We have discussed the general aspects of police–media relations; now we turn our attention to police–community relations and how its link with the media fits in. Police–community relations is a complicated and changing relationship between the police internal communities and its external communities. The media is the primary link between the police organization and its external environment. The media is instrumental to the police as they attempt to manage their image and create support for programs and strategies. Community- and problem-oriented policing initiatives to be successful must have the support and involvement of community members. The public must know about the programs and the problems addressed, and then must be willing to give up their time and participate. Support and involvement once created are maintained by a steady flow of information. Unfortunately, information on police–community relations topics, particularly on community policing, does not receive the same media attention as crime topics. Furthermore, it appears that police agencies are not adequately publicizing their community- and problem-oriented efforts, or if publicizing them, many citizens do not receive the publicity (Chermack and Weiss, 2006). Also, the police–community relationship may be so strained that the public do not believe that the police are serious. The media is in the position to be an important partner in assisting the police to identify problems and communicate community and problem-solving efforts to the public and community leaders. The success and growth of "Crimestoppers" programs mentioned earlier is evidence of a successful police–media partnership. Therefore, the police turn to proactive strategies to involve the media as a partner in building and sustaining good police–community relations. One of those strategies is the appointment of public information officers (PIOs) (Chermak and Weiss, 2005).

Public Information Officer

Most large agencies, those serving over 100,000 population, have chosen to communicate with the media through a designated public information officer (Chermak and Weiss, 2005). A **public information officer** (PIO) maintains liaisons with the media, thus relieving department administrators of some of the burden of working with reporters. The duties of PIOs include responding to media inquiries, developing media releases, scheduling press conferences, and conducting training throughout the organization (Surett and Richard, 1995). PIOs as one of several "gatekeepers," others include crime reporters and newspaper editors, determine which crimes become news (Chermak and Chapman, 2007). They do so while performing a public relations role in promoting the best image of the department. PIOs also respond proactively to scandals, create public and political support for new department activities, and satisfy media requests for information. The PIO is not necessarily a sworn police officer. In the Chermak and Weiss (2005) study of 239 law enforcement agencies, over 50 percent of the departments used sworn personnel as PIOs, 17 percent used personnel who had other duties along with public information responsibilities, 14 percent used civilians, and 16 percent used a combination of sworn and civilians acting as PIOs. The PIOs in the study were very busy individuals meeting daily with the chief and were contacted by approximately 15 reporters daily and 13 different media agencies each week. Their busy schedule often prevents them from conveying information on police initiatives. Some departments have decentralized the publications of community policing and crime prevention programs to the units involved. The media also had reasons for not publicizing community policing stories. Crime stories were easier to produce than stories evaluating community policing programs. The reporter would have to interview community-policing officers, residents, and community leaders. The majority of the police and the media personnel in the study agreed or strongly agreed that the relationships were cordial but had the potential to change dramatically because of unpredictable events such as scandals or misrepresentations by either party. Nevertheless, the study concluded that police agencies should consider other marketing strategies to increase public awareness and involvement in community policing activities. The study also pointed to a need for additional personnel and resources to market community policing.

BOX 11.3
Fort Lauderdale, Florida, PD Office of Media Relations

Media Relations Coordinator

The duties of the Media Relations Coordinator include, but are not limited to, preparing written news releases on incidents that are of public interest, meeting with media personnel on the scene of high profile incidents, responding to media and public inquires, and publishing information related to progressive programs established to enhance relations between the community and its police department.

Source: www.fortlauderdale.gov/police/media.html

Seattle PD-Media Relations Office

The Seattle Police Department believes a responsible and effective partnership with the media is vital to our mission. We depend on that partnership—as well as community trust and confidence—in carrying out our responsibilities. There is one sergeant and three media relations officers assigned to this office, who respond to media requests as early as possible, release public safety information in a timely manner, and accommodate other media requests when needed.

Source: www.seattle.gov/police/contact/media.htm

The PIO's skill is a critical factor in moving the agency from an adversary position to one of cooperation. The PIO is a critical person during demonstrations and protests who should not condemn the cause, which is usually protected by the U.S. Constitution, but should denounce illegal tactics and acts if they occur (King, 2000). In a newsworthy event, the PIO frequently use a news briefing to disseminate the facts to the public as quickly as possible, allowing the media to report the facts accurately (Sparks and Staszak, 2000). Sparks and Staszak state that a well-conducted news briefing conveys information and assures the citizens that the department serves the community. Anyone who watched television during the Columbine High School massacre in Colorado is familiar with Deputy Steve Davis, the PIO for the Jefferson County Sheriff's Office. He arrived on the scene eighteen minutes after the call went out, and for the next two weeks, he held news briefings every hour (Rosenthal, 1999b).

The PIO office is also the ideal unit in which to set up internal training programs in press relations. The Fairfax County (Virginia) Office of Public Information established in 1974 has a field PIO program that provides four weeks of training for selected officers (Rosenthal, 2001b). The trained officers fill in for the Office of Public Information (OPI) as needed. All Fairfax County Police Department first-line supervisors receive a one-day orientation on the department's media and public information policies. In recognition of the area's cultural diversity, the department communicates information in Spanish, Korean, Farsi, Vietnamese, and English. The OPI is also a member of the Metropolitan Washington Public Safety Media Relations Council. This association of public safety and media professionals established in 1968 meets monthly to air grievances and exchange information.

The National Association of Public Safety Information Officers (NAPSIO), set up by PIOs in 1974, became a major forum for exchanging ideas and programs. NAPSIO has conducted training workshops in all facets of professionalizing police–press liaison and maintains a network of correspondence among PIOs throughout the country, with beneficial results.

NAPSIO no longer exists as an organization. PIOs now are associated through the Public Information Office Section of the International Association of Chiefs of Police (IACP) and through that affiliation have worked together to develop international standards for police–media relations. PIOs from various criminal justice agencies have formed regional associations, such as the Lake County (Indiana) Public Information Officers Association, founded by the PIO of the Lake County Prosecutor's Office (Rosenthal, 2001a). There is a statewide PIO association in Colorado. The Emergency Services Public Information Officers of Colorado had 80 members in 1999 (Rosenthal, 1999a).

Marketing Police–Community Relations

Publicizing police efforts in order to create a partnership between the police and the community and to involve community members in community policing, problem solving, or crime prevention programs is not the same as producing crime statistics and traditional crime reports for the media. Police agencies have to go beyond the media and traditional outreach strategies. The agency's outreach strategies must be designed to compliment and supplement the media (Chermak and Weiss, 2003). In other words, police departments must be creative in marketing police–community relations.

Chief Mark Fazzini, College of DuPage Police Department in Glen Ellyn, Illinois, has a unique approach to reaching citizens in the community and educating them to available police services that has implications for public relations and police–community relations. He calls his plan Marketing Available Police Services (MAPS). Marketing, he says, consists of understanding, creating, communicating, and delivering services to obtain members' satisfaction. For police purposes, this begins with understanding the communities and the need and expectations that citizens have of their police services. This includes meeting with the diverse community entities and have them provide input into problem identification and problem-solving strategies. The department then communicates the developed initiatives to affected groups. Chief Fazzini realizes that if the department has services but the community does not know of them, they are a waste of resources. Communication between the police and the community is the key to the MAPS concept and can develop positive relationships between the police and the community.

Creative outreach programs have been successful in other police agencies according to Chermak and Weiss (2003). Chicago PD, when they began their community policing program, used multimedia and multilingual initiatives such as brochures, newsletters, billboards, and television and radio ads and set up informational hotlines. The New Haven, Connecticut, community policing outreach effort included a public TV program, workshops for residents, and a documentary film profiling the city's police and community policing. The Corcoran, California, a city of 26,000, created Amigos de la Comunidad, a Spanish-language police academy which led to a Spanish-language unit in the department's volunteer community patrol. These examples and the other presented throughout the book demonstrate creative marketing of programs through the media and other outlets to improve police–community relations.

REALITY CHECK

The Media Comes Through

In Rome, Georgia, the District Attorney is Leigh Patterson. Ms. Patterson has been accused of zealously prosecuting people without power or influence, while overlooking felonies committed by those who are affluent or politically connected (and in at least one case, employed by her). Despite her reputation, Ms. Patterson is strongly supported by the local Democratic Party and influential members of the local bar. She also has been astute enough to employ one of the better attorneys in the area in responding to recall efforts.

On February 10, 2003, Marcus Dixon (then 18) had sex with Kristie Brown, a 15-year-old girl at a local high school. Two days later Dixon was arrested on charges of statutory rape and sexual battery. Dixon is African American; the alleged victim is white. At the time of his arrest, Dixon claimed that the sex was consensual and that the victim claimed rape when it was discovered that she had lost her virginity to a black male. On March 14, 2003, Dixon was indicted on the rape and sexual assault charges as well as an additional charge of aggravated child molestation. On May 15, 2003, he was acquitted of rape, false imprisonment, sexual battery, and aggravated assault. He was convicted of aggravated child molestation and misdemeanor statutory rape. On May 23, 2003, he was sentenced to 15 years in prison, to serve at least 10 behind bars.

Some of the jurors in the case later indicated that they were not convinced that the sex was not consensual but had convicted Dixon on what they understood to be lesser charges because of the three-year age difference. At least one juror indicated that she was shocked to learn that the child molestation charge carried a mandatory prison sentence. Dixon appealed the child abuse conviction on the grounds that the law (which was created to deal with sexual predators that had harmed children) was wrongly applied to his situation.

Civil rights groups took up the case as an example of racial injustice. An Atlanta attorney, David Baltzer, took up the appeal at no charge to Dixon. Ms. Patterson claimed that the vaginal bruising and tearing from the loss of virginity constituted injury and the statute was correctly applied. On January 22, 2004, oral arguments were heard before the Georgia Supreme Court.

Media coverage of the case intensified after the case was discussed on the *Oprah* broadcast of February 26, 2004. During this time local African American leaders sought to initiate a recall petition of Ms. Patterson. Her attorney successfully argued that the recall document was improperly worded and had to be dismissed. Under Georgia Law it could not be brought back up for six months (this time frame was extended due to another portion of the law that prohibits recall petitions during apolitical campaigns).

On May 3, 2004, the Georgia Supreme Court ruled that the aggravated child molestation charge was inappropriate. Following the decision, Superior Court Judge Walter Matthews ordered Dixon to be released on recognizance while the statutory rape charge was reviewed. He later noted that Dixon had served a longer period in prison than the maximum required for the statutory rape conviction and ordered him released. Ms. Patterson criticized the Georgia Supreme Court for making a bad decision and turning a "sexual predator" loose. She also criticized Judge Matthews because he allowed bond before receiving written confirmation of the higher court's ruling. She indicated that she would file a motion for reconsideration and would also seek charges against Dixon on another case. Her motion was denied, and additional charges against Dixon were not pursued.

There is no doubt in the minds of Marcus Dixon's family, friends, and supporters that if the media had not provided intense coverage of his case, he would still be sitting in prison on wrongful charges by a racist, malicious, and unscrupulous prosecutor.

Conclusions

The media represent a principal link between police agencies and the public they serve. Media impact on virtually every citizen is enormous, and crime news is a major media topic. Except for the relatively few people who become directly involved with the police, private citizens learn of police activity, crime prevention, the pursuit and apprehension of criminals, and their disposition in the courts by what they read in their newspapers and see and hear on television and radio. What a citizen reads, hears, and observes in the local media largely define the citizen's perception of the police.

Easy generalizations about whether the media help or hinder law enforcement and "heat up" or "cool off" civil disorders should be avoided: It is too easy to cite evidence on either side of the issue. However, both the police and members of the media have an interest in the security of all citizens and the preservation of order. The U.S. system has a built-in conflict between the freedom of the press guaranteed by the First Amendment to the U.S. Constitution and

the right to a fair trial guaranteed by the Sixth Amendment; there is often accurate information that could prejudice jurors if it were known to them. The police are in the center of this conflict, and therefore should develop—with or without the cooperation of the media—guidelines for disseminating information about crime.

During the crisis situations (e.g., riots, demonstrations, and terrorist actions) that have become so characteristic of today, the police and the media have sometimes found themselves working at cross-purposes; here again, guidelines are needed so that neither party tramples on the rights or responsibilities of the other. Fortunately, several means exist for improving police–media relations, including regularly scheduled police–media meetings; press councils; working with a press, radio, or TV ombudsman; mutual education programs; and mutual projects and goals.

The police–media–community link is a critical one. The nature of a community's police–media relationship helps to define police–community relations in that community.

Student Checklist

1. Overview media commitment to the reporting of crime news.
2. Contrast the responsibility of the press and the police.
3. Justify the need for guidelines in reporting.
4. Establish police–media guidelines for routine information release, crisis situations, and hostage situations.
5. Identify ongoing blocks to positive police–media relations and strategies for resolving them.
6. Contrast individual constitutional rights and the public's right to know.
7. Describe the duties and responsibilities of a public information officer.

Topics for Discussion

1. Should there be a code of conduct for all the media, not just professional journalists? Support your answer.
2. What information, in your opinion, should police not volunteer to the media about a crime?
3. How responsible is the press in your community?
4. How is information disseminated to the press by police agencies in your community?
5. How could your local police department market its community policing programs?

Bibliography

Abrams, D. (2009). "Presumed Innocent? Bernie Madoff?," *The Wall Street Journal*. http.//online.wsj.com/article.

Arango, T. (2009). "Death Row Foes See Newsroom Cuts as Blow," *The New York Times*. www.nytimes.com

Barker, T., and Carter, D. L. (1994). *Police Deviance*, 3rd ed. Cincinnati, OH: Anderson.

Chermak, S., and Weiss, A. (2003). *Marketing Community Policing in the News: A Missed Opportunity?* U.S. Department of Justice Office of Justice Programs, National Institute of Justice.

Chermak, S., and Weiss, A. (2005). "Maintaining legitimacy using external communications strategies: An analysis of police-media relations," *Journal of Criminal Justice*, Vol. 33, pp. 501–512.

Chermak, S., and Chapman, N. M. (2007). "Predicting crime story salience: A replication," *Journal of Criminal Justice*, Vol. 35, pp. 351–363.

Crawford, K. A. (2000). "Media ride-alongs," *FBI Law Enforcement Bulletin*, Vol. 69, No. 7, pp. 26–31.

Edwards, A. L. (2009). "Florida laws upon book on Casey Anthony's life," *OrlandoSentinel.com*. www.orlandosentinel.com/news.

Goodman, W. (October 29, 1990). "How much should t.v. tell and when?" *New York Times*.

Katzenbach, J. (September 1980). "Overwhelmed in Miami," *Police Magazine*, pp. 7–15.

King, T. R. (2000). "Managing protests on public land," *FBI Law Enforcement Bulletin*, Vol. 69, No. 9, pp. 10–13.

Lazin, F. A. (1980). "How the police view the press," *Journal of Police Science and Administration*, Vol. 8, pp. 148–159.

Lofton, J. (1966). *Justice and the Press*. Boston, MA: Beacon Press.

MacDougall, C. D. (1964). *The Press and Its Problems*. Dubuque, IA: W. C. Brown.

Morgan, R., and Newburn, T. (1997). *The Future of Policing*. Oxford, England: Clarendon Press.

Rosenthal, R. (1999a). "Portland cements media agreement," *Law & Order*, Vol. 33, No. 11, pp. 22–23.

Rosenthal, R. (1999b). "Lessons from Littleton: Managing the media in a crisis," *Law & Order*, Vol. 47, No. 6, pp. 25–26.

Rosenthal, R. (2001a). "Chicago trains the media," *Law & Order*, Vol. 49, No. 8, pp. 20–21.

Rosenthal, R. (2001b). "Winning media strategies," *Law & Order*, Vol. 49, No. 6, pp. 23–24.

Rosenthal, R. (2001c). "One of the best PIOs," *Law & Order*, Vol. 49, No. 3, pp. 21–22.

Schmid, A. P., and DeGraaf, J. (1982). *Violence as Communication: Insurgent Terrorism and the Western News Media*. Beverly Hills, CA: Sage.

Siegel, L. J., and Senna, J. J. (2007). *Essentials of Criminal Justice*, 5th ed. Pacific Grove, CA: Thomson/Wadsworth.

Sotelo, M. (2000). "Exploring police, media's vexing problem of relationships," *New Photographer*, Vol. 55, No. 2, pp. 12–14.

Sparks, A. B., and Staszak, D. D. (2000). "Fine tuning your news briefing," *FBI Law Enforcement Bulletin*, Vol. 69, No. 12, pp. 22–24.

Staszak, D. (2001). "Media trends and the public information officer," *FBI Law Enforcement Bulletin*, Vol. 70, No. 3, pp. 10–13.

Surette, R., and Richard, A. (1995). "Public information officers: A descriptive study of crime news gatekeepers," *Journal of Criminal Justice*, Vol. 23, pp. 325–326.

Trigoboff, D. (2000). "Stations restrained, or manipulated," *Broadcasting & Cable*, Vol. 130, No. 3, p.14.

Toufexis, A. (June 28, 1993). "A weird case baby? Un huh," *Time*, p. 41.

USA Today. (December 12, 1991). "Smith trial offers mixed message about date rape," Editorial, p. 10A.

Vetter, H. J., and Perlstein, G. R. (1991). *Perspectives on Terrorism*. Pacific Grove, CA: Brooks/Cole.

Worral, J. L. (2000). "Constitutional issues in reality-based police television programs: Media ride-alongs," *American Journal of Criminal Justice*, Vol. 25, No. 1, pp. 41–64.

Walsh, M., Vice-Chairman, Public Information Officers Section, International Association of Chiefs of Police (April/May 1983). Interview.

CHAPTER 12

Special Populations and the Police

"The graying of America" has been a popular phrase in recent years as the number of older people continues to grow. Statistics project that by 2030, Americans 65 and older will actually outnumber their younger counterparts.

—National Association of Social Workers

His [the adolescent's] delicate masculinity is at stake. He must save face and prove himself to his companions.

—DeSanto and Moore

KEY CONCEPTS

Citizens on Patrol
Dependency Issues
Elderly Department
   Volunteers
Learning Disorders

Mental Illness
Mental Retardation
Personal Identity
Physical Incapacitation
Physiological Disorders

Self-Image and
   Self-Esteem
Special Populations
Stereotyping
TRIADs

LEARNING OBJECTIVES

Studying this chapter will enable you to:

1. Identify how the special populations in a community pose special problems for the police.
2. Describe some of the developmental characteristics of adolescence and how they impact interactions of the young with police.
3. Describe some of the developmental characteristics of maturation and aging and how they impact interactions of the elderly with police.
4. Contrast the needs of the young, elderly, and disabled.
5. Identify the major elements that contribute to resolving or compounding the problems of special populations.
6. Suggest several ways through which the effectiveness of services to special populations might be improved.

Every day, every minute, police are first on the scene. They must decide if a child is in imminent danger of abuse and needs to be removed from his or her surroundings. They must comfort the elderly woman or man whose spouse has died. They must search for the mentally handicapped person who has wandered away from home and is in danger. They must confront a teenager who held up a convenience store at gunpoint, bludgeoned a blind 79-year-old, crippled woman to death, or ran away from an intolerable home situation. They must confront a 60-year-old man who molests children, and they must arrest an elderly woman who has somehow survived a failed suicide pact. After being called every name known to people, police officers must maintain their composure and act in the best interest of the youth who insult them.

It is a police responsibility to help children, elderly, and disabled people protect themselves from crime, while also protecting them from themselves and from the sense of isolation and alienation that comes with the fear of being victimized, a fear that is detrimental to quality of life.

Community relations efforts, especially crime-prevention programs, often target the needs of these groups. Even efforts considered successful often do not reach the populations they purportedly seek to reach. Many efforts are undermined by individual officers in personal interactions with young, elderly, and disabled persons. Existing problems also may be escalated by officers who are poorly trained in working with these populations. Sometimes understanding is misunderstanding because myths regarding the young, elderly, and disabled are common in our society. These myths act as barriers to positive police relations with major segments of the community.

Information in this chapter helps to debunk some of the myths and to increase understanding of needs of these **special populations**. Strategies for increasing the effectiveness of community relations efforts are also suggested.

SPECIAL PROBLEMS FOR THE POLICE

The young, the elderly, and the disabled represent three major groups in society for whom the police must provide specialized services. All need the protection of police, sometimes even from members of their own families, each other, and themselves. The young and the elderly are more vulnerable to almost all types of abuse than other age groups in our society. Estimating conservatively from the findings of national studies, more than 1 million children (birth to age 18) and another million elderly people (65 and over) are abused yearly in the United States. No one knows for sure how many die from abuse and neglect.

Youths between the ages of 11 and 18, more than any other age group, confront and are confronted by police. More than half of the arrests made by police are of people under the age of 18. Most police–youth contacts do not result in arrest. In fact, were police to formally act upon every police–youth contact that legally could be said to involve a juvenile offense, the number of arrests would more than double.

Studies suggest that young peoples' future attitudes and behavior toward police and the law are influenced by the way police handle encounters with them. A discretionary decision by the officer to divert a child to other resources or make a field adjustment (although a right not legally granted to police in some states) is exercised at some level in every state. Such decisions are often made based on the following factors: the officer's confidence in the local juvenile court; the seriousness of the offense; circumstances surrounding the offense; the attitude and demeanor of the child; the presence of clear evidence; and the wishes of a complainant (Siegel and Senna, 2007). Departmental policy and the attitudes of parents are also influential in such decision making. Such a decision is difficult to make under the best of circumstances. Prejudice, lack of understanding of youth, and any number of other factors could negatively influence the outcome.

The number of people age 65 and over in our society now stands at 34 million. That number is expected to surge to 69.4 million in 2030 or 20 percent of the population (Anonymous, 2000a, p. 14). Police must deal with an increasing number of crimes by and against the elderly and offer protection, patience, and resolution of what may be the most serious problem of all to the elderly—fear. How to best develop and use resources on behalf of the elderly requires an understanding of the problems of the elderly and of the strengths and limitations an elderly person can bring to their problems and their solution.

UNDERSTANDING THE YOUNG

The First Ten Years

Interactions between police and children who are 10 or younger are for the most part positive. Children move through several developmental stages during this period, as they gain new skills and independence and learn about the world. From infancy, when children are totally dependent on others to meet their needs, through the toddler stage, when they gain a greater sense of autonomy and more self-awareness, their world is relatively small because most of their interactions are with family and close friends. As they reach preschool age, however, they interact with more people outside the family group and increase their range of experiences. They are curious and imaginative during this time. They like to imitate and observe.

Middle childhood, the period from about 7 to 11 years of age, builds on the previous years. The primary people in children's lives are at home, in the neighborhood, and at school. If children have been encouraged to be imaginative, to be curious, and to observe, they can learn good work habits. The world of these children is much larger and the range of their experiences greater than ever before.

MEETING BASIC NEEDS For many children, police can be a role model, a powerful authority figure, a protector, an adult friend, a hero, and an avenue to adventure and excitement. Relationships between police officers and children are important (Figure 12.1). "Clancy, the Talking Police Car," "Officer Friendly" programs, station-house tours, bicycle safety programs, crime-prevention poster competitions, and other projects target preschool and elementary school students to deliver safety and crime-prevention information and guidance to them and to establish police as a positive force in society. Programs such as these are important ones. They are

FIGURE 12.1   DARE Program, Birmingham, Alabama.
Courtesy of Birmingham Police Department.

most successful when conducted by officers who are patient, have a sense of humor that young children can appreciate, and understand and like children. Other programs designed to prevent child abuse and to help children to recognize danger and protect themselves from abuse (or further abuse) are also very useful for school-age children (Doerner and Lab, 2005). Special training for officers is mandatory for properly conducting such programs (Carter, 2002).

The Teenage Years

Much of the potentially negative interaction between young people and police occurs between the ages of 11 and 17, because this is the period during which most delinquency and incorrigibility take place. If we were to search for one word to describe the youth developmentally, the word would have to be "change." This is a period of transition from childhood to adulthood, from dependence to independence. No two children proceed through this period and deal with these changes in exactly the same way.

A TIME OF RAPID CHANGE   "Human development is defined as physical, emotional, and social changes in structure, thought, or behavior which are functions of biological and environmental influences" (Mayhall and Norgard, 1983, p. 67). Adolescence is the final stage before adulthood in human development, and it is probably more than one stage. It is a time of rapid changes in all areas of development. It begins with the onset of puberty, which for most people occurs between 11 and 13 years of age, and is marked by physical and sexual maturing.

Mental ability changes during adolescence. Piaget suggests that it becomes more operational. The youth gains the capacity (but not necessarily the practical experience or the information) to reason in more formal ways, analyze problems, sort through possible outcomes or consequences, make complex moral analyses, and arrive at reasonable solutions and moral judgments (Piaget, 1968). Relationships with family members may become more distant and relationships with peers, both male and female, become closer.

DEVELOPMENT TASKS   Havighurst (1972) suggested the following as the developmental tasks of the adolescent:

1. Achievement of new and mature relations with age mates of both sexes.
2. Achievement of masculine or feminine social roles.
3. Acceptance and effective use of one's body.
4. Achievement of emotional independence from parents and other adults.
5. Preparation for marriage and family life.
6. Preparation for a career.
7. Acquisition of a set of values and an ethical system.
8. Acquisition and utilization of socially responsible behavior.

In the view of many, and sometimes of themselves, teenagers are "too" in almost everything—too emotional, too calm, too big, too little, too sexually interested or disinterested. They are concerned with "body image" and with the opinion of their peers. They seek ways of testing changes—physically, emotionally, and socially. They act on the need to test new strength, new maturity, new freedom and to "prove" knowledge and toughness, especially for the benefit of peers. If unresolved in other arenas, their conflicts between authority and freedom, dependence and independence seem to be a natural source of police–youth confrontations. As youth take risks and act in disrespectful ways, they set up power struggles with authority figures who need to "teach them a lesson." Power struggles decrease goodwill and increase distrust. They underscore mutual self-esteem issues. If enough encounters with police end negatively, outright mutual hatred may result and tensions in a community may increase.

MEETING BASIC NEEDS   Programs for youth are often designed to divert them from the juvenile justice system (as police–social work teams, mental health and social service referral projects, crisis hotlines, runaway houses, time-out programs, and drug and alcoholism diversion projects). They may also strive to encourage positive behavior within juvenile gangs and in programs geared toward changing juvenile attitudes toward police and teaching youth about police organization and function (e.g., station-house tours, junior police, and youth ride-along programs).

The most difficult questions facing police officers regarding teenagers often are not addressed by these programs: How can the officer deal with youthful misbehavior in a way that both protects the public, discourages the behavior, and yet does not negatively label the youth unnecessarily? How can the officer help a youth to master the tasks of adolescence and encourage maturity? How can the officer help a youth to satisfy the need for excitement and risk and "prove" him- or herself in positive, constructive ways? These are the problems that programs for youth must address. They are also the problems that every officer who encounters youths on a regular basis must personally solve.

UNDERSTANDING THE ELDERLY

A Profile

Currently, more than 60 percent of the elderly in the United States live in metropolitan areas. Many reside in high-crime areas because rents are lower and fixed incomes stretch further, which may actually add to the isolation of the elderly. Crimes committed by the elderly, once considered to be almost nonexistent, are increasing. Although the increase is occurring in many crime areas, the greatest problem appears to be petty larceny offenses, such as shoplifting. In one Florida city, for example, 44 percent of the shoplifting cases against people over age 60 involved theft of food items (valued less than $10) (National Institute of Law Enforcement and Criminal Justice, 1981, p. 2). This increase is not due to a "geriatric delinquent" class. As the U.S. population becomes older, we can expect greater increases in its crime involvement during the next several decades (Schmalleger, 2007).

FIGURE 12.2   One of New York's finest giving assistance to an elderly citizen.

Courtesy of New York Police Department.

BOX 12.1
The Problem of Toxic Agers

The vast majority of seniors are honest law-abiding citizens. However, as we indicate within this chapter, not all are. As with any group, there are certain segments that will participate in unlawful behavior. And as the "baby boomers" continue to age, these numbers will increase within the overall population. Gerontologists identify these elderly offenders as toxic agers. According to Davenport (1999, p. 8) "Toxic agers are older adults, usually in their 70's and 80's who consistently act out defensive, negative behavior that is based upon ego-distorted perceptions, values, beliefs, messages and experiences. These perceptions then are projected onto others in varying degrees and levels of intensity and skill depending on the relationship and susceptibility of the other person to the toxic ager."

The development of toxic behavior in elder adults is seen as being a product of life events going all the way back to the individual's youth. Or in the words of an elderly woman assessing a particularly malicious octogenarian, "I knew her when she was a child, a teenager, a young woman, a middle-age woman, and now as an old woman. She has always been a self-serving jerk. Now people cater to her whims because she is old, and it has made her even worse."

The behaviors of a toxic ager may not just impact on relatives and caregivers. In a small northwest Georgia town, it actually has perpetuated corruption and delayed progress for an entire community. A city park board decided not to renew a lease with their local historical society. This decision was based on the society's noncompliance with prior lease agreements, their refusal to account for past monies (approximately $300,000 raised in the park that had been misappropriated or were totally unaccounted for), as well as their stated intentions to use new monies raised in the park on external projects. Most of the members of this group were elderly people who had dropped out of the historical society years before but had rejoined to help take over the society from

"outsiders" (and to prevent an audit of their past financial activities).

The ringleader of the group was an elderly woman (the octogenarian referred to above) who had previously controlled the historical society and who had manipulated the prior park board to allow her to control the park's assets for many years. Under her influence the group began a public effort to discredit the park board. They threatened legal actions, pressured other local officials to try to influence the board, created chaos at board meetings, and used other means to coerce the board into relinquishing control of the park to them. Two board members capitulated under the pressure (each had some indiscreet actions in their past that they did not wish to have publicized). The group then began a concerted effort (including slander, extortion attempts, and physical threats) to force the other member to resign from the park board.

Once the other board members surrendered, they began carrying out the wishes of the historical society. They would meet frequently with one another and historical society directors without the other board member being present. These meetings violated Georgia Public Meeting and Georgia Public Records laws (felonies) on both the park board's part and on the part of the historical society (in that more than a third of their income came from their control of public properties). When the board member went to the local district attorney for assistance, the DA informed him that enforcing public meeting and public records laws were not her responsibility. She also chided him for having disappointed one of her employees (who was a member of the historical society's board of directors and actively involved in the above activities). The DA then warned the board member not to pursue the matter and informed him that she would use her prosecutorial discretion to not press charges because "No one in this county will convict a bunch of 80-year-olds."

Transitions into Late Adulthood

There is no "typical" older person developmentally, socially, or economically. Although we have determined that development does not stop with becoming an adult, we are just beginning to learn about the subtleties of the aging process. Many factors are involved in aging, and most are complex. Environment, biology, diet, lifestyle, and any number of other factors vary the process of aging. (Women generally live longer than men; some people are more susceptible to disease than others; etc.)

Parent (1977) suggests that people must solve three developmental tasks in the transition into late adulthood: (1) completion of one's life goals; (2) evaluation of one's life performance and the resolution of conflict about one's failures and disappointments; and (3) preparation for decline.

According to Peck (1968, pp. 88–92), the transition into late adulthood is the retirement process: integration versus despair; ego differentiation versus work-role preoccupation; body transcendence versus body preoccupation; and ego transcendence versus ego preoccupation.

An elderly person has likely relinquished a parental role, lived through loss of many family members and friends, confronted in some ways the successes and failures of his or her life thus far, and prepared for old age. This preparation is usually done by simplifying lifestyle, preparing for future financial security, arranging for physical care, and so on. On an emotional level the elderly person becomes more aware, consciously, of death.

What factors help to ease the transition? Golan (1992) stated, regarding women, "psychologists feel that the critical variable is ego strength or emotional autonomy, while sociologists tend to believe that social connectedness or ties to a network of social relationships are most likely to help. For some women, the two factors may be mutually reinforcing; for others, one set may serve as the substitute for the other" (p. 211).

Facts about the Elderly

PHYSICAL FACTS Generally older people are more affected by chronic disease than by acute illness. The most prominent health conditions are heart disease, arthritis, and diabetes. Physical limitations and reduced functioning are generally present, and the aged are more prone to accidents than are younger people. Crisis tends to precipitate debilitating accidents.

The physical changes in the elderly have been used to fuel a tremendous amount of health care fraud (Ford, 1992). Health care is the second-largest U.S. industry, next to education. Ford states that every level of this health care system is affected by fraud—from a doctor who charges exorbitant fees and authorizes unnecessary tests, to a hospital or nursing home that overbills Medicare, to pharmacists who dispense generic drugs at brand-name prices (Ford, 1992, p. 2).

EMOTIONAL AND FUNCTIONAL FACTS Functional disorders most frequently observed in the elderly center around depression. Physical and mental health are usually closely related. Organic disorders, often due to strokes (blocking of brain tissue), may cause a wide range of behavioral symptoms, from irritability and confusion to paralysis.

Although declining health is a fact of late adulthood, level of function depends largely on the individual's determination to remain active in order to retain his or her functioning and on the availability of medical and social service resources in the community that can support this level of functioning (Golan, 1992). Other important considerations are nutrition as an integral part of health care, living areas that meet the needs of the older person, social interaction, and meaningful work or activity. These are very important considerations as programs for the elderly are planned by police.

Patricia Moore, a noted gerontologist, traveled over a three-year period throughout the United States and Canada disguised as a woman in her eighties. She reported on her findings in 1988 at a national symposium on "Violent Crime against the Elderly," cohosted by the American Association of Retired Persons (AARP), the International Association of Chiefs of Police (IACP), and the FBI (Lent and Harpold, 1988). The thesis of her argument was that there is a need for better services and programs to facilitate a better future quality of life and that the law enforcement community needed to become involved in this movement. This assessment remains valid as we enter a new century.

MEETING BASIC NEEDS Helping the elderly to meet their basic needs may require a wide range of programs, including federally funded public housing; local city- and county-funded special-needs transportation; housekeeping and visiting nurse services; increased medical assistance through Medicare and Medicaid; and supplemental programs, Meals on Wheels (a program that provides hot meals to elderly people), and reduced senior citizen rates for prescription medicines. Police projects might include programs for crime prevention and citizen safety and should also focus on programs that offer opportunities for the elderly to participate on their own behalf and also on behalf of police projects (victim–witness advocacy programs and police volunteer organizations).

UNDERSTANDING THE HANDICAPPED

Just as the young and the elderly pose special problems for the police, so do people who are physically or mentally impaired. Individuals who are challenged due to such infirmities are often misunderstood by other members of society and are too frequently disenfranchised by governmental entities. Despite the equal protection guaranteed by the Americans with Disabilities Act of 1990, many disabled citizens are not properly served by the police. This is not due to a lack of caring on the part of police officers as much as it is a lack of knowing what to do. Most U.S. police officers have simply not been adequately trained to deal with citizens suffering from physical or mental disabilities (Carter, 2002).

In this section, we refer to a number of categories of individuals who are handicapped. Several terms may be used: "infirm," "disabled," and "challenged" come to mind immediately. We use the term "handicapped" because we feel it is the most accurate. The individuals we discuss have ailments or disorders that are detrimental to their well-being. "Challenged," although it may sound nicer, does not factually depict the difficulties that many have to face. Nor does "disabled" reflect the abilities of millions of Americans to lead whole and productive lives by overcoming the infirmities that they suffer.

The Physically Handicapped

Millions of Americans suffer from physical maladies that make their lives more difficult than those of other citizens. For these individuals, diseases, injuries, inherited traits, and birth defects have resulted in loss of vision, hearing, and/or mobility. Police officers may find themselves providing services to citizens who are bedridden, wheelchair-bound, blind, deaf, or a combination of the preceding. And just as the elderly and the young make attractive victims for many criminals, so do the physically disabled.

Handicapped individuals who do not need police protection may still need police services. By monitoring handicapped parking spaces, officers may ensure that wheelchair-bound citizens can move about more readily. Ensuring that warning devices designed to aid the blind or the deaf are operational can guarantee the safety of pedestrians that rely on them, and taking the time to communicate with these individuals (particularly the deaf) may aid in their sense of belonging within the community. Some of the more common physical handicaps are discussed in the following section.

PHYSIOLOGICAL DISORDERS   Forty types of muscular diseases currently affect more than 1 million Americans, according to the Muscular Dystrophy Association (MDA, 2006). Neurological disorders, such as multiple sclerosis and cerebral palsy, make life difficult for others. Epilepsy, although not a continuously debilitating condition, can also create problems for those who experience periodic seizures.

Tourette syndrome is a neurological disorder characterized by nervous tics (sudden movements that occur repeatedly). Persons who suffer from it may experience any of the following types of uncontrolled outbursts: *copropraxia*, the making of obscene gestures; *coprolalia*, the vocalizing of obscene or other socially unacceptable words or phrases; *echopraxia*, mimicking the movements of others; or *Palilalia*, repeating the same words over and over again (Ottinger, 2006). Needless to say, an officer who is not knowledgeable about this physiological disorder could take a very wrong course of action in dealing with the situation.

Autism is a developmental disability that usually occurs by age three in as many as one in a hundred people. This disorder causes difficulties in both verbal and nonverbal communication. The efforts of professional football player Doug Flutie and the sales of Flutie Flakes have helped to educate Americans about this disease.

Down syndrome is another **physiological disorder** that is very common in the United States. One out of every thousand births results in a child with Down syndrome (Pueschal, 2006). Due to a chromosome abnormality, these individuals are slower than other children in physical and mental development. They tend to have distinctive features that some describe as mongoloid in appearance.

(a)

(c)

(d)

(b)

(e)

FIGURE 12.3 (a) North Carolina School for the Deaf's main building, the beautifully refurbished administration office, is one of the oldest structures in Burke County; (b) selecting a new Homecoming Queen; (c) yes, the deaf can play football; (d) the ladies show they can also play volleyball; (e) a high school learning group.

Courtesy of North Carolina School for the Deaf.

They are often susceptible to other diseases and frequently have poor hearing and/or eyesight. Although they make excellent victims for the unscrupulous, they rarely engage in criminal activity.

PHYSICAL INCAPACITATION   Individuals who are immobile or limited in mobility may be so for many reasons. Disease, birth defects, and heredity cause many individuals to be physically incapacitated. In addition, spinal cord injuries disable thousands of persons each year. Individuals who are limited in mobility do not pose as many challenges for the police as do others. Most wheelchair-bound citizens ask only that they be granted reasonable access to buildings and public spaces. Others ask only that they be given assistance if and when they should need it. Many do not come into contact with the police, unless they happen to be employed within a police agency or other organization that generates frequent contacts on a professional or business basis. Many citizens who suffer from limited mobility are extremely successful. Former U.S. Senator Max Cleland of Georgia (who lost an arm and both legs in Vietnam) is such a person.

THE BLIND   Americans who suffer from vision disorders include those who have total vision loss as well as those who experience partial loss of vision. Vision loss or deterioration is usually the result of inherited traits, birth defects, injuries, diseases, and aging. Those who have impaired vision may require assistance in avoiding physical hazards such as open utility access holes and busy intersections that do not have warning devices. They may also require protection from those who would consider them easy targets for ordinary street crimes such as theft or robbery. They are less likely to be involved in the commission of crimes but may be quite capable of doing so, depending on the nature of the crime. Blindness—although a severe impediment—does not hold back most who suffer with it from successful careers and full lives.

THE DEAF   Deafness, like blindness, may be the product of a birth defect, heredity, disease, injury, or aging. Partial hearing loss is quite common for older Americans as well as for younger people who have been subjected to loud noises for extended periods of time. Interestingly, deafness tends to have more of a cultural effect than do the other physical handicaps. Although the blind tend to deal with their situation on a more individual basis, the deaf tend to adopt a group identity. Indeed, when a hearing person attempts to learn sign language, one of the first things that is taught is that there are cultural norms within the "deaf community" that differ from those of the hearing.

Because of their ability to move about more freely within the community, the deaf are more likely to come into contact with the police as victims, witnesses, and offenders than are other physically handicapped individuals. Officers who fail to understand that a person is deaf can find themselves being embarrassed by the media for harassing someone they thought was being difficult when actually that individual could not hear them. More tragically, officers may use deadly force against a deaf person who has failed to heed their verbal commands and then, in an effort to communicate, reaches in his or her pocket for a writing pad.

In order to deal fairly and appropriately with the approximately 26 million Americans who are deaf or hearing-impaired (Crispen, 1999), the police must have programs that facilitate communication. Every 9-1-1 facility must have a Telecommunication Device for the Deaf (TDD), as should large police stations. Cities that have large deaf communities, such as Morganton, North Carolina, where the North Carolina School for the Deaf is located, should provide training in sign language and deaf awareness to every officer. Police agencies that serve communities with smaller deaf populations should have prompt access to interpreters.

Like those with other physical handicaps, the deaf are frequently quite successful in their careers and family lives. The selection of Heather Whitestone as Miss America is an example of the deaf's ability to succeed within U.S. society.

The Mentally Handicapped

The need for the police to understand the needs of the physically handicapped is no less true regarding the mentally handicapped. Millions of individuals in the United States suffer from some type of mental impairment. It is estimated that 200,000 people with mental illness are jailed or imprisoned in the United States every day (Peak and Glensor, 2004, p. 204). Most of those who are mentally handicapped have no contact with the police; the majority of those who do are victims. However, in domestic violence situations and some sex offenses, the mentally handicapped may be offenders.

LEARNING DISORDERS   **Learning disorders** should more correctly be classified under physical handicaps with Tourette syndrome and Down syndrome. However, since their physical aspects are less (if at all) noticeable, they are grouped here with mental disabilities.

Attention deficit hyperactivity disorder (ADHD) is a disability that affects many Americans. Inattention difficulties, hyperactivity, and impulsiveness exemplify this disorder. School failure and emotional difficulties are frequent by-products of this disorder when it is not properly treated (Goldstein, 1997).

Other learning disorders include *dyslexia*, letter reversal that makes reading comprehension difficult; *dyscalculia*, which makes understanding math difficult; and *dysgraphia*, which is difficulty with written work or handwriting. Lastly, *auditory processing difficulties* make it difficult to process and comprehend auditory information (Johnson, 1995). The effects of learning disorders may result in truancy and juvenile delinquency due to frustrations with school failures and could lead to severe emotional difficulties if left untreated.

MENTAL ILLNESS   **Mental illnesses** range from mild emotional distress to outright insanity. At some point in our lives, most of us experience periods of depression and frustration that cause us to think and act irrationally. Such irrational behavior, although notable to friends and family members, may not be severe and may not have lingering consequences. When such behavior does interfere with our abilities to function within our work and social situations, intervention may be necessary. If behaviors could be harmful to ourselves or others, compulsory intervention may be appropriate. The police may come into contact with people affected by (or might themselves suffer from) a vast range of mental disorders. Every experienced officer can tell of problems they have had dealing with violent mentally ill people who were going to harm themselves or someone else. In actuality, veteran officers will have dealt occasionally with people who were depressed, paranoid, or suicidal. Less frequently they will have dealt with individuals who were totally out of touch with reality. Rarely will they have dealt with a deranged person who is committing acts of mayhem against others. However, such incidents when they do occur, such as the infamous shootings at the University of Texas Tower many years ago, catch the attention of media and public alike.

Most acts of violence by mentally ill individuals are assaults on family members within the home (Monahan, 1995). They are usually the result of the mentally disturbed individual's inability to cope with what is to him or her an adverse situation. When these situations become explosive and weapons are available, they can be extremely dangerous.

BOX 12.2
Facts About the Mentally Ill

In large U.S. cities, 7 percent of all police contacts involve a person with a mental illness.

There are three times as many people with mental illness in prisons as there are in psychiatric hospitals.

One in every six people imprisoned in the United States has a severe mental illness.

People with mental illness are three times more likely to be victims of violent crimes than the rest of the population.

People with mental illness are four times more likely to be killed by law enforcement officers than are the rest of the population.

Law enforcement officers are more likely to be killed by a person with mental illness than by other assailants, including those with a prior arrest for assaulting police or resisting arrest.

Source: American Psychiatric Association (2006).

Today's police officers receive training in dealing with mentally ill and/or emotionally disturbed individuals. Courses in crisis counseling are quite common. For more extreme situations, training in hostage negotiations and other means of peacemaking and conflict resolution are also available (Fuller, 2005). In addition, crisis intervention teams (CIT) are trained in several police agencies to respond to incidents involving the mentally ill: Albuquerque, New Mexico; Memphis, Tennessee; Portland, Oregon; San Jose, California; Seattle, Washington; and Waterloo, Iowa. They are modeled after the CIT team first established in Memphis in 1983 (Vickers, 2000). Of the 900 uniform patrol officers in Memphis, 213 have received special training and are designated CIT officers.

MENTAL RETARDATION   The physiological handicaps discussed earlier frequently result in diminished mental abilities of those afflicted by them. The effects of Down syndrome and similar maladies have already been noted. People who suffer from **mental retardation** are not able to solve intellectual problems as well as the average person. This does not mean that they cannot lead full lives. Indeed, many individuals with limited intellectual capacities hold jobs and have happy family lives. Although some mentally challenged individuals may engage in criminal behaviors, they are much more likely to be the victims of such actions.

UNDERSTANDING THE HOMELESS

A Profile

We do not have an accurate measure of how many homeless people reside within the United States (for a variety of reasons, they are usually not found on census roles). Estimates are that their numbers range from 300,000 to 3 million (Peak and Glensor, 2004). In any large city (and even in small towns and rural areas), we can see them sleeping in alleys and abandoned buildings, panhandling on the sidewalks, loitering in parks, scavenging through garbage, drinking in front of businesses and homes, and urinating in public view. Sometimes we are moved to sympathy; sometimes we are moved to disgust; often it is a mixture of both. Unfortunately, these visions of the homeless being filthy, lazy, drug addicted, or criminal too frequently cause us to stereotype homeless people as public nuisances.

FACTS ABOUT THE HOMELESS   Among the homeless you will easily find individuals from the following three categories: growing numbers of elderly people who have no pensions or inadequate retirement incomes and no family members who can (or will) assist them; runaways under the age of 18 who have fled their homes and feel that they have nowhere to go; and people who suffer from mental disorders. You will also find military veterans, entire families, and people who are actively working but are employed in low-paying jobs. In reality, the majority of homeless people are no different from you or me except that situational factors have resulted in their having no home.

Following are some facts regarding the homeless in America:

- 30 percent of the homeless are military veterans.
- 37 percent are families with children.
- 25 percent are children.
- 25–30 percent are mentally disabled.
- 40 percent are drug or alcohol dependent.
- 25 percent of crimes committed by homeless people are against property or persons compared to 35 percent committed by nonhomeless people ("A Place to Call Home," 2006).

The current economic crisis has added numerous individuals and families to the ranks of the homeless and there is growing concern that violence against the homeless has increased nationwide. There is no nationwide tracking of crimes against the homeless, but Los Angeles

County has reported that homeless individuals in 2008 have been set on fire, stabbed, shot, and beaten with baseball bats (Hennessy-Fiske, 2009). County supervisors are calling for these attacks to be classified as Hate Crimes, allowing for enhanced sentences. At this time, only one city and two states have such legislation: Seattle, Maine, and Alaska. Legislation is pending in 10 states and Washington, D.C.

MEETING BASIC NEEDS   The growing number of homeless people in America creates a major challenge for police agencies. The number of needy individuals and families has increased while available monies from local, state, and federal agencies have declined or become restricted. Charitable organizations are bearing the brunt of providing assistance and have limited resources. When no one knows whom to turn to, it is the police who are called. Providing assistance is especially daunting when those needing assistance also suffer from mental disorders. Innovative programs that provide training for police officers and assistance for the homeless are desperately needed.

YOUTH, THE ELDERLY, THE HANDICAPPED, AND THE HOMELESS: SHARED PROBLEMS

Dependency Issues

Although the traits may vary dramatically, there are some intriguing similarities in the experience of being young and of being elderly. The most apparent of these is that a large percentage of the population of both groups is dependent on other persons or on social agencies for most or all of their basic needs. This is also true of the severely disabled. The young are dependent on their parents for food, clothing, shelter, discipline, and training. As they grow, they are dependent also on schools, over which they have little or no control, for their continued socialization and education. In some families, children gain increased decision-making power as they develop, and thus gain increased power over their own lives. In other families, however, the power is retained by parental figures, courts, and/or other external decision makers.

The elderly and the severely handicapped are dependent, in varying degrees, on their families, on social security payments, and often on various welfare agencies for food, clothing, shelter, and general health care. They, too, often seem to have little control over many of the decisions made on their behalf.

All three groups, according to the degree of their dependence and/or vulnerability to victimization, require special protection from the justice system. All persons have the right to a safe environment and to have their lives and property protected. This has always been one of the primary justifications for the existence of government. The elderly have the legal and human rights of any citizen and may have been very active in exercising these rights in the past. As dependence on others increases, however, the ability to independently exercise rights decreases. The young are sometimes not aware that they even have rights, nor do they understand the appropriate avenues for exercising them.

> The child is a citizen of the State. While he "belongs" to his parents, he belongs also to his State. Their rights in him entail many ties. Likewise the fact the child belongs to the State imposes upon the State many duties. Chief among them is the duty to protect *his right to live and to grow up with a sound body*, and to permit no interference with that right by any person or organization (*In re* Sampson, 317 N.Y.S. 2nd 611). [Italics added]

The constitutional rights of a child to due process in juvenile court proceedings were clarified in *In re Gault* (1967). *Parens patriae*, the court acting in the best interest of the child, can no longer be interpreted as a means of depriving a child of these express rights. Other recent court decisions have extended and clarified the rights of children in a number of other areas, including their right to receive treatment for venereal disease and treatment for the use of dangerous drugs without parental knowledge or consent. Although many protections for the young, the disabled, and the elderly exist, intervention on the part of others on their behalf (advocacy) is necessary in order for their rights to be protected.

Dependency, vulnerability, and *protection* are all terms that infer a limit on the ability of a person to choose for himself, to have charge of life decisions. The more limited the choices a person feels he or she has, the more powerless a person believes himself or herself to be. A child who is removed from his or her own home and "in his best interest" is placed in a series of foster homes—none of which he chose or participated in choosing—is in a position of increased powerlessness. In a similar position is the elderly woman, accustomed to driving her own car, who has to admit that she can no longer drive and must depend on others for transportation. Her choices have been limited and her powerlessness increased.

Personal Identity Issues

When the young, the elderly, the severely handicapped, or the homeless (as well as others not in these groups) feel powerless, this feeling is often acted out in one of the following ways: (1) the person defers to the powerlessness and agrees to be helpless or (2) the person finds ways of publicly asserting power (e.g., through power struggles with family members and/or authority figures or other activities that may require police intervention).

Where Do I Fit?

The young, the disabled, the elderly, and the homeless often wrestle with opposite sides of the same identity problem: Where do I belong? How can I fit into society or the community? The young are seeking ways to increase their independence while retaining, with or without their consent, a part of their dependence. They wish to have an independent place in the world but are not prepared to give up the security they have in the family system. Parents contribute to the ease or difficulty with which this problem is resolved, but much of the burden rests with the youth. The disabled and the elderly face similar difficulties in either establishing or maintaining their independence.

Self-Image and Self-Esteem

The elderly, in particular, struggle to retain a part of their independence while their dependency needs increase. As with youths, the frustration of the struggles is compounded by the fact that many of the changes they experience occur, to a large degree, without their voluntary consent. The issue in both instances is one of personal identity. It is an issue of **self-image** and **self-esteem**, and it is resolved (or unresolved) on an individual basis.

The young, the severely disabled, the elderly, and the homeless share another experience. Often all are treated "like children" in society. They are talked at, talked about, and planned for, but often they are not included in the decision making about their lives. Sometimes they are "taken care of" so well that their dependence on others increases without their consent or realization.

In acting as the parental authority for these persons, we achieve the following:

1. We strip them of a part of their independence and their self-respect.
2. We increase their vulnerability and encourage the assumption that these persons are unable to choose for themselves.
3. We decrease, even more than necessary, their right to make decisions for themselves and their responsibility for their own actions.
4. We increase their feelings of powerlessness.
5. We fail to provide positive ways in which they can experiment with decision making.

Essentially, if police act like the authoritative parent, they encourage others to act like children. "Children" have license to pout, complain, defer decisions, feel persecuted, and blame the consequences of their actions on others. The likelihood of "misbehavior" is increased.

Stereotyping Issues

The young, the handicapped, the elderly, and the homeless in our society share at least one more experience. Perceptions about them are seldom based on their individual characteristics. Instead, they are based on some generalized perception that has become the stereotype of their group. Often this perception is based on a negative, disabling stereotype. Elsewhere in this book, we have discussed in much detail the problems created by **stereotyping** and destructive or negative perception. Certainly all these apply to stereotyped perceptions of these special populations. Hostility invokes hostility and also perpetuates stereotyping.

Myths about Youth

MYTH 1: ALL TEENAGERS WHO COMMIT DELINQUENT ACTS ARE GOING TO BE ADULT CRIMINALS   Actually, a very small percentage of all youths who are referred to juvenile courts for delinquent acts become adult criminals. When it is considered that most (if not all) youths commit at least one delinquent act (whether or not they are caught and/or referred), that small percentage is significantly reduced.

MYTH 2: ALL TEENAGERS HAVE SEVERE ADJUSTMENT PROBLEMS DURING ADOLESCENCE
Some teenagers are better able to adjust to adolescence than others. Most are not referred for delinquency or incorrigibility. Many are school, church, and community youth leaders and move without major disruption into adulthood.

MYTH 3: TEENAGERS CANNOT BE TRUSTED   As are all people, teenagers are individuals. Treating teenagers with respect encourages trustworthy behavior.

MYTH 4: ALL TEENAGE GROUPS ARE GANGS   Gangs, by definition, have some specialized features. They are organized and have a leadership, symbols, common goals, and criteria for membership. In this definition, the Boy Scouts, Campfire Girls, 4-H Clubs, and church groups would all qualify as gangs. What usually separates gangs from other organizations is the nature of their goals, and their illegal and sometimes violent activity. However, many modern-day juvenile gangs are separated even further.

In the past, young people joined gangs for a sense of personal identity; however, today many gangs are motivated by financial interests. They are in the business of acquiring and selling stolen goods or of drug trafficking, and they apply ruthless violence to protect their illicit enterprises. Some members of large-city gangs have ready access to semiautomatic weapons and submachine guns. The largest number of current gang members who fall into this category belong to the "Crips" and the "Bloods," two juvenile gangs organized around drug trafficking who got their start in Los Angeles. Gangs create special problems for the police that require extensive training (and, in larger cities, the creation of specialized units), but officers should be careful about stereotyping.

Myths about the Elderly

MYTH 1: PEOPLE OVER SIXTY-FIVE ARE MORE OFTEN VICTIMIZED BY CRIME THAN THE REST OF THE POPULATION   Persons over 65 are actually victimized by crime less than the rest of the population. It will be interesting to see how the aging of the "baby boomers," who started entering their sixties in 2006, will affect crime and victimization rates. Senior citizens do tend to be frequent victims of certain types of personal larceny crimes, such as purse snatching, pick pocketing, consumer fraud, and con games. Also, older people, when victimized, are more vulnerable to physical and psychological harm than people in other age groups, and the loss of what might seem to be a minimal amount of money or property might create a greater hardship on the elderly than on people in other groups. Particularly disturbing for the elderly is that they are more likely to fall victim to strangers in or near their homes. This increases the fear level of the elderly.

MYTH 2: WOMEN OVER THE AGE OF SIXTY-FIVE ARE FREQUENTLY RAPE VICTIMS   Actually, the opposite is true. In fact, only about 1 percent of all known rape victims are women who are over 50 years of age. Unfortunately, fear of rape and of other violent crimes may create a sort of self-imposed isolation and may restrict an elderly person's lifestyle dramatically.

MYTH 3: THE ELDERLY ARE TOTALLY DEPENDENT ON OTHERS FOR THEIR CARE AND OFFER NO CONTRIBUTION TO SOCIETY   The elderly are often an untapped resource of information and service in our communities. They may serve as consultants to business and industry and to the criminal justice system. They are often skilled and conscientious volunteers in the system. They are some of the best community relations links that an agency can have.

MYTH 4: THE ELDERLY CANNOT ENJOY SEX BECAUSE OF PHYSIOLOGICAL DIFFICULTIES   A person's attitude toward sex and the availability of a sexual partner are by far the most important factors influencing presence or absence of a continued and gratifying sex life (Masters and Johnson, 1966, pp. 241–242).

MYTH 5: INTELLIGENCE REACHES A PEAK IN THE TWENTIES AND DECLINES AT A STEADY RATE   So long as health is generally good, research indicates that intellectual stability and growth can be an important part of middle and old age. Where problems occur they are usually caused by illness or marked inactivity. In fact, recent studies suggest that the adult brain may not really be a "finished product" after all. It may continue to be capable of structural change, or a sort of "rewiring," or the formation of new synapses following some forms of damage.

Myths about the Handicapped

MYTH 1: HANDICAPPED PEOPLE CANNOT TAKE CARE OF THEMSELVES   People who suffer from physical and mental handicaps may be found in all walks of life. Many notable people have overcome physical and mental handicaps to become quite successful.

MYTH 2: THE MENTALLY ILL ARE DANGEROUS AND CANNOT BE TRUSTED   Far more harm is perpetuated on the U.S. populace by "sane" offenders than by the mentally ill. Only a small percentage of violent crimes are committed by mentally ill offenders.

MYTH 3: THE MENTALLY RETARDED DO NOT KNOW WHAT IS GOING ON   Those who suffer from mental retardation are keenly aware of their limitations; they have had them pointed out on numerous occasions. They are just as human as you and I and deserve to be treated accordingly.

MYTH 4: THE POLICE SHOULD NOT TREAT THE HANDICAPPED DIFFERENTLY FROM ANYONE ELSE   The handicapped deserve to be treated in an equitable manner. They aren't asking for preferential treatment, just fair treatment that takes the effects of their disability into consideration. It is not only the right thing to do; it is the legal thing to do.

Myths about the Homeless

(Adapted from National Law Center on Homelessness, www.nhchc.org/curriculum/module1DH3)

MYTH 1: HOMELESS PEOPLE COMMIT MORE VIOLENT CRIME THAN HOUSED PEOPLE   Homeless people commit *less* violent crimes than housed people.

MYTH 2: MAGNET THEORY: SETTING UP SERVICES FOR HOMELESS PEOPLE WILL CAUSE HOMELESS PEOPLE FROM ALL AROUND TO MIGRATE TO A CITY   Studies have shown that homeless people do not migrate for services. To the extent that they do move to new areas, it is because they are searching for work, have family in the area, or other reasons not related to services. A recent study found that 75 percent of homeless people are still living in the city in which they became homeless.

MYTH 3: THE CHRONIC THEORY: HOMELESS PEOPLE ARE A FIXED POPULATION WHO ARE USUALLY HOMELESS FOR LONG PERIODS OF TIME   The homeless population is quite diverse in terms of their length of homelessness and the number of times they cycle in and out of homelessness. Research on the length of homelessness states that 40 percent of homeless people have been homeless less than six months, and more than 70 percent of homeless people have been homeless less than two years. Another research has identified three categories of homeless people:

transitionally homeless, who have a single episode of homelessness lasting an average of 56 days,

episodically homeless, who have four to five episodes of homelessness lasting a total of 265 days,

chronically homeless, who have an average of two episodes, lasting a total of 650 days,

MYTH 4: HOMELESS PEOPLE ARE MOSTLY SINGLE MEN   Families constitute a large and growing percentage of the homeless population.

MYTH 5: HOMELESS PEOPLE DON'T WORK AND GET MOST OF THEIR MONEY FROM PUBLIC ASSISTANCE   Homeless people do work, and a relatively small percentage of them receive public assistance.

MYTH 6: ALL HOMELESS PEOPLE ARE MENTALLY ILL OR SUBSTANCE ABUSERS   Around a quarter of homeless people are mentally ill, and about 40 percent are alcohol or substance abusers, with around 15 percent suffering from disabilities.

YOUTH, THE ELDERLY, THE HANDICAPPED, AND THE HOMELESS: A FEW CONTRASTS

Interactions with the Criminal Justice System

Although an increasing number of elderly and handicapped people encounter the criminal justice system as offenders, most interact with this system as victims of or witnesses to crime. A larger number of youths interact with the system as juvenile offenders. Those who encounter the system as victims are usually victims of abuse and neglect rather than victims of other types of crime (Doerner and Lab, 2005).

Maturity and Life Experience

The elderly and physically handicapped adults, although faced with problems of declining health, increasing vulnerability, and dependence, and possible lack of self-esteem, possess a level of maturity and life experience that the young and the mentally handicapped often do not have. Their resources may be greater. They have also had the opportunity to plan for this period in their lives and may therefore be prepared for some of the difficulties they may encounter. In contrast, the very immaturity, impulsiveness, and lack of experience of youth contribute to adjustment problems.

Looking Toward the Future

The young and the elderly see life and its opportunities from two different perspectives—one with anticipation and one with hindsight. Health issues are different; health problems of the young are usually acute; those of the elderly are usually chronic. Differences in health and life perspective also influence decision making. Depending on the nature of the disability, the outlook of handicapped people may approximate that of the elderly, regardless of their age.

THE PROBLEMS WITH PROGRAMS

Knowledge of Resources Available

Resources are usually available in areas of recreation, public assistance, information, counseling, crime prevention, and support services. Often the difficulty in finding a program that might match the needs of a young, elderly, disabled, or homeless person is not that they do not exist, but that the officer is not aware of the resource. Police–community relations must include knowledge, use, and constant updating of available community resources.

Some Do Not Reach the Population They Hope to Serve

Obviously, a great variety of programs is available to provide services to young, elderly, disabled, and homeless persons. In practice, however, many of these programs do not reach the population they purportedly serve, even though they appear to be successful programs. Sometimes the difficulty lies in the fact that they are time-limited or funding-limited projects, which may be phased out before many people know that they exist. Other times the problem is the degree of enthusiastic commitment on the part of the provider. Many programs responding to the same need for services never reach and involve the populations who need them most. Because of a poor knowledge of the population served, inadequate information dissemination, a lack of transportation services, and financial limitations, the following may be true about a number of persons who most need to be involved in prevention–protection programs:

1. They are not aware that such programs exist.
2. They have no means of transportation to and from the location where the programs are available.
3. They are afraid to hear any more about crime because they might not be able to sleep at night ("If I ignore it, maybe it will go away").
4. They do not feel the program applies to them.

As discussed in the previous section, there is danger in some of the ways we choose to meet the needs of young, elderly, disabled, and homeless persons. We may actually contribute to new problems by our approach to solving old ones.

A NEW APPROACH

With this new information and a different perspective, perhaps it is possible for us to approach these special populations differently. The content of the programs we provide for these groups may be valid, although sometimes neither dynamic nor far-reaching enough. *The greatest problem is in how service is provided.*

It is important that a young person, a handicapped person, a homeless person, or an elderly person be approached in the following ways:

1. As an individual.
2. With respect for that individual, no matter what his or her needs or views.
3. In a way that involves the person being served in the assessment of the need to be addressed, in the planning of the action to be taken, and in the action itself.

Without such an approach, our programs will fall short of their potential. Worse, we may compound the problems of the people we intend to help and, as a result, compound the problems of the police and the community.

The Community Oriented Policing Services (COPS), U.S. Department of Justice School-Based Partnership (SBP) grant program funds law enforcement and school partnerships that address crime and disorder problems in and around schools (Varano and Bezdikian, 2001). Specifically, these partnerships must address one of the following problems: bullying/threat/intimidation; drug dealing on school grounds, including alcohol use and related problems; problems experienced by students on the way to and from school; assault/sexual assault; vandalism/graffiti; loitering and disorderly conduct directly related to crime or student safety; disputes that pose a threat to student safety; and larceny. The involved police agencies reported that they had partnered (provided intelligence, financial, and/or political support) with students, school administration and faculty, bus drivers, school support personnel, parents, and local businesses.

An innovative program started by the Fort Myers, Florida, Police Department addresses the needs of the elderly and the young. The program, called Getting Retirees Actively Motivated to Policing Again (G.R.A.M.P.A.) Cops, uses retired police officers to work in the schools with school resource officers (SROs) in drug prevention programs (Spurlin and Schwein, 1990). These G.R.A.M.P.A. Cops also assist in other programs, such as for bicycle safety or to prevent child molestation awareness. According to Spurlin and Schwein, the program has benefited both the police department and the schools. It has allowed experienced police officers to reenter the police profession and has decreased operating expenses for the department, which no longer has to assign regular police officers to the schools. It has also allowed the police department to double its budget for SROs.

A problem faced by all police agencies is the misuse of handicapped parking spaces. Departments have instituted targeted crackdowns and increased the fines for violations of parking norms. The Omaha, Nebraska, Police Department has instituted a volunteer program to assist officers in parking enforcement patrol with aims to achieve the following:

- To prevent the unauthorized use of handicap parking stalls by promoting community awareness.
- To promote cooperation between the volunteers and the police in resolving the problem.
- To aid the police, freeing them to respond to higher risk calls. (http://co.douglas.ne.us/omaha/police/services)

The volunteers must be 21 years old, U.S. citizens, and pass a background check and an interview. They must pass a certification training course and refresher courses and have a completed application on file with the police department's coordinator of volunteers.

The Fort Lauderdale Model response to homelessness is based on the understanding that "the homeless are not 'problem people' but rather 'people with problems'" (Pusins, 2000). The model is a problem-solving approach to the issue of homelessness and was begun when it was recognized that the traditional police strategy of strict enforcement of local laws and rules was not effective and did not provide long-term solutions to the problems created by homelessness. A partnership was formed between the Broward Coalition for the Homeless and the Fort Lauderdale Police Department. The coalition developed a two-hour Homeless 101 training program for police officers. The program introduces officers to the reality of homelessness, its causes, and the most effective ways to deal with this serious social problem. The training is an example of community policing and problem solving and relies on a partnership with the homeless community as well as homeless advocacy groups and social service providers. The department's homeless policy supports this partnership, with officers being encouraged to refer the homeless to an appropriate social service provider in lieu of arrest.

POLICE–SENIOR PARTNERSHIPS

TRIAD Programs

TRIAD is a national community policing effort that partners senior citizens with sheriff's deputies and police officers for the purpose of promoting safety among the elderly (Anonymous, 2000b; Burkett-Dreggors, 2001; Frady, 2001; Gaines, 2000; see also, www.monticello.avenue. org./jaba/silver/apr99/triad.html; www.oag.state.ny.us/seniors/triad.html; www.planopolice.org/crimeprevention/Triad.htm; www.vbe.com/~jonvon/triad-1.htm; and www.tcpa.org/triad/). A TRIAD consists of a three-way effort among a sheriff, the police chief(s) in the county, and AARP or older/retired leadership in the area. The goals of TRIADs are to enhance law enforcement services to area seniors, to reduce unwarranted fear of crime, and to create learning opportunities for seniors and law enforcement alike.

TRIAD was first formed in 1988 as a volunteer effort between the National Sheriff's Association, the International Association of Chiefs of Police, and AARP. Since then, it has grown to 755 TRIADs in more than 47 states, England, and Canada. The National Association of TRIADs, Inc. (NATI), a tax-exempt affiliate corporation of the National Sheriff's Association, was formed in 1999. Public Law 106-546—Protecting Seniors from Fraud Act—also known as the TRIAD Law, signed by President Clinton on November 22, 2000, enables NATI to request $1 million a year for funding. This funding was provided through 2005. Funding has continued and in 2009 TRIAD celebrated its twenty-first year.

TRIADs have sponsored activities on the following:

Crime

Information on how to avoid criminal victimization

Expanded involvement in Neighborhood Watch

Home security information and inspections

Personal safety tips

Knowledge of current frauds and scams

Training in coping with telephone solicitations and door-to-door salesmen

Elder abuse prevention, recognition, and reporting information

Training for deputies and officers in communicating with and assisting older people

Reassurance programs for older citizens

Telephone call-in programs by and for citizens

Adopt-a-senior visits for shut-ins

Buddy systems for shut-ins

Emergency preparedness plans by and for seniors

Senior walks at parks or malls

Victim assistance by and for seniors

Court watch activities

Refrigerator cards with emergency medical information

Older persons volunteering within law enforcement agencies

Central to the success of each TRIAD are the senior advisory councils, or Seniors and Lawmen Together (SALT). The SALT council assesses the needs of the elderly in the community and provides a forum for the exchange of this information between seniors and law enforcement.

Specialized Units

Some police departments have created specialized units to handle cases involving senior citizens. In Texas, at least four departments specialize in senior citizen units: the Harris County Sheriff's Department's Community Services; Grand Prairie Police Department's Victim Assistance Outreach; San Antonio Police Department's Sex Crimes and Family Violence Unit; and the Houston Police Department's Elderly Crimes Prevention Unit (Anonymous, 1999). The Grand Valley Police Department employs four citizens to provide victim assistance duties.

R.U.O.K. (Are You Okay?)

R.U.O.K. programs, such as those operated by the La Marque Police Department and the Fort Bend County Sheriff's Department in Texas, are computer programs that phone senior citizens who live alone at least once a day (Anonymous, 1999). Senior citizens fill out an application listing next of kin and personal information. If there is no answer from the computer-generated call and redials, an officer is sent to investigate.

Citizens on Patrol

Citizens on Patrol is an important part of the community policing efforts of many police departments. According to the Web site of the National Association Citizens on Patrol (NACOP), the term actually describes a number of citizen volunteers such as "Citizen Observer Patrols," "Community Action Patrols," "Police Auxiliary Citizens Team," "Retired Senior Volunteer Patrol," "Volunteers in Policing," and "Volunteers on Patrol." Founded in 1999, NACOP represents 5,000 citizen volunteers in 80 cities across 18 states. Citizens on Patrol comprises groups of senior citizens (55 and over) such as the Senior Patrol in Milford, Delaware; the P.R.O.U.D. (Picayune Retired Organized, United and Dedicated) senior patrol in Picayune, Mississippi; the Senior Volunteer Patrol (SVP) in Chula Vista, California; the Retired Senior Volunteer Patrol (RSVP) in Chula Vista, California; the Senior Police Partners (SPPS) in Long Beach, California; and the Senior Volunteer Patrol in Oceanside, California. Although the duties of these groups vary, they generally include crime victim assistance; home security inspections; parking enforcement, including handicapped parking; traffic control; vacation home security checks; patrolling business districts parking lots and school zones; making personal contact with business owners, patrons, residents, and visitors; calling and/or visiting homebound seniors; documenting graffiti sightings; and having reception greeter at police front counters. As one can see from the list of duties, Senior Citizens on Patrol can be and is a vital part of a police department's police–community relations.

Senior Citizens Police Academy

We have already discussed citizens police academies and their use in a police department's police–community relations efforts. Many departments have citizens police academies specifically for senior citizens. The Jersey City, New Jersey, Police Department Senior Police Academy was developed to help keep senior citizens safe and educate them about resources and services available to them. Among the topics addressed are reporting crime and using 911, avoiding flimflams and identity theft, home and personal safety, and pedestrian safety. The academy runs for 3–4 weeks and to date has graduated 550 seniors. The Senior Citizen Police Academy of the Washington, D.C., Metropolitan Police Department was started in 2005 in partnership with the DC Office on Aging with the purpose of enriching and enhancing the quality of life in neighborhoods around the city. Upon graduation from the six-week curriculum taught in three-hour sessions twice a week, the seniors sign up for volunteer positions and/or community organizing around the city. The Orlando, Florida, Police Department's Senior Citizen Police Academy was started in 2000 and it holds classes in the community usually at a Senior Center to make the academy more accessible to seniors. The training highlights what seniors can do to prevent their own victimization and contribute to crime prevention in their communities.

REALITY CHECK

In a departure form the previous Reality Checks, we provide an example of a progressive police policy dealing with deaf and hard of hearing persons.

Cincinnati Police Department Policy Statement Regarding Effective Communication with People who are Deaf or Hard of Hearing

Overview

It is the policy of this law enforcement agency, the Cincinnati Police Department to ensure that a consistently high level of service is provided to all community members, including those who are deaf or hard of hearing. This Agency has specific legal obligations under the Americans with Disabilities Act and the Rehabilitation Act. To carry out these policies and legal obligations, the Agency instructs its officers and employees (hereinafter "officers") as follows:

- People who identify themselves as deaf or hard of hearing are entitled to a level of service equivalent to that provided hearing persons.

- The Agency will make every effort to ensure that its officers and employees communicate effectively with people who have identified themselves as deaf or hard of hearing.
- Effective communication with a person who is deaf or hard of hearing in an incident—whether as a victim, witness, suspect or arrestee-is essential in ascertaining what actually occurred, the urgency of the matter, and the type of the situation.
- Various types of communication aids—known as "auxiliary aids and services—are used to communicate with people who are deaf or hard of hearing. These include use of gestures or visual aids to supplement oral communication; an exchange of written notes, use of a computer or typewriter; use of assistive listening devices (to amplify sound for persons who are hard of hearing); or use of qualified oral or sign language interpreters.

On-Call Interpretive Services

- The Agency will maintain a list of sign language and oral interpreting services that are available (on-call 24 hours per day) and willing to provide qualified interpreters as needed. Each of these services will be chosen after having been screened for the quality and skill of its interpreters, its reliability, and other factors such as cost. The Agency will update this list annually.

Source: Modified from www.cincinnati-oh.gov/police

Conclusions

Many resources are available to help police meet the needs of special populations. Some may be used intact; others will require adjustments to meet specific needs. New resources will be developed. The agency that truly wishes to successfully meet the needs of the young, the elderly, and the disabled will need to address the following areas when planning and delivering services:

1. Increased training of officers in developmental issues of special populations, in self-awareness, and in strategies for meeting the needs of even difficult-to-reach individuals in these populations.

2. Ongoing awareness of community resources.
3. Planning and implementation of programs that actively involve special populations and foster their input and interaction in a meaningful way in all stages of development and delivery.
4. Planning and implementation of programs that do not increase fear or reduce quality of life.
5. Increased efforts on the part of all officers to build interpersonal relationships with special populations within the community.

Student Checklist

1. Identify how special populations in a community pose special problems for the police.
2. Describe some of the developmental characteristics of adolescence and how they impact on interactions of the young with police.
3. Describe some of the developmental characteristics of maturation and aging and how they impact on interactions of the elderly with police.

4. Contrast the needs of the young, elderly, and disabled.
5. Identify the major elements that contribute to resolving or compounding the problems of special populations.
6. Suggest several ways through which the effectiveness of services to special populations might be improved.
7. Describe the police programs directed toward senior citizens. How do these programs improve police–community relations?

Topics for Discussion

1. Are the basic human rights of young, elderly, and severely disabled persons different from those of other persons?
2. How do suggestions made in this chapter for increasing the effectiveness of programs for special populations compare with suggestions made for increasing effectiveness in police–community relations?

3. What is your perception of the needs of special populations who live in your community? How can you ascertain whether or not your perception is correct?
4. What are your local police department's policies on dealing with special populations?

Bibliography

American Psychiatric Association. (2006). *The Criminal Justice Mental Health Consensus Project*. http://consensusproject.org.

Anonymous. (February 2000a). "Today's seniors," *Builder*, pp. 14–16.

Anonymous. (2000b). "Sheriffs in the heartland," *Sheriff*, Vol. 52, No. 4, pp. 16–19.

A Place to Call Home. (2006). *The Homeless*, http://aplace2callhome.tripod.com/homeless/id5.html

Burkett-Dreggors, D. (2001). "Crime prevention for an aging America: A stepping stone to comprehensive response," *Sheriff*, Vol. 53, No. 5, pp. 30–32.

Carter, D. L. (2002). *The Police and the Community*, 7th ed. Upper Saddle River, NJ: Prentice Hall.

Crispen, M. (1999). "Critical issues for the hearing impaired and the criminal justice community," Paper presented at the 1999 Annual Meeting of the Academy of Criminal Justice Sciences in Orlando, Florida.

Davenport, G. M. (1999). *Working with Toxic Older Adults: A Guide to Coping with Difficult Elders*. New York: Springer Press.

Desanto, J. A., and Moore, E. M. (March 1981). "Aggression and excessive force in the police portrait," *The Police Chief*, p. 49.

Doerner, W. G., and Lab, S. P. (2005). *Victimology*, 4th ed. Cincinnati, OH: Anderson.

Ford, J. L. (October 1992). "Health care fraud: The silent bandit," *F.B.I. Law Enforcement Bulletin*, pp. 2–7.

Frady, R. (2001). "How law enforcement responds to senior victims," *Sheriff*, Vol. 53, No. 5, pp. 32–33.

Fuller, J. R. (2005). *Criminal Justice: Mainstream and Cross Currents*. Upper Saddle River, NJ: Pearson/Prentice Hall.

Gaines, J. (2000). "President's message," *Sheriff*, Vol. 52, No. 4, p. 6.

Golan, N. (1992). *Mental Health and the Elderly: Social Work Perspective*. New York: Free Press.

Goldstein, S. (1997). *Managing Attention and Learning Disorders in Late Adolescence and Adulthood: A Guide for Practitioners*. New York: Wiley Interscience Press.

Havighurst, R. J. (1972). *Developmental Tasks and Education*, 3rd ed. New York: David McKay.

Hennessey-Fiske, M. (2009). L.A. County seeks to classify violence against the homeless as hate crimes. *LA Times*. www.latimes.com/news.

In re Gault, 387 U.S. 1, 87 S. Ct. 1428, 18 L.Ed. 1967.

In re Sampson, 317 N.Y.S. 2d 611.

Johnson, D. J. (1995). "An overview of learning disabilities," *Journal of Child Neurology*, January, Vol. 10, Suppl. 1, pp. S2–S5.

Lent, C. J., and Harpold, J. A. (July 1988). "Violent crime against the elderly," *F.B.I. Law Enforcement Bulletin*, pp. 11–19.

Masters, W., and Johnson, V. (1966). *Human Sexual Response*. London: Churchill.

Mayhall, P. D., and Norgard, K. E. (1983). *Child Abuse and Neglect: Sharing Responsibility*. New York: Wiley.

MDA. (2006). Muscular Dystrophy Association Web Page: www.mda.org.

Monahan, J. (1995). *Mental Illness and Violent Crime*. Video presentation prepared for and distributed by the National Institute of Justice.

National Association of Social Workers. (2006). *Issue fact sheet on aging*. Available at http://www.socialworkers.org/pressroom/features/issue/aging.asp.

National Institute of Law Enforcement and Criminal Justice. (1981). *A Mutual Concern: Older Americans and the Criminal Justice System*. Washington, D.C.: U.S. Department of Justice.

Ottinger, B. (2006). *Tourette Syndrome Tics*. Available at www.tourettesyndrome.net

Parent, M. K. (1977). "The losses of middle age and related developmental tasks," in E. R. Prichard, et al. (Eds.), *Social Work with the Dying Patient and the Family*. New York: Columbia University Press, pp. 146–153.

Peak, K. J., and Glensor, R. W. (2004). *Community Policing and Problem Solving*, 4th ed. Upper Saddle River, NJ: Prentice Hall.

Peck, R. C. (1968). "Psychological development in the second half of life," in B. Neugarten (Ed.), *Middle Age and Aging*. Chicago, IL: University of Chicago Press.

Piaget, J. (1968). *On the Development of Memory and Identity*. Worcester, MA: Clark University Press.

Pueschal, S. M. (2006). *Down Syndrome*. Available at http://thearc.org/faqs/down.html.

Pusins, B. (2000). *The Fort Lauderdale Model: Police Response to Homelessness*. Available at http://ci.ftlaud.fl.us/police/homeless5.html.

Schmalleger, F. (2007). *Criminal Justice Today*, 9th ed. Upper Saddle River, NJ: Prentice Hall.

Siegel, L. J., and Senna, J. J. (2007). *Essentials of Criminal Justice*, 5th ed. Pacific Grove, CA: Thomson/Wadsworth.

Spurlin, J., and Schwein, S. (May 1990). "G.R.A.M.P.A. Cops," *FBI Law Enforcement Bulletin*, pp. 2–4.

Varano, R., and Bezdikian, V. (2001). *Addressing School-Related Crime and Disorder*. Washington, D.C.: U.S. Department of Justice—Office of Community Oriented Policing Services.

Vickers, B. (2000). "Memphis, Tennessee, Police Department's crisis intervention team," *Practitioner Perspective*. Washington, D.C.: U.S. Department of Justice.

Works in Progress. (2006). *The Homeless*, http://www.olywa.net/wip/feb2002/homeless.html.

CHAPTER 13

Community Relations in the Context of Culture

I have a dream that one day my children will be judged by the strength of their character and not by the color of their skin.

—MARTIN LUTHER KING JR., 1963

Racial classifications of any sort pose the risk of lasting harm to our society. They reinforce the belief, held for too much of our history, that individuals should be judged by the color of their skin.

—SANDRA DAY O'CONNOR, 1993

KEY CONCEPTS

Cognitive Scripts
Community Relations Service
Cross-Cultural Factors
Cultural Citizens Police
 Academies
Cultural Diversity

Cultural Relativism
Cultural Universals
Discretionary Decision
 Making
Ethnocentrism
Multiculturalism

Police Multicultural Advisory
 Committees
Stereotyping
Xenophobia
Xenophiles
Xenocentrism

LEARNING OBJECTIVES

Studying this chapter will enable you to:

1. Define *cultural context*.
2. Describe the cultural context of community relations.
3. Contrast characteristics of different cultural groups.
4. Analyze several cultural factors that may be misunderstood by police.
5. Describe several community relations strategies for improving community relations in the context of culture.

This chapter examines the impact of culture in the United States, and how cultural considerations affect police–community relations.

Culture is the way of life shared by members of a society. It includes not only language, values, and symbolic meanings but also technology and material objects (Brinkerhoff, 1998). When applied to the United States, this definition would allow for individual and group differences according to region, ethnicity, religion, political orientation, class, and gender but would hold that, despite these differences, Americans share a common culture based on a national heritage of personal freedom and democratic principles. While encouraging individuality, U.S. citizens and resident aliens are expected to adhere to basic societal values and beliefs.

Other definitions of culture are not as inclusive. Rather than seeing a society in which there is great consensus despite regional, ethnic, religious, political, class, and gender diversity, these definitions stress the conflicts that occur within such a broad-based nation. They tend to see culture as all that human beings learn to do, to use, to produce, to know, and to believe as they grow into maturity and live out their lives in the social groups to which they belong (Tischler, 2007). Such a definition would view the United States not as a cultural melting pot but as a complex mixture of diverse groups engaged in competitions that too frequently boil over into cultural conflicts.

Both of the definitions are accurate and both are somewhat misleading. U.S. culture may be distinguished from European, African, or Asian cultures. The American people, however (as is true of most large social groups, including European, Asian, and African), are not culturally homogeneous. In fact, the United States is culturally diverse. There are numerous ethnic groups, religious groups, and many age and sex attributes of communities across the United States that help to make them unique. Immigrants—newcomers who may have difficulty in understanding the common characteristics shared by U.S. citizens (particularly our traditions and norms)—comprise still another culturally diverse group.

In this chapter, we seek to understand how culture influences human behavior, on the part of both the police and the communities they serve. Our view is that neither the common values and beliefs of U.S. society as a whole nor the competing views produced by **cultural diversity** within it can be ignored. Both the commonality of the former and the distinctions of the latter contribute to our strength as a nation.

Understanding and appreciating individuals within a cultural context—within the framework of the way their language and behavior express their feelings and beliefs as part of a cultural group—will provide new opportunities for police and citizens to increase the effectiveness of their interpersonal communication, open avenues for increased mutual respect, and form a realistic base for clarifying common values and areas of mutual concern.

THE CULTURAL CONTEXT OF COMMUNITY RELATIONS

A *context* is a framework for understanding meaning. It is the environment, or the conditions in which something is said or done. Contexts are very important. Without them, what people mean by what they say and do would rarely be clearly understood. The media is often accused of quoting people "out of context," that is, of selecting some portion of a speech and using it in a way that infers a meaning that the speaker did not intend. Because people usually behave in culturally defined ways, culture is a part of the meaning of every interpersonal interaction.

Being Culturally Appropriate

It is possible to have excellent counseling skills and yet apply them in culturally inappropriate ways (see Weaver, 1992). It is possible to make decisions precisely by the letter of policy and procedure and to commit acts that are inappropriate and inhumane. Understanding the cultural context of our own beliefs and actions and the beliefs and actions of others can help to prevent such tragedy.

In order to understand how to deal with people of different cultures (or of divergent sub-cultures within a dominant culture), one must seek to examine the context of that particular culture. Weaver (1992) demonstrated that failure to understand the dynamics of another culture could cause police officers to misinterpret the intentions of others. The seeking of contextual understanding of different cultures is defined by sociologists as cultural relativism. **Cultural relativism** means that we seek to understand different cultures from their particular perspectives or on their own terms rather than imposing preconceived standards from our own cultural development (Tischler, 2007).

Achieving cultural relativism is not an easy task. We all have biases and preconceptions that we bring to every situation we encounter. Psychologists use the term **cognitive scripts** to refer to the application of past experiences to new situations or encounters (Bartol, 1998). How we approach these situations is thus colored by our personal development, which is largely influenced by our own cultural environment. How we respond to influences from our cultural environment shapes how we respond to other cultures. When we perceive cultures other than our own as flawed or inferior, we are being *ethnocentric*. People within a nation who see all other nations as inferior, individuals who see other races, religions, or regions as having lesser morality or intellect, are practicing **ethnocentrism** (Bucher, 2004; LeMay, 2005). Ethnocentrism is a form of **xenophobia** in that those things with which we are familiar and therefore perceive as preferable are influenced by cultural considerations. Catholics who have contempt for Baptists, African Americans who hate Hispanics, Northerners who perceive Southerners as inferior, and upper-class elitists who consider those of other classes to be unworthy are all examples of ethnocentrism.

Cultural biases are not always to the detriment of those who are different from us. Frequently, people are so concerned about being fair to others that they discriminate against their own kind. **Xenophiles** are people who are ashamed of who or what they are. They feel that people who are different from them are either superior or warrant preferential consideration. When these feelings are applied to other cultures they are referred to as **xenocentrism** (Bucher, 2004; LeMay, 2005). If we have come to perceive our culture as flawed or inferior to others, we are being *xenocentric*. Such perceptions can be just as detrimental to cultural relations as those of ethnocentrists. Americans who are anti-American, Southerners who are anti-Southern, Native Americans who are ashamed of their ancestry, and individuals who are ashamed of their social class are examples of xenocentrism.

To deal fairly and objectively with other people within a culturally diverse society, one must be both accepting and understanding of his or her own culture, as well as others. We must be sensitive to the norms and traditions of others, but we must also understand that there are **cultural universals** that are dictated by the overall society in which we live (Popenoe, 2000). Determining and applying those behaviors or values that are appropriate universal standards (i.e., U.S. ideals of individual freedoms, social equality, order under law, and democratic values) can be extremely difficult. People must come to terms with their own moral and social perspectives, as well as understand how compatible their views are within society as a whole. As we discuss in more detail in the following chapter, there is considerable disagreement on what behaviors are culturally appropriate. What is often perceived as being a societal standard is "often only a common strand found among the diverse elements of which it is composed" (Popenoe, 2000).

In the following sections we discuss many of the cultural influences that the police must consider to properly enforce universal standards in a diverse U.S. society.

Understanding Crime

In order to understand crime in minority communities we must take into account the ideas, feelings, and experiences of the people in the community (Shusta et al., 2005). Weis and Sederstrom (1981) stated, "In essence an individual learns criminal behavior, particularly within social groups or social areas where there is a culture conflict or inconsistency surrounding the violation of the law." They argue for getting families, schools, peer groups, youth gangs, local officials, and social organizations involved in healthier social development opportunities for young people, and effectively organizing the community against crime. Accomplishing such a goal requires an understanding of cultural contexts.

Providing Services to the Community

New immigrant communities and other communities in transition need special police attention. Officers can help to ease the shock of entering a new culture by offering protection and informal education. But such work requires close personal contact, not remote observation through the windows of patrol cars (Shusta et al., 2005). Services to any community must be matched to the citizen's perception of need and to the resources of the community. Distrust of established agencies, expectations of community members, different languages and different symbols, and many other factors must be considered in planning and providing for effective services (Colvard, 1992; Pitter, 1992). Many new immigrants, both legal and illegal, suffered abuses at the hands of government officials in their native lands. A product of those abuses is a strong distrust of government institutions in general and the police in particular (Pitter, 1992). These immigrants tend to perceive the police as oppressors rather than public servants (Colvard, 1992). Their fears are heightened by cultural conflicts and language barriers that block effective communication between the police and many ethnic communities.

These blocks to effective communication (discussed in detail in Chapter 8) are experienced not only in immigrant communities but are also observable within communities comprising English-speaking ethnic minorities. In those areas, the language may appear on the surface to be the same, but cultural variations in linguistic patterns and semantic meanings impair understanding and heighten tensions between officers and citizens. The results are police–citizen encounters in which individuals "talk at" one another rather than communicating.

FIGURE 13.1 Cultural diversity is not pleasing to everyone.
Courtesy of Birmingham Police Department.

Overcoming Stereotypes

Stereotyping of police by the community and of the community by the police interferes with effective community relations. Stereotyping is often based on prejudice. Prejudice creates and is created by hostility and mutual fear, and distrust is intensified in the process.

Officers and community members who can appreciate and respect cultural differences are less likely to be fearful and judgmental of people from cultures other than their own. They can be more open to assessing their own biases and achieving mutual respect.

Understanding beliefs and behavior in a cultural context may help to debunk stereotypes about members of that culture, but even in the process of gaining understanding, a new danger exists. Because characteristics must be generalized to place them in a cultural context, we must take care not to replace the old stereotypes with new ones.

Discretionary Decision Making

Three major factors that influence decision making in the field are space, time, and appearance (Greenlee, 1980, p. 50). Perception and use of these are often culturally defined.

SPACE   The suspect's use of physical and personal space both during an alleged offense and during questioning influence decision making by the officer. Finally, the officer's decision is usually based on his or her own cultural definition of the proper use of space in such a situation, even though that definition may not be understood by the suspect.

TIME   Time of day, elapsed time, and use of time on the part of the suspect are decision-making factors. "Proper" use of time usually is culturally defined. Time may be perceived specifically or globally, depending on the cultural context of the perceiver.

APPEARANCE   Males are more likely than females to commit some types of crimes (e.g., rape and voyeurism). Age, too, may be a factor in determining who to stop and question about a specific crime. The person who looks "out of place" in a neighborhood may be considered a primary suspect, as may a person who is stereotyped as a potential problem. Care must be taken not to mistake poverty and its impact on a group of people for culture.

As Greenlee states, "a discretionary decision resulting in a just action depends on the officer's ability to assess cultural norms accurately and to be, in effect, the cultural and social engineer at that moment" (Greenlee, 1980, p. 51).

Characteristics of Culture

Culture comprises all of the following characteristics:

- *It is organic and supraorganic.* It depends on people acting, thinking, and feeling to exist, but it outlives individual people and generations.
- *It is overt and covert.* Overt parts of culture, such as language and houses, can be observed, but attitudes, philosophies, and spiritual elements are inferred.
- *It is explicit and implicit.* Explicit culture can be described by the people who perform the behavior that is a part of it (e.g., playing football, brushing teeth). Implicit culture is more difficult to describe objectively (e.g., adults speak a common language but may not be able to explain objectively its grammar and syntax).
- *It is ideal and manifest.* The ideal culture is what people believe their behavior should be; manifest culture is how people really behave.
- *It is stable and changing.* System principles apply to cultures. Both change and a need for structure and predictability are constants.

No person adheres to all the values in a given culture; socialization is seldom complete. Within every culture there are distinctive subcultures (Popenoe, 2000). As a result, diversity within a culture is common. Hispanic culture includes Cuban, Puerto Rican, Mexican, Spanish, and other subcultural groups. Southeast Asian culture includes Laotian, Vietnamese, and Cambodian groups. It is possible to describe basic traditions and standards, or touchstones, of a culture because these are less subject to area variation. It is not possible, however, to define a culture precisely, nor to find a person who perfectly represents a given culture.

CROSS-CULTURAL FACTORS

The following factors should be viewed only as examples of the variety of **cross-cultural factors** that lead to cultural understanding and misunderstanding.

African Americans

The term *African American* has supplanted *black* as the preferred terminology by which to refer to Americans who fall within the Negroid categorization of racial groups. This terminology can be misleading, in that there are Americans of African descent who are not black and there are blacks residing in the United States who are neither American nor of direct African descent. Despite those distinctions, in this book the term *African American* is used to refer to U.S. residents who are Negroid or identify themselves as being African American, Afro-American, Negro, or black.

African Americans are no longer the majority minority within the United States; they have been surpassed by Hispanics or Latinos. However, African Americans number 34,658,190 (U.S. Bureau of the Census, 2001), and comprise 12.3 percent of the U.S. population. The majority of African Americans reside within urbanized areas of the nation. They also represent 22.1 percent of all persons living below the poverty level (U.S. Bureau of the Census, 2001). These figures may be interpreted to mean that African Americans are overrepresented both within the lower class and within inner cities. The products of these findings are that large numbers of African Americans live under both economic and social hardships. The existence of such hardships places a direct burden on the relations between African Americans and the police who serve them.

Despite considerable progress in regard to race relations within U.S. society, African Americans continue to be dramatically overrepresented within U.S. correctional institutions. At the end of 2000, there were 1,381,892 black prisoners in federal and state prisons (Bureau of Justice Statistics, www.ojp.usdoj.gov/bjs/prisons.htm). This translates into 3,457 imprisoned black males per 100,000 black males in the United States. This overrepresentation will continue until such time as economic and social conditions for African Americans improve. Although African Americans have for the most part become *culturally assimilated*—adopted behaviors, customs, language, dress, and values consistent with the norms of the overall society—large numbers are still striving to be *structurally assimilated*—integrated into the common institutional and social life of the country (Rothman, 2005; Schaefer, 2007). This resistance to structural assimilation is a product of lingering ethnocentrism among both the white majority and African Americans.

African Americans have experienced more difficulty in becoming assimilated into U.S. society than have many other ethnic minorities, for two primary reasons: (1) clearly notable racial characteristics, and (2) the legacy of slavery. The first difficulty has been reduced as U.S. society has become less color conscious due to the civil rights movement, laws barring racial discrimination, and the continued deepening of human understanding. The second difficulty is actually more challenging. Even in a society committed to social equality that utilizes governmental programs to redistribute wealth and enhance the quality of life and opportunities for the lower class, change comes slowly. The change is hindered by political disagreements with regard to the appropriateness of change strategies utilized by governments and individuals.

FIGURE 13.2 The Birmingham Police Department, which once symbolized racial intolerance toward African Americans, is now reflective of cultural diversity.

Courtesy of Birmingham Police Department.

Within both African American communities and U.S. society as a whole, constant disagreements occur over what should be done to enhance the quality of life for African Americans (LeMay, 2005). Should we follow the model of Martin Luther King Jr., who sought an integrated, color-blind society in which all citizens were treated equally? Or, do we follow the Malcolm X model, which demands enhanced economic opportunities while maintaining separation of the races? Is racism only a white problem? Or is anyone who dislikes members of other races or seeks treatment distinctive from other races guilty of racism? Are affirmative action programs still beneficial? Or have they become more divisive than beneficial? These are but a few of the complex and difficult questions with which we as a society continue to wrestle.

Within the ranks of African Americans, the perspectives are as varied as those found within American society as a whole. Many African Americans call for continued understanding and cooperation among the races. They stress mutual respect and opposition to racism and bigotry on the part of both blacks and whites. Others, such as the National Coalition of Blacks for Reparations in America, argue that peaceful coexistence cannot be achieved until "white society" atones by apologizing for the enslavement of African American ancestors and subsequent injustices that have continued to the present and then pays reparations to every African American. Still others hold more moderate positions as to what is best for both African Americans and other Americans (Healey, 2003; Macionis, 2006).

The end result of the foregoing debates is that the police will continue to be seen by many African Americans as representatives of an unjust and oppressive society (Cole, 1999). Unfortunately, African Americans will continue to be a large part of the police clientele (both as victims and offenders). The police must therefore seek to understand the perspectives and problems of African Americans, and they must do so with true concern and sensitivity. This is best achieved through the enhanced selection, training, disciplinary, and accountability strategies discussed in previous chapters. It is also supported by continued emphasis on equitable minority representation at all levels within police agencies and increased community involvement in the police decision-making process. Hopefully, the successful implementation of these strategies will prevent racial riots such as those experienced in Los Angeles in 1992 and Cincinnati in 2000.

NEW IMMIGRANTS   The complexity of African American relations within U.S. society (and with the police in particular) is further compounded by the diversity of immigrants (both legal and illegal) who have begun arriving in the United States from Africa and the Caribbean. Most Africans have little in common with African Americans beyond racial similarities. The cultural norms, values, history, and traditions differ significantly. Tribal and family influences, language difficulties, religious differences, and divergent attitudes regarding democracy and legal order make assimilation into both U.S. society as a whole and within African American communities quite challenging for all but the better educated Africans.

The influx of Caribbean refugees who are Negroid is creating a similar dilemma. Although many refugees speak English, most are poorly educated and can neither read nor write. Like African immigrants, they have distinctive cultural traditions and values that conflict with U.S. societal norms. This has led to heated debates as to what immigration policies should be regarding specific island nations. Haiti, where many of the poorly educated, French-speaking populace seek to escape abject poverty and political turmoil by entering the United States is a classic example (Macionis, 2006).

Hispanic Americans

Hispanic Americans comprise the majority ethnic group in America. The 2000 census found 35,305,818 residents of Hispanic descent, comprising 12.5 percent of the total population (U.S. Bureau of the Census, 2001). It is thought that this number is grossly underrepresentative due to the fact that many Hispanics are undocumented aliens who avoided contact with census takers and many individuals did not identify themselves as Hispanic.

Hispanic Americans are unique among U.S. ethnic minorities in that they are categorized not by race but by ethnic heritage. Hispanics are a very diverse ethnic group whose racial membership includes individuals who could be racially classified as Negroid, American Mongoloid, or Caucasoid, with most being varied mixtures of Caucasoid and American Mongoloid, or Caucasoid and Negroid. According to the U.S. Census Bureau, Hispanics are those persons who identify themselves as being of Mexican, Puerto Rican, Cuban, Central or South American, or other Spanish-culture origin. Many do not choose to identify themselves under the umbrella of Hispanic, which they consider to be too broad, preferring designations more specific to their particular origins (Schaefer, 2007). Others prefer to be referred to as Latinos. Still others prefer to be identified solely as Americans.

There are many differences among the ethnic subgroups that Hispanic Americans comprise. However, they share several common difficulties that set them apart from others in U.S. society. The most notable distinction for many Hispanics who have recently immigrated to the United States or have lived their lives within segregated enclaves is that of the Spanish language. There are many Hispanic dialects, some so different from others that they may appear to be another language. However, except for some variations in the definition and use of specific terms, they are similar enough to be mutually understood. Unfortunately, to those who do not understand the language's subtle nuances and reliance on nonverbal gestures, the different use of surnames and last names to indicate heritage, the closer proximity of communications, the greater use of touching, and its heightened expressiveness, the Spanish language may appear to be both foreign and threatening. This can lead to serious misunderstanding between Spanish-speaking citizens and English-speaking police officers (Colvard, 1992; Shusta et al., 2005; Weaver, 1992).

While language is a major distinction for Hispanics, other important cultural differences deserve comment. Hispanic males tend to exhibit a strong sense of *machismo*, in which they place great emphasis on their personal honor and their position of power within traditionally male-dominated families (Tischler, 2007). Hispanics have very strong commitments to family and often live within large familial groups that include three or more generations. Religion (predominantly Catholicism) plays an important role in their lives, and many have a fatalistic view of life ("If it is God's will, it will occur") (Bucher, 2004). Like other ethnic minorities, Hispanics place a greater emphasis on the welfare of the group rather than of individuals. Hispanics have traditionally been less materialistic than other U.S. ethnic groups, which combined with discrimination contributes to their being overrepresented within the lower class. Like other ethnic minorities, their frustration with limited social and economic opportunities has frequently led to negative relations with the police.

There are more than five million Hispanics from Central America, South America, or other Spanish cultures or origins. However, we confine our discussions to the three largest categories of Hispanic Americans: Mexican Americans, Puerto Ricans, and Cuban Americans.

MEXICAN AMERICANS   Mexican Americans are by far the largest Hispanic group in the United States. There were 20,640,711 Mexican Americans identified by the 2000 Census, comprising 7.3 percent of the total population (U.S. Bureau of the Census, 2001). Like African Americans, Mexican Americans (or Chicanos) have a long history of oppression in U.S. society. While we may tend to think of Mexican Americans as being recent (often illegal) immigrants from Mexico seeking better economic conditions, many have historical connections within the United States that are far older than those of all other ethnic groups except Native Americans (Rothman, 2005). They became Americans because their homelands were forcibly annexed by American colonialism. As a Chicano living in New Mexico informed one of the authors, "My family never moved. The United States moved." This perspective is also held by many Mexican immigrants who feel that they have merely moved to lands that rightfully belong to their people (LeMay, 2005).

Mexican Americans see themselves as quite distinct from other Hispanics both in racial composition and cultural history (Schaefer, 2007). They are a racial amalgamation of European and Native American, which while distinctly different from "Anglos" is the least divergent of all non-Caucasian groups. Their cultural development was shaped by early Spanish and Native American historical events that took place in Mexico and the American Southwest.

Mexican Americans have not created nationwide political organizations to promote their group interests as have African Americans and some other ethnic groups (Schaefer, 2007). Nor have they been quick to use social unrest as a weapon against injustice. The 1977 drowning of a handcuffed Chicano by six white Houston police officers led to demonstrations by Mexican Americans and calls for reforms but did not lead to riots. Chicanos have seemed more content to use the established political process to address their grievances than have other ethnic groups. It has been argued that this is due to successful assimilation on the part of many Mexican Americans (Shusta et al., 2005).

PUERTO RICANS   Puerto Ricans make up the second-largest grouping of Hispanics within the United States. In the 2000 census, 3,406,178 Puerto Ricans (1.2 percent of the total population) were identified (U.S. Bureau of the Census, 2001). This figure does not include people living in Puerto Rico, which is a U.S. possession. Like many Mexican Americans and all Native Americans, Puerto Ricans are Americans because their lands were incorporated into the United States (Mobasher and

Sadri, 2004). Puerto Rico became a U.S. possession in 1899 following the Spanish-American War. All Puerto Ricans are considered U.S. citizens who may freely move back and forth from the island to the continent, which many frequently do (Kitano, 1996). The privileges and responsibilities extended to Puerto Ricans (i.e., voting in presidential elections and paying federal income tax) vary depending on whether they reside in Puerto Rico or elsewhere in the United States.

Approximately one-third of all Puerto Ricans are black, with the majority being varying mixtures of Caucasoid, American Mongoloid, and Negroid (Schaefer, 2006). As a result of this ethnic and racial mixture, white Puerto Ricans may suffer from discrimination against Hispanics, while black Puerto Ricans also may suffer from racial discrimination. Due to discrimination and other cultural influences that make assimilation into society on the U.S. mainland difficult, many Puerto Ricans move back to Puerto Rico.

The attitudes of Puerto Ricans toward the United States varies considerably. Many Puerto Ricans view the United States as a colonial power that wrongly holds their island. They feel that Puerto Rico should be granted independence from the United States. Others feel that Puerto Rico is a distinct region within the United States and that as such it should be granted statehood. Still others feel that Puerto Rico is best served by being an American possession but having a degree of autonomy as currently provided by its status as a commonwealth. This debate has raged for several years, and at this writing it appears that the status quo will continue into the foreseeable future.

CUBAN AMERICANS   Cuban Americans numbered 1,241,685 persons, or 0.4 percent of the total population in the 2000 census (U.S. Bureau of the Census, 2001). They are mostly concentrated within southeast Florida near their original homeland. While there was some migration to the United States during the 1800s and early 1900s due to the close proximity of Florida to Cuba, most did not immigrate until Fidel Castro took power in 1959. The initial Cuban immigrants were predominantly well-educated members of the upper and middle class who were light skinned and either spoke English or readily learned to do so. These individuals maintained their Cuban identity but were easily absorbed into southeast Florida society. Later immigrants fleeing from Cuba's Communist society were less affluent, and more racially diverse; few spoke English, but they were able to adapt due to American acceptance of refugees from Communism and resources provided by previous immigrants. As the Cuban American community grew in the Miami area, many immigrants were able to adapt without learning English or adopting "American" customs (Rothman, 2005).

In 1980, Castro agreed to allow more than 100,000 Cubans to leave Cuba from the port of Mariel. In addition to political refugees, most of whom were poor, lacking in job skills, and unable to speak English, the Cuban government included several thousand people who had been imprisoned for committing nonpolitical crimes, being mentally ill, or being homosexual. The inclusion of this relatively small number of individuals resulted in a negative reaction toward the "Marielitos," which previous Cuban immigrants had not experienced. This negativism also heightened discriminatory attitudes by other ethnic groups toward Cuban Americans in general. Today, the Miami region is an ethnically and racially diverse area in which Cuban Americans comprise almost half of the populace (U.S. Bureau of the Census, 2001).

The political and social influence wielded by Cuban Americans in southeast Florida has provoked considerable resistance on the part of non-Cubans living there. Relations with lower- and middle-class whites, African Americans, and other Hispanics not of Cuban descent have frequently become strained. Twice during the 1980s, riots occurred as the result of police actions that led to the death of African Americans. One was precipitated by the death of a motorcyclist at the hands of a predominantly white group of police officers. The second occurred after an African American was killed by a Cuban American officer. In 1991, another riot occurred after a Hispanic officer of Colombian descent shot an African American motorist. The fact that riots did not occur following the officer's acquittal on manslaughter charges in 1993 is testimony to enhanced efforts to mediate grievances within Miami's multicultural community.

Asian Americans

Asian Americans are a highly diverse group made up of persons of Chinese, Japanese, Filipino, Korean, Vietnamese, Cambodian, Hmong, Laotian, Thai, Asian Indian, Bangladeshi, Burmese, Indonesian, Malayan, Okinawan, Pakistani, Sri Lankan, and other nationalities. In 2000, Asians comprised 3.6 percent of the American populace or 10,242,998 persons (U.S. Bureau of the Census, 2001). As categorized by the U.S. Census Bureau, Asians include persons classified both by racial characteristics (i.e., individuals displaying Mongolian features) and geographic origin (areas in which the inhabitants reside are considered to be a part of Asia, but like Asian Indians, the residents do not display Mongolian features).

Like other immigrant groups, Asian Americans have suffered from discrimination due to differences in race, religion, culture, language, and social organization (Popenoe, 2000). During the 1800s, Asian immigrants were used when cheap labor was desirable but abused when they and their children were perceived as being in economic competition. In California, citizenship was denied to immigrants who were not white. As recently as 1952, the California constitution forbade the employment of Asian workers. This "fear" of Asians flooding the country led the U.S. government to impose restrictive immigration laws that severely limited the number of Asians that could enter the country (Schaefer, 2006).

In addition to discrimination based on fear of economic competition by both whites and other ethnic groups, Asian Americans suffered from the view that they had unbreakable ties with their homelands that were stronger than any attachments they might have for the United States. This view was erroneous in that descendants of Asian immigrants had readily adopted mainstream American customs (including the use of English as a primary, if not a single, language) (Farley, 2005). Their adherence to cultural traditions and heritage was in effect no stronger than what might be found among white ethnic groups. Another difficulty faced by Asian Americans is that members of other ethnic groups who have had little exposure to Orientals (other than Hollywood stereotypes) tend to look upon all Asians as being the same. This has often led to spillover bigotry from persons who dislike an Asian nation or another Asian American group (Henslin, 2007). Such bigotry caused the 1982 beating death of a Vietnamese American by unemployed autoworkers who thought he was Japanese (Tischler, 2007).

The largest Asian groups in American society are Chinese Americans, Filipino Americans, Japanese Americans, Asian Indians, Korean Americans, and Vietnamese Americans. Other Americans of Asian descent make up only a small percentage of U.S. ethnic minorities. The following sections focus on the larger categories of Chinese Americans, Filipino Americans, Japanese Americans, and to a lesser degree, Asian Indians, Vietnamese Americans, and Korean Americans.

CHINESE AMERICANS   Chinese Americans were the earliest of the Asian groups to begin immigrating to the United States. They were first imported in the 1850s to work in mines, to help build railroads, and to perform duties that were considered inappropriate for white males (LeMay, 2005). Today they remain one of the largest groupings of any new immigrants. There were approximately 2,432,585 Chinese Americans identified in 2000 (U.S. Bureau of the Census, 2001). Many of these citizens are descendants of immigrants who came to this country more than 100 years ago. Others (both legal and illegal) are recent arrivals. The majority of Chinese Americans reside in California and Hawaii, but they may be found living throughout the United States.

Like other Asian Americans, Chinese Americans tend to have strong family ties, strict discipline, and a deep-seated respect for heritage and traditions. As mentioned earlier, Chinese Americans have historically experienced severe oppression within American society. They were denied both citizenship and work because of their race (Popenoe, 2000; Schaefer, 2007). They were specifically excluded from immigration to the United States (Tischler, 2007). They were also barred from testifying against whites. Despite these handicaps, Chinese Americans as a whole have persevered, in large part, because of strong commitments to both educational and economic success.

Despite the successes of many upper- and middle-class Chinese Americans, large numbers continue to live in poverty in racially segregated "Chinatowns." Racial discrimination and cultural conflict continue today. Although current stereotypes depict Chinese Americans as having economic affluence and political influence, large numbers (particularly recent immigrants) have not been assimilated into U.S. society.

FILIPINO AMERICANS Filipino Americans numbered 1,850,314 in the 2000 Census, making them the second-largest grouping of Asian Americans (U.S. Bureau of the Census, 2001). Like other Asian Americans, their numbers tend to be clustered in California and Hawaii. Unlike other Asian American ethnic groups, Filipinos are more racially diverse. They are predominantly of Malayan descent with varying mixtures of other races, due to various times during which the Philippines were controlled by other nations (i.e., Spain, the United States, and Japan). Indeed, Filipino Americans are frequently mistaken for Hispanic Americans due to their physical appearance and Spanish surnames (Mobasher and Sadri, 2004).

The Philippines were annexed by the United States following the Spanish-American War. Like Puerto Ricans, they had a unique status as both U.S. nationals and subjects. This ended when the Philippines was officially granted independence in 1934. Easy immigration to the United States was halted following independence, but a large number of Filipinos had already migrated in search of better economic conditions in Hawaii and California. Their lives as workers on Hawaiian plantations and West Coast farms were harsh, and they were paid meager wages (Popenoe, 2000). They were also segregated from other ethnic groups due to cultural differences and discrimination (Healey, 2003).

Following World War II, restrictions on Filipino immigration were loosened, and a second wave of immigrants came to the United States (Popenoe, 2000). Like other immigrants they experienced hardships both in adjusting to and being accepted into U.S. society. Despite these obstacles, Filipino Americans have been able to achieve a median family income that is one of the highest among Asian American groups (Popenoe, 2000).

ASIAN INDIANS Asian Indians comprised the third-largest Asian group according to the 2000 census, which found residents of Indian ancestry. Like neighboring Pakistan, Bangladesh, Burma, and Sri Lanka, India is populated by people with a very complex mixture of racial, ethnic, and religious groups who are in constant competition and, frequently, open conflict with one another. These conflicts are exacerbated by the population density of India. In addition, widespread poverty may be found within the rigid class system that still exists within Indian society (Mobasher and Sadri, 2004). Due to these conditions, many Asian Indians have immigrated in search of a better life.

In that they have dark skins but Caucasian features, Asian Indians are an "in-between ethnic group" that differs from other racial classifications (Henslin, 2007). This means that they are not readily assimilated into other groups that tend to have predominantly Caucasoid, Mongolian, or Negroid features. In addition, their religious beliefs (Hinduism, Islam, Sikhism, Buddhism, and Jainism) and traditions are seen as threatening by many Americans. This has led to segregated communities and limited opportunities for Asian Indians of less affluence.

VIETNAMESE AMERICANS The fourth-largest Asian group in American society is that of Vietnamese Americans. In a manner similar to that of Korean Americans, the immigration of Vietnamese to the United States was largely the product of U.S. involvement in an Asian conflict. Unlike Korea, war immigrants were not limited to American brides, orphans, and students. The fall of South Vietnam to Communist North Vietnam led to thousands of Vietnamese citizens seeking asylum in other countries (Popenoe, 2000). The initial wave of Vietnamese refugees immigrating to the United States consisted primarily of upper- and middle-class individuals, predominantly Catholic, who left Vietnam to escape reprisals from the Communists (Schaefer, 2006; Schaefer, 2007). Assimilation for this group, while challenging, was not as difficult as for those who came later.

The second wave of Vietnamese refugees began arriving in the United States after 1975. As a whole they were less educated, poorer, younger, Buddhist, and less prepared for entry into American society (Schaefer, 2006; Schaefer, 2007). Many of these refugees were "boat people" who had endured extreme hardships to escape Vietnam and eventually gain entry in the United States. The combined number of Vietnamese Americans that resulted from these immigration processes was 1,122,528 in the 2000 census (U.S. Bureau of the Census, 2001).

Like some other Asian groups, those Vietnamese who spoke English, were better educated, and had economic assets and/or marketable skills experienced considerably less difficulty in gaining acceptance in the communities in which they settled. The poorer, less affluent refugees have experienced challenges more similar to those of earlier Asian immigrants. Prejudice and hostility toward Vietnamese immigrants have been extremely severe in areas in which Vietnamese customs and economic competition have brought them into direct conflict with working-class persons of other races.

The outcome of the Vietnam War did not result only in mass immigration from Vietnam. Other Asian groups who had supported U.S. involvement in Southeast Asia also fled their countries as political refugees. These groups were predominantly Cambodians, Hmong (a separate ethnic group living in Laos), Laotians, and Thais. Their immigration added greatly to the numbers of Cambodians, Hmong, Laotians, and Thais living in the United States.

KOREAN AMERICANS   Korean immigration has taken place in three waves. The first began in 1882 with the signing of the Shufeldt Treaty and ended in 1905 when Japan took control of Korea. The second took place during and after the Korean War (between 1950 and 1953) when

FIGURE 13.3 Sgt. Cheng Her of the Western Carolina Police Department.

Courtesy of Western Carolina Police Department.

immigration policies were relaxed for war brides, war orphans, and students. The third wave began following the Immigration and Naturalization Act of 1965 and continues today (Bucher, 2004). The product of these successive waves is that there were 1,076,872 Korean Americans identified in the 2000 census (U.S. Bureau of the Census, 2001).

Korean Americans have experienced difficulties similar to those of other Asian immigrants. Like Chinese Americans and Japanese Americans, Korean Americans have been relatively successful in adapting to American society (Tischler, 2007). A willingness to learn English and adopt Christianity has aided their success. Some may even argue that they have been too successful. These "hardworking, striving, studious people living in closely knit families" have begun to suffer from the same domestic problems (divorce, abuse, alcoholism, etc.) that plague the white majority (Henslin, 2007). It should be further noted that the success of Korean Americans has led to strained relations with other minorities, as evidenced in the Los Angeles riot of 1992.

JAPANESE AMERICANS   Japanese Americans began arriving in the United States in fairly large numbers during the 1870s. Their experiences were very similar to those of Chinese Americans in regard to mistreatment and prejudice at the hands of the white majority and other ethnic groups (Popenoe, 2000). Although they were the objects of bigotry and discrimination, Japanese Americans were more readily adaptable to American society than were many other immigrant groups. Like Chinese Americans, they were industrious and sought to attain both educational and economic success. Unlike Chinese Americans and other Asian groups, the Japanese are less likely to segregate themselves within ethnic communities (Schaefer, 2007) and are more likely to intermarry outside their ethnic group (Farley, 2005). As a result, they have been more easily assimilated than Chinese Americans.

Due to the war with Japan, one of the more shameful exhibitions of racism in U.S. history was perpetrated upon Japanese Americans during World War II, when more than 110,000

FIGURE 13.4   Officer with a citizen in front of a community police ministation.
Courtesy of Delray Beach Police Department.

Americans of Japanese descent were forcibly removed from their homes and placed in "relocation camps" (LeMay, 2005). Included were people whose families had lived in the United States for nearly a century. Anyone of one-eighth or greater Japanese blood was considered a potential Japanese sympathizer (Henslin, 2007). It was not until 1988 that survivors of the Japanese relocation programs received an official apology and partial compensation from the U.S. government (Tischler, 2007).

Although they did not arrive in the United States in large numbers until after 1900, the Japanese American population has grown steadily. Today they comprise the fifth-largest group of Asian Americans, numbering 796,700 in the 2000 census (U.S. Bureau of the Census, 2001). As a group, Japanese Americans have been very successful in both economic and educational achievements (Henslin, 2007), yet they continue to suffer from discrimination and bigotry. Much of this discrimination is based on racism, but a great deal may also be attributed to envy by other groups. Japanese Americans are resented not just because of their (exaggerated) success within American society but also because of Japan's success in the world economy (Farley, 2005).

Native Americans

The previous sections focused on those persons who have immigrated to the United States and the difficulties they have experienced in adjusting to and being accepted into American society. The racial and cultural distinctions among those ethnic minorities have significantly influenced how they interact with one another and with the white majority. Ironically, the challenges those groups have faced are overshadowed by those endured by the indigenous peoples of the lands that now comprise the United States.

PACIFIC ISLANDERS   Until 1980, Pacific Islanders were classified among "Other Races" within the U.S. census. In the 1980 and 1990 censuses, Pacific Islanders were grouped with Asians. We have not classified them as such for two reasons. The first is that such a grouping was based more on geography than on race or culture. Pacific Islanders are predominantly Polynesians, Micronesians, or Melanesians (Mobasher and Sadri, 2004). These racial groups are distinct from

FIGURE 13.5   Tribal police officers at the San Juan (New Mexico) Pueblo.

others discussed previously. The second reason is that the vast majority of Pacific Islanders residing within the United States are not immigrants from other nations but from lands that are part of the United States. In that these peoples are Americans due to American imperialism rather than to immigration, they are more correctly classified as Native Americans.

HAWAIIAN AMERICANS   The majority of Pacific Islanders residing in the United States are Hawaiian Americans. Hawaii was a separate kingdom until 1893, when American businessmen, aided by the U.S. Navy, led a successful revolt against the Hawaiian monarchy. In 1900, Hawaii became a territory of the United States despite considerable opposition by native Hawaiians. Efforts to make Hawaii a state were resisted by Congress until 1959, primarily due to fears of its heavily Oriental population, which had been imported during the late 1800s and early 1900s to work on the plantations (Lind, 1980). Today, Hawaii is a prosperous state noted for its natural beauty, its mild climate, its friendly treatment of visitors, and its cultural diversity. However, the negative impact of the American experience on native Hawaiians tends to be overlooked.

Hawaiian Americans numbered 140,652 in the 2000 census (U.S. Bureau of the Census, 2001). True Hawaiian Americans are of Polynesian descent. Today they are a minority population in the state of Hawaii. That few pure Hawaiians remain is the result of diseases transported to the islands by visitors, which nearly decimated the native populace during the 1800s, and Hawaiian intermarriage with Asian and white immigrants. The social product is a "melting pot" of diverse cultures and traditions (Schaefer, 2006). Unfortunately, within this "multicultural society," native Hawaiians have suffered discrimination and abuse at the hands of both white Americans and Asian Americans. Native Hawaiians (who were traditionally friendly and trusting) discovered that their lands had been taken over, their economic opportunities limited, and their cultural heritage repressed by other ethnic groups. Many native Hawaiians residing in the "American Paradise" today are currently experiencing economic and social adversities similar to those of other ethnic minorities.

SAMOAN AMERICANS   The Samoan Islands were an independent kingdom in the South Pacific until 1899, when they were partitioned by the United States and Germany. The western islands, which had been seized by Germany, were administered by New Zealand following World War I. In 1962, Western Samoa became an independent nation. American Samoa, as the smaller group of eastern islands is known, has remained under the control of the United States since 1899 (Schaefer, 2006).

The residents of American Samoa are of Polynesian descent and are predominantly Catholics. They are not U.S. citizens, but as U.S. nationals they are free to travel to the United States. As the result of unrestricted immigration, mostly in search of better economic conditions, there were 91,029 Samoan Americans included in the 2000 census (U.S. Bureau of the Census, 2001). Many Samoans immigrate to Hawaii, where they are more readily assimilated than on the U.S. mainland (Schaefer, 2007). The Samoan American experience has been similar to that of other ethnic minorities.

GUAMANIAN AMERICANS   Guam is located within the Marianas Islands and is now a part of the Commonwealth of the Northern Marianas. The United States obtained control of Guam in 1898 at the conclusion of the Spanish-American War. Most Guamanians are "Chamoros," a mixture of native Guamanians, Filipinos, Mexicans, Anglos, and Japanese (Bucher, 2004). Increased economic competition caused Guamanians to begin immigrating to the U.S. mainland in 1970 after the U.S. government opened immigration to Guam for other Asian groups. The 58,240 Guamanian Americans identified in the 2000 census (U.S. Bureau of the Census, 2001) have encountered difficulties similar to those of other Pacific Islanders.

AMERICAN INDIANS   We use the term *Native American* as an umbrella under which all the indigenous peoples of America are categorized. To distinguish others from Pacific Islanders,

Eskimos, and Aleuts, we use the term *American Indian* to refer to the 308 tribes of Native Americans residing within the continental United States (Magleby et al., 2006). Some Native Americans object to the label *American Indian*, citing its derivation from the erroneous assumptions of early European explorers (Cummings and Wise, 2005). However, in that the term is still in use by the U.S. Census Bureau, the Bureau of Indian Affairs, and the American Indian Movement, we shall utilize this terminology. (The authors of this current edition are one-sixteenth Sioux and one-quarter Chickasaw, respectively, so we assure the reader that no disrespect is intended.)

Thus far we have discussed American Indians as if they are a homogeneous group (a practice that the U.S. government too frequently followed). Nothing is further from the truth. Like Asian Americans and Hispanic Americans, American Indians are comprised of culturally diverse peoples who have little in common. The depiction of "bloodthirsty" half-naked warriors riding across the Plains made great Hollywood hype but bore little resemblance to reality. To discuss the diversity among the many tribes and their various cultures and traditions would require volumes. However, the reader should be aware that American Indians had (and continue to have) many different lifestyles that were greatly influenced by their tribal traditions and geographical area. Many were fishermen, farmers, shepherds, ranchers, and craftsmen who lived in permanent and well-governed communities (Bucher, 2004). In fact, the model used by Benjamin Franklin in drafting the Articles of Confederation, which originally governed the United States, was based on the League of the Iroquois (Tischler, 2007).

American Indians are the most disadvantaged minority group in the United States. They have suffered harsher and more prolonged discrimination than has any other minority group. Almost every ethnic group in America has been grievously exploited but none to the degree of American Indians. The enslavement of Indian tribes began in New England prior to the importation of African slaves and continued in the Southwest for several years after the freeing of African slaves (Barker, Hunter, and Rush, 1994). Entire Indian tribes were driven from their lands, confined to lives of poverty on dreary reservations, and/or massacred at the hands of white settlers and the U.S. government. The "Trail of Tears," in which members of the Eastern tribes were forcibly removed to lands west of the Mississippi River, the 1864 Sand Creek Massacre of peaceful Indians in Colorado, the 1890 Massacre at Wounded Knee in South Dakota, and countless other acts of wanton aggression against American Indian men, women, and children (Farley, 2005) exemplify one of the more shameful periods in the history of the United States.

Even in today's enlightened society, which seeks to promote ethnic harmony and which vigorously enforces laws prohibiting discrimination against ethnic minorities, approximately half of American Indians live on government reservations (Schaefer, 2007). Conditions on those 278 reservations are predominantly poor, with most residents living in poverty and lacking decent health care (Magleby et al., 2006). Of those who live off reservations, nearly one-fourth live in poverty (Cummings and Wise, 2005).

American Indians are estimated to have numbered as high as 10 million at the time that Europeans began settling in North America. By 1850 their numbers had declined to approximately 250,000 as a result of starvation, disease, and deliberate massacre (LeMay, 2005). It has only been within the latter portion of this century that the number of American Indians has experienced sizable growth. In the 2000 census, American Indians and Alaskan Natives numbered 2,475,956, or 0.9 percent of the U.S. population (U.S. Bureau of the Census, 2001). This increase has been attributed to high birth rates and somewhat improved living conditions (Popenoe, 2000). It is also due in part to a greater willingness on the part of respondents to identify with their American Indian heritage (Tischler, 2007).

Due to increasing awareness of the continued plight of American Indians and the efforts of organizations such as the American Indian Movement and the National Indian Youth Council, it is hoped that the economic and social conditions of American Indians will improve. But when one realizes that these first Americans were not granted U.S. citizenship until 1924, it appears that change will come slowly.

ESKIMOS AND ALEUTS Like American Indians, Eskimos and Aleuts are considered Native Americans. These groups have distinct racial and cultural features similar to those of Siberian Asians, which distinguish them from American Indians (Cummings and Wise, 2005). In the 1990 census, when they were classified apart from American Indians, there were 57,152 Eskimos and 23,797 Aleuts residing in the United States (U.S. Bureau of the Census, 1991). Due to their segregation from most of American society in the Alaskan Arctic, Aleuts and Eskimos did not share the long history of oppression experienced by American Indians. However, with the coming of white settlers in the late 1800s and the development that has followed, they have experienced difficulties similar to those of other ethnic minorities.

White Americans

Based on the preceding sections, the reader might assume that all ethnocentric wrongs have been perpetuated on minorities by the "white majority." This view is incorrect for two reasons:

1. All peoples tend to be somewhat xenophobic. The products of this xenophobia are racism, bigotry, intolerance, and discrimination against other groups. Just as minorities have suffered from these social evils, so have they imposed them on one another, as well as on whites. Historically, those within positions of power in the United States have been predominantly white. This has led to the false impression that all whites have power and that all minorities are powerless. It has also led white xenophiles and minority xenophobes to overlook, or too readily excuse, minority misconduct.
2. There is no cohesive "White America." White Americans are as culturally diverse as any other racial category. Indeed, white Americans are varying mixtures of many Caucasoid ethnic groups. To classify all whites as Anglo Americans would be equivalent to labeling all Asians as Japanese, all Hispanics as Chicano, all Pacific Islanders as Samoan, or all American Indians as Cherokee. "European American" is a more accurate designation but still fails to note that many whites, while predominantly of European descent, also have the blood of other races.

In the 2001 census, whites listing one race numbered 274,595,678 or 97.63 percent of the U.S. population. Those listing race in combination with one or more races were 216,930,975 or 77.1 percent (U.S. Bureau of the Census, 2001). There has been an increasing interest in ethnic heritage among white Americans during the past decade, which ironically gained impetus due to the televised presentation of Alex Haley's *Roots*, a history of an African American family. Later films, such as Ron Howard's *Far and Away*, have aided in keeping white ethnic interests alive. Heightened awareness of cultural heritage among whites has also resulted from the current push for multicultural education by minorities and white liberals.

Due to the past success of "Americanization," which emphasized learning to speak English and abandoning national origin or cultural identity in favor of becoming an American (Tischler, 2007), many whites have only limited knowledge of their cultural heritage. Despite this loss, the majority of white Americans are still able to identify their national, if not specific area of, origin.

EUROPEAN AMERICANS The original European immigrants to America were primarily from the colonial powers of England, France, Holland, and Spain. By 1700, the English culture was dominant along the East Coast (Schaefer, 2007). Later immigrants (both before and after the American Revolution) were expected to adopt the social standards of this earlier group of White Anglo-Saxon Protestants (WASPs). Affluent WASPs controlled the political and social environment of early America (many non-WASPs argue that they still do). As non-English immigrants from western Europe arrived, they were indoctrinated as to how to conduct themselves. For Protestants from Scotland, Wales, Ireland, Sweden, Norway, Germany, France, and Switzerland, this was not a particularly difficult task. For Catholics from those same nations, the adjustment was more difficult due to religious persecution. Irish Catholics, in particular, were the recipients of severe harassment and oppression at the hands of the WASP power structure (LeMay, 2005).

As masses of non-Protestant immigrants began arriving in America from southern and eastern Europe, they also suffered from bigotry and discrimination. These "White Ethnics," as they are called (Healey, 2003), did not assimilate as readily as had previous white immigrants. Even in the 1990s, despite the constant pressures of Americanization, strong cultural identification can be found among their descendants. In addition to their cultural identification, one can also find a resentment among this group toward those who would declare that their "whiteness" has made for easy assimilation into American society. This resentment appears to be well founded if one considers that 66.5 percent of the nation's poor are white (U.S. Bureau of the Census, 1992, p. 12).

JEWISH AMERICANS   Approximately 6,500,000 Americans identify themselves as being Jewish (Schaefer, 2007). Unlike the other non-Protestant ethnic groups identified above, Jewish Americans did not identify with a common homeland. Nor can Jews be identified as a distinct racial group (despite the efforts of anti-Semites to do so). Their intermarriages with other ethnic cultures and the adoption of Judaism by members of diverse racial groups preclude such a racial identity. However, being Jewish transcends mere religious identification. Many people who do not practice Judaism still strongly identify with being Jewish. This strong cultural identification has been both beneficial and detrimental to Jews. Their adherence to a specific ethnic identity has enabled them to preserve their unique cultural heritage. Unfortunately, it has also led to their being targeted by others for being "different."

Jewish immigration to America began during the colonial period and continues today. The earliest Jewish immigrants came from Spain and Portugal. They were followed by immigrants from Germany and later from eastern Europe. In recent years, Jewish immigration into the United States has been primarily from Russia. As a group, Jewish Americans have achieved economic success and considerable political power, yet they have suffered from prejudice and discrimination throughout American history (Macionis, 2006). Anti-Semitism is no longer as common in the United States, but it continues.

Middle-Easterners and Northern Africans

Another cultural grouping that may be found in the United States is that of Middle-Easterners and Northern Africans. Members of this group either immigrated from or are descendants of immigrants from the Middle East or Northern Africa. Included in this grouping would be Arab Americans, Iranian Americans, and Turkish Americans. The exact number of Americans of Middle Eastern or Northern African descent is difficult to ascertain in that some members of this grouping are categorized as "Other Asian," others are classified within the general category of "White," and still others may be found within the category of "Other Race." However, utilizing data from the 2000 census (U.S. Bureau of the Census, 2001), it appears that their numbers would exceed 1 million. While many practice other religions, the majority are Muslim.

Immigration from Northern Africa and the Middle East has been a fairly recent phenomenon. Northern Africans and Middle-Easterners did not begin arriving in the United States in large numbers until the relaxing of immigration restrictions by the Immigration and Naturalization Act of 1965. Although their numbers are relatively small in comparison to other ethnic groups, they have received considerable attention in recent years due to the hostile relations that the United States has had with Iran and Iraq, and due to terrorist activities by a variety of Arab and Middle Eastern groups. The product of this attention has been a dramatic increase in hostility, discrimination, and assaults on U.S. citizens and resident aliens of Arab and Middle Eastern descent, particularly since the events of September 11, 2001.

A Perspective on Diverse Cultures

The United States is comprised of numerous ethnic groups that are actively engaged in social and economic competition in a pluralistic society. Racism, ethnocentrism, and discrimination continue. Too frequently, we experience racial unrest in our urban areas. "Hate crimes" are perpetuated by frustrated individuals who act out against groups or persons who differ from them. A casual observer may wonder why outright cultural conflict such as that currently found in regions of eastern Europe and Africa does not break out.

Although the authors cannot assure the reader that such incidents will never take place in the United States, we can offer hope that they will not. We will always have individuals who fear and hate peoples who are different from them, and there will always be individuals and groups who will play on those fears and hatred for their own political and/or economic gain. Some will blatantly preach their bigotry, others will seek to conceal it within noble-sounding rhetoric. Despite the existence of those who harbor resentment and animosity toward other races or ethnic groups, the majority of Americans are actually quite tolerant of one another. The reason for this is quite simple: *We are more alike than we are different.*

IMPROVING COMMUNITY RELATIONS IN THE CONTEXT OF CULTURE

Generally, the following elements must exist in order for strategies designed to improve community relations in the context of culture to be successful, especially since we have such diverse cultural groups in most U.S. cities.

Appreciating Culture

Understanding and appreciating the cultural patterns and characteristics that exist in the community are prerequisites to making positive decisions in a cultural context. Developing a strategy in which the community can participate and retain a sense of community ownership and self-help must begin with this step.

Understanding Language

Lack of a common language creates the likelihood for misunderstanding, increased fear, and increased distance in interpersonal relations. It is not possible to be fluent in each of the many languages and ethnic dialects that exist in our larger, multicultural cities. It is possible, however, to learn key street-applicable phrases in the language, to have translators available in major language groups, and to appreciate some of the cultural values expressed in language. As members of the community teach new language skills to police officers, they may also learn from the officers some of the same elements of English.

Getting Involved in Meaningful Ways

Getting involved can reduce isolation and stereotyping and increase community morale and participation in policing. Those who live outside the community and spend little free time there are outsiders, even if they once were community residents. Face-to-face contact is important. A new immigrant may come to the United States with a view of the police based on an old-country value, which is one of fear and distrust. Police must understand that view and appreciate its cultural context if change is to be possible.

In another sense, the community will have to make the same commitment in reverse and seek to understand the police view and appreciate its cultural context. Rather than leading to stereotyping and distrust, such efforts could lead to helping both officers and the community achieve their goals. If it is true that the values of police officers are lower in context than the communities they serve, this understanding of context can be used by police and the community to build cooperation. Reward can be attached by the agency and the community to community relations projects, gaining social recognition for the officers. The challenge of confronting barriers and building a legacy of cooperation can be both exciting and lead to inner harmony. In this way, meeting community needs can also meet the needs of the officers.

Affecting Public Policy

Community members can be encouraged by police officers to get involved in the formation of public police policy that affects their lives. Police can help build a supportive network that involves the leadership of more than one cultural group.

Making a Firm, Full Commitment

The agency and its officers must make a firm, full commitment to improving relations in the context of culture if the effort is to be successful. It must be firm in the sense that what is promised is what is delivered; the commitment is not just rhetoric but real. It must be firm also in the sense that it will be supported over a long period of time and will not be abandoned at the first sign of problems. It must be full in the sense that energy, money, and time must be committed to the effort. This includes rewards for officers and enough flexibility within the program to meet new challenges as they arise.

Multicultural Advisory Committees

Multicultural advisory committees that form partnerships with the diverse ethnic communities and their police agencies are examples of community policing in action and should be put into place by police agencies at all levels of government. Our neighbor to the North, Canada, is a nation of diverse cultures. Canadian police agencies practice community policing at all levels and have multicultural advisory committees in them. The Royal Canadian Mounted Police (RCMP), an agency similar to the FBI and Canada's federal police, are committed to serving the needs of their diverse communities. For example, the Richmond, British Columbia, RCMP state on their Web site that they are "reaching out to and partnering with a cross section of Richmond's diverse multicultural groups to strengthen existing partnerships and build positive relationships with representatives from local cultural organizations" (www.richmond.ca/safety/police/cprograms/multicultural.htm). The agency's multicultural advisory committee is the vehicle for this outreach effort and its mission is to "advance and promote positive relations between the Richmond RCMP and Richmond's diverse multicultural community by:

- creating an open, equitable, and sensitive organization, and
- encouraging an effective RCMP response to diversity issues and to reaching the goals of our national Bias-free Policing policy."

Bias-free policing involves decisions based on reasonable suspicion or probable grounds (probable cause) rather than on stereotypes about race, religion, ethnicity, gender, or other prohibited grounds.

The Canadian police agencies at the local level also have multicultural advisory committees. The Victoria and Vancouver Police Departments have police diversity committees. The Vancouver Diversity Advisory Committee, created in 1996 and composed of police and community members, meets monthly to discuss and implement improvements with respect to the relationships between the police and the community. The Greater Victoria Police Diversity Committee is a consultative and advisory committee to police departments in the Greater Victoria area. Their Web site says that the goal "is to help police members better understand the diverse cultures, value systems, unique perspectives, and conditions and religious beliefs" of the minority groups they serve (http://vicpd.ca/diversity.html).

Australia, another country that practices community policing and has widely diverse groups, has a long history of police–community multicultural advisory committees. The first

Australian police multicultural advisory unit (MAU) was established by the Victoria police in 1983. The unit within the police department is staffed by bilingual/bicultural sworn and unsworn members who are responsible for the following:

- Advising police on multicultural issues
- Providing cross-cultural training for police members
- Providing information on the role of police to Victorians from culturally and linguistically diverse backgrounds (www.police.vic.gov.au).

In 1985 the Police and Community Multicultural Advisory Committee (PACMAC) was established. This is a joint committee between the Victoria police and the Victorian Multicultural Commission. The members for this advisory committee are drawn from the Victoria police and Victoria's culturally and linguistically diverse communities. In 1993 the National Police Ethnic Advisory Bureau was established. This bureau recommends to all the police commissioners of Australia national policies, programs, and initiatives for improving police–ethnic community relations in Australia. This has led to state and local agencies forming their own police ethnic advisory groups made up of police and members from the multicultural communities.

In the United States, at the federal level, regional office of the Federal Bureau of Investigation establishes multicultural advisory councils composed of community representatives from ethnic and religious groups and law enforcement agencies. The goals of these councils are to build relationships and intergroup knowledge to improve community safety. The Los Angeles FBI office with their multicultural advisory committee (MCAC) holds town hall meetings to discuss community issues. In 2008, the New Orleans Field Office created a multicultural advisory council composed of community leaders and representatives from the diverse groups in the city to promote understanding and communication between the New Orleans community and the FBI (http://new orleans.fbu.gov/pressrel/2008/no073008.htm). Among the participating groups are representatives of the City of New Orleans Human Relations Commission, Children's Bureau of New Orleans, the Human Rights Campaign, the Anti-Defamation League, Catholic Charities Archdiocese of New Orleans, the Hispanic Chamber of Commerce, Reaping the Harvest Church, Unity of Greater New Orleans, the Loyola Center for Intercultural Understanding, the Better Business Bureau, Mary Queen of Vietnam Church and the Vietnamese community, the Jewish Federation of Greater New Orleans, Advocacy Center, the Times Picayune-Asian Affairs, the Indian community, the Ninth Ward community, and the Mid-City Neighborhood Organization.

Local police multicultural advisory committees are not as numerous and well developed as those found in Canada and Australia. However, there are some good examples: The Richfield, Minnesota, police multicultural advisory committee "will provide advice, suggestions, and assistance to the Richfield Police Department to aid them in better serving, communicating with, and understanding the many cultures that reside in, work in, or visit the Richfield area" (www.ci.richfield.mn.us).

Specific Targets

RECRUITMENT It is generally accepted that recruitment of officers must reflect the racial/cultural makeup of the community. The agency must seek the best candidates within these groups and then assist them to be culturally appropriate and to translate their understanding of their culture into positive action.

A three-year national advertising campaign to support local police recruitment, especially women and ethnic minorities, was undertaken in the United Kingdom (England and Wales) in 2000. The campaign sought to demonstrate the challenges the police face and to raise the status of policing in the public's eye and among the police themselves (Anonymous, 2000). Advertisements by celebrities and others ran on TV, in newspapers, on radio, and in theaters. The first year results showed a 77 percent increase in police recruits (Anonymous, 2001a). Such a national advertising program might work well in the United States, especially in conjunction with the federal COPS program.

The minority recruiting efforts of many police departments have dramatically changed the demographics of the departments. Shifting demographic patterns and an aggressive recruitment program have changed the New York City Police Department from 86.6 percent white in 1979 to 52.3 percent white in 2005 (Lee, 2005). The rest of the department in 2005 was 17.4 percent black, 25.5 percent Hispanic, and 3.8 percent Asian. In fact Asian Americans are the fastest growing group in the department. The 2005 academy graduating class of 1,750 recruits was the first time that minorities made up the majority of recruits (www.nyc.gov). More than half of the class, 54.06 percent were minorities—28.17 percent Hispanic, 17.7 percent black, 8 percent Asian, and 0.22 percent other. The graduating class was also the most educated in the department's history, with 57 percent having either an associate's or baccalaureate degree; 68 recruits had a master's degree and three were attorneys. The fire department is still 92 percent white, demonstrating that changing demographics is not solely responsible for the shift in the NYPD.

Progressive U.S. police departments like the NYPD, and those in many other countries, no longer hire at the minimum level—that is, they pursue a process of screening in, not screening out applicants (Cordner, Scarborough, and Sheehan, 2004). Basically, the screening-out process considers all applicants who meet the basic qualifications of high school diploma or GED, background checks, and so on. In the screening-in process, the department considers all those who meet the minimum qualifications, but only hires those who meet identified needs. For many departments these needs include ethnic diversity. Therefore, many police departments are specifically targeting minority/ethnic communities to ensure that women and men recruited by such efforts come from various racial and ethnic backgrounds (Prussel and Lonsway, 2001). Targeting minority communities is the best, and maybe the only, way to increase diversity in policing. In Long Beach, California, community leaders assist in recruiting efforts by training cultural groups to qualify for positions with the police department and other city agencies. In addition, several police departments are paying language incentive pay. The Dallas Police Department pays an additional $75–100 per month to officers fluent in Spanish, Cambodian, or sign language. San Jose, California, gives hiring preferences to applicants who speak eight certified foreign languages (Bennett, 1999). Regular officers who speak these languages receive incentive pay.

TRAINING The United States has become more multicultural and it is necessary that all police training (preservice and in service) must reflect the demographics of the community served. To accomplish that, training must reflect the following six principles (Himelfarb, 1991, pp. 53–55):

1. Respect for and sensitivity to the diverse communities served is essential for effective policing.
2. Respect for and sensitivity to ethnocultural communities can best be achieved through a broad-based multicultural strategy.
3. Training must be an essential element of such a strategy.
4. Training must be ongoing and built into the experience of policing; that is, it must be more than a course or two on **multiculturalism.**
5. A multicultural strategy that supports it will be most effective if perceived as integrated aspects of the philosophy and operations of policing.
6. A multicultural strategy and training program must be created in consultation with the ethnocultural communities served by the police.

The training must emphasize that the police are not "apart from" the community but are "a part" of the community (Coderoni, 2002).

The Santa Ana Police Department was instrumental in setting up the Task Force on Police–Asian Relations (TOPAR) in Orange County, California. Several departments joined to produce a series of videotapes for both officers and immigrants. They held a series of seminars explaining Southeast Asian culture with the goal of increasing communication and understanding between refugees and police. Problems still exist, but most feel that progress has been made (Taft, 1982, pp. 17–21).

Language skills may be taught through the use of key words, role-play situations depicting cross-cultural incidents, and case studies that demonstrate values, beliefs, and lifestyles. Involvement of community members and practice are critical to the success of language training. Crash courses usually have little long-term use.

The Houston Police Department's academy and in-service program incorporates many of the key strategies discussed in this chapter in an effort to improve community relations with the Hispanic population. The program includes information about Hispanic culture and its variations and information and activities regarding stress—what causes it and how to recognize it. Part of the training also includes discussion about Hispanic culture and cultural differences at Ripley House, a community center in a Hispanic area. This encourages communication between police officers and members of the Hispanic community. Confronting stereotypes through asking and answering anonymous questions of officers and learning a basic system of communication in Spanish that is geared toward street use are also part of the overall program. Input from officers is an important part of the training. A fiesta attended by officers and community members concludes one part of the training. Attendance is supported by the department. Each officer is rewarded with points toward certification, an insignia, and an opportunity to make changes in the program.

Rockland County, New York, because of its borders (Connecticut, New Jersey, and Westchester County, New York) and its proximity to New York City, has 15 different cultures (including Jamaican, Korean, Hasidic, Filipino, Cambodian, Haitian, Chinese, and Ramapo Mountain Indians) within its borders. With input from individuals from each culture and assistance from the Rockland County Chief's Association, the sheriff's office developed a 200-page sensitivity training manual (Merla, 1996). The manual, used in the police academy, provides information on each culture's religion, language, characteristics, and community dynamics. The manual also contains cultural taboos (e.g., a female officer touching an Hasidic male is considered offensive).

Since early 1990, the California cities of San Jose, Long Beach, Stockton, and Garden Grove have provided cultural diversity training to their officers. Stockton and Garden Grove provide such training to all employees. African Americans, Asian Americans, and Hispanic Americans make up almost 50 percent of each city's population (Bennett, 1995). The Roanoke, Virginia, Police Department has made efforts to build relationships with the Vietnamese community (Chapter 8). An integral part of this program is cultural awareness training for Roanoke police officers (Coventry and Johnson, 2001).

PUBLIC INFORMATION BULLETINS FOR LANGUAGE MINORITIES   The U.S. Department of Justice has published a brochure containing ideas for developing materials for people who do not speak fluent English. The materials are geared toward involving such people in the nation's social, political, economic, and legal mainstream to avoid isolation and frustration.

ONGOING COMMUNITY PARTICIPATION   Involving the community in training programs and in volunteer and citizen review efforts helps to secure continuing input. Police can be personally involved in community activities, particularly in outreach activities with youth. Foot patrol and/or team policing in designated areas may also be helpful. Close personal connections with the community must be maintained both on duty and off. The Los Angeles Police Department storefront center in Korea Town is the joint effort of the department and the community.

In St. Paul, Minnesota, the police chief meets with leaders of the Hmong, a group of 10,000 Laotian hill people who have settled there. His goal is to stay up to date on community developments and provide meaningful in-service training in the police department on Hmong culture (Taft, 1982, p. 17). On July 12, 2001, the Houston Police Department held its ninth Multicultural Reception at a local restaurant (Anonymous, 2001b). Citizens representing African American, Hispanic American, Asian American, and other ethnic and cultural groups attended. All were encouraged to wear attire that represented their culture or ethnicity.

Cultural Citizens Police Academies

The success of citizens police academies (CPA) has led many police departments to offer the same instruction in the group's native language or special topics that affect the minority groups. The Orlando, Florida, Police Department has offered a citizens police academy in Spanish since 2003. The Corcoran, California, Police Department offers a Spanish-language CPA entitled "Amigos de la Comunidad" or "Friends of the Community." The instruction is translated from the English-language CPA. In 2002, there were 20 Spanish-language CPAs in 12 states (Walker, Herbst, and Irlbeck, 2002).

Sacramento, California, is the most racially and ethnically integrated major American city, with 48 different cultures, including Hmong, Vietnamese, Slavic, and Mien (www.policevolunteers.org). The Sacramento Police Department conducts cultural academies for the Mien, Hmong, and Slavic communities. These academies are held once a week for three hours over a six-week period. The topics are more or less the same as in the English-language CPA and include additional topics of concern to the cultural group.

THE COMMUNITY RELATIONS SERVICE (CRS) CRS is an agency of the U.S. Department of Justice, created by the Civil Rights Act of 1964. The purpose of the agency is to assist in resolving community racial conflict, and the method is through noncoercive, third-party intervention. The service has regional offices in Atlanta, Boston, Chicago, Dallas, Denver, Kansas City, New York, Philadelphia, San Francisco, and Seattle. CRS conducts formal negotiations and offers informal assistance to facilitate resolution of conflicts, frequently assisting communities in resolving disputes arising from alleged police use of excessive force.

ADVOCACY "Action" committees can be formed that work with community social and legal services, civil rights, and other groups to promote police–citizen communication and citizen participation in formulating and monitoring police policies and practices that reflect the cultural needs of the community. For example, Hispanic Americans are becoming increasingly involved in and committed to influencing public policy in justice areas.

POLICE–COMMUNITY RELATIONS COMMITTEES Whenever minority groups voice concern that they are not receiving fair treatment form their police force, police–community relations committees can be established that include representatives from these alienated groups. This is exactly what happened in New London, Connecticut, in 1984 when complaints came from the black and Hispanic residents about the lack of fair treatment by a predominately white New London Police Department. A nine-member committee was formed with representatives from the NAACP and the Hispanic community, at least one woman, a council member, two nonvoting representatives for the high school, a member of the police union, and a police member designated by the chief. Recently, a member from the gay community was added. The original purpose of the committee "was to recommend to the city administration and City Council methods and programs designed to foster better understanding between citizens and police officers." The committee has had a rocky past but it is still functioning.

REALITY CHECK

Coping with Cultural Diversity

In light of the many racial and ethnic groups in the United States, how do we as a nation deal properly with cultural diversity? In the 1990s, three distinct perspectives were held by Americans in regard to cultural diversity. Each of these three perspectives offers a solution for coping with cultural diversity that is contradictory to the solutions offered by the others.

Leftist advocates of cultural pluralism claim that since the United States is a multicultural society, the political, economic, and educational systems must reflect that diversity. This "politically correct" group argues that straight, white, Anglo males have wrongly dominated American society (Gates, 1993). This wrong must be corrected by providing preferential treatment for females, ethnic minorities, and homosexuals until true equality of results has been achieved.

Political correctness (PC) calls for downplaying traditional studies of Western culture in favor of studies that emphasize the views of ethnic minorities, non-Christian religions, females, and gays (Eshleman, Cashion, and Basirico, 1993). PC advocates also support bilingual education by asserting that forcing immigrants to learn English is demeaning to minorities. Quotas designed to achieve equal results are considered both appropriate and necessary. They respond to allegations of reverse racism, sexism, and "straight bashing" by declaring that these actions are needed to pay back white males for their past oppressions of others. In short, not only must equality of results be accomplished, but atonement for past injustices must be made.

Conservative proponents of Americanization claim that PC is racist, sexist, anti-Christian, and heterophobic. These "fundamentalists" see the overemphasis of multiculturalism and discrimination against white males as harmful to all of society in that they promote separateness, bigotry, and intolerance. Actions that took place in the past cannot be undone in the present, particularly when those now targeted either had nothing to do with past injustices or were themselves victims of injustice. This group argues that English must be the official language of the United States in order to maintain the American culture (Eshleman, Cashion, and Basirico, 1993). They argue further that traditional American values must be upheld to protect our national identity, thwart moral decline, and prevent society from breaking down into cultural enclaves such as those currently found in eastern Europe and Africa.

Americanization proponents partially agree with the concept of equal opportunity for individuals but oppose the use of quotas or other mechanisms to ensure equality of results. They state that ethnic minorities and females are being assimilated into the economic and political power structure, and that time will eventually remove any inequities. Stressing multiculturalism is seen as rewarding activists who are motivated by selfish desires for economic and political gain rather than contributing to society. They further argue that efforts to redistribute wealth and expand welfare programs stifle individual initiatives and lead to overreliance on government (Brookhiser, 1993). Finally, these American fundamentalists view homosexuality as a deviant lifestyle that should be repressed rather than accepted by society. Critics of this extreme conservatism argue that it is close-minded, racist, sexist, classist, and homophobic.

A third view is held by *moderates, joined by a mainstream coalition of both liberals and conservatives.* This group disagrees with the extremism of the two other perspectives. Multiculturalism is seen as reasonable and healthy, but it is felt that societal norms and shared values must be preserved to protect all groups and maintain order within a pluralistic society. Affirmative action programs designed to provide equality of opportunity by ensuring a "level playing field" for women and minorities are felt to be appropriate. However, absolute guarantees of equal results are viewed with skepticism. Bilingual education is seen as beneficial in preserving ethnic identity as long as it does not ignore the competency in English needed to be competitive in American society (Tischler, 2007). Homosexuality is seen as a personal matter that should be used neither for nor against gays.

This moderate approach to multiculturalism is based on a desire to create an equitable, color-blind nation that is tolerant of differences among its diverse population. All groups, regardless of cultural heritage, gender, or sexual persuasion, are seen as contributing to American society. In this perspective, past injustices should be acknowledged in order to guard against similar unfairness in the future. However, efforts to exact vengeance for past evils (real or imagined) are seen as meaningless and divisive. Instead, cooperation based on education, tolerance, and a desire for a common good is seen as the appropriate means for coping with cultural diversity. Both left- and right-wing critics of moderation tend to see it as being allied with their ideological opponents at the opposite extreme.

Which of the foregoing perspectives is most compatible with your own views on culture? Why?

Conclusions

People usually behave in culturally defined ways, and their behavior can often be understood in the context of culture. Positive police–community relations are easiest to achieve in a community that is relatively culturally integrated. They are most difficult to achieve in fragmented communities that are culturally diverse and where cultural rules are in transition and unclear.

We rarely have the ideal as an option, but even in the most fragmented community an aggressive ongoing program for improving community relations in the context of culture can be effective. The key elements of a successful program include appreciating the culture(s); understanding the language(s); getting involved in meaningful ways; making a firm, full commitment; and creatively overcoming barriers.

It is important to remember that we are one culture as well as many. We have some basic values and goals in common. We share common feelings of anger, sadness, happiness, and fear. We also wish to be valued and to belong. Ruth Benedict (1934) wrote this:

> What really binds men together is their culture— the ideas and the standards they have in common. If instead of selecting a symbol like common blood heredity and making a slogan of it, the nation turned its attention rather to the culture that unites its people, emphasizing its major merits and recognizing the different values which may develop in a different culture, it would substitute realistic thinking for a kind of symbolism which is dangerous because it is misleading. (p. 16)

Student Checklist

1. Define *cultural context*.
2. Describe the cultural context of community relations.
3. Contrast characteristics of different cultural groups.
4. Analyze several cultural factors that may be misunderstood by police.
5. Describe several community relations strategies for improving community relations in the context of culture.

Topics for Discussion

1. List five values that you share with other members of your family. Are these values commonly held by all members of your community?
2. Discuss the cultural contexts that exist in your community. How has your community worked to resolve conflicts in values among these contexts?
3. What training is offered to police officers in your community that could improve community relations across cultures?
4. What are the possible benefits to be obtained from forming police multicultural advisory committees?
5. Does your local police department have any special minority recruitment programs? If so, what are they?

Bibliography

Anonymous. (August 30 2000). "UK Government: Home secretary launches first ever national advertising police campaign," *M2 Presswire*, Coventry.

Anonymous. (April 23 2001a). "UK Government: Police recruits up 77%," *M2 Presswire*, Coventry.

Anonymous. (2001b). "HPD recognizes diversity at multi-cultural reception," *The HPD News*, Vol. 1, No. 8, p. 1.

Barker, T., Hunter, R. D., and Rush, J. P. (1994). *Police Systems and Practices: An Introduction.* Upper Saddle River, NJ: Prentice Hall.

Bartol, C. R. (1998). *Criminal Behavior: A Psychosocial Approach,* 5th ed. Upper Saddle River, NJ: Prentice Hall.

Benedict, R. (1934). *Patterns of Culture.* Boston, MA: Houghton Mifflin.

Bennett, B. R. (1995). "Incorporating diversity: Police response to multicultural changes in their communities," *FBI Law Enforcement Bulletin,* Vol. 64, No. 12, pp. 1–6.

Bennett, B. (1999). "Beyond affirmative action: Police response to a changing society," *Journal of California Law Enforcement,* Vol. 33, No. 2, pp. 10–15.

Brinkerhoff, D. B. (1998). *Essentials of Sociology,* 4th ed. St. Paul, MN: Wadsworth.

Brookhiser, R. (March 1, 1993). "The melting pot is still simmering," *Time,* p. 72.

Bucher, R. D. (2004). *Diversity Consciousness: Opening Our Minds to People, Cultures and Opportunities*, 2nd ed. Upper Saddle River, NJ: Pearson/Prentice Hall.

Coderoni, G. R. (November 2002). "The relationship between multicultural training for police and effective law enforcement," *FBI Law Enforcement Bulletin*.

Colvard, A. L. (1992). "Foreign languages: A contemporary training requirement," *FBI Law Enforcement Bulletin*, Vol. 61, No. 9, pp. 20–23.

Cole, D. (1999). *No Equal Justice*. New York: The New Press.

Cordner, G. W., Scarbourgh, K., and Sheehan, R. (2004). *Police Administration*, 5th ed. Cincinnati, OH: Anderson Publishing.

Coventry, G., and Johnson, K. D. (2001). "Building relationships between police and Vietnamese community in Roanoke, Virginia," *Bureau of Justice Assistance Bulletin*, Washington, D.C.: U.S. Department of Justice.

Cummings, M. C., Jr., and Wise, D. (2005). *Democracy under Pressure: An Introduction to the American Political System*, 10th ed. Pacific Grove, CA: Thomson/Wadsworth.

Farley, J. E. (2005). *Majority-Minority Relations*, 5th ed. Upper Saddle River, NJ: Pearson/Prentice Hall.

Gates, D. (March 29, 1993). "White male paranoia," *Newsweek*, pp. 48–53.

Greenlee, M. R. (February 1980). "Discretionary decision making in the field," *Police Chief*, pp. 50–51.

Healey, J. F. (2003). *Race Ethnicity and Gender*, 3rd ed. Thousand Oaks, CA: Pine Forge Press.

Henslin, J. M. (2007). *Sociology: A Down-to-Earth Approach*, 8th ed. Boston, MA: Pearson/Allyn and Bacon.

Himelfarb, F. (November 1991). "A training strategy for policing in a multicultural society," *The Police Chief*, pp. 53–55.

King, M. L., Jr. (August 28, 1963). "I have a dream" speech, in Washington, D.C.

Kitano, H. H. L. (1996). *Race Relations*, 5th ed. Upper Saddle River, NJ: Prentice Hall.

Lee, J. (2005). *In Police Class, Blue Comes in Many Colors*. www.michaelsaray.com.

LeMay, M. (2005). *The Perennial Struggle: Race, Ethnicity and Minority Group Relations in the United States*, 2nd ed. Upper Saddle River, NJ: Pearson/Prentice Hall.

Lind, A. W. (1980). *Hawaii's People*, 4th ed. Honolulu, HI: University Press of Hawaii.

Macionis, J. J. (2006). *Society: The Basics*, 8th ed. Upper Saddle River, NJ: Pearson/Prentice Hall.

Magleby, D. B., O'Brien, D. M., Light, P. C., Burns, J. M., Peltason, J. W., and Cronin, T. E. (2006). *Government by the People*, 21st ed. Upper Saddle River, NJ: Pearson/Prentice Hall.

Merla, M. (March/April 1996). "Fair treatment for all: Equal opportunity police training," *Community Policing Exchange*, p. 3.

Mobasher, M., and Sadri, M. (2004). *Migration, Globalization and Ethnic Relations: An Interdisciplinary Approach*. Upper Saddle River, NJ: Pearson/Prentice Hall.

O'Connor, S. D. (June 28, 1993). Supreme Court majority opinion written by Justice O'Conner, in *Shaw v. Barr* 92–357.

Pitter, G. E. (1992). "Policing cultural celebrations," *FBI Law Enforcement Bulletin*, Vol. 61, No. 9, pp. 10–14.

Popenoe, D. (2000). *Sociology*, 11th ed. Upper Saddle River, NJ: Pearson/Prentice Hall.

Prussel, D., and Lonsway, K. A. (2001). "Recruiting women police officers," *Law & Order*, Vol. 49, No. 7, pp. 91–96.

Rothman, R. A. (2005). *Inequality and Stratification: Race, Class and Gender*, 5th ed. Upper Saddle River, NJ: Pearson/Prentice Hall.

Schaefer, R. T. (2006). *Racial and Ethnic Groups*, 10th ed. Upper Saddle River, NJ: Pearson/Prentice Hall.

Schaefer, R. T. (2007). *Race and Ethnicity in the U.S.*, 4th ed. Upper Saddle River, NJ: Pearson/Prentice Hall.

Shusta, R. M., Levine, D. R., Wong, H. Z., and Harris, P. R. (2005). *Multicultural Law Enforcement: Strategies for Peacemaking in a Diverse Society*. Upper Saddle River, NJ: Pearson/Prentice Hall.

Taft, P. B., Jr. (July 1982). "Policing the new immigrant ghettos," *Police Magazine*, pp. 10–26.

Tischler, H. L. (2007). *Introduction to Sociology*, 9th ed. Pacific Grove, CA: Thomson/Wadsworth.

U.S. Bureau of the Census. (1992). *Income, Poverty, and Wealth in the United States: A Chartbook*. Washington, D.C.: U.S. Government Printing Office.

U.S. Bureau of the Census. (2001). *2000 Census of Population: General Characteristics of the United States: 2001*. Washington, D.C.: U.S. Government Printing Office.

Walker, S., Herbst, L., and Irlbeck, D. (2002). *Police Outreach to the Hispanic/Latino Community: A Survey of Programs and Activities*. A Report by the Police Professionalism Initiative University of Nebraska at Omaha and the National Latino Peace Officers Association.

Weaver, G. (1992). "Law enforcement in a culturally diverse society," *FBI Law Enforcement Bulletin*, Vol. 61, No. 9, pp. 1–7.

Weis, J. G., and Sederstrom, J. (1981). *The Prevention of Serious Delinquency: What to Do?* Reports of the National Juvenile Justice Assessment Centers. Washington, D.C.: U.S. Department of Justice.

CHAPTER 14

The Dilemmas of Dissent and Political Response

We hold these Truths to be self-evident, that all Men are created equal, that they are endowed by their Creator with certain unalienable Rights, that among these are Life, Liberty, and the Pursuit of Happiness—That to secure these Rights, Governments are instituted among Men, deriving their just Powers from the Consent of the Governed, that whenever any Form of Government becomes destructive of these Ends, it is the Right of the People to alter or abolish it, and to institute a new Government, laying its Foundation on such Principles, and organizing its Powers in such Form, as to them shall seem most likely to effect their Safety and Happiness.

—Declaration of Independence, 1776

KEY CONCEPTS

Acceptable Dissent	Human Dynamics	Right to Dissent
Civil Disobedience	Legalistic Position	Strategies of Dissent
De-escalation of Conflict	Neutralizing Disorder	Strategies of Response
Escalation of Conflict	Power Tactics	Upward Spiral of Violence

LEARNING OBJECTIVES

Studying this chapter will enable you to:

1. Define the parameters of the right to dissent under the U.S. Constitution.
2. Present contrasting views of acceptable dissent.
3. Describe the interaction of the strategies of dissent and response.
4. Identify the significant aspects of escalation and de-escalation.
5. Analyze the ways in which police, courts, and corrections become instruments of power in relation to dissent.
6. Describe the necessary components for effectively neutralizing disorder without increasing violent dissent.

C hange and resistance to change are part of every system. For change to occur, some amount of "deviance" takes place and the "normal way of things" is disturbed or—as perceived by some—threatened.

The rights guaranteed to individuals and groups by the First Amendment to the Constitution of the United States reflect a commitment to allowing dissent as a means of bringing about needed social, legal, and political change. However, powerful social and political forces everywhere have always been resistant to change, so dissent has often led to intense and even violent confrontation. In 2009, the entire world was watching as peaceful dissent was violently repressed in the Islamic Republic of Iran. The brutal actions of the ruling theocracy demonstrated that its rhetoric of democracy is a sham. Freedom is never free, someone pays for it.

Dissent may be active or passive, nonviolent or violent, individual or mass. In a democratic society, the major dilemma becomes how to avoid social disorder, while at the same time avoiding total social control.

To better understand the dilemmas of dissent and political response, we must first understand the concept of dissent. Toward that end, in this chapter we consider contrasting views of dissent and study current social conflicts as they relate to both the strategies of dissent and response and the consequences for all parties involved. We address the processes of escalation, de-escalation, and resolution of social conflicts, and the involvement of police, courts, and corrections in them.

DISSENT: CATALYST OF PROGRESS

Change versus Order

One of the problems in political history is the conflict between change and order. It is difficult to say that any specific historical time was in a "state of order" because the patterns of conflict and resolution that were current then have led to new conflicts. This process will continue to occur. Our present society is complex, technologically communicative, and composed of many groups of people who have different interests, lifestyles, and values. Our political reality is that we are essentially a society of groups rather than of persons. These groups are pressing for change at an accelerating rate because more and more individuals feel they cannot bring about change unless they represent, or are represented by, a power base (Cummings and Wise, 2005).

Why Seek Change?

Why are so many groups seeking change? The answer, perhaps, can be found by examining our culture. Our contemporary culture places great emphasis on achievement, but it also emphasizes dissatisfaction with one's present state. Thus, achievement and its companion value, individual self-determination, promote the right to protest and to have grievances addressed—indispensable elements of a "free society."

The Right to Dissent

The First Amendment protects the freedoms of speech, the press, the right of the people to assemble peacefully, and the right to petition the government for a redress of grievances (Figure 14.1). The amendment protects not only the *individual's* **right to dissent** but also the right of *groups* to dissent, assemble, petition, and demonstrate. The First Amendment is a principle—a symbolic commitment

FIGURE 14.1 First Amendment to the U.S. Constitution.

Congress shall make no law respecting an establishment of religion, or prohibiting the free exercise thereof; or abridging the freedom of speech, or of the press; or the right of the people peaceably to assemble, and to petition the Government for a redress of grievances.

by our government to permit dissent and debate on public issues. Dissent, in the words of the National Commission on the Causes and Prevention of Violence, is the "catalyst of progress."

Keeping Dissent Peaceful

The survival of our democratic system is dependent on accommodating dissent, solving disagreements, peacefully containing social conflicts, righting wrongs, and modifying the structure of the system as conditions change. Although these changes are necessary to keep the government alive, the organization of government itself is fundamentally resistant to change. This resistance by the government to peaceful change leads to violence, a problem that the National Commission on the Causes and Prevention of Violence found has occurred throughout the history of the United States. The commission's conclusions remain accurate:

1. America has always been a relatively violent nation. Considering the tumultuous historical forces that have shaped the United States, it would be astonishing were it otherwise.
2. Since rapid social change in America has produced different forms of violence with widely varying patterns of motivation, aggression, and victimization, violence in America has waxed and waned with the social tides. The decade just ending, for example, has been one of our most violent eras, although probably not the most violent.
3. Exclusive emphasis in a society on law enforcement rather than on a sensible balance of remedial action and enforcement tends to lead to a decaying cycle in which resistance grows and becomes ever more violent.
4. For remedial social change to be an effective moderator of violence, the changes must command a wide measure of support throughout the community. Official efforts to impose change that is resisted by a dominant majority frequently prompt counterviolence.

FIGURE 14.2   Religious extremists protesting against gay rights.

Tim Boyle, Getty Images Inc.–Liaison.

5. Finally, Americans have been, paradoxically, a turbulent people that have enjoyed a relatively stable republic. Our liberal and pluralistic system has historically both generated and accommodated itself to a high level of unrest, and our turmoil has reflected far more demonstration and protest than conspiracy and revolution (The National Commission on the Causes and Prevention of Violence, 1969, pp. 1–2).

Acceptable Dissent

Our current concern with militant and dissident groups involves the strategies they use to apply pressures in an attempt to bring about changes in society (see Figure 14.3). The men who wrote the Constitution did not define "**acceptable dissent** tactics" in the First Amendment. Therefore, the meaning of what is considered acceptable strategies of dissent constantly changes. For example, the acceptability of such protest strategies as civil disobedience, direct action, violent confrontation, sit-ins, boycotts, parades, and draft-card burnings varies greatly, depending on who is defining these actions. Such tactics may be acceptable to a protest leader or even a bystander, but not to a Supreme Court justice or a police officer. Even legal scholars concede that drawing constitutional lines on acceptable dissent procedures is a difficult task (Magleby et al., 2006). The U.S. flag desecrations of the 1960s, 1970s, and 1980s produced varied definitions of acceptable and unacceptable dissent practices, depending on the state where they happened, the law enforcement agency that arrested the offenders, the court that tried the offenders, and whether or not the convictions (and not all were convicted) were appealed (Welch, 1999). The U.S. Supreme Court declared in 1989 that desecrating the flag constitutes a form of political protest that is protected by the First Amendment. This set off a storm of protest and several attempts by the U.S. Congress to pass federal statutes to ban flag desecration (one passed and was declared unconstitutional by the Supreme Court) (Welch, 1999). The effort by Congress to pass a constitutional amendment against flag desecration still continues.

FIGURE 14.3 Birmingham, Alabama. American Nazi Party demonstration.
Courtesy of Birmingham Police Department.

A Legalistic Position

A MODEL DEFINITION   A model definition of acceptable dissent was developed by former Supreme Court Justice Abe Fortas, who wrote the following:

> The First Amendment protects dissent if it is belief and not acts, if it is speech and does not create a clear and present danger of injury to others, if it is against a specific law or enforcement thereof by silent and reproachful presence, in a place where the dissenter has every right to be. Violation of a valid law is not justified by either conscience or a good cause. (1968, pp. 106–111)

SUPPORTIVE LEGALISTIC VIEWS   A similar position was taken by Archibald Cox, special prosecutor during the Watergate scandal, who said that the Constitution guarantees a wide variety of public actions to express sentiment, dramatize a cause, and demonstrate aroused indignation, power, or solidarity. As Cox explained, "One may disregard with legal impunity the commands of civil authorities if what the authorities forbid is in truth only the exercise of a privilege guaranteed by the Constitution" (1971, p. 386). Such action does not involve a violation of law in the ultimate sense because the orders given by the authorities are not law at all. However, the Constitution does not give us the right to disobey *valid* laws. Conducting a sit-in demonstration in someone's office, for example, would plainly violate valid and constitutional laws. The Constitution does not give anyone the privilege to violate a law even if the protest demonstration is designed to test the law's constitutionality. Citizens cannot pick and choose which laws they will obey without destroying the whole concept of law. The privilege of freedom and the right to peaceful change are eroded by such lawbreaking, although some changes have occurred as a result of such tactics.

Most of the members of the Violence Commission took a similar position. They said that no matter how a person feels about the dissenters' cause, he must not violate valid laws. In their views, "respect for the judicial process is a small price to pay for the civilizing hand of law, which alone can give abiding meaning to constitutional freedom" (*Walker* v. *Birmingham*). The Violence Commission suggests that the best way to challenge the constitutionality of a law is by initiating legal action, and while the judicial test is in progress, all other dissenters should abide by the law (National Commission on the Causes and Prevention of Violence, 1969, pp. 90–91). Every time a court order is disobeyed and each time an injunction is violated, the effectiveness of our judicial system is eroded. Defiance of the law is the surest road to tyranny. Disobeying valid laws does not contribute to the emergence of a more humane society, but leads instead to the emergence of a totalitarian state.

THE LEGALISTIC POSITION: A SUMMARY   Under this view, protesters are justified in disobeying the commands of civil authorities who try to forbid actions that exercise privileges guaranteed by the Constitution. Those who hold this view, however, insist that no one has the right to disobey valid laws. Three important corollaries of this position are as follows:

- Protest actions that break valid laws weaken the legal system, thus creating a threat to the privilege of freedom and the right to peaceful change, and compel the state to resort to its power.
- A distinction must be made between laws violated through protest actions (e.g., trespass and traffic laws) and laws violated because they are the object of dissent.
- The law and legal institutions are the only viable mechanisms for change in a democracy. Consequently, the best way to challenge the constitutionality of a law is through legal action; while the judicial test is in progress, all other dissenters should abide by the law.

CONTRASTING POSITIONS   In contrast to the legalistic positions taken by Fortas, Cox, and the Violence Commission, others feel that (1) the traditional methods of dissent are insufficient or have fallen on deaf ears; (2) dissent is often focused on organizational policies or administrative decisions and not laws; and (3) the dissent issue is often not negotiable to those in the power structure. Thus, one cannot legally protest those procedures or institutional practices that the legal system assumes to be "correct." For example, few legal options are available to people who want to alter school curriculums or textbooks that devalue the role of minority groups in U.S. history. Conversely, a person can protest discriminatory employment practices through the law but not through the economic system itself.

A KEY ISSUE   Both the legalists and the advocates of dissent agree that creative disruptive tactics are legitimate, yet they also realize that many protest strategies pose a serious political problem: *how to avoid social disorder while at the same time avoiding total social control.*

A CLASSIC ARGUMENT   Howard Zinn, an advocate of civil disobedience, argued that government has abdicated its duty to meet the needs of the people in order to serve the needs of those in power (1968). To right the balance, therefore, he urged strategies of dissent that go far beyond what is legally acceptable. He also argued that the Constitution should be interpreted boldly and broadly in order to augment what he called "the natural rights of the citizen."

> Why should not the equal protection clause of the Fourteenth Amendment be applied to economics, as well as race, to require the state to give equal economic rights to its citizens: food, shelter, education, medical care? Why should not the Thirteenth Amendment barring involuntary servitude be extended to military conscription? Why should not the cruel and unusual punishment clause of the Eighth Amendment be applied in such a way as to bar all imprisonment except in the most stringent of cases, where confinement is necessary to prevent a clear and immediate danger to others? Why should not the Ninth Amendment, which says citizens have unnamed rights beyond those enumerated in the Constitution, be applied to a host of areas: rights to carry on whatever family arrangements (marriage, divorce, etc.) are desired, whatever sexual relationships are voluntarily entered into, whatever private activities one wants to carry on, so long as others are not harmed (even if they are irritated)? (Zinn, 1968, pp. 115–116)

Zinn suggested some guidelines for deciding when to disobey the law through protest activity:

1. **Civil disobedience**—the deliberate violation of the law for a vital social purpose—is not only justifiable, but necessary whenever a fundamental human right is at stake and the right cannot be secured through existing legal channels.
2. Government and laws are *instruments* to life, liberty, and happiness, not ends in themselves. Consequently, obeying "the rule of law" has *no* social value—and has *negative* social value if laws are bad ones.
3. Civil disobedience can involve violating laws that are not in themselves wrong in order to protest an important issue (e.g., illegally occupying a building, although normally wrong, is justified as part of a protest against, say, racism).
4. If a specific act of civil disobedience is morally justifiable, then jailing those who performed the act is *immoral* and should be opposed.
5. The tactics used in civil disobedience should be as nonviolent as possible, and the distinction between harm to property and harm to people should be a paramount consideration. However, the appropriate degree of force or disorder must be determined in light of the significance of the issue at stake.
6. The degree of disorder in civil disobedience should be measured not against some misleading degree of "peace" or "order" associated with the status quo, but against the real disorder or violence produced by the abuse that led to protest.
7. The state and the citizen have opposed interests. The state seeks power, influence, and wealth as ends in themselves and is in a favored position to obtain them, even if this means depriving individuals of the health, peace, creative activity, and love they seek. Each citizen, therefore, must learn to think and act on his or her own or in concert with fellow citizens against the state (Zinn, 1968, pp. 119–122).

ARENAS FOR DISSENT

The United States is a politically diverse nation. The numerous cultural influences discussed in Chapter 13, in conjunction with a wide variety of perspectives in regard to what the role of government and the extent of individual freedoms should be, frequently lead to bitter conflicts among competing political parties and interest groups. The major disagreements in the U.S. political system tend to occur between liberals and conservatives. Liberals seek to increase governmental (particularly federal) control over the modes of production and to promote social programs designed to help the poor. Conservatives argue for limited government and promotion of self-reliance by individuals. Both liberals and conservatives claim to cherish individual freedoms but tend to interpret them differently. Liberals argue that government must provide protections to ensure that the poor, minorities, and those living alternative lifestyles are treated fairly and equally. Conservatives argue that government intervention discriminates against the middle and upper classes, the white majority, and those who hold traditional American values (Magleby et al., 2006).

The nature of the liberal–conservative debate is not as easily defined as the preceding might cause one to believe. There is not one type of conservative, nor is there one type of liberal. Instead, liberalism ranges from socialists on the far left, who make American social policies similar to those found in "democratic socialist" nations such as Sweden (Basirico, Cashion, and Esheleman, 2005), to "neoliberals," who are skeptical of welfare programs and governmental bureaucracies (Magleby et al., 2006). Conservatives range from "ultraconservatives" on the far right who favor religious fundamentalism and strict enforcement of morality in addition to strongly opposing a "welfare state" to "neoconservatives" who support limited government involvement in solving social problems but fear that "excessive liberalism" threatens individual liberties and social stability.

A great many Americans occupy the middle of the political spectrum in that they consider themselves to be neither liberals nor conservatives. These citizens hold divergent views that cannot readily be classified by political scientists. Such persons might favor both capital punishment and abortion. They might vote for a Republican for one political office and a Democrat for another, and they would feel no obligation to abide by the wishes of a particular political party or interest group in making political decisions (Cummings and Wise, 2005).

Other Americans may have political ideologies that are far more extreme than those found within the liberal–conservative spectrum. Communists (and many remain despite the decline of Communism in the former Eastern bloc nations) feel that even the welfare capitalism found in the United States is evil and must be eliminated. Anarchists (a limited few) argue that all government is evil. Libertarians, who are considerably more moderate, criticize both liberals and conservatives as abusing the power of the government and infringing on individual liberties. Like conservatives, libertarians would sharply limit the size and power of the federal government. Like liberals, libertarians are very concerned with protecting individual freedoms.

Due to the nature of democracy in the United States, many compromises are made in order for the political system (and subsequently, the social and economic systems) to function. This compromise causes many (on the left, on the right, and in the middle) to feel that their views are being ignored by those in power. When this occurs, many Americans frequently utilize dissent in an effort to effect change. In U.S. society, dissent can be said to occur in at least five major areas: political, social, economic, religious, and environmental. Although these are not mutually exclusive, they often serve individually as primary targets for dissent.

Political Dissent

Political dissent is concerned primarily with effecting change in political policy. Power is sought in political decision making. Examples of nonviolent political dissent include the historic protests that were waged during the 1960s in opposition to the Vietnam War and in support of civil rights protection for minorities. More recent demonstrations in the United States have resulted from the efforts of opponents seeking to eliminate lawful abortions within the United States and from gay rights advocates seeking to eliminate laws and regulations that are considered discriminatory against homosexuals.

When advocates of political change resort to violence, it is frequently the activities of a single person or a small group of extremists within a predominantly peaceful organization. However, it may be calculated actions of an organization that is willing to use terrorism to bring attention to themselves or their cause (White, 2006). While most civilized peoples deplore terrorism, a person classified as a terrorist by one group may be considered a hero or freedom fighter by others (Fagin, 2006). For example, to most Americans (including opponents of abortion), the bombing of abortion clinics and/or the murder of doctors who perform abortions are acts of terrorism, but to some they are morally justified acts taken in defense of unborn children. However, those same persons would define terrorism quite differently if their churches were attacked by pro-abortion forces.

Social Dissent

Social dissent is concerned primarily with gaining social equality. Often, the conflict is over the counting and discounting of minority-group concerns in our society (Henslin, 2007). Social acceptance and rejection, changes in public opinion and social institutions, and having a "viable place" in the community are all social concerns. Social dissent in the United States was pioneered by Martin Luther King Jr., who utilized nonviolent protests as a means of drawing attention to inequitable treatment of African Americans (Greenberg and Page, 2005).

During the 1990s, the groups that most frequently utilized social dissent were gay rights advocates, feminists, and ethnic minorities. Many of these groups are also involved in political dissent, because changes in the law, a part of structuring social change, are a political prerogative.

Economic Dissent

Economic dissent is concerned primarily with effecting change in the economy and meeting material needs. Economic dissent addresses in general issues of unemployment; underemployment; poverty; and food, clothing, and shelter. Strikes and protests regarding unfair labor practices and demonstrations on behalf of the homeless may be considered economic dissent. One example was the Los Angeles Riot of 1992. Although the initial spark was the acquittal of the police officers accused in the videotaped beating of black motorist Rodney King, the real issues dealt with living conditions, unemployment, lack of opportunity, and what residents saw as social and economic oppression.

Religious Dissent

Religious dissent is concerned primarily with effecting change in the definition of religious freedoms or specific religious practices that may violate existing law. In this instance, conflict may be between opposing values or religious beliefs or between church and secular law. Much antiabortion dissent is couched in a religious context. Other examples include the ongoing debate over prayer in the schools, atheist–religious conflicts, Catholic–Protestant and Jewish–Gentile conflicts, and the refusal of religious groups such as the Amish and Mennonites to comply with compulsory school attendance laws. The attacks on doctors and abortion clinics by supporters of "Operation Rescue," the dramatic events that led to the 1993 deaths of approximately 90 people in the Branch Davidian compound near Waco, Texas, during an FBI assault, and the 1993 bombing of the World Trade Center by Muslim fundamentalists demonstrate the extremes that religious dissent in the United States can reach.

Freedom to believe is absolutely protected by the First Amendment to the U.S. Constitution, but freedom to act is not totally free from interference (Cummings and Wise, 2005). This is particularly true if those actions obstruct the rights of others, are seen as detrimental to the health and well-being of group members (especially juveniles), if the group or individual is found to be only incidentally religious, or when fraud or deception is involved (Lucksted and Martell, 1982).

Environmental Dissent

Environmental dissent is concerned primarily with effecting change in the surroundings or settings in which we live. Issues might include zoning changes, health hazards, and threats to wildlife. Recent environmental debates have ranged from preserving endangered species, halting the inappropriate disposal of chemical waste, eliminating pollution of air and water, guarding against radioactive or toxic risk to populations, and the harvesting of public forests. This dissent can range from community resistance to building chemical incinerators, to assaults on hunters or people wearing furs by animal rights extremists, to acts of sabotage and terrorism against perceived environmental offenders.

STRATEGIES OF DISSENT AND RESPONSE

Legalists and advocates of dissent differ in many critical respects, but they all recognize the need for "justice," "order," and "change" and agree that dissent must be analyzed in relation to crises in American institutions. This factor was also recognized by the National Commission on the Causes and Prevention of Violence. In a staff report, the commission suggests that mass protest is an outgrowth of social, economic, and political conditions and the violence that occurs in these protests arises from an interaction between protesters and the authorities.

Commission observations include the following:

- Political processes establish what "violence" is. Whoever has the power to disseminate and enforce their definitions blames the other party for the violence.
- Both the authorities and the protesters often exaggerate the violence committed against them in order to discredit the other party, gain sympathy from third parties, and deflect attention from their own violence.

FIGURE 14.4   Dissenting shipbuilders on strike in Newport News, Virginia.
Courtesy of Newport News Police Department.

- The interplay of protest and violence must be seen in light of the surrounding structure of power and authority and the conceptions held by the authorities of the nature of protest and the proper uses of official violence.
- Participants in mass protest today see their activity as political action aimed at the existing arrangements of power and authority that produced their grievances (Popenoe, 2000; Tischler, 2007).

The Labeling Process

In most issues of social conflict, a variety of groups and individuals with differing demands and differing strategies of dissent wish to be heard. These dissenters, however, generally have much less power than the political authorities or other parties whose actions, beliefs, policies, or laws the dissenters are protesting. Because dissenters usually have the least amount of power in a social conflict, the views of the more powerful authorities or organizations generally become the accepted ones.

The authorities, or those who have power (the "establishment"), generally label dissenters as "militants." This label may be applied to whole groups of dissenters or to individual spokespeople for a particular group of dissenters. No clear-cut definitions exist for the word "militant." This label has been used by the opponents of a movement to discredit everyone in the movement; it has also been used selectively by persons who partially agree with the objectives of the movement but who regard some of its demands as nonnegotiable. It is generally agreed that militants (1) approve of violence as a protest tactic, (2) are hostile toward their adversaries, and (3) do not accept the legitimacy of the structural system or its institutions.

Strategies of Dissent

Strategies of dissent differ with regard to three concerns: (1) the nature of the desired changes, (2) the means of achieving change (specifically, the degree of adherence to the rules of the system), and (3) attitudes toward the people who defend the system. Three strategies can be distinguished: strategies of order, disorder, and violence.

In the strategy of order, dissidents divide their attention between the changes to be accomplished and the accepted rules regarding legitimate ways of bringing about change; dissidents who use this strategy follow the rules.

In the strategy of disorder, dissidents have less interest in both the given rules and the powerful persons who stand in the way of change; they focus strongly on the changes needed.

In the strategy of violence, dissidents divide their attention between the changes needed and the powerful persons who stand in the way of change; dissidents who use this strategy attack their enemies.

Presumably, we can define any particular dissident group's strategy at any given time simply by analyzing its rhetoric and observing its deeds.

Strategies of Response

To understand the dynamics of dissent strategies, we must also understand the **strategies of response** utilized by political authorities or other parties who are the targets of dissident groups (Table 14.1). These can vary as widely as the strategies of protest groups and generally differ with respect to the same three concerns: the nature of desired changes, the means of achieving change, and attitudes toward the people who defend the system. The strategies of response are the response of law, of order, and of violence.

In the response of law, authorities do not respond at all or only respond in a protective manner as long as dissenters adopt legal strategies of protest (i.e., strategies of order). If the dissenters adopt illegal means of protest, however, the response of law strategy involves arresting dissenters and processing them in a legally acceptable manner. In this response, authorities follow proper legal procedures.

TABLE 14.1 Strategies of Dissent and Response

Dissent		Response	
Concerns		**Concerns**	
1. The nature of desired changes		1. The nature of desired changes	
2. The means of achieving change		2. The means of achieving change	
3. Attitudes toward people who defend system		3. Attitudes toward people who defend system	
Strategies	*Focus On*	*Strategies*	*Focus On*
1. Of order:	legitimate ways of bringing about change	1. Response of law:	no response or protective response
2. Of disorder:	changes needed; less concern with rules or powerful persons who stand in the way	2. Response of order:	arresting and processing dissenters in legal and acceptable manner
3. Of violence:	attacking enemies; change needed and powerful persons who stand in the way of change	3. Response of violence:	issue in conflict and people who are dissenting; attack enemies

Possible Interactional Outcomes

Changes in orientation and strategy

Violent action

Resolution of conflict

In the response of order, authorities make no response or only a protective one to legal protest (strategies of order). Illegal dissent, however, is met by attempting nonviolent bargaining over the social issue. The authorities place less emphasis on the demanded change than on maintaining order or preventing violence.

In the response of violence, authorities are concerned with the issue in conflict and focus on the people who are dissenting (regardless of what strategy of dissent they use). In other words, they attack their enemies.

Interaction between Strategies

When the strategies of dissent and response meet head-on, three outcomes are possible: changes in orientation and strategy, violent action, or resolution of the conflict.

CHANGES IN ORIENTATION AND STRATEGY   Those who adopt a given strategy of dissent usually expect it to have a specific effect on third parties or to elicit a specific strategy of response from the authorities. Thus, the civil disobedience of Martin Luther King was a strategy of order designed to draw attention to a particular issue and to educate the public about it; to a large extent, it succeeded. Problems arise, however, when dissidents and those in power find that their efforts are not producing the results they want. Their strategy may change toward greater use of violence.

VIOLENT ACTIONS   Some dissident groups seem committed to violence from the outset, engaging in guerrilla warfare and terrorist activities. Moreover, many law enforcement officials favor violent response to dissent; if they disagree with the dissenters on the issues, they are likely to consider acts of civil disobedience as simply another type of crime, and they often try to divert attention from the issues by defining the dissidents as terrorists, "crazies," or common criminals.

Guerrilla warfare, as a strategy of violence, exists throughout the world. Underground armies and terrorist organizations are particularly prevalent in underdeveloped nations that are ruled by dictatorship.

Terrorism and guerrilla insurgency have appeared in all segments of major U.S. cities. The use of terrorism as a tactic of dissent usually is directed at persons who exercise power and at the symbols of that power. The goal of this form of dissent is often terror and anarchy.

Some observers predict that the police officer on the street in the future will be required to deal with criminal violence arising from violent political dissent. The National Advisory Commission on Criminal Justice Standards and Goals (1976) and subsequent presidential commissions on terrorism have encouraged local police to increase their ability to deal with such activity.

A key element in violent dissent is that the dissenters seek to achieve their goals by whatever means necessary. Some domestic terrorist groups that are active or have been active in the United States in recent years include the Aryan Nation; the Black Liberation Army; the Christian Patriots Defense League; The Covenant, the Sword, and the Arm of the Lord (CSA); the Jewish Defense League; the Ku Klux Klan; Macheteros; Move; Neo-Nazis; the New World Liberation Front; Alpha 66; Omega 7; The Order; Posse Comitatus; Puerto Rican Armed Forces of the Revolution (FALN); the United Freedom Front; the Weather Underground; Fuqra; the Armenian Secret Army for the Liberation of Armenia (ASLA); Justice Commandos for Armenian Genocide (JCAG); the Croation National Liberation Forces; the Animal Liberation Front; and, arguably, Operation Rescue (Poland, 2005; Simonsen and Spindlove, 2007; White, 2006). In addition to these politically motivated groups, many individuals and criminal gangs engage in activities that could also be classified as terrorism. As if there were not enough of a harm potential from these "homegrown terrorists," the number of international terrorists operating in America is increasing. Due to the events of September 11, 2001, local and state law enforcement in the United States have had to assume responsibility for "Homeland Security" along with the federal agencies (Fagin, 2006; White, 2006).

RESOLUTION OF THE CONFLICT   This outcome, of course, would seem the most desirable, and it is often possible, although the struggle to reach it may be long. Those who adopt strategies or responses of violence, however, may not want any resolution other than the complete surrender or destruction of the other side.

The Role of Third Parties

Both dissidents and authorities plan tactics, publicity, and media communications to win over third parties. This is especially important when power differences are great between the conflicting parties, and the weaker party can obtain a compromise or achieve its goals only if strong third parties become its allies. In the civil rights movement in the South, the goal the protesters sought was inclusion in the political system; thus, these groups aimed their messages not only at the persons directly affected but also at third-party persons sympathetic to these goals and at those who believed in the legal inclusion of African Americans in the political system. As a result, media coverage and the violent response of political authorities to the civil rights movement had the consequences of affecting third-party intervention by the federal government, expanding the issues in conflict, and obtaining participants in the movement as well as allies.

The Role of the Media

Because media coverage is so necessary for reaching third parties, all parties try to influence the way conflict and the parties to it are portrayed in newspaper and magazine articles and on radio and television. Dissenters create events for media that will draw attention to the conflict and hopefully build bargaining power for them. Political authorities, on the other hand, attempt to control what the media present by exercising power through regulatory agencies and political pressure. They attempt to control sources of information by making government documents secret, infiltrating dissident groups with agents of the government, cutting off dissident groups from media visibility, and attacking the media for their "underdog" bias. When political authorities are pressed by dissent, freedom of the press comes under increasing fire.

ESCALATION AND DE-ESCALATION OF CONFLICT

Once conflict has started, each party tends to undergo changes that make the conflict more intense. Conflict, however, cannot escalate indefinitely. Sooner or later, forces or events that de-escalate conflict will influence the behavior of the parties involved.

Escalation Factors

INCREASE IN LOYALTY AND COMMITMENT   Feelings of loyalty and commitment to one's position increase if the other side responds with coercion, threats, or injuries. Increased commitment leads to and justifies further efforts toward the attainment of one's goals, creates anxiety, and heightens a sense that *now* is the time to act. For example, dissident or militant leaders state, "Seize the time!" "Freedom now!" "Peace now!" or other rhetoric emphasizing urgency:

> This is our last gasp as a sovereign people, and if we don't get these treaty rights recognized, then you might as well kill me because I have no reason for living. (Means, 1973)

He was not killed. And at this writing, more than 40 years later, Mr. Means has not given up on living.

> My hunger is for liberation of my people, my thirst is for the ending of oppression. I am a political prisoner, jailed for my beliefs that black people must be free. . . . Death can no longer alter our path to freedom. For our people death has been the only known exit from slavery and oppression. We must open others. Our will to live must no longer supersede our will to fight, for our fighting will determine if our race shall live. . . . Brothers and sisters, and all oppressed peoples, we must prepare ourselves both mentally and physically, for the major confrontation is yet to come. We must fight. (Brown, 1968)

Fortunately, the race war that Mr. Brown (who is now in prison for murdering an African American deputy sheriff) called for has not taken place. Despite frequent setbacks and the combined efforts of both white and black militants, race relations in the United States continue to progress.

PERSISTENCE IN A COURSE OF ACTION   Once conflict begins, it often escalates because leaders acting as representatives of an entire group usually persist on a course of action, even if no success is achieved. Mistakes are rarely admitted by either the dissenters or the responders. However, admission of mistakes does tend to occur when the group's constituency changes, when the futility of the strategy becomes apparent, or when escalation and reaction reach the point where survival of the group is threatened. Thus, the Black Panthers party retracted its focus on the police when party programs were seriously threatened by police actions. Party leaders recognized that other authorities are more important than the police and began to concentrate more deeply on other issues.

WITHDRAWAL OF MODERATE MEMBERSHIP   Another factor influencing the escalation of conflict is the withdrawal of members who are unwilling to participate in more intense conflict, leaving the group to those who are more eager to engage in hostile actions. With the withdrawal of moderates, dissident groups that have previously been viewed as peaceful activists (e.g., Operation Rescue) may begin to emerge as terrorist threats.

AN UPWARD SPIRAL OF VIOLENCE   Hostility and aggression from one side will very likely be answered in kind from the other side, so that an **upward spiral of violence** is created. Once the spiral begins, a relatively weak response from one side is unlikely to stop it; the other side will react with even more violence in order to defeat a seemingly "weakened enemy." If the police see a group of dissidents as a threat or as a source of violence and respond with violence, the dissident group tends to increase its violent activities. Once intensely engaged, even efforts by police to de-escalate the conflict may be interpreted as retreat and evidence of weakness. Therefore, such efforts will require careful planning and execution in order to avoid increasing the level of violence.

De-escalation Factors

Conflict cannot escalate indefinitely. The processes of de-escalation are embedded in those of escalation. Although participation in conflict behavior produces greater commitment to the group and willingness to escalate conflict, it also becomes increasingly costly if the attainment of the group's demands is not in sight.

SUPERIOR COERCIVE POWER   One side may use its superior coercive power to repress the opposition through harassment or by imprisoning its leaders. However, actions that are perceived as too extreme can lead to both heightened resistance on the part of the dissidents and increased sympathy from those who were neutral or somewhat opposed to dissent.

DIVIDE AND CONQUER   One side may split the conflict by being conciliatory in a divisive way (e.g., by granting the demands of some members of the opposition and thus removing their reasons for continuing the conflict). Placating the more moderate factions within the opposition may seriously weaken those who hold more extreme positions. The product is a deeply divided opposition that may force extremists to either capitulate or be rejected by their previous allies.

THIRD-PARTY INVOLVEMENT   One side may introduce issues that involve third parties who then either act as negotiators or increase one side's power to the point where the other side can no longer bear the cost of intense conflict. For example, during the Vietnam War, raising the POW issue brought new third parties into the peace movement. The intervention of third parties also can have a de-escalating impact on the authorities by increasing the political costs of continuing the practices being protested.

A REDEFINITION OF "REASONABLE"   The struggle may become so intense that leaders who formerly seemed militant now appear "reasonable"—an appearance that can only increase their bargaining power, if authorities have not repressed the entire movement.

Success Factors

In general, dissident groups are more likely to be successful if they have the following:

1. A specific goal or a broad goal (e.g., equality of job opportunity) that can realistically be achieved (e.g., by reserving a specific percentage of construction jobs for minority group applicants).
2. A specific, identifiable target (e.g., a particular political leader, landlord, or company).
3. Demands that realistically can be met. Some demands are defined as nonnegotiable by the conflict authority (e.g., state sovereignty, capitalism, or student control of school administration), and some demands are not grantable by the targets chosen (e.g., police and mayor).

OUTCOMES

Determinants of Outcomes

DIFFERENCES IN POWER Power differences seem to be the major determinant in the outcome of social conflict. Extreme power differences almost invite domination and repression if the conflict has escalated to highly coercive strategies. In general, the greater the power difference, the more the outcome is likely to be withdrawal or domination of the dissidents (Eitzen and Zinn, 2007).

PERCEIVED PERMANENCE OF CONFLICT The outcomes of different conflicts also vary according to the perceived permanence of the conflict. The Vietnam War has long since ended; mass rioting does not prevail over periods of weeks and months. Underlying social conflicts, however, such as the status of black, brown, and Native American citizens in our society seem to be continuing and painfully direct issues (Skolnick and Currie, 2007).

In a sense, the call for "black power" during the 1960s grew out of the perception that there would have to be many years of resistance and protest against white institutions and attitudes for African Americans to gain equality. In this view, to bargain from a position of strength, blacks first had to establish group solidarity. This same strategy is currently being utilized by advocates of gay rights, who are seeking to establish a group identity based on sexual preference.

Enhancing group solidarity to improve bargaining position is the objective of many other groups in our society with similar issues. Group solidarity is often defined in terms of self-defense, cultural autonomy, a sense of community, and community control.

The role of "militant" groups where conflict is perceived to be ongoing or permanent might include the following:

1. Correct the illusions of progress through critical, pessimistic attitudes.
2. Identify unresolved issues through confrontations.
3. Radicalize membership of the movement and increase polarization between the movement and its opposition.
4. Create an awareness of injustice among nonmovement third parties.

Schools and the police are among the primary targets of such movements; other targets involve issues such as housing, welfare, and social services.

PERCEIVED INSTRUMENTS OF POWER In the midst of conflict, police, courts, and corrections administration and personnel are often seen as political instruments of power rather than as instruments of law.

The Police

In the drama of dissent, police frequently find themselves acting as substitutes for necessary political and social reform. Labor history demonstrates that the police served as the main bulwark against the labor movement. Picket lines were violently dispersed; meetings were disrupted; and organizers and activists were shot, beaten, and jailed. Police harassment of unions, such as the United Farm Workers, was common. Denial of strikers' legal rights; physical and verbal abuse; detaining organizers for long periods; encouraging workers to cross picket lines; and arresting strikers for trespass, unlawful assembly, secondary boycott, and illegal picketing were common practices. The police have also sought at times to prevent the political organization of Native Americans, Chicanos, and blacks by harassing and intimidating organization members and arresting leaders.

RESPONSES OF VIOLENCE In some of our larger cities, tenant groups, students, war protesters, gays, browns, and blacks have drawn similar responses from the police. For example, some of the most highly publicized responses of violence occurred in Chicago at the 1968 Democratic

National Convention and in police confrontations with the Black Panther party. The shooting outbreaks between Panthers and police in San Francisco, Oakland, New Orleans, Detroit, Toledo, Philadelphia, New York, Houston, and Chicago were touched off by harassment (the Panther view) or minor offenses (the police view). These incidents involved the selling of a Panther newspaper on a Detroit street corner, the assault upon two police infiltrators in New Orleans, and the stockpiling of weapons in the other cities. The Black Panthers argued that police respond violently for a number of reasons:

- Many of them are "racists."
- Few minority persons serve on police forces.
- The police are isolated from the people they serve.
- Police are ill-trained for sensitive peacekeeping jobs.
- Police have a special view of dissent and dissenters.

This same theme was echoed in the Los Angeles Riot of 1992 and the Cincinnati Riots in 2000.

POLICE VIEW OF DISSENT   Many police officers (and administrators) view protest as unequivocally illegitimate. They tend to regard organized protest as the conspiratorial product of authoritarian agitators, Communists, rabble-rousers, spoiled kids, outsiders, or anarchists. This view does not distinguish dissent from subversion and lumps all dissent strategies into one category (Skolnick, 1969, p. 199). As a result, police may tend to be hostile to most strategies of dissent and make the reduction of dissent their goal. The dangers of such a position are many. The police may underestimate both the number of people involved and the emotionality of dissent. They may arrest leaders or speakers at mass rallies, thereby heightening the cycle of escalating violence. They may equate the law with their own situational use of power. As the police have become more comfortable with their role as protectors of individual rights rather than as strictly law enforcers, this view of protest has become less prevalent (Barker, Hunter, and Rush, 1994).

DISSENTERS AS DELIBERATE PROVOKERS OF VIOLENCE   Violent dissent and violent response are generally an interactional product of short-term situational escalation or a product of a history of unsuccessful dissent and/or response strategy. Some dissenters, however, purposely provoke hostility and violence in order to gain attention, increase membership, enlist third-party support, or simply show how "violent" the system is. Thus, the greater the resistance the groups encounter, the greater their motivation to continue their "just" struggle. Threats of punishment have little deterrent value on dissenters of this type, because they can use such threats to increase sympathy for their cause (Simonsen and Spindlove, 2007; White, 2006).

POWER AND THE RESPONSE OF ORDER   The response of order is more likely to occur if the power of the dissenting group approaches that of the powerful group. When a large number of people become involved in dissent and when their goals become specific and clear, police response of order is more frequent. If negotiation is on side issues that are not seen as critical by a majority of the dissenters, the strength of the dissent becomes diffused.

THE POLICE AND "DIRTY WORK"   The police frequently provide the most visible direct response to dissent. It is a response that the powerful and/or larger segments in society wish to see made, even though they themselves do not wish to be personally involved in the response. In such instances, the police find themselves doing the "dirty work" of larger political and social forces. As the police have become more representative of the communities they serve, many are beginning to resent that position (Barker, Hunter, and Rush, 1994). The accepted approach today is an attempt to balance the rights of protesters with the need to maintain law and order. Law enforcement officials are encouraged not to condemn the cause but, rather, to denounce the illegal acts and tactics of the protestors (King, 2000, p. 12).

Sometimes police seem to have been forced unwillingly into violent confrontations by the actions of legislative and judicial bodies over which they had no control. For example, city officials may decide to take steps to block what might have been a peaceful demonstration. The dissenters, with increased commitment, decide to demonstrate anyway. The police are caught in the middle.

POLITICAL SURVEILLANCE   The FBI, CIA, IRS, Army, Secret Service, Civil Service Commission, Department of Justice, and other government agencies sometimes, like the police, equate dissent with subversion. As a result, they maintain surveillance of the activities of dissidents. One major purpose of this surveillance is political control of dissent. Fortunately, the misuse of surveillance has led to congressional inquiries and the imposition of restrictions on those agencies with surveillance capabilities (Cummings and Wise, 2005).

Agents Provocateurs   To keep tabs on dissident groups, law enforcement agencies often have tried to infiltrate them with undercover agents, who may well commit provocative acts—or encourage others to commit them—to gain the dissenters' confidence and to obtain concrete evidence of illegal activity. The need for undercover agents is quite clear. Without them, terrorist acts would be extremely difficult to prevent. The 2006 arrests of terrorists in Canada who were planning on planting bombs and the arrests in Great Britain of a group of terrorists planning to blow up airliners flying to the United States were due to excellent intelligence gathering and the use of undercover operatives.

NATIONAL SECURITY   When the national security is believed to be at stake, political intelligence sweeps up dissenters of all styles. To protect the national security, all groups and individuals committed to social or political change, however peaceful, nonviolent, or legal, must be scrutinized because they may be "subversive." These intelligence activities are designed to demoralize, intimidate, and frighten citizens into not dissenting. The harassment, invasion of privacy, prosecution on drug charges, vandalism of offices and homes, blacklisting, and illegal searches by these intelligence services are chilling. When a covert force plays an important role in political decisions, the selection of candidates, the publication of false opinion polls, and the conducting of "smear" campaigns, then this nation's stated democratic political processes cease to exist. The First Amendment becomes meaningless when dissenting individuals are not allowed to exercise their rights. If there are great personal costs involved in the process of dissent, then there is no freedom. Driving political activity underground tends to escalate strategies to the more organized forms of violence, paramilitarism, terror, sabotage, assassination, guerrilla warfare, espionage, counterintelligence, and extreme political repression (Henslin, 2007; Simonsen and Spindlove, 2007).

NEW LIMITS ON POLITICAL SURVEILLANCE   To the concern of those who believe intelligence efforts are important, the trend in the recent past has been for legislatures, courts, and administrators to establish a tighter rein on police intelligence units. Some of the most restrictive guidelines have been placed on the FBI. After the guidelines went into effect in 1976, domestic security investigations by that agency fell dramatically. Most state guidelines are not as restrictive as those of the FBI. For those who believe that every "scrap of information" should be kept, such guidelines are a great handicap to police. For those who believe that intelligence gathering should be a highly selective activity and should exclude much political information, the new rules are a means of streamlining and professionalizing the intelligence process.

The Courts

The passage of laws that attempt to stifle dissent, such as riot conspiracy laws, mob action laws, and administrative laws, all make the court an arena for the politics of protest. Intelligence gathering, selective prosecution, and the response of violence tend to underwrite the perception that the courts are also political instruments of power.

The court process assumes that the activities defined as crimes are disapproved of by the community as a whole. In contemporary dissent situations, however, these conditions may not be met. As dissent increases and as a strategy of dissent gains acceptability, a majority of the citizens may not define the activity as criminal. Moreover, they may not accept the court's authority to decide the dispute. This presents a crisis for the courts and the legal system. The court becomes a political arena in which actors attempt to win third parties to their side (Skolnick, 1969, p. 243).

THE ISSUE OF IMPARTIALITY   It is difficult for the court to function as an impartial arbiter of conflict when the government itself is a party to the conflict. In the United States, lower courts have often set aside their independence and become instruments of political need, without regard for legality. In the civil turmoil of the 1960s and early 1970s, courts often took the following view:

1. Civil disorders were emergency situations that required extraordinary measures of control and resistance.
2. The courts must support the police and other public agencies acting to restore order.
3. Because of the emergency, defendants must be presumed guilty (until proven innocent).
4. High bail is required to prevent rioters from returning to the riot.
5. The niceties of due process cannot and should not be observed while an emergency lasts.
6. Due process should be restored as soon as the emergency passes (Skolnick, 1969, p. 237).

No recent period in history has provided such powerful examples of the courts as political arenas than the decade in which the government moved in several dramatic trials against well-known dissidents such as Dr. Benjamin Spock, the Chicago Seven, the Panther Twenty-One, and Angela Davis. The government sought conviction; the defendants sought acquittal. Both parties also had other, perhaps greater, concerns. The dissenters were willing to accept the legal penalties for their acts to raise the moral justice of their cause. The government's main purpose, particularly in the Spock trial, was probably to deter draft resistance and adult support of this resistance. However, the event was also used to discredit these dissenters symbolically, to blame dissent on Spock for his permissive child-rearing philosophy, and to rally patriotic third parties to the government's side. Actually, the Spock trial may have produced the opposite effect: It became a rallying point for the entire movement. Through the trial, citizens were informed about the issues of war.

ATTACKS ON THE COURTS   During their trials, dissidents of that period frequently tried not only to publicize their grievances, but also to attack the courts themselves, the criminal justice system, and, ultimately, the entire U.S. socioeconomic and political system.

Corrections: The Prison

THE REALITIES OF PRISON LIFE   Citizens want those whom they consider to be "deviants" to be "disposed of" safely, quickly, and invisibly. This invisibility creates a need for prisoners to escalate the strategy of dissent if they wish to obtain attention. Most prison dissent—in the form of hunger strikes, building takeovers, and hostage taking—is directed toward making third parties aware that "just" ideals are perverted both inside prison and out. Prisons are the breeding grounds of the strategy of violence and the marketplace of the response of total control.

Dissenters often claim that prisons, like the courts, are instruments of political oppression. Whether or not the claim is justified, punitive confinement is the essence of American penal institutions.

REACTIONS TO PRISON LIFE   Reactions to prison life may be docility, cooperativeness, and un-complaining conformity, or it may be rebellion in the name of liberty. Often prisoners feel that to be subject to the arbitrary exercise of power is to be a slave (Zimbardo, 1972, p. 8). Prison authorities may feel that prison dissent is caused by a small band of militants, the circulation of militant revolutionary literature, the influence of militant lawyers, and the strategies of dissent occurring outside the institution. They respond to threat by transferring inmates, placing them in solitary confinement, censoring mail and reading materials, and limiting contacts.

Systems for Solution

The Task Force on Disorders and Terrorism, whose report was released in late 1976, addressed setting standards and goals for the criminal justice system and for the nonofficial community in prevention, evaluation of threats, and management strategies for riots, urban disorders, prison disorders, and terrorism (National Advisory Commission on Criminal Justice Standards and Goals, 1976).

Currently, much emphasis is being placed on the use of negotiation, which stresses human dynamics, rather than "power" tactics, as an effective means of **neutralizing disorder**. However, as exemplified by the 1993 FBI assault on the Branch Davidian compound near Waco, Texas, authorities tend to revert to the use of force when negotiations fail. Whether or not that FBI response was correct will remain a matter of debate for many years.

AWARENESS   The best solution is prevention. If the police maintain close, ongoing contact with community members and help to keep channels for communication open, mutual trust will help to open legitimate peaceful options for dissent and deter the escalation of dissent to violent action. Close positive contact will also allow the police and community members to be aware of increasing tensions in a community, the factors involved in that tension, and ways to diffuse it.

Police officers also need to be self-aware. Their own assumptions and reactive behavior may increase the intensity of problems. Their level of hopefulness that what they do can make a difference influences the behavior of dissenters.

Agency administrators affect the officer's level of hopefulness and his or her ability to deal with fear and anxiety. They affect the officer's emotional and physical preparedness for situations of dissent. Support for the officers in the form of guidelines, education and training, planning, and coordination of function is a key element of success.

EDUCATION   Officers who understand human dynamics and mass behavior (e.g., that riots have a classic lull between 3:00 and 9:00 A.M.), the interaction of strategies of dissent and political response, the element of surprise, how to deal with their own fear and anxiety, and how to gain consistently reliable information are better prepared to respond to dissent in ways that prevent violence. In addition to gaining information as a resource, officers need to gain response skills. This may be accomplished through role play and should be provided over a period of time so that skills can be acquired, tested, and sharpened.

PLANNING AND PREPARATION   Planned, practiced tactical response can be successful. If police agencies are prepared, they can effectively use the wide range of options that they have and seize the initiative in a situation. Perhaps many different responses will be needed. If planning has been effective, the roles of each cooperating agency and jurisdiction are defined, and coordination of resources exists, disorder can be neutralized without extinguishing dissent or imposing excessive social control.

Cooperation and coordination among units in a single police agency (e.g., those trained in the various tactics of countersniper, assault, negotiation, and intelligence) are critical. Just as critical is cooperation of police with other agencies. A system response must be an organized one. Usually such response is from the "bottom up." The local agency is the key decision maker, and other agencies provide support. If this division of responsibility is not followed, procedures may be imposed from the "top down" (e.g., federal agencies making decisions for the local police).

Jealousies, conflicting philosophies, and poor planning can lead to immobility and disaster. Many of these problems can be avoided if police–community relations are conducted effectively with members of the justice community and clear guidelines for cooperation are developed. This includes not only other police agencies, but also courts and corrections.

HUMAN DYNAMICS VERSUS POWER TACTICS   Political response to dissent may shape the intensity of the dissent. Restraint on the part of the police will help to prevent violent confrontation. In contrast, heavy-handed harassment increases anger and invites violence.

Establishing dialogues with dissenting groups and applying an understanding of **human dynamics** are much more effective than **power tactics** in maintaining long-term peace, even if it is somewhat uneasy. Further discussion of human dynamics as a part of conflict management is found in the next chapter.

THE BATTLE OF SEATTLE

Background

The most serious incident involving the police and political dissent in the United States since the Age of Dissent (1965–1975), maybe in U.S. history, occurred in a city where it should not have happened: Seattle, Washington, a city known for its liberal lifestyle. It involved a police department well known for its community policing philosophy and style, and a department commanded by a well-respected police chief with a Ph.D.: Chief Norm Stamper. While with the San Diego Police Department, Chief Stamper introduced a community-oriented policing program, considered by many to be the first in the nation. His undergraduate senior thesis was titled "The Community as DMZ: Breaking Down the Police Paramilitary Bureaucracy." Stamper's doctoral dissertation described how civil service and paramilitary structures contribute to police losing touch with communities (Wilson, 1999). However, the city, the chief, and the police department became caught up in a situation they neither asked for nor created.

President Bill Clinton volunteered the city of Seattle as the site for a meeting of the World Trade Organization (WTO). Clinton wanted the WTO meetings to be held in the United States to spotlight the benefits America receives from international trade (Beveridge, 1999). This controversial organization was opposed by environmentalists, unions, and human rights groups around the globe. The WTO was well known as a "lightning rod for critics on the left and right, nationally and internationally, and had caused bitter diplomatic tensions" (Collier, 1999). The president himself had publicly criticized the actions of the WTO one month before the meeting:

> The WTO has been treated for too long like some private priesthood for experts where we know what's right and we pat you on the head and tell you to go along and play by the rules that we reach. (Collier, 1999)

It was known well in advance of the meeting that tens of thousands of protesters, some estimates said 50,000, would show up. The nature of the WTO allowed protesters to pick their cause from protecting clean air, sea turtles and dolphins, job exports and pest imports; curbing child labor; to eliminating beef hormones and genetically modified food (Postmand and Mapes, 1999). Protest organizers hoped for a "protest of the century" (Phillips, 1999). By the time the meeting ended, demonstrators had come from a Ralph Nader group, Greenpeace, the Sierra Club, Direct Action Network, the United Steel Workers of America, the Teamsters, the AFL–CIO, Students Against Sweatshops, an anarchist group calling themselves the Black Bloc, and numerous other self-proclaimed protest groups. The majority of the protesters were expected to be peaceful, but even they had forewarned the police that small radical fringes were planning violence (Collier, November 24, 1999). "Battle in Seattle" T-shirts had been on sale a week before the meeting (Postman and Mapes, 1999). Six thousand delegates from 135 countries were expected for the meeting.

Events

The morning of the first day, Tuesday, November 30, 1999, Teamsters Union President James Hoffa Jr. spoke at the organizing site and said, "We're basically putting a human face on the WTO. It has to consider human rights and workers' rights along with trade" (Beveridge, 1999). As he was speaking, 9,600 workers of the International Longshore and Warehouse Union began shutting down cargo movements up and down the West Coast in solidarity with the anti-WTO protests. Twenty thousand labor activists walked along a designated parade route from the organizing point to downtown. Their march was peaceful and uneventful.

Downtown the protests had turned ugly. Thousands of people, estimates range from 6,000 to 10,000, gathered in two locations and began to march toward the convention center where the meetings were to be held. They linked arms and prevented the delegates from entering the convention center. Some of the more radical demonstrators lay down in the streets, and some even chained themselves together. Beveridge (1999) says the police say they fired red pepper gas into these groups of chained demonstrators. The resulting clash between the demonstrators and the police and pepper spraying prevented the delegates from reaching the convention center. U.N. Secretary-General Kofi Annan and U.S. Secretary of State Madeline Albright were scheduled to talk at the opening ceremony; however, neither could reach the convention center. By the end of the day, police had fired their entire supply of pepper spray and tear gas at the demonstrators, forcing them to borrow from other agencies (*Seattle Times* staff and news services, 1999). The police had also used rubber bullets and batons to control the demonstrators. By the end of the day, protesters had defied the police, lit small fires, smashed windows, and scrawled graffiti; the opinion session of the WTO had been canceled; the mayor had declared a civil emergency and imposed a curfew; the governor had called up 200 unarmed National Guardsmen; and 300 Washington State Patrol troopers were on their way (Cook, 1999). The clashes between the police and demonstrators continued until the end of the meeting on Friday, December 3, 1999.

There is no question that the majority of the protesters in Seattle were nonviolent, but it appears also that they were gassed, pepper sprayed, shot with rubber bullets, and hit with batons along with a number of residents not engaged in the demonstrations. Residents were gassed and arbitrarily stopped, and some claim brutalized, when the downtown area was declared a protest-free zone, thereby driving the protesters into the Capitol Hill residential neighborhood. The minority demonstrators, such as the black-clad anarchists, the Black Bloc, who were more interested in violence and riot than political dissent, triggered the violent confrontations between the police and the demonstrators and the vandalism that occurred. There was also looting by criminal elements attracted, as they always are, to such chaotic situations.

Thankfully, no one was killed during the Battle of Seattle. However, a number of injuries occurred (to police and demonstrators), and almost 600 persons were arrested. Almost all arrested were charged with misdemeanors and out of jail in a week, released on their own recognizance (Rahner, 1999). Chief Norm Stamper resigned four days after the Battle of Seattle ended, acknowledging that his officers did not get all the support they needed and that he and the city had pursued a policy of negotiation, not confrontation, with the demonstrators (Wilson, 1999). The ranking officer in charge of the departments planning for the WTO meeting would retire in less than a year. Chief Stamper also confirmed that the trained anarchists were behind the violence. Stamper admitted that his department did not have enough staff, even with the help of the National Guard and the Washington State Patrol, to cope with the tens of thousands of protesters (Wilson, 1999). The cost to the city was more than $9 million. The city's reputation was damaged throughout the world, and numerous agencies—including the FBI—began investigations.

What Can Be Learned from the Battle of Seattle

The U.S. Constitution guarantees citizens freedom of speech and the right to assemble as long as they do so peacefully. The delegates to the WTO meeting also had constitutionally protected rights of free speech and assembly. In failing to get the WTO delegates through the protesters and into the opening ceremony on Tuesday, the badly outnumbered police gave the demonstrators the upper hand, caused the police to overreact and set in motion the events that followed (*Seattle Times* staff and news services, 1999). Mayor Schell said that a massive police presence at a peaceful demonstration, which he expected at the WTO conference, would create unruliness. Los Angeles Sheriff's Department

Captain Richard Odenthal, a veteran of the Rodney King riots, says that he advised Seattle officials they needed to have an adequate perimeter around the conference site (*Seattle Times* staff and news service, 1999).

The situation spiraled out of control because of a lack of preparation, adequate staff, and coordination with other agencies. Jerome Skolnick in defense of the Seattle Police Department is quoted thus:

> The Seattle Police Department has a reputation as a very fine, community-oriented department, but because we haven't had that much recent experience with civil disorder, they may have underestimated the need for preparation, for intelligence, for manpower. Obviously, they were caught unprepared, and I think it's because everybody looked upon this as a very positive occasion, a chance to promote the city as an international trading place. (*Seattle Times* staff and news service, 1999)

The Seattle Fire Department even criticized the Seattle Police Department for its lack of preparation. "Several months before the WTO conference, the Seattle Fire Department, based on information it had received, was preparing for the worst. SFD told the police department to do the same and was ignored" (Henderson, 2000, p. 43). The Seattle Police Department also turned down offers for assistance from several law enforcement agencies before the WTO conference took place. This lack of coordination with other agencies, inadequate planning, and insufficient manpower had tragic results.

REALITY CHECK

Privacy versus Security?

On March 9, 2006, the PATRIOT Act was renewed by Congress and President Bush. Despite the efforts of Senate Democrats and libertarian-leaning Republicans who had sought to amend portions of the Act thought to undermine civil liberties, the Act was passed without revision.

The PATRIOT Act makes it easier for federal agents to gather and share information in terrorism investigations, install wiretaps, and conduct secret searches of households and businesses. Civil libertarians have voiced concerns about the PATRIOT Act since it was first proposed as part of the government's Homeland Security efforts after 9/11. These concerns have been highlighted by revelations that the Bush administration has authorized wiretaps and is monitoring e-mails of individuals thought to be communicating with terrorists.

The PATRIOT Act received approval without concessions to protect civil liberties. Despite the best efforts of the national media to create opposition among the American populace to the Bush administration "excesses," polls continue to show that Americans are willing to sacrifice some of their privacy in order to be safer from terrorism. The fear of civil libertarians (and of the authors) is that once personal freedoms are lost (or devalued) they will not only be difficult to regain, but will also serve as precedent for further losses. What do you think?

Conclusions

Change and resistance to change are part of every system. For change to occur, some amount of "deviance" takes place, and the "normal way of things" is disturbed. Dissent—acts designed to bring about needed social, legal, and political change—grows out of people's desire to shape their own

destiny and to be more active in the processes and structures that shape their lives.

Political authority can, if it chooses, adapt and be responsive to change by encouraging solutions that will alleviate the conditions that have led to dissent. Political authority can also respond to dissent by trying to control it, either through persuasion, reward, compromise, or force. The latter alternative will induce some people to be docile, but may drive others to violent resistance.

If authority recognizes the issues raised by dissent, institutions may be transformed; if authority defines these issues as nonnegotiable and tries to control or stifle dissent, democratic political institutions will turn into prisons that are run without the consent of the governed.

When political dissent turns to demonstrations and protest in the community, the responsible officials must plan, prepare, and coordinate with all community agencies and outside agencies to meet the possible threat of violence and disorder.

Student Checklist

1. Define the parameters of the right to dissent under the U.S. Constitution.
2. Present contrasting views of acceptable dissent.
3. Describe the interaction of the strategies of dissent and response.
4. Identify the significant aspects of escalation and de-escalation.
5. Analyze the ways in which police, courts, and corrections become instruments of power in relation to dissent.
6. Describe the necessary components for effectively neutralizing disorder without increasing violent dissent.
7. Describe the events leading up to the Battle of Seattle. How could the city and the police department have been better prepared?

Topics for Discussion

1. Discuss the conflict between the right to dissent and the need to maintain order.
2. Discuss several positive ways of resolving social conflict.
3. In what ways is power a central issue in dissent and political response?

Bibliography

Barker, T., Hunter, R. D., and Rush, J. P. (1994). *Police Systems and Practices: An Introduction.* Upper Saddle River, NJ: Prentice Hall.

Basirico, L. A., Cashion, S. G., and Eshleman, J. R. (2005). *Introduction to Sociology*, 2nd ed. Redding, CA: Best Value Books.

Beveridge, D. (November 30, 1999). "Pepper gas fired on demonstrators against World Trade Organizations," *Seattle Times.*

Brown, R. (1968). March speech on "The Black Panther."

Collier, R. (November 24, 1999). "World-Trade Showdown: Wide-ranging WTO summit will spotlight division, dissent," *Seattle Times.*

Cook, R. (December 1, 1999). "City struggles to regain control of downtown streets after rampage," *Seattle Times.*

Cox, A. (1971). "Direct action, civil disobedience and the Constitution," in J. B. Grossman and M. H., Grossman (Eds.), *Law and Change in Modern America.* Pacific Palisades, CA: Goodyear.

Cummings, M. C., Jr., and Wise, D. (2005). *Democracy under Pressure: An Introduction to the American Political System*, 10th ed. Pacific Grove, CA: Thomson/Wadsworth.

Eitzen, D. S., and Zinn, M. B. (2007). *In Conflict and Order: Understanding Society*, 11th ed. Boston, MA: Pearson/Allyn and Bacon.

Fagin, J. A. (2006). *When Terrorism Strikes Home: Defending the United States.* Boston, MA: Pearson/Allyn and Bacon.

Fortas, A. (1968). *Concerning Dissent and Civil Disobedience.* New York: New American Library.

Greenberg, E. S., and Page, B. I. (2005). *The Struggle for Democracy*, 7th ed. New York: Pearson/Longman.

Henderson, J. (November 24, 2000). "Demonstrating success," *Police.*

Henslin, J. M. (2007). *Sociology: A Down-to-Earth Approach*, 8th ed. Boston, MA: Pearson/Allyn and Bacon.

King, T. R. (September 2000). "Managing protests on public land," *FBI Law Enforcement Bulletin*, pp. 10–13.

Lucksted, O. D., and Martell, D. F. (April 1982). "Cults: A conflict between religious liberty and involuntary servitude? Part I," *FBI Law Enforcement Bulletin*, pp. 16–20.

Magleby, D. B., O'Brien, D. M., Light, P. C., Burns, J. M., Peltason, J. W., and Cronin, T. E. (2006). *Government by the People*, 21st ed. Upper Saddle River, NJ: Pearson/Prentice Hall.

Means, R. (1973). "American Indian movement," *Chicago Express*, p. 1.

National Advisory Commission on Criminal Justice Standards and Goals. (1976). *Disorders and Terrorism: Report of the Task Force on Disorders and Terrorism.* Washington, D.C.: U.S. Government Printing Office.

National Commission on the Causes and Prevention of Violence. (1969). *To Establish Justice, To Insure Domestic Tranquility.* Washington, D.C.: U.S. Government Printing Office.

Phillips, K. (November 29, 1999). "Is the World Trade Organization a blessing or a curse? Con: More Power and Wealth for the Elite," *Seattle Times.*

Poland, J. M. (2005). *Understanding Terrorism: Groups, Strategies, and Responses*, 2nd ed. Upper Saddle River, NJ: Pearson/Prentice Hall.

Popenoe, D. (2000). *Sociology*, 11th ed. Upper Saddle River, NJ: Pearson/Prentice Hall.

Postmand, D., and Mapes, L. (December 6, 1999). "Why WTO united so many foes," *Seattle Times*.

Rahner, M. (December 6, 1999). "Most jailed WTO protestors are no longer behind bars," *Seattle Times*.

Seattle Times staff and news services. (December 6, 1999). "How did the police do? Everyone has an opinion," *Seattle Times*.

Simonsen, C. E., and Spindlove, J. R. (2007). *Terrorism Today: The Past, the Players, the Future*, 3rd ed. Upper Saddle River, NJ: Pearson/Prentice Hall.

Skolnick, J. (1969). *The Politics of Protest: Violent Aspects of Protest and Confrontation*, a staff report to the National Commission on the Causes and Prevention of Violence. Washington, D.C.: U.S. Government Printing Office.

Skolnick, J., and Currie, E. (2007). *Crisis in American Institutions*, 13th ed. Boston, MA: Pearson/Allyn and Bacon.

Tischler, H. L. (2007). *Introduction to Sociology*, 9th ed. Pacific Grove, CA: Thomson/Wadsworth.

Welch, M. (1999). "Social movements and political protests: Exploring flag desecrations in the 1960s, 1970s, and 1980s," *Social Pathology*, Vol. 5, No. 2, pp. 167–186.

White, J. R. (2006). *Terrorism and Homeland Security*, 5th ed. Pacific Grove, CA: Thomson/Wadsworth.

Wilson, K. A. C. (December 7, 1999). "Embattled police chief resigns," *Seattle Times*.

Zimbardo, P. G. (April 1972). "Pathology of imprisonment," *Society*, p. 8.

Zinn, H. (1968). *Disobedience and Democracy: Nine Fallacies on Law and Order*. New York: Random House.

CHAPTER 15

Conflict Management

Police are called to resolve disputes, arbitrate impasses, correct injustices, and calm contentious disputants. The incensed, the infuriated, and the belligerent are the habitual clientele of the police.

—FINK AND SEALY, 1974

KEY CONCEPTS

Alternatives to Arrest
Civil Disturbances
Concept Management
Conflict Intervention Teams

Conflict Management
Crisis Negotiations
Community Conflict
  Intervention

Defusement Process
Hostage Negotiations
Individuals in Crisis

LEARNING OBJECTIVES

Studying this chapter will enable you to:

1. Contrast conflict-management approaches with traditional police policy.
2. Contrast the difference between crisis negotiations in hostage and nonhostage incidents.
3. Identify several alternatives to arrest.
4. Describe the defusement process.
5. Apply the concept management approach and its application to the variety of disputes that the police encounter.
6. Understand why civil disturbances were avoided in some cities after the first Rodney King verdict.

Conflict management (also known as peacemaking) emphasizes alternatives to arrest. However, in many cases arrest may be the last resort when all other alternatives have been exhausted. This is an important but sometimes neglected aspect of police–community relations. Society is continually striving to understand the proper position of arrest in the fulfillment of its needs. No one believes that arrest can be completely discarded, but in many situations the usefulness of arrest is questionable.

315

The power to arrest is a necessary and useful tool in police work, but many times arrest, particularly mass arrest and arrest relating to civil disobedience, is likely to be inconsistent with the responsive, effective, considerate police operations so essential to police–community relations. Mass arrest has always been associated with the suspension of individual rights. In terms of mass dissent and civil disobedience, the line that separates the positive and negative impact of arrest is unclear, especially because the ranks of dissenters have been joined by college professors, members of Congress, religious leaders, and other community leaders. Mass arrests of the tens of thousands who participated in the Battle of Seattle (discussed in the previous chapter) would have been a disaster, even if possible. Many arrests may aggravate, rather than resolve, impending problems.

Conflict management focuses on working with the community to identify areas of conflict, defusing problems when (or before) they arise, minimizing or preventing property damage and violence through communication, education, and/or advocacy of community interests. This approach emphasizes policies, procedures, and attitudes that are different from the punitive policies and procedures traditionally associated with police work. Community relations is an important part of and a beneficiary of conflict-management approaches (Fuller, 2005).

MAINTAINING AN ORDERLY COMMUNITY

How do we maintain an orderly community? Since the late 1950s, police agencies in the United States have been especially attuned to the difficult and critical problem of doing so. Unfortunately, there is no prescribed formula to tell us how to accomplish this task. Each situation is unique and must be resolved through intricate knowledge of the community, its concerns, and its priorities.

A New Philosophy for Conflict Management

Before a police agency can develop an effective order-maintenance program, it must first initiate a program of self-critical analysis; the goal of this program is to scientifically and rationally place the police role into proper perspective as it relates to community needs, tolerances, and expectations. Such an analysis must include the realization that police–community relations means responsive, effective, and considerate police operations.

Community Concerns and Changing Priorities

The primary consideration of police operations should be the concerns and changing priorities of the community's citizens. The police department must make an effort to provide the community with staff assistance directed toward identifying and resolving the causes of crime and violence, whether those causes are legal or social.

A Partnership

Police officers are involved in a balancing act between rigid enforcement and community tolerances, which is complicated by their own personal beliefs. Before any alternatives, contingencies, or strategies are developed, the department must first acquire an in-depth knowledge of the community and its problems, which can only be accomplished by police operating as a part *of*, and not apart *from*, the community. In addition, the community must be convinced that its police department is operating objectively and is serving the community's legitimate interests to the best of its ability. A partnership must exist between the police and the community. This partnership is one step in laying the groundwork for an accommodation within the department and the community organization, information, and education efforts initiated by the police.

Exemplary Projects

Many departments are becoming more committed to developing conflict-management policies and procedures, usually targeting certain types of problems, individual problems such as mental illness and suicide, episodic problems between people who do not have a history of ongoing relationships, problems between parties with ongoing relationships such as domestic violence, crisis incidents involving hostage situations and nonhostage incidents, mass dissent, and civil disobedience. The Family Crisis Intervention efforts of the New York City Police Department was one of the first programs to demonstrate that trained police officers could be successful not only in defusing the conflict, but also in protecting the lives of the officers who respond to such crises (Peak and Glensor, 2004). Hostage negotiation units begun in the New York City Police Department in 1972 have been one of the most successful innovations in law enforcement. The crisis negotiation concept is used to resolve violent and potentially violent situations whether or not there is a hostage (Noesmer, 1999).

The above project is but one of many exemplary projects found in agencies around the country. Others include the following: Memphis, Tennessee, has a Crisis Interaction Team created to deal specifically with mentally ill individuals; Clearwater, Florida, actually runs a homeless shelter and coordinates social services with other organizations to aid the needy; and Portland, Oregon, made a creative alliance with retailers to regulate the type of alcoholic beverage containers sold in a successful effort to reduce public drunkenness (Peak and Glensor, 2004).

CRISIS NEGOTIATIONS

Traditionally police **crisis negotiations** have meant hostage negotiations. While the skills required for both types of negotiations are similar, crisis negotiations involve far more incidents than securing the release of hostages and surrender of the hostage taker. Crisis negotiations are best viewed as an umbrella of activities in which hostage negotiations are but one component. While specialized training is required for hostage negotiators, *all police officers* should receive regular training in dealing with individuals, couples, and groups of people in crisis situations. This training should provide officers with the skills and insights necessary for defusing potentially volatile situations.

Historically police responses to conflict management have been to use all due force necessary to end the threat as quickly as possible. Unfortunately, hasty actions have too frequently led to death and injuries to police officers, participants, and innocent citizens. They have also been catalysts for future conflict. And, they have caused long-term harm to police–community relations. What is needed (and what is being used by more progressive police agencies) is a new philosophy that stresses the need for fair and just resolution of conflict with the focus being the protection of human life rather than an expeditious closure to a particular incident.

BOX 15.1
Conflict Management Compared to Traditional Police Responses

Traditional Police Response

1. Prompt response with strong show of force.
2. Use threat of arrest to curtail unrest.
3. Strict enforcement of all laws.
4. Time is money; resolve it quickly!
5. Use the experience to enhance riot training for future events.

Conflict Management Response

1. Prompt response based on prior planning with minimal force needed to contain the conflict.
2. Seek to open channels of communication.
3. Use discretion in enforcement to avoid creating "greater harm."
4. Life is precious; take time to do it right!
5. Use the experience to revise tactics and training as well as build relationships to avoid future conflicts.

Qualities of a Good Negotiator

Qualities of crisis negotiators and crisis counselors are similar. Gettinger (1983, p. 17) stated that the qualities of a good negotiator are "patience, an ability to keep the conversation going, and an ability to suspend value judgment." According to Lowenberg and Forgach (1982), a crisis counselor shows respect, warmth, and empathy through words, tone, and actions. Personal qualities include maturity, honesty, and genuineness, because people with these qualities are more likely to be able to handle crisis situations with objectivity and confidence (Lowenberg and Forgach, 1982). These sources agree that the best person for the job is one who can make genuine connections with others. Most references suggest that the best crisis negotiator is a police officer with these qualities and "street knowledge" and one who has been trained in crisis negotiation techniques.

Key Elements of Negotiation Training

Central to most emergency situations is a need for planning and preparation; achieving contact; clarifying needs and hopes; exploring possible mutually acceptable solutions; and contracting for a solution and feedback. Gaining skills in these areas is part of negotiation training.

Nielson and Shea suggested that effective negotiators need to be self-confident; recognize that negotiating is more than bargaining; focus on needs rather than on solutions; work toward agreements that can be mutually acceptable; and seek creative alternatives to impasse. Extensive training using role play and situations that are designed to challenge the officer's creativity in seeking alternatives is critical, as is continued practice after training in order to maintain skills (Nielson and Shea, 1982). These guidelines were created with hostage negotiations in mind but are actually necessary for all police problem-solving activities.

FIGURE 15.1 **Conflict management in the extreme situation.**
Courtesy of Birmingham Police Department.

DOMESTIC DISTURBANCES   Nowhere is this more evident than in the handling of domestic disturbances. According to Sherman (1992), domestic assault is the most frequent form of violence that police officers encounter. At least 8 million times each year police officers will confront a victim who has been beaten by a spouse or lover. One police trainer has said that "Living in a home racked by domestic violence is like living in a POW camp" (Benson, 1993). Another trainer has said that "American women are safer in the streets than in their homes" (Benson, 1993). The public and the police have long recognized the need for skilled crisis intervention in these police calls. However, police alternatives for dealing with these incidents is now subject to debate.

In the mid-1980s, mandatory arrests of suspects in misdemeanor domestic violence arrests became widely accepted. Numerous states passed laws that allowed police officers to make misdemeanor arrests in domestic disturbance when they did not view the assault or did not have a warrant. Up to that time, the police hardly ever made an arrest unless there was serious visible injury or they had a warrant. This was an expansion of police powers and seen as a breakthrough in the handling of domestic disputes.

Several factors combined to make mandatory arrest the most feasible alternative. A research study conducted by Sherman and Berk in Minneapolis during the years 1981 and 1982 on the effects of mandatory arrests showed that it was successful in reducing the violence and repetition of domestic disturbances. The Sherman and Berk report recommended that police in all 50 states be allowed (not required) to make warrantless arrests in misdemeanor domestic violence cases (Sherman, 1992). In 1984, the U.S. Attorney General's Task Force on Family Violence urged police departments to adopt arrest as the preferred response to domestic violence. At this same time the police department of Torrington, Connecticut, lost a $2.6 million lawsuit to Tracy Thurman, whose husband had continued to assault her while police officers hesitated to act. These events combined to make mandatory arrest the preferred police alternative (Benson, 1993, p. 37).

Recent research has convinced Sherman (1992) and others that mandatory arrests may have been doing more harm than good. Replications of the Minneapolis research have shown that arrest deters domestic violence in some cities but not others based on a combination of factors, such as race, socioeconomic status, and the history of violence among the participants (Doerner and Lab, 2005). Instead of requiring mandatory arrest, Sherman suggests, state statutes should require mandatory action from a list of options. The options would be determined by the needs and makeup of the community and could include choices such as transporting the victim to a shelter, transporting either victim or suspect to a detox center, letting the victim decide whether or not the suspect is to be arrested, or providing short-term protection. In any event, this recent research has shown that there is no one answer to conflict management in domestic settings and that the police must combine training with policy and use the law along with other social service agencies to reduce the violence and manage the conflict.

The Milwaukee, Wisconsin, Police Department uses a combination of mandatory arrests and social services to handle domestic violence. The department has had a policy of mandatory arrest since 1986, three years before the state made it a law. In addition, the department works closely with two battered women's shelters. Police officers are instructed to call the shelters from the scene and social workers assess the victim's condition and need for counseling, emergency shelter, or a protection order. The Sojourner Truth House, the city's largest battered women's shelter, also participates in police training and Batterers Anonymous, a 20-week program to which offenders may be diverted (Benson, 1993, p. 39).

Individuals in Crisis

Individuals in crisis are persons who demonstrate inadequate coping skills when faced with stressful life events and endanger themselves or others, for example, the mentally ill or those who have ingested too much alcohol or drugs. Some intend to die at the hands of the police, a tactic known as "suicide by cop" (Bower and Petit, 2001). The police departments of Memphis, Tennessee, and Albuquerque, New Mexico, have crisis intervention teams (CIT) to deal with these individuals (Bower and Petit, 2001; Vickers, 2000). The Albuquerque program is fashioned after the Memphis model. Both grew out of a cooperative arrangement with police agencies and community mental health agencies. CIT members are specially trained officers who complete a 40-hour certification course in how to deal with individuals in a mental illness crisis.

The CIT officers (213 out of 900 uniformed officers in Memphis; 108, or 25 percent, of the field patrol in Albuquerque) respond to all calls involving the mentally ill. All 9-1-1 calls are screened by trained operators; those possibly involving mental illness are dispatched to a CIT officer. In 1999, Albuquerque CIT officers responded to 3,257 calls (Bower and Petit, 2001, p. 3). Of the calls, 48 resulted in the individuals being transported to a mental health facility. Less than 10 percent of the subjects were arrested. Fifty percent of the calls involved mental illness and 45 percent were suicide attempts or threats. Alcohol was present in 27 percent of the incidents. Since the programs have been in existence, both cities have experienced a drop in SWAT callouts, police shooting deaths, and officer injuries.

HOSTAGE NEGOTIATIONS

The field of **hostage negotiations** has expanded from its first appearance in the New York City Police Department in 1972 to now include both hostage and nonhostage incidents in which negotiations are necessary to prevent violence. Hostage situations are those where the subjects hold another person or persons and make demands on a third party, usually law enforcement (Noesmer, 1999). The demands are usually for money, a means to escape, a chance to air grievances (common in prison and jail riots), and political and social change (terrorist incidents). The hostage takers make direct or implied threats against the hostages if their demands are not met.

In most hostage situations, the hostage takers realize that the value of their hostages remains in them staying alive. Hostage takers understand harming the hostages increases the risk that the police will use force to resolve the crisis (Noesmer, 1999). Law enforcement officials have learned to handle these situations by stalling for time, lowering the subjects' expectations, and reversing their sense of empowerment and control. The negotiators buy time by using stalling tactics and engaging in give-and-take bargaining (Noesmer, 1999, p. 8). The subjects must work for everything they get. During such negotiations, the tactical team is planning and getting into position should force be needed. The majority of all hostage incidents are resolved without force because the hostage takers prefer life to their demands.

Crisis negotiations not involving hostages are more difficult to negotiate and have a higher probability of violence. These involve incidents in which the subjects hold victims with whom they have had a prior relationship: former employers or coworkers; former lovers or spouses; or neighbors; or in which subjects are mentally disturbed (Noesmer, 1999). The subjects are unable to control their emotions and are motivated by anger, rage, frustration, hurt, confusion, or depression. They have barricaded themselves or hold their victims against their will, and they make no demands on the police other than to be left alone to express their anger against the person or persons they hold. The negotiator must use all of his or her skills to contain the situation and respond to the subject in a careful and thoughtful manner.

Loss of life is more likely to occur in a nonhostage crisis than in a hostage incident (Noesmer, 1999). Time remains the best ally of the police; rash action is likely to involve loss of life.

A BROADER CONCEPT

Conflict management is not limited to crisis negotiations and domestic crisis situations. Police departments of every size are recognizing the importance of applying conflict-management strategies to disputes that may involve a single person, a few people, disputes between hundreds of people, and conflicts that occur over the use of public space (Goldstein, 1990, pp. 111–112).

In some agencies, conflict management is still a very narrow concept that is packaged for delivery by one unit to a specific category of problems (such as crisis negotiation). This unit, because it is "different," may be an agency stepchild and may not receive general officer and administrative support. There may be little coordination between this unit and other police units within the department, and even less coordination between this unit and other members of the justice community. Lacking the supportive resources that can be gained through this sort of coordination, the success of the unit may be limited, even though its officers have excellent personal rapport with community members.

Disputes between a Few People

The disputes between a few people that police officers deal with could involve people who live with one another, tenants and landlords, customers and merchants, or neighbors. The typical reaction to any incident that disturbs the public peace or involves a dispute between two or more persons is to "call the cops." As Egon Bittner pointed out:

> In place of the freedom of self-help we have devised an exceedingly cumbersome and time-consuming method of dealing with transgressions and omissions, known as the administration of justice. For most purposes this method works, if not well, at least well enough. Thus, if I desire to prevent my neighbor's dog from tearing up my flower bushes, I can go to court to obtain some satisfaction for past damages and an injunction against future trespasses. But if the neighbor sics his dog on me and threatens to do it again, then I can scarcely be expected to wait for the wheels of justice to turn. Instead, I will do what every American would, namely, "Call the cops!" (Bittner, 1972, p. 95)

DISPUTES BETWEEN NEIGHBORS Tasker Street in Philadelphia, Pennsylvania, is similar to a number of streets in large urban cities throughout the United States. It runs through a one-mile-square area of the city known as Grey's Ferry. This section of the city is mostly a lower-income African American community with a predominantly African American housing project, and it is surrounded by pockets of middle-income white neighborhoods. In 1989, when Captain Arthur Berry, an African American police officer, assumed command of the 17th District, which included the Grey's Ferry area, it was a racial battlefield where "neighbors really hated each other" (Parker, 1992).

Soon after Captain Berry took command, a racial incident resulted in the tragic death of a 16-year-old white youth. To resolve this incident and lessen the conflict in the area, Berry approached the leaders of the main community groups: the Grey's Ferry Community Council, which represented the white neighborhoods; the Stinger Square Council, which represented African Americans in surrounding communities; and two Tasker home associations, one representing African Americans in surrounding communities and the other representing African Americans in the housing project (Parker, 1992, p. 26). It was Berry's intention to have these groups meet to determine a cooperative solution to the conflict between neighbors.

The first attempts to meet were less than successful, but Berry continued to meet individually with the leaders of the groups. Before long, the leaders began to meet on a regular basis and discuss community conflicts. The program has been a success, violence has been curtailed, and African American and white neighbors are beginning to get along (Parker, 1992, p. 27).

A problem faced by all communities with colleges and universities is the noise created by the young students in the neighborhoods and public spaces they share with nonstudent neighbors. There are house parties, celebrations after sporting events, and walk-by traffic that often keep residents up at night and create a large trash problem. This noise creates grief and frustration and often motivates homeowners to sell and move out or constantly complain to police or university authorities. Burlington, Vermont, has a unique method of dealing with this noise issue—Neighborhood Walk. In the Neighborhood Walk program, police officers, residents, University of Vermont officials, and volunteers walk the streets in the complaining neighborhoods asking the partiers to quiet down, clean up graffiti, and meet their neighbors.

The "Walkers" are specially trained and cautioned that their job is not to do police work but to remind the students that they are a part of the neighborhood.

DISPUTES BETWEEN YOUTHS AND MERCHANTS   A particularly disturbing source of neighborhood conflict is the presence of large groups of youths, particularly teenagers "hanging out" on business property at all hours. The majority of the teenagers who hang out cause no serious problems. However, some drink and fight with one another and litter on private property. The police can rely on a strict law enforcement approach or they can try to resolve the conflict in a manner that is agreeable to both the youths and the property owners. In 1992, officers from the Joliet, Illinois, Police Department took the latter approach (Parker, 1992).

Officers developed a trespassing agreement to be signed by owners and managers that would allow the police to arrest trespassers without having the owners and managers verbally warning trespassers to get off their property. The officers also had school liaison officers explain the trespass agreement in school and solicit anonymous comments from teenagers. The officers also located areas for the youths to hang out. This combined effort resulted in less conflict between youth and merchants and increased interaction between the police and the youths.

LANDLORD–TENANT DISPUTES   Traditionally, there has always been friction between tenants and landlords. Tenants often take advantage of landlords who do not carefully supervise and maintain rental property, and landlords often take advantage of tenants who do not understand the legal technicalities of rental contracts or landlord obligations. Disputes involving tenants and landlords are common occurrences. The police have traditionally regarded such disputes as strictly civil matters that do not call for police involvement, and often one of the participants falls victim to the other. The tenants may suffer unfair landlord practices, ranging from illegal rent increases to eviction, or the landlords may have their rental property completely destroyed by the tenants. When landlord–tenant disputes continue over a period of time, criminal acts often

FIGURE 15.2   Conflict management could be the simple act of being present in crowd situations to ensure order at "purely recreational" events.

Jeff Greenberg, PhotoEdit Inc.

occur. These include property destruction, assaults that may result in serious injury or death, and other types of violence. Disputes in many cities reach proportions where angry groups of tenants or a civil rights organization enter into large-scale demonstrations against the landlord; as a result, there is a breakdown in order. Thus, in many landlord–tenant disputes police become involved, with a considerable expenditure of labor to conduct investigations or quell disorder.

The Dayton Police Department's conflict-management unit established a program to intervene in landlord–tenant disagreements at the initial stage. The program is an ongoing crime and violence prevention project, a definite police responsibility.

This program requires part of one conflict-management officer's time. Upon being notified of a dispute (either by a beat officer who identifies a dispute during his or her course of duty or by a call from one of the parties involved), the officer meets with the tenant and landlord to find out what the problem is. Then, employing the training received, the officer informs both participants of their mutual obligations and what they legally can and cannot do. The officer keeps in contact to ensure that both sides reach reasonable and satisfactory agreements. Often the officer is able to handle a dispute quickly by referring the tenants and landlords to the proper service agencies or by informing the agency that a dispute exists.

This program deals with police responsibilities (crime and violence prevention) at a level traditionally ignored by police. The program saved the Dayton Police Department countless hours that would otherwise have been expended (Ritchey, 1992).

Disputes between Hundreds of People

The police are often called upon to handle disputes between hundreds of people whenever there are political disputes or disputes over such current social issues as abortion, gay rights, environmental issues, and other highly charged topics (Figure 15.3). They are also present at civil rights demonstrations, labor–management disputes, rallies of extremist groups, and urban riots. Such events require the police to assume a conflict-management approach emphasizing mediation and negotiating skills.

FIGURE 15.3   Crowd control in New York City.
Rob Crandall, The Stock Connection.

The issues that bring about these disputes and their locations have changed in the last 30–40 years. Civil rights protests were predominant in the 1950s and 1960s, and Vietnam was the issue behind most protests in the late 1960s and 1970s. In the 1990s, the majority of the protests and demonstrations occurred as a result of environmental issues and over such social issues as abortion and the right to life. The demonstrations of the 1990s were not as likely to occur in urban areas as they were in the 1960s, 1970s, and 1980s. The 1999 demonstrations in Seattle were a special case, and it is extremely unlikely that such an event will occur in the near future. Demonstrations today increasingly occur in rural and small-town America (Fanton, 1990). Unfortunately, many of the departments in rural and small-town America are ill-equipped and not trained in handling disputes between hundreds of people.

CIVIL DISTURBANCES FOLLOWING THE FIRST RODNEY KING VERDICT   The April 29, 1992, acquittal of the four Los Angeles police officers charged with the beating of Rodney King unleashed a riot of burning, looting, killing, and general mayhem in Los Angeles and led to disturbances in many other U.S. cities. This incident created an image of urban unrest not seen in the United States since the 1960s. However, several large urban cities—particularly Boston, Chicago, Miami, and San Diego—were able to avoid these disturbances through strategic planning and deployment of police forces, the willingness of police and city officials to maintain close communication with their constituents, the debunking of rumors, and good old-fashioned luck (Clark, 1992).

In each of these four cities, the police had contingency plans ready in the event they were needed to maintain calm and quell disorder. Police administrators in these cities recognized that an acquittal verdict would produce disturbances, so in each of these cities, police and city officials made public pronouncements voicing their dismay about the verdicts and asking for calm. Chicago Police Superintendent Matt Rodriguez released a public statement conveying his "amazement and concern" over the verdict (Clark, 1992, p. 6). Other police executives met with community leaders and spoke at the spontaneous demonstrations that sprang up in their cities. The San Diego Police Department let residents know that they could protest the verdicts peacefully, but that they would not allow opportunists to engage in violence, looting, or burning.

FIGURE 15.4   Anatomy of a rural demonstration.

The first environmental demonstration in Allegheny County, New York, occurred May 31, 1989, caught everyone by surprise, and took place on the front steps of the county courthouse. Several hundred demonstrators assembled in front of the courthouse, and forty-eight of them surrounded a car carrying two members of a state commission who had come to inspect the site of a nuclear dump site. The protesters blocked the wheels and refused to let the commission members out of their car.

"It presented a big problem," Allegheny County Sheriff Larry Scholes said later. His department consisted of twenty-one full-time staff whose primary duties were maintaining the county jail. Scholes recalls, "I walked out there with one uniformed deputy. As soon as that vehicle pulled in and was surrounded by forty-eight people, I asked my office to get additional staff."

Two civil deputies were called in, and then the New York State Police were summoned when it became clear that the objective of the people surrounding the car was to be arrested. Eventually, the demonstrators were arrested and the two shaken commissioners were allowed to leave. Sheriff Scholes stated, "I feel like Andy of Mayberry on a bad day."

Following the initial demonstration of May 31, Sheriff Scholes met with representatives of the protest groups to advise them of his concerns about violence and the need for communications. "We set up a rapport right from the very first meeting," the sheriff reported. "They feel comfortable calling and asking me something, knowing that if I can't give the information, I'll tell them so, and if I do give them the information, it's going to be accurate. They, in turn, have done the same thing for me." Sheriff Scholes's approach did not stop the demonstrations; that was not his intent. However, his handling of the demonstrations did lessen the potential for violence and reduced the likelihood of surprise for both parties.

Source: Adapted from B. Fanton, "Rural demonstration," *Law & Order,* November 1990, pp. 92–97.

Each of the cities set up networks to control the spread of rumors and keep community leaders informed of police activities. Community leaders in each of the cities were praised for their part in keeping the cities calm. In fact, the relationships created between police and community leaders during this crisis have led to positive developments in conflict management. The San Diego Coalition for Equality—Year 2000 was formed by residents and the police department after the immediate crisis was over. There have been meetings in Chicago between community leaders and the police to explore solutions to other possible sources of conflict.

Disputes over the Use of Public Space

The police are often involved in conflict situations when there are disputes over the use of public space. Sometimes these disputes involve the illegal use of public space, such as when prostitutes or drug pushers use public streets to engage in illegal enterprises. However, peddlers, alcoholics, the mentally ill, and the homeless may compete with merchants, shoppers, pedestrians, and others for public space that all feel entitled to use. In the latter instances, the police would prefer to resolve the conflict whenever possible without resorting to arrest.

HOMELESS PEOPLE   As discussed in Chapter 12, although the homeless have a high arrest rate, they are not involved in crimes that involve violence or threats of violence against others (Snow, Baker, and Anderson, 1989). Their crimes mainly involve acts that indicate personal dysfunction, such as public intoxication, theft and shoplifting, and violation of city ordinances. Nevertheless, a survey by the Police Executive Research Forum (PERF) indicated that the responding police officers view the homeless as a source for concern because they increase the fear of crime among citizens and the conditions in which they live pose a public health hazard (Carter and Sapp, 1993).

FIGURE 15.5 **Officer attempting to reason with illegal protestors.**

AP Wide World Photos.

Although respondents to the PERF survey were aware that the police are often the only resource available to provide aid to the homeless, they recognized that a law enforcement response was not the answer.

> [This] is not strictly a police problem and requires, like domestic abuse, a multidisciplinary approach. Police are strictly a stopgap measure dealing with immediate problems and are not equipped to deal with root causes. (Carter and Sapp, 1993, p. 7)

More than 80 percent of the police officers reported that their departments provided transportation when they came in contact with homeless persons requiring shelter. The majority of the contacts the police had with the homeless involved "public nuisances," such as panhandling, public intoxication, or problematic behavior indicating mental illness.

Although the use of public space by the homeless receives more attention, there are other groups that also create (and receive) grief for accessing public space. We have already alluded to organized protests within a previous section. However, there are two groups that warrant consideration.

YOUNG PEOPLE   As discussed in Chapter 12, young people need to get out and interact with one another. Having limited financial resources means that much of this socialization is spent "just hanging out." Unfortunately due to fears of vandalism and theft, as well as liability for harm that the youths may incur on their property, business owners are generally not receptive to their presence. If public spaces are not available, these young people will be forced to move to other areas (where unlawful activities may be allowed or actually promoted by older youths or unethical adults). Young people may also resort to dangerous use of public properties for street racing, graffiti art contests, and other acts of vandalism, as well as petty thefts for scavenger hunts or from just plain boredom. Lastly, they may cruise in their cars looking for other youths doing the same.

Some communities respond to the activities of young people by closing off downtown areas, enforcing curfews, prohibiting "after-hours loitering," or regulating traffic patterns. One of the best solutions that we are aware of is presented in Box 15.2.

POOR AND WORKING-CLASS PEOPLE   Just as young people often don't have the financial resources needed for movies, concerts, sporting events, and so on, neither do poor and working-class adults. Like teenagers many of these adults are young, active, and need to socialize with others their own ages. This is particularly true for ethnic minorities who are underemployed, or who are spending large portions of their salaries to support family members. Police

---

BOX 15.2
Dealing with Excessive Cruising in the Dallas-Fort Worth Area

During the 1990s cruising was a serious problem in the Dallas-Forth Worth area. A particular section between the two cities was known for the hundreds (and later thousands) of teenagers who would drive into the area on weekends. Preliminary efforts to restrict cruising on the main thoroughfare created a greater problem by pushing the young people onto side streets and into neighborhoods where their noise, partying behaviors, and the subsequent traffic congestion were not appreciated. In an innovative move, local police agencies decided that rather than try to stop the kids from coming into the area to socialize, they would actually encourage them to do so. Instead of writing tickets to stop cruising, the police invited young people to park and party. Huge parking lots were rented from the local university, and teen traffic was diverted to these lots. Vendors provided legal food and beverages while various types of entertainment were also supplied under the watchful eyes of local police. The result: Thousands of teenagers were able to socialize in a safe and socially acceptable manner.

BOX 15.3

"Entertaining Themselves," Hispanic Workers Playing Soccer

Many communities within the Southeastern United States are finding themselves with increasing numbers of Mexican and South American migrant workers. These workers are usually employed in agriculture, construction, and factory jobs that Americans don't want to do. While some workers are fortunate enough to settle down with their families, many cannot do so. Often they share living quarters with several other workers in order to save money. They send most of the money they make back home to Mexico or South America to help take care of their families. That frequently leaves them alone and with little money when they are not working. In areas where public or at least semi-private spaces are available, these young adults meet with others to have soccer matches. On weekends and holidays, groups of young adults may be seen playing soccer (with organized teams in matching uniforms) on grassy fields in public parks, on open school playgrounds, and at unused community recreational facilities, while several hundred spectators watch.

recreational leagues (discussed in Chapter 12) are excellent solutions, as are municipal and county recreational leagues. However, these have time and availability constraints. Sometimes the best solutions are to simply allow these adults access to public space where they can create their own recreational activities. This is best done by ensuring that spaces in public parks and playing fields are available for unscheduled activities by unorganized groups of individuals. By allowing these poor and working-class adults to congregate in well-lighted and safe areas patrolled by the police, conflict- and frustration-induced criminal behavior may be avoided. An example of such an activity is provided in Box 15.3.

CONFLICT INTERVENTION AT THE COMMUNITY LEVEL

Although the conflict-management unit of the police department of Dayton, Ohio, no longer exists, it has been incorporated into its community policing strategy (Ritchey, 1992). Thus, the conflict intervention team of this unit still provides a useful model.

Conflict Intervention Teams

The **conflict intervention team** of the Dayton conflict-management unit was responsible for seeking, identifying, and intervening in potential conflicts before they became serious disruptions. Police departments may not be able to recognize conflict before it reaches major proportions unless the department develops close communication and contact with the community. The primary responsibility of the Dayton CIT was to develop and nurture this kind of close contact. Team members spent most of their time in the community in an effort to create the open exchanges of opinion that are necessary for a working police–community interaction. The team members met with ministers, presidents, and leaders of neighborhood organizations and service clubs, directors and staff members of service agencies, business and industrial leaders, school administrators and faculty, leaders and members of paramilitary and youth groups, gang members, and others who had no formal connections to anyone or any group but who could still exert influence over a large number of people.

The Defusement Process

The relationships mentioned above gave team members a chance to learn about the conflicts and community problems that might lead to violence and confrontation situations. These relationships played a major role in the **defusement process**—a conflict-management technique employed to smooth over potentially abrasive police–community interaction when a large group forms, either spontaneously or as a planned demonstration.

Major Aspects of Conflict Intervention

The first aspect of conflict intervention is to identify conflict and potential conflict in the community and to respond to potentially explosive situations as they arise in the community.

The second aspect is actual intervention in a conflict and working out a solution so that the need for forceful police response is eliminated. This includes keeping command officers informed as conflicts develop and preparing a number of alternatives that the department can adopt in handling each situation. During this stage, the conflict intervention team acts as a resource and research arm for the department, attempting to find a means of responding that will maintain a maximum of order, yet not result in an open confrontation.

At other times, intervention may mean going immediately into the problem area and bringing initial relief to the community through defusement before developing the longer-term solution. This permits the department to control a situation through conflict-management techniques using as few as six officers (the number on Dayton's conflict intervention team) and to alleviate problems that might otherwise call for a more extensive use of force. The ability of the team to defuse potentially dangerous situations illustrates the value of a conflict-management approach toward law enforcement at the community level. The conflict intervention unit cannot be only a specialized task force that acts as a planning source for the department; it can also be a practical, on-the-street operation that intervenes in crises as they arise. Its approaches are those of mediation, communication, and advocacy. When a conflict and its participants have been identified, a meeting or series of meetings is arranged between the team and those community members who are parties to the conflict. The Dayton CIT intervened in such varied disputes as two quarreling neighbors, two youth groups, labor and management during a strike situation, and a group of college students hostile to the school administration.

In many cases, a conflict could result from lack of proper services from some other public agency. Advocacy by the CIT could be used to ensure that the proper service is rendered. This concept could also be employed during intensive conflict situations when an in-depth study is necessary to discover the causes of the conflict and develop recommendations for action.

SLO Solutions Program: A Community Conflict Resolution Partnership

The SLO program administered by the San Luis Obispo, California, Police Department is a free conflict resolution service offered to all San Luis Obispo residents. The community partnership program is funded by the City of San Luis Obispo; the California Polytechnic State University (Cal Poly); Cuesta College, a large community college; and Creative Mediation, a local nonprofit organization (Linden, 2008). Originally conceived to handle disputes between college students and neighborhood residents and landlords, it is now a city-wide program, with each partner paying their portion of the costs; Cal Poly University and Cuesta College paying for the estimated number of their students living in the city; and the city paying for the remaining nonstudents. Creative Mediation staffed by professionals and volunteers is a nonprofit organization that has been delivering conflict resolution and mediation services to community residents for over 13 years.

The kinds of conflicts resolved include those involving noise, parking, trash, parties, security deposits, lease agreements, communication, expectations in lifestyle choices, and financial concerns. The program is intended to deal with the problems underlying the symptoms (repeated police calls) of the conflict situations encountered by all police organizations, such as neighbor–neighbor, landlord–tenant, and roommate–housemate disputes. The mediation is a voluntary nonadversarial process involving a neutral third party facilitating a negotiated settlement. In fiscal year 2006–2007, 563 residents were served and 63 mediation sessions were held, resulting in 52 written agreements. A survey of those served revealed that 99 percent responded that the services were helpful to them. This exemplary program provides the community and the police an alternative way to handle conflict.

REALITY CHECK

Try Your Hand at Conflict Management

Problem 1

Situation. Several paramilitary and loosely organized youth groups are responsible for considerable apprehension in the city's neighborhoods and for assaults and destruction to property.

Potential. Because of the quick, "hit-and-run" nature of gang activities, only rarely are witnesses and victims able to identify assailants or provide enough information to effect arrests. It is virtually impossible for the department to legally halt such activities.

However, all gangs do not engage in antisocial behavior, nor are all members of a gang that engages in antisocial behavior destructive or violence oriented. Indeed, some of these groups have assisted the department in keeping tense situations from exploding. Therefore, an attempt by the department to "get the gangs off the streets" by gathering intelligence information and making arrests will be both unfair and of little value in reaching the real sources of trouble. Additionally, such police action has proven to be disastrous; it serves as a recruiting mechanism for the gangs and, as experience across the country has shown, further alienates young people, drawing police into an imaginary "war" with the youths. Neither does such action offer more than stopgap measures. It only commits the department to respond to gang activities again and again.

What Would You Do? Actual Conflict-Management Unit Response

The conflict-management unit recognized its double predicament. The gangs were becoming more influential in Dayton, and a confrontation with them would heavily drain the department and the city of vital resources. Therefore, the conflict-management unit sought to develop a longer-lasting solution to this problem.

Operating under the premise "If you can't beat 'em, join 'em," two conflict intervention team officers practically became gang members. But this was not an intelligence or undercover operation. The two officers wore their police uniforms and rode marked police motorcycles in their interaction with the gangs. This gave the team a chance to meet the gangs "on their own ground," developing an honest relationship with them that allowed the officers to become familiar with gang leaders, their habits, and other related matters. The officers cautioned the gang members if they were causing trouble and explained the consequences of their behavior.

Evaluation. This relationship between the officers and the gangs proved to be valuable. The department was able to reduce the late-night noise created by gangs, the general vandalism and littering, and the roughhousing that often led to assaults on innocent people. It prevented a potential gang–police confrontation and reduced the need to investigate complaints due to gang activities. In addition, the conflict-management operation provided the community with a visible police presence, assuring residents that the department was monitoring gang activity.

Problem 2

Situation. Growing urban schools, beginning to integrate, and the complex problems of young people experiencing the first challenges of responsibility have been a source of difficulty. This is complicated by racial antagonisms, often reflected in homes and carried into schools by the students, by apprehension on the part of city residents who live in school neighborhoods, and by the fear of "new" people (integration).

Potential. There is a real strain on intergroup relations among students in the public school system, and even unintentional acts can produce confrontations between African American and white youngsters. Traditional responses—sending in "troops" to separate and disperse youngsters—have resulted in making the police the object of the confrontation and creating just as serious a problem. In many cases, this type of response only aggravates the situation and makes it necessary for the department to return to the school on a continual basis, which places an exhausting strain on departmental resources. It also irritates students, who resent massive police presence at the schools and are drawn more and more into the situation.

What Would You Do? Actual Conflict-Management Unit Response

Recognizing that the Dayton Police Department could not afford to respond day after day to such situations, yet realizing that the department had an obligation to ensure that the schools remain peaceful learning centers, the conflict-management unit sought to develop longer-lasting solutions.

Conflict intervention team members met with students in seminars, assemblies, conferences, workshops, classrooms, and street parties to explore and dissect myths, rumors, false and malicious statements, and ignorance. This brought about an understanding on the part of both African American and white students that the fast-moving pace of our times calls for interdependence. These discussions were expanded to include parents and residents of the school neighborhoods. In addition, the team members promoted the establishment of student–faculty–administration councils, which brought usually separated people into a more positive alliance.

The team also developed a special course that was taught to high school students in civic classes. This course was led by a conflict-management officer who discussed such topics as the laws of search and seizure, the U.S. system of justice and constitutional rights, police responsibilities and limitations, and basic police operations.

Evaluation. The Dayton Police Department was able to maintain a healthy learning atmosphere in the schools, reducing the negative attitudes that students often have toward police. Racial tensions and hostilities among students and in school neighborhoods were reduced, and the department no longer has to contend with continuous, abrasive contacts between students and neighborhood residents.

Conclusions

Conflict management will become an increasingly vital area of police work in the new century as the U.S. population expands and changes. Disputes between persons, hundreds of persons, and others over the use of public space will increase. The public and the police will seek alternatives to arrest whenever possible. Police departments, rural and urban, will be forced to examine the inventory of tools and resources they have at their disposal to deal with conflict. Departments will consider their coercive powers, their discretionary powers, and the power to arrest and to issue warrants or warnings when dealing with conflict.

Police departments will also call on other community resources, such as the news media, churches, and civic organizations, regulatory agencies, neighborhood organizations, and social service agencies, to assist them in the management of conflict. These departments will have to provide training and specialized personnel in conflict management.

It is imperative that arrest be viewed from a reasonable and proper perspective. There are too many persons in the police service and within our communities who view arrest as the final problem solver. This simplistic point of view has served as an inhibiting factor in allowing police to increase their options for response. The coercive powers of the police are certainly necessary for the performance of their duties; however, these same coercive powers (arrest) sometimes contribute to the chaotic conditions in today's communities. Police, as the community's resource in control of deviant behavior, must look beyond traditional ways so that their contribution to society may be even more effective.

Student Checklist

1. Contrast conflict-management approaches with traditional police policy.
2. Describe crisis negotiations.
3. Identify several alternatives to arrest.
4. Describe the defusement process.
5. Describe several strategies for developing close communication between the police and the community.
6. Apply conflict-management strategies to typical situations needing police intervention.

Topics for Discussion

1. Set up a conflict-management program in your class. "Respond" to the situations described in Reality Check.
2. Discuss the advantages to police of having such a program.
3. Discuss alternative ways for the police and the community, such as the SOL program, to handle conflict.

Bibliography

Benson, K. (March 1993). "Domestic violence: The house divided," *Police*, pp. 32–36.

Bittner, E. (1972). *The Functions of the Police in Modern Society.* Washington, D.C.: National Institute of Mental Health.

Bower, D. L., and Petit, G. W. (2001). "The Albuquerque Police Department's crisis intervention team: A report card," *FBI Law Enforcement Bulletin*, Vol. 70, No. 2, pp. 1–6.

Carter, D. L., and Sapp, A. (March 1993). "Police response to street people: A survey of perspectives and practices," *FBI Law Enforcement Bulletin*, pp. 5–9.

Clark, J. R. (May 31, 1992). "Keeping a lid on things," *Law Enforcement News*, pp. 6ff.

Doerner, W. G., and Lab, S. P. (2005). *Victimology*, 4th ed. Cincinnati, OH: Anderson.

Fanton, B. (November 1990). "Rural demonstrations," *Law & Order*, pp. 92–97.

Fink, J., and Sealy, L. G. (1974). *The Community and the Police—Conflict or Cooperation.* New York: John Wiley & Sons.

Fuller, J. R. (2005). *Criminal Justice: Mainstream and Cross Currents.* Upper Saddle River, NJ: Pearson/Prentice Hall.

Gettinger, S. (1983). "Hostage negotiations bring them out alive," *Police Magazine*, Vol. 6, pp. 10–18.

Goldstein, H. (1990). *Problem-Oriented Policing.* New York: McGraw-Hill.

Linden, D. (2008). *SOL Solutions Programs: A Community Conflict Resolution Partnership.* Submitted to Alliance for Innovation: 2008 J. Robert Havlick Outstanding Achievement in Innovation Award Submission.

Lowenberg, D. A., and Forgach, P. (1982). *Counseling Crime Victims in Crisis.* Washington, D.C.: Aurora Associates.

Nielson, R. C., and Shea, G. F. (August, 1982). "Training officers to negotiate creatively," *The Police Chief*, Vol. XLIX, pp. 65–67.

Noesmer, G. W. (1999). "Negotiation concepts for commanders," *FBI Law Enforcement Bulletin*, Vol. 68, pp. 6–14.

Parker, P. (August, 1992). "Starting with the kids," *Police*, pp. 26–27.

Peak, K., and Glenser, R. W. (2004). *Community Policing and Problem Solving*, 4th ed. Upper Saddle River, NJ: Prentice Hall.

Ritchey, D., Officer, Dayton, Ohio, Police Department (September 9, 1992). Personal telephone conversation.

Sherman, L. W. (1992). *Policing Domestic Violence: Experiments and Dilemmas.* New York: Free Press.

Snow, D. A., Baker, S. G., and Anderson, L. (1989). "Criminality and homeless men: An empirical assessment," *Social Problems*, Vol. 36, No. 5, pp. 532–549.

Vickers, B. (2000). "Memphis, Tennessee, Police Department's crisis intervention team," *Practitioner Perspectives*. Washington, D.C.: U.S. Department of Justice.

CHAPTER 16

Community Participation in the New Millennium

Perhaps, the most significant aspect of police-community relations remains as the context in which the police and the community work together in an effort to reduce criminal activity and insure the safety of citizens.

—MILLER AND BRASWELL, 1997

Policing is too important an aspect of public policy to be left to the police. It is fundamental to our quality of community.

—MORGAN AND NEWBURN, 1997

KEY CONCEPTS

Civilian Oversight Agencies
Civilian Review Boards
Community Participation
Community Problem
    Solvers
Community Values

Crime Prevention
Globalization
    of Crime
Guardian Angels
Homeland Security
Local Strategies

National Association for
    Civilian Oversight of Law
    Enforcement
Regulatory Participation
Supportive Participation
"War on Terror"

LEARNING OBJECTIVES

Studying this chapter will enable you to:

1. Define the concept of community participation.
2. Describe the factors that influenced the development of community participation efforts.
3. Describe the factors that create resistance to community participation.
4. Contrast several methods of community participation in the provision of police services.
5. Compare the effectiveness of different styles of community participation.
6. Describe the world and national events affecting the police and their communities.
7. Describe what is necessary for improving police–community relations in the new millennium.
8. Describe how one chooses a community-specific strategy for police problems.

Throughout this book, the word "community" has included all the many environments where police work. As a term, community means "common unity," common goals meeting common needs, but such a definition seems out of place in most urban settings. Small towns, too, may be separated into many communities with sometimes conflicting needs. Group interests and values are varied and complicated and have a direct impact on the working environment of the police officer.

There is little argument today that citizen participation in the justice process is crucial to its effectiveness. Never before in this country has each individual citizen been so aware of crime and its personal cost. Citizens are also more aware that they must participate in their own protection and be responsible for their own actions. We have come to appreciate Greenberg's urging that "there is something magical about the power of self-help" (1977, p. 60). But at what level should this participation exist? Do we need modern-day vigilantes? Should we spend huge sums of money on security devices and security personnel? Should we have civilian review boards to control police misconduct? What should volunteers be allowed to do within justice agencies?

This chapter addresses the concept of community control, for the purpose of providing the reader with an objective description and analysis of some of the methods of community participation currently being considered or implemented in criminal justice.

THE CONCEPT OF COMMUNITY PARTICIPATION

Little agreement exists on a definition of **community participation**. The term is generally defined to suit the purposes of a specific analysis, and depends to a large extent on what subject is being investigated. Definitions range from the community's absolute control over an organization (of which there are few examples) to the ability of a community to exercise some degree of input into the organization (of which there are many examples) (Figure 16.1).

What Is a Community?

To understand the concept of community participation, we must first review the major characteristics of community:

1. Group interaction that may be deliberate or unintentional, positive or negative, ranging from conflict to cooperation.
2. Shared boundaries that may be largely geographical (simply a common physical location), common interests (professional, social, economic, or political), or common history, values, goals, needs, or some combination of these.

FIGURE 16.1 Community participation continuum: The need for balance.

Not Enough Community Participation	Appropriate Community Participation	Too Much Community Participation

Not enough community participation results in isolation of the police from the communities they are supposed to serve. This may lead to inappropriate behavior on the part of the police, which is detrimental to democratic principles and the welfare of citizens.

Appropriate levels of community participation result in crime prevention strategies and involvement in police decision making and serves the best interests of both the police and citizens.

Too much community participation results in power struggles among competing interest groups, which may lead to discriminatory practices, corruption, and ineffectiveness on the part of the police.

The environment in which police work is fragmented and segmented, and sometimes many "communities" with competing goals make up a larger community of people living together within a common geographical area and sharing some common needs. The justice community is described as systems within systems interacting with one another within legal boundaries. One of the key problems of community relations is that all of these communities are part of the relationship and their uncommon needs, as well as their common ones, must be defined and addressed.

What Is Participation?

The use of the word "participation" is difficult to pinpoint. Some writers have used participation as absolute control in "the ability to impose one's views upon others by the threat or use of power." Participation can also mean the "opportunity to check, regulate, or keep within certain limits the actions of others" or "the legitimate authority and power to govern." Defined in this manner, participation is used in the context of providing an equilibrium and a measure of accountability. Finally, participation can be used more indirectly to include the ability to communicate with, to influence, to vote for, to participate in, or to exercise impact with important decision makers. Used in this manner, participation emphasizes the ability to interact with people. Each of these definitions of participation can be found to some extent in the criminal justice system. Prisoners' riots can be reviewed as attempts to exercise control by threat or use of force. Civilian review boards, developed to handle citizen complaints against the police, are examples of a community's attempt to control by way of regulation and accountability. Recent citizen voting initiatives to reinstate the death penalty, citizen support of community-based correctional and diversionary programs, and citizen participation on criminal justice advisory councils are examples of community control by interaction.

What Is Community Participation?

Community participation is a continuum of citizen participation. It is multifaceted, is ever-changing, and encompasses a wide range of citizen involvement. Degree of participation varies with community characteristics and community goals. If the intent is to destroy the political system, threat or use of violence might be considered an effective use of control. If improving the

FIGURE 16.2 Citizens participating at a police–community fair.

Courtesy of Oceanside Police Department.

relationship between police and citizens is the goal, efforts might be centered around assessing mutual needs and fears and opening new avenues of communication. The continuum of citizen participation includes a wide range of activities pursued at various levels of the criminal justice system.

Several key questions may be helpful in analyzing the nature of existing citizen participation (Altshuler, 1970, pp. viii–ix). From what community is the demand for increased involvement coming? How likely is it to persist or mushroom? What type of increased participation does the community desire? How does the demand for increased participation fit into the general framework of U.S. culture and politics? What types of interest are affected by increased community control? How is the community defined? What mode of representation or accountability does it seek?

DEVELOPMENT OF COMMUNITY PARTICIPATION

New Demands

Today, more and more citizens are demanding a greater voice in the decisions that affect them. Citizens feel that government has become too far removed from their needs and from public accountability. They want public institutions to empower them rather than simply serve them, and this includes pushing control of the government bureaucracy into the community (Osborne and Gaebler, 1993). This also includes government agencies that measure outcomes not inputs, that are measured by their goals and missions and not rules and regulations, that redefine their clients as customers, and that prevent problems before they occur and decentralize authority.

The criminal justice system has not remained isolated from these accusations. The police, who are the most visible arm of the government at the community level, are often accused of representing the force of the dominant white class and of employing differential treatment and unnecessary brutality. The courts, too, have been criticized, with accusations ranging from uneven justice to a questioning of judicial standards and accountability. The bail system, plea bargaining, and sentencing criteria are viewed as arbitrary decisions that are no longer responsive to the changing mores of the communities being served. Attacks aimed at the correctional system center around its perceived inability to rehabilitate the criminal so that he or she is no longer a threat to society (Fuller, 2005).

The demand for increased participation by various communities comes from an apparent realization on the part of citizens that they have a stake in making the components of the criminal justice system operate at a level responsive to their needs. This realization of citizen responsibility is being translated into citizen action. No longer is the aroused citizen content to permit the professionals to solve alone the problems of the police, courts, and corrections. Instead, the emphasis has seemingly switched from "*They* should do more" to "*We* can do more." Examples of this are numerous. Groups of citizens have organized to monitor the performance levels of the police, courts, and corrections.

When the community is dissatisfied, pressure to improve the performance is generated from the community to the relevant administrator or elected official. The pressure is sometimes direct in the form of filing numerous complaints against a specific agency; at other times, it is more indirect and takes the form of citizen ballot initiatives or community support of alternative candidates. Judging from recent municipal, state, and national elections, "law and order" has become a visible issue that few office seekers can afford to ignore.

A Clear Necessity

As the National Advisory Commission on Criminal Justice Standards and Goals pointed out:

> Government programs for the control of crime are unlikely to succeed all alone.
> Informed private citizens, playing a variety of roles, can make a decisive difference in

the prevention, detection, and prosecution of crime, the fair administration of justice, and the restoration of offenders to the community. (National Advisory Commission on Criminal Justice Standards and Goals, 1973, p. CC-7)

Citizen and community involvement in the justice system is not viewed as merely desirable: It is a necessity.

An Old Concept

Community participation in the justice system is not a new or radical concept. It dates back to when peace was kept by the entire community (e.g., when citizens spotted crimes, they were supposed to notify their neighbors so that they all could apprehend the criminal). As time passed and society became more complex, communities delegated these responsibilities to criminal justice specialists, but they did not abdicate them. Thus many feel that responsibility and accountability for planning, decision making, and action regarding criminal justice should be returned, insofar as is practical, to the community.

SYSTEMS AND COMMUNITY VALUES

The police occupy a strategic position in any society because they are charged with enforcing the norms of society. In order to perform this role, they must interact with the members of society. The importance of this interaction and cooperation varies with the nature of the total society. In a strictly regulated society, conflict in values becomes less important because individual values tend to be less important. In societies where the individual member is considered important, value conflicts become vital to the system's maintenance of the community, and the police value system must accommodate **community values** to a greater degree.

Problems of Community Participation

COMMUNITY RESISTANCE TO COMMUNITY PARTICIPATION   The recognition of the usefulness of citizen involvement or community participation is not universally accepted by either the average citizen or the professionals employed in the criminal justice system. By its very nature, community control is reactive. It is only when conditions become unacceptable that citizens are aroused from apathy and are motivated to devote time, imagination, and energy to a particular cause. The civil rights movement of the 1960s; the college student demonstrations over the invasion of Cambodia in 1970; and demonstrations by women's rights organizations, Gay Liberation, Gray Panthers, Women Against Rape; antinuclear groups; and others that have represented various issues in the 1990s are examples of an aroused citizenry.

The Rodney King incident in Los Angeles, the Abner Louima and Amadou Diallo incidents in New York City, the Malice Greene slaying in Detroit, and the Cincinnati riot have all resulted in citizen demands for more control over their respective police agencies. Since 1994, Congress has authorized the Civil Rights Divisions of the Department of Justice to bring civil suits for declarative or injunctive relief against police departments for acts of misconduct. These acts can include excessive use of force; false arrests, charges, and reports; and improper stops, searches, and seizures. Since 1994, the Pittsburgh, Pennsylvania, Police Department; the Steubenville, Ohio, Police Department; and the New Jersey State Troopers have entered into consent decrees to avoid civil action by the U.S. Department of Justice (Barker, 2002, p. 20). Each of these consent decrees has included increased accountability to the citizens served by these agencies.

Even most of the organized Neighborhood Crime Prevention efforts occur after several people in a neighborhood have been victimized, rather than as true primary prevention. Communities react when the services provided are no longer acceptable to them. Even then, it is not the entire community that responds, but rather only the energetic and sufficiently aroused citizen. It is a difficult task to enlist the support of the unaffected citizen. The National Advisory Commission on Criminal Justice Standards and Goals emphasized this point and its implications:

> There appears to be a widespread assumption that it is the business of the criminal justice system to respond to this demand and to marshall all available resources to choke off crime at its roots. This viewpoint neglects the certainty that unless a worried citizenry can translate its indignation into active participation in the search for and implementation of an effective solution, the criminal justice system must inevitably fall even farther behind in its crime control and rehabilitation efforts. Awakening the conscience of America is a necessity because if the multiplicity of factors that produce crime and delinquency are not recognized and remedied, more crime will occur, more of it will go undetected, and the inadequateness of the system will thus become even stronger incentive to further illegal activity. (National Advisory Commission on Criminal Justice Standards and Goals, 1973, p. CC-2)

PROFESSIONAL RESISTANCE TO COMMUNITY PARTICIPATION   Beyond marshaling citizen support and involvement in the criminal justice system, advocates for increased citizen participation point out the need to instill a willingness on the part of the police, courts, and corrections to use available citizen input effectively. Many studies indicate that the three components of the justice system are reluctant to involve citizens in their operations. Many employees view such participation as an attempt to minimize their professional expertise (Trojanowicz et al., 1998). Every year, while working on one of the author's assignments, students are often met by resistance from police agencies who say that any request for the department's mission statement, a copy of a policy, or examples of police–community relations programs must be made through the Freedom of Information Act. These are matters of public record and the community has a right to know about its police agency.

In addition, there is a natural suspicion of outsiders on the part of any organization. As was pointed out earlier, scientific management is, of itself, sometimes a barrier to citizen participation. It is established public administration theory that much organizational energy is spent in self-sustaining activities. Proposed reforms tend to be evaluated in terms of their efficiency in protecting the organization's welfare and their ability to minimize the required expenditure of energy (Roberg, Kuykendall, and Novak, 2002). The organization's employees reinforce this tendency by developing patterns of behavior that further insulate the organization from the community. Their members often prefer to maintain the status quo despite public demands for change. They may be more resistant to community input than members of other organizations, because of the fragmentation of their services into separate local units, their method of recruitment and promotion, and their degree of isolation from the general public, as well as from one another.

TWO TYPES OF COMMUNITY PARTICIPATION

According to the role assigned to citizens, community participation can take two general forms: regulatory and supportive. In regulatory participation, members of the community regulate operations of components of the criminal justice system. In supportive participation, the community supplements and complements operations of the system. The following discussion describes examples of regulatory and supportive community participation.

Regulatory Participation

Regulatory participation has been directed primarily at the police, as policing agencies are the most visible form of government at the community level, and police officers the primary initiators of action in the entire justice system. When police officers make the decision to arrest, they are making a formal determination of whether or not the potential arrestee should be processed into the criminal justice system. What happens at the police level determines to a greater degree what the rest of the criminal justice system is capable of doing. The initial and most expansive sorting out of "criminals" from "average citizens" is done by the police: Only those arrested by the police can be adjudicated by the courts and rehabilitated by corrections. For these reasons, much public attention and concern center around the operations of law enforcement agencies.

The following sections review briefly five major developments in the area of regulatory participation of the police. These developments are (1) the attempt to establish civilian complaint review boards, (2) the attempt to create an ombudsman to review citizen complaints against the police, (3) the attempt to decentralize the police politically and administratively, (4) the attempt to ride patrol on the police in the community, and (5) the attempt to affect the establishment of enforcement priorities.

CIVILIAN REVIEW BOARDS

Origins.   Most law enforcement agencies have some internal machinery for reviewing allegations of misconduct against their agents. Dissatisfaction with this machinery, particularly among members of minority groups, has led to the establishment of **civilian review boards** in several U.S. cities, usually in the face of severe police opposition. They were usually established after allegations of excessive use of force or racial profiling by the police, or a string of police shootings. They were seen as a way to check against abuse and to restore the community's trust in its police department. The typical civilian review board consisted of seven to nine members, including some members of the police, but with a civilian majority. Usually, the civilians were appointed by the mayor and the police members were named by the police commissioner. The size of the administrative and investigative staffs varies from board to board.

The Controversy over the Boards.   Wherever they were proposed or implemented, civilian review boards provoked controversy. Below are some of the leading arguments pro and con:

1. *Pro.* Advocates of the boards claim that they have the following merits:
   a. Create a climate in which citizens can freely state their complaints about police misconduct.
   b. Educate the public about their legal rights.
   c. Provide for public exoneration of police officers by an impartial agency.
   d. Are primarily concerned with getting at the truth (not with protecting the police department).
2. *Con.* Opponents of the boards argue that they have the following demerits:
   a. Destroy police administrators' authority to investigate and discipline their officers.
   b. Demoralize police officers and make them hesitant to act on complaints.
   c. Are probably biased against the police and, in any case, are staffed by civilians unqualified to judge the performance of police officers.

Civilian Oversight Agencies

NEW CONCEPT   The new policing philosophy that ushered in community policing stressed that the police are accountable to their community and that civilian oversight is not only necessary but required in a free society. Today, the new concept of civilian review is known as civilian oversight. Since 1995 a nonprofit organization, the National Association for Civilian Oversight of Law Enforcement (NACOLE), has brought "together individuals and agencies working to establish or improve oversight of police officers in the United States" (www.nacole.org). NACOLE promotes greater police accountability by means of the following:

- organizing an annual training conference to increase the knowledge and skills of staff members and volunteers who work in oversight.
- providing technical assistance and advice to jurisdictions that are considering the creation or revitalization of oversight bodies.
- identifying best practices as they emerge from the experiences of members.

FIGURE 16.3 **A variety of community participation strategies.**
Courtesy of Pelham Police Department.

- encouraging networking, communication, and information sharing to counter the isolation inherent in the profession.
- furnishing information to government officials and community representatives that will support their advocacy of oversight in their state, counties, cities, and towns.

In addition to the annual training meetings NACOLE publishes newsletters, reference and resource lists, investigative tips, and suggested qualifications for civilian oversight staff and volunteers. They also list a roster of 80 civilian oversight agencies in 31 states.

NATURE OF AGENCIES   There is not one model for citizen oversight agencies and they found in municipal and county agencies (see NACOLE, Roster of U.S. Civilian Oversight Agencies). Some monitor citizen complaints only against the police and several monitor complaints against both police and fire department employees, such as the Office of Public Safety Accountability in Sacramento, California, and the Public Safety Auditor in Omaha, Nebraska. They are appointed by a variety of elected authorities—mayors, and city and county councils or boards. Throughout the United States, civilian oversight agencies have a range of duties: some receive and investigate all complaints of police misconduct against sworn police officers; others may only receive and investigate use of force and complaints of racial bias; many only investigate officer-involved shootings or deaths in custody. Some cities such as Chicago have an independent civilian oversight agency and a police internal affairs which share or have distinct duties as described in the following example:

BOX 16.1

City of Chicago Independent Police Review Authority

The Independent Police Review Authority (IPRA) is an independent department of the City of Chicago staffed with civilian investigators. IPRA was created in 1974 in response to public and internal concerns about the integrity of excessive force investigations. [Actually called the Office of Professional Standards at that time.] In 2007, by ordinance, the City of Chicago re-structured IPRA creating an independent City department.

IPRA performs the intake function for all allegations of misconduct made against members of the Chicago Police Department.

IPRA is directly responsible for conducting investigations into allegations of the use of excessive force,

police shootings where an officer discharges his/her weapon and strikes someone, deaths in custody, domestic violence, verbal abuse including bias and coercion. IPRA also investigates allegations of off-duty misconduct relating to excessive force and weapons discharge incidents.

Headed by a civilian Chief Administrator and staffed entirely with civilian investigators, IPRA is charged with the mission of maintaining the highest level of integrity while conducting objective, thorough investigations, striving to reach a sound and just conclusion.

Source: Adapted from www.iprachchicago.org/about.html

In addition to the separate and independent citizen oversight IPRA department, the Chicago Police Department has its own internal affairs division within the Bureau of Professional Standards that is "responsible for investigating alleged or suspected violations of statutes, ordinances, and Department rules and directives, and for detecting corrupt practices involving Department members" (http://portal.chicagopolice.org).

THE OMBUDSMAN   Some cities and states have established an ombudsman as, or a part of, their civilian oversight for all government agencies. The ombudsman concept in government is fairly new to Americans, but it has been in existence in Sweden since 1809.

The ombudsman concept is external to the police department and has the power to act upon any complaints received from aggrieved citizens. It differs from the civilian review board in the sense that it handles complaints lodged against all governmental agencies, including the city manager's office, fire department, and department of public works. The department or agency named in the complaint is obligated to assist the ombudsman in the investigation of the complaint. If the complaint is found to be justified, the ombudsman notifies the concerned agency and advises the proper administrator of the action required to relieve the situation. The administrator reports back to the ombudsman when the corrective steps have been taken, at which point the ombudsman notifies the complainant of the disposition of his or her complaint.

The ombudsman concept has applications for all types of police agencies and their communities. For example, an independent ombudsman was recommended by a panel examining the sometimes contentious relationships between the Harvard University Police Department and the university's diverse student body and faculty (www.boston.com/news). Black students and faculty have complained for years that they have been treated unfairly by the largely white police force. The recommended public safety ombudsman would report to the president and review results of investigations into complaints against officers.

The ombudsman approach appears to have several advantages in terms of the community. It provides the opportunity for citizen complaints to be aired in an environment of seeming impartiality. A measure of government accountability is inherent in the process.

The opposition to the concept has been primarily from law enforcement. The police argue that their work is unique, especially when compared with that of firefighters, public works employees, the city manager's office, or even city council members. Many law enforcement administrators question whether someone unfamiliar with police practices can adequately appraise what would constitute correct police procedure in a given situation.

COMMUNITY POLICING In response to various communities' demands for greater participation in the functioning of law enforcement agencies, many police administrators have initiated changes designed to bring officers into closer contact with the communities being served. These changes have taken a number of forms, many of which fall under the name "community policing." The basic goals of community policing are to return greater responsibility to those doing the actual policing at the community level and to provide for increased citizen involvement in crime prevention and police service delivery. (Community policing was discussed in detail in Chapter 10.)

CITIZEN AND COMMUNITY ALERT PROGRAMS In August 1966, a civic group was organized in San Francisco called "Citizens Alert." Its program was developed as an alternative to police review boards and was composed of people interested in police work. Its purpose was to facilitate communication between the police and the community and to collect, analyze, and report police misconduct. One method used was to have someone on call day and night who could respond to complaints of alleged police misconduct. Legal and medical services were also available. The organization investigated the complaint independently and registered its findings with the relevant police agency.

The proponents of the group emphasize the importance of its independent status and its grass-roots appeal. The opponents stress its ineffectiveness in handling complaints; because the group is not present at the incidents, investigations are based solely on the testimony of the complainants.

The "Community Alert Patrol" is similar in some ways to the "Citizens Alert." The former has augmented its approach by using community residents to follow police cars in the neighborhood to observe and document police activity. The participants use "community alert" cars and carry flash cameras, tape recorders, and two-way radios. This approach was developed in the Watts community of Los Angeles and has been implemented with varying degrees of success in several other communities.

Supportive Participation

Supportive participation may be defined as the community's willingness to function in the capacity of supplementing and complementing the operations of the criminal justice system. Four key roles may be identified as being central to community participation. They are the volunteers—those who work directly with the person being assisted; the social persuaders—persons of influence or elite status in the dominant social system who are willing to persuade others to support criminal justice programs; the gatekeepers of opportunities—those who control the access to important social systems; and *intimates*—persons who possess a common background or understanding of the problems confronting the person to be assisted (O'Leary, 1969, p. 99). The effective balancing of these roles by a program coordinator can be of valuable assistance in generating a successful program in the community.

Unlike regulatory participation, supportive participation is directed toward augmenting and providing supportive services to the justice system. The most obvious examples of supportive participation are found in the support and development of diversionary and community-based treatment facilities.

VOLUNTEERS IN CRIMINAL JUSTICE AGENCIES Volunteer work in justice agencies has increased tremendously in recent years. Some programs for police volunteers are limited to specific areas of service (e.g., search and rescue), whereas others are much more broadly based. Some police agencies now use volunteers in records, patrol, traffic control, community liaison, and crime prevention functions. The Tulsa, Oklahoma, Police Department has a unique volunteer system working on "gray cases," those that are in the gray area of not being solved and not being active (Smith, 1999). The Gray Squad is made up of citizen volunteers from all walks of life: doctors, accountants, veterinarians, computer experts, and so on. A dentist served as forensic odontology

C.O.P. Program
Citizen/Police Interaction Form

Name:_____   Date:_____

Address:_____   Area of Town:_____

Resident   Business   Other:_____

Officer:_____

Problems or Information Related to Your Community Area:

_____

_____

_____

_____

Recommendations and/or Suggestions for Community Improvement:

_____

_____

_____

_____

_____

Once completed, please forward to the C.O.P. Coordinator as designated on the business card that you have been provided. All information will be treated as confidental.

FIGURE 16.4   C.O.P. program citizen–police interaction form.

Courtesy of Rome Police Department.

consultant on a homicide case. Reserve officer programs are now found in most major U.S. cities. Although the training and duties of these volunteer officers vary from agency to agency, they are generally extensively trained and function in most of the ways paid officers function. Many agencies draw their officers from this volunteer pool. Most citizens in reserve programs, however, are not seeking full-time police service. They come from many professions, usually with above-average incomes. They volunteer to provide a public service and to enjoy the challenge of the job.

Volunteers now have a place in most justice agencies. Many juvenile courts have well-organized volunteer programs. Corrections agencies, prosecutors' offices, and adult criminal courts are, as a group, less consistent in their use of volunteers than are police and juvenile agencies. Even here, however, acceptance of volunteers has increased, and their services are now being utilized in a wide range of functions. Volunteers are an important element in working with victims, the most neglected persons in the criminal justice process. Victim-advocate volunteers provide short-term crisis to victims of crime and their survivors (Jungle, 2001).

SELF-PROTECTION OUTSIDE THE SYSTEM

Volunteer Patrols.   Volunteer patrols have been formed in some neighborhoods to patrol the area on a regular schedule. Their function is said to be preventive, and if they observe suspicious behavior, they are to report it to the police. Although many patrol members follow such guidelines very well, others take the responsibility for apprehension and/or meting out justice into their own hands. It is this latter action that concerns the police.

Private Security.   According to a *New York Times* estimate, $12 billion is spent annually on private security in the United States. Many police officers are allowed by their agencies to provide individual guard service (but usually not private investigation). Many sources estimate that the private security officers in the United States now outnumber public police officers by more than two to one. Many large companies now hire and train their own security forces. Hospital security has been among the fastest-growing areas.

Environmental or target-hardening crime prevention efforts for personal property protection have led individual citizens to invest large sums of money for security devices, attack dogs, firearms, and so on.

BOX 16.2
One Style of Participation: The Vera Institute of Justice

Merely involving the community is not sufficient. When a community is contemplating making a change in the system, it must recognize the importance of selecting an appropriate method for exerting influence and control. The Vera Institute of Justice in New York City provides a positive example of a private group of citizens working together to improve the criminal justice system. A brief review of their approach to improving the criminal justice system may serve as a model to others who are considering similar actions.

Vera's control strategy was to identify specific problem areas and to experiment with changes that could benefit both the defendant and relevant criminal justice agencies (police, prosecution, courts, and corrections). The efforts of the Vera Institute have resulted in several successful projects in the New York City Police Department. Their collaborative effort resulted in the establishment of the Community Patrol Officer Program (CPOP) in the 72nd Precinct in Brooklyn. This program is currently being expanded to include other precincts in New York City (McElroy, Cosgrove, and Sadd, 1993).

The style of participation selected by the Vera Institute is an important facet of its success. Basically, the approach has five steps:

1. The Vera staff identifies the problem, considers the alternatives, and proposes a solution to the affected criminal justice agencies.
2. The institute then provides the personnel to operate the project on a trial basis, thus minimizing the concerned agencies' expenditure of valuable resources.
3. The institute assumes responsibility for the trial phase and continues to remain in close contact with the involved agencies.
4. When the trial phase has been evaluated and is considered to be a success, the institute assumes an advisory role and permits the involved agency to take control of the project.
5. Although no longer formally involved with the project, the institute remains in close association with the agency, available to discuss problems as they arise.

The Vera example illustrates that bureaucratic inaction or citizen apathy need not hamper the development of effective community involvement in the criminal justice system.

Guardian Angels.   The Guardian Angels began as a community safety patrol in New York City in 1978 and has grown into the most well-known citizen volunteer group in the world (www.guardianangels.org). Its community safety patrols are considered the model for Neighborhood Watch programs. In 1979, the volunteer group established its first subway patrols. The Guardian Angels are easily recognized by their distinctive red berets. The Guardian Angels has 125 chapters throughout the world, including chapters in Puerto Rico (1987), London (1989), Australia (1992), Japan (1996), Brazil (2002), and Africa (2005). The Guardian Angles and its volunteer efforts have been recognized by presidents Richard Nixon (1971 Commendation of founder Curtis Sliwa), Ronald Reagan (1983—President's Volunteer Action Award), Bill Clinton (1998—President's Service Award), and George W. Bush (2004—praised for actions during Florida hurricanes; 2004–2006—Hollywood, Florida, chapter received three President's Service Award). In addition, NYC Mayor David Denkins proclaimed Guardian Angels' week (1992), Mayor Wellington Webb proclaimed Guardian Angles' Day (09/02/1994) in Denver, and Mayor Rudy Giuliani proclaimed Guardian Angles' Days in NYC (1994–1995, and again in 2001).

In each safety patrol chapter, Guardian Angels volunteers patrol streets, subways, and other public areas unarmed from dusk to dawn. They also attend community festivals and other large gatherings to deter criminal activity. They are credited with reducing criminal activity in target areas. They are generally well trained and disciplined, and they intervene to protect citizens (physically, if necessary). They make a citizen's arrest and hold the suspect for the police (Barker, Hunter, and Rush, 1994).The Guardian Angels also sponsor school programs designed to prevent bullying and raise gang awareness.

In response to citizens' concerns for assistance in dealing with online threats to children, the Guardian Angels created CyberAngels in 1995. The award-winning program addresses issues like pedophilia, child pornography, privacy, and online crimes. The CyberAngels is international in scope and has multilanguage capability. Its current mission is divided into three areas of activity:

- Prevention through education.
- Assistance of victims by helping to trace and identify the perpetrators of online crime.
- Monitoring of Internet issues that affect the public.

Even though the Guardian Angels cooperate with all types of police agencies at the federal, state, and local levels, including the FBI and Interpol, they are not without opposition from some police agencies.

POLICE ATTITUDES TOWARD THESE GROUPS   Generally police are critical of these groups, usually citing such problems as the lack of professionalism in private security and the danger of overzealousness in the volunteer patrols. They argue that the Guardian Angels are a potential problem because they are not held accountable for their actions in the ways that police are. They also are unable to screen prospective members adequately and could therefore allow someone with excessive power needs into the group.

Family Crisis Intervention Projects.   The New York City Police Department established a unit to intervene in conflict-ridden family situations and mediate or resolve them before they escalated into violence that would require arrests. The project achieved its designated objectives and also helped to improve police–community relations. Consequently, it has been emulated in other urban areas.

Community Responsibility Programs.   Frequently located in low-income, ethnic, and racial communities, these projects provide an alternative to the official juvenile justice system. Thus, instead of going to court, a juvenile offender in these communities may appear before a panel of residents—adults and youths—who determine his or her responsibility. If found guilty, the

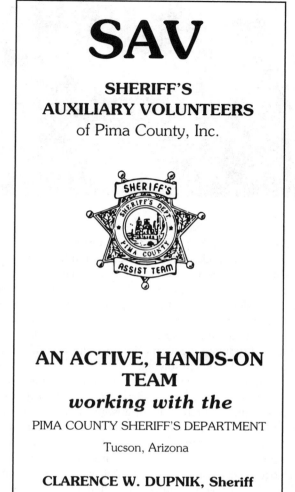

FIGURE 16.5 A community involvement program.

Courtesy of Pima County Sheriff's Department.

juvenile offender may be asked to do supervised work for the good of the community and perhaps also participate in a counseling program.

Victim–Witness Advocate Programs.   Victims and witnesses are often the "forgotten men and women" of the criminal justice system. In 1976, Pima County, Arizona, set up a program to provide them with short-term counseling, social service referral, and court information. Later the program added a juvenile unit, a mobile unit to deal with family crisis situations, and other programs. Similar models now exist in many areas.

POLICE–COMMUNITY RELATIONS IN THE NEW MILLENNIUM

The themes throughout this book are embodied in the idea expressed at the beginning of this chapter by Morgan and Newburn: Policing is too important an aspect of public policy to be left to the police. For that matter, the operation of the justice process in its entirety is too important an aspect of public policy to be left to the members themselves. There is little argument today with the statement that citizen participation is crucial to the effectiveness of the justice process.

FIGURE 16.6 Police ferry residents to higher ground in New Orleans after Hurricane Katrina pounded the city in August 2005.

Marko Georgiev, *The New York Times.*

Therefore, all free citizens are, or should be, involved in policing the community in which they live. The Peelian Principles expressed the truism of policing in a democratic and free society: The police are the public and the public are the police. We have stressed the idea that the police and the community are inseparable, that a police force is the people's police. Police–community relations has always depended on the process of developing and maintaining meaningful, two-way communication among the agency, its service area, and specific populations served. Policing a community involves the police and the community in partnerships and consultations that create a sense of safety, problem solving, and quality living through crime prevention and control, emergency responses during crisis situations, and problem solving.

We have stressed that the police–community partnerships involve an increasingly diverse consortium of internal and external communities. The exchange relationships with these internal and external communities define police–community relations for any given police agency, no matter what the size. Even in rural communities, we have seen that there are various community groups with whom the police must interact: the young, the old; minority, ethnic and racial groups; the disabled; and others. Every police agency, no matter how large or small, must deal with political groups, other criminal justice agencies, and the media. Police agencies, except the very small, must contend with the reality of internal communities with often differing views, and with minority officers, gender differences, differences in sexual preferences, and police unions.

The relationships between the police and their communities must be one of cooperation, not conflict. Therefore, the exchange relationships between the police and their communities must allow for meaningful feedback. Furthermore, these relationships must be real and not rhetorical; the presence of programs is not proof of good police–community partnerships and problem solving. We are not yet at the stage where we can say that all or even a majority of U.S. police agencies are engaged in meaningful partnerships with their communities. Altering a long-standing tradition of isolation from the community they serve will take time, years, decades or even longer. Furthermore, these community–police partnerships will always be evolving partnerships, altered and changed by persons and events occurring outside the local community.

There are several examples of police–community partnerships that could serve as models for police–community relations in the new millennium. One is the Seattle Police Department's Community Outreach Program, whose motto is *Building Bridges One Community Member at a Time* (www.seattle.gov/police/programs/advisory).

SFD Community Outreach Councils

Seattle's community outreach program is composed of three advisory councils—precinct advisory councils, demographic advisory councils and a city-wide advisory council. These councils have developed incrementally since the late 1980s. The department's first efforts to establish community policing resulted in the creation of precinct advisory councils in the late 1980s. The goal of these councils was to allow groups of citizens at the geographical level to partner with the police department on public safety issues and become more knowledgeable about law enforcement in their communities. In the mid-1990s, the police department observed that the precinct advisory councils were not reflective of the diverse communities in Seattle; therefore, demographic advisory councils were created.

Demographic advisory councils allowed the Seattle Police Department to reach out to and develop relationships with the minority communities and give them a voice in public safety issues. In 2002, one police officer was assigned as a liaison officer with each of the 11 demographic advisory councils. Soon after this, a designated command staff member was also appointed to the demographic advisory councils. Seattle PD says that this structure "provides council and community members with access to the Department not only at the 'street' level but at the command 'policy and decision making' level." This allows for better sharing of concerns and problem solving. The goals of demographic advisory councils are as follows:

- Create and strengthen programs and communication efforts that build trust between police and minority communities.
- Increase participation of individuals from minority communities working in partnership with Seattle police on public safety issues.

In 2003, a city-wide advisory council was created. This council is composed of members from the demographic and precinct advisory councils and meets with the chief of police quarterly. This council discusses broad issues that affect all the diverse communities in Seattle.

Public Safety Project—Burlington, Vermont

The Public Safety Project (PSP) of Burlington, Vermont, emphasizes community partnerships to combat blight, crime, and quality-of-life issues. First established in one of the city's most diverse and impoverished neighborhoods, Old North End (ONE), it has now spread city-wide. ONE had high rates of crime and poverty and low rates of pride and ownership. The city's Community and Economic Development Office and the police department convened nonprofit agencies, neighborhood residents, city staff, the University of Vermont, and elected officials together to develop methods to deal with ONE's problems. Twelve neighborhood associations were created in the ONE neighborhood. The first year accomplishments included a bike safety day and helmet distribution, street parties, greenbelt gardening, cleanups, and leadership development workshops. In 2001, public safety projects expanded to include Section 8 housing developments, a mobile home park, low-income neighborhoods, student neighborhoods, and highly transient neighborhoods. The PSP effort is an aggressive community organizing initiative that allows residents to take ownership of their neighborhoods and provides the tools for problem solving. PSP is staffed by AmeriCorps*Vista volunteers and driven by community members (see Box 16.3 and MetLife Foundation, n.d.).

BOX 16.3
AmeriCorps*Vista Volunteers

Volunteers in Service to America (VISTA) was founded in 1965 to fight poverty and incorporated into the AmericaCorps network of programs in 1993. AmeriCorps Vista is the national service program to fight poverty. VISTA members commit to serve full time for a year at a nonprofit organization or local government agency, working to fight illiteracy, provide health services, create businesses, and strengthen community groups. During their year of service the volunteers receive a modest living allowance, health care, and other benefits. At the end of the year, they can choose an education award worth $4,725 to pay for college, or $1,200 in cash.

THE IMPACT OF WORLD AND NATIONAL EVENTS ON COMMUNITIES

We have always known that national and world events affect all of us and our communities. However, at least three world and national events may become more of an issue in the twenty-first century than ever before in our nation's history.

Globalization of Crime and Criminal Groups

The twenty-first century will be an age of increased **globalization of crime** and criminal groups. International drug dealers engaged in a multibillion-dollar industry will impact an increasing number of communities in rural and urban America. In addition, immigrant smuggling, trafficking in weapons and stolen vehicles, and money laundering will become problems in more American communities. Organized crime groups, gangs, and money launderers will seek outlets for their activities in rural and urban areas. The response to these community problems will require exchange and feedback from all the internal and external communities of the police.

Globalization of Protest Issues and Protest Groups

In the new millennium, the police in all American communities will face the likelihood that social protests will be carried out by groups better prepared and organized than they are today. Anarchists, peace advocates, environmentalists, workers' representatives, and supporters of every possible social issue connect with each other in cyberspace. These groups can come together from outside the community and from outside the country to participate in a social protest and demonstration. The 1999 Battle in Seattle occurred in a city well known for its police–community relations and a police department led by a community policing pioneer. The events in Seattle point to the globalization of protest issues and protest groups, with 50 groups—including labor unions—participating in that disturbance. In the new millennium, police departments and their communities must plan for such events occurring in their locales.

THE WAR ON TERROR AND IMPACTS OF HOMELAND SECURITY

The attack on the United States on September 11, 2001, changed the nation, and its impact on policing in America will be felt for many years. The very real threat of additional terrorist attacks has increased the need for national and community security. Security has increased at all large public gatherings. We are all becoming accustomed to being screened, searched, and prodded when we travel and attend sporting events or other mass gatherings. The effects of new laws passed in response to the terrorist attacks will undoubtedly affect our lives and civil liberties. We are not as free as we once were. Police in the United States could become more militarized and more war oriented, depending on the advent of more attacks.

Traditionally, U.S. police isolated themselves from their communities because they were professional crime fighters engaged in a war on crime. One can only speculate on the isolation from the public that would occur if the police at the federal and local levels had wrapped themselves in secrecy because of a war on terror. We also know that the events of September 11, 2001, have exacerbated the tenuous relationships between certain ethnic groups and the police. Allegations of racial profiling have expanded beyond the black community.

A residual effect of the events of September 11 and the **"War on Terror"** conducted by the United States has been the drying up of federal monies to support police innovations at the local level. This has included monies for community-oriented policing initiatives. This was not necessarily a bad thing. For many agencies, C.O.P. was more talk than action anyway (Hunter and Barker, 1993). Many agencies were into community policing as long as there were federal monies available. This was a real disservice to the many police leaders trying to improve police relations with their communities. Whatever the future of the funding sources, a need for improved police–community relations will still exist, and police departments and police leaders will still be willing to move in that direction.

Warring Against Foreign Terrorists

AL-QUAIDA   Al-quaida (also known as Alquaida, Al Quaida, or Al-qaida) is the radical Islamic terrorist organization headed by the elusive Saudi billionaire Osama bin Laden. Allegedly bin Laden ordered the attacks on the World Trade Center Towers and the Pentagon on September 11, 2001. International efforts to eradicate the organization have seen limited success. The U.S. invasion of Afghanistan, which resulted in the overthrow of the Taliban that had harbored bin Laden, has seriously hampered Al-quaida's operations. However, they are still operating in the border areas of Afghanistan and Pakistan and are very active among insurgents in Iraq.

IRAQ   While there are bitter debates among Americans as to whether the United States should have invaded Iraq, the fact remains that our nation has a moral obligation to rebuild the Iraqi national infrastructure before we can withdraw from Iraq. How long our troops remain in Iraq during this rebuilding will continue to create a major division within American society.

IMPRISONING "FOREIGN COMBATANTS"   In addition to the divisive issues of Iraq and Afghanistan, within America's "War on Terror," yet another issue has caused severe criticisms within America and from abroad. The imprisonment of "Foreign Combatants" at Guantanamo Bay in Cuba has brought condemnation of the U.S. policies by international human rights groups. Whether the president had legal authority to imprison enemy combatants without trial continues to be debated as this is being written. President Obama has said he will close Guantanamo Bay but that has not stopped the controversy of what to do with those being held there.

Homeland Security

The Department of Homeland Security was created following the attacks on America by Al-quaida on September 11, 2001. To better coordinate efforts at preventing future acts of terrorism on American soil, the U.S. Border Patrol, U.S. Customs Service, U.S. Secret Service, the Transportation Safety Administration, and the Federal Emergency Management Agency were merged. This huge organization was seen as the means to enhance intelligence capabilities and to better protect the nation. This focus on **homeland security** has not been without controversy. According to some Bush administration critics, the organization is ineffective in its antiterrorist activities, and it neglects natural disaster preparedness (see this chapter's Reality Check). However, the absence of subsequent attacks by Al-quaida or similar organizations has been hailed by supporters as evidence that this emphasis is correct.

INCREASED SECURITY EFFORTS   Anyone who has flown on a commercial airline since September 11 is well aware of the increase in security precautions that must be endured while traveling. In addition to travel restrictions, the simple act of mailing a package to a friend or loved one has become more difficult. Participating in public events, attending sporting contests, riding on public transportation, and other activities have become more complicated because of security concerns. These security requirements are not expected to decline but are thought to become a part of everyday life as we move further into the twenty-first century.

DOMESTIC EAVESDROPPING   While Americans have indicated a willingness to make some privacy concessions in order to be safer, the extent that civil liberties may be infringed upon is a matter of great concern for many. As we noted in the Chapter 14 Reality Check, there is currently a great debate about limiting the invasive powers granted to federal law enforcement agencies by the Patriot Act. These arguments are heightened by the revelations that the Bush administration ran domestic eavesdropping operations against those suspected of communicating with terrorists. The exact nature of and extent of this domestic spying is unclear. Advocates claim that only a small portion of the population is under surveillance and that these actions are both necessary and lawful. Critics argue that this is an unnecessary and unconstitutional violation of civil liberties.

Regardless of where one stands in regard to America's "War on Terror" and the federal government's "Homeland Security" programs, these efforts will continue to impact our communities and local police efforts for many years to come.

IMPROVING POLICE–COMMUNITY RELATIONS IN THE NEW MILLENNIUM

Understanding What the Police Do for Their Communities

Any strategies suggested or recommended to improve police–community relations must be based on what the police do, or should do, for their communities. Without trying to come up with an exhaustive list, in the following sections we outline what we consider to be the most salient aspects of what the police must continue to do for their communities.

CRIME PREVENTION AND CONTROL   The great American police reformer August Vollmer, writing in 1936 stated, "The original purpose of police organizations was protection against the occurrence of major crimes and the apprehension of perpetrators of such offenses" (Vollmer, 1971, p. 1). This has not changed. **Crime prevention** and law enforcement will always be major objectives of the police. They will always be involved in proactive and reactive strategies to prevent and control crime. What has changed is the recognition that the police are not in the crime prevention and control business by themselves. As stated in Chapter 10, the police and the public are learning that law enforcement requires a cooperative effort, not alienation and isolation from each other. Or has this changed or just been forgotten for a time? Vollmer recognized the importance of the community in crime prevention efforts when he called for the police to act as a coordinating agency for the resources of the community to prevent crime (Vollmer, 1971, p. 235). He recommended that crime prevention efforts "may be achieved through a committee of representative citizens, or a representative council of the appropriate community agencies . . ." (Vollmer, 1971, p. 235). Today's thinking expands community involvement from representative "elites" to giving the opportunity to every law-abiding citizen in the community. Vollmer also recognized that crime fighting was not the only service that the police performed for their communities.

EMERGENCY RESPONDERS TO CRISIS SITUATIONS   Vollmer recognized that as one of the only 24/7, 365-days-a-year public agencies, the police would be called upon to aid the sick, the injured, the missing, the insane, and the feeble minded. They would also be called to disasters, strikes, and riots "to preserve, if possible, or to restore peace and order" (Vollmer, 1971, p. 3). He added that citizens at any time of day or night could report suspicious persons or circumstances to the police and request action by the police. Later scholars would add to this list the peacekeeping, order maintenance, and conflict resolution duties of the police in crisis situations. Vollmer went on to say that the public thinks of the police as "thief takers," but "few know them as the useful and versatile servants that they actually are" (Vollmer, 1971, p. 186).

COMMUNITY PROBLEM SOLVERS   Vollmer and all of the early police reformers recognized that the police have, and have always had, a problem-solving role in the community. However, those problems usually have been crime- or delinquency-related problems, and the police have traditionally chosen what community problems should be solved. As outlined in Chapter 3 and throughout this book, this has changed dramatically. Today, the police and the community are cooperative problem identifiers and solvers in many, but not all, instances. Goldstein (1990) states that the objective of problem-oriented-policing is "to focus on problems of concern to the community" (p. 70). However, problems to be solved can be identified by the community, police management, or rank-and-file officers.

CHOOSING COMMUNITY-SPECIFIC STRATEGIES

No One Solution

As stated in Chapter 1 and stressed throughout this book, police–community relations are complicated and constantly changing interactions between representatives of the police organization and an assortment of government agencies, public groups, and private individuals representing a wide range of competing and often conflicting interests. There is no one community with whom the police interact. Rather, there is a consortium of internal and external communities. Therefore, there can be no one strategy that fits all problems.

Problem-Solving Policing and Community Policing

Mark Moore (1992) states that problem solving and community policing as alternative organizational strategies define general approaches to policing rather than a definitive set of activities. Furthermore, any particular program that reflects these organizational strategies might differ in particular localities. For example, a problem-solving approach to domestic violence in Kansas City might be different from the one in another city. Community policing approaches to drug dealing may be different in different cities (Moore, 1992, p. 120). This does not mean that problem-solving policing (problem-oriented policing) or community policing (community-oriented policing) should not be embraced as organizational strategies, or guiding philosophies, by police agencies. Both recognize the importance of community partnerships and exchange and feedback from the police's internal and external communities. However, Moore makes clear that there may be "no one best way to deal with each of the problems facing policing. The best response will often depend on local circumstances" (Moore, 1992, p. 120).

Local Strategies for Local Problems

U.S. policing is a fragmented system composed of numerous agencies of various sizes. Our system of federalism, which ensures a distribution of powers between the federal government and the states, dictates a fragmented system. Therefore, our national and historical tradition reflects that policing will always be a local responsibility. Consequently,

> the mark of an effective police department will not be how successful it is in implementing the most recent national model of a successful program but instead in how thoughtfully it crafts a local solution to a local problem, taking into account the local character of the problem and the local means of dealing with it. (Moore, 1992, p. 120)

Those **local strategies** will be crafted to meet local problems of a crime prevention and control nature (e.g., reactive or proactive strategies that target places or offenders); emergency responses to crisis situations (e.g., responding to domestic violence, the mentally ill, or social protests); or solving community problems. The community problem to be solved may be a crime prevention or control problem or a crisis situation, but it does not have to be. It may be a quality of life issue unrelated to crime or crisis issues, but it doesn't have to be. It may be discovered in consultation with the community, but it doesn't have to be. Its resolution may be evaluated by feedback from the community. It has to be. That is what police–community relations is all about. Police–community relations is the process of developing and maintaining meaningful, two-way communication between the agency, its service area, and specific populations served.

REALITY CHECK

Homeland Security versus Disaster Preparedness

In Chapter 14 we addressed civil libertarians' concerns about the Bush administration's focus on Homeland Security. As we discussed previously, the creation of the Department of Homeland Security resulted in the Federal Emergency Management Agency (FEMA) being absorbed along with the Border Patrol, Secret Service, Customs, and Transportation Safety Administration into this gargantuan organization. Critics of this reorganization argue that many of the billions of dollars that have been spent on Homeland Security have been wasted on ineffective and unnecessary programs. However, their greatest criticisms are not about its abilities in regard to protecting the country from terrorism. They argue that the overemphasis of Homeland Security resources on terrorism has resulted in monies being wrongly removed from planning and preparation for natural disasters.

The failure of the FEMA to respond to Hurricane Katrina's devastation of New Orleans in August 2005 brought enormous criticism of the Bush administration in general and the then Secretary of Homeland Security Michael Chertoff in particular. Subsequent fraud and waste within FEMA response and recovery programs for New Orleans have kept the criticisms flowing.

As this is being written, there are calls by politicians and the emergency management community to remove FEMA from the Department of Homeland Security and position it within the federal government so that its director reports directly to the president. What do you think?

Conclusions

As long as the criminal justice systems fails to do what citizens expect it to do, demands for community control will exist. Because the police, or indeed the justice system as a whole, cannot function properly in a free society without the help and support of the people it serves, community participation is essential for success.

At every point in the system, concerned citizens can become involved in the justice process. The stage, manner, and level of involvement are determined both by the sources available and by the individual's area of interest and level of motivation.

Many models of community control exist. Choosing the "best" model in a specific situation is a matter of understanding the unique characteristics of the community, its citizens, and its criminal justice clientele.

The new millennium presents new challenges for the police and the criminal justice system. Our world has shrunk, and each local community will be affected by the globalization of crime and criminal groups and the globalization of protest issues and protest groups. We still have no way of determining the long-term effects of the September 11 attacks on America. However, we are certain that each of us as individuals and members of communities that interact with the police and the justice process will be affected.

Improving police–community relations in the new millennium requires an understanding of what the police do for their communities and a realization that there is no one solution that will fit all police–community relations problems. We have tried to make that clear throughout this work. Solutions must be tailored to local problems and local needs.

Student Checklist

1. Define community participation.
2. Why are some communities more desirous of control than other communities?
3. How has the federal government become a part of community participation in police agencies?
4. Contrast several different methods of community participation in the criminal justice system.
5. How is police organization a factor in police resistance to community participation?
6. Compare the effectiveness of different styles of community participation.
7. Why are volunteers important to the criminal justice process?
8. Investigate the various types of programs available in your community.

9. Why is policing too important to be left to the police?

10. What is meant by the globalization of crime and criminal groups?

11. What is meant by the globalization of protest issues and protest groups?

12. What are some of the possible effects of September 11?

13. What do the police do for their communities?

14. Why are problem-oriented policing and community policing not the solutions for all police–community relations problems?

Topics for Discussion

1. What degree of community participation do you believe is appropriate in your community?

2. How would you know that a method of community participation was effective?

3. Based on your answer to topic 2, what methods of community participation mentioned in this chapter are most effective?

4. Can we continue to have community participation and also promote homeland security? If so, how?

Bibliography

Altshuler, A. A. (1970). *Community Control: The Black Demand for Participation in Large American Cities.* Indianapolis, IN: Pegasus.

Barker, T. (2002). "Ethical police behavior," in K. M. Lersch (Ed.), *Policing and Misconduct.* Upper Saddle River, NJ: Prentice Hall.

Barker, T., Hunter, R. D., and Rush, J. P. (1994). *Police Systems and Practices: An Introduction.* Upper Saddle River, NJ: Prentice Hall.

Fuller, J. R. (2005). *Criminal Justice: Mainstreams and Crossroads.* Upper Saddle River, NJ: Pearson/Prentice Hall.

Goldstein, H. (1990). *Problem-Oriented Policing.* New York: McGraw-Hill.

Greenberg, M. A. (April 1977). "Volunteer crime prevention program: A proposal for survival in the third century," *The Police Chief,* Vol. XLIV, pp. 60–61.

Hunter, R. D., and Barker, T. (1993). "BS and Buzzwords: The new police organizational style," *American Journal of Police,* Vol. XII, No. 3, pp. 157–168.

Jungle, T. (2001). "Helping victims helps everyone," *Sheriff,* Vol. 53, No. 1, pp. 28–30.

McElroy, J. E., Cosgrove, C. A., and Sadd, S. (1993). *Community Policing: The CPOP in New York.* Newbury Park, CA: Sage Publications.

Miller, L., and Braswell, M. (1997). *Human Relations and Police Work,* 4th ed. Prospect Heights, IL: Waveland Press.

Moore, M. H. (1992). "Problem-solving and community policing," in M. Tonry and N. Morris (Eds.), *Modern Policing.* Chicago, IL: The University of Chicago Press.

Morgan, R., and Newburn, T. (1997). *The Future of Policing.* Oxford, England: Clarendon Press.

National Advisory Commission on Criminal Justice Standards and Goals. (1973). *Working Papers for the National Conference on Criminal Justice.* Washington, D.C.: Law Enforcement Assistance Administration.

O'Leary, V. (January 1969). "Some directions for citizen involvement in corrections," *The Annals,* Vol. 381, No. 1, pp. 99–108.

Osborne, D., and Gaebler, T. (1993). *Reinventing Government.* New York: Penguin Books.

Roberg, R. R., Kuykendall, J., and Novak (2002). *Police Management,* 3rd ed. Los Angeles, CA: Roxbury.

Smith, C. A. (1999). "Tulsa's Gray Squad solves cold cases," *Law & Order,* Vol. 47, No. 11, pp. 48–49.

Trojanowicz, R. C., Kappler, V. A., Gaines, L., and Bucqueroux, B. (1998). *Community Policing: How to Get Started,* 2nd ed. Cincinnati, OH: Anderson.

Vollmer, A. (1971). *The Police and Modern Society.* Montclair, NJ: Patterson Smith reprint. Originally published in 1936.

RECOMMENDED POLICE-RELATED WEB SITES

Civil/Constitutional Rights Sites

American-Arab Anti-Discrimination Committee	www.adc.org
Anti-Defamation League (ADL)	www.adl.com
Center for Constitutional Rights	www.ccr~ny.org/v2/home.asp
Constitution Society	www.constitution.org
U.S. Commission on Civil Rights	www.usccr.gov
U.S. Department of Justice	www.usdoj.gov/civilliberties.htm
U.S. Department of Justice, Civil Rights Division	www.usdoj.gov/crt/crt-home.htm

Community Policing Sites

Carolinas Institute for Community Policing	www.cicp.org
Center for Problem-Oriented Policing	www.popcenter.org
Child Development-Community Policing Program	www.cd-cp.org
Community Justice Exchange	www.communityjustice.org/exchange
Community Oriented Policing Service	www.cops.usdoj.gov
Community Policing Consortium	www.communitypolicing.org

Federal Law Enforcement Sites

Bureau of Alcohol, Tobacco, Firearms and Explosives	www.atf.treas.gov
Drug Enforcement Administration	www.usdoj.gov/dea
Federal Bureau of Investigation	www.fbi.gov
Federal Law Enforcement Training Center	www.fletc.gov
Immigration and Naturalization Services	www.ins.usdoj.gov
Internal Revenue Service	www.ustreas.gov/irs
Office of the United States Attorney General	www.justice.gov/ag
Offices of the Inspector General	www.ignet.gov
U.S. Customs Service	www.customs.treas.gov
U.S. Department of Homeland Security	www.dhs.gov/dhspublic
U.S. Department of Justice	www.usdoj.gov
U.S. Department of the Treasury	www.ustreas.gov

Legal Organizations Sites

American Bar Association	www.abanet.org
American Judges Association	www.ncsc.dni.us
American Judicature Society	www.ajs.org
National Association of Criminal Defense Lawyers	www.nacdl.org
National College of District Attorneys	www.law.sc.edu/ncda
United States Supreme Court	www.supremecourts.gov

Legal Reference Sites

Cornell Law School Legal Information Institute	www.law.cornell.edu
Findlaw	www.supreme.lp.findlaw.com
Kansas Cop Law	www.kscoplaw.com
Lawyers Weekly, Inc.	www.lawyersweekly.com
Legal Aspects of Search and Seizure	www.kscoplaw.com/outlines/ssoutline.htm
Legal Information Institute	www.law.cornell.edu/topics/constitutional.html
National Association of Attorneys General	www.naag.org
National District Attorneys Association	www.ndaa.org

Police Accreditation Sites

Commission for Florida Law Enforcement Accreditation	www.flaccreditation.org
Commission on Accreditation for Law Enforcement Agencies, Inc.	www.calea.org
Commission on Accreditation for Law Enforcement Agencies, Public Safety Communications Accreditation Program	www.calea.org/newweb/PSCAP/PROGRAM.htm

Police Employment Sites

Law Enforcement Careers	www.911hotjobs.com
Law Enforcement Jobs	www.lawenforcementjob.com
Officer Employment	www.officer.com
Police Jobs	www.policeemployment.com

Police Ethics Sites

Ethics Links	www.hailesgp.com/Ethicslinks.html
Florida Officer Discipline Bulletin	www.fdle.state.fl.us/cjst/officer_dis/professionalism_bulletin/index.html
The Institute of Law Enforcement Administration/ Center for Law Enforcement Ethics	www.theilea.org/ilea/ethics.html
Police Ethics	www.kirkwood.cc.ia.us/faculty/mpenrod/police_ethics

Police Fraternal Organizations Sites

Florida Police Benevolent Association	www.flpba.org
Fraternal Order of Police	www.grandlodgefop.org
Los Angeles Police Protective League	www.lapd.com/main/home.asp?topic=HME&IngKey=en
Southern States Police Benevolent Association	www.aspba.org

Police History Sites

The Constabulary	www.constabulary.com
Guardian Angels Safety Patrol	www.mit.edu/people/ericldab/ga.html
The London Metropolitan Police	www.victorianweb.org/history/police.html
Sir Robert Peel	www.met.police.uk/history/peel.htm

Police Information Sites

Cop Links	www.coplink.com
Cop Net	www.cop.net
Cops on Line	www.copsonline.com
International Police Association	www.policenet.org
John Walsh's Sex Offender Viewing Site	www.familywatchdog.us/
Police Headquarters	www.firstcop.com
Police Officer's Internet Directory	www.officer.com

Police Professional Organizations Sites

The American Polygraph Association	www.polygraph.org
Asian American Law Enforcement Association	www.aalea.org
Federal Hispanic Law Enforcement Officers Association	www.fhleoa
International Association of Campus Law Enforcement Administrators	www.iaclea.org
International Association of Chiefs of Police	www.iacp.org
National Association of Black Law Enforcement Officers	www.blackcops.net
National Association of Police Organizations	www.napo.org
National Association of Women Law Enforcement Executives	www.nawlee.com/index.html
National Black Police Association	www.blackpolice.org
National Center for Women and Policing	www.womenandpolicing.org
National Organization of Black Law Enforcement Executives	www.noblenatl.org
National Sheriffs Association	www.sheriffs.org
South Carolina State Constables Alliance	www.scconstable.org

Police Publications Sites

9-1-1 Magazine	www.9-1-1magazine.com
Police Magazine	www.policemag.com
Police Week	www.policeweek.org
The Police Marksmen	www.policemarksmen.com

Police Research Sites

Criminal Justice Policy Foundation	www.cjpf.org
Directory of Law Enforcement Agencies	www.officer.com
Federal Bureau of Investigation, Law Enforcement Officers Killed and Assaulted	www.fbi.gov/ucr/killed/2001leoka.pdf
Federal Justice Statistics Resource Center	www.fjsrc.urban.org
Florida Law Enforcement Research Coalition	www.flerc.org
National Archive for Criminal Justice Data	www.icpsr.umich.edu/NACJD
National Criminal Justice Reference Service	www.ncjrs.org
Officer.com (resources and articles)	www.officer.com
Police Executive Research Forum	www.policeforum.org

Police Foundation	www.policefoundation.org
United Nations Crime & Justice Information NetworkInformation Network	www.uncjin.org
United States Department of Justice	www.usdoj.gov
U.S. Bureau of Justice Assistance	www.ojp.usdoj.gov/BJA
U.S. Bureau of Justice Statistics	www.ojp.usdoj.gov/BJS
World Justice Information Network	www.jin.net

Police Retirement Sites

American Association of Retired Persons	www.aarp.com
Houston Police Retired Officers Association	www.hpdretired.com
New Jersey Police and Firemen's Retirement System	www.state.nj.us/treasury/pensions/pfrs1.htm
New York City Police Pension Fund	www.nyc.gov/html/nycpp/home.html
Social Security Cost of Living Adjustments	www.ssa.gov/OACT/COLA/latestCOLA.html
Society of Former Special Agents of the FBI	www.socxfbi.org/design5.htm

Police Stress Sites

Central Florida Police Stress Unit	www.policestress.org
Corrections and Law Enforcement Family Support	www.ojp.usdoj.gov/nij/clefs/welcome.html
National Police Suicide Foundation	www.psf.org
Police Officers and Post-Traumatic Stress Disorder	www.home.socal.rr.com/jpmock/ptsd/ptsd.htm
Police Stress Line police_stressline.htm	www.geocities.com/stressline_com/

Police Support Sites

Concerns of Police Survivors	www.nationalcops.org
Gay Officers Action League of New England	www.goalne.org
Gay Officers Action League of New York	www.goalny.org
National Law Enforcement Officers Memorial Fund, Inc.	www.nleomf.com
Officer Down Memorial Page	www.odmp.org
Public Safety Officers Benefits Program	www.ojp.usdog.gov/BJA

Police Training Sites

American Society of Law Enforcement Trainers	www.aslet.org
Americans for Effective Law Enforcement	www.aele.org
California Peace Officer Standards and Training	www.post.ca.gov
FBI National Academy	www.fbi.gov/hq/td/academy/na/na.htm
Institute of Law Enforcement Administration	www.theilea.org
International Law Enforcement Educators and Trainers Association	www.ileeta.org
Mesa (AZ) Police Department Training Officer Program	www.ci.mesa.az.use/police/fto
Multicultural Law Enforcement Training Resources Center	www.MulticulturalLawEnforcement.com
National Association of Field Training Officers	www.nafto.org
Office of the Police Corps	www.ojp.usdoj.gov/opclee

Ondra Berry Law Enforcement Cultural Diversity Training	www.betances.com/consultants.htm
San Diego Regional Training Center (RTC)	www.sdrtc.org
Simulations Training Systems	www.simulationstrainingsystems.org
Southern Police Institute	www.louisville.edu/a-s/ja/spi

Police Watch Organizations Sites

American Civil Liberties Union of Florida	www.aclufl.org/index.html
American Civil Liberties Union, Police Practices	www.archive.aclu.org/issues/policepractices/hmpolice.html
"Broken Windows" and Police Discretion	www.ncjrs.org/pdffiles1/nij/178259.pdf
The NAACP	www.naacp.org
Principals for Promoting Police Integrity	www.ncjrs.org/pdffiles1/ojb/186189.pdf
U.S. Commission on Civil Rights	www.usccr.gov
U.S. Department of Justice	www.usdoj.gov/civilliberties.htm
U.S. Department of Justice, Civil Rights Division	www.usdoj.gov/crt/crt-home.htm

INDEX